THE

LAYING OF THE CABLE,

OR

THE OCEAN TELEGRAPH;

BEING

A COMPLETE AND AUTHENTIC NARRATIVE

OF THE

ATTEMPT TO LAY THE CABLE ACROSS THE ENTRANCE TO THE GULF OF ST. LAWRENCE IN 1855,

AND OF THE

THREE ATLANTIC TELEGRAPH EXPEDITIONS

OF 1857 AND 1858:

WITH A DETAILED ACCOUNT OF

THE MECHANICAL AND SCIENTIFIC PART OF THE WORK, AS WELL AS BIOGRAPHICAL SKETCHES OF MESSRS. CYRUS W. FIELD, WILLIAM E. EVERETT, AND OTHER PROMINENT PERSONS CONNECTED WITH THE ENTERPRISE.

ILLUSTRATED WITH PORTRAITS, ENGRAVINGS OF THE MACHINERY, AND SCENES IN THE PROGRESS OF THE GREAT WORK.

BY

JOHN MULLALY,
HISTORIAN OF THE ENTERPRISE.

NEW YORK:
D. APPLETON AND COMPANY,
346 & 348 BROADWA-
1858.

PREFACE.

It was the good fortune of the author to have been on board the U. S. frigate Niagara during the Atlantic Telegraph expeditions of 1857–'8, and to have been present on the occasion of the landing of the cable in Newfoundland on the memorable 5th of August. While on these expeditions he acted in the capacity of special correspondent of the New York Herald, and in that position collected a large amount of information in regard to the history, progress, and successful completion of the great enterprise. This he embodies in the following pages, and it is enough to say that he was present at every scene therein described, and was acquainted with every step in the progress of the undertaking; that he knew the men by whom it was so successfully carried on, and that he has faithfully endeavored to deserve the title which he has received of "Historian of the Enterprise."

He takes advantage of this opportunity to return his thanks to the ward-room officers of the Niagara for the many kindnesses and courtesies which he received at their hands during the eleven months he spent on board that ship as their guest, and to Captain Hudson for the privileges he was permitted to enjoy on the two cruises which he made with that gallant commander. To Mr. Cyrus W. Field, from whom he obtained much of the information herein presented, he desires also to express his sincere acknowledgments for the many acts of personal friendship for which he is indebted to that gentleman. He would likewise take this occasion to return his thanks to Messrs. Markwell and Arcedeckne of London, who were unremitting in their kind attentions during his visit to that city.

CONTENTS.

LIST OF ILLUSTRATIONS.

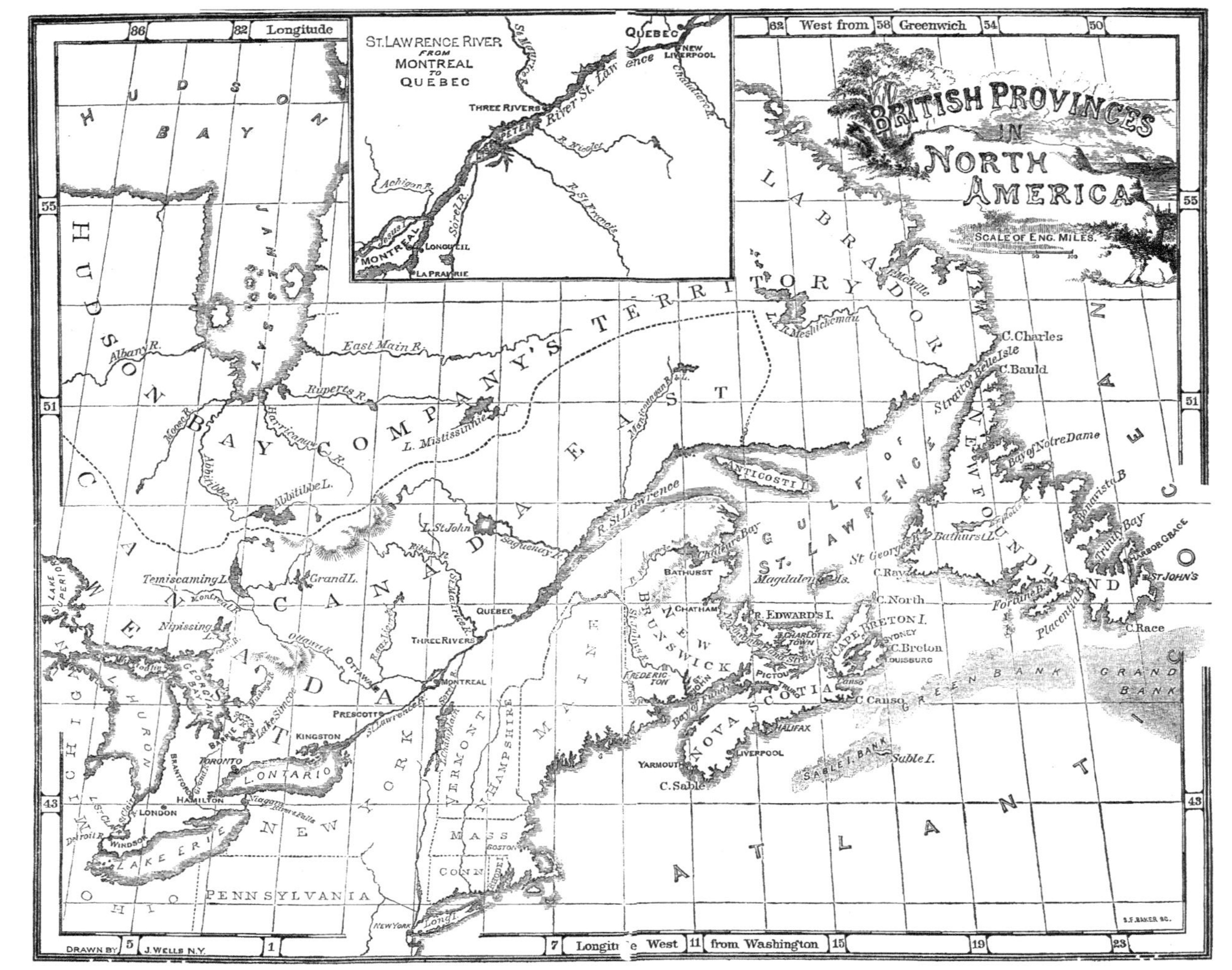
BRITISH PROVINCES IN NORTH AMERICA
SCALE OF ENG. MILES.
ST. LAWRENCE RIVER FROM MONTREAL TO QUEBEC
QUEBEC
NEW LIVERPOOL
THREE RIVERS
MONTREAL
LONGUEIL
LA PRAIRIE
River St. Lawrence
HUDSON BAY
JAMES BAY
LABRADOR
HUDSON BAY COMPANY'S TERRITORY
EAST
CANADA EAST
CANADA WEST
East Main R.
Ruperts R.
Albany R.
Moose R.
L. Mistissinnie
Abbitibbe L.
L. St John
Saguenay R.
R. St Lawrence
ANTICOSTI I.
GULF OF ST. LAWRENCE
NEWFOUNDLAND
C. Charles
C. Bauld
Strait of Belle Isle
Bay of Notre Dame
Trinity Bay
HARBOR GRACE
ST JOHN'S
C. Race
Placentia B.
Fortune B.
Bathurst L.
St Georges B.
C. Ray
Magdalen Is.
C. North
CAPE BRETON I.
SYDNEY
C. Breton
LOUISBURG
C. Canso
PR. EDWARD'S I.
CHARLOTTE TOWN
NEW BRUNSWICK
BATHURST
CHATHAM
FREDERICTON
PICTOU
NOVA SCOTIA
HALIFAX
LIVERPOOL
YARMOUTH
C. Sable
Sable I.
SABLE I. BANK
GREEN BANK
GRAND BANK
ATLANTIC OCEAN
QUEBEC
THREE RIVERS
MONTREAL
OTTAWA
PRESCOTT
KINGSTON
TORONTO
HAMILTON
BRANTFORD
LONDON
WINDSOR
BARRIE
Grand L.
Temiscaming L.
Nipissing L.
Lake Simcoe
GEORGIAN BAY
HURON
L. ONTARIO
LAKE ERIE
LAKE SUPERIOR
MICHIGAN
NEW YORK
VERMONT
N. HAMPSHIRE
MAINE
MASS
BOSTON
CONN
PENNSYLVANIA
OHIO
New York
Long I.
Longitude
West from Greenwich
Longitude West from Washington
DRAWN BY J. WELLS N.Y.
S.F. BAKER SC.

ORIGIN AND HISTORY OF THE ATLANTIC TELEGRAPH.

In 1852 an act was passed by the Legislature of Newfoundland, incorporating certain parties for the organization of a company to construct a telegraph line across the island, extending from St. Johns on the eastern coast, to Cape Ray at its south-western extremity. Their object was to place New York and every city of the United States and British provinces within six days' communication of Europe, for the idea of a submarine telegraph had not yet taken practical form and shape. The better to carry this plan into execution, it was proposed to run a line of steamers from Galway in Ireland to St. Johns, Newfoundland, and to send the intelligence which was received on the arrival of the steamers at the latter port to Cape Ray, and thence by a small steamer connecting with the nearest available point on Cape Breton, from which it would then be transmitted by the land lines to all parts of the continent. This company failed, however, to fulfil the terms of their charter, and finally became utterly bankrupt, leaving some fifty thousand dollars unpaid, and this owing chiefly to the operatives on the line. While the company was in this insolvent condition, its engineer, Mr. Fred. N. Gisborne, applied to Mr. Matthew D. Field, who was at that time in New York, to aid them in procuring a loan for the continuance of the work. Mr. Field immediately presented the subject to his brothers Cyrus W. and David Dudley Field, and urged them to buy bonds of the company convertible into stock, or to subscribe for stock, and induce their friends to do the same. Mr. Cyrus Field took the subject into earnest consideration, and struck with the idea of establishing telegraphic communication between Europe and America by a submarine cable stretching from Newfoundland to Ireland, he wrote two letters, one to Lieut. Maury, with a view of consulting him about the practicability of submerging such a cable between the points proposed, and the other to Professor Morse, in regard to the electrical difficulties of the undertaking. In reply to these letters he received the most gratifying assurances of the practicability of the scheme from both these high scientific authorities. This correspondence took place in February of 1854, and thus satisfied of its feasibility, the two brothers resolved that an effort should be made to get up an association for the purpose of carrying it through. In reflecting upon the plan to be pursued, they came to the conclusion that it was better to confine the organization to a limited number of persons, in order to secure greater unity and decision. The following gentlemen were accordingly invited to Mr. Field's residence: Peter Cooper, Chandler White, Moses Taylor, and Marshall O. Roberts; and here we will let Mr. David Dudley Field relate this part of the history.

"They met Mr. Cyrus W. Field and myself at his house, where, around a table covered with maps, plans, and estimates, the subject was discussed for four successive evenings, the practicability of the undertaking examined, its advantages, its cost, and the means of its accomplishment. The result of the conference was the agreement of all the six gentlemen to enter upon the undertaking. Mr. Cyrus W. Field, Mr. White, and myself were to proceed to Newfoundland to procure a charter, and such aid in money and privileges as the government of that island could be induced to give. The agreement with the Electric Telegraph Company, and the formal surrender of its charter, were signed on the 10th of March, and on the 14th we left New York, accompanied by Mr. Gisborne. The next morning we took the steamer at Boston for Halifax, and thence, on the night of the 18th, departed in the little steamer Merlin for St. Johns, Newfoundland. Three more disagreeable days voyagers scarcely ever passed than we spent in that smallest of steamers. It seemed as if all the storms of winter had been reserved for the first month of spring. A frost-bound coast, an icy sea, rain, hail, snow and tempest, were the greetings of the telegraph adventurers in their first movement towards Europe. In the darkest night, through which no man could see the ship's length, with snow filling the air and flying into the eyes of the sailors, with ice in the water, and a heavy sea rolling and moaning about us, the captain felt his way around Cape Race with his lead, as the blind man feels his way with his staff, but as confidently and as safely as if the sky had been clear and the sea calm; and the light of morning dawned upon deck, and mast, and spar coated with glittering ice, but floating securely between the mountains which form the gates of the harbor of St. Johns. In that busy and hospitable town, the first person to whom we were introduced was Mr. Edward M. Archibald, then Attorney General of the colony, and now British Consul in New York. He entered warmly into our views, and from that day to this has been an efficient and consistent supporter of the undertaking. By him we were introduced to the Governor (Kerr Bailey Hamilton), who also took an earnest interest in our plans. He convoked the Council to receive us, and hear an explanation of our views and wishes. In a few hours after the conference, the answer of the Governor and Council was received, consenting to recommend to the Assembly a guarantee of the interest of £50,000 of bonds, an immediate grant of fifty square miles of land, a further grant to the same extent on the completion of the telegraph across the ocean, and a payment of £5,000 towards the construction of a bridle path across the island, along the line of the land telegraph. Mr. Cyrus W. Field, thereupon, on the 25th of March, took the return steamer from St. Johns, on his way to New York, in order to fit out a steamer for the service of the company, while his two associates remained in Newfoundland, to obtain the charter and carry out the arrangements with the former company. They continued there nearly five weeks, during which, after many discussions and negotiations, the charter was at length obtained, and the $50,000 of debt of the old company was thereupon paid. The charter was liberal and provident. After declaring that it was 'advisable to establish a line of telegraphic communication between America and Europe, by way of Newfoundland,' it incorporated the associates for fifty years, established perfect equality in respect to corporators and officers, between citizens of the United States and British subjects, allowed the meetings of the stockholders and directors to be held in New York, or in Newfoundland, or in London, conceded the exclusive right to establish a telegraph from the continent of America to Newfoundland, across the ocean, granted fifty square miles of land; and, further, provided that 'so soon as the said company shall have actually established a communication across the Atlantic ocean, by means of a submarine cable or wire from this island, the said company shall receive from the government of this island a grant of fifty square miles of ungranted and unoccupied wilderness land, to be selected by the said company, in addition to the grants hereinbefore mentioned,' a provision subsequently extended, so as to permit the company, to establish the communication by an auxiliary or associate company. In the early part of May, the two gentlemen who had remained behind in Newfoundland rejoined their associates in New York, and there the charter was formally accepted and the company organized. As all the associates had not arrived till Saturday evening, the 6th of May, and as one of them was to leave town on the morning of Monday, it was agreed that we should meet for organization at six o'clock of that day. At that hour they came to my house, and as the first rays of the morning sun streamed into the windows, the formal organization took place. The charter was accepted, the stock subscribed, and the officers chosen. Mr. Cooper, Mr. Taylor, Mr. Field, Mr. Roberts and Mr. White were the first directors. Mr. Cooper was chosen president, Mr. White vice-president, and Mr. Taylor, treasurer. Thus was inaugurated that great enterprise whose completion we celebrate to-day. The plan was formed, the arrangements made, and the work begun. What followed was the execution of the great design. From the 8th of May, 1854, to the 5th of August, 1858, there scarcely passed four years and three months; but they were as fruitful of anxiety and toil as of successful results. The land line across the island of Newfoundland—upwards of four hundred miles —was first to be made. This was a work of incredible labor. The country was for the most part a wilderness of rock and morass, 'a good and traversable bridle road eight feet wide, with bridges of the same width,' had to be made the whole distance; men, materials, and provisions had to be transported first from St. Johns to the heads of the different bays on the southern coast, and afterwards chiefly on men's backs to the line of road. The first year Mr. White, as vice president, directed in person the operations; the second and third years superintendents were sent down. In addition to the land line in Newfoundland, another of one hundred and forty miles in Cape Breton was constructed, and contracts made with companies in Nova Scotia, New Brunswick, Maine, New Hampshire, Massachusetts, Connecticut and New York, to connect their lines with the Newfoundland line. Then there was the submarine line between Newfoundland and Cape Breton, eighty-five miles in length, and another thirteen miles long across Northumberland Straits to Prince Edward Island. To procure these Mr. Cyrus W. Field visited England twice—once in December 1854, and again in January 1856. The first attempt to lay the submarine line across the Gulf of St. Lawrence was made in 1855, and was unsuccessful. A second attempt made the next year succeeded. Thus was completed the chain of Telegraph from New York to the eastern coast of Newfoundland, and the projectors now stood upon the shore of the Atlantic in their progress eastward.

" The whole expense thus far with very trifling exceptions, had fallen upon them—Mr. Cyrus W. Field having made the largest contributions —amounting to more than two hundred thousand dollars in money— and Mr. Cooper, Mr. Taylor and Mr. Roberts each a little less. No other contributors beyond the six original subscribers had come, except Professor Morse, Mr. Robert W. Lowber, Mr. Wilson G. Hunt, and Mr. John W. Brett. The list of directors and officers remains to this day as it was at first, except that Mr. Hunt, as director, has taken the place of Mr. White, who died in 1856, and that Mr. Field is vice president and Mr. Lowber secretary. In all the operations of the company thus far, the various negotiations, the plan of the work, the oversight of its execution, and the correspondence with the officers and others, mainly devolved upon Mr. Cyrus W. Field.

"The greatest and most difficult part of the original design still remained to be executed, and that was the submarine cable from Newfoundland to Ireland. The distance was 1,950 statute miles; the sea was stormy and uncertain; no submarine line of more than three hundred miles had then been attempted. In anticipation of the task now to be undertaken, Mr. Field, on his first visit to England in 1854, had invited manufacturers to furnish him with specimens of cable which they would recommend, and estimates of its cost, and he had entered into correspondence with various persons on the subject. In 1856, he procured an order from our government under which Lieutenant Berryman made soundings of the Atlantic between Newfoundland and Ireland. Lieutenant Berryman sailed on that service on the 18th of July, and the next day Mr. Field sailed for England, having received the formal consent of the company to make arrangements in England for the submarine line, either by a subscription to this company, or by organizing a new company as auxiliary or associated with this. In England he had invited the co-operation of Mr. Brett, a gentleman of great experience, who in 1851 formed a company which had laid the first submarine cable from England to France. He afterwards brought in Mr. Edward O. W. Whitehouse, electrician, and Mr. Charles T. Bright, engineer—both gentlemen of high scientific attainments. These four gentlemen on the 29th of September, 1856, entered into a formal agreement to use their exertions for the formation of a new company, to be called the Atlantic Telegraph Company; the object of which should be 'to continue the existing line of the New York, Newfoundland and London Telegraph Company to Ireland, by making or causing to be made, a submarine telegraph cable for the Atlantic.' This done, Mr. Field issued on the 1st of November, 1856, a circular signed by him, as Vice President of the New York, Newfoundland and London Telegraph Company."

The following is the circular referred to by Mr. Field:

THE ATLANTIC TELEGRAPH.

'Fifteen years have barely elapsed since the success of the first line of electric telegraph demonstrated the immense practical importance of that invention.

'Its rapid adoption by almost every civilized nation, already gives promise of even greater things than it has yet accomplished in the furtherance of social and commercial intercourse.

'It is, however, only within the last five years that practical men have wrought out successfully the application of the same principles to the still later problem of the submarine telegraph.

'Surrounded by every species of difficulty which besets a new and untried path, Mr. Brett, with the aid of a few associates, achieved in 1851 his first success in the electric union of France and England.

'The result of this decisive experiment, favorable alike in its national, commercial, social, and, though last not least, in its remunerative aspects, has been such as to disarm all prejudice, and to encourage a desire for the utmost possible extension of similar undertakings.

'England is now united by six distinct submarine cables to adjacent coasts, and other countries have not been slow to catch her spirit of enterprise in this important application of science to the wants of man.

'America alone, the greatest and most progressive of all the nations with whom we have intercourse, has hitherto been debarred from participating with us in the advantages of electric intercommunication, while the daily increasing requirements of the two nations render such an institution more than ever necessary to the well-being of both.

'The genius of science and the spirit of commerce alike demand, that the obstacles of geographical position and distance alone shall no longer prevent the accomplishment of such a union.

'Under the influence of these considerations, the subject of establishing a telegraph to America has been largely and anxiously studied on both sides of the Atlantic.

'The careful and elaborate investigations of Lieutenant Maury, of the U. S. Navy, into the physical geography of the sea, threw a new light upon what had been supposed to constitute the chief engineering difficulties of such an enterprise. His clear and accurate definition of the currents of the ocean, and the soundings of the Atlantic deeps—imperfectly known previous to his researches—have developed an extraordinary, and, to speak with reverence, a providential fact. The two conditions to be chiefly desired for the successful submersion of a telegraphic cable are, the absence of currents interfering with the steady descent of the line; and a level bottom with a stratum likely to remain undisturbed, and adapted for its subsequent security and preservation. These conditions, though first elucidated for philosophic objects other than those of telegraphic science, have been shown to exist in a remarkable degree throughout a plain extending between the coasts of Ireland and Newfoundland; which possesses the additional advantage of being the shortest possible route between the shores of the Old and New Worlds. So marked, indeed, are those features, and so favorable is their bearing on the great project, that they seemed to the discoverer at the time so providential, as to justify his designation of it as the Telegraph Plateau.

'The mighty current which takes its rise in the Gulf of Mexico, and flows northward as far as the banks of Newfoundland, washes the eastern shores of the United States with great force; and the precipitous hollows existing in its course would render a route to the south of the banks impracticable for telegraphic purposes. Immediately to the north of the great banks these abysses cease to exist. Stretching away in a direct line from St. Johns, Newfoundland, to the bay of Valentia, on the Irish coast, lies the vast sub-oceanic plain already referred to, which is situated in the line of nearly absolute rest of the waters of the Atlantic, the bed of which has been shown, by the specimens obtained on sounding, to consist throughout of the most minute microscopic shells, which, from their delicate organism and the perfect state in which they are found, prove the utter absence of all motion in the water surrounding them. To use the words of the highest authority on the subject,*—" this plateau is not too deep for the cable to sink down and rest upon, and yet not so shallow that currents or icebergs or any abrading force can derange the wire after it is once lodged upon it."

'In April, 1854, a company was incorporated by act of the Colonial Legislature of Newfoundland for the purpose of establishing a line of telegraphic communication between America and Europe. That government evinced the warmest interest in the undertaking, and in order to mark substantially their sense of its importance, and their desire to give to it all the aid and encouragement in their power, they conferred upon it, in addition to important privileges of grants of land and subsidy, the sole and exclusive right of landing telegraphic lines on the shores within their jurisdiction, comprising, in addition to those of Newfoundland, the whole Atlantic coast of Labrador from the entrance of Hudson's Straits to the Straits of Belle Isle. This act of the Colonial Legislature was subsequently ratified and confirmed by Her Majesty's Government at home. The company also obtained in May, 1854, an exclusive charter from the government of Prince Edward's Island, and afterwards from the State of Maine, and a charter for telegraphic operations in Canada.

'The exclusive rights absolutely necessary for the encouragement of an undertaking of this nature, having thus been secured along the only seaboard eligible for the western terminus of a European and American cable, the company in the first instance commenced operations

* Maury's Physical Geography of the Sea, p. 256.

by proceeding to connect St. Johns, Newfoundland, with the widely ramified telegraph system of the British North American provinces and the United States. This has been recently completed by the submersion of two cables in connection with their land lines: one, eighty-five miles in length, under the waters of the Gulf of St. Lawrence, from Cape Ray Cove, Newfoundland, to Ashpee Bay, Cape Breton; the other, of thirteen miles, across the Straits of Northumberland, connecting Prince Edward's Island with New Brunswick. Electric communication is thus established direct from Newfoundland to all the British American Colonies and the United States.

'On the Irish side, lines of telegraph have been for some time in operation throughout the country, and are connected with England and the Continent by submarine cables. The only remaining link in this electric chain, required to connect the two hemispheres by telegraph, is the Atlantic cable.

'The New York, Newfoundland, and London Telegraph Company being desirous that this great undertaking should be established on a broad and national basis, uniting the interests of the telegraph world on both sides of the Atlantic, have entered into alliance with persons of importance and influence in the telegraphic affairs of Great Britain: and in order, at the same time, to obtain the fullest possible information before entering upon the crowning effort of their labors, they have endeavored to concentrate upon the various departments of the undertaking the energies of men of the highest acknowledged standing in their profession, and of others eminently fitted for the work, who were known to have devoted much time and attention to the subject.

'The route between the two shores had already been minutely surveyed by Lieutenant Maury, whose name alone amongst nautical men is a sufficient guarantee for the accuracy of the results obtained, and whose personal counsel and co-operation the promoters are authorized to say will be given to the undertaking in bringing it to completion. The data obtained by him have received the most ample corroboration in the recent special soundings taken by order of the United States Government, at the instance of the New York, Newfoundland, and London Telegraph Company, by Lieutenant Berryman, U. S. steamer "Arctic," whose valuable and able assistance the company wish to acknowledge.

'It is with the highest satisfaction that the company are able to refer to the aid which Her Majesty's Government are inclined to give to their labors. A line of soundings taken at spots intermediate between those effected by Lieutenant Berryman, has been ordered by the Lords of the Admiralty to be made forthwith; and the readiness and cordiality with which every suggestion on the part of the promoters has been met by their Lordships, and by those at the head of the several departments, call for the warmest thanks of all concerned in the undertaking.

'In the engineering department, advantage will again be taken of Lieutenant Maury's invaluable advice in connection with the machinery employed in paying out the cable, and of the co-operation of others who have carried out the submersion of the submarine lines already laid. The soundings of the ocean along the plateau, which gradually increase from 1,000 fathoms to 2,070 fathoms at the middle and deepest part, present no obstacle in depositing a cable with regularity along a soft and almost level plain of such a nature—and the question of submerging a cable in depths almost equal, and under less favorable conditions, has been already surmounted without difficulty.

'In order to determine various points connected with the electrical department of the undertaking, a continued investigation of all the phenomena connected with the use of long submarine circuits has been carried on during the last two years; and Professor Morse, who has recently visited England, has, for many days consecutively, gone into a rigid series of demonstrations on this subject in connection with those gentlemen who have devoted so much energy and patience to this department of the work. He declares his conviction that the problem is conclusively solved, and that the attainment of full commercial success is no longer doubtful.

'It may be mentioned here, that the possibility of readily and rapidly transmitting telegraphic signals beyond a certain distance by submarine wires, had been thrown into some doubt by the discovery of certain phenomena of induction and retardation, described by Professor Faraday.

'In the year 1854, at the instance of Mr. Brett, Mr. Wildman Whitehouse first took up the subject of the effects of induction in long submarine conductors, in its relation to practical telegraphy, by commencing a series of preliminary experiments upon a cable containing 660 miles of submarine wire. In the following year, when the great project of Transatlantic communication came more prominently into view, these experiments were continued more fully on 1,125 miles of similar wire, the results being obtained and recorded with the utmost care and accuracy, by means of apparatus contrived for the purpose, and new both in character and principle. Several facts of the highest importance to electrical science, and of the most encouraging nature as regards the undertaking, were thus determined; and in a still more extended series of experiments this year on 1,020 miles, conducted conjointly by Mr. Whitehouse and Mr. Bright, Engineer to the Magnetic Telegraph Company, these two gentlemen have been enabled to realize and amplify every previous encouraging result, and at the same time to perfect instruments suitable for practical telegraphic use, and capable of working through almost unlimited lengths of submarine wire. The size of the conducting wire required for such distant operations has formed the subject of special inquiry with these gentlemen. They have finally established a claim to the foremost position in the scientific department of the undertaking, by practically demonstrating to Professor Morse and others, on an unbroken length of over 2,000 miles of subterranean wire, the fact of telegraphic operations carried on with an amount of accuracy and at a speed which determines at once the certainty of full commercial success.

'Nothing can be more satisfactory than the result of these experimental demonstrations, which have been verified by Professor Morse,—proving, as they do—First, that telegraphic signals can be transmitted without difficulty through the required distance; Secondly, that a large conducting wire is not required for the purpose; and Thirdly, that the communication can be effected at a thoroughly satisfactory speed.

'All the points having a direct practical bearing on any part of the undertaking have thus been subjected to a close and rigid scrutiny; and the result of this examination proving to be in every respect of the most favorable character, it remained only that those possessing the required power should take the initiative.

'The New York, Newfoundland, and London Telegraph Company, possessing, in virtue of their charter, all the necessary powers, deputed their vice president to visit England in the summer of the present year; and they gave him full authority to make on their behalf such arrangements as should seem to him best fitted to carry forward the great work.

'The outline of the formation of the "Atlantic Telegraph Company" sufficiently explains the nature of these arrangements.

'The expenditure to be incurred in carrying out the undertaking is small, compared with the magnitude and the national importance of the work.

'The Projectors confidently anticipate having the cable completed in time to lay it in the summer of 1857, and under any circumstances, not later than the spring of 1858. It is proposed to employ two steamships in the submersion, each laden with half the cable, and that they shall proceed together to a point half way between the two coasts. The two ends of the cable having been carefully joined together, the vessels will start in opposite directions, one towards Ireland and the other towards Newfoundland, uncoiling the cable and exchanging signals through it from ship to ship as they proceed. By this means, the period ordinarily required for traversing the distance between the two coasts will be lessened by one-half, each vessel having only to cover 820 nautical miles in order to finish the task assigned to it. It is expected that the operation of laying the cable will be completed in about eight days from the time of its commencement.

It is no less fortunate than remarkable that the greatest depth and difficulty will thus be encountered *first;* hence, should any accident occur, it can only involve the loss of a very few miles of cable; this part safely accomplished, the progress of the vessels in the process of submersion will be hourly attended with less and less difficulty and risk.

The grandeur of the undertaking constitutes a sufficient guarantee for its commercial success when carried out; as, in addition to the great use of the cable by the governments on each side of the Atlantic, and in ordinary social intercourse, it will constitute the chief medium through which all the important business transactions between the Old and New World will be effected. The transmission of intelligence for the press in both Continents will also form a most important feature of its usefulness.

It will readily be admitted that the number of messages at present passed along the wires to or from a single capital like London,* where the rapidity of railway transit renders the Post Office a powerful competitor, will scarcely constitute any criterion of the probable amount of traffic through a cable affording the only rapid means of communication between two vast and civilized Continents, and which in its operation will shorten the period of an interchange of correspondence almost from a *month* to an hour, and to which the whole of both networks of telegraph lines, already established throughout Europe and America, amounting to not less than 100,000 miles, will act as feeders. A very limited number of commercial messages forwarded from each side daily, occupying the cable but a few hours, will, without any other sources of revenue, produce a large return on the entire capital.

The difference of longitude between the two Continents presents another important consideration connected with the advantageous working of the line; for, owing to the time in America being nearly five hours later than in Europe, the whole of the business messages of the day transmitted from this side between 10 A.M. and 3 P.M. will have arrived in America by the time the mercantile community in the various

* Not less than 3,000 messages are transmitted in and out of London, and a larger number in and out of New York, daily.

cities and towns throughout the New World have commenced business, and the cable be thus perfectly clear for the return flow of messages to Europe.

Whilst, however, the revenue of such a line must, on the lowest estimate, be exceedingly remunerative, the working expenses, being limited to the two terminal stations, will necessarily be very small. Under such circumstances, it appears difficult to over-estimate the commercial returns that will accrue from this undertaking.

(Signed) CYRUS W. FIELD,
Vice-President of the New York, Newfoundland, and London Telegraph Company.

LONDON,
November 1st, 1856.

" Without waiting for the formation of the new company," continues Mr. Field, " my brother, on behalf of the Newfoundland Company, made application to the British government for its aid in ships and money, and received on the 20th of November a letter from the Treasury, which I am tempted to read, promising ships to assist in laying the cable, and a fixed yearly sum in payment for government messages. He also personally solicited bankers and merchants in London for subscriptions, and, with Mr. Brett, visited Liverpool and Manchester to address public meetings. He subscribed £100,000 towards the capital of £350,000, and Mr. Brett followed with a subscription of £25,000. A day or two after the Treasury letter was received, the subscriptions were closed, when it was found that the applications for stock exceeded the capital by about £30,000, so that on the final allotment Mr. Field had eighty-eight shares and Mr. Brett twelve."

The Treasury letter referred to, reads as follows:

TREASURY CHAMBERS, *November* 20, 1856.

SIR: Having laid before the Lords Commissioners of her Majesty's Treasury your letter of the 13th ultimo, addressed to the Earl of Clarendon, requesting, on behalf of the New York, Newfoundland, and London Telegraph Company, certain privileges and protection in regard to the line of telegraph which it is proposed to establish between Newfoundland and Ireland, I am directed by their lordships to acquaint you that they are prepared to enter into a contract with the said Telegraph Company, based upon the following conditions, viz.:

1. It is understood that the capital required to lay down the line will be (£350,000) three hundred and fifty thousand pounds.

2. Her Majesty's Government engage to furnish the aid of ships to take what soundings may still be considered needful, or to verify those already taken, and favorably to consider any request that may be made to furnish aid by their vessels in laying down the cable.

3. The British Government, from the time of the completion of the line, and so long as it shall continue in working order, undertakes to pay at the rate of (£14,000) fourteen thousand pounds a year, being at the rate of four per cent. on the assumed capital, as a fixed remuneration for the work done on behalf of the Government, in the conveyance outward and homeward of their messages. This payment to continue until the net profits of the company are equal to a dividend of six pounds per cent., when the payment shall be reduced to (£10,000) ten thousand pounds a year, for a period of twenty-five years.

It is, however, understood that if the Government messages in any year shall, at the usual tariff-rate charged to the public, amount to a larger sum, such additional payment shall be made as is equivalent thereto.

4. That the British Government shall have a priority in the conveyance of their messages over all others, subject to the exception only of the Government of the United States, in the event of their entering into an arrangement with the Telegraph Company similar in principle to that of the British Government, in which case the messages of the two Governments shall have priority in the order in which they arrive at the stations.

5. That the tariff of charges shall be fixed with the consent of the Treasury, and shall not be increased, without such consent being obtained, as long at this contract lasts.

I am, sir, your obedient servant,

James Wilson.

Cyrus W. Field, Esq., 37 Jermyn street.

" Too much praise cannot be awarded," continued Mr. David Dudley Field, " to the English government and people for the zeal with which they came forward in answer to the call made upon them. Money was obtained from individuals as freely as it was wanted, and the government outran even the people. (Applause.)

" Returning then to America, Mr. Field, with his American associates, made application to the Government of the United States for aid, similar to that given by the English Government, and he applied to individuals for a participation with him in the stock he had taken. Congress voted the aid requested after a vehement opposition, against which the measure was carried in the Senate by a majority of one. Of the stock twenty-seven shares were taken in the United States."

And here closes the account of the organization of the enterprise. The biographical sketches of the men who were engaged in its successful accomplishment, and the narrative of the expeditions commencing with the first attempt to lay the Newfoundland cable, and ending with the final one on the 5th of August, will be found in the following pages.

THE MEN OF THE ENTERPRISE.

In an undertaking of such magnitude as that which forms the subject of this work, it would be unjust and invidious to give all the credit to any one man, for an enterprise of this kind requires such a combination of rare faculties and varied talents as is rarely, if ever, found in one individual. In the following necessarily brief sketches of the men who played a prominent part in the managerial, the scientific, and nautical departments of the enterprise, the author has endeavored to show their different relations with it, and to present a simple statement of the facts to the public.

CYRUS W. FIELD.

Cyrus West Field was born in Stockbridge, Massachusetts, in November, 1819. His father was the clergyman of that place, and is still living at the advanced age of seventy-eight. His mother is also alive, and although but a few years younger than her husband, is a woman of remarkable energy and vitality, both of which qualities seemed to have been inherited to the fullest extent by the subject of this sketch. In 1853 nearly all their children were assembled beneath the old homestead to celebrate their golden marriage, and among them was Mr. Cyrus W. Field, who had arrived just in time for the purpose from an extended tour in South America. We should have said that all their children, consisting of seven sons and two daughters were present, and a still larger number of grandchildren.

The eldest of the brothers, David Dudley Field, is a lawyer, and occupies a high position at the New York bar.

Matthew D. Field, who is by profession a civil engineer, was a State Senator of Massachusetts, and is now in connection with Major Ripley, late of the U. S. Army, proprietor of a valuable lead mine on the land of the New York, Newfoundland, and London Telegraph Company, within some fifteen miles of Trinity Bay.

Jonathan Edwards Field is a lawyer at Stockbridge, and stands at the head of the bar in his native county. He has also been a State

CYRUS W. FIELD.

Senator, and was at one time nominated for the office of Secretary of State of Massachusetts.

Stephen Johnson Field is now Justice of the Supreme Court of California, and has lately distinguished himself by two dissenting opinions from the court—one in favor of the constitutionality of the law for the observance of the Sabbath, and the other in regard to the Frémont claim.

Another brother, Timothy Field, entered the U. S. navy as a midshipman, and was lost at sea.

Henry Field is a clergyman, and was pastor of a church in St. Louis, and of another in West Springfield, Massachusetts. He is now one of the editors of the New York Evangelist, and a literary man of much ability. A book which he wrote some years ago, entitled, "The Irish Confederates of 1798," is one of his best efforts.

Cyrus W. Field, the subject of this sketch, resolved, when quite a boy, to become a merchant, and with this determination came to New York in 1835, being about sixteen years of age. His brother David Dudley procured him a situation in the store of Mr. A. T. Stewart, with whom he served his apprenticeship. He remained with Mr. Stewart about four years, and when he left the establishment his fellow clerks testified their appreciation of his many good qualities by giving him a dinner, at which were a large number of his friends. Soon after leaving Mr. Stewart he engaged in the manufacture of paper in Westfield, Massachusetts. In 1840, three months before he reached his majority, he married Miss Mary Bryant Stone, of Milford, Connecticut. He remained at Westfield about two years, at the end of which time he returned to New York, and established a paper warehouse, but failed when he had been a comparatively short time in the business. A compromise, however, was obtained with his creditors, and having succeeded in procuring a release from his obligations, he again started in business. This time he was successful, and in 1852 had realized a large fortune. But his creditors were not forgotten, for, having kept a strict account of the balance which he believed was still due, notwithstanding the fact that they had released him from the obligation, he sent each of them a check for the amount. Having amassed a competency for life, he gave up the business to Mr. Stone, his brother-in-law, and started on a tour to South America with Mr. Church, the well-known artist. The first place at which they arrived was Carthagena, at the mouth of the Magdalena River, from which they went to Honda, and thence to Bogota. From Bogota the travellers proceeded across the Andes to Quito on the backs of mules, and from Quito to Guayaquil. At Guayaquil they took the steamer to Panama, and reaching Aspinwall by the shortest route, took passage at once for New York—Mr. Field arriving at home in time for his father's golden wedding.

During the summer of 1854, the death of his brother-in-law, Mr. Stone, rendered it necessary for him to resume his business relations with his former partners, and he once more entered upon the active duties of the establishment which he had left but a comparatively short time before.

Mr. Field's connection with the great work, the successful termination of which has brought him so prominently before the public, commenced in the year 1854, from which time up to the present he has been the very life and soul of the enterprise. As all the facts and details of his connection with both the Newfoundland and Atlantic telegraphs are given in the history of the two companies, it is needless to repeat them here. There are some facts, however, which we cannot avoid giving in detail. In the summer of 1856 Mr. Field arrived at Liveopool en route for London, in order to procure specimens and samples of cable from which to select one for the Atlantic Telegraph Company. In August of the same year, Lieut. Berryman, commanding the Arctic, entered Queenstown, having surveyed and sounded the plateau between Ireland and Newfoundland. As soon as Mr. Field was apprised of it he set out for Cork, and having consulted with Lieut. Berryman, returned to London by way of Milford Haven, Wales. In the cars that started from Milford Haven was Mr. Brunel, the celebrated engineer, whom Mr. Field recognized, and to whom he introduced himself. The subject of conversation was the cable, and in course of it Mr. Field brought forward a portion of the cable submerged in the Gulf of St. Lawrence, the core of which is composed of seven twisted strands, which form the conductor. "Why not have the outer covering of the Atlantic cable formed of twisted strands as well as the conductor," said Mr. Brunel. "By that means you will have a stronger, lighter, and more flexible cable than if you retain the outer covering or armor of solid wire." By one of those strange coincidences that often happen in every-day life, Messrs Glass and Elliott, the well-known gutta percha manufacturers, were also in the cars, and overhearing the conversation, joined in. During a ride of three hundred miles, the party so opportunely thrown together discussed this subject, and the result was an order to Glass and Elliott to manufacture a specimen cable after the plan suggested by Mr. Brunel.

Mr. Field is, as the public are already aware, a man of the most indomitable energy and success; a man who seems to delight in meeting obstacles, that he may have the pleasure of overcoming them. No defeat, no matter how discouraging, disheartens or sways him from his purpose, to which he holds with remarkable tenacity. An illustration of this was presented on the 11th of August, 1857, when the cable parted. The disaster had just occurred when the news spread over the whole ship, creating a most painful excitement. Mr. Field, who had more at stake in the enterprise than any member of the whole company, and who might be supposed to feel the effects of the failure more than any one aboard, proved himself equal to the emergency. Losing no time in vain regrets, he called a meeting at once on board the Niagara, at which Captain Hudson and the commanders of the other ships were present, and it which it was resolved to make a series of experiments in view of the resumption of the undertaking the following October, or in the summer of 1858. These experiments were intended to test the practicability of splicing and laying the cable from mid-ocean, and it is enough to say that they were successful. Having made the arrangements for these experiments and ascertained the amount of cable paid out, Mr. Field started for England on board the Cyclops, one of the British ships of the squadron, and on landing proceeded at once to London. When Mr. Field reached London he found that the news of the failure had got there before him, and the directors and shareholders met him with what it would require a terrible latitude of expression to call encouraging looks. A meeting of the Board was immediately called, at which Mr. Field set forth the prospects and condition of the enterprise, and showed, whatever doubts there might have been, there could be none now regarding its practicability. He infused new hope into the company, and arrangements were immediately entered into to renew the attempt during the present summer. We should state that at this time Mr. Field was simply a director, but at the particular and special request of the company he subsequently accepted the position of general manager. His appointment to this office was made when he was in the United States, and as soon as he secured the consent of the Government giving Mr. Everett, the Chief Engineer of the Niagara, leave of absence, for the purpose of designing and superintending the construction of the paying-out machinery, he returned to England, where he arrived on the 16th of January. But there are some other points which should be mentioned here, showing the nature of Mr. Field's connection with the undertaking. About four years ago, as we have said, he interested himself for the first time in telegraphic enterprises, and with an energy that appears to characterize every thing he undertakes, entered upon this new field. It was through his efforts and the efforts of Mr. David Dudley Field, Mr. Chandler White, Mr. Moses Taylor, Mr. Marshall O. Roberts, and Mr. Peter Cooper, that an association, called the "New York, Newfoundland, and London Telegraph Company," was organized, for the purpose of laying a cable across the Gulf of St. Lawrence, and of connecting with the line which the Atlantic Telegraph Company intended to lay between Europe and America. Mr. Chandler, who was one of the most active and energetic of the early members, has since died, and his place is now occupied by Mr. Wilson G. Hunt, a merchant of high reputation and standing in New York. This latter company had been organized, but the capital was not subscribed. Mr. Field determined, however, that the enterprise should not be delayed on this account, went to England and held meetings in London, Liverpool, Manchester, and other places, where, by his speeches, he created such an enthusiasm, that in the course of a few weeks the whole amount of the stock was taken up. He had previously, in connection with Mr. White and David Dudley Field, as we have stated, obtained a charter from the Colonial Government of Newfoundland, granting the

American Company the exclusive privilege for fifty years of running a telegraph across that island and through any of the adjacent waters In addition to this the company were secured the interest on two hundred and fifty thousand dollars for fifty years, and a present of fifty square miles of land, which they were at liberty to select in any part of the island. Through the efforts of Mr. Field, there were other minor and less substantial marks of favor bestowed upon the company by the Newfoundland government. Charters had been previously granted by the governments of Prince Edward Island and New Brunswick, also giving the company exclusive privileges and benefits. Every thing had been thus favorably settled to prepare the way for the great work of the age. Through the same manager, the governments of the United States and Great Britain were induced to grant the use of six national ships with which to perform the task of submerging the cable. As a proof of the services which were rendered by Mr. Field, from his connection with the great undertaking, it is only necessary to quote the following incontrovertible testimony.

Mr. P. Christopher Bushell, President of the Liverpool Chamber of Commerce, addressing a meeting of the Atlantic Telegraph Company on the 18th of February, 1858, made use of the following language:

"We know that the greatest sacrifices have been made—I think I may say by all the gentlemen connected with this enterprise, especially by the great originator of it, Mr. Cyrus W. Field."

And at the same meeting the following resolution was unanimously adopted:

"*Resolved*, That the warm and hearty thanks of the company be tendered to Mr. Cyrus W. Field, of New York, for the great services he has rendered to the Atlantic Telegraph Company, by his untiring zeal, energy, and devotion from its first formation, and for the great personal talent which he has ever displayed and exerted to the utmost in the advancement of its interests."

In seconding the resolution, Mr. Brooking, the Vice-Chairman, said:

"It is now about a year and a half ago since I had the pleasure of making the acquaintance of my friend Mr. Field. It was he who initiated me into this company, and induced me to take an interest in it from its earliest stage. From that period to the present I have observed in Mr. Field the most determined perseverance, and the exercise of great talent, extraordinary assiduity and diligence, coupled with an amount of fortitude which has seldom been equalled. I have known him cross the Atlantic in the depth of winter, and, within twenty-four hours after his arrival in New York, having ascertained that his presence was necessary in a distant British colony, he has not hesitated at once to direct his course thitherward. That colony is one with which I am intimately acquainted, having resided in it for upwards of twenty years, and am enabled to speak to the hazards and danger which attend a voyage to it in winter. Mr. Field no sooner arrived at New York, in the latter part of December, than he got aboard a steamer for Halifax and proceeded to St. Johns, Newfoundland. In three weeks he accomplished there a very great object for this company. He procured the passing of an Act of the Legislature which has given to our company the right of establishing a footing on those shores, which ere long, I hope, will result in connecting us with Ireland. You have now the right to go on the shores of Newfoundland. Without that right conceded by the Legislature of that island you would not have been enabled to go there; and that right which we have secured is confined exclusively to our company. That is only one of the great acts which Mr. Field has performed with a desire to promote the interests of this great enterprise. (Hear, hear.) I have worked early and late with Mr. Field, and can speak to his diligence with the greatest possible satisfaction: and I feel persuaded that in selecting that gentleman to assist the Directors in the general management of the company there has been imparted into it an element of success which has given to me and to others a large increase of confidence in the result of our undertaking. I have in him and in his judgment every possible faith, and I believe that my colleagues repose equal confidence in his ability."

To this high compliment Mr. Field responded as follows:

"I feel, gentlemen, that I have scarcely time to eat, drink, or sleep, and none to make a speech; but I assure you that all the energy and little talent which God has given me shall be bestowed between now and next June in endeavoring to carry out this enterprise; and it will give me great pleasure, when I am in America, to talk through the cable with any of you upon this side of the Atlantic. (Loud cheers.) Before you separate I hope you will pass one resolution for me—it is a vote of thanks to the directors of this company. I am not a director: but I know something of companies on both sides of the Atlantic, and I may safely say that I never knew a company in which the directors worked so hard, and exhibited so little of selfish motive, as in this. Your Board comprises gentlemen in London, Manchester, Liverpool, and Glasgow, and day after day I have seen almost every member attending the meetings of the directors, not for the sake of putting a guinea a day into their pockets; for they are above that; but from higher motives and loftier considerations. (Cheers.) Your directors have never received a farthing of your money, and I hope that the meeting will unanimously pass a vote of thanks to those gentlemen." (Applause.)

Extract from the Minutes of the Board of Directors, dated January, 27, 1858.

"The Directors having for several months felt that it would greatly advance the interests of this enterprise, if Mr. Cyrus W. Field of New York, could be induced to come over to England, for the purpose of undertaking the general management and supervision of all the various arrangements that would be required to be carried out before the sailing of the next expedition; application was made to Mr. Field, with the view of securing his consent to this proposal, and he arrived in this country on the 16th instant, when it was ascertained that he would be willing if unanimously desired by the Directors, to act in behalf of the Company as proposed, and Mr. Field having retired, it was unanimously resolved to tender him in respect to such services, the sum of £1000 over and above his travelling and other expenses, as remuneration."

Mr. Field declined to accept any thing in compensation for his services, at the same time that he complied with the request of the Company. Whereupon the following resolution was passed:

"*Resolved*, That Mr. Field's kind and generous offer be accepted by this Board; that their best thanks are hereby tendered to him for his devotion to the interests of this undertaking."

Extract from the Proceedings of the Meeting of the Managing Committee, dated at London, 26th of March, 1858.

"*Resolved*, That Mr. Cyrus W. Field, General Manager of the Company, is hereby authorized and empowered to give such directions and orders to the officers composing the staff of the Company, as he may from time to time deem necessary and expedient with regard to all matters connected with the business proceedings of the Company, subject to the control of the Directors."

"*Resolved*, That the Staff of the Company be notified hereof, and required to observe and follow such directions as may be issued by the General Manager."

On the reception in London of the news of the success of the undertaking, the Secretary of the Company, Mr. George Saward, addressed a letter to Mr. Field, from which the following is an extract: "At last the great work is successful. I rejoice at it for the sake of humanity at large. I rejoice at it for the sake of our common nationalities, and last but not least, for your personal sake. I most heartily and sincerely rejoice with you, and congratulate you, upon this happy termination to the trouble and anxiety, the continuous and persevering labor, and never-ceasing and sleepless energy, which the successful accomplishment of this vast and noble enterprise have cost you. Never was man more devoted—never did man's energy better deserve success than yours has done. May you in the bosom of your family reap those rewards of repose and affection, which will be doubly sweet from the reflection, that you return to them after having been under Providence the main and leading principal in conferring a vast and enduring benefit on mankind. If the contemplation of fame has a charm for you, you may well indulge

3

in the reflection, for the name of Cyrus W. Field will now go onward to immortality, as long as that of the Atlantic Telegraph shall be known to mankind." For some time after the return of the fleet from the second unsuccessful expedition, it was doubtful whether another attempt would be made at once or whether the enterprise would be postponed indefinitely. Many of the directors, discouraged by repeated disappointments, were in favor of selling the cable and giving up the idea altogether, rather than risk all their capital by a disastrous failure. A despatch was sent to Mr. Field, at Queenstown, informing him of the feeling prevailing among the directors, and the probability that they would abandon the enterprise. He lost not a moment in indecision, but hastening to London, called together the directors and endeavored to infuse among them his own high hopes and sanguine expectations. One director left the meeting, refusing to take any part in the proceedings; but the other members who were present at last concurred in his views, and gave their sanction to another and final attempt.

PROF. S. F. B. MORSE.

The inventor of the electro-magnetic telegraph is so well known, not only in his own country, but throughout the civilized world, that it would appear almost unnecessary to say any thing further of him than that he acted as electrician on the first Atlantic telegraph expedition. There are, however, some circumstances connected with his invention which are of such particular interest at this time as to justify a relation of them here. Before, however, entering into these, it may be well to state a few facts in connection with the earlier life of Professor Morse. It is not, perhaps, generally known that at the time he invented the magneto-electric telegraph he was engaged in the active pursuit of his profession as an artist, in which he had obtained a high reputation for some original works. He was a sculptor as well as a painter, and his model of the Dying Hercules, which was made in England in the year 1813, gained for him the highest medal of the Adelphi Society of Arts. This model was intended simply as a copy from which to paint his picture of the same subject—a work of art which received at the time the greatest praise, and which was selected from among the first for particular notice by the critics.

Professor Morse left England in the year 1815, having resided in that country about four years, and returned to his native land, where he continued the active pursuit of his profession as an artist. In 1829 he again visited England and remained till 1832, in which year he went home in the ship Sully. It was during the passage in this ship that he first conceived the idea of the electro-magnetic recording telegraph, the invention of which has given him so prominent a place among the great scientific men of the world. Among the passengers on the Sully was Hon. Wm. C. Rives, United States Minister to France, and a number of other gentlemen who have since been the most ardent friends of the Professor. In one of the many social gatherings which took place among the company, a conversation arose in regard to a subject which was at that time extensively discussed among scientific circles—the obtaining of a spark from the electro-magnet, which showed the identity of electricity and magnetism, a fact which had often been supposed to exist, but the existence of which had not been conclusively proved by actual experiments. In the course of conversation the well-known circumstance of Franklin's having caused electricity to pass through three or four miles of wire, for the purpose of measuring its velocity, was related, and it was this particular circumstance which led the Professor to an investigation of the subject, with the view of employing the subtle agent as the messenger of man. He made the observation, that "if electricity can be made visible in any desired part of the circuit, there is no reason why a system of signs could not be devised by which intelligence might be transmitted between distant points." The remark excited little or no attention at the time, but the idea took such firm possession of his mind that he devoted the greatest part of his leisure time to the invention of an instrument by which, what was before but an idea, was to be converted into a fixed fact. The result was the invention of a machine of which an illustration and description are presented on another page. In the year 1835 he exhibited this model to his class of pupils in the New York University, where he had his studio, and gave an explanation of the purpose for which it had been constructed; but it was not till the month of October, 1837, that he entered a caveat at the Patent Office in Washington. This caveat contained a detailed description of the invention. In 1838 he applied to Congress for an appropriation for the erection of a telegraph line between Washington and Baltimore, a distance of thirty miles, the sum required being thirty thousand dollars. The application was before Congress about five years before it was acted upon, and it was not till the month of May, 1844, that the line was in operation. The first message sent over the wire was by Miss Annie Ellsworth, the daughter of the Commissioner of Patents, who had taken an active interest in the passage of the bill granting the appropriation. Miss Ellsworth was the first to convey the intelligence of the fact to the Professor, who had despaired of the passage of the bill that year, as the close of the session was at hand and there was no prospect of its being taken up before the next session. At the last hour, however, it was passed, and the following morning the Professor, who was in ignorance of the circumstance, and was preparing to leave Washington, was informed by Miss Ellsworth of the final success of the application.

"Annie," said he, when she had imparted the welcome tidings—"Annie, the first message that goes over the wires shall be sent by you." And, true to his promise, the first message was sent by her. This corresponded with the high character of the event, and has connected her name with it forever. In answer to the Prefessor's notification, she sent the following as the message which she deemed should be transmitted from Washington to Baltimore:

"What hath God wrought!'

The establishment of this telegraph was soon followed by the construction of others, and from that time to the present they have increased with such rapidity that there are now about forty-five thousand miles in operation in the United States.

In 1838, while the application for an appropriation was pending before Congress, he went to England and applied for a patent for his invention there, but it was denied on the ground that a description of it, as it had been exhibited to his class, was copied from an American into an English publication, and it had thus become public property. It is needless to say any thing further to show the absurdity of such a reason—a mere statement of the grounds upon which the denial was based is sufficient for that. Various claimants have since risen to dispute his right to the invention; but, after a tedious litigation and a display of the most bitter hostility, the justice of his claims has not only been recognized, but his instrument is now almost universally used and acknowledged as the most perfect that has been invented.

It was a matter of regret to all connected with the undertaking, to whom Professor Morse had endeared himself by his many admirable qualities, that he was not on board the Niagara during the final expedition, but he had previously withdrawn from the enterprise. He is now in Europe receiving the well-deserved rewards of his labor from the crowned heads who have thus honored themselves by honoring genius in the person of the inventor of the Electro-Magnetic Telegraph. We cannot better close our sketch of this distinguished gentleman, than by giving descriptions of the first model of his recording machine:

THE FIRST ELECTRO-MAGNETIC RECORDING INSTRUMENT.

The Morse system is based upon the important discovery made by Professor Oersted, of Copenhagen, in the winter of 1819, which laid the foundation of the science of electro-magnetism. He ascertained that when a wire conducting electricity is placed parallel to a magnetic needle properly suspended, the needle will deviate from its natural position, and place itself at right angles with the conducting wire. Other new and important facts were soon after discovered.

The following illustration and description of the model of the first electro-magnetic recording machine, invented by Pro. fessor Morse, possesses much intorest in this connection :

(Fig. 1.) A is a juncture frame, nailed upon a common table to serve for the building up of the machinery. B is a sort of trough simply for sustaining the three drums, C, B, and E.

C is the paper drum, on which the paper is rolled.

E is moved by a cord passing over the little pulley-wheel on the outside of the axle of the second wheel of the clock train of F, and is moved by the train when in motion. F is a clock train of wheels moved by the weight G, and regulated by a fly.

G is the weight passing over a pulley elevated for the purpose of a longer run.

H (figs 1 and 2) is a pendulum lever, having the fulcrum at A, and a limited movement of about a quarter of an inch at the other extremity, which carries a pencil made to be in constant contact with the paper strip passing over the drum D. About half way up on the lever is attached the keeper *d* of an electro-magnet *e*, fixed upon a small bracket from the cross bar of the frame, and on the other side is the fixture for a spring and regulating screw, to retain the lever or withdraw it, when the magnet is not in motion.

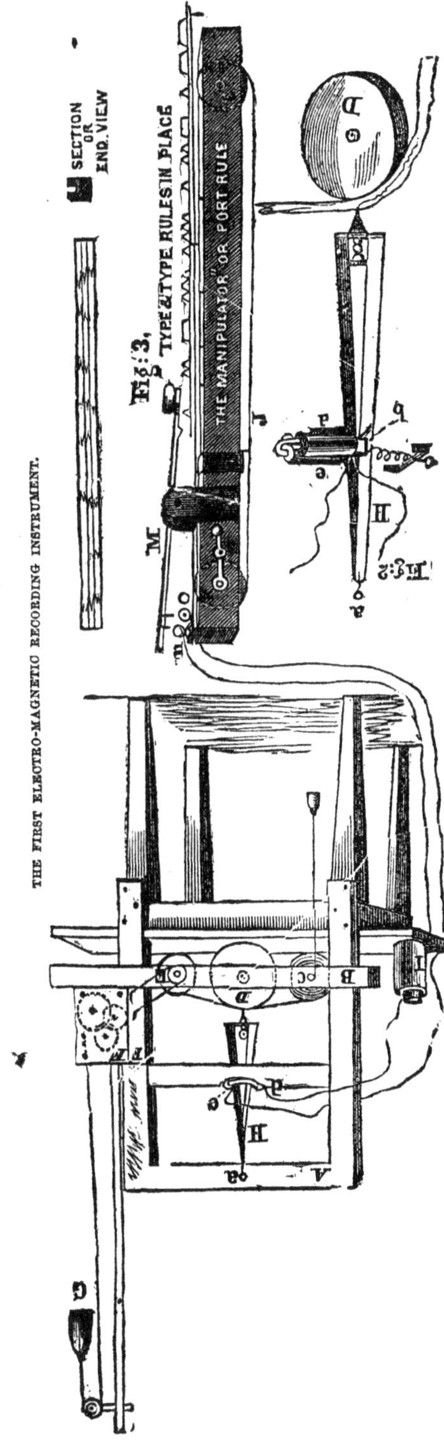

THE FIRST ELECTRO-MAGNETIC RECORDING INSTRUMENT.

I is a galvanic battery of copper and zinc, from one pole of which one end of the conjunctive wire, which is continuous around the electro-magnet forming its helices, is attached. From the other pole the conjunctive wire goes to the mercury cup (fig 3) *n*, at one extremity of the port rule J, while the other end of the conjunctive wire from the electro-magnet goes to the other mercury cup *o*, leaving the only broken part of the circuit of battery I between the two cups *n* and *o*.

J is the port rule (fig. 3) which carries the type rules. The port rule is composed of a contact lever M, whose fulcrum is supported from the sides of the frames, and has upon one end of the lever a forked wire for bridging the broken space between the mercury cups *n* and *o*, and upon the other end a weight, and beneath it a cog.

At each end of the port rule frame is a drum (K and L), carrying an endless band (which was 06.1½ inch carpet binding) whose motion is regulated by the crank and handle K.

Figure 4 is a side view of the rule in which the type were set up, having pins underneath to stick into the endless band; there were many of these made to follow each other by simply placing a second behind the first until the whole message is sent.

Figure 5.

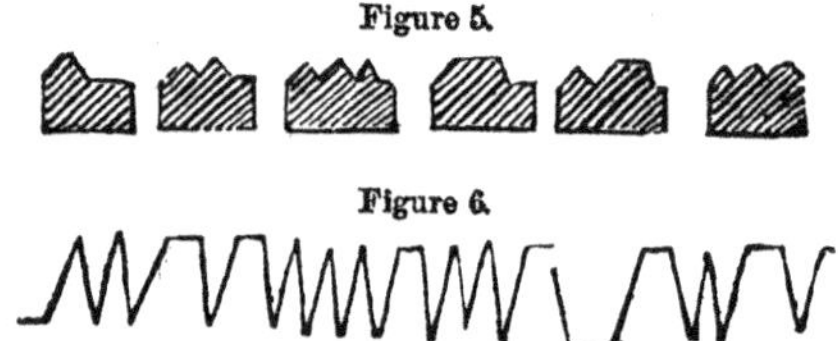

Figure 6.

[The characters in the alphabet that would be marked by the type in the above port rule.]

The clockwork being set in motion by releasing the fly wheel of the clock train, the paper begins slowly to be unrolled from the drum C, over the drum D, and to be rolled upon E, after passing under the pencil which is at the end of the lever H. The lever H has a motion of about one-fourth of an inch at the pencil end; the pencil is held by the spring (see figure 2) on one side (the left) of the paper strip, and while thus held makes a continuous line on that side.

Now, the crank handle, K, of the port rule (figure 3) is turned, and the endless band brings the type rule, with its type, under the cog upon the lever M. The first type lifts the cog and lever, and plunges the fork at the other end into the two cups, N and O, closing the circuit of the battery, I, and charging the magnet, *e*, which, attracting the keeper, *d*, upon the lever H, draws the pencil to the other (right) side of the paper, making a mark across; and now the first type having passed the cog of the lever M, the weight causes the lever to fall, and withdraws the fork from the mercury cups, breaking the circuit and discharging the magnet, leaving the spring again to act and restore the lever H, with its pencil, to its position on the left side of the paper, having in its retreat made another mark across the paper and completed the first character, which is in the form of a V. Thus, by the continuous movement of the port rule, with its type, the forms of the type, whether dots or lines, are similarly marked upon the paper. (An example of the characters thus marked is seen in figure 6.)

This plan and history of the recording telegraph of Prof. Morse is from the evidence in the courts of the United States, proved by several witnesses to have been in operation in 1835. It may well be asked, then, why in every history of the telegraph published in England or elsewhere, this date of 1835 should be ignored, and the injustice towards Prof. Morse perpetrated by constantly giving the date of his invention 1837. He planned it in 1832, and executed it in 1835. The date of the caveat or patent is not the date of the invention, for it will scarcely be maintained that the invention was not made if he had not taken his patent.

Prof. Morse, in 1835, conceived the idea of making an electro-magnet record words by having a steel point fixed to the end of a lever, upon which was attached an armature—the armature, in being attracted by the electric-magnet, to indent paper, which should be drawn forward at an uniform rate of speed. Prof. Morse found himself unable to make use of his instrument for great distances, from the resistance to and dissipation of the electrical current along the conductors. To overcome this difficulty he adopted, in the spring of 1837, a receiving magnet, and a relay or repeating circuit. Prof. Morse made application for a patent in April, 1838, and in December, 1842, Congress appropriated $30,000 for the purpose of testing its practical application. In the month of June, 1844, the instrument was working in an eminently successful manner for a distance of forty miles, between the cities of Baltimore and Washington. Prof. Morse has obtained for his instrument several patents—the first was dated June 20, 1840. This was re-issued January 15, 1846. A second patent was taken out on the 11th of April, 1846. These were both re-issued on the 13th of June, 1848; and another patent, containing improvements, was taken out on the 1st of May, 1849.

MR. WM. E. EVERETT.

The subject of this sketch is a native of Watertown, in the State of New York, and was born on the 17th of April, 1826. He obtained

WILLIAM E. EVERETT.

his present commission as Chief Engineer in the United States Navy at the close of the Mexican war, throughout the whole of which he served both on sea and land. Although but a junior in the service, he was often intrusted in important and responsible positions.

Entering the navy in 1845 as Assistant Engineer, his promotion was very rapid, and he was intrusted with the performance of important and responsible duties by the government. While Assistant Engineer, Mr. Everett served a considerable time under Mr. Haswell, a gentlemen to whom he considers himself much indebted for his proficiency in the science in which he has obtained such an enviable reputation. Mr. Everett was one of the members of the Board of Engineers appointed to examine and report upon the construction of the engines for the six war steamers, of which the Niagara was one. In the beginning of 1857 he received his appointment as Chief Engineer of that vessel, and acted in that capacity during the first Atlantic Telegraph Expedition.

It was while holding this position that he rendered the efficient service to the undertaking that brought his mechanicals kill and ingenuity into such prominence. When it was decided by the committee appointed by Capt. Hudson last year, and consisting of Mr. James H. North, the first Lieutenant of the Niagara, Commander Pennock and Mr. Everett, that there was sufficient space in the ship for the reception of the cable, he (Mr. Everett) contributed largely towards her preparation for the coiling of the great sea line. Subsequently his suggestions, when followed out by the Chief Engineer of the company, were attended with the most satisfactory results. When the cable parted and the vessels returned to Plymouth, he was requested by the directors to make a report in regard to the machinery, and to suggest whatever alterations and improvements he considered necessary to adapt it to the work. In the performance of this task, he called in to his assistance Messrs. Penn, Lloyd and Field, three engineers of distinction in England, with whom he consulted and made a joint report. After this, the Niagara having discharged the remainder of the cable, returned to New York, arriving on the 20th of November, 1857. She was some days after put out of commission, and on the application of Mr. Field, again granted by the government for the renewal of the attempt this summer. From what they had seen and known of Mr. Everett, the company resolved on applying, through the general manager, Mr. Cyrus W. Field, to our government for "the loan" of that gentleman, as an English paper expressed it. The application was not only a high compliment to Mr. Everett personally, but a high compliment to the character of our country. Not only by the expressed desire, but at the earnest solicitation of the Board of Directors, leave of absence was asked for him, that the enterprise might have the advantage of his abilities. The engineering department was to be placed under his direction; he was to draw up the plan of the machinery, and the whole was to be constructed under his supervision. The application being a somewhat unusual one, our government hesitated for some time before granting it, but on due consideration acceded to the request. Mr. Everett obtained the required permission and started for England with Mr. Field, the 6th day of January last, in the Persia, arriving in Liverpool on the 16th of the same month. No time was to be lost. The two proceeded at once to London, where they found that nothing had yet been done towards making the experiments preliminary to the adoption of the required form of machines for paying-out the cable, although it had been explicitly understood before Mr. Everett's departure from England, that the experiments would be announced to him on his arrival. Nothing, however, as we have said, had been done, and he was obliged himself to enter upon the experiments, the results of which were of such consequence. Night and day he worked in the dirty, miserable-looking, out of the way factory, in a dirty, miserable-looking, out of the way place, called Gravel lane, and in some four or five weeks had developed the plan of the admirable machine, copies of which are now on board the Agamemnon and Niagara, and a detailed and illustrated description of which is placed before our readers. The machinery was tested for several days, and at an appointed time a number of the most distinguished engineers of England were invited to its inspection. It is almost needless to state what is already known, that it met with general approval, and that it was decided to be the best adapted to the purpose for which it was designed. About three weeks before the departure of the expedition, it was sent down to Plymouth and put on board both ships, Mr. Everett attending more especially to that which had been designed for the Niagara. The same expedition which had marked the whole work attended its fitting up at Plymouth, where it was also tried with equal success. Mr. Everett having thus far performed the work, was further requested by the company to take charge of the paying-out on the Niagara, as it was impossible for him to superintend it on board of both ships. In the labors incident to this position, he was assisted by Mr. Henry Woodhouse, a gentleman who occupies a distinguished position among the scientific men of England, of which country he is a native.

Before taking charge of the paying-out machinery on the Niagara, Mr. Everett received the following official letter:

ATLANTIC TELEGRAPH COMPANY,
22 Old Broad street, London, April 24, 1858.

DEAR SIR:—As you have now reported to the managing committee that the paying-out machinery for H. M. ship Agamemnon is completed, and that it has been working satisfactorily during the last three days, and that you do not consider any alteration necessary to increase its efficiency; and as another set is required for the United States frigate Niagara, the managing committee have authorized and instructed me to request that you will immediately give directions to Messrs. Easton & Amor to put another set in hand for that ship; and I am further to request that you will continue your supervision over the construction of the machinery, and also undertake to superintend and direct its being properly fixed and fitted on board the Niagara.

I am further instructed to request, that you will take charge of the operation of experimenting upon, and subsequetly of paying out the cable from that ship; in doing which you will have the cooperation of Messrs. Woodhouse, Follansbee, and of such assistant engineers as you may consider it requisite to appropriate to such service. You are also authorized to make such preparations and arrangements as are necessary to enable you to carry out the foregoing instructions.

I remain, yours truly,

GEO. SAWARD, Secretary.

To W. E. Everett.

MR. WOODHOUSE.

Mr. Woodhouse is Assistant Engineer of the Telegraph Company, and was appointed to aid Mr. Everett in the laying of the cable. He was on the first expedition, and has been ever since retained in the service of the company. The work which came under his charge has always been thoroughly performed, and his efficiency and practical talent have rendered him an invaluable *attaché* to the undertaking. Mr. Woodhouse has had a most extensive experience in the work of submerging cables, having being engaged in the business since he laid that across the Black Sea from Varna to Balaklava. He attended more especially this time to the construction of the coils and other work on the Niagara; and it is sufficient to say that he was one of the most efficient officers connected with the company. He was also on the Niagara last year, and, when his services were demanded, was always prompt, self-possessed and efficient.

MR. CANNING.

This gentleman is an English Engineer, and was one of the scientific corps of the expedition of August, 1858, who had charge of the work on the Niagara. Like Mr. Woodhouse, he has had a good deal of experience in the laying of submarine lines, having had the direction and superintendence of the first but unsuccessful attempt to submerge the cable across the Gulf of St. Lawrence, the undertaking having been defeated by a gale. Previous to this, however, he was engaged in connecting Spezzia with Sardinia by a line across the Straits of Bonfacio, and in superintending the union of Prince Edward Island with New

Brunswick by the same means. While in the Niagara, during the expedition of 1857, Mr. Canning was always ready in every emergency, and when the cable surged off the wheel, he succeeded by his quickness in getting it on twice without damage. In the final expedition, he was one of the numerous staff of the Agamemnon, and was among the most energetic and the most skilful.

MR. DE SAUTY

Is one of the most practical electricians in the employment of the company, and has had considerable experience in the working of both land and submarine lines. He was on the Niagara during the first expedition, Dr. Whitehouse having been too unwell to go to sea. Mr. de Sauty has been over six years engaged in telegraphing, the greater portion of which time he devoted his attention more especially to the laying of submarine lines and the construction of those erected on poles. The laying of the submarine cable across the Gulf of St. Lawrence was successfully accomplished under his superintendence—the first attempt, which was made in 1855, under the direction of Mr. Canning, having failed in consequence of a storm, during which they were obliged to cut the cable. Mr. de Sauty is entitled also to the credit of having put down the second Black Sea cable, which connected Varna with Balaklava. We may add that he was the first to employ the Morse instrument in submarine telegraphing. Mr. de Sauty is an Englishman.

MR. CLIFFORD.

Although occupying a comparatively subordinate position, Mr. Clifford is an engineer of great skill and ingenuity, and a draughtsman of more than ordinary ability and acquirements. He was connected with Mr. Everett as an assistant in superintending and forwarding the construction of the present machinery, in which work he rendered material service. The experience which he obtained from his connection with the engineering department of the enterprise during the first expedition was of great advantage to him, as it has proved indeed to all who were then connected with the undertaking. The putting up of the machinery on board the Agamemnon was effected under his direction, and he had partial charge of the laying of the cable from that ship. One of the main features in Mr. Clifford's character is his good, sound practical common sense, to which he appears to subordinate every thing, and which enables him to see things in their right light. Mr. Clifford is also a native of England.

MR. J. C. LAWS

Was at the head of the practical members of the electrical department, and has considerable ingenuity in mechanical matters. Mr. Laws is quite a young man, and has not long commenced his education in the science of electricity, but from the knowledge he has already acquired, he promises to become prominent among the electricians of England. He accompanied the Niagara on the last expedition.

MR. CHAS. T. BRIGHT

Is the Chief Engineer of the company, although he had nothing to do with the construction of the paying-out machinery used in the last expedition. He is a native of England, where he occupies a prominent position among scientific men. He is one of those who joined with Mr. Field in the formation of the Atlantic Telegraph Company, and rendered considerable service to the enterprise in the early stages of its history.

MR. WHITEHOUSE.

This gentleman is one of the principal electricians of the Atlantic Telegraph Company, and has devoted a great deal of time and attention to the submarine telegraph instruments and submarine telegraphing. He was originally a physician, but his devotion to this particular branch of science led him to abandon the practice of his profession, and to apply himself exclusively to electric telegraphing, particularly to experiments, having in view the invention of an instrument, by which to ascertain and register the velocity of electric currents through submarine cables, and the result of which has been the production of a machine, by means of which the possibility of transmitting messages through two thousand five hundred miles has been proved so conclusively, that it has put to rest all doubts that might have been entertained upon the subject. The instrument by which the speed of the "lightning" is calculated, is a triplicate Morse registering machine, upon which marks are made by means of an astronomical clock or pendulum, and by which signals are produced on the entering of the current into and its passage out of the wires, showing the retardation of the last current in going through great lengths. This is accomplished by a pendulum arrangement, beating seconds and making marks on the upper part of a strip of Morse registering paper, the middle marking style or electric pen being connected with the near end of the cable, and the bottom style being connected with the distant end. On a current being sent into the wire, it registers its passage immediately on the middle style, and, coming out of the wire, shows its passage by registering on the lower part of the strip of paper.

PROF. THOMPSON

Is a native of Scotland, and a man of high scientific attainments. He has devoted many years to the science of telegraphing, in which he has made some improvements. Prof. Thompson was at the head of the Electrical corps on the Agamemnon during the second and third expeditions. He is one of the Directors of the Company.

MR. J. W. BRETT.

From the prominent part this gentleman has played in the organization of submarine telegraph companies, he is known in England as the father or founder of them. This is in fact his great forte, and the many successful companies which have been established through his instrumentality is the strongest proof that can be presented of his ability in this important department. He obtained the first privilege from the French government of landing a cable on the shores of France, and connecting that country with England. He was present at the making and laying of it down, and assisted in the establishment of the Dover and Ostend, the Dover and Calais, the Spezzia and Corsica, the Sardinia and Corsica, and other lines of which he was mainly the originator. He was specially interested in the success of the Atlantic Telegraph, being one of the original projectors of the company.

MR. APPOLD

Is the inventor of the brakes, which have been so modified by Mr. Everett as to adapt them to the paying-out machine. He is an amateur mechanic, and possesses more than ordinary inventive powers. Having plenty of money, plenty of time, and nothing else to do, he occupies himself mostly in experiments of a mechanical nature. Mechanics are his hobby, and a machine shop has attractions for him that are irresistible. He is always inventing something, and is never satisfied except when working with iron. In fact this feature in his character is carried to such an excess as to become an eccentricity. His own house is full of evidences, of his peculiar inclinations. By some peculiar contrivance every gas burner is lit at the same time, and every window shutter closes with a simultaneous bang. These are but a few of the achievements of his genius when applied to domestic purposes, and his outdoor triumphs in the display of his inventive faculties are no less remarkable.

CAPTAIN W. L. HUDSON.

THE CAPTAIN OF THE NIAGARA.

Captain W. L. Hudson is already well known to our readers on account of the prominent part he played in the first expedition, and the important service he rendered on one occasion in saving the cable. Throughout the whole undertaking he took a most active interest in every thing that tended to promote its success. On the memorable evening of the 7th of August, 1857, when it seemed almost impossible to save the cable from slipping overboard after it had parted, and when the then chief engineer, Mr. Bright, had made no provision to meet such an emergency, he held the broken end on board for an hour with a hawser, until the splice was effected, and the work of paying-out could be resumed. Captain Hudson is one of the oldest and most respected officers of the American navy, and enjoys a high reputation for his abilities and judgment as a seaman, which are said to be of the first order.

During the forty-two years which he spent in the service of his country he was noted for his probity of character and true benevolence of heart. He has a high sense of the responsibilities which his position devolves upon him, and endeavors to meet them as an honest man should. During the terrible cholera year of 1832 he was a resident of Brooklyn. Seeing the fearful extent of its ravages—that it was impossible by ordinary means to keep it in check, and believing that it was the duty of every man to do all in his power towards the relief of the sufferers—he devoted himself to the noble work of attending on the sick. In this heroic task he was assisted by Mayor Hall, of Brooklyn, Bishop McIlvaine, and two other gentlemen. This committee of five would sally out every day to find out new objects for their assistance, and in their search would enter such houses as were inhabited by the poorer classes, who they rightfully supposed were most in need of their aid. If they found any of the occupants afflicted with the cholera they had them removed to the hospital or attended by a physician at their own homes. Each day the captain and the other members of the committee would visit their patients, note their condition, and when any of them died, see that the last rites were properly performed. At that time blood-letting was practised to some extent as a remedial measure; but as it was found to terminate fatally in many cases, it was abandoned. The Visiting Committee were, it is understood, among the first to adopt the use of ice, which was generally successful. Captain Hudson was never in active service, but who imagines that his claims to courage or heroism want higher evidence than what we have given? He was promoted to the position of Post Captain by the late Retiring Board, having served through all the grades. When the pirates of the Grecian Archipelago had become so bold and audacious in their depredations upon American commerce as to call for determined and prompt action on the part of our government, he occupied the post of sailing master on board the sloop of war Warren. After this he made a four years' cruise in the Peacock, one of the vessels of the Exploring Expedition under Commodore Wilkes, which was subsequently lost in the quicksands of Columbia river. Not a soul on board, however, was lost. While on this cruise the Peacock was placed in many a perilous position, and on several occasions would inevitably have been wrecked amid the ice but for the coolness, self-possession and seamanship of her commander. Previous to his taking command of the Niagara, Captain Hudson held the post of Commander of the Brooklyn Navy Yard, which he occupied over six years.

THE CAPTAIN OF THE AGAMEMNON.

A change took place in the command of the Agamemnon since 1857, her former commander, Mr. Noddall, having been recently appointed to another post. The gentleman who now occupies this responsible position is George W. Preedy, who holds the rank of Post Captain, and who is some twenty odd years younger than Captain Hudson. The difference in age and yet the quality in rank in both these cases is explained by the fact that while in our service seniority is almost always the only rule for promotion, favoritism, and distinction in service of any consequence, generally leads to elevation in rank in the British navy. The difference in the ages of the two Post Captains need not therefore be a subject of astonishment. Captain Preedy has served over twenty years in the British navy, and is now about that middle age which those who profess to know every thing about the matter—and who, it is to be hoped, are fully informed—say that a man is in full possession of all his physical and mental powers. The age is fixed somewhere between forty and forty-five, the very summit of the hill, which is always regarded as an emblem or figure of life. The captain of the Agamemnon was in the Baltic fleet during the Russian war, and served in the capacity of commander on board the Duke of Wellington, one of the largest propellers in the English navy. He is regarded in the service to which he belongs as an admirable seaman and navigator, independent of which his many fine qualities as a man have acquired for him a well deserved popularity. He takes a special pride in the work to which he has been appointed, and to which his qualifications as a commander have been one of his principal recommendations.

During the fearful gale of eight days which overtook the telegraph squadron while on their way to mid ocean, his ship was placed in imminent peril. There never was an occasion that required more coolness and self-possession, and Captain Preedy proved himself fully equal to the emergency. For eight long and anxious days and nights she was buffeted by the fierce storm, but the gallant captain and his brave officers battled with it to the end, and saved their ship and its precious freight in the midst of dangers that might well appal the stoutest hearts. All honor to the heroic commander and to the gallant officers and crew who so nobly seconded his efforts.

THE CAPTAIN OF THE GORGON.

The British Admiralty have certainly shown a great deal of judgment in the appointment of the commander of the Gorgon. It was a matter of some importance to the Atlantic Telegraph Company that this officer should be assigned to the post, in consequence of the prominent part he performed last year. He rendered important service by soundings which he took on the plateau, and the new sources of information which he opened to scientific investigation. In the report which he made of the work, he has shown himself to be a man of extensive acquirements and of a liberal and generous mind—a character which is rarely met with, and is, therefore, the more to be prized. After referring in a modest and moderate manner to the way in which he acquitted himself of the task he was intrusted with, he speaks of his indebtedness to Lieut. Brook and the use of his "ingenious sounding apparatus;" alludes to the assistance he obtained from his own officers in complimentary terms, and acknowledges the aid he received from the mechanics in the preparation of the machinery for the work. It was Commander Dayman, it may be remembered, who made the sounding at the time the cable broke in August, 1857, and reported the depth at 1,950 fathoms. Soon after his return and the presentation of his report he was promoted from the rank of lieutenant to that of commander, and still further rewarded by being appointed to the command of one of the vessels detached for the expedition. Exclusive of the service which he has performed in connection with the present enterprise, he is looked upon as one of the most accomplished officers in the British navy, and is reputed to be a gentleman of very fine scientific attainments. The result of his soundings on the plateau are very clearly set forth in his report, which is an unpretending, unaffected statement of all the details. He is the only one of the English commanders of last year's expedition who has been reappointed.

CAPTAIN W. C. ALDHAM.

This gentleman is the captain of her Majesty's steamship Valorous, which accompanied the Agamemnon while laying the cable. He is considered one of the most efficient officers in the British navy, and is a general favorite among all who know him in the service.

CAPTAIN HENRY C. OTTER

Is one of the junior Post Captains of the British navy, being about forty years of age. He commanded one of the surveying steamers in the Baltic during the Russian war. He has but recently been assigned the command of the Porcupine, which is one of the smallest steamers in the English navy. Captain Otter met the Niagara while on her way up Trinity Bay, and piloted her up the Bay of Bulls Arm, the landing place of the cable.

THE NEWFOUNDLAND SUBMARINE TELEGRAPH.

THE AUXILIARY TO THE ATLANTIC LINE.

The laying of the submarine cable across the Gulf of St. Lawrence would have been accomplished in August, 1855, but for a most unfortunate accident, or rather series of accidents, which postponed the completion of the work for another year. The steamer James Adger was chartered by the New York, Newfoundland, and London Telegraph Company to tow the vessel in which the cable was coiled, and which it was supposed was then awaiting her arrival at Port au Basque, a small fishing village on the southern coast of Newfoundland. The James Adger left New York at ten o'clock on the morning of the 7th of August, and as it was intended by the Company that the voyage should be one of pleasure as well as business, they invited a large party of their friends, to whom we shall without further ceremony introduce our readers:— Peter Cooper, Mrs. Cooper, Prof. S. F. B. Morse, Mrs. Morse, Master A. B. Morse, Cyrus W. Field, James S. Sluyter, Robert W. Lowber, Mrs. R. W. Lowber, Miss Ann Redfield, Rev. Gardiner Spring, Rev. D. D. Field, Rev. H. M. Field, Miss Gracie Field, Miss Alice Field, Miss Allen L. Herndon, Dr. Lewis A. Sayre, Mrs. Lewis A. Sayre, David A. Sayre, Wm. M. Swain, Master W. J. Swain, John Thornley, Prof. F. Sheppard, Bayard Taylor, Miss Lizzie Alger, John Conger, Rev. J. M. Sherwood, Mrs. Ann Palmer, Mrs. Edward D. Jones, Miss Mary Sterns, Marshall Brewer, F. N. Gisbourne, Chas. T. Middlebrook, John Mullaly, T. W. Strong, D. C. Hitchcock, S. A. Richards, B. F. Ely, H. W. Barron, Geo. H. Brown, A. A. Raven, F. O'Brien, F. H. Palmer, J. P. Palmer, Chas. J. Smith, Dr. P. A. Bruyere, John G. Kip, Chas. H. Houghton, J. W. Kennedy, Francis Winton, L. P. Palmer, Joseph Jones, Miss Cooper, Robert Russell.

The weather on the morning of which we have spoken was all that could be desired; the sun shone out in an almost cloudless sky, and the light breeze that rippled the surface of the water served only to moderate the intensity of the summer's heat. Every thing seemed to favor the enterprise, and the crowd that thronged the deck of the steamer were buoyant with bright and hopeful anticipations of the future. There was an unusual bustle on Pier No. 4, North River, that morning; carriages came dashing down with heavy luggage and light-hearted passengers; every body was in every body else's way; people stood upon each other's toes, and, strange to say, smiled good humoredly; porters with atlantean shoulders carried off trunks and portmanteaus of all imaginable shapes and sizes, and deposited them in the most out-of-the-way places; newsboys were eagerly soliciting customers for the morning papers; venders of light literature were loud in their praises of "the Blood-red Avenger," "The Desperate Burglar, or the Miser's Fate," "The Bandit's Cave, or the Robber's Oath," and a host of other works equally taking and terrible; friends congratulated friends, and wished each other a happy voyage and safe return; scientific men looked graver and more important than ever, and pronounced their opinion for the hundredth time how "that cable" should be laid; and loud above the din and bustle and confusion rose the shrill whistle of the steam-pipe, announcing that the moment of departure was near.

"Let go that hawser there," shouted several of the hands as they made ready to start, and the passengers, who had till this time been in complete possession of the deck, at once gave way. Then there was a general shaking of hands, "a hurrying to and fro," the last passenger arrived on board after losing his hat and cane in his desperate struggle to be in time, the last rope was unfastened, the steam whistle gave out its last warning note, every body was told for the last time to "look out," and the James Adger commenced slowly moving out into the river. Three hearty cheers greeted her as she swung loose from the pier, and were repeated again and again as we swept past. A salute of three guns was fired from her bow, which was responded to by another from one of Spofford & Tileston's Steamers, and the United States frigate Potomac honored the company and the enterprise in which they were engaged, as far as the strict rules of the Navy allowed, by running up the Stars and Stripes to her peak. Again and again we were cheered by our friends who crowded the end of the pier, until only the faint echo of their voices could be heard, and again and again we responded with a rivalry of friendship that was determined not to be outdone.

We were soon under full headway down the bay, and in a few minutes our friends became indistinguishable in the lengthening distance. The last we saw of them was through a telescope, and there they still stood at the end of the pier waving their adieus. Gradually we lost sight of the large public buildings, and then the city itself began to disappear below the horizon. And now we have left Staten Island behind us, and sweeping past Nevisink are out upon the open sea.

Our first night on the water was marked by a grand display of celestial pyrotechnics that illuminated the whole heavens, and converted the liquid element through which we ploughed our way into an ocean of fire. It appeared as if the powers of the air had determined to signalize our mission, and they did so in a peculiarly appropriate manner. The scene was one of those which could never be forgotten. During the evening an electric machine was brought upon the upper deck, and it was there when the night set in. Beside it sat Professor Morse, its inventor, who had been explaining the principle of its construction to the company but a few hours before. Here and there were little groups, some on the bow, some on the wheel-house, and others scattered about the deck enjoying themselves in pleasant social intercourse. The sweet music of woman's voice singing some favorite melody gave a new attraction to the scene. At first the lightning flashed in broad sheets along the horizon, then rapidly extending towards the zenith it lit up the sky with an almost dazzling brilliancy. From behind the dense heavy masses of black clouds that hung on the ocean's verge were flung, as if by unseen hands, huge balls of fire that left a track of flame to mark their course along the heavens. At intervals gigantic fiery serpents darted from their place of ambush, writhing and twisting in their tortuous way through the ebon vault above, and then again all was dark as midnight. Gradually the clouds spread over the sky, shutting out the pale and twinkling light of the stars, and the flashes of lightning became more vivid and more frequent until the whole heavens was one mass of flame. For two hours we gazed on this magnificent spectacle, until the heavy drops of rain warned us of the coming storm and drove us unwillingly to seek shelter from its fury.

That night we had a concert in the after cabin at which every body was present, and in which all who had voice for music and some who had not, joined. Some of the best airs from Robert Le Diable, and other popular operas, were sung with the most exquisite taste by one of our lady passengers, and then, to give variety to the entertainment, we had the choicest selection from Negro Minstrelsy. "Robert toi que j'aime," was followed by the "Dandy Broadway Swell;" and "The Colored Fancy Ball," shared the applause with "Come per me Sereno." The sailor's farewell to his lady-love was sung by a votary of the comic muse, and although evidently a pathetic subject, and one in which the aforesaid fair one and her "galliant" lover claimed the sympathy of the hearers, the tale of their distress was heard with the most unfeeling indifference, and the end of each verse was the signal for an outburst of laughter. This from a company, too, that should have known better was, as Dogberry says, "most tolerable and not to be endured." There was one portion of the song which in justice to the composer we must quote, as it is in its way a perfect gem, and will serve to show the reader at a glance the sad plight of the lovers:

> "While you are on your shentle bed ashleepin' fast ashleep,
> Zen we poor jolly sailors are ploughing on ze zeep."

The reader will perceive from this that the song is slightly foreign, and that "the Sweet German accent" is one of its most attractive features.

But the concert like all other sublunary things had an end, and all retired for the night to dream over the pleasing scenes and incidents of the day. The strains of music gradually died away, the merry laughter of the gay and light-hearted company was hushed, and the only sounds that broke the stillness of the night were the monotonous dash of the waves and the ceaseless din and clangor of the mighty machinery.

Early on Sunday morning, the 12th of August, we came within sight of Newfoundland, and as may be supposed, there was considerable excitement on board. There it lay like a dark cloud on the horizon, and there were sage speculations among those who professed to be learned in nautical matters, as to whether it was really a cloud or the Island itself. Grave arguments were held on the subject, always terminating, however, with the unsatisfactory conclusion of "wait and you'll see," which we all philosophically concluded to do, as it was the only course left. Gradually the cloudy indistinctness of the land disappeared, and as the more prominent points of the coast became visible, not a soul could be found who didn't believe it was real, genuine, *bona fide* terra firma from the very commencement. About five hours before we reached Port au Basque, where it was expected we would find the Cable Ship, the bold promontory of Cape Ray, which is the extreme south-western limit of Newfoundland, was visible from the deck of the steamer. All the telescopes on board were brought into requisition, opera glasses were in great demand, and those who were not so fortunate as to possess either, strained their eyes looking through spectacles and spy-glasses in the vain hope that they would see something like a ship twenty miles off, and firmly believing that that ship when found would be the very one we were in search of. We could perceive the fishermen's huts when within a distance of eight or ten miles, but no vessel except a few fishing smacks greeted our anxious gaze. It was suggested that as a portion of the harbor was hidden from the view by high rocks, she might not be visible from sea; but even that hope was dispelled when we arrived at its entrance. Two schooners were lying at anchor there, but the Cable Ship had not made her appearance, although they were expecting her arrival over two weeks. A vessel was seen on the morning of Saturday answering to the description of our ship standing off Port au Basque; it was blowing so hard, however, and the wind was so adverse, that she was obliged to put to sea again.

This was a great disappointment, as the weather was most favorable for the laying of the cable, and as we intended to begin work at the earliest hour on Monday morning. In this dilemma we could do nothing but either await the arrival of the Sarah L. Bryant, or go direct to St. Johns, which we intended to visit before our return to New York, pay our respects while there to the authorities of Newfoundland, and after a brief stay, call at Port au Basque again, where it was confidently expected we would find the object of our search if she had not foundered at sea. We lay outside the harbor three or four hours to land some articles which were required in the construction of the telegraph at that point. Some of the members of the Company went ashore, where they were met by Mr. Canning, an experienced engineer from London, who was engaged to superintend the laying of the cable. He confirmed what we had heard about a vessel having been seen off the coast the day before.

As our stay here was very brief, and as many of us only saw the land from the deck of our steamer, we could form no correct idea of its character. It had a wild, bleak and inhospitable look, however, and the account that our pilot, who had visited it frequently, gave us of it was any thing but pleasing. It was, he said, nothing but rock and bog, interspersed here and there with deep holes and quagmires, which, he jocularly informed us, it would be much easier to get into than to get out of. But after all, the majestic hills that towered to the height of fifteen hundred feet above the ocean, the huge masses of rocks that lined the coast, and the restless sea, whose waves broke in foam at their feet, imparted to the scene a sublimity that all the bogs and quagmires and holes could not affect.

The greater portion of the southern coast of Newfoundland was visible from the deck of our steamer during nearly the whole period of our passage from Port au Basque to St. Johns. The character of the coast scenery was the same throughout, presenting to the eye of the voyager nothing but bold rugged cliffs, which in some places rose precipitously out of the water to the height of three or four hundred feet. On the morning of the 14th of August, about seven o'clock, we were within a few miles of our place of destination. Every body was up early, for we had heard so much of the harbor of St. Johns and the approach to it, that we determined to see all that was to be seen.

The morning of our arrival, unfortunately, was rainy, and, as may be supposed, the city did not appear to the best advantage; but the grandeur of the surrounding scenery, and especially that of the coast, more than made up for the annoyance we felt in consequence of the weather. The island is protected on the east by the same bold mountainous line of coast which we had observed all along its southern extremity. Steep rocks rise to the height of seven and eight hundred feet almost perpendicularly out of the water, which is so deep that the largest vessel might pass alongside within a few feet with perfect safety. In some places their front is scarred by deep seams which extend from their very summits, not unfrequently terminating in huge caves at their base. We felt the strongest curiosity to enter some of these, and make explorations in their hidden recesses, but had no opportunity of doing so, and were obliged to leave without gratifying our desire. They were just such caves as we had read of long ago in our days of novel reading, recalling to mind the thrilling adventures of pirates and smugglers, with their long, low, black schooners.

ENTRANCE TO ST. JOHN'S, N. F.

The entrance into the harbor is so concealed from the view at sea, that we could not perceive it till within a distance of half a mile. On the right rises Signal Hill, to a height of at least six hundred feet, overlooking the town, and commanding a fine view of the country, which extends behind it like a gigantic panorama. The summit of this hill is crowned with a fortification, and at its base is another, neither of which, in their present condition, would be capable of resisting a well sustained attack by sea and land. The entrance or Narrows, as it is called, is, however, well defended by other forts, and in the last war, it was protected by an immense iron chain extending across and fastened to the rocks on either side. The marks left by drilling holes in the rocks are still visible, as are also the remains of an old cannon and anchor which had served as holdfasts for the chain. Opposite Signal Hill, on the other side of the Narrows, rises another hill, or mountain, as it should more properly be termed, to an elevation above the level of the water of over six hundred feet. On the other side of this, and about one hundred and fifty feet from its base, another fort has been erected, in the centre of which stands the light-house. While passing this point we were hailed by a soldier, who inquired where we were from, and how many days we were out, and having answered him, we gave the good people of St. Johns notice of our approach with a thundering salute that was repeated a hundred times by the echoing hills. The Narrows is about a third of a mile in length, while it varies in width from three to fifteen hundred yards, and was doubtless formed in one of those terrible convulsions to which the whole island seems to have been subjected, and to which it probably owes its origin. It appeared as if the mountain had been torn apart, leaving a safe passage open to the harbor. The city is built on the side of a hill that ascends gradually to a height of about a hundred and fifty feet, and presents an exceedingly picturesque appearance. It overlooks the harbor, which is a little over a mile in length, and a quarter of a mile in width; and which is one of the best in the world, affording at all times a safe anchorage for ships of the largest dimensions. The first thing that strikes the visitor is its peculiar formation. After you have passed the entrance it has the appearance of a lake, so completely is it shut in from the ocean. Gigantic hills tower above you on every side, except that on which the city stands, and on their rough and rugged declivities little patches of gardens have been made by the more industrious of the fishermen, whose cottages help to subdue the natural wildness of the scene. Near the water's edge, and all around the harbor, are erected the stages or "flakes" as they are termed, on which the codfish are cured.

The town of St. Johns has no public buildings that can lay claim to architectural pretensions, with the exception of the Catholic Cathedral, which is a large and imposing edifice, built in the style of the Roman Basilica, and capable of holding ten thousand persons, or little less than half the population of the whole city. It cost about five hundred thousand dollars, and has several fine pieces of sculpture, among which are two or three of the best productions of Hogan, the celebrated Irish sculptor.

The Colonial Building, as the structure in which the legislative business of the Island is transacted is called, was built a few years ago at an expense of about two hundred thousand dollars. It is a square granite building, two stories high, with a large portico in front, supported by six Ionic pillars. It contains the chambers of the two legislative branches, the House of Assembly and the Legislative Council, besides the library and a number of smaller apartments. A short distance from the Colonial Building is the Governor's house, in which Chas. H. Darling, the then Governor of the Island, resided. The country around St. Johns is remarkable for the diversity as well as the beauty of its scenery. In the afternoon of the day on which we arrived, a party of us enjoyed the luxury of a ride along an exquisite little valley called the Vale of Riverhead. The roads, which branch out in every direction from the city are, without the least exaggeration, among the finest in the world; and Topsail Road, which runs along the side of one of the hills that form the boundary of this valley, affords one of the most delightful drives in this part of the country. As you ascend the more elevated parts of it you can see the whole town of St. Johns, the harbor which lies at its feet, and the lofty crest of Gibbet and Signal Hills, towering in the more remote distance, beyond which the deep blue of the Atlantic is visible through the huge gaps of the coast mountains. Below you, almost at your feet, lies the Vale of Riverhead, forming in its quiet beauty a marked contrast with the wild mountain scenery by which it is surrounded. A small stream fed by tiny rivulets from the rough sides of the mountains pours its clear waters through the centre of the valley, making sweet music as it sweeps sparkling over its rocky bed. In some places its course is broken by miniature cascades, that glitter like a shower of diamonds in the warm sunlight, while in others it is almost wholly concealed from the sight by overhanging trees, beneath whose shade its waters become black as midnight. It is a trout stream too—just such a one as Walton would have delighted to angle in. Beautiful little cottages dot its banks, and here and there may be seen, through the jealous foliage that clings around them, the more imposing mansions of the wealthier inhabitants of St. Johns. It is a lovely scene, and might have tempted a less ardent admirer of the beauties of nature than we professed to be, to linger a few weeks among its attractions. But necessity—"stern necessity," as the poet calls it—interposes: the cable must be laid, and in a few days more the charming Vale of Riverhead will be lost to our view, perhaps forever.

Saturday, the 18th, was the day fixed for our departure, but still we were unwilling to leave till we had made some return for the hospitality we had received from the people of St. Johns. The Company, therefore, invited over two hundred of the principal inhabitants of the city on an excursion about ten miles outside the harbor; and about twelve o'clock we set out with one of the most pleasant and sociable parties that was ever collected on the deck of a steamer. The day was as fine as could be desired, and the scenery of the coast magnificent. We saw the "Spouting Rock" as it is called, which is one of the greatest natural curiosities in the island, and, perhaps, in the world. The rock itself is not more than thirty feet above the surface of the water, and has a cavity in its centre which runs through it to the base, and which is from six to seven feet in diameter. A small stream of fresh water flows from an overhanging hill into this cavity, and when the tide is out finds its way through an opening in the rock into the sea. When the tide is coming in the waves rush with such force into this hole as to throw the fresh water in the cavity to a height of twenty, and sometimes forty feet.

SPOUTING ROCK, NEAR ST. JOHNS.

After a pleasant trip of two or three hours along the coast we returned with our guests to the harbor, where we parted with many mutual regrets. Cheer after cheer was given and returned, handkerchiefs were waved, and when we could hear each other no longer, the cannon thundured out our adieus. While passing through the narrows, Mr. Huested, who was engaged by the Company to blast the Merlin Rock, which lay right in the way of vessels entering the harbor, and which was very dangerous to those of the largest class, got up a grand submarine explosion for our especial entertainment. We had hardly passed over the rock when the explosion took place, throwing up a vast body of water to the height of sixty or seventy feet, and shaking the mountains on either side like an earthquake. Our vessel trembled with the concussion, and the spray fell in a shower upon the deck, sprinkling a number of our passengers, to the great amusement of those who escaped. On clearing the Narrows a parting salute was given as our bow turned in the direction of Port au Basque, where we expected to find the Sarah L. Bryant awaiting our return.

About five o'clock on the morning of the 20th of August, we came within sight of Cape Ray, and about seven o'clock were sufficiently near to Port au Basque to discern objects through the telescope. Some of our company went aloft, and gave us the cheering intelligence that they saw a large vessel lying behind the high rocks which protected the entrance to the harbor, but we were afraid to hope lest we should be doomed to a second disappointment. There was no doubt, however, as to a vessel being there, for she had been seen also through the telescope; but it was confidently believed by some that it would prove to be the French frigate, Iphigenie, which, it was said, took a northern course after leaving Halifax. In fact, every one, even the most sanguine, feared to hope. While we were speculating on the probability of its being the Sarah L. Bryant, a small row boat was observed approaching our steamer and in less than half an hour we were within hailing distance. Among those in it was Mr. Sluyter, the captain of the Victoria, which could also be seen lying in the harbor. Mr. Field, who, with several others, was on the bow of the steamer anxiously awaiting their approach, now hailed them.

HARBOR OF PORT AU BASQUE.

"Has the bark arrived?" he cried out, in a stentorian voice.

A wave of the hat was the only reply; but it was enough, and one wild, enthusiastic hurra broke from those on board the James Adger.

"Hold on, hold on," said Mr. Field, "wait till we are certain."

Then repeating his question, he was answered in the affirmative. The company were all impatience to give vent to their enthusiasm, but they restrained their feelings for a few moments longer.

"When did she arrive?" he asked.

"On Wednesday," was the reply.

This was sufficient, we were amply repaid for the anxiety we suffered, and three such cheers as followed the glad tidings has seldom been heard. After all, we had not come from New York on a fruitless errand, and we would yet, if favored a little longer, be enabled to lay the cable which is to be the first link in connecting the Old World with the New, and bringing the people of both continents into instant communication with each other. After all, we could tell our friends on our return that we had accomplished the great undertaking, and that the first important submarine telegraph had been laid on this side of the Atlantic.

We had now reached the entrance to the harbor, and could distinctly see the masts of the long expected vessel towering above the rocks, with the stars and stripes flying from her mizzen peak. In a few minutes more we gave her a salute from our cannon, and ere the echoes died away among the distant hills, the little Victoria responded again and again, till she was completely enveloped in a cloud of smoke. It was a grand sight for the people of Port au Basque, the quiet of whose little village was never before disturbed with such boisterous rejoicing. A number of children were amusing themselves on the side of the hills which bound the harbor, and enjoying the scene before them with the greatest zest, but the first report set them scampering like a flock of frightened deer, and fearing a second attack, they disappeared like magic. In a few minutes we were anchored alongside the bark, and all was excitement and bustle among the passengers. We all wanted to go ashore, but as the number of boats was not equal to the demand, many had to remain on board. It was soon ascertained that it would be impossible to commence the work of laying the cable for two or three days, so that there would be an opportunity for every one to gratify their desire. The Sarah L. Bryant had, it appeared, very tempestuous weather, and for twenty-six hours was exposed to all the fury of a terrible gale, during which her hatches were battened and she was running under bare poles.

On the arrival of the James Adger at Port au Basque, we found that the mechanical arrangements on board the Sarah L. Bryant, for the laying of the cable, were not completed. It was resolved, under these circumstances, that the steamer should go to Cape North and select the best and nearest portion of the coast to Cape Ray, the point of connection. Mr. Field and some sixteen or eighteen of the passengers remained at Port au Basque till the return of the steamer, and as we

PORT AU BASQUE.

were among those we took advantage of the earliest opportunity to visit the bark, which was about five hundred tons burthen, and strongly built. The cable itself weighed four hundred tons, and was seventy-four miles long, while the distance between the points of connection on Newfoundland and Cape Breton is sixty-five. The extra nine miles were allowed to make up for the inequalities in the bottom of the ocean, and any variation that might be produced in the direct line by the wind or currents. The cable lay in immense coils in the hold of the vessel, and the operation of coiling alone took fourteen days. The machinery was very simple in its construction, and was the same that was used in laying the Mediterranean cable. The cable as it came out of the hold passed over iron rollers, and from these between vertical guide rollers, from which it passed again over two large wheels, each eight feet in diameter. As these revolved it was thrown out on a cast iron saddle, over the stern of the vessel. The wheels were supplied with four brakes, worked by two long levers and two compressors, which were employed to prevent the cable from surging as it passed round the wheels, as well as to prevent it from running off by its own weight. These completed the whole of the machinery.

The morning of the 22d of August the Sarah L. Bryant was towed by the Victoria up to Cape Ray Cove, which was decided upon as the starting place, being nearer by five miles to Cape North. There was also another great advantage it possessed over Port au Basque: it had a fine sandy beach, which experience has proved, forms a better and safer resting place for the cable than rocks. Once it becomes imbedded in sand, it may lie there for a century, but if exposed to friction on rocks, it would be worn away or cut through in less than a year.

It was found necessary to remove the telegraph instruments from Port au Basque to the point selected on the beach of Cape Ray Cove, which in itself was a most tedious and laborious work. As a number of

THE TELEGRAPH FLEET IN A GALE.

the passengers volunteered their assistance, however, it was expedited, and by twelve o'clock every thing was transported to the place designated. Here it was decided to erect a frame house, which was an undertaking of no small magnitude when the limited means and facilities of the place are considered. The Victoria was employed in carrying the frame and timber for the purpose from Port au Basque, but when she arrived with them at the Cove it was found that she could not approach within several hundred feet of the shore on account of the shallowness of the water. They were obliged under these circumstances therefore to form a raft, and on it to land all the timber required for the building of the house. The largest planks were accordingly thrown over the propeller's side, lashed together with ropes in the form of a square, and on this was placed the frame work, the shingles and the other parts of the structure.

CAPE RAY.

After an hour's hard work, in the course of which the raft gave way two or three times, they succeeded in getting all the timber upon it and attaching it to a boat prepared to tow it ashore. The progress made in rowing was rather slow, but they at last succeeded by hard tugging and pulling to get it within fifty or sixty yards of the beach. Here, however, the waves were so high, that it was considered by some exceedingly perilous to land in the midst of them; but as the whole shore was lined with breakers, and it became evident that there was no other resource, they went to work in utter defiance of the danger.

"Row ahead," said Captain Sluyter, who was on the raft with one of his crew, "row ahead." The fishermen pulled with might and main, and in a few minutes after the order was given, they were in the midst of the breakers, which threatened every moment to swamp the boat. They saw they were in for it now, and as there was no retreating, they rowed with redoubled energy; but the raft, which had held together better than was expected after leaving the side of the steamer, now exhibited strong symptoms of going to pieces, and it had hardly got in among the breakers before it parted in the centre, leaving Captain Sluyter on one portion and his assistant on the other. Their position became every moment more dangerous, as the planks on which they stood were very slightly secured, but by the most unremitting exertions they succeeded in keeping them together, and in getting safely ashore. A large portion of the timbers would doubtless have floated off with the receding tide had it not been for those on shore who rushed up to their armpits in the water, and not without some risk, hauled them up on the beach. In this they were assisted by the dogs, which seized the planks in their teeth, and although sometimes over a hundred feet out, swam ashore with them.

TAKING THE RAFT ASHORE.

When all the timber was landed the frame of the house was put up, and in an incredibly short space of time it was prepared for the reception of the batteries and other telegraph instruments. A deep hole was dug in the centre of the building, and in this was sunk a heavy piece of timber about the thickness of an ordinary capstan. A hogshead was placed over this again, and the intermediate space between it and the capstan, as we shall call it, being filled up, it was rendered so firm that it would hold the largest vessel in a gale of wind. Around this the cable was to be wound, and although the straining produced by it was comparatively slight, it was considered necessary to have it well secured in case of emergency.

Every thing was now prepared and in readiness for the laying of the cable, which was commenced on Thursday, the 23d of August.

It was a most exciting scene, although attended with little danger to those employed in the laying and paying out of the line. The Sarah L. Bryant was lying a little less than a mile from the shore, and the steamer Victoria about half that distance. A sufficient quantity of the cable was taken from her hold and placed in the form of a coil upon two boats lashed together. This was performed with little difficulty; but the towing of it ashore was a most critical task, and required all the attention and care of Mr. Canning. It was impossible, without imminent risk, to employ either the James Adger or the propeller in this part of the work, as neither could approach sufficiently near the shore to land the cable. It was therefore decided, as the only safe and practicable plan, that the boats should be towed ashore by two others manned by fishermen, and some of the hands from the steamers. As soon as the cable was placed on board the boats, they were taken in tow, and then commenced the tedious process of paying out. Its whole weight was about four tons, and as it had to be paid out with more caution than would be required in laying it from the ship, at least five hours were consumed in landing and placing it in connection with the batteries.

TAKING THE CABLE ASHORE.

When the boats having the cable on board commenced paying it out, they moved so slowly that their progress was hardly perceptible from the deck of the steamer. It was known that the work had begun, but, unfortunately, the James Adger was too far off to allow the company on board to see what was doing. A portion of the most enthusiastic volunteered their services, and having procured one of the steamer's boats, assisted in towing. They were determined on sharing the glory of the undertaking, that they might hereafter have the gratification of saying that they were among those who laid the great submarine cable on this side of the Atlantic. They worked hard for two or three hours, and did not give up till they saw it successfully landed; then giving three enthusiastic cheers, which were answered in the same spirit by those on shore, they started for the steamer with the gratifying intelligence.

"Now boys," said one of the party, "let us be the first to bring the news, and we will call ourselves the Submarine Telegraph Express, for the occasion." A general assent was given to this proposal, and away they started for the James Adger, making their little boat fly over the waves in their impatience to reach the vessel. As they passed the propeller one of the hands hailed them and asked the news.

"What is the matter?" he inquired. "Have they got through? Is all right?"

"Yes," they all replied in one voice; "the cable is landed—all right. Let us have three more cheers—hip, hip, hurra." And three more cheers were given that made the welkin ring. While passing the Sarah L. Bryant the same question was asked, and the response greeted with another burst of enthusiasm. In ten minutes they were on board the James Adger, where, however, they found the gratifying intelligence had preceded them. Little did they imagine then that their efforts would be rendered worse than useless, and that in the course of a week one-half the cable would be lost.

The end of the cable having been secured by several coils around the capstan, we remained at anchor that night, and made ready to start early the following morning. That morning, however, we were prevented by a dense fog, which rendered it exceedingly dangerous for us to attempt such an undertaking. In fact, if we felt ever so much inclined, it would have been almost impossible, as we could not discern objects at a distance of a hundred yards. We were obliged, therefore, to remain where we were during the greater part of the day, anxiously watching every sign of a change in the weather. One of our boats, containing seven or eight persons, ventured out, and having mistaken the direction of the land, came very near being lost. The error, however, was discovered before the steamer was out of sight, and corrected immediately. Up to eight o'clock that evening no change had taken place in the weather; and we began to lose all hope of the fog clearing away that night. About nine o'clock, however, we caught faint glimpses of the moon through the murky atmosphere, and in a few minutes more we could see her dimly, as through a veil. Slowly the fog began to disappear, and in the course of an hour we discerned the ship and propeller lying on our larboard bow, and about one-fourth of the distance between us and the shore. A light breeze sprung up which assisted in clearing the atmosphere, and there was every indication that we would have fine weather in the morning for the prosecution of our work. At last, after knocking about here for four or five days, we had a favorable prospect of getting away, and we congratulated each other on our good fortune. In two days more, and with a continuance of such weather, we would be at Cape North with the end of the cable, and ready to start for home. But here, again, we were doomed to disappointment and to a longer stay off this bleak and desolate coast. The breeze to which we were indebted for clearing away the fog, freshened near midnight, and before daybreak blew a perfect gale. Notwithstanding the state of the weather, it was decided to start in the morning, and about six o'clock we accordingly weighed anchor and made ready to tow the ship to sea. All this time we were under shelter of the land, and although it blew with great violence, the waves ran low. Having succeeded, after the greatest difficulty, in attaching the Sarah L. Bryant with a hawser, we prepared to tow her, but in this we were prevented by another obstacle. It was found, after repeated attempts, impossible to raise her anchor; and, having no other alternative, her captain was obliged to slip it, having previously attached a buoy to the chain to mark its location. All this time the submarine cable held on securely to the ship, although subjected to a great strain. In the midst of the intense excitement which prevailed on board the steamer, it was rumored that it had given way, but it had only disappeared from our view for a few moments, and when we looked again, there it was, holding on with a death-like tenacity. In the midst of all the trouble it was encouraging to see this; we felt grateful that our labor had not been in vain, and re-assured as to the strength it was said to possess.

We now endeavored to get into a proper position to tow the bark, but after several ineffectual attempts, we were obliged to give it up in despair. Both the steamer and the bark were almost completely at the mercy of the elements; the hawser got under our wheels, and serious apprehensions were felt that it would interfere with their action. Fortunately, they escaped without damage; but we had hardly got clear of it when the ship was observed drifting down upon us with such rapidity as rendered a collision inevitable. From the moment her anchor was slipped she became unmanageable, and although every effort was made to get her bow in a straight line with our stern, it was found impossible to do so. There seemed to be some terrible fatality hanging over her, and as she came down stern foremost upon our bow, our worst fears were excited for the safety of both vessels. The propeller was lying off at a distance of two or three hundred yards, but she could render no assistance, and any attempt she might make would only render the matter more serious.

The scene on board our steamer was painfully exciting; every one crowded to the larboard side, awaiting the collision in breathless anxiety. The captain, as soon as he discovered the imminence of the danger, gave orders to reverse the wheels, and we were now moving out of the way of the ship, but so slowly that we appeared to make no progress. "Back her! back her!" he cried out to the first mate, who passed the order to the engineer. "Back her! why don't you back her?" roared the captain of the Sarah L. Bryant; but the ships appeared to be drawn together by some irresistible attraction, and in a few minutes after the order was given they struck. The larboard bow of our steamer came in contact with the stern of the bark; but not with such violence as we anticipated. None of our timbers were started, the only damage we received being two slight scratches about five feet above the water line, while the bark was uninjured. Our escape appeared almost miraculous, for at one time it seemed as if nothing could save us, but now that the fearful suspense was over the excitement died away. The ladies were not on deck when the accident occurred, as they had in compliance with the request of the captain retired to the cabin a short time before. They were ignorant of our danger, therefore, till it was all over.

We escaped, as we have said, almost by a miracle, a serious catastrophe; but we were not as yet clear of the bark, and more than once we were near coming in contact again. It was found necessary to cut the hawser on board our ship, and to let her take care of herself until we could get into a better position. As soon as we parted from her she dropped her remaining anchor, still holding on to the submarine cable, and we also came to anchor about the same time. We remained in this state for about an hour, when we saw two or three flags or streamers run up at half mast on board the bark—a signal of distress. Shortly after she unfurled some of her sails, and stood out to sea. She had lost her anchor, and to save herself from drifting on the rocks, was obliged to cut the submarine cable, and stand off from the shore. In a few minutes we were after her, and by a series of most skilful manœuvres attached her to our stern by a hawser. When we first approached, several efforts were made to throw a rope over her side, but without success, when our captain changed the position of our vessel so as to let her drop under our stern, and allow a rope to be flung to one of the men on her bowsprit. The rope was caught, the hawser hauled on board, and in less than a quarter of an hour we had her safely in tow.

THE JAMES ADGER AND SARAH L. BRYANT LEAVING CAPE RAY.

During this difficulty the bark lost two of her anchors, and the steamer was obliged to part with one of hers, leaving only two between both vessels. Both of these belonged to our steamer, but as it was impossible for her to return near the land without some security, our captain was obliged to give her one of his own.

The 26th being Sunday we did not move from the Cove, and a part of the day was spent in repairing the cable, which broke again soon after. It was evident now that the portion which had been laid must be abandoned, and that it should be relanded and secured anew to the fastenings in the telegraph house.

At an early hour on Monday morning the 27th, the Victoria took the bark in tow, and brought her within a distance of about six hundred yards from the beach. The cable was then placed upon the boats, as described in the preceding chapter, successfully landed, and placed in connection with the batteries. A stiff breeze from the north-west however prevented the prosecution of the work, and it was deemed advisable to defer it till the next morning. Outside the Cove the waves ran so high that any attempt to land the cable would have endangered the safety of both vessels. That day therefore we remained at anchor, and flattered ourselves with the hope that the weather would soon prove more auspicious.

The following morning was all that could be desired; the waves had subsided to a gentle ripple, there was scarcely a cloud to dim the brightness of the sun, Cape Ray appeared resplendent in his beams, and every thing seemed to favor the enterprise. As the first dawn of morning tinged the eastern horizon, the bark raised her anchor and was towed out to our steamer, which lay at a distance of half a mile from the beach. In less than an hour she was attached to the James Adger with a hawser, and the process of laying the cable was commenced in earnest. All our delay seemed trifling in view of our certainty of success—for no one entertained any doubts now of its success, so long as the weather proved favorable. The first two miles of the cable were laid without an accident, but just as they were commencing on the third a kink occurred, and it was found necessary to stop the steamer to repair the damage. In the course of an hour all was set right and we were under way again; but in a few minutes more the white flag which had been agreed upon as a signal before starting, was displayed, and we were obliged to stop. Mr. Canning afterwards said, that the speed of the steamer, even at its lowest rate, was too fast for the purpose, and that it was almost impossible for his men to pay out the cable with sufficient rapidity. Eight were employed in the hold turning out the coils, and eight more in attendance on the machinery. The position of those in the hold was one of considerable danger, and two or three were severely bruised by the cable as they were in the act of uncoiling it. It required their constant vigilance, and greatest activity to keep clear of it as it swept up through the hold, for if once caught within its folds, the consequence would have been serious, if not fatal. To avoid this, they stood on the outside of the coil, raising it up and passing it out at the rate of two, and sometimes, three miles an hour.

Several kinks occurred up to twelve o'clock on Tuesday night, and it was reported on board of our steamer at one time that the cable had parted. This report, however, was found to be incorrect, and it was ascertained that it only required splicing, and that it had to be cut to splice it successfully. This was a tedious task, and took till seven o'clock the following morning to accomplish. From this till four in the afternoon they had very few stoppages—the machinery worked admirably—and although our steamer was still somewhat too fast, the cable was paid out with less difficulty than had been experienced before. Up to this time they had to pay it out from the small coil in the bow of the vessel, but the work was not so arduous when they reached the larger one, which lay in the main hold. The kinks, therefore, became less frequent; and as we were now within sight of St. Paul's, which was about fourteen miles distant, we felt elated at the prospect of landing it there in a few hours more. We were, it is true, somewhat discouraged by a break taking place in two of the three copper wires, one only having remained perfect. Still, strong hopes were entertained that when once landed, all the wires would be in good working order. Forty miles of the cable had been paid out from the time we started, while the actual distance traversed did not exceed thirty-two at the utmost. It was, therefore, considered advisable to land it at the island of St. Paul's, instead of Cape North, as was at first proposed, and to make the connection next year. Not more than thirty-three miles of the cable remained, and it was on making the allowance for the loss of this, that Mr. Canning reluctantly concluded to give up the design originally entertained of running to Cape North.

At four o'clock the wind, which had been increasing for the last two or three hours, blew with such violence as to render it impossible to continue the work on board the bark. The sea ran so high that it was only at intervals we could discern those on her deck. The sky looked wild and threatening, and the waves broke in spray over the decks of both vessels. The ocean was covered with a mist that rendered objects, at the distance of four or five miles, invisible, and St. Paul's Island could no longer be seen. To render our position still more critical, another kink occurred in the cable, and both vessels were compelled to lay to. They made several attempts to repair the damage, but all was useless, the bark rolled with such violence that the men could not work, and it was with the greatest difficulty they could even stand on the deck. Every eye was now fixed on Mr. Canning, and they all waited with feverish anxiety for him to give the order to cut the cable. They had for more than an hour abandoned all hope of being able to land it, and their fears were aroused for their own safety and that of the vessel. But Mr. Canning was unwilling to give the word, still hoping, even against hope, that the gale would abate, and that before morning he would be able to resume work. Although both vessels were holding on by the cable, it showed no sign of parting, and would doubtless have remained whole to the end, had it been considered prudent to hold on by it. It was at this juncture that its strength was tested, and successfully proved. We had heard that it was capable of holding a seventy-four in a gale of wind, but it seemed hardly possible that even a rope of iron wire, not much more than an inch in diameter, could hold two vessels under such circumstances.

When Mr. Canning refused to cut the cable, and there appeared to be no prospect of the gale abating, the captain of the bark, Mr. Pousland, told him he would have to give the order, as the safety of his ship was now endangered.

"Mr. Canning," said he, "I shall be obliged to cut the cable."

"You can do as you please," said Mr. C. in reply, for he would persist no longer in his attempts to save it, as it had now become a matter of life and death. The next minute the cable was cut, the white flag which had been displayed on the bow for the last two hours was lowered, and we were once more in motion with the bark in tow.

On board our steamer the paying out of the cable was regarded with the greatest interest, from the moment we started from Cape Ray Cove. A watch of two hours was organized among the company, to be kept up till we reached the place of destination. Two persons were appointed on each watch, whose duty it was to attend to the signals on the bark, and to stop our steamer when required. During the daytime, the chief engineer, Mr. Scott, assisted in this part of the work, and the passengers will never forget the feelings with which they heard him call out to the man at the engine to "Stop her," or the relief they felt when he gave the word to "Hook her on, and let her go slow." We dreaded the appearance of the white flag, for it was an indication that something was wrong on board the bark, and when it was lowered it seemed as if an oppressive weight had been removed from our minds. But when the gale came on, and the lives of all on board the Sarah L. Bryant appeared to be in imminent danger, the interest became painfully intense. Although not more than five hundred feet from us, we could only see those on her deck at brief intervals. She plunged violently, and as she rose at times on the crest of the waves, we could see at least one half of her keel. For two long hours we watched her tugging at the cable, anticipating with impatience the word to cut it; but still she held on, and there seemed to be no intention on the part of those in command to give the order. At last the white flag disappeared, after an hour of painful suspense, and we soon perceived that the cable had been cut. The order was immediately given to our engineer to go ahead, but as there was some danger of the hawser breaking, our steamer was not put under full headway. At one time we were ourselves in a most critical condition, and were laboring heavily in the trough of the sea. It was only for a few minutes, however: our steamer was placed head to the waves, and we were soon out of danger. We now made as direct as possible for

Sydney, going at the rate of from two and a half to three miles an hour, and expecting to reach that port on Thursday.

The evening previous to the day on which the cable was cut the British war steamer Argus, Captain Purvis, which had been visible for the last two hours, came alongside the propeller, and was spoken by Captain Sluyter. Orders had been received by Admiral Fanshawe of the North American station, from the British Board of Admiralty, to render any assistance in his power to the vessels employed in laying the cable. The order was transmitted to Capt. Purvis, who immediately set out from Halifax, but unfortunately arrived too late for the purpose. He asked Capt. Sluyter if he required any assistance.

"Are you in want of assistance?" he inquired, when the propeller came within speaking distance.

"No," was the reply.

"Are you short of coal?"

"Yes, rather."

"Is the other steamer short of coal also?" he again asked

"Yes, we are both short."

"Then I shall lie by you all night, and if you should need assistance you shall have it."

True to his word, Captain Purvis remained by us, and as we saw the green and red lights of his steamer gleaming through the darkness of that long and weary night, we enjoyed a feeling of security for those on board the bark we had not felt for hours before.

About seven o'clock on Thursday morning, the Argus came alongside again, and we observed one of her men holding a black board on her paddle box, having the following inscribed in large letters upon it:

CAN WE RENDER YOU ANY ASSISTANCE?

Our captain shook his head in reply, but the Englishman was not satisfied with this, and taking a short turn, came back and again displayed his black board, with the following words:

ANSWER—YES, OR NO! AS I AM ON MY PASSAGE.

This was definite enough and required an explicit answer, which was given promptly. A piece of chalk was produced, and the significant monosyllable "No" written in gigantic characters on the side of our smoke stack. This was sufficient, and in a few minutes more the Argus left us; but long after she disappeared beyond the horizon we could trace her course by the black line of smoke which she left along the sky.

On Thursday afternoon, about four o'clock, we took a pilot on board, and an hour after we were safely anchored opposite the coal wharf of

North Sydney. Our stay here was much longer than we anticipated, but we made the best use of our time, and before our departure had formed numerous acquaintances, and were tolerably well posted up in the character of the place and its people

The Sarah L. Bryant was left at Sydney, where the remaining thirty-three miles of the cable were taken ashore, and the propeller Victoria took her departure for St. Johns at an early hour on Sunday morning, September 2d. A few hours later we started for home, and after a favorable passage of three days, we arrived within sight of Long Island, about five o'clock on the morning of the 5th. Our pilot, Mr. Thomas Vail, who came with us from New York, now took charge of our steamer, which arrived safely at pier No. 4, North River, on Wednesday, September 5th. This ended the first attempt to lay the cable across the Gulf of St. Lawrence. The following year, however, a second attempt was made, and with complete success.

THE FIRST ATLANTIC TELEGRAPH EXPEDITION.

The United States Frigate Niagara, which had been detailed for the purpose of assisting in the work of submerging the Atlantic Submarine Cable, left New York on the 22d of April on her trial trip, and two days afterwards, set out for England. Never before had a vessel sailed on so grand an enterprise, an enterprise which taxed the faith of the most credulous, and afforded the scientific sceptic another field for the display of his argumentative powers. The impracticability of the work had been shown again and again, but the men by whom it was undertaken were not to be dismayed by vague fears or idle predictions. They were called enthusiasts, and cautious capitalists wondered that men whom they had previously regarded as possessing sound common sense should have been so far led astray by a splendid impossibility. To lay a cable almost two thousand miles across the bed of the ocean seemed to them as chimerical as the idea of establishing communication between the earth and its attendant planet by means of a line of aerial steamers. Besides the known difficulties which stood in the way of the accomplishment of such a work, who could tell what strange obstacles impossible to foresee and impossible to guard against, lay in the unknown depths of the wild and stormy Atlantic? True, the ocean had been sounded, and specimens taken from a depth of two miles exhibited, but what of that? Were there not men who contended, and who were ready to prove by scientific reasoning, that the ocean had no bottom, and that those who made the so-called soundings were the dupes of their own imaginations, or something worse? Then there were others who were dismayed by the magnitude of the enterprise, and who shrank from its contemplation as they would from the full glare of the midsummer sun. Human genius had worked wonders, but it could not achieve impossibilities. And so they argued, that the idea of the Atlantic telegraph never could be realized. But the announcement has been made to the believing and the unbelieving, that the Niagara has sailed from the port of New York to assist in the work of uniting two worlds by an electric chain, along which the thoughts of men will fly with the speed of the lightning itself. Our Government, to its credit be it said, had acted generously in the matter in selecting the largest and best appointed ship for the great experiment, and the English Government on its part displayed no less liberality. And now that the Niagara is fairly off, we will introduce the reader to her commander and officers :—

Captain, W. L. Hudson; Commander, A. M. Pennock; Lieutenants, Jas. H. North, J. D. Todd, John Guest, Clark H. Wells, W. D. Whiting, E. Y. Macaulay, Beverley Kennon; Surgeon, J. C. Palmer; Purser, Joseph C. Eldredge; Passed Assistant Surgeon, A. M. Lynah; Assistant Surgeon, T. W. M. Washington; Captain of Marines, J. C. Rich; Lieutenant of Marines, W. S. Boyd; Chief Engineer, W. E. Everett; First Assts., John Faron, T. A. Shock; Second do., M. Kellogg, John W. Moore; Third do., Alex. Grier, Thos. R. Ely, J. McElwell and H. Kutz; Boatswain, Robt. Dixon; Carpenter, H. P. Leslie; Gunner, John Webber; Sailmaker, Wm. B. Fugitt; Captain's Clerk, J. W. Hudson; Purser's Clerk, Edward Willard.

There were a few gentlemen who went out on the expedition as passengers on board the Niagara. These were: Professor Morse, Captain Schwartz, and Lieut. Kolobnin, of the Russian Navy, and the author. Mr. Field subsequently joined the vessel in England.

And now, as the Niagara is fairly entered upon the expedition, and may be said to have an individuality of her own, we will invite the attention of our readers to the character of the vessel herself and the little world which moves within her. They will thus be better enabled to understand more perfectly many of the details which are represented in the course of this narrative. Very little in fact is known about life on board a naval vessel, except what is obtained from novels, and that is so interwoven with romance, that it is not to be relied on. For those, therefore, who have obtained their information only from such sources, or who have no knowledge whatever on the subject, there may be some interest in the following sketch of the ship:

LIFE ON BOARD THE NIAGARA.

To begin, then, at the beginning, the spar deck is the first part of the ship that claims attention. It is the principal deck on the vessel, and is so named from the fact that all the masts and rigging are visible from it. The spar deck of the Niagara differs in many particulars from that of other vessels of war in the American navy, and presents perhaps a greater extent of clear and unobstructed space than is to be found in any other ship of war in the world. In nautical language it is what is called "a flush deck," which, reduced to plain English, means that it is as free from all obstructions as it is possible to make it on a vessel of such a character. This is a most essential object in the case of a ship like the Niagara, which differs in many points from war steamers. She is the largest steam frigate in the world, and exceeds in tonnage the heaviest of the line of battle ships in the British navy. While, however, she surpasses them in size, she numbers but twelve guns; but these are of such great calibre, and are capable of doing such terrible execution, as to place her, it is claimed, on a perfect equality with any of them, if they should not render her superior. Each of these guns weighs fourteen tons, including the carriage, and is capable of throwing a shell of one hundred and thirty pounds a distance of three miles. These terrible engines of destruction can be fired with as much accuracy as a rifle, and possess a great advantage over other kinds now in use, not merely on account of their great size, but from the fact that they can throw a shell to a distance which is beyond the range of those employed on the other vessels of our navy. The art of throwing projectiles has reached such a state of perfection that from the moment the shell leaves the gun the time which must elapse before it strikes the object is so nicely calculated that it explodes immediately on reaching its destination. Each of these guns is worked by twenty-five men, and from this number a "captain of the gun," a second captain, first and second loaders, first and second spongers, and others, are selected for special duty. The shell itself is loaded with six pounds of powder, and the quantity required for a charge is thirty pounds. The total weight of the twelve guns, with their carriages, is one hundred and sixty-eight tons; and if to this be added the shells and powder required for one hundred rounds to each, we will have an aggregate of about two hundred and seventy tons. To support such a weight of guns the spar deck, which on the Niagara is also the gun deck, is constructed of the strongest timber, and is strengthened by both wooden and iron stanchions. As these guns would only serve to encumber the vessel and interfere with the work for which she has been detached from the regular service, they were not taken on board. Their place, however, was supplied by four signal guns of less than one half their size, but which twenty or thirty years ago would have been regarded as gigantic specimens of their kind.

For the purpose of securing all the clear space possible on this deck, the poop and forecastle were greatly reduced in size, compared even with vessels of one-third the tonnage of the Niagara. In fact, on both there is hardly sufficient standing room for forty men. Some idea, however, of the great size of the vessel and the area of the spar deck, may be formed from the fact that in walking from the poop to the forecastle and from the forecastle to the poop eight times, you traverse a distance of about a mile. Of a summer's evening—such evenings as some of those we have had since our departure from New York, with a sea so calm that there was hardly a ripple on its surface, and the long swells were scarcely felt on our ship—a walk upon the deck is a luxury which Broadway, with all its varied beauties and attractions, could not surpass. Abaft the bridge or gangway, which divides the deck into two parts, is the officers' promenade or quarter-deck. As the executive authority reposes in the officer of the deck or the officer on watch, which is the same thing, and as the representative of the captain, he is supreme in his decision on all matters that do not require the arbitration of the commander himself; every outward mark of respect is to be paid to him by all who present themselves on this part of the quarter-deck. In compliance with this regulation every officer or man attached to the ship raises his cap when stepping on the quarter-deck, in deference not merely to the officer to whose charge the vessel has been consigned for the time being, but to the government of the United States, whose representative he is, and to the great people whose will has called that government into existence. This officer may be distinguished from the rest by his carrying in his hand a trumpet, by which he is enabled to give his orders to the men in the most distant parts of the ship. Forward of the bridge—that is, from the bridge to and including the forecastle—is that portion of the ship assigned particularly to the men, although of course they are restricted to no particular part in the performance of their duty; but this portion is free to those who are not on watch, and who are at liberty to pass their time in any way that may not conflict with the rules. Here, when the weather permits, they are to be seen employed as taste or inclination dictates; some engaged in reading, some in telling yarns, some in relating the adventures of their last cruise, some in making or mending their clothes, and others of a less sociable or industrious turn of mind dozing away their leisure time, like many of the same disposition on shore, who are too sluggish or indolent either to think or work. It must not be supposed, however, that their leisure cannot be broken in upon, or that they are entirely free from duty while off watch; for, properly speaking, a sailor is always at the command of his superior, and necessarily so, as his services may be required at any moment. When the order is given to have "all hands on deck," all who are on and off watch must be prepared to take in sail or perform any other duty that is required of them. This done, they are at liberty to enjoy the rest of their leisure time, subject, however, to be called upon again whenever their services may be required.

From the spar deck a part of the engine is visible, and looking down through the hatch you see the machinery by which this immense mass is propelled through the water at a speed of from ten to twelve miles an hour. This hatch is situated about midships, but on walking forward a few feet nearer to the forecastle you discover two other hatches, by means of which the fire room is supplied with pure air and light. This room is at least twenty-five feet below the spar deck, and a few feet still further down is the keel of the vessel. Rising above these hatches are the two smoke-pipes, both of which are capable of being lowered, by some telescopic contrivance, so as not to be higher than ten or twelve feet above the level of the deck. This arrangement is absolutely necessary, as they would otherwise be in the way of the mainsail; but all danger from fire is avoided by the consumption of the caloric, which in nearly all other steamers passes through the smoke-pipes. In fact, so little danger is to be apprehended from fire, that the temperature of the air at the top of these pipes never exceeds 130 degrees, and is generally much lower. Forward of the fire room hatches is the launch, a large open boat, about thirty feet long, and capable of holding one hundred and twenty men in case of shipwreck. Inside of this is another launch somewhat smaller, and inside of this again a cutter smaller still. They are all well secured to the deck by iron chains, but are so moored, or, to use a less nautical term, so firmly secured that in an emergency they can be detached in less than five minutes, and made ready in a very few minutes more for the important work for which they are mainly designed. The launch is also employed to water the ship—that is, to supply her with fresh water, and if necessary with provisions. There are besides these three boats another, called the dinkey, which is also placed in the launch, and six cutters which are secured to the davits on each side of the vessel. In all, there is room for between four and five hundred men. These, ample as they may appear, are not the only means for saving life, as in many cases they would of themselves be entirely useless for the purpose without some auxiliary. In the event of a man falling overboard, for instance, even five minutes would be too long, and the best swimmer might not be able to keep himself above water till a boat could reach him. To meet such an emergency, there are two life buoys attached to the stern, and connected by means of wires to two handles, which are within the reach of either of the two men stationed at this part of the vessel. By pulling this handle the buoy is immediately detached, and falling into the sea is, in nine cases out of ten, effective in the saving of life. The instant the cry of "a man overboard" is heard by the watch upon this station, his hand is on the handle, the buoy falls from its place, and it not unfrequently happens that it is seized before it is a minute afloat. All this is accomplished in less time than is taken in the description. During this operation, the ship is arrested in her course, the gang of men who are stationed at the life-boat are engaged in unmooring and launching it, and in about ten minutes from the moment the man has fallen overboard he is rescued and restored to his shipmates. As the life buoy would not be visible at night, it is lighted by means of a trigger, which ignites a sort of roman candle or blue light, that continues burning ten or fifteen minutes. To prevent the possibility of mistake, the following words are inscribed above both handles—" LIFE BUOY—PORT FIRE."

At night, the handle under the words " port fire " is the first that is pulled, and immediately after the life buoy with the light thus produced, must be set afloat. This admirable invention has been the means of saving many lives, and all vessels, whether belonging to our commercial marine or navy, ought to be provided with one at least.

Descending from the spar deck to the depth of ten or twelve feet, you reach the main or berth deck, which may not improperly be termed the domestic department of the ship. The captain's cabin, the officers' wardroom, the petty officers' mess, the cook's galleys, and in fact every thing that is required in the household arrangements of so large a number of men, are all on this deck. Here, too, they eat and sleep, while nearly all the work of the vessel is done on the spar deck. The captain's cabin is situated, of course, nearest to the stern, and is fitted up and furnished with a degree of neatness and taste that you might look for in vain in some of the best hotels in New York. Here is the ship's library, and here, too, all the orders are issued to, and reports received from, the various officers in command. Every day the doctor sends in his account of the number of sick in the hospital, and every day the sailing master submits the result of his observations and calculations in regard to the sailing and position of the ship, while the first lieutenant, who is his chief executive officer, reports to him every thing of importance that comes under his charge. Matters which a landsman might regard as trifling are sometimes made the subject of a detailed report, and entered upon the ship's journal with the same care that would be given to the entry of a debt in a ledger. If a piece of timber is observed floating past the vessel, official information of the fact is conveyed to the captain by the orderly, who keeps guard near the cabin, or one of the crew despatched by an officer for that purpose. Unimportant, however, as such things may appear to those who have but a limited knowledge of life at sea, they are sometimes of the utmost consequence. Beside the scientific works required for the use of the ship, there is a library for the sailors, containing principally books of a moral and religious tendency, with some histories, lives of celebrated men, adventures by sea and land, and a few works of fiction. These afford excellent and instructive reading to such of the crew as are disposed to spend their leisure time in that way, and are certainly a great improvement upon the yellow covered literature and other trash that too often find their way on board both men of war and merchant vessels. This library is also in the cabin, and is fitted up with that regularity and regard to order which should characterize all the departments of a ship-of-war. As a general thing, the opportunity which it affords to sailors for mental improvement is very seldom taken advantage of, while the Life of Jack Sheppard, Dick Turpin, and the biographies of celebrated pirates and buccaneers, are read with the most intense interest. Occasionally, it is true, there are to be found fine, sterling, good-hearted, simple-minded, honest fellows, whom all the vicious associations and evil influences to which they have been exposed are unable to corrupt or deprave, and to such libraries of this kind are among the favors that they prize most. Every way it is regarded, the ship's library is an institution that should be sustained, as one of the means by which the moral and mental standard of our seamen is to be improved and elevated.

The wardroom of the officers is the most spacious apartment, not only in the Niagara, but is said to be the largest and most commodious in the American or any other navy. It is about fifty feet by thirty, and between nine and ten feet from the floor to the ceiling. The furniture is of a simple and unpretending character, but there is an appearance of elegance about the style of the apartment itself which more than makes up for the absence of mahogany, or more costly rosewood. An engraved portrait of Washington, in a plain gilt frame, hangs in the most conspicuous place in the apartment, and this is the only work of art by which it is embellished. But the visitor must not take this as an indication of a want of appreciation of the fine arts in the officers, for nothing would be more incorrect or more unjust. Enter almost any of the fifteen snug and neatly furnished little eight-by-ten bedrooms, and you will see more than one painting, and among these perhaps copies of some gems of the old Italian masters and articles of *vertu* obtained during a cruise in the Mediterranean. And there, prized still more, hanging beside these, is some present from dear friends at home, whom absence and distance have only served to render dearer than ever. Wherever you turn your eyes you see evidences of woman's taste and ingenuity; it may be in a beautifully wrought watch-pocket, or pincushion, or other trifle, all giving an air of taste, if not of luxury, to the little bedroom. The government in its bounty has furnished it with a tolerably good bureau, a washstand, a chair and a bedstead, or rather some contrivance to place a bed on, but here its liberality has stopped; and the officers have to supply the hundred other necessaries that make up the sum total of a well regulated, well provided household. They have to purchase bed clothing, looking-glasses, towels, pitchers, basins, soap, knives and forks, spoons, cooking utensils, plates, tables, table covers, coffee and tea pots, plates and dishes, cups and saucers, bowls and all the other articles which are considered indispensable in the proper management of domestic matters. The experience which they obtain in this way gives them a decided advantage over landsmen, and makes them, as may be supposed, somewhat of a domestic turn. In fact, the close and intimate connection into which they are brought with each other binds them together like members of one family, and the friendship which is formed in the wardroom and at the mess table often lasts through life, and with a firmness and sincerity sometimes exceeding that which exists in the family relations.

The mess fund is formed by equal contributions levied on each member of the wardroom, and with this is purchased the provision necessary for the cruise. The caterer of the mess is selected from among the officers, and to his charge is consigned the direction and management of all those things which fall to the care of caterers generally. This office is purely an honorary one, but, unlike most offices of an honorary kind, there is considerable responsibility attached to it. He looks after all the table appointments, and requires of the steward an account of the breakages, takes notes of the consumption of provisions, and at the end of the cruise renders an account of his charge.

The wardroom is exclusively the officers' apartment, and not even the captain is privileged to enter it, except for the purpose of official inspection, when it is of course thrown open to him. While, however, it is their own, indeed as much as any gentleman's house is his, and no one can force himself uninvited into the mess, it would be wrong to suppose that there are, therefore, no interchange of courtesies, or that it is enclosed by a sort of Chinese wall for the exclusion of all but those who are members of the mess. So far from this being the case, it is a common thing, I understand, in our navy, for the officers to invite the captain to partake of their hospitality, and some of the pleasantest hours which are spent on board a man-of-war, are those passed by the officers and the captain in the interchange of mutual courtesies and friendly feeling. During the passage of the Niagara I had the pleasure of being present at one of these re-unions, the company consisting of all the wardroom officers, the captain, Professor Morse, and the two Russian officers, Captain Schwarz and Lieutenant Kolobnen, and I had a full opportunity of realizing the fact that the amenities of social life are as well understood and as much appreciated at sea as on land.

According to the rules of the ship all the lights in the berth-room are extinguished at ten o'clock, but permission can be obtained from the officer of the deck to keep them lighted for one or two hours after that time if necessary.

After ten o'clock, also, all conversation or noise that may disturb the sleep of the officers who have kept watch or are going on watch is strictly prohibited, and only one light is allowed in the wardroom. Whatever may be said about late hours and dissipation ashore, there can be very little if any at sea, and however men may be inclined to indulge while on land, they have certainly no opportunity for it on board a ship of war.

The messrooms of the warrant officers are not equal in appearance to that which has just been described; but their rooms are hardly inferior in point of accommodations and general appearance to those of the wardroom officers. In this particular the Niagara differs from nearly every other ship in our naval service, and for this point of difference the warrant officers are indebted, to a considerable extent, to Mr. George Steers, who was determined that his fellow-mechanics should have no reason to complain of limited or inferior accommodation. The warrant officers are so called on account of their being appointed by a warrant signed by the President, and differ from the lieutenants in their not being confirmed by the Senate. They are also inferior in rank, and are out of the line of promotion. Their mess consists of the carpenter, the sailmaker, the boatswain, the gunner and assistant engineers, the chief engineer being one of the wardroom officers.

Forward of the mess and berth rooms is the part appropriated especially to the sailors and marines, and it extends on either side of the masts and hatchways, which occupy nearly the whole of the central space, about two hundred feet each side, by from fifteen to twenty in width. It is in this portion of the berth deck that the marines and sailors sleep, eat, and transact nearly all their little domestic affairs. At twelve o'clock some two hundred men here sit down to dinner, all divided into separate messes of fifteen men, each of which has its own cook, who is generally selected on account of his qualifications in the culinary department. Let a man obtain a character among his messmates for superior attainments in cooking, and he is at once elevated to the position. He must understand thoroughly the making of dunderfunk, be *au fait* in the cooking of lobscouse—two very favorite dishes among sailors—and if his abilities are of so high an order as to comprehend the baking of puddings or pies, so much the better for his own standing and the palates of his messmates. Lobscouse, which, as has been stated, is a dish in great favor among sailors, is a kind of stew, and is usually composed of salt beef, potatoes, onions, a liberal sprinkling of pepper, and the due allowance of water. It was supposed by the ignorant, and those who had an undue appreciation of Jack's digestive powers, that its flavor was strengthened by the addition of pieces of sole leather, some old buttons, and occasionally a piece of tarpaulin or hemp cuttings; but it is all a mistake, for although Jack, in the vicissitudes to which all who follow a seafaring life are subject, is sometimes compelled to put up with the hardest fare, and sometimes obliged to do without any at all, he has no particular relish for a compound that would try even the stomach of an ostrich. Dunderfunk is made of hard bread, beef, or pork and beans, a little molasses and a small quantity of vinegar; and, notwithstanding its startling title, is, after all, as simple and as easily made as fish, or any other kind of chowder. The fare which is given to the seamen in our naval service, although not of the best description, is far superior to that which the laborers in our cities and on our farms receive. Every mess has a liberal supply of beef, pork, potatoes, onions, flour, coffee, sugar, tea, and all the little etceteras which are so essential to the complete success of all cooking operations. These are served out every second or third day by the Purser's steward, who keeps an exact account of the amount distributed among the different messes. As our Government is very liberal in regard to rations, each man receives more than he can dispose of, unless endowed with unusual gastronomic powers, and as a general thing the amount supplied to every twelve men is abundantly sufficient for a whole mess of fifteen. On the principle, it is to be supposed, that "enough is as good as a feast," they draw rations for twelve, and in exchange for the surplus receive its full value in money, with which they are enabled to supply their table with many delicacies which are not to be found on the provision list. It is not uncommon, therefore, to find a mess occasionally sitting down to as good a dinner as the officers themselves; and plain puddings, apple pies and roast beef, have long ceased to be unknown luxuries to the common sailor. Their household appointments are not, it must be acknowledged, of the best description, and in lieu of tables and chairs they are obliged to eat off, and sit down on, the deck. A piece of tarpaulin serves all the purposes of a table-cloth, and although some fastidious tastes might object to the peculiar odor which it gives the smoking viands, yet it is a healthy odor, to which only landsmen would think of objecting. Upon this the dinner is spread, each man supplying himself from the large dish in the centre, which contains pork, or beef, or lobscouse, or dunderfunk, or whatever other fare they may have. At eight o'clock in the evening the hammocks are slung up, each man having a certain space allowed him to swing from during his four hours off watch; but he is liable at any moment to be roused from his slumbers by the cry of "all hands on deck," and is sometimes obliged to postpone his sleep till the next night if the weather should prove stormy. In such cases, however, he generally manages to make up for lost time by snatching a moment of rest on the deck, or wherever and whenever he can during any intervals that he may have. With all his troubles and labors, Jack is, perhaps, one of the most cheerful of men, and if he is sometimes too ardent a votary of the jolly god, he is not a stranger to the finer sentiments and feelings. He has a strong love for music, and indulges it whenever he has an opportunity. There is not, perhaps, a vessel in the American navy whose crew numbers over thirty or forty men that has not a musician of some kind among them, and they are generally held in the highest estimation.

As for the Niagara, she has quite a large force of them, independent of the two official musicians, if they may be so called, that the government of the United States has provided. These are entered upon the ship's list as musicians, but lest there should be any misapprehension in regard to their particular grade, or the instruments on which they perform, it may as well be stated that the musicians in this instance are simply a fifer and drummer. It will, however, satisfy all true and patriotic Americans to know that their abilities are fully equal to the performance of "Hail Columbia," and "Yankee Doodle," and the American who after that would stop to inquire into their knowledge of the works of the great composers has not a spark of feeling in his whole composition. These are the official musicians, but there are, as I have said, a number of others on board, amateurs, who play for the love of it, and without hope or prospect of pay. It was my good fortune to be a witness of a concert which took place here a few evenings ago, and although not one of the assembly I had still a fair chance of seeing and hearing all that was going on. The concert came off on the berth deck, within a few feet of the cook's galley; the performers were two rival violinists, who have been contending for the palm ever since they came on board, and the audience consisted of some three or four of the cooks, two or three powder monkeys, and some twenty or thirty sailors. The performers sat opposite each other, and suspended between them was a large ship's lamp, which threw a dim and clouded light on the admiring faces around. One of the fiddlers entertained his audience with the wonderful performances of the "Bob-tailed Nag," while the other played "Villikins and his Dinah," with an expression that even Jem Baggs himself could not surpass. The contest was maintained with about equal success on both sides, and when the change of watch called the rivals away to the spar deck and broke up the assembly, it was impossible to decide which had the advantage. The affair furnished a topic for conversation many days after, and I believe the remembrance of it will remain with the hearers long after the cable is laid.

This sketch of the main deck and social life among the sailors would be incomplete if I failed to mention one of the most important institutions in the vessel—the ship's dispensary. The dispensary is situated at one end of the warrant officers' mess and berth rooms, on the starboard side, and is supplied with all the medicines necessary for the treatment of every disease. It is under the charge of the surgeon's steward, who makes up all the prescriptions, and who is to all intents and purposes the same as an apothecary. There have been very few cases of sickness among the crew of any consequence, but were it not for the course which has been pursued by the ship's physicians they would have more patients on the list than they could well attend to. On board of almost every man-of-war there are a number of good-for-nothing idle fellows who endeavor on every occasion to shirk their work by feigning sickness. Sometimes they succeed, but the detection of one or two generally leads to the discovery of the rest, when their names are at once taken off the sick list, and they are obliged to perform their duty.

The orlop deck is almost exclusively used for the storage of provisions, water, the ship's ammunition, extra hawser, ropes, sails, and all the other articles that constitute a ship's stores. The part appropriated to the provisions is protected from the invasion of rats or mice by a casing of tin, and the magazines, besides being carefully locked and sealed, have a sentry always on guard near them. At the extreme forward end of the orlop deck is the hospital, which has accommodations for fifteen or twenty patients, but fortunately there are not more than two or three in it at present, and those are not seriously sick. The engine and fire rooms are situated about the centre of the vessel, and extend from the bottom of the ship to the spar deck. In comparison with her immense size, they take up very little space. The firemen, whose watches, like the sailors, are divided into four hours each, sleep on the orlop deck, have separate messes, and are never, except in cases of emergency, required to do any work upon deck.

According to naval discipline, every man on board a ship of war is supposed to be always ready for duty, unless prevented by sickness; but, as sailors require rest, as well as other men, their hours of labor are so divided, that while one-half of the crew are on watch or duty, the other half are at leisure. There are two watches, which are known by the names of port and starboard, each of which are four hours long. As this system, however, if followed out, would only give one-half the crew four hours' sleep every night, another watch, called the dog-watch, which is intended to obviate this difficulty, was established. This is a watch of two hours, and extends from four to six and from six to eight in the evening, and by this means each of the two watches of the ship are enabled every second night to get eight hours' sleeep. Thus the watch which is relieved from duty at eight o'clock in the evening, can sleep till twelve, and being again relieved at four, may at that hour take possession of their hammocks and sleep till eight in the morning. These watches are stationed in different parts of the ship, both day and night, some in the foretop, an elevated position on the foremast about a hundred feet from the deck, and some in the main and mizzen tops, while others are placed on the forecastle or poop, by the ship's boats, a: the helm, and other stations, where they are always ready when their services are required. One of the men on the foretop keeps a look-out for all vessels, and on account of his position is able to see them half an honr or more before they are visible from the deck. The moment he descries a sail, though it looks like a mere speck on the horizon, he announces it to the officer of the deck. "Sail ho!" he cries aloud, from his station, when the officer, if he desires to know the direction in which he has seen it, asks, "Where away?" and is told in reply that it is on the weather quarter or lee bow, as the case may be. But in mid-ocean the announcement that a vessel is in sight is received with the greatest interest. Every one is anxiously looking out for her, and all the telescopes and opera glasses on board are in immediate demand.

The men stationed at the poop are required to be particularly vigilant, so that if a man should fall overboard, they may be ready at a moment's warning to detach the life-buoy. There are several other watches for the reefing, furling, and setting sails, and for various other duties, the details of which possess little interest for the general reader.

The force of marines on the Niagara does not exceed sixty men, but they are among the most effective and the best drilled in the service. They are the sentry of the ship, and are always placed on guard over the grog, the ship's stores, the provisions, and on the different decks. The marine, besides being the sentry of the ship, is also a soldier, and his drilling and training differ in no material respects from the drilling and training of the soldier in our military service.

Every ship of war in our navy is provided with sailors' clothing of all kinds, sufficient to supply their demands during the cruise, and longer if necessary. These are given to the men at cost price, and the total amount deducted from their wages. In this respect the seamen on board a man-of-war have a great advantage over those who ship on a mere merchant vessel, and who are obliged to purchase their outfit at exorbitant rates in retail establishments. In addition to this the clothing furnished by the government is of a superior quality, and Jack has the satisfaction of knowing that he gets the full value of his money. If he is of a saving, economical nature, this is a great consideration to him; and as his means are limited, and he is not very judicious in the expenditure of them, it is the best thing the government can do, as long as it deals only with honest contractors, and not with men who never scruple to make money even by frauds upon those who labor hard for a living.

The clothes are served out by the purser on a specified day, when all who have applied for various articles of dress must be in attendance. This officer has their names written on a schedule opposite the different pieces of clothing of which they are in want, and as he calls them out in their turn, they step forward and receive them from one of the purser's assistants. One pile of clothing consists entirely of pants, another of drawers, another of caps, another of socks and stockings, another of pea-jackets, another of flannel overshirts, another of boots and shoes, and so on to the end of the list. As they are not very particular about the exact size of the pants or pea-jackets, it is easy to suit them, but the chief trouble is in the fitting on of the shoes. He has, however, an immense number of all sizes to select from, and he generally finds his measure some time between five minutes and half an hour. The flannel and cloth he converts into a shirt or trousers, as taste or necessity may dictate, and when he wants to lay in a good supply he obtains from ten to twenty yards of it for the purpose. Some are not so expert at the needle as others, and those will pay three or four yards of their flannel for the making of a pair of pants or a shirt, and more in proportion for a pea-jacket or other article of dress that requires a larger expenditure of time and labor in its manufacture. The tailoring is carried on principally on the forward parts of the spar deck, in favorable weather, when as many as twenty or thirty may be seen sitting under the bulwarks and working away as if they had served a regular apprenticeship to the trade. There, in the midst of that group of lookers-on, is an experienced hand at the work, chalking out the various parts for the sleeves, the collars and the body, before cutting it out; while here, in the centre of another little knot of spectators, is an amateur in the same business, employed in embroidering a star of various colors, for the top of a cap, or the collar of a flannel shirt. They are not only supplied with cloth and clothing, but with thread, needles, thimbles, bodkins and every thing necessary to carry on the tailoring successfully. And this is not all. The ingenious sailor is not only able to make his own clothes, but he can turn out of his hands as good hats as he can purchase in the store. They are made of straw, or some similar material, which he first plaits and afterwards stitches together without even a fitting block, and yet with as much neatness and success as if he had all the appliances of a manufactory at his control. From all this it will be seen that however different they may appear, it is not impossible to combine the two occupations of sailor and tailor in the one person, and that the same man who is accustomed to handle a marlinspike can use a needle with as much skill and dexterity.

That particular hour of the whole twenty-four which possesses the most interest for sailors, and which is always looked forward to with pleasure, is that appointed for serving out the grog. No matter how dilatory they may be on all other occasions, they are always on the alert when Uncle Sam, as they say, is going to "stand treat." All hands are on deck then, and collected in an eager, expectant throng before the grog tub, ready to "stand by" when their names are called. The vessel used for serving out the liquor is a small tin cup called a "tot," which contains somewhat more than a glass full, which is emptied by each man with a rapidity that would astonish any one ignorant of the ease with which Jack disposes of such welcome favors. Occasionally some men are to be found among a ship's crew who are strictly temperate, and to these the government always makes an allowance in money when paying their bills, equal to the value of their grog rations. In the course of a year this amounts to nine or ten dollars to each man, sufficient to keep him in shoes for nearly the whole of that time. By saving in this and other rations he is enabled to add, if he is so disposed, at least twenty dollars to his twelve months' pay, which at the rate of eighteen dollars a month for a good seaman, is over two hundred dollars. The green hands, who come under the title of landsmen, and of whom there are a large number on board the Niagara, are not so well paid. Whatever saving or economy they may exhibit in the consumption of their mess rations is very rarely extended to their grog, and one of the severest penalties you can inflict upon them is to deprive them of their daily allowance. When other punishments for minor offences have failed, "cutting off the grog" has almost invariably succeeded in bringing the culprit to his senses. Notwithstanding all the efforts of the temperance advocates for the abolition of this particular institution on shipboard, it seems destined to a long life; and it is much to be feared that although Jack is the party whom their efforts are intended to benefit, he is so far unable to appreciate their kindness that he would prove one of their most strenuous opponents.

ARRIVAL OF THE NIAGARA IN ENGLAND.

The Niagara arrived in the Thames on the 14th of May, and came to anchor off Gravesend, a small port about twenty-five miles from London. She remained here till the 5th of June, when she left for Portsmouth, to undergo the alterations necessary to fit her for the reception and laying of the cable. While lying in the Thames she was an object of much interest, and was visited daily by a large concourse of people.

The inhabitants of Gravesend flocked in crowds to see the ship, and when it was reported that we would not remain more than a week, received the announcement as they would the departure of old and cherished friends. The first and second day after we had anchored opposite their picturesque little city, only a few of them came to see us. There would, however, have been a large number, had it not been generally believed that they would not be allowed on board; but as soon as they learned that they were not only allowed on board but that they were not restricted to any part of the ship, we were almost overwhelmed with visitors. The weather was favorable, and they took advantage of it, determined that it should not be their fault if they did not see us and ascertain for themselves what kind of people the Yankees are. The river in the immediate vicinity of our ship swarmed with small craft of every description, and from early morning till eight in the evening a steady, constant stream of men, women, and children poured in and out over her sides. They flocked in throngs into the officers' wardroom, the captain's cabin, the engine-room, and all parts of the vessel, and appeared as if they would never weary in looking at every thing they saw. It was the first American man-of-war, they said, that had ever anchored in the Thames, and as they had never seen one before, their curiosity was excited to the highest pitch. They wanted to know if all our vessels were of the same size, and were astonished that we should allow persons to visit every part of her. The boatmen, who hailed her appearance with general joy on account of the impulse she gave to their business, were unbounded in their praises of her immense size, and the symmetry of her model. One of these, a tough, weather-beaten old fellow who had, he told us, been in many a hard blow off the English coast, had quite an interesting conversation with one of a party belonging to the Niagara, whom he was taking out to the vessel.

"What kind of a ship is that?" said the gentleman, professing to be ignorant of her character.

"That? Vy that's a Hamerican ship," he replied.

"Well," said his questioner, "are the people civil aboard of her? Will they let you see her?"

"Yes," he said, "they're wery good—wery civil; their civility is n'countable—they're so civil."

"Well, I see," the other rejoined, "I see she's a very large ship for a frigate."

"Aye, you may say that. Ecod, I believe you sir. If they calls such a ship as that a frigate, I dunna what their liners be. Ha! ha!"

The women are in raptures with both officers and men, and sometimes give pretty free expression to their feelings.

"I really thought," one of them said the other day to an officer who was showing her the vessel and explaining all the parts of it to her, "I really thought that they didn't allow people to look about the ship. But we find the officers and the men so very civil and so willing to oblige us that we were quite taken by surprise. Indeed," she continued, "I like the officers so much that if I had a chance I think I'd run away with one." Here was a female kidnapper with a vengeance; but she did not show any desire to carry out her design then and there.

Among the celebrities who visited the ship was Lady Franklin, who was, of course, a great object of interest on account of the position in which her melancholy loss, her self-devotion, enduring hope and noble fortitude have placed her before every lover of true womanhood in both the Old World and the New. She is now about sixty-five years old, and in stature is rather below the medium height. Her face is peculiarly expressive, and every feature of it is indicative of that remarkable tenacity of purpose and undying hope which have buoyed her up in the midst of her affliction and which at this time still characterize her. It is said that she has at last abandoned all hope of ever seeing her husband alive, but believes that his body and the records of his cruise will yet be found. A proper feeling of delicacy forbade all allusion to the subject among the company; but those who were present could not avoid seeing the emotion which she endeavored to subdue. She had visited the Resolute when in London, and her presence again among Americans awoke recollections of a pleasing but still of a painful character, recalling to her mind the efforts which our countrymen have made for the discovery of the lost navigator and the early death of one of those who was foremost in the ranks of Arctic explorers.

Before leaving for Portsmouth the Agamemnon, which was appointed by the British Government to take one-half the cable at Greenwich, arrived in the Thames. As she passed us on her way up the river, three thundering cheers burst from her decks and shrouds, that roused the slumbering echoes on either shore, and before they died away they were answered by our men with one long sustained hurrah, that seemed to pierce the very clouds. The three that greeted and came thundering to us from the British ship were as distinct and as nicely graduated as if they were timed and marked by the roll of a drum; but ours appeared to be under no restraint, and blended and mingled in one long wild hurra like the sound of a whirlwind. After one more cheer—a parting one before the British vessel passed beyond hailing distance—the riggings were cleared, and we watched her as she ploughed her way up the Thames, part of her hull looming above the banks, even as she turned the bend in the river.

It was supposed that the Niagara would take her half the cable from the manufactory at Greenwich, and that the Agamemnon would ship the other half from the manufactory at Birkenhead, opposite Liverpool, but this order was reversed on account of the great size of our ship and the difficulty of procuring sufficient room for her near the wharf in front of the cable works.

The arrival of the Susquehanna in the Thames was daily expected, as she had some time before received orders to join the Niagara and to act as her escort during the expedition. It was known through private letters that she had left Spezzia on the 18th of May, and she was therefore looked for several days previous to her arrival. On her way, however, she stopped five days at Lisbon, from which she made the passage to Cowes in four more. While lying in this part of the British Channel she was passed by the Osborne, the British Admiralty yacht, on board of which was the Grand Duke Constantine of Russia, who was on a brief private visit to the Queen, and the details of whose reception were given at length in the English papers. There was considerable consumption of gunpowder on the occasion, but not quite such an expenditure of the article as took place during the eleven long and weary months that the allies lay before Sebastopol. But a comparatively brief period has elapsed since the celebrated siege of that city, and now we see the two royal families who at that time were at deadly feud with each other, meeting on terms of apparently the most friendly social intercourse. It appears that the Grand Duke was somewhat jocular on the occasion of his introduction to Mr. Bower, who at the time of the siege was sailing master on board the Agamemnon, one of the vessels of the immense fleet with which the English assailed the great Russian naval dépôt of the Black Sea. It is said that he asked Mr. Bower if he did not find himself in a "very hot berth," but the future historian is left in complete ignorance of Mr. B.'s answer, for the journalist, while he has recorded the pleasantry of the Grand Duke, has said nothing about the reply of the sailing master. There was, as has been already stated, a considerable consumption of gunpowder at the reception of the distinguished visitor, and it may not be unworthy of notice that the Susquehanna was the first to salute him. Her yards were manned, and twenty-one guns fired, a compliment which, it is said, the Grand Duke expressed his high appreciation of as tendered by a nation with which Russia had always been on the most friendly terms.

The Susquehanna arrived in the Thames about 7 o'clock on Sunday morning, the 31st of May, and a few hours after was seen from our deck. As she neared our ship our signals were run up, and after she had passed and anchored within a few hundred yards of us, one of our officers was sent on board of her. Captain Hudson subsequently visited Captain Sands, her commander, according to the rules of our naval service, which require the junior captain to pay this mark of respect to the senior on all such occasions. This was the only demonstration which was made—there was no cheering, nor any of those manifestations of feeling which were displayed on both sides the Sunday before, when the Agamemnon passed us on her way up the river. It is only, it appears, when our ships are parting company that they cheer each other. But if our men were not permitted to indulge in those friendly demonstrations, the gratification which they felt at seeing another of our national vessels in a foreign port, with the flag of the republic flying from her peak, was none the less sincere and heartfelt. This was the first time that two American war vessels had been seen in the Thames, and it is gratifying to be able to state that they were the largest vessels of their class in the world, the Niagara being the largest propeller, and the Susquehanna the largest side wheel steamer. The officers of both vessels soon made or renewed acquaintance with each other, for some were formerly old companions in the service, and their meeting, as may be supposed, was of the most pleasant character.

PREPARATION OF THE NIAGARA AT PLYMOUTH.

The Niagara left the Thames for Portsmouth on the 5th of June, where she arrived the following day. She was detained here two weeks, while the necessary alterations were being made for the coiling of the cable at Birkenhead. Those who were on the ship before she left New York the previous April, would have been astonished at some of the changes she underwent during her stay at this port. The officers' wardroom was broken into, three of their state-rooms on each side of it taken down, and the partition which divided it from the rest of the main or berth deck completely removed. The open space which extended outside of this apartment, away beyond the steerage, is called "the country" among the sailors, but the barrier once removed, the officers' wardroom might now properly be said to form a part of the rural districts, and the whole mess enjoyed all the

NIAGARA AND TENDER.

pleasures of rustication for several months. They sacrificed whatever conveniences they had to the success of the enterprise, cheerfully abandoned their berths for a hammock, and turned out of their state-rooms, that there might be sufficient space for the coiling of the cable, which was spread over a large tract of "the country." The moment the carpenters and other workmen made their appearance, there was a general moving among those whose quarters were invaded, which, on a small scale, might not inaptly be compared to the first of May in New York. Looking-glasses were intrusted to the hands of careful waiters, and stowed away in places of safety; little libraries taken down from their shelves above the berths, and packed in trunks for the time being; then followed the wardrobe in all its variety—the naval uniform and the dress of the civilian, the cocked hats of the officers in three-cornered japanned boxes, all by themselves, and the beavers of the citizens, with and without boxes; the three or four dozen shirts and the five or six dozen collars, carried as carefully on the outstretched arms of the waiters as if they were so many new-born babies; India-rubber overcoats, India-rubber overalls, and India-rubber boots, forming an impervious armor against the rain; combs, brushes, razors, bootjacks, hat brushes, pin cushions, needles, scissors, and all the other great and little things without which no domestic establishment can be carried on either on ship or ashore. Various contrivances were resorted to by those who lost their state-rooms, and the ingenuity exhibited under the circumstances would have astonished a landsman. Here is a little corner which was set apart for a water jar, but which has been converted into a sort of dressing chamber. The jar has been removed, and in its stead a basin stand is erected, while upon a little hook above it hangs a towel, and the whole three-cornered concern is enclosed by a curtain formed of canvas, behind which the owner performs his morning ablutions and arranges his toilet. The oil carpet furnished by Uncle Sam's agents (and it's a very poor affair) was taken up, the bulkheads torn down, and the stanchions soon shared the same fate; but in their stead were placed strong iron braces, or arches, to support the immense beams which extended under the spar deck, from side to side of the vessel. In some places, while the state-rooms were torn down, just enough of the berths were left to allow the occupant to lie upon one side, making it absolutely necessary for him to get up altogether before he could turn on the other. But after all the inconvenience and annoyance which attended these alterations, there was a novelty in the change which gave it a sort of attraction. The carpenters made a tremendous noise when at work, and the confused sound of hammering, sawing and filing, was any thing but pleasant; but it was nothing compared to a good strong patriotic democratic mass meeting in the Park, or an excited, belligerent and pugilistic crowd in Tammany Hall.

Other changes and preparations were made on the Niagara at Portsmouth, among which was the attachment of a cable guard to her stern, and of which a description will be found in the more advanced pages of this work.

THE NIAGARA AT LIVERPOOL.

The necessary alterations having been made in the ship during her stay at Portsmouth, she left that port for Liverpool on the 20th of June, where the cable was to be coiled and the machinery fitted up previous to her departure for Queenstown, Ireland, which had been decided on as the place of rendezvous for the Telegraph Squadron. The Niagara arrived in the Mersey on the 22d, where she attracted as much attention as she received during her detention in the Thames. The Captain and officers were overwhelmed with attentions, and found it impossible to meet all the demands of public and private hospitality. The Chamber of Commerce gave them a dinner, the Mayor of Liverpool another, and the American residents a grand banquet on the Fourth of July.

It was the first celebration of the national anniversary which had ever taken place in that city, and from beginning to end was a most successful affair. There are only twenty-five American residents in Liverpool—a small number, it must be acknowledged, but they were not, as they proved, too small numerically for what they undertook, and what there is no doubt will serve as a precedent for future imitation.

The officers of the Niagara were all dressed in uniform, and as the steamboat which conveyed them from the ship landed at the pier, they became the subject of the most intense curiosity to all who saw them, and wondering eyes displayed their anxiety to know what the whole thing meant. As they passed on their way up the pier, the following colloquy took place between two of the most curious.

"What are all these officers doing here?—what does it all mean, I wonder?" inquired one of these of the other.

"That's what I've been trying to find out myself," he replied, "but nobody seems to know. I hear that they're the officers of the great Yankee man-of-war that's agoin' to take that 'ere cable, but what they're a goin' to do I don't know."

"I'll tell you what they're about" said a third chiming in—"I'll tell you what they're about: this is the Fourth of July, and they re going to a great dinner."

But this did not enlighten them any the more, so the third party had to give them some of the particulars regarding the day, and informed him that all the American flags were displayed in honor of the occasion.

On the arrival of the officers at the hotel, they were received by the committee, by whom they were introduced to the rest of the company. When the ceremony of introduction was over, the whole party proceeded to the dining hall. This apartment was handsomely ornamented for the occasion. Over the entrance the American flag was displayed : at the opposite end was a rather fierce looking specimen of the bird of Jove, while upon the walls around the apartment were hung engravings of the telegraph fleet, the signers of the Declaration of Independence, a portrait of Washington, the American Senate in session, and a fac simile of the Declaration itself. When the dinner was thoroughly discussed, the company passed the rest of the evening in speech making and the interchange of friendly sentiments.

Among those who visited the ship while in the Mersey was Prince Napoleon, the son of Jerome, and another of the nephews of his uncle. He was attended by his suite, consisting of the following gentlemen :—Le Baron de la Ronciere, capitaine; le chef d' escadron d' état Major Ferri; Disant, aide-de-camp du Prince chef d' escadron de cavalerie; Clerc, écuyer du Prince; M. Regnault, membre de l'Institut; M. de Chaucourtais, engénieur des mines; M. Arago, son of the astronomer; Inspecteur Général des Beaux Arts; le capitaine de frégate Silva; commandant le yacht Reine Hortense; Hamelin, lieutenant de vaisseau, and Miet, enseigne de vaisseau. It was understood that the prince was to visit the ship *incog.*—that is, every body, from the captain down to the powder monkeys, were to know who he was—at least such is the meaning of the word, as established by royal usage and custom. The young English Prince is to make his tour of Europe in the same style; and when all the other members of the royal family set out on their travels, it is to be presumed they will adopt a similar course.

The Prince and his suite came alongside in a steamboat, and his Imperial Highness was the first to come on board. The captain invited the whole company into the cabin, where he explained the different features of interest in the enterprise to them. The Prince is said to be a remarkable likeness of his great uncle, but he is much taller, being about five feet eleven. He has certainly the Napoleonic face, and might easily be picked out in a crowd as a member of the family; but that imperial expression which is seen in all the portraits of the First Napoleon, is wanting in the nephew. He is about thirty-five years of age, and resembles his uncle, not only in the face, but in the peculiar stoop of the shoulders by which the Little Corporal was distinguished. The Prince is exceedingly affable in his manners, and although his knowledge of English appears to be somewhat limited, he manages to carry on a tolerably animated conversation with the partial aid of an interpreter. Captain Hudson posted him up in all the particulars about the cable, the way it was made, the way it was to be laid, and, last of all, the way the ships were to take when engaged in paying it out. He then took the Prince and suite around the vessel, and showed them all that was worth seeing, and when he was taking his departure manned the rigging and gave him three cheers. The Prince was very much gratified with his reception, and invited the captain to dine with him the same afternoon.

The Niagara was as great an object of curiosity and wonder here as she was to the people of Gravesend, when she was lying in the Thames, and her fame extended far and wide throughout the country. Captain Hudson, for the purpose of giving all who desired to see her an opportunity of doing so, permitted one of the ferry companies to bring passengers alongside, but issued an order that they should not be allowed to go below the spar deck, or in any part of the ship where they might in any way interrupt or interfere with the workmen while employed in coiling the cable and putting up the machinery. As a large number of persons availed themselves of this privilege, the ferry company reaped quite a harvest, and of course took every means to keep up the public interest in the ship. They issued large posters, which stared at one from the walls near the wharves, and ornamented the wheel-houses of the steamboats plying to and from the ship. The public were notified, through the means of these, that "the Leviathan United States frigate Niagara is to be seen from nine o'clock A. M. to eight P. M.;" and further, knowing that no visitors were permitted to come aboard on Sunday, they endeavored to attract passengers by announcing that such and such boats pass the Leviathan American Ship on their way to such a place, and that they would go round her for the purpose of letting them have a full view of this "monster of the deep." For the privilege of visiting the ship the ferry company charged one shilling sterling a head—about twenty-five cents of our money—the price of admission to any of the negro operatic entertainments in New York. With some of the people a shilling is quite a large amount of money, and it is often as much as many receive for half a day's labor. It is easy to imagine from this what an event they considered the appearance of a vessel of this description in their waters, and that a visit to her is something to look forward to as a treat which they might enjoy only once in half a century. In this state of mind they came on board, and were astonished that they were not allowed to go all over, even into the cabin and officers' wardroom, both of which are as private as any gentleman's house could be, and which it is really a privilege to be permitted to enter. Some of them did not understand this, but, supposing that the shilling entitled them to the right of going wherever they pleased, were considerably disappointed when they found that they were confined to the spar deck, and that the other parts of the vessel were shut against them. One of these went up to the officer of the deck, and, with a look of extreme disgust and dissatisfaction, said he desired to go below.

"I should certainly allow you to do so with pleasure," replied the officer, "but there is an order against permitting persons to go below this deck, as they might interfere with the operatives."

"But I want to see it, you know," said the visitor; "I paid my shilling to look at every part of the ship. I was promised that I should see the berths below and all the ship underneath, when I gave my money."

This was said with a manner and in a tone of voice which would lead a person to suppose that he had been swindled out of his shilling, and that the officer himself was a party to the transaction.

This ended the conversation, and the visitor left the ship in high dudgeon, leaving an undecided impression on the mind of the officer whether he intended to sue him for obtaining money under false pretences, or that his indignation had so far got the better of him as to deprive him utterly of the power of replying in a manner that would do justice to his feelings.

THE COILING OF THE CABLE.

The coiling of the cable at Liverpool occupied three weeks, and although a somewhat tedious operation, possessed many features of interest.

The men employed in the work were, with the exception of half a dozen who were engaged by the Atlantic Telegraph Company, sailors on the Niagara, who volunteered for the purpose, as none but such as were willing to serve and freely offered themselves, were drafted from the crew for this service. They were informed that none but volunteers should be employed, and of its nature and character; the difficulties by which it would be attended; the wear and tear of clothes, and the tedious task on which they were about to enter—explaining, in fact, all its objectionable features, so that after they should have entered upon it they might not be able to say they did so in ignorance of what they were required to do. The objectionable features, however, did not seem to deter them from coming forward in large numbers, and offering their names, from which a strong force was made out for the work. They were perfectly enthusiastic about it, and it seemed to be a matter of rivalry among them as to who should be accepted. About one hundred and twenty were enlisted for the service, and these, with ten of the operatives of the company, formed the great corps of cable coilers on the Niagara. The day was divided into watches, and as there were about thirty men on each watch, they were required to work only six hours out of the twenty-four.

A visit to the coil when all hands are engaged in packing the cable, and when it is coming down through the hatch into the circle or circus that is prepared for its reception, is full of interest. To make your way successfully into that part of the ship is no easy task, and if not acquainted "with the ropes," one must expect to receive many a knock in the head or legs, by running foul of planks, or chains, or ringbolts, and twenty other things, the names of which are known only to the initiated. After a descent of some twenty feet you find yourself in the lower hold of the vessel, looking over the little wooden wall that bounds the circus and keeps the outer part of the coil in its proper place, on a large mass of what appears at first sight to be solidified tar, with a cone rising in the centre like a miniature representation of a mountain peak. Thirty men, with blackened hands, blackened feet, and clothes that are rapidly changing to a deep mourning color, are standing in a circle about half way between this same cone and the outer edge of the coil. There is one who is constantly walking round this circle with somewhat of the steady jog trot speed of an old mill horse, and who, in his revolutions, pays out the cable to each man as he passes him. He just gives him sufficient for his share, for if he were to give him a foot over the exact amount required, the separate coils would be unevenly laid, and great delay would be caused by having to go over the work again. If he walks fast, therefore, he is obliged to pay out in proportion to his rate of speed, but both walking and paying out are so nicely proportioned in this respect that he is very seldom obliged to correct any mistakes.

This is the simple process of coiling the cable—the mere mechanical part of the work, and nothing can be more dull or monotonous, or stupidly uninteresting. It has, however, a social aspect which it would be unjust to overlook. The thirty operatives who sit around the cone, sometimes a few inches, and at other times twelve or thirteen feet from it, are not mere automata, but men, and a good jolly set of fellows they are, with the ready joke, the quick repartee, budgets bursting with yarns, and riddles, and conundrums, and Joe Millerisms, mixed up with an abundance of mother wit that if possessed by one individual would immortalize him forever in the annals of the comic and humorous. There is one who stands high in repute among the particular watch to which he belongs, and whose fame has spread to such an extent among the the other watches that they would raise a subscription to buy his time for their own especial amusement. He is a prince of good fellows—a regular Jack Tar—well stocked with yarns that leave even the inventive powers of Munchausen in the shade, and as full of fun as an egg is full of meat—provided it be a good one, which makes all the difference in the world, so far as the accuracy of the comparison is regarded. But with all their jokes, and riddles, and yarns, and conundrums, they do not neglect their work, for while in their merriest mood, the cable is packed away with as much rapidity as if they bestowed their undivided attention on it, and kept as silent as a congregation at a prayer meeting. They call themselves the telegraph watch, and it is with no little feeling of pride they regard their position as coilers. The superintendent, who is placed over them to see that they do not neglect their work, and who sits in that little box outside of the circle, has no occasion to display his authority, for they are so willing, and so active, and so quick, and so earnest, too, that there is really no necessity for his supervision. He may now and then throw in a word by way of showing that he is in his box; but his occasional requests or exhortations to the men to "be lively now," are entirely unnecessary; they are both active and lively, and he knows it as well as a man ever knew any thing with which he was thoroughly acquainted. He has his part to perform, however, and when he tells them about once every half hour the same thing that he has been telling them ever since the first yard of the cable was taken on board, they know that after all it is only a matter of form, and no insinuation or hint that they are not attending to their work. They know, too, that he is just as good a fellow as any one of their own number, and that he enjoys a joke as well as those inside the circle. After all the dulness and monotony of the work, there is no dulness about the workmen, and the time passes so rapidly with them, that they are sometmes astonished when a fresh "telegraph watch" comes to their relief.

The cable men of the Niagara were like so many Mark Tapleys, and came out most creditably under circumstances that would have damped the ardor of any other body of men. The circle of coilers, as they sat round the ring piling up flake on flake, were more like a social party assembled for amusement than a body of operatives who had a monotonous work to perform. They amused themselves with conundrums, both good and bad, related yarns as long as the maintop-bowline, and laughed at jokes that they had heard for the twentieth time. But withal there was no neglect of the work, which went on unceasingly from morn to night, and from night to morn, till the twenty-first day saw the last mile of it placed on board. Nearly one-half the time, too, they

COILING SCENE ON BOARD THE NIAGARA.

were reduced to a stooping posture, for, as the coils increased in height, the space between the top of them and the beams of the deck overhead gradually diminished so as to render it impossible for them to stand, or even sit upright. In this extremity they resorted to a contrivance which was no less novel than it was ingenious, and which afforded them an inexhaustible fund of mirth and humor. The operative who travelled round the circle, paying out the cable which he hauled down through the opening above him, was obliged by the increasing height of the coil, not only to stoop like his fellow-workmen, but was compelled to go down upon his hands and knees. As it was impossible, however, for him to use his hands while upon all-fours, it became necessary to devise another way of paying out to the coilers. The inventive faculties were now called into play, and the result was the contrivance which is represented in the subjoined engraving.

A belt, it may be observed, is fastened round his body, and to this again is attached an iron ring through which the cable passes, and by means of which it is thus paid out to the operators. When this ingenious contrivance was introduced, it was welcomed amid a shower of jokes from every part of the circle, and when harnessed to the "payer out," the provocation was so perfectly irresistible, that from that time to the end of the work there were enough yarns spun and stories told to make a dozen such volumes as Baron Munchausen, with a whole library of Joe Millers to boot. He was called "a fast hoss," "a bob-tailed nag," "a full-blooded racer," &c., &c., &c., and small bets were offered on his trotting round the course in less than two forty. "Hey—get along there—what 're you about—trot round, my filly—jee up now and show your training," and such like exclamations greeted him as he proceeded on all fours round the cone. "Give me a grip of your tail, old Joey." "There he goes off in a canter—ten to one on his pacing," and so the fun was kept up, the fast nag himself occasionally joining in with the company. Take it altogether, there was never such a combination of humor, fun, genius and art, as was to be found in the submarine cable circles of the Niagara, and if the circles of the Agamemnon had only half the complement, they must have been as jolly a set of fellows as ever assembled on a British man of war.

While the Niagara was receiving the cable in the Mersey, a meeting of the members of the Atlantic Telegraph Company was held in London to decide upon the debated question, whether the laying of the cable should be commenced from Valentia Bay or from mid-ocean. The engineers were in favor of the latter course, but they were overruled by the electricians, who advocated the former. And so it was decided, that the cable should be landed at Valentia Bay, and paid out across the ocean to Newfoundland. According to the plan adopted, the Niagara was to pay out her portion of the cable first, and then to splice the end to that on board the Agamemnon, which was to lay the remaining half, and land her end at Trinity Bay, the point of connection on the American side. Whatever doubts there may have been as to the greater feasibility of the mid-ocean plan, there certainly can be none now in view of the results which have attended the first and last expeditions.

THE NIAGARA AND THE TELEGRAPH FLEET AT QUEENSTOWN.

The coiling of the cable on the Niagara at Liverpool occupied three weeks, as we have said, but her departure was delayed by the fitting up of the machinery. She left Liverpool, however, on the 27th of July for Queenstown, Ireland, where she arrived on the 29th of the same month. While at Queenstown several electrical experiments were made, and satisfactory results reported, although it was subsequently admitted, that, if the cable had been successfully submerged on the first expedition, the electricians could not have sent messages through it. The Agamemnon arrived at Queenstown on the 30th of July, three days after the Niagara; and while the vessels were lying within a few hundred yards of each another, the ends of the cable on both were joined so as to make one continuous line of twenty-five hundred miles. The insulation was found to be perfect, and about ninety currents were sent through the conductor in a minute, but the electricians had not attained that perfection in their instruments necessary to secure the correct transmission of words and messages.

The whole telegraph squadron, consisting of the following vessels, sailed from Queenstown:

The U. S. Steam Frigate Niagara, to lay the half of the cable from Valentia Bay, Ireland.

The U. S. Steam Frigate Susquehanna, to attend upon the Niagara.

H. M. Steamer Agamemnon, to lay the half of the cable on the American side.

H. M. Steamer Leopard, to attend upon the Agamemnon.

H. M. Steamer Cyclops, to go ahead of the steamers, and keep the course.

The steamers "Advice" and "Willing Mind," to assist in landing the cable in Valentia.

In Trinity Bay the U. S. Steamer Arctic and the Telegraph Company's steamer Victoria were to await the arrival of the fleet, and assist in landing the cable there.

DEPARTURE OF THE SQUADRON FOR VALENTIA BAY—THE MACHINERY AND OTHER APPLIANCES FOR LAYING THE CABLE.

The squadron left Queenstown for Valentia Bay on Monday, the 3d of August, and arrived there the following day. Advantage was taken of the passage to experiment with the machinery, which up to that time had not been tested on board the Niagara. Before referring more particularly to these experiments, however, it becomes necessary at this stage of the undertaking, to lay before the reader a detailed description of the various points which are necessary to an understanding of the whole subject. And, first of all, let us look at that wonderful plateau—that great submarine prairie, which lies between Ireland and Newfoundland, and which seems to have been placed there by the hand of Providence for this great end.

THE ATLANTIC TELEGRAPH PLATEAU.

In the course of this work reference has been made to the many things which appear to have conspired in favor of this, the greatest enterprise ever undertaken by man. The discovery of the value of gutta percha as an insulator happened at the most opportune moment, and proved of the most vital importance; and still later, at a time when the prospect of an Atlantic telegraph was not only discussed but was absolutely undertaken, a great plateau, it was asserted, extended along the bed of the ocean, exactly between the two points which it was proposed to connect. In both these instances—that is, in the discovery of this peculiar use of gutta percha and in the existence of this grand ocean level—nature seems to have given her powerful assistance towards the successful accomplishment of the undertaking. While every other part of the bed of the Atlantic is marked by the same inequalities, the same abrupt declivities and mountain heights, this is like an immense prairie, stretching over an extent of fourteen hundred miles from east to west, with an average depth of seventeen hundred fathoms, and never exceeding twenty-five hundred, entirely free from under currents, lying directly between the most advanced posts of the Old and New Worlds, and as it approaches the Newfoundland coast, north of the Great Bank, entirely free from the effects of icebergs, which ground on the shallow bottoms. It seems not only peculiarly adapted for the purpose, but as if it were absolutely designed by Providence for this very object.

The existence of this plateau was believed in some years before it was proved by actual test. Sea captains who had made frequent passages over this route, came to the conclusion that the depth of the water in this part of the ocean was not so great as that to the north and south of it—a conclusion which was based upon the indications in the difference of color. One of the theories in regard to the formation of this ocean prairie is based on the revolutions which some scientific men say were effected during the ice period. The immense granite boulders which are found on the limestone prairies of Iowa and Illinois, are supposed to have been deposited where they now are when the sea covered those vast plains. There are no rocks of a similar description, it is alleged, nearer than from five hundred to a thousand miles to the north of them, and their remarkable appearance at this distance is accounted for in a rather ingenious manner. It is believed that they were conveyed southward from the Arctic regions in the frozen embraces of gigantic icebergs, and that on reaching a more genial climate they were literally thawed out and deposited where they are now seen. By the deposits of these and other materials, it is argued the prairies of Illinois and Iowa have been formed in the course of those incalculable, unknown ages which passed before the earth was considered by the Creator a fit habitation for the last and most perfect of his creatures. Now, whether true or false, the theory is very plausible, and should receive a fair consideration. Here, however, it does not rest—its application comes next. If far stretching plains, which it is believed once formed the bed of the ocean, were thus built up, why should not the action of a similar agency produce a similar result? Here we have gigantic icebergs floating down every year from the north—some of them carrying with them immense rocks which they have torn from the Arctic mountains on their descent into the sea. As these icebergs have floated down into milder latitudes they have gradually become weaker and weaker, until, unable any longer to carry their weighty burdens, they have deposited them in the bed of the ocean, and on that particular part of it which has been mapped out in the charts of Lieut. Berryman, of the United States Navy, and Captain Dayman, of H. M. Navy, as the line of the telegraph plateau. Although there is no proof either for or against this statement, and cannot be so long as the depths of the sea remain unrevealed to the eye of man, it is a well ascertained fact, that large quantities of earth and heavy fragments of rock are carried down yearly from the polar regions by the huge icebergs, which descend in such numbers as frequently to render the ocean almost impassable in some latitudes. The Gulf Stream is, however, said to be the great agent by which this plateau has been built up, and but for it the Atlantic Telegraph Company would be under slight obligation to those same icebergs for the part they have performed. The Gulf Stream meets them every year just in the right spot, and, wending off in a northeasterly direction, immediately above the line of the plateau, carries with it the more solid matter with which they were freighted, and which it scatters along its route. This matter, combined with what is held in solution by itself, forms in the course of thousands of years an immense mass, sufficient, perhaps, to make an island larger than that of Great Britain. The telegraph plateau has been called a plain; but it is, more properly speaking, an immense table-land, like the steppes of the Andes, rising up from the bed of the ocean. To the south of it the Atlantic is four, five, and six miles deep, while on the plateau alone is there any thing like a uniform level. In addition to the rocks which have been deposited by the melting or melted icebergs, there is, as has been stated, a large quantity of other matter, consisting, if we are to judge from the soundings of the two officers of the United States and British navies, just named, in great part of exceedingly minute shells, so minute indeed, as to be imperceptible to the naked eye. The finding of these is considered an infallible indication of the absence of currents at the bottom of this part of the ocean. This belief is further sustained by the fact, that in the soundings of Captain Dayman and Lieut. Berryman, the slack line would be coiled and kinked over the lead, showing plainly that it had reached the bottom after the lead had become detached, which could not have been the case if the plateau were swept by currents.

The first soundings which were made were taken by Lieut. Berryman in the summer of 1853, and the second and last in the fall of 1856. These were very successful, establishing, beyond all peradventure, the existence of the plateau. In June and July of 1857, Captain Dayman, of H. M. S. Cyclops, also made soundings on the line of the proposed telegraph, and with the same satisfactory result. Some exceptions had been taken in regard to the reliability of Lieut. Berryman's soundings, but those of Captain Dayman were strongly corroborative of their correctness, making allowance for the variations of locality in the soundings of the two officers.

It must not be forgotten that the soundings of Capt. Dayman and Lieut. Berryman were made at distances of from five to thirty miles apart, and were seldom if ever taken within a mile of each other. In view of this fact the reader will at once perceive their remarkable coincidence. Capt. Dayman states in his report that whatever errors there may be in the depths given by marked lines, they are on the side of excess. The reason for this is twofold: "Firstly, the loss of time (and consequently loss of line also) in estimating at great depths, by the intervals, the exact moment when the sinker ceases to descend. Secondly, the loss of line which may be caused by the deviations from the perpendicular of certain portions of it in passing through water moved by under currents." He is of opinion that soundings in depths above 1,000 or 1,500 fathoms can be depended upon as strictly as within twenty or twenty-five fathoms, except with very small and light lines. In regard to the disputed existence of under currents, he relates the following interesting incident: "On the evening of the 16th of July, the sea being too high for the employment of smaller lines with any chance of bringing up the bottom, I sounded with the tapered whale line and a sinker of ninety-six pounds weight, trusting for the depth to the sounding machine attached, corrected for index error, ascertained with the same line. The depth thus found was 2,176; but 2,400 fathoms of line had been paid out, to make sure of detaching the weight, and, to our surprise, the 200 fathoms next to the sinker came up to the surface in one tangled coil. The sinker was detached, and the valve (as usual in the deepest water) full of soft ooze; but that part of the line which had lain at the bottom in a coil was in many places covered with the same kind of ooze, which had adhered to it throughout its passage to the surface. Subtracting 200 from 2,400, the amount of line out, we obtain by the marks the approximate depth of 2,200 fathoms, or about twenty-four fathoms more than that shown by the machine. As the ship was kept throughout the operation exactly over the line, and the depth marked thus (minus the 200 fathoms foul on the bottom) agrees within twenty-four fathoms of that recorded by the sounding machine, the indications of which may fortunately in this instance be depended upon, it would appear that the line must have been carried down nearly perpendicularly, and that, therefore, no under current affected it."

This ought to be a sufficient answer to those who insist that the whole bed of the ocean is swept by currents, and that in consequence thereof it is impossible to lay a cable ever in the great depths.

The specimens of the bottom which were brought up by Capt. Dayman and Lieut. Berryman are exceedingly interesting in more than one point of view. They show that the plateau is covered almost throughout its whole length by a soft kind of mud, which has been called ooze, and which is composed mainly of the remains of the smallest form of marine life—of creatures so minute as to require the strongest powers of the microscope to make them visible to the human eye. The plateau must not be understood as stretching across the ocean from Newfoundland, but lies rather between the 15th and 48th degrees of west longitude. The greatest depth is 2,400 fathoms, according to Capt. Dayman, while according to the soundings of Lieut. Berryman, it does not exceed 2,070. The most remarkable, and indeed almost the only declivity which has been found along the line, is that lying under the 15th degree of west longitude, where, within the course of a few miles, the depth varies from 550 to 1,750, and the nature of the bottom changes from rock to ooze, the latter having been taken up from the greatest depth.

It should be remembered here, however, that these soundings were made at such a distance from each other that the declivity may not be so great as is supposed, and that the descent, instead of being abrupt or precipitous, is rather in the form of a gentle slope. Whatever may be its character, there can now be no dispute in regard to the possibility of laying the cable in this particular part of the plateau. This has been proved in the most satisfactory manner by the result of the expedition of 1857 and and the final expedition of 1858, which showed that there were none of those sudden runs of the cable which formed the chief obstacle in the laying of the Mediterranean cable from Sardinia to Algeria.

An attempt was made to lay the line between those two points in September, 1855, and it was proceeding most favorably, when a most alarming flight of the cable occurred. "About two miles, weighing sixteen tons, flew out with the greatest violence in four or five minutes, flying round even when the drums were brought to a dead stop, creating the greatest alarm for the safety of the men in the hold, and for the vessel." In the laying of the Atlantic cable in August of 1857 there was, as has been stated, no difficulty of this kind, although they had passed the abrupt declivity alluded to the day before the cable parted, through the mismanagement of the then chief engineer, Mr. Bright, and the defective character of his machinery. If there was one fact favorable to the success of the enterprise, which was proved more clearly than any other, it was the ease with which the line was laid on this particular part of the plateau.

From Valentia Bay to 15 degrees 6 minutes west, the bottom consists of rock, of sand, and of mud. The bottom between the forty-fifth degree of west longitude and the Newfoundland coast is irregular, and is made up of stones and gravel, but by steering to the north of the arc of the great circle, this is changed, and a thick mud, peculiarly adapted for the reception of the cable, is obtained. The same muddy bottom is found in Trinity Bay; so that no danger need be apprehended in regard to the safety of the line. On one occasion, while in latitude 52degrees 14 minutes north, longitude 30 degrees 45 minutes west, the depth being 1,675 fathoms, "broken shells of large size, which unfortunately disappeared in the hands of the surgeon who was washing," were taken up. These were the only "shells of large size" which were brought to the surface, and their disappearance is to be regretted from the new scientific facts or information which their discovery might have established. "The sounding machines," says Captain Dayman in his report, "were by Massey, with dials graduated from 160, the usual deep sea lead, to 1,500 and 3,000 fathoms." Captain Dayman also says that "the detaching sounding apparatus used was a modification of that invented by Mr. Brooke, an officer of the United States Navy." The specimens of the soundings were brought up in a tube, which being the first to strike the bottom, seldom failed to secure a portion of the material of which it was formed. Of course there was no means of ascertaining the depth or thickness of the stratum of ooze or the nature of that on which it rested, whether it was one foot, a hundred or a thousand feet; and it is doubtful whether this point will ever be embraced in the discoveries of science; nor does there seem to be any means of ascertaining whether the telegraph plateau has been built up by the deposit of immense boulders borne down from the Arctic regions by gigantic icebergs. Until science has penetrated into the profoundest depths of the ocean, and laid them as open to us as the surface of the earth, nothing satisfactory or definite, we suppose, will ever be known in regard to this theory. One fact which is at present of the greatest importance, is that the telegraph plateau, which was at one time considered a myth, does really and actually exist; and that fact being established, we can afford to wait for the solution of those other questions which have arisen from its discovery.

THE INFUSORIA OF THE PLATEAU.

The specimens which have been brought up from the plateau, and which to the unaided vision appear when dried of a white or reddish white color, bear a very strong resemblance to very fine chalk. Their appearance as they lie at the bottom of a glass vessel is that of a light brown muddy sediment, in which are observed minute hard particles, hardly any of which exceed one-fiftieth of an inch in diameter. The explanation which Mr. Thomas H. Huxley, F. R. S., to whose inspection they were submitted, has furnished us, is nearly all the information we have upon this interesting subject. We have seen the highly magnified specimens which the illustration is intended to represent, and to the perfect accuracy of which we can bear testimony. Those specimens which have just been referred to were obtained from depths ranging from 1,700 to 2,400 fathoms, and of these specimens "fully nine-tenths consist of minute animal organisms, called *foraminiferæ*, provided with thick skeletons composed of carbonate of lime." Proof of their composition is found in the fact that the application of a dilute acid produces a violent effervescence and the disappearance of the larger portion of the matter. The use of the acid is not attended with such a result if the specimen be previously exposed to a full red heat. The species of the *foraminiferæ*, of which eighty-five per cent. of the specimens consist, is called *globigerinæ*.

The specimens shown have been magnified about three hundred times their natural size, and are, as may be seen, of various dimensions and shapes, yet with general points of resemblance.

These *foraminiferæ*, as found in the soundings, vary in size from one-thousandth to one-sixtieth of an inch in diameter; and as the scientific part of our readers may desire to know something more about their construction, they will read the following description by Mr. Huxley, with profit and interest: "In the very young *globigerinæ* the wall of the cell, or cells, of which it is composed, is smooth and thin, but as it adds cell to cell the older ones become beset externally with tubercles, the wall at the same time thickening and exhibiting narrow canals which run perpendicularly to its plane and open between or in the tubercles. The tubercles multiply in number and elongate, so as eventually at first to resemble close set and sharp-pointed palisades, and then by the rounding off of their outer ends, to constitute a more smooth, enamel-like coat, which attains a three hundred and fiftieth of an inch, or more, in thickness. The smallest *globigerinæ* are either clear or have but slightly granular contents, but a very large proportion of the larger ones are rendered opaque by a reddish brown granular mass contained in their interior. When such specimens are treated with very dilute acids which dissolve away the calcareous skeleton, a delicate pale membrane is left enclosing the granular mass, which seems to be held together by a continuation of the same substance. The granular contents have the same form as the skeleton, and are quite soft and easily crushed. I can hardly doubt that these are the soft and once living parts of the animal itself, with or without imbedded foreign matters. The other five per cent. of the calcareous organisms are *foraminiferæ*, of, at most, not more than four or five species. The remaining ten per cent. of the whole deposit consists partly of granular matter, partly of animal, and partly of vegetable organisms, provided with siliceous skeletons and envelopes. The other specimens consist of broken fragments of *diatomaceæ*, so imperfect and so broken that they can with difficulty be distinguished among the mass."

A considerable difference of opinion exists among scientific men in regard to the birthplace of these singular forms of life. It is contended by some that they have been carried to that part of the ocean where they are now found by the Gulf Stream, and by others that they have sunk from the surface of the ocean, where they have lived and died. Both these positions, however, are assumed, as we understand, merely as a matter of speculation, in the absence of such information as further and fuller research may give. If they have drifted into their present bed by the action of the Gulf Stream, they must have had their birth in shallow waters; but then it is argued in opposition to this view that none of the *echini* which inhabit shallow water are found with them. In regard to the idea advanced that they have lived and died at the surface, from which they have gradually sunk to the bottom, it is said that some *globigerinæ*, or something that resembles them, have been found in the Western Pacific. In opposition to this, however, it is denied that these are *globigerinæ*, and so that speculation is disposed of. There is yet another proposition, which, as we have entered upon the scientific explanation of the subject, should not be forgotten. We have given the two positions—that is, that these minute organisms have lived and died in shallow waters, from which they have been carried by that wonder-working agent which performs such an indispensable part in the economy of nature—the Gulf

Stream—and that they have lived, died, and been deposited from above where they are now found; but there is yet another which must be stated. The existence of any form of life in the great depths of the sea was supposed to be impossible, but it appears now that it is not, and it is argued that if animals of a higher organization can live three or four hundred fathoms below the surface, "the difference in the amount of light and heat at 400 and at 2,000 fathoms is probably, so to speak, very far less than the difference in complexity of organization between these animals and the humble *protozoa* and *protophyta* of the deep sea soundings."

Here then we have presented the various theories to which the discoveries of these microscopic specimens have given rise, and the scientific explanations by which they are enforced. These may or may not be interesting, as the reader may determine, but they are subjects of the greatest importance to naturalists, who, it is to be hoped, will some day render them sufficiently clear and intelligible to the unscientific portion of the civilized world by divesting their description of those technicalities which, however gratifying they are to the learned writers, are generally heavy, dull, stupid, unintelligible, and sometimes alarming to the uninitiated and unlearned readers. When they know that these *infusoria*, or (not to be scientific ourselves) when these minute forms of life, some of which are not larger than the point of a pin, are just the things to form a bed for the cable to rest on or in, where there are plenty of them, as there are; that they will in course of time enter into combination with the iron wire of the cable when it is in process of oxidization, thus form-

HIGHLY MAGNIFIED INFUSORIA TAKEN FROM THE TELEGRAPH PLATEAU.

ing a concrete mass around the gutta percha insulation, and protecting it beyond possibility of injury; and that finally, no matter whether they have lived and died above the spot whence they have been taken, or have drifted there with the Gulf Stream, they are just in the very place where they are wanted—understanding these things, the people will realize their importance to the great enterprise, no matter how much naturalists may dispute regarding their birth-place.

These engravings represent the infusoria magnified three hundred times their natural size, which are so infinitesimal as to be the merest mites on the surface of a microscopic glass. Notwithstanding they are so perfect in form, so delicate in construction, and so minute in size, the bed of the plateau is so quiet and undisturbed from the action of the ocean that scarcely any of them, comparatively speaking, are injured or broken by abrasion or attrition. They do, indeed, form a sort of bed of down for the cable to rest upon.

THE GREAT OCEAN CABLE.

The manufacture of the Atlantic Telegraph Cable is one of the most interesting and at the same time one of the most simple processes it is possible to conceive. The cable is formed of the strand of seven copper wires which compose the conductor and which occupy the centre; the gutta percha insulator, the hempen serving, and the outer wire covering or protecting armor.

The discovery of the peculiar properties of gutta percha, dates back to the year 1842 or 1843, but its application to submarine telegraphing did not take place till about the year 1850, when its value as an insulator was proved by the laying of a cable across the English channel. Up to this period, the manufacture of the raw material was confined to the making of water pipes, machine belts, picture frames, and innumerable other articles for which it was considered especially adapted; but the impulse given to the trade by the new use which was found for it created an increased demand, and it eventually became one of the most valuable and important articles of import.

The tree from which the gutta percha is obtained grows in the East Indies, and the principal market is at Singapore, from which the London Gutta Percha Company procure their supply. It is sent to them in its crude state, and has to be subjected to the several processes of mastication, boiling and kneading, before it can be employed in the manufacture of the submarine cable. In this condition, as it lies in the storehouse of the company, you discover among the mass several rough specimens of the skill of the natives. Here is something that was evidently intended for a camel, although there is no trace of a hump on his back, and he has lost a leg during his long sea voyage, but the artist has still left sufficient evidence by which to tell the species to which he belongs. There are quite a large number of animals besides this, but the task of classifying them would exceed even the powers of Cuvier himself. This one has the bill of a duck on a head that otherwise resembles that of a monkey, and that other is a combination of bird and quadruped, for the like of which you might search in vain among all the fabulous mythological or manufactured animals that were ever created by the inventive genius of ancient poet or modern showman. All these—the animal with the monkey's head and duck's bill; the three-legged and humpless camel—in a word, the whole menagerie—are put into immense cauldrons, with the common mass, and boiled, and boiled again, until they are rendered as soft as dough. In this state the gutta percha is thrown into a machine called a masticator, in which it is literally torn into shreds, and from which it is again taken to be again boiled. By this process it is purified and freed from all foreign materials which may have entered into it while it was being collected by the Hindoos. But it is not yet fit for the work for which it is designed, and must be again masticated, cleansed, and kneaded several times before it can be used in the covering or insulation of the copper wire along which the electric current is to pass. When it has been thoroughly kneaded, it is so perfectly plastic, that it can be joined with the greatest ease, and in such a manner that it cannot be torn apart at the point of adhesion. The two parts being joined, become as completely one, as united and blended as two glasses of water when poured into the same vessel. This property which it possesses is peculiarly valuable, when it is found necessary to repair any defects in a cable during the process of paying it out. In such cases it is only necessary, after splicing the internal copper wire or conductor, to heat the parts of the gutta percha which are to be joined. When this is done, the open space or break is covered by layers of gutta percha as thin as the page on which we write, and eight or ten of which layers are required to make the broken part uniform with the rest.

Over twenty tons of the raw material are manufactured every week in the factory, and in the boiling department alone, some forty or fifty vats or cauldrons are constantly in use. On entering the first floor, you see them throwing out their little jets of steam on every side, while the boiling waters bubble up through the openings on top, reminding you of the descriptions which travellers in Iceland have given of the hot springs of that strange country. Passing from this department to the floor above, the finishing room is reached, and here the process of coating the conductor is performed. The conductor is composed of seven copper wires, six being wound spirally round theseventh, which is perfectly straight and occupies the centre. The conductor itself, on account of its peculiar spiral form, is capable of being extended twenty per cent. of its own length before breaking, and the seven wires of which it is composed give it a decided and important advantage over that formerly used. In the case of the first cable, which the New York, Newfoundland and London Telegraph Company attempted unsuccessfully to lay across the Gulf of St. Lawrence, one of the greatest difficulties they had to contend against, was the breaking of the three conductors, which, it is more than probable, would never have occurred had they been composed of seven wires each, instead of one. Should the whole seven break under an excessive strain, the continuity or electric connection will not necessarily be destroyed unless they all give at one point, an occurrence which may be almost regarded as beyond probability. The advantage which it has over the single wire conductor cannot be doubted, since it has been practically tested with the most gratifying success. It has been proved that the drawing out or attenuation of a mile of the copper wire to ten-elevenths of its thickness reduces its power of conduction only a thirty-seventh part.

The covering or insulating process is effected by means of a cylinder, in one end of which a die of the required size is placed, and through which the gutta percha is forced with a piston. As it passes through this die in the form of an elongated pipe-stem, or maccaroni, the core is forced through its centre at a uniform rate of speed, and the now insulated conductor is cooled by drawing it through a water conduit some fifty feet in length. To insure its perfect insulation the core is covered with three coats of gutta percha, after which it is ready to receive its additional protection of prepared hemp and iron wire. The shore part of the cable, which will be about an inch and a-half in diameter, or twice the thickness of the portion intended for the deep sea, has five coverings of gutta percha, and each one of the outer wires which are to serve as an armor for it, is at least a quarter of an inch thick. It is a massive affair, and capable of resisting a strain equal to forty or fifty tons. Some idea may be formed of the quantity of iron consumed in the work, when it is known that the protecting armor requires 379,312 miles of wire about the thickness of a common pin, while the length of the copper wire required for the conductor is 21,084 miles. The protecting armor is composed of eighteen strands, each strand consisting of seven wires, wound round the insulated core in a spiral form, and being about the twelfth of an inch thick.

The following engravings show the exact thickness of the deep sea and shore end cables.

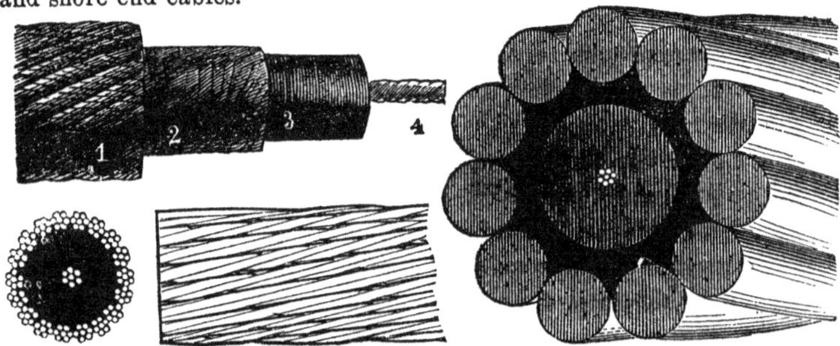

END AND SIDE SECTIONS OF CABLE AND END OF SHORE CABLE.

1. Wire—Eighteen strands of seven wires. 2. Six strands of yarn.
3. Gutta percha—Three coats. 4. Telegraph wires—Seven in number.

The manufacture of this part of the cable is very simple. The conductor having been thoroughly tested, to prove its complete insulation, the cable is sent to the factory, where it is covered with the iron wire and prepared for coiling. Before the insulated wire leaves the gutta percha factory, every sixty miles of it are thoroughly examined. Should any flaw be found it is immediately repaired, and the cable is again subjected to the electric test, when, if it prove perfect, it is allowed to remain undisturbed until such time as it is placed on shipboard. The break of continuity or connection in the core from imperfect insulation, or a parting of the copper wire, is made known by the ringing of a bell, which sounds the alarm the instant the interruption takes place, and continues ringing so long as the battery sends the electric stream along the conductor. The author was an observer of this test, and saw it applied with the most perfect success. The connection was temporarily destroyed; but the moment the battery was brought to bear upon the conductor, the unerring indicator, the little bell, commenced ringing, and kept it up till the battery was detached. Through the means of that same infallible detective every mile of it is not only proved before leaving the factory, but as it goes into coils on shipboard.

The covering of the Atlantic cable with its wire protection or armor is performed by a separate establishment, and is an entirely different process from that just described. There are in fact two of these manufactories, one at Birkenhead, opposite Liverpool, and the other at Greenwich, about five miles from London.

The factory at Greenwich is situated on the banks of the Thames, and about a mile from the hospital for superannuated sailors. It is in the very centre of a manufacturing district, and in view of the mammoth iron steamer Great Eastern. There is nothing in the external appearance of the building which would give any indication of the character of the work performed within its walls, and the only intimation which the spectator who is not privileged to enter has of it, is that conveyed in the immense sign on the roof, which informs him that the submarine telegraph cable is manufactured there. The whole establishment is surrounded by a wall eight or ten feet high, to keep out that spirit of inquiry which, whether laudable or not on the part of the public, does not receive the same amount of toleration, or the same opportunity in England that it does in the United States. There is, in addition to this wall, a porter at the gate, who is one of the most polite of Cerberuses, and who guards it as well against all unprivileged applicants as did the Russians the fortress of Sebastopol. The only approach to it is by a gravelled pathway which is terribly destructive to shoe-leather, and a journey over half a dozen miles of which would use up the best pair of boots ever made; and yet, strange to say, these gravel footpaths are so common about London, and all over England, as to give rise to the belief that the interest of the shoemakers is among the strongest in the kingdom, and that the authorities who have the charge of the making and repairing of roads, must have a strong sympathy with that time-honored and indispensable class of tradesmen. Happening fortunately to be one of the privileged few who were permitted to enter the factory, I visited it during my stay in London. On passing the gate, I discovered on each side a circus, thirty or forty feet in diameter, which had been dug to the depth of about four feet. In both there were eight coils, each containing from twenty to three hundred miles of the cable, and some three or four of which were receiving it as it came freshly made out of the factory. The men who were engaged in packing or coiling it had their hands and feet besmeared with tar, and the whole establishment was redolent of the same material. But no matter how objectionable the tar may be, it is an excellent preventive of rust, and absolutely indispensable in the manufacture of the cable.

The two circuses, or basins, as they are, perhaps, more properly called, are so constructed, that they can be filled to the top with water, to allow of the complete submersion of the cable.

The machinery in the cable factory is very simple, and although at the first glance it appears rather intricate and complicated, a few minutes' inspection makes it all perfectly plain. The first process is the serving or covering of the gutta percha insulation with hemp steeped in a composition of tar and pitch, after which it receives the external protection or wire armor. The preparation of the hemp and the winding of it on bobbins engage the services of a dozen boys, who work from morning to night, and from Monday to Saturday, with all the steadiness and regularity of their older fellow operatives. Hundreds of miles of this hemp passes through their hands every week, and although it is the least important of the different materials of which the cable is composed, still it could not well be done without. The serving of the hemp on the core is accomplished by means of a revolving machine, on the periphery of which are placed seven or eight of these bobbins, the core of the cable passing directly and perpendicularly through the centre. As this machine revolves, the bobbins also revolve on their own axes, paying out the hemp, which is thus served on the core. The process can perhaps be more simply illustrated by taking two flat circular pieces of wood of the same size, say about three feet in diameter, and each having a hole in the centre. Let these be joined by three or four upright bars of wood or iron set at equal distances apart, all placed within about an inch of the periphery. This done, the next thing is to get the requisite number of spools, each spool representing a bobbin, seven being sufficient for the purpose, and to fasten them on axes to the lower one of the two circular pieces of wood. The machine is now finished and in working order. Through the central holes run a small rope, and wind upon each one of the spools enough twine to illustrate the process. The machine having been set on a pivot must now be put in motion, the ends of the twine joined to the rope about an inch above the top of the spools, and the rope itself drawn slowly through the central holes. Then, as the machine revolves and the rope is drawn upward, the spools will also revolve, paying the twine out and serving it on the rope. Here you have a tolerably fair illustration of the manner in which not only the gutta percha is covered with the hemp, but in which the last or wire protection is laid on. The velocity with which these machines revolve is somewhat calculated to startle nervous people on a first visit to the factory, and should some of the bobbins happen by any chance to fly off while they are in motion, they would make wild work with any thing with which they might happen to come in contact. But fortunately they are so well secured that accidents of the kind seldom or never occur. While the cable is being paid out from the machine in its finished state, it passes over several small wheels and through vats of tar, as it is drawn out by the men who are engaged in coiling it in the basins. Five of the wire-covering machines were in operation at the time of our visit, and these gave about twelve miles as the aggregate of their day's work.

THE PAYING-OUT MACHINERY.

The machinery which was put up on the Agamemnon is a duplicate of that on the Niagara, and a description of one will therefore answer for both. In addition to the winding-in and paying-out part of it, there was an engine of twenty horse power, which was always to be kept in readiness should it be found necessary to use it in taking up the cable, an operation which had always failed.

This portion of the machinery was made the subject of severe criticism, and it was asserted, in advance of its trial, that it was too heavy and too powerful for the work for which it was constructed.

The machine was composed of four V sheave wheels, which are indicated in the following engraving by the letters a a a a.

The cable passes over these in the manner exhibited in the engraving first entering the groove or sheave in the second sheave wheel, passing over and under it. It then passes over the first sheave wheel, and taking a turn over the greater part of its periphery, is carried to the fourth, from which it is delivered to the third, passing finally from that to the sheave wheel at the stern, and over that again into the ocean.

The brake wheels, which are shown by the

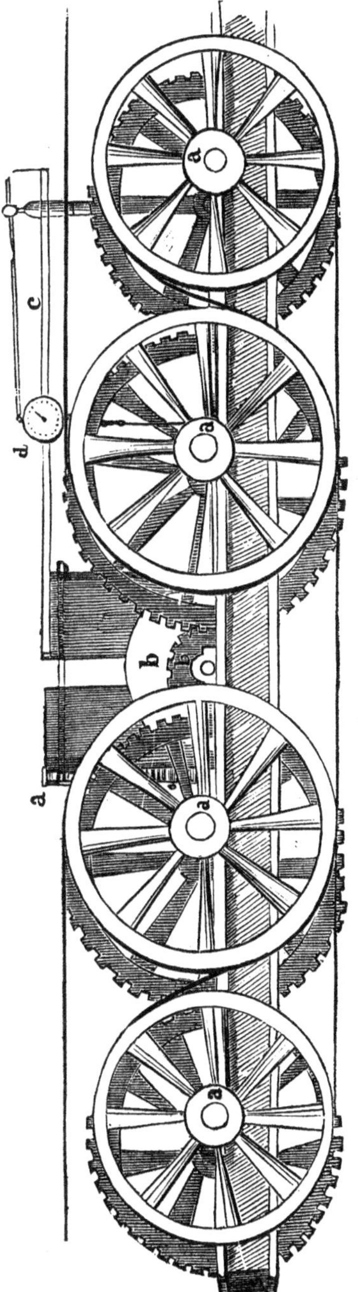

THE PAYING-OUT MACHINERY.

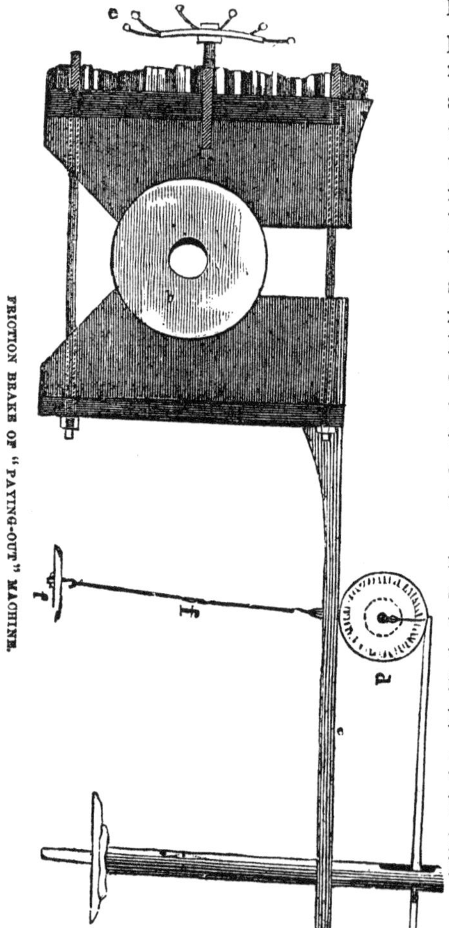

FRICTION BRAKE OF "PAYING-OUT" MACHINE.

letter *b*, are turned by a pinion, as in the winding-in machine, and revolve with a velocity proportioned to the size of the sheave wheels, each of which is five feet in diameter. The brake wheels are acted upon by wooden blocks, screwed together as represented in the Friction Brake, and when compressed, act upon the lever *c*, which is connected with the indicator *d*. This indicator shows the strain on the cable.

The brake is worked by means of the handle *e*, beside which there was always a man stationed to work it when required. The indicator is similar to a patent spring scale, and *f*, *f*, is simply a line and weight to keep it from being pulled out of its place by the action of the lever.

THE MACHINERY FOR WINDING IN.

Although it was hoped that there would be no occasion for the use of this machine, yet it would have been a culpable want of foresight to have neglected providing one for each of the cable ships. One of the most serious difficulties which was to be apprehended in the work of paying out was that which might arise from the kinking of the cable. But the ease with which it was coiled on the Niagara—frequently at the rate of three miles an hour, and on one occasion at the rate of five miles—was certainly most auspicious and promising for the success of the final operation. There was no strain, no tendency to kink, and with the exception of a slight twist which would be perceptible even on a thread when unwound from a spool, there was nothing to justify the fear that there would be any obstacle in the way of the successful accomplishment of the work from such a cause. Still, as has been said, it would have been culpable in the engineers to have neglected to make provision for such an emergency. The winding-machine, although it added considerably to the weight of the machinery for paying out, was, according to the opinion of the engineers connected with the enterprise, as compact and as light as it could possibly be, considering the work which it had to perform. The following representation gives a correct view of it, and with the explanations of the various parts, will render it clearer to the popular understanding than any unaided verbal description.

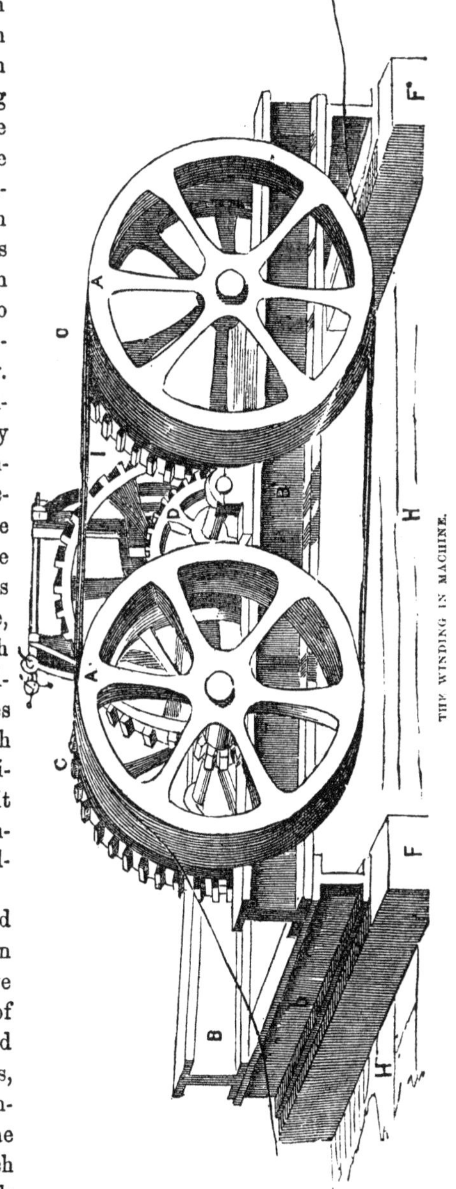

THE WINDING IN MACHINE.

A A are two grooved drums, sheaves about seven feet in diameter, having five grooves on the periphery of each. The cable is wound round each drum five times, passing from one to the other in succession till all the grooves are filled, when each revolution of both wheels pays it out to the hands of the men who stand ready to coil it as it is taken up from the ocean. The object of passing it round these drums so often is to render it easier for the engineer to check it by the application of the brake, which is indicated by letter E, and which is presented more in another engraving. The winding-machine is so constructed that it can be made to perform the work of the paying-out machine should it be found necessary to employ it in that way. In the event of its being

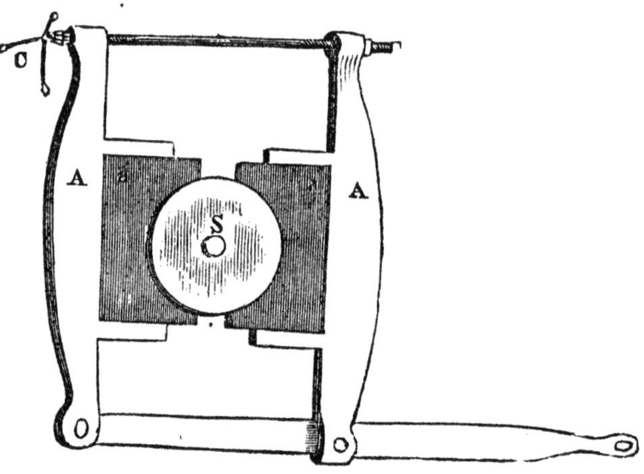

SECTION OF THE FRICTION BRAKE.

used for such a purpose the brake becomes absolutely necessary to restrain the speed of the cable in going out over the stern. The grooves are for the purpose of keeping the cable from becoming entangled, or rather from crowding and cutting the outer wire, which would be very liable to occur were the periphery of the drum perfectly flat. The five grooves are seen to advantage in the following engraving, the letter *a* showing the groove in which the deep sea line rests, and the letter *b* that in which is represented the shore cable, the end sections of both deep sea line and shore cable being represented by proportionately sized circles, the first of which (*a*) fills up only a part of a groove, and the second (*b*) nearly the whole of one.

On the same shafts as the groove drums of the winding-in machine are the spur wheels C C, in gear with the pinion placed between them, and which is indicated by D. The shaft on which this pinion is fixed also carries the brake alluded to, and which, as has been stated, was only to be used when the winding-in machine was employed in paying out. The two iron levers A A, which are seen in the engraving of the friction brake, hold the blocks of wood *a a* to the brake wheel S. By screwing the nut C, which is connected with a right and left hand screw, the levers A A are pressed together on the wheel C, which stops the large wheels, and by which of course the whole machine is checked when sufficient pressure is employed. There are two brakes, one of which is immediately behind the other, and cannot, therefore, be seen. The whole weight of the winding-in machine is about five tons.

The grooved wheels, it was calculated, would run with a velocity of ten revolutions to the minute, and at this speed would wind up the cable over the wheel at the stern at the rate of three miles an hour. The paying out is regulated in the same way—that is, for every three miles of the cable passed over these grooved wheels to the wheel at the stern and from it down into the ocean, each of the grooved wheels would make ten revolutions a minute. In the winding up of the cable, which is a much slower process than the paying out, on account of the greater strain produced by the operation, the length of cable taken in would not exceed one mile and a half an hour, and the revolutions would be reduced, therefore, to five per minute.

On the same shaft with the brakes is represented the third large spur wheel I, which is worked by a pinion driven by the engine.

STOWAGE OF THE COILS ON THE NIAGARA.

The following engraving is designed to show the stowage of the coils on board the Niagara.

The paying-out and winding-in machinery is shown on a small scale by letter *a*, and the coils by the numbers 1, 2, 3, 4, 5, and 6, which also present the order in which they were to be paid out, No. 1 being the ten

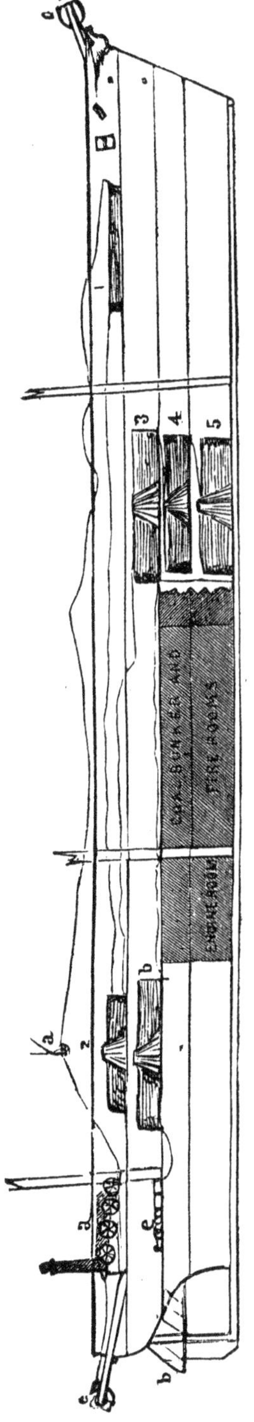

SECTION OF THE NIAGARA WITH THE CABLE ON BOARD.

miles of the shore cable. Letter *f* is a similar sheave wheel to that over the stern, and was to be used when it became necessary in consequence of a gale, to remove the cable to the bow, so as to enable the vessel to steam up against the wind, as it would inevitably have been broken otherwise.

The length of miles in the different coils on board the Niagara, the remainder being on board the Agamemnon, is presented in the following tables:

			Miles.
Coil No. 1—Shore cable;			10
No. 2—Deep sea cable,			130
No. 3	do.	do.	294
No. 4	do.	do.	181½
No. 5	do.	do.	352
No. 6	do.	do.	297
Total,			1,264½

The shore and deep sea cables were to be passed to the paying-out machinery over a series of small-sized drums, placed at regular intervals between the coil from which it was taken and the machine.

THE CABLE GUARDS.

Among the most important parts of the machinery which was required in the laying of the cable, were the guards for the propellers of the Agamemnon and Niagara, and without which its successful accomplishment was considered doubtful, these being absolutely necessary to prevent the fouling of the submarine cable in the event of the ship being obliged to back out of the way of icebergs, or from other causes. It was a point to which the greatest attention was very properly given, as the breaking of the cable, after several hundred miles of it had been paid out, would postpone the completion of the enterprise for a year, in addition to the great pecuniary loss by which such a disaster would be attended. It was proposed to avoid such a disaster by surrounding the screw with a cage, which would effectually prevent the cable from coming in contact; but as the two vessels were differently constructed, and as it would be absolutely necessary to place the Niagara in dry dock before

STERN OF THE NIAGARA SHOWING CABLE GUARDS.

a.—Horse shoe guard.
b.—Vertical braces.
c.—Horizontal braces.
d.—Section of guard and vertical brace.
e.—Water line.

the cage could be fastened to her, it was decided to abandon it in her case, and to adopt a guard in its stead. The cage was, therefore, only used on the Agamemnon, which was docked for the purpose. From the subjoined drawings the reader will perceive at once the difference between the two contrivances.

In this drawing it will be seen that there are two guards of iron which sweep round the stern of the Niagara, in the form of a semi-circle or horseshoe, enclosing both the propeller and the rudder, the lower being about a foot above the water line, and the other at an elevation of some seven or eight feet from it. As the ship drew three or four feet more when loaded with the cable, the lower guard would, of course, be submerged to a corresponding depth, forming a still better protection when in the process of backing. This guard was placed about three feet from the flange of the screw, and between eleven and twelve from the side of the rudder post, so that its full diameter at this point was from twenty-two to twenty-four feet. The length of the perpendicular bars varied from seven to fourteen feet, and the whole presented so small a surface to the action of the water, and was so well fastened with bolts and screws, that it was expected to resist all the pressure to which it might be subjected, either from the inside or outside.

In the case of the Agamemnon, to which the cage was applied, and of the stern of which the following is a correct drawing, the difference will at once be seen when compared with the Niagara. The counter or under rounding of the stern is much nearer to the water mark than that of the Niagara, and to this cause is owing the difference in the open space which is so apparent in a comparison of the sterns of both ships.

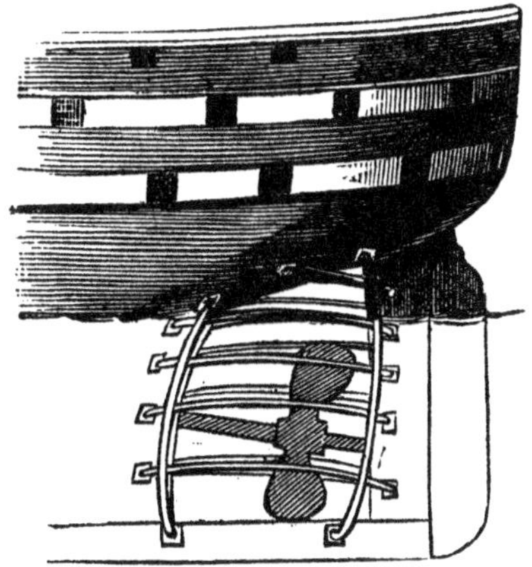

THE STERN AND SUBMARINE CABLE GUARD OF THE AGAMEMNON.

The cable protector presented in this drawing is, literally speaking, a cage made of bars of iron placed almost at right angles with each other, and inside of which the screw is observed. It descends below the water-mark; the perpendicular bars, of which there are two on each side, being screwed to the counter and the keel of the ship, not more than three or four feet of the whole cage being visible above the surface of the water. The horizontal bars are rounded out so as to form a section of a circle, the diameter of which is about twenty-four feet, leaving a space of about two feet and a half between them and the sweep of the screw. The horizontal bars in this instance, instead of being brought round the rudder, are screwed into the rudder post, and the whole cage was subjected more to the action of the water than the guard of the Niagara, on account of its deeper submersion. Both the guard and the cage were the best that could be devised at the time, and proved efficient for the purpose they were intended to subserve.

PASSAGE TO VALENTIA BAY, AND TRIAL OF THE MACHINERY.

The day of the departure of the Telegraph Squadron from Cork, was not as auspicious as could have been desired, but there was no time to be lost, and, fair or stormy, it was absolutely essential that they should leave. Five o'clock was the hour fixed for their departure, but it was past six before the whole squadron was under way and out of the harbor. The British side wheel steamer, the Leopard, was the first to move, and about half an hour after she had got out to sea the Agamemnon followed. Next in order was the Susquehanna, the Niagara bringing up the rear. Soon after we passed the entrance the order of the procession underwent a complete change, for the Niagara in a few hours took the lead, leaving the other three behind. In less than an hour after we had left the Cove of Cork we lost sight of the entrance, behind the bold headlands which mark nearly the whole of the Irish coast; and early the following morning we had passed Cape Clear, the most southern point of the island. The Susquehanna and the Leopard were the only two vessels in sight, the Agamemnon having disappeared during the night. We proceeded, however, on our course, and at eleven o'clock were off the Skelligs, two bluff rocks which stand out a mile or so from the mainland, and which are about eight or nine miles from Dingle bay. In a little more than an hour we were at its entrance, and before running in made three experiments upon ten miles of discarded cable, which had been put on board our ship while lying in the Cove for the purpose. It was the same wire with which the machinery on the Agamemnon had been tested, and which, although somewhat defective, served almost as well as that which had not yet been used. The cable was passed round the sheave wheels of the paying-out machine, and then, as it was passed over the stern, a kedge anchor was tied to the end to sink it, and thus by bringing a weight upon the wheels, caused them to revolve until a sufficient portion of the cable was paid out to enable the vessel to proceed at the desired speed. The anchor having been fastened, was dropped into the water, but the weight was not heavy enough to produce the desired result. The wheels of the ponderous machinery refused to move, and the anchor, after swinging to and fro from the stern for a few moments, dropped sluggishly into the water, but without effect. The shafts were oiled, and about forty men were put to work to pull the cable over the wheels by main strength, and pay it out until such time as there should be enough of it over the stern to bring the strain necessary to set them in motion, without the aid of any other force than that exercised by the weight and strain of the cable itself. It was a slow and tedious process, and to some who were impatient of delay, it was doubtless a most vexatious one. The first half hour passed, and still the men continued hauling it over the sheaves and passing it overboard, without effecting the slightest change, but in less than five minutes the wheels began to move, slowly at first, and then with increased speed, till the rate of paying out reached from two to three miles an hour. All this time there was no apparent tendency to kink, and there was now an opportunity after all the trouble, and all the pulling and dragging, to test the machinery in a satisfactory manner. There was no difficulty about paying out, but there was one most essential point to be settled before its success could be finally established. It was necessary to try the action of the brakes, and to do that the cable would be most probably subjected to a strain which it might be found too weak to resist. It was, however, valueless for any other purpose, and so it mattered little what strain it might be subjected to. So the brakes were put on, and the wheels over which it passed having been stopped in this way, it broke in a very few minutes. The object of the brakes, as has been explained, is to stop the cable when a kink takes place, or when any defect is discovered before it passes over the wheel, so that it may be repaired before it descends into the water.

A second experiment was tried and with the same result, and a third ended in the same manner. The Niagara now proceeded on her way into Valentia Bay, which is three or four miles from the entrance of Dingle Bay. While on our passage in we had a magnificent view of this part of the coast, and a fine opportunity of judging of its scenery. The County of Kerry is one of the most southern counties of Ireland, and its whole line of coast is remarkable for its rugged character, and for the deep indentations which the action of the sea, from age to age, has made upon it. Huge mountains rise up on almost every side, and great masses of rock, in a thousand fantastic shapes, stand out miles from the land, terrible as those of which the Greek mariners stood in such awe, and of which such tales of horror have been handed down to us. Two immense rocks, which look as if they had been flung from the huge mountain that guards the left side of the entrance of Dingle Bay, stand there like grim and weather-beaten sentinels. On the other side is a long mountain range, the face of which, looking seaward, is worn with deep fissures, while its base is hollowed out at irregular intervals by caves, some of which extend, as we were told, several hundred feet into the very heart of the mountains. The bay is between two and three hundred fathoms deep, but it is so open to the sea, and the anchorage is so bad, that it is one of the worst places which a vessel could select in a storm. The waves break with terrible force on the rocks, throwing their spray far up the bleak mountain sides, and the wind sweeps with relentless fury on the ill-fated vessel that may be caught here on a lee shore. But Valentia Bay is more protected, and although not safe in a storm, affords much better anchorage. The land for miles into the interior is very rocky and barren, and affords a poor pasturage for the diminutive but hardy race of cattle for which the County of Kerry is famous. It is a difficult matter to distinguish the huts of the peasantry on the great hillsides; but here and there can be seen the ruins of churches, which were built by pious Christians of the fifth and sixth centuries, and whose walls have long since crumbled into decay. This Island of Valentia suffered fearfully during the famine in Ireland, and hundreds died of starvation on the roadside or in the miserable dwellings, some of which still remain, and in which their bodies were found many weeks after their death, unburied. Within the last few years it is said the condition of the people has considerably improved, but if what I saw is called improvement, they must have been in a terrible state before the process of amelioration commenced. Some of them live at present by fishing, some by cultivating the ungrateful soil, and some by quarrying slate from the hillsides. About three miles from the head of Valentia Bay is the village of Caherciveen, and at the same distance from where our ship now lies is Knightstown, a small village of one thousand inhabitants, called after the Knight of Kerry, a gentleman who has been one of the strongest advocates of the Atlantic Telegraph. From the deck of our ship we could see a small sandy cove, which was selected as the place for the landing of the shore end of the cable, and a hundred yards from which a temporary tent was erected for the batteries and other telegraph instruments. In front of it was displayed an attempt at the stars and stripes, but it was only an attempt, and it would require one of the most shrewd guessing Yankees that ever lived in or came out of Connecticut to tell what it was intended for. It was soon replaced by

VALENTIA BAY, THE EASTERN TERMINUS OF THE ATLANTIC TELEGRAPH

another, of a more unmistakable kind, however, and that ought to be sufficient to satisfy the most exacting patriot.

Although it was certain that we could not take the shore end of the cable out, yet it was concluded to employ our spare time in trying another experiment with a part of the 1,250 miles of the deep sea line which made up our half of the Atlantic telegraph, and which was free from defects. The Willing Mind, a steamer which came round from Cork as an additional tender to the Advice, took the end of this on board, and securing it firmly, started off from the Niagara at a speed of about four miles an hour, and when about five or six hundred yards from her the brakes were put on. The little steamer tugged and pulled away, but the wheels refused to turn while the brakes remained as they were, and after tugging and pulling for about five minutes the cable parted, having given way at last to a dragging force equal to a weight of three tons and a half. This was regarded as very satisfactory, but there is one thing which I think it proves—that the brakes could not be brought to bear upon the cable with such an immense mass as the Niagara hauling on it. The only plan was to let it run free, and if a kink should occur, to take the chances rather than put on the brakes, which appeared to be certain destruction.

We arrived and anchored in Valentia Bay on the evening of the 4th, but at too late an hour to commence operations other than described. The work of landing the shore part of the cable was deferred therefore until the following morning at eight o'clock. At the appointed time every thing was prepared for the work, the Willing Mind came under our stern ready to tow the heavy shore line, and in addition to this there were some half dozen boats from the Susquehanna and Leopard, with two or three from the Niagara, all prepared to assist in the work. The engineers, however, before beginning, at once decided on testing both the shore cable and machinery, and for that purpose got the Willing Mind to tow out some five or six hundred yards. This preliminary operation was attended with such success that it was determined to commence work without further delay. Two of the launches of the Leopard and one from the Susquehanna were brought under the stern of the Niagara, and about a mile and three-quarters of the cable coiled upon them; then another mile or three-quarters was put on board the Willing Mind, and the whole four towed by the Advice, went off in procession towards the point indicated as the landing place by the American flag, already alluded to. On the shore there were about two thousand persons, the whole population of the place, and large contributions from miles around, waiting there from seven in the morning till seven in the evening for the arrival of the fleet of cable boats, whose progress they had watched with so much anxiety and impatience. It was five o'clock when we started; never before was such a scene presented in Valentia Bay, and the poorest spectator there, though he could not tell what strange agency it was that lay in that cable, understood what it was intended to effect, and his face beamed with joy as he heard his comrades say that it brought them nearer to that great land that had so generously stretched out the helping hand to their starving countrymen, and that had given a shelter and a home to those who had found neither the one nor the other in the land of their birth. It was a happy day for them, and when later in the evening that cable was landed, and it was proposed to give three cheers for America, there were none there who responded with more sincerity and honest enthusiasm than the poor peasantry.

It took about two hours to land the cable, but the shallowness of the water prevented the Advice from running close to the shore. The passengers, therefore, consisting of a number of friends of the enterprise, got into one of the small boats, and rowed in as near as they could, but still not near enough for us to get ashore without wetting our feet. We were not long left in doubt, however, as to what we should do, for we had hardly run our boat aground before there was a whole crowd of men in the water, regardless of wet clothes, proffering their assistance, and offering as many backs as there were passengers in the boat. It was one of the incidents of the great scene which was being enacted, and occasioned considerable merriment among the bystanders. Here a little fellow presented himself to a gentleman of the most portly dimensions, and insisted upon his ability to take him ashore. It was no use, however, for had he the strength of Atlas he could not have persuaded the passenger that he was able to carry him, and so he had to call another to his help, when both of them succeeded in landing him safely, to his great satisfaction and relief. These two performed the job so well, that the rest of the passengers at once entered into a contract with them, and were landed high and dry upon the beach. About half an hour after we got ashore the small fleet of cable boats were observed rapidly approaching, headed by one bearing the united unions of England and the States —that is, the Union Jack and the Stars alone on a blue ground, while the words "Atlantic Telegraph" were inscribed upon it in large letters.

Among those on shore were the Lord Lieutenant of Ireland, (Lord Morpeth, of anti-slavery proclivities,) Lord Hillsborough, the Knight of Kerry, and nearly all the gentlemen connected with the enterprise. But here comes the cable in the hands of the crew of the Niagara's boat, who rush up the beach with it dripping with water, for in their haste to carry it ashore they have to wade knee deep. Mr. Cyrus W.

Field is there beside Lord Morpeth, or, as he is now called, Lord Carlisle, and as Captain Pennock comes up in advance of his men with the cable he introduces him. There is no time for the passage of formalities, and the introduction and meeting are therefore free from them.

"I am most happy to see you, Captain," says Lord Morpeth; and the Captain most appropriately replies:

"This, sir, is the betrothal of England and America; and I hope in twenty days the marriage will be consummated."

The crowd now press around, all eagerness to help in pulling up the cable, and when the work is through, those who have been fortunate enough to put their hands to it show the marks of the tar to those who have failed in the attempt, as a proof of their success. By dint of pulling and hauling, they get it into the trench in which it is to be laid, and take up the end to the top of a little hill, where they secure it by rolling it around a number of strong stakes driven fast into the earth, and placed in the form of a circle. This is the centre of the site marked out for a house, in which the batteries and instruments are to be placed, and which was used as a temporary station till a better and more substantial one could be erected. When the cable was placed here, and the enthusiasm of the people had somewhat subsided, the rector of the parish made an appropriate prayer.

At the close of the prayer, Lord Carlisle addressed the people as follows:

"My American, Irish, and English friends, I feel at such a moment as this that no language can be becoming, except that of prayer and praise. However, it is always allowable to any human lips, though they have not been specially qualified for the office, to raise the ascription of 'Glory to God on earth, peace, good-will to men.' That, I believe, is the spirit in which this great work has been undertaken; and it is this reflection which encourages me to feel the strongest hopes of its final success. (Hear, hear.) I believe the great undertaking, now so happily begun, will accomplish many great and noble purposes of trade, of national policy, and of empire; but there is only one view in which I will now present it to those whom I have the pleasure to address. You are aware—you must know, some of you, from your own experience, that many of your dear friends and only relations have left their native land to receive hospitable shelter in America. (Applause.) Well, then, I don't expect you can all understand the wondrous mechanism by which this great undertaking is to be carried on, but this I think you will all of you understand. If you wish to communicate some piece of intelligence straightway to your relations across the wide world of waters—if you wish to tell those whom you know it would interest in their heart of hearts, of a marriage, a birth, or a death among you, this little cord which we have piled up on the shore will impart those tidings quicker than the flash of the lightnings. (Applause.) Let us now hope, let us now pray, that the hopes of those who have set in operation this great design may be rewarded by its entire success, and let us hope further that this Atlantic cable will, in all future time, serve as an emblem of that strong cord of love which, I trust, will always unite the British Islands and the great continent of America, and join with me in my fervent wish that the great Giver of all good, who has enabled all his servants to discern so much of the workings of those mighty laws by which he governs the universe, will further this wonderful work, and will further so bless its operation, as to make it serve the high purposes of the good of man and his own great glory. (Hear, hear.) And now, my friends, as there can be no project or undertaking which ought not to receive the approbation and applause of the people, let all join with me in giving three hearty cheers."

Three cheers were given with a will; but it was not enough, and they cheered and cheered until they were obliged to give up from exhaustion. "Three cheers," said Lord Carlisle, "are not enough—they are what they give on common occasions. Now, for the success of the Atlantic cable, I must have at least one dozen." The crowd responded with the full number, and then cheered the following:

"The Lord Lieutenant of Ireland."

"The United States of America."

"Mr. Cyrus W. Field."

Mr. Field, in reply, spoke as follows: "Ladies and gentlemen—words cannot express to you the feelings within this heart. It beats with affection towards every man, woman and child that hears me; and if ever on the other side of the water one of you present yourselves at my door, and say you had a hand in this, I promise you a true American welcome. (Cheers.) 'What God hath joined together let no man put asunder.'" (Cheers.)

And more cheers were given for the following:

"For the sailors."

"For Yankee Doodle."

"For the officers and sailors on board the ships that are intended to lay the cable."

"The Queen."

"The President of the United States."

"The American Navy."

Captain Wainwright, of the Leopard, returned his thanks on the part of the officers of the squadron, and said that there was not a man who would not be ready to make almost any sacrifice to promote the success of this undertaking.

This closed the great ceremony of landing the first Atlantic submarine cable, and if we had been as successful in taking it ashore at Newfoundland, we certainly would have had reason for congratulation and rejoicing. On our return to the wardroom of the Niagara, we had a pleasant social gathering of all the officers, at which Lieut. Boyd brought out an immense cake, with which we celebrated the event.

THE LAYING OF THE CABLE FROM VALENTIA BAY.

THE FIRST DAY—AUGUST 6.

The landing of the shore cable in Doulus Bay was successfully accomplished, as has been stated, on the evening of the 6th of August, a day which will be ever memorable in the minds of all who were present on the occasion. To the people of that part of Ireland it was an event of the most absorbing interest; and although there were many there to whom the scientific character of the work was an inexplicable mystery, it was, as we have said, enough for them to know that it brought them nearer to that great nation where myriads of their countrymen had found a home, and where by honest industry they were enabled to obtain an independent livelihood. Never before had such a mass of people assembled on the shores of that bay, and never did people regard any spectacle with deeper interest. They came from miles around—from their huts on the steep hill sides and the dark mountain passes, from the storied scenes of Killarney in the interior, and the bleak-iron bound coast for which the south as well as the north of Ireland is so celebrated. It was a great day for all—from the Lord Lieutenant down to the poorest man who quarried slate for eight pence or a shilling a day, on the side of the hill that overlooks the harbor of Valentia. From seven in the morning till seven in the evening they awaited with impatient eagerness the landing of the cable; and when the boats which bore it to the beach were within a hundred feet of the place designated, they could with difficulty be restrained by the police from rushing into the water and pulling it ashore. People may talk about the popular enthusiasm which is manifested at coronations, the visits of monarchs, and all that, but he must indeed have been a great monarch who was received with such heartfelt welcome as the crowd gave to that electric chain. The moment the cable boats touched the shore, the people, animated by one impulse, ran forward, and the guardians of the public peace, unable to restrain their eagerness, were swept aside by the rush. A hundred hands seized the cable, and running up the elevated ground which fronts the bay, landed it about fifty feet above the water mark. Then followed the scene which has been already described, a scene of the wildest enthusiasm, in which the name of America was hailed with cheers that made the mountains ring. They never tired of cheering, and the man who proposed "three more for Yankee Doodle," when each voice was hoarse from the extraordinary duty it was called upon to perform, was answered with a deafening hurrah, that was repeated again and again, till the crowd could almost cheer no more from sheer exhaustion.

That night there was a grand ball at the little village of Knightstown, and the day dawn caught the merry-makers still engaged in their festivities. A bonfire of peat, piled up as high as a good-sized two-story house, sent its ruddy and cheerful light far out into the darkness, brightening up the black crevices in the frowning rocks, and throwing a glow on the faces of the light-hearted peasantry that gathered around it in a huge circle. There was a fiddler among them, and though his music was not quite so scientific as Paganini's, and he would occasionally throw in a few dubious notes of his own by way of improvement on the composer, yet to that crowd it was as acceptable as the best that cultivated ear ever listened to, or that was ever applauded by kid-gloved hands at the Academy of Music. "The wee sma' hours ayont the twal" were fast passing away when they dispersed to their several homes, but the bright fire kept it up still longer, and had a terrible battle with the daylight before it was subdued. The bright red glow which but a few hours before illuminated and made cheerful every thing it touched, became paler and paler, till it was lost in the still brighter light of day, and before night, there was nothing left but a mound of white smouldering ashes, beneath which the fire gradually expired. The following morning, about four o'clock, the author was making his way in a small boat from the Niagara up to the scene of the festivities of the evening before, with his last letter for friends at home, but he found the little village of Knightstown sound asleep, and even the owner of the inn, which in this part of the country rises into the dignity of a hotel, was as oblivious as ever wearied and worn-out traveller could desire to be.

It may be as well to state here, lest the reader should mistake the object of the visit, that the innkeeper was also the postmaster of the village, and that, in his official capacity, he was a great man in Knightstown. On this occasion, he seemed to be somewhat put out by being roused from his slumbers at such an early hour; but when he learned that it was a visitor from the Niagara, his door was thrown wide open, and the letters, having received the postage stamps, were dropped through the little crevice in the huge slate that stands like a door in front of the Knightstown Hotel. Feeling considerably relieved, the writer returned to the Niagara, which was to have started at five o'clock that morning, and which, when he had cleared the harbor of Valentia, he saw standing out to sea at the rate of two miles an hour, with her bow turned westward. The cable was over her stern, and the process of paying out appeared to be progressing with perfect success; when she commenced suddenly blowing off steam, and her stoppage soon after gave evidence that there was something wrong on board. In a few minutes more the cause was explained.

In paying out, the cable slipped off the wheel, through the want of proper caution on the part of one of the men who had charge of it at this point, was caught between the wheel and the journal, and became wedged so tight that it was impossible to extricate it in time. The motion of the vessel was arrested in a few moments, but it was too late; the strain was more than the cable, strong as it was, could bear, and in less than five minutes from the time it was caught in the machinery it parted in the water, leaving the loose part swinging over the stern. As may well be supposed, this was a most trying time; but as every hour lost only made the difficulty worse, preparations were immediately made for the recovery of the broken end, which lay on the bottom at a depth of between thirty and forty fathoms, and at a distance of about four miles from the point where it had been landed the evening before amid such enthusiastic rejoicings. Mr. Woodhouse, Mr. Canning, and Captain Kell, started off the Niagara; and by the aid of two paddle-box boats from the Leopard, one from the Susquehanna, and the little steam-tug the Willing Mind, they accomplished the tedious and difficult task of under-running the cable from the shore to the place where it had parted, and where they took up the end for the purpose of making a splice. Unfortunately the roughness of the sea prevented this, and after several ineffectual attempts they were obliged to give it up till the following day, when it was hoped the elements would prove more favorable. Accordingly our ship's head was turned once more towards Valentia, and in less than an hour she was anchored in the bay. That night it was arranged that the cable should be again underrun from the shore, and spliced under the shelter of the headland which protects the entrance on the left of the bay. This was to be done as early as possible on the following morning.

Up to this time we had met with nothing but reverses, and the prospect, to say the least of it, did not appear very promising. We had lost a day by this accident, and any further delays might cause the postponement of the enterprise till the following year. All felt, therefore, that not an hour could be spared, and that every minute should be carefully economized if we expected to succeed at all. There were many anxious minds on board the Niagara that night, and many an inquiring look was taken at the barometer, which had shown some indications of an unfavorable change in the weather; but about 12 o'clock the wind moderated and the barometer again rose.

For three-quarters of an hour only was the electric connection complete, and during that time some signals and a few messages were transmitted through the cable. The test, so far as the continuity was concerned, was as perfect as could be desired, but it must be observed that the current did not pass through the whole wire, but only through one hundred and forty miles, consisting of the coil of the shore cable and the spar-deck coil of the deep sea line. It is proper to state here that the paying out of the shore cable, which is an inch and a-half in diameter, and weighs about eight tons to the mile, was a rather difficult operation, and attended with considerable risk. While the deep sea line is remarkable for its great flexibility, this portion of the cable is as much the reverse as it is possible to conceive. It was made with the view of resisting all the strain to which it might be subjected by the fouling of anchors or otherwise, and the wires of which the outer covering or protection was composed are each about one-eighth of an inch in diameter. While, therefore, great strength was obtained, it was impossible at the same time to have the additional advantage of great flexibility, and the consequence was, that when it came to be wound round the wheels for the purpose of paying out, it could not be made to run clear into the sheaves, but was constantly bulging out somewhere, requiring unremitting care and attention on the part of the workmen to prevent it from running off altogether. It was through the neglect of one of these, as has been stated, that it really did run off, and that it became necessary to splice it a second time. How much we longed to see the last yard of it overboard and the process of paying out the deep sea line commence! We felt confident, from its pliability, that there would be little or no difficulty experienced in its manipulation; that on this account particularly there would be no danger of its running off the sheaves, and thought that the power of the brakes could be so nicely graduated as to bring little if any strain upon it. Had we it once safely down, we were confident that, if favored with fair weather, we would be able to pay out our twelve hundred and fifty miles successfully.

The Second Day—August 7.

This was in reality the third day on which the work of laying the cable was continued, but as the mere landing of the shore portion of it cannot fairly be entered to the account of paying it out, it should more properly be called the second. It is, therefore, in this order that it is recorded, and it is for this reason that the mere process of landing is not included in the regular minutes of the expedition, which may be said to have commenced only when the ship herself was under way and paying out the cable over her stern. After all, however, this may be regarded as an immaterial point, although it may be well to state it in this connection, if for nothing else than the sake of accuracy.

The work was commenced about half-past five o'clock in the morning, when the Willing Mind, which played such a conspicuous part in nearly all the preliminary operations in and about this place, proceeded, with a number of workmen on board, to the buoy which marked the spot where the cable lay. She was accompanied by two boats from the Leopard and Susquehanna, each of which had a strong force to assist whenever they might be required. For three or four hours, during which they worked with might and main, they endeavored to raise it, but finding it impossible to accomplish their purpose within any reasonable time, they concluded to underrun it once more from the shore. About an hour was taken to do this, and the only thing that now remained to be done was to splice the end on board the Niagara with that which had been recovered. The Willing Mind started once more for our ship, taking one end with her to the boats of the Susquehanna and Leopard, which were lying under the lee of the land, and where the work of splicing could be carried on with less risk and greater despatch. We could see them from the deck of the Niagara working hard and fast, and during the two or three hours they were employed in this way they were objects of the most eager curiosity. The splicers were surrounded by a portion of the crew of both boats, and were almost concealed from our view, so that we had no chance of seeing what was going on. At last, after three of what appeared the longest hours, the Willing Mind and the other boats parted company, the latter returning to their separate ships. This was proof positive that the cable had not only been spliced, but that the spliced portion had been laid. By seven o'clock the anchor was up, and we were once more under way, paying out as if nothing had occurred to interrupt our progress. For the first five or ten minutes the machinery did not run as well as could be wished, and a thumping sound, that excited the most unpleasant sensation, was made by its passage over the wheels. But the ear soon became accustomed to this, and so long as it passed safely into the water every one was satisfied. The coil from which it was paid out was in the forepart of the ship, within a few feet of the forecastle, and as the distance from that to the stern was nearly her whole length, a number of men were stationed at intervals, like sentinels, between the two points, to see that every foot of it reached its destination in safety. Every thing that could be done was done to give it a safe and easy passage, but it still continued to thump away at the machinery, and before the last part of it left the ship, it created such an excitement on board that all we had previously gone through in that line seemed trifling in comparison. The part where the shore cable is joined to the deep sea line gave way as it was passing over one of the wheels, and in a minute more the broken portion would have been out over the stern, and lost beyond all hope of recovery, at least in time to permit of the seasonable prosecution of the work that year.

This was the most critical moment of the enterprise. The provision which was made for such an emergency saved it, and the admirable management of the ship, by which the strain was taken off it during the process of splicing, is worthy of all praise. The captain had ordered a strong hawser, of sufficient length, to be placed near the stern of the vessel, where it could be used at any moment, and then awaited with no small degree of anxiety the time when it should be announced that they were ready to pay out that portion where the two cables were joined. At last it was reached, and the speed of the vessel having been reduced to a fraction of a mile, so that she could only be said to be moving through the water, it was passed through the hands of the men as carefully as if it were the most tender fabric in the world, and had just gone over one of the wheels, when it was observed giving way at the joint. The men in charge were at once on the alert, and in a moment had it firmly secured to the hawser. Mr. Everett, the chief engineer of the ship, seemed ubiquitous, and rendered most efficient service at this part of the enterprise. With a coolness and self-possession deserving of all praise, he observed every thing that was going on around him, and was ready for every emergency. His conduct on this occasion pointed him out as the proper man to take charge of the cable on the next expedition; and Mr. Field never showed his foresight and judgment to better advantage than when he mentioned Mr. Everett to the Telegraph Company as the engineer who should construct the paying-out machinery. The accident occurred at half-past eleven, and the ship was about seven miles from the point from which she started that afternoon. The other vessels of course could not have been aware of its exact nature, but they must have known from the stoppage of the ship that there was something wrong. Whatever may have been their anxiety during the long and weary hour and a half which it took to renew the splice, it certainly did not exceed what we felt during that time. Not a word was spoken except by those in command, and the orders were promptly and quietly obeyed. Those who could take no active part in the work, looked on with something of the feeling with which a man awaits the result of a chance on which his very life may depend. Many an inquiring look was directed to that portion of the cable that hung over the stern, and at the men who were employed at the work of splicing. It seemed as if it would never be finished, although the joiners went at it with a will, knowing how much depended on their expedition, and performed it in half the time that would be given to it under other circumstances. The hemp serving and gutta percha insulation were cut off, leaving both ends of the copper wire or conductor perfectly bare. This was done in almost less time than it takes to relate the circumstance. The two conductors were then laid together, bound up with a single wire, and the whole soldered together. After this the gutta percha was placed over the conductor in a perfectly plastic state, and the insulation having been thus effected, the hempen strands were served upon it, the iron protecting wire or external armor placed over that again, and the whole securely bound with strong hemp. Having been spliced in this way, it was lowered down cautiously over the stern by the same hawser, so that there was little or no strain brought upon it, and in less than half an hour more the ship was on her course, going at a rate of from two to three miles an hour.

Many an impatient look is directed toward the splicer, but he performs his duty well; he is working with all possible dispatch, and although we wish he were quicker, he is doing all a man can do; if the cable be lost, it will certainly be through no fault of his. In the midst of the subdued excitement—for as I have said, no one attempted to speak but in whispers, except those in command—we could not but think, when we looked out upon the calm sea as it sparkled under the bright light of the full moon, with a feeling of gratitude upon the auspicious weather with which our enterprise had been blessed thus far. Never was a vessel more favored than ours, and if we are only permitted to lay this cable, what a time of rejoicing we will have when we get back to New York. It is almost too much to hope, and as we think what we have yet to go through, our sensations become painful in the extreme. Let us, when we return to the Empire City, be able to tell our friends that the cable is laid, and the United States, big as they are, will not be able to hold us.

Let us lay this cable successfully and we will—but it is useless saying what we wil do. After all our anxiety, after all the excitement, it may be that we are not destined to accomplish our great work this time, but our hopes are strong, and I know that there is not a man on board, from the captain to the humblest hand, that is not wrapt up heart and soul in the enterprise. So strong is the feeling, that I believe there would be less excitement among them at the cry of "man overboard" than there would at the announcement that the cable had parted, perhaps it is because they think the man might be picked up, but that the cable never could.

The cable meantime has been paid out, and in less than an hour we are at least two miles off from where the splice, which had put every one into such a terrible state of anxiety, is lying safely upon its ocean bed. We are glad to get rid of it, for it was one of the worst customers with which we had yet to deal, and every body congratulates every body else that it is safely overboard. "I tell you what," says one of the quartermasters, two or three hours after; "I tell you what, that was a hard tug, and I hope we won't soon have such another"—a hope in which it is almost needless to say every one who heard him joined.

The next point of interest now is the telegraph office, the door of which is beset with eager inquirers, all desirous of knowing how the cable works, and a considerable number of these with messages for friends not only in Valentia, Liverpool and London, but away off in the United States. Among these was the writer, who took advantage of the first opportunity to transmit the following despatch to the New York Herald, and which he feels considerable pride in being able to say was the first sent to any newspaper over the Atlantic Telegraph, or that portion of it which was laid. And here it is:

United States Frigate Niagara,
At Sea, off the Coast of Ireland, August 8—1 P. M.

To James Gordon Bennett, Esq., New York *Herald Office.*

The cable is being paid out over the stern in capital style, and the ship is going at the rate of two miles an hour. We have just paid out the twelfth mile most successfully, and are getting on admirably. The insulation was found to be perfect after a splice had been paid out, and the cable is in such excellent working order that messages are transmitted between the ship and the shore with the greatest ease. All are well on board the Niagara, and sanguine as to the result of the expedition. We can see the lights of the other steamers as they hover around us, and can imagine what intense anxiety they must feel to know how we are getting on. J. M.

The subjoined despatch was received from the telegraph office at Valentia Bay:

We see the Niagara broadside on. Is there any thing wrong in the paying out?

To which the following reply was received:

All is right. Every thing is going on well. The ship's broadside being on arises from her drifting, as she was going very slowly—only a mile and a half an hour.

The messages that were sent by the officers to their friends and relatives in different parts of the United States would fill nearly a volume, and the operatives were kept busy at the instrument the whole time.

Third Day—August 8.

Since the Niagara left New York, she was not and could not have been favored with fairer weather than she had to-day. The sun rose in an almost cloudless sky, and the wind was so light that it hardly raised a ripple on the water. The rest of the telegraph squadron had spread a part of their canvas in the hope of being able to save their coal; but they made nothing by it, and were obliged to furl their sails which were hanging loosely from the yards. Even the light ensigns hung from the peaks in folds, and there was hardly strength enough in the breeze to shake out the still lighter streamers that floated from the main. We heard the bells of the Susquehanna as she stood off about half a mile on our starboard quarter, and, were it necessary, could have hailed her at that distance without any great straining of lungs. The Leopard was taking it easy away off four or five hundred yards on the port side, and the Agamemnon, with her massive and warlike-looking hull, although a mile and a half away, loomed up as visibly as if she were not more than one-third that distance off. The Cyclops amused herself running ahead of the rest of the squadron, as if on the look-out for something which she never succeeded in finding. She had a jolly, rollicking way of her own, that contrasted strongly with the rolling gait of the bluff Agamemnon and the dashing style of the Leopard, which pitched into every sea, no matter how small, as if it had some insidious designs upon her, throwing it from her in showers of spray. The Susquehanna took it quietly enough, and seemed as perfectly satisfied at going two miles an hour as if she had been going a dozen in the same time. About twenty miles astern of the squadron the Skelligs, two high rocks that stand out from the main land like gigantic outposts, were distinctly visible, and although the little light-house at the entrance to Valentia harbor had sunk below the horizon some hours before, we could still tell its position by the high landmarks by which it was surrounded. There were the Blasketts, an island mountain, and one of the first of the many highlands which the mariner sees on this part of the Irish coast before he enters Dingle bay; and those low, half-sunken, treacherous-looking rocks, with which the waves are at perpetual war, are the Foze, and are the dread of all the shipmasters who trade about this part of the island. Away off beyond the Foze and the Blasketts, among those highlands of the county Kerry, is some of the most magnificent scenery that ever delighted the eyes of a traveller; and as those highlands sink gradually below the horizon, the valleys darken with the evening shadows, and the mountain peaks, suffused with the red glow of the descending sun, look more like the creations of dreamland than a living, actual reality.

It is Captain Pennock's watch to-day, although Captain Hudson may be said to be always on, with the exception of the few hours which he gives to rest. The Captain's first question is in regard to the cable, as it is in fact the first with almost every one when they have got the sleep out of their eyes.

"What is the rate at which the cable is being paid out?" he inquires, addressing Mr. Fugitt, the sailmaker, who is one of the guardians of the coils.

"Three miles, sir," is the response. This is not so fast as had been expected, but it is doing very well for the present, although the intention is to do much better before a hundred miles of the cable shall have been passed over the stern. A visit to the coil proves that the report of Mr. Fugitt is correct, and also proves another thing, that whatever fears might have been felt in regard to kinks, or any thing of that kind, are entirely groundless. Nothing could be more gratifying than the way in which it comes up out of the coil—so flexible, and yet possessing so much strength. There is no trouble whatever with it—no twisting into knots nor entangling of the flakes—but the whole process of uncoiling goes on without the slightest difficulty. The men who stand around the circle looking out for accidents have an easy time of it, and might be in New York or Liverpool, or away in the Punjaub, for all their services are required That cable couldn't kink if it tried; and so long as it passes out of the ship safely, and is deposited securely on the bottom, it may twist as much as it pleases. The iron wires which form the outer covering or protection may become so corroded with the action of the salt water as to afford it no longer any protection; but while the insulation remains intact, the essential part of the cable requires no other protection than that given it by the gutta percha. It has been urged, as an argument in favor of the success of the Atlantic telegraph, that the iron wire, in the process of decomposition to which it would be subjected after its submersion, would enter into combination with the calcareous substances, which, as has been shown by the soundings of Lieut. Berryman and Capt. Dayman, form a part of the deposit of the bed of the ocean. Once the cable is down, however, and down securely, who cares whether it does or not, or whether there is not a particle of the protecting wire left?

The first coil will be all run out some time to-morrow (Sunday) morning, and then what a time there will be in passing the second splicing safely out of the ship, and how we shall rejoice at having even one-tenth part of our half laid! Various speculations are afloat as to the length submerged and the distance run; and when it is announced from some quarter or another that the twenty-five hundred miles aboard both ships will fall short before the Agamemnon reaches the Newfoundland terminus, a rather uneasy feeling takes possession of some, although the engineers express their confidence that two or three days' reckoning will show there is not only enough, but plenty to spare. The only thing that remained now to be done was to get rid of the cable as fast as we could, for although we might have been satisfied with three miles when we started, now that we had attained that, we would not be content till we reached four or five. The only objection to this was that it might bring too great a strain upon it, and that in our impatience to get through with our part of the work we might lose the cable—a catastrophe, the very dread of which haunted us like a nightmare. True, the strain at the present rate, as appeared from the indicator, did not exceed four hundred pounds, while the cable, as had been proved by the experiment in Valentia Bay, was capable of bearing a strain of three and a half tons.

It has just been proved from a calculation of the distance run and the amount of the cable paid out, that there is at present no reason to fear we shall not have enough. The ship is thirty-nine miles from the point at which the shore end of the cable was landed, while the number laid does not exceed forty-one, showing that only two miles more than the actual distance traversed have been expended, and that if they continue at this rate they will have sufficient with which to lay a submarine telegraph line from Cape Race, Newfoundland, to Cape North, the most northern part of Cape Breton. But all this is premature. When we reach mid-ocean, if ever we succeed in getting so far, we will be better able to tell.

This day closed with fine weather, and a promise of its continuance. In the evening, about seven or eight o'clock, the remarkable color of the sea attracted general attention. But only a few hours previous it had a deep blue, but it was now a very light pea green, and, looking closely at the surface, we discovered that it was strewed with dead medusæ. For miles and miles we passed through these, and would doubtless have continued to see them had we not been prevented by the darkness of night. Another visit to the coil and the telegraph office before going to bed, satisfied us that the cable was going out in fine style, and that the continuity was perfect. That word "continuity" had become quite a pet on board; and if any thing went wrong with the cable, the first question was always of course in regard to its safety, and the next as to the continuity being all right. Once at ease on both these points every one slept more soundly, but the moment the slightest breath was whispered of any thing wrong with either, the greatest anxiety was manifested till the cheering intelligence was given that the work was going on successfully. If the "old coffee-mill" stopped for a minute, all hands in the cabin and wardroom were on deck to know the cause of it, and did not go below again till it went on as before. The "coffee-mill" was the name given to the paying-out machine, from the peculiar noise made by the wheels, and which bore somewhat of a resemblance to that which would be produced by a mill for grinding coffee. The sound became as familiar to us as that of our own voices, and so long as we heard it, we knew that every thing was safe—that is, that the cable, which was every thing to us, was going out without difficulty. The first thing we heard in the morning was the paying-out machine grinding away above our heads, and although it made what some might consider a disagreeable racket, to us it was more pleasing than the best opera ever produced by Italian, German, or any other composer. This night, particularly, it seems more noisy than ever, but instead of interfering with our rest, it will only make us sleep the sounder.

Fourth Day—August 9.

The now familiar sound of the paying-out machine, which never ceases except when there is something wrong with the cable, kept on through the whole night without interruption, and was the first thing that greeted our waking senses. We were doing wonders, and so long as the brakes were not applied, the machine showed no sign of halting in its work. At our mess table it was the principal subject of conversation, and all were of the opinion that the laying of a cable across the Atlantic was not only feasible, but that it would be accomplished in this present month of August, and by the ships Niagara and Agamemnon. There were some, it is true, who thought that there might be a difficulty when we came to the great depths, and that the increased weight and strain which would then be brought upon the cable, with the pitching and rolling of the ship in a heavy sea, might be more than it could bear; but after all, there was little danger to be apprehended from this, if the brakes were not put on, for it was observed that when they were employed for the purpose of checking its speed, they very frequently stopped the wheels from turning, and brought upon it the strain produced by the speed of the vessel—a strain which would part the strongest cable ever made, as it parted the shore cable but a few days ago, and only a short time after we got out of Doulus Bay. Those brakes, in fact, are the only things that we have to dread; and if they were once overboard, there is no difficulty, so far as our experience has yet proved, in the way of the successful accomplishment of this enterprise.

We are in high humor at the progress we have already made, as well as the fine weather we have had, and being on the second coil of the deep sea line which was put on the berth deck, are now looking forward to the time when we shall get rid of that too. The coil which had been formed on the spar deck, and the last mile of which was paid out at a quarter to 8 o'clock this morning, contained one hundred and thirty miles, which, with the ten miles of heavy shore cable, made one hundred and forty, or about one-ninth of the whole amount on board. It was known last evening that if no accident occurred, we would reach the foremain deck coil some time this morning; and as the critical moment arrived, all who could were up on deck to see the splice by which the two were connected go over the stern. This moment was looked forward to with considerable interest and anxiety. It was thought that the strain produced by the machinery on the joint, which is certainly not so strong as the other parts of the cable, would be too much for it, and that it would give on being paid out. Every precaution was therefore taken to prevent such an occurrence. The speed of the ship was reduced to a mile an hour, and the spliced portion lowered gently from the stern. About thirty men were stationed about the coil and at the machinery, while a dozen stood near the stern, all ready for any emergency that might arise. Standing by the circle from which the cable was now going up with greatly diminished speed, we watched flake after flake and turn after turn as it was unwound from about the cone, until the last turn—the spliced part—was reached, and following it up to the machinery, saw it pass safely over the five wheels and down into the water. In a half hour more all danger was over; a few more revolutions were given to the propeller, and we were soon going at the rate of three miles an hour towards Trinity Bay, Newfoundland. This speed was increased to three and a half, and before night we were going at the rate of five, the highest we had reached yet. The rest of the squadron were somewhat astonished, for having graduated their speed by what we had been running, they began to fall astern very rapidly for two or three hours. They soon found out the cause, however, and putting on a little more steam, took their former position. The ease with which the cable was paid out at this rate convinced all of the practicability of continuing it with perfect success, and with such favorable weather as had attended the enterprise up to this time, of laying the cable inside of sixteen days. All that was necessary was to look out for the splices, to reduce the speed at the proper time, and especially to avoid the use of the brakes except when imperatively necessary. The accumulation of tar in the grooves or sheaves it was feared might have a tendency to throw the cable off the wheels, but as it was brushed away again by the cable almost as quick as it gathered, little attention was paid to it.

In the early part of the day divine service was celebrated, the captain performing the duties of chaplain. There was not, however, any interruption in the work; the men were at their stations as usual, and mingled with the captain's voice was the din of the machinery. At the close the prayer for the success of the expedition, which was read at the celebration of the landing of the cable, was repeated, and the earnest amen which followed, showed how deep an interest every one felt in it.

The greatest depth over which we had passed was four hundred fathoms, but to-morrow we expect to be paying the cable out into two thousand fathoms of water, or somewhat over two miles. This will test the practicability of laying it in great depths, and settle forever one of the most serious questions to which this enterprise has given rise. It is supposed by some, in opposition to the "telegraph plateau" theory of Lieut. Maury, that the bottom of the ocean, instead of being of one uniform level between Ireland and Newfoundland, has the same depressions and heights, the same abrupt declivities and mountain ranges, which are to be found upon the surface of the earth.

The soundings of Lieut. Berryman, of the United States navy, and Commander Dayman, of the British navy, have proved the existence of this plateau; but still it is urged that, as these soundings were taken at intervals of thirty, forty or fifty miles, it is impossible to tell the exact character of the bed of the sea from them, or to form any thing more than a speculative opinion in regard to the subject. The laying, therefore, of this cable will do much towards putting an end to all doubts whatever regarding it, as well as towards proving the practicability of the present enterprise. One of the great difficulties which Mr. Brett had to contend with in laying a cable across the Mediterranean, was caused by the great depth of water, which in parts equals the deepest soundings found on the telegraphic plateau, but those were abrupt and not gradual descents, like what we shall have. We will not be alarmed by any of those rapid runs of the cable that threaten destruction to all in its way, for the descents over which we shall pass will not be greater than one thousand feet to the mile, while the average will be perhaps about three hundred. This is certainly most promising, and if the promise holds good and the cable don't part, we may have an opportunity of realizing it to-morrow.

During the day we signalled the squadron that "all was right," which meant that the cable was going out safely, that the continuity was perfect, and, in a word, that we were getting along as well, if not better, than could be expected. They were satisfied, and during the remainder of the day kept on their westward course without interruption, while we pursued ours steadily, paying out the cable at the rate of from five to six miles per hour. The electricians said the cable was in good working order, and messages were sent through it to America by the officers of the Niagara to their friends and relatives, all of whom will doubtless have received them before we reach the other side of the Atlantic. There is evidently a determination not to let it remain idle for want of work, and the operators have enough to do if they get through the pile of manuscript which lies on their desk before morning.

Fifth Day—August 10.

There was a pretty heavy sea on during the whole of this day, and it was evident that there had been a gale somewhere in the immediate vicinity, judging from the size of the waves. The rate of paying out varied from four and a half to six knots an hour, and the cable came up from the coil as easily as if the ship were only making two knots. It is certainly a wonderful cable, and those coils are admirably adapted to the work. There was, it must be confessed, a prejudice against them at first, and when they were suggested as the best form that could be devised, some objected to them, on the ground that they would be so liable to kink. This opinion has now been proved to be erroneous, and those who opposed the circles are convinced by practical demonstration that they were the best that could be adopted.

This morning about ten o'clock a sail hove in sight, when the squadron, in addition to their own national colors, displayed the Telegraph flag. Our quartermaster, when she was some three or four miles off, proclaimed her to be "a Dutchman." In half an hour he took another observation of her; said he could see her colors, that she was Norwegian, adding, in a triumphant tone, that he knew "she was some kind of Dutch," but he guessed it was "pretty high up."

About eleven o'clock the Agamemnon signalled to us, desiring to know if we had any news, through the cable, from the East Indies, a part of the British dominions which at this particular time excites the most painful interest throughout England. We replied that we had not. There were, we understood, some on board who had relatives there, and who naturally felt anxious to hear about the condition of things in that country. At this time we were in 2,150 fathoms water, and the cable was going out in magnificent style. There were none of those sudden alarming runs which had been predicted for us when our ship should come to the great depths, and had we not known from the chart of the soundings where we were, we could not have told the difference, so far as its effect upon the line was concerned. We could partly tell the strain by the angle which it made with the water, while the speed at which it went out was marked upon an indicator connected with the machinery. The strain was shown more accurately by another indicator, so that we could tell the exact number of pounds it was subjected to at any particular time. This hardly exceeded three hundred, except when the brakes were put on, and then it was increased to fifteen and twenty hundred, and sometimes more. In all cases, however, it would not do to take the indicator as a true guide, as the pitching of the vessel produced a strain which is not always, if it is ever, correctly marked upon it.

There was a great deal of excitement created by the cable getting off the wheels twice this evening, but fortunately it was put on again without any other accident. It was to a considerable extent a repetition of the same scene that took place when the cable broke off the coast of Ireland. The ship was backed immediately, the cable released from the strain, and in five minutes, which seemed so many hours, it was put on the wheels again. When the order was given to the engineer to "go ahead slow," it is impossible to describe the scene which followed—the relief from a feeling of terrible suspense and painful excitement to which every one was wound up, the warm and hearty congratulations that were interchanged, and the eagerness with which we still continued to watch the wheels, fearful of a repetition of the accident. The engineers kept near the machine, ready in case of emergency to go over the work again; but fortunately there was no call for their services in the same way this night, after the second catastrophe.

The throwing of the cable off the wheels was caused by the accumulation of tar in the sheaves, which are not so deep and so wide as experience has proved they should have been. The tar, which is pressed out of the iron or protecting wire as the cable passes over the wheels, sticks in the sheaves until it gathers in some parts in large lumps, which become hardened by exposure to the air. The effect of this is to throw the cable off altogether, as occurred in the two cases just mentioned.

We had hardly recovered from the alarm created by these accidents, when the whole ship was thrown into another state of excitement by the report that the continuity was gone—that the cable refused any longer to transmit the electric current; in a word, that all communication between the ship and the shore had ceased, in consequence of some accident to the copper wire or conductor, of which no one knew the cause.

For two hours and a half the continuity was lost; and we believed that all was over, that the three hundred and odd miles which had been laid were laid in vain, that we would be obliged to return, and report our own failure, when the eyes of the whole world were turned upon us, and at a time, too, when we confidently hoped that success was within our reach if we only exercised a due amount of vigilance and caution. The Engineers, Captain Hudson and Professor Morse had all agreed that the only thing to be done was to cut the cable for the purpose of getting it off the paying-out machine, and transferring it to that which was to be used for winding up, and in regard to the successful operation of which there were very serious and well-founded doubts.

Mr. De Sauty, the assistant electrician, and Mr. Bright, consulted with Professor Morse as to the best course to be pursued, when he expressed the opinion that the strain to which the cable had been subjected at the time it slipped off the wheels had opened the gutta percha, and thus destroyed the insulation. This certainly seemed the only reasonable explanation that could be given of the affair, and the cause stated was generally accepted as the true one. About two miles of the cable had been paid out since that accident occurred, and the only question that now remained to be decided was whether the winding-in machine could be safely employed in under-running this length. This, as Professor Morse said, was for the chief engineer, Mr. Bright, to determine, and it rested with him to give the order to have the cable cut, in case he should so decide. Mr. Bright did so decide, and preparations were being made to carry his order into execution, when Mr. De Sauty informed Professor Morse that the continuity had been restored, and that the insulation had not been destroyed. In five minutes more the intelligence would have come too late, for in that time the cable would have been cut, and the conductor thus detached from the telegraph instrument could not have given any indication of its being perfect up to the terminus on the vessel. The glad news was soon circulated throughout the ship, and all felt as if they had been imbued with a new life. A rough, weather-beaten old sailor, who had assisted in coiling many a long mile of it on board the Niagara, and who was among the first to run to the telegraph office to have the news confirmed, said he would have given fifty dollars out of his pay to have saved that cable. "I have watched nearly every mile of it," he added, "as it came over the side, and I would have given fifty dollars, poor a man as I am, to have saved it, although I don't expect to make any thing by it when it is laid down." In his own simple way he expressed the feelings of every one on board, for all are as much interested in the success of the enterprise as the largest shareholder in the company. They talked of the cable as they would of a pet child, and never was child treated with deeper solicitude than that with which the cable is watched by them. You could see the tears standing in the eyes of some as they almost cried for joy, and told their messmates that it was all right. They did not know any thing about the scientific definition of the word "continuity," for to them it was a mystery which was incapable of explanation, but when they heard it was gone, they seemed to understand it as if by instinct, and to appreciate the full extent of the loss.

I have said that it was a great relief to all to learn that the electric connection was still perfect, but each man, as he retires for the night, has a feeling of nervousness and uncertainty, lest the morrow should have something still worse in store for us.

Sixth Day—August 11.

This has been a sad day. We had retired full of hope, not, it is true, unmixed with a sort of dread that there was something still worse than what had yet happened impending over the enterprise. This morning, about four o'clock, we were awakened out of our sleep to hear the cable had parted in over two thousand fathoms water. Five minutes after it had been announced every one was out of his bed to ascertain for himself if it was indeed true. There was, however, no reason to doubt, for there hung the broken end over the stern swinging loosely, and there were the wheels as motionless as a rock. The other end had not yet sunk to the bottom; it had to descend more than two miles before it reached the plateau, and it would require more time to accomplish that. The noise that sounded like pleasant music in our ears had ceased, and the machine which had caused us such anxiety had now become as so much useless lumber, blocking up the quarter deck. The cause of the calamity was the application of the brakes, at a time when it was fatal to use them. There was a pretty heavy swell on, and as usual under such circumstances, the stern of the vessel was elevated or depressed as she rose on each wave. It was while her stern was down that the brakes were put on, so that in addition to the strain produced by its rising again, the cable had to bear an additional strain of three thousand pounds, as marked upon the indicator. This was more than it could bear, and the consequence was that it parted. The moment the brakes were used the wheels stopped, and when the stern rose again they remained immovable, so that, between the strain brought upon the cable by the vessel and that caused by the application of the brakes, it had, as I have said, to bear more than it was ever calculated to sustain. The indicator showed a strain of three thousand pounds; but it is impossible to calculate the strain by which it was broken.

Had the brake not been applied, there is no doubt whatever that the cable would have remained perfect to the end, unless we were compelled by very great stress of weather to cut it. The circumstance, to say the least of it, was most unfortunate; but if the enterprise has failed, the expedition has proved one thing beyond all possibility of doubt, the practicability of laying a submarine telegraph cable across the Atlantic between Ireland and Newfoundland. Of this every man on board is as fully convinced as he is of his own existence, whether it be laid next year, or its accomplishment be postponed for fifty years to come.

The order to put on the brakes was given by Mr. Bright at this critical moment, and there is no doubt whatever on the mind of any one conversant with the facts, that it was that order that caused the fracture of the cable. The author, however, confidently believes that it was impossible to lay it successfully with that machinery, and that some such accident must have inevitably occurred before the arrival of the fleet at Newfoundland.

This morning, soon after the catastrophe, a consultation was held in the cabin of the Niagara, at which Captain Hudson, Captain Pennock, Captain Wainwright, Mr. Bright, Mr. Woodhouse, Mr. Canning, and Professor Morse were present, when the question of commencing the work over again with what cable remained on board both vessels was discussed, but as it was found, after due calculation, that there was not enough to connect the two points, the proposition of course did not prevail. The following table and statement show the amount paid out and the balance of cable on hand:—

	Statute miles.	Nautical miles.
Upper deck	130	111
Main deck	294	255
Lower deck	182	157
Lower hold	352	305
Wardroom	297	257
Total	1,255	1,085

This, with ten miles of shore cable, made a total of 1,095 nautical miles. Of this, 334 were paid out when the cable parted, leaving 759 miles on board the Niagara, which, with the half in the Agamemnon, left 1,847, or a surplus of 207 over 1,700 miles—the distance between the termini at Newfoundland and Ireland—an excess of 12 per cent. This was, as has been said, considered insufficient, and the proposition was accordingly rejected as impracticable. Indeed, it was deemed doubtful whether, if the cable had not parted, there would have been enough to reach Trinity Bay.

Another proposition was made, that when the vessels returned to England an additional length of cable be procured, and with this and new machinery the work be recommenced in October. This, however, was to be decided by the directors, and in the mean time it was understood that the Niagara was to lie at Plymouth until further orders. It was believed that if this proposition should not be carried out, our ship would be detained till the following year, when the Telegraph Squadron were to take a fresh start.

Soon after the meeting Mr. Field, with his usual promptitude, left the squadron in the Cyclops—the rest of the vessels, with the exception of the Leopard, remaining to make some experiments to test the practicability of splicing the ends of the cable from both the Niagara and Agamemnon. This occupied another day, and proved that it was perfectly practicable to join the ends of the cable in mid ocean.

BOUND FOR PLYMOUTH.

Having made the experiments suggested by Mr. Field, and which, as has been stated, were entirely successful, the Telegraph Squadron started for Plymouth, one of the first naval depots in Great Britain. On their way to that port a trial of speed took place between the Niagara, the Agamemnon, and the Susquehanna. Properly speaking it could hardly be called a race, for we were all so confident of the superior merits of our own vessel in point of speed, that we looked upon such a thing as competition or comparison as not only out of the question, but absolutely preposterous. True, we had heard a great deal of the qualities of the Agamemnon under sail and steam, and we certainly felt no inclination to depreciate her either as a sailing ship or a steamer; but at the same time the superiority which was claimed for her over our vessel we were not prepared to admit. We were told that she was the "crack" ship of the British fleet; that she could steam from twelve to fourteen knots an hour; and that she was, in a word, the fastest propeller on either side of the ocean; but all this we took with a certain degree of latitude, and while we listened to the relation of her wonderful performances, our opinion of the Niagara underwent no change. The fact is, as I have said, that we felt so confident of the superiority of the Niagara, as to regard such a thing as a trial of speed perfectly preposterous. There was then, literally speaking, no race between the two ships, for several reasons:—in the first place the vessels were not in proper trim or condition; in the second, we had only three boilers in operation, being deprived entirely of the use of our fourth by the proximity of the furnaces to the coils of cable, which might have been damaged by the heat of the fires; and in the third, we knew that the Agamemnon had frigates' masts instead of her own spars, which had been taken out the better to qualify her for the work of laying the great sea line. Yet I have no doubt that she made an effort to outrun us, if it be fair to judge from her increase of speed and the indications afforded by the dense columns of black smoke which occasionally issued from her pipes, that they were piling on the coal below. This is not all, however, for there was still stronger evidence in the frank acknowledgments of her men as to the great qualities of the Niagara, and the astonishment which they unfeignedly express at her speed and steadiness. And now let me state what it was that caused this change of opinion in men who were so full of praises of their own ship, and who, with a pardonable pride, believed she was superior to any other, although that other was the Niagara.

The day on which the cable was broken—that ill-fated 11th of August—some experiments were tried, all of which, as has been stated, proved successful. The following day, Wednesday, the 12th of August, we were on our way to Plymouth, and desiring to keep company with the Agamemnon, we kept under steam alone, while she was under both sail and steam. It was not, however, till the 13th, that what has been called the race between the two ships took place, and then the fact is, the Susquehanna was the only competitor we had. About 10 o'clock Captain Sands made the following signal to us:—"Going to Plymouth," intimating that he was bound for that port, and if we intended to keep company we had better "hurry up our cakes." We thoroughly understood the meaning of this signal to be a reflection upon the speed of our vessel, for on board of the Susquehanna they were rather inclined to depreciate her in this particular. They had been talking some time before about her failure, and in proof of it referred to the length of her passage from New York to England. It was upon this that they based their estimates of her qualities, and under the impression that their own was her superior, they gave us a challenge in this indirect way. At this time, that is, about 10 o'clock, the Susquehanna was a few hundred yards ahead of us, on our starboard bow, and as if to clear up any doubt we might have had in regard to the signal being a challenge, she slowed down until she was right abeam with our ship. In reply to the signal of Captain Sands, Captain Hudson made the following:—"We can only use two boilers, in consequence of cable."

Only two boilers were in use, but as a portion of the other two could be used without risk to the cable, we also got them under steam, so that three boilers may be said to have been in operation.

There was no doubt on the Susquehanna that they were certain of beating us, and although laboring under all the disadvantages already referred to, we were determined to lower their pride and punish them for their presumption. It must be remembered that we had the cable guard attached to our stern, that we were below our regular bearings with the cable, and that we had but three boilers in use; while the Susquehanna was in admirable condition, and there is no doubt was under a full head of steam when she dropped down and came abeam with the Niagara. As soon as she took that position, her wheels, which before this had being going at an ordinary rate, began to revolve with accelerated velocity, and finally with a rapidity that cleared up whatever doubts we might have had of her intentions. All the sails that were of any service were put on, and every evidence was given that she was doing her very best under the circumstances. Her rate of speed was about ten miles an hour.

All the steam that could with safety be used was raised, and we also made as much sail as was considered profitable. For twenty minutes or half-an-hour the Susquehanna occupied the same position, so that her gangways were within our line of vision during that time. We had not, however, got properly under way for the first fifteen or twenty minutes, but after this it became evident that the gangways were closing up—that is, they were falling below the line of vision, so that we could only see the gangway on the port side, or the side next to our ship. It was now apparent they were doing all in their power to maintain their position, but from this time the Susquehanna gradually began to fall astern, until her foremast was brought in a direct line with our mizen. In a few minutes more we were ahead of her, and an hour from the time she dropped down and came abeam with us she was about half-a-mile astern. Still she kept at it, although Captain Sands must have been pretty well satisfied regarding the comparative merits of both ships. From ten o'clock till four they kept it up, the Agamemnon doing her best also. At four, the Agamemnon was about twelve miles astern, and the Susquehanna about five. As we did not wish to run away from them altogether, and as Captain Hudson desired to keep company with the former, we hove too and let off steam till she came up. At twenty-five minutes past four the Susquehanna passed us, and at half-past-five the Agamemnon went by us under sail and steam. The race was over, and the Susquehanna displayed no more signals after this about going to Plymouth.

Notwithstanding all this the Agamemnon proved herself, with all the disadvantages under which she labored, and to which we were also subject, both a good steamer and a fast ship. She could hardly be expected to equal the Niagara in speed, for the two are constructed on very different models; and the only wonder is that any doubt could be entertained with regard to their qualities. Whatever may be said about her sailing and steaming abilities, the Agamemnon is one of the finest line-of-battle ships in the world; and it is no wonder that she is the pet of the British navy after her gallant performances before Sebastopol, when she distinguished herself by the fearlessness with which she steamed up to within eight or nine hundred yards of the frowning batteries of that terrible fortress.

The officers of the Susquehanna not only acknowledge that their ship was well beaten, but express their belief that the Niagara is one of the swiftest vessels in the world—that she is, in fact, without an equal. Since their conversion we have pardoned them for their presumption in thinking that they could beat us, and accept their voluntary praises of the Niagara as a proof of their sincerity. There is no doubt whatever that the long passage—a passage which was made under the most unfavorable circumstances—of our ship from New York to London in April, 1857, disappointed every one regarding her character as a steamer and sailing vessel; but those who knew her, and who have witnessed her performances under all circumstances, are satisfied that she will realize the high expectations that were formed of her.

ARRIVAL AT PLYMOUTH.

The Niagara arrived at Plymouth on the 13th of August, 1857, where she remained till the 5th of November following, when she sailed for New York. Mr. Field had arrived sometime before, and had called a meeting of the Board of Directors at London, at which Mr. Everett and the commanders of the expedition were present. The result of these meetings was, that Mr. Everett was requested to examine and report upon the form of machinery best adapted to secure the success of the next expedition.

While occupying this position, he was literally deluged with plans of proposed machines, suggestions in regard to the laying of the cable, and advice from every quarter as to the manner in which the work should be performed. Some of those correspondents offered their suggestions and advice without hope of pay, or at least without saying any thing about it, but it must be confessed that the majority were worldly minded and looked after the almighty dollar. Machines of the most remarkable structure were presented on paper for consideration, accompanied with detailed descriptions and explanations covering whole reams of foolscap. Take them all together they were rich specimens of literature, and should not be allowed to pass into that obscurity to which the efforts of aspiring genius are so often consigned. They were from clergymen, artists, mechanics, engineers, sailors, soldiers, officers, and gentlemen of leisure—that is, those who are supposed to have plenty of money, and plenty of time to spend it in. The following is one of the volunteer letters, and, as will be seen, the suggestions which it contains are the joint production of two parties, although, according to the laws of the church, they should properly be regarded as one:—

"I was talking to my wife in bed last night, whose brother was in the navy, as to depositing your Atlantic telegraph rope, when she suggested whether you would not have difficulties with the currents, which she had heard her late brother speak of as interfering with the soundings. It immediately struck me that you were beginning at the wrong end, and that the rope ought to start from the American side, so that the Gulf Stream might act on the concave, or inside of the curve of descending rope and facilitate its deposit, instead of acting on the convex side and tend to throw it down—it curves and renders a much longer length as necessary. If there be weight in this suggestion, and you begin at the American end, the course of your vessel should curve southward to allow for or compensate the northward tendency of the Gulf Stream. As you know the depths and the surface rates of the current, and its angle with the ship's course, you may guess the rates and the direction of the current at different depths, or average them, and thus get across with the shortest possible amount of rope, and therefore in the straightest line. If these suggestions reach you before you sail, but too late to be directly of use, they may put you on methods of reducing the evil I have anticipated."

Whatever "weight" there may be in the suggestions of this correspondent, he is certainly entitled to the credit of originality, and it is to be hoped that in the laying of the next cable the engineers will have a proper regard for the concavity and convexity of the curve of the descending rope and the northward tendency of the Gulf Stream. But here is another, and although not quite so clear as that already given, still it is a remarkable production:—

"GENTLEMEN—Permit me to suggest to your notice the fact, as time will prove, that you will never lay your electric cable complete till you adopt very different means to those at present employed. When you find the broken cable you will find it broken at a knot, and many more knots may be found tied. This I consider to be self evident. There has been a hundred miles of the cable used beyond the actual distance laid—nearly two-thirds I compute more than shown by the main depths of soundings. I can give an efficient method of how to lay safely, without strain, the cable in a direct line without any waste in angles, at a greater saving in cost. I will say no more at present in justice to myself."

Every one who reads the foregoing will no doubt appreciate the sense of justice by which the writer was actuated, although they may not clearly understand the "angle" difficulty to which he alludes.

Some of the letters were very elaborate, and began usually with an essay on some subject that was supposed to have an intimate connection with the enterprise. Of this character was one which gave some curious particulars concerning the habits of whales, and all of which was intended to show how much easier the cable could be laid by the plan proposed. Conspicuous among the applicants figured a clairvoyant, who expressed a strong desire to be employed by the company for a proper consideration, in return for which, she engaged in cases of break of continuity, to tell exactly in what part the break had occurred, and in the event of fracture of the cable, where the end could be found. All these disinterested applicants, clairvoyants, inventors and all, were summarily disposed of; but not at all discouraged, they kept up their applications and correspondence to the end, and some even threatened to sue the company if they did not adopt their suggestions. It will be strange hereafter if some of them do not lay claim to the credit of having invented the machinery, and seek to deprive Mr. Everett of the fame to which he is so justly entitled.

Mr. Everett having signified his intention of complying with the request of the Atlantic Telegraph Company, associated with himself Messrs. Penn, Lloyd and Field, three English engineers of high reputation, with whom he conjointly made the following report:—

LONDON, SEPTEMBER, 1857.

GENTLEMEN:—Having examined, agreeably to your request, the apparatus and arrangements on board the Niagara for paying out the Atlantic telegraph cable, and given the whole subject our careful consideration, we beg to lay before you the conclusions at which we have arrived.

We consider the paying out sheaves require no alterations except those suggested by Mr. Bright in a memorandum which he was good enough to place in our hands, a copy of which we append, namely:—To have one groove only in each of the sheaves, to make the groove deeper and wider at the periphery, and fit them with guards, to prevent the cable coming off, to apply scrapers for removing the tar from the grooves, and to make the circumference of each successive sheave which the cable passes over as much larger than the preceding one as the cable is found to stretch by the application of the increasing strain which it has to bear in passing round the several sheaves when it is being paid out with the maximum strain, and thus greatly diminish, or perhaps entirely obviate, the slipping of the cable on all the sheaves. We may add, that we see no reason why this apparatus should not also be used for hauling in the cable when necessary, if sufficient engine power be provided for that purpose.

The most important consideration, however, to which we have directed our attention, is how to guard against the strain being brought on the cable while paying out, greater than it is considered capable of bearing without risk of damage—that is, having determined the maximum strain, how to counteract the numerous causes which have a tendency to increase it; and which, especially when brought into operation simultaneously, would otherwise endanger or destroy the cable.

The means which we recommend for this purpose are the substitution for the present brakes of two others, moving with the same regular velocity, but of twice the diameter, and having their rubbing surface of gun metal, about twelve inches wide; each brake to be capable of doing the whole work; but both may be in operation together if found convenient. They should be constructed on the plan patented some years ago by Mr. Appold. Their rims should be lined with slips of lignum vitæ, about three inches broad and half an inch apart, and immersed about one-third of their diameter in cisterns of salt water, it being found by experience that brass and lignum vitæ work together under great pressure with no appreciable wear. Mr. Appold's brake has the advantage of insuring a uniform holding power, so long as the pressure on the lever remains unaltered, capable of being increased or diminished to any required degree with certainty.

A light movable sheave of the same size as those on the paying-out apparatus should be introduced, and be arranged to move horizontally on the deck through a space of about twenty feet, by the action of strong springs of vulcanized India rubber. The cable by passing over that on the stern of the ship would be relieved from the great inequalities of strain to which it would otherwise be subject, and the position of this sheave would at all times be the surest indication of the maximum strain on the cable—a matter of the utmost importance to be known, as upon it should depend the adjustment of the brakes and other operations for ensuring the safety of the cable itself.

The importance of carrying this principle into operation is enhanced in our minds by our conviction that any injury sustained by the cable in deep water, would in all probability be irreparable, it being exceedingly doubtful whether the cable could by any contrivance be safely arrested if broken while running out, or raised from the bottom of the sea.

As an additional means of obviating the danger of breaking the cable, we recommend the adoption of some kind of compensating arrangement to allow for the rise and fall of the stern of the ship in a sea way, which may be controlled either by springs or weights. We have seen at Mr. Hodges', of Southampton Row, vulcanized springs which we feel satisfied would answer perfectly. We think, with these additions and alterations, the apparatus would be greatly improved, and might be confidently expected to answer its intended purpose.

We now beg to offer some observations on matters which, although of comparatively minor importance, ought, in our opinion, to be attended to in order to ensure, as far as may be practicable, the success of an undertaking so novel, great, and difficult; correct instruments should be provided for indicating the speed of the ship and the distance run, as well as the rate at which the cable may be running out, and the whole quantity expended. By means of these instruments and the adjustment of the paying-out apparatus, the rate of the cable above that of the ship may, we think, be regulated with considerable exactness, and the excess, we venture to suggest, should not be less than one-third. This appears to be the only means of allowing the cable to sink into the hollows at the bottom of the sea, instead of hanging, as it might otherwise do in some places, in long loops, supported only at their ends, and consequently having to bear strains which, if not at first, might ultimately produce fracture when the strength of the iron wire became impaired by oxidation. All the machinery should be covered by a kind of house on deck, to protect the attendants from the weather. It should be well lighted at night, and proper accommodation provided for the men when off duty. An adequate number of efficient attendants should be hired to superintend the machinery, who should relieve each other at short intervals, and the greatest care should be taken to keep all the indicators and other instruments in good working order.

In conclusion, we beg to say that we think no practical difficulty would be found in carrying out all the mechanical arrangements we have suggested, and we also think that they should be carried out under the special superintendence of the officer intrusted by the company with the important duty of laying the cable, assisted by the most able, practical machinist, who may be willing to undertake the execution of the work, who should make an experiment ashore on the proposed brake as soon as one can be finished, and such other experiments as he may deem necessary to enable him to arrange the details in the most effectual manner. We are, gentlemen, your very humble servants,

T. Lloyd,
Joshua Field,
John Penn,
W. E. Everett.

Alterations recommended to be made in the Paying-out Machinery.

The sheaves should have single grooves, deeper than those at present fixed, and a slight difference should be made in the diameter of each sheave, the largest leading off to the stern of the vessel, and the smallest of the sheaves leading from the coil. By this the adhesion of the cable to the sheaves will be considerably increased.

Guards should be placed at the lead to the sheaves over the grooves capable of being readily opened to put the cable in its position, or take it out if required, and scrapers should be provided to remove the superfluous tar.

Experiments should be tried in the lubrication of the brakes and of the material of the surfaces in contact, with the view of obtaining the most regular drag.

A travelling pulley should be placed between the stern wheel and the paying-out machine, by which the unequal pull occasioned by the pitching of the vessel will be much reduced, at the same time that an additional indication is given of the strain upon the cable.

Charles T. Bright.

Some of these suggestions were adopted by Mr. Everett, but, as may be seen by the description of the machinery employed on the final expedition, the plan adopted and followed out was almost entirely different from that which had been used on the first unsuccessful attempt.

On the fifth of November, as has been stated, the Niagara left Plymouth for New York, but it was understood before her departure that Mr. Everett should take charge of the construction of the machinery, and for this purpose should return as early as possible the following year. A few days before the departure of the vessel a grand ball and entertainment was given by the officers to the many friends whose hospitality they had enjoyed while in England, and the officers themselves partook of a sumptuous banquet which Capt. Stewart, of H. M. S. Impregnable, gave in their honor. Fifteen days after leaving Plymouth the Niagara arrived in New York, and soon after was put out of commission till she should be again required for the resumption of the great work in 1858.

THE SECOND ATLANTIC TELEGRAPH EXPEDITION.

THE NIAGARA AGAIN AT PLYMOUTH.

THE experience which had been gained by the results of the Expedition of August, 1857, led to many changes in the plan of operations for the expedition which was to sail in the month of June. The machinery, as has been shown, had proved utterly inadequate to the performance of the work for which it was constructed, and it was therefore determined, as the reader is aware, that this important matter should be entrusted to the skill and ingenuity of Mr. W. E. Everett. The vessels which had been detailed for the laying of the cable before, were again detached for the renewal of the attempt. Mr. Field had accepted the position of General Manager of the Company at the urgent solicitation of the Board of Directors, and the services of Mr. Everett were also secured on application for leave of absence to the United States Government. Both these gentlemen entered upon the duties before them with all the energy and zeal which so great a work demanded. Some delay attended the application of Mr. Field for the appointment of the Niagara; but that point satisfactorily settled, they started for England in the Persia, on the 6th of January, 1858, and arrived at Liverpool the 16th of the same month. As the subsequent movements of Mr. Field are given in detail in the biographical sketch of that gentleman, we will proceed at once in our narrative of the Second Atlantic Telegraph Expedition.

The U. S frigate Niagara, having received her complement of officers and men, started from New York for Plymouth on the 9th of March, 1858. As some changes had been made in the appointment of the former, the following list will enable the reader to recognize the names of those who were re-appointed :—

Captain Wm. L. Hudson; Lieutenants, Jas. H. North, J. D. Todd, John Guest, Wm. A. Webb, E. Y. Macauley, B. Gherardi; Surgeon, D. S. Green; Purser, J. C. Eldridge; Lieutenant commanding Marine Guard, Wm. S. Boyd; Passed Assistant-Surgeon, F. M. Gunnell; Assistant-Surgeon, Wm. C. Hay; Chief Engineers, J Follansbee,

J. Farren; First Assistant-Engineer, Wm. B. Stamin; Second Assistant-Engineers, G. R. Johnson, M. Kellogg; Third Assistant-Engineers, Wm. G. Buehler, Jas. H. Bailey, J. McElwell, H. Kutz; Captain's Secretary, J. W. Hudson; Purser's Clerk, Edward Willard; Boatswain, Robert Dixon; Gunner, J. Webber; Sailmaker, Wm. B. Fugit; Carpenter, H. P. Leslie; Acting-Master's Mates, J. W. Goodrich, W. W. Brooke, Stephen B. Hudson, A. M. Mason, G. Keyworth, A. Stockholm.

The Niagara arrived at Plymouth on the 23d of March, after a passage of a little over thirteen days. She experienced very heavy weather during the greater part of the passage, and never did she display her splendid qualities to better advantage. From the 9th to the 16th it was unpleasantly rough, and on the 13th, 14th, and 15th it blew a perfect gale. There is no doubt that this was the equinoctial, and it did full justice to itself so far as heavy blowing is concerned. Those who have crossed the Atlantic in the months of March and September can form some idea of the nature of equinoctial gales and of the terrific force with which they sweep over that ocean. Under the heaviest stress of weather, however, the Niagara behaved magnificently, and went through the storm at the rate of ten and eleven knots an hour, and this, too, while other ships were hove-to. Her quickest day's run was three hundred and four miles, and there is no doubt that she would have accomplished the passage in ten days but for the head winds which prevailed from the 17th to the 22d. During the gale she had the wind from the south and south-east, from which it changed to the east, and stuck there with the most dogged obstinacy. While blowing from this quarter we had, however, no complaints to make in regard to the quality of the weather, which, with this one exception, was as fine as could be desired.

A rather melancholy circumstance occurred when the ship was three days out from port. A sailor, named William Wilson, fell from the maintop and was instantly killed. It is supposed that he was struck on the head with a boom, and was thus thrown from the yard. He was engaged at the time in clewing the yard down. Another death took place later in the passage, but it was from a protracted sickness. The name of the deceased was Samuel Scudder, and the disease of which he died pleurisy. They were both buried in a seaman's grave, and had the funeral service read over their remains. Poor fellows, whatever pleasing prospects they may have had when they entered on this special service were doomed to a fearful disappointment. One man fell over the fore-topsail-yard, but fortunately was caught by another who was on the same yard, and held there till he was relieved from his perilous position.

The Niagara, as I have said, arrived in the channel opposite Plymouth on the night of the 22d instant, and entered the Sound the following morning. Hardly had she anchored before a number of the officials of the place made their appearance on board, and among these, strange to say, two revenue officers. What their object could have been in thus thrusting themselves on a national vessel of another country, and outraging the rules of international courtesy it is impossible to say, but it is to be presumed that their conduct in this instance was attributable to ignorance—certainly the only reasonable explanation that can be given for such a breach of all the rules of international etiquette. After making their abode on the ship for about two days, they took their departure, and that was the last we saw of them. The Niagara lay in the Sound till the 24th instant, when she weighed anchor and proceeded up the harbor, preparatory to going into dock for the reception of the cable. After her arrival the numerous friends which the officers made during their stay here the year before, paid a welcome visit, and again tendered their hospitalities. Invitations were extended by nearly all the regiments stationed at this port to the officers of the Niagara. I should state here that as an evidence of the friendly feelings which were manifested towards them, all, or nearly all the vessels lying in the harbor cheered them as the ship passed up to her anchorage. The rigging of the Impregnable and other vessels were manned by their crews, who gave three cheers that waked all the slumbering echoes of the surrounding hills. The welcome was responded to with an enthusiasm on the part of the Niagara's men which proved that they were determined not to be outdone in this demonstration of friendly feeling.

Besides the attentions which the officers received from their friends, they were honored with others of the most pressing character. The wardroom was almost literally deluged with circulars and business cards of every description. Tailors, shoemakers, washerwomen, hotel keepers, hatters, &c., &c., were most assiduous in their attentions and solicitations for patronage. Among the business applications was the following gem, which is worthy of publication on this side of the ocean:

" Mr. Wm. H. Westcott (pupil of Coulon and nephew of Mrs. Williams, the Octagon), professor of dancing, Princess street, Plymouth, teacher for the nobilities' balls, &c., begs to announce to the officers of the army and navy, and his friends generally, that he continues to receive daily adults, irrespective of age, for private tuition in all that is prevailing among the *élite.*"

As our readers might imagine that Mrs. Williams is the octagon, it may be as well to state that she is nothing of the kind, but that the particular part of the city in which her nephew receives "daily adults," and teaches "all that is prevailing among the *élite*," is dignified with that title.

It was rumored that the Queen intended to witness the departure of the telegraph squadron from Plymouth, but as there was no certainty about the matter, and as many of us naturally felt desirous of seeing for ourselves what the head of so great a nation looked like, a nation that was to be brought next door to us by the successful termination of the enterprise in which we were engaged, we were determined to go to London and see her, not only in her capital, but in her palace. We were desirous of seeing a real, genuine, *bona-fide* queen, one who wore a crown, for though we were accustomed every day to see sovereigns in our own country, they were without that indispensable adjunct of royalty.

To come to England and go away without having seen the queen is indeed a terrible oversight, a crime, for the commission of which every traveller from the United States must expect to meet with the stern censure of all those curious and wonder-loving friends who expect to be informed on the minutest points. Fortunately, I have seen the queen, and although I was not at her drawing-room, nor honored with an introduction by our minister—for the simple reason that the favor was not requested of him—I had just as fair an opportunity as those who were, and who were graciously permitted to bend the knee before the royal lady, and to kiss her royal hand. By the kindness of a friend I was placed in possession of the following ticket of admission to Buckingham Palace, through the grand hall of which the Queen always passes on her way to hold her drawing-rooms in St. James's:

ADMIT THE BEARER TO THE

GRAND HALL ON THURSDAY,

The 22d of April, 1858, at a quarter past one o'clock.

EXETER, Lord Steward.

BUCKINGHAM PALACE.

*** The parties are to retire after her Majesty has passed.

Provided with this, I started out at least half an hour before the appointed time, and made my way to the palace, in front of which I arrived about one o'clock. The next point was to make out the precise part of that building to which it would afford me admission, and which I succeeded in finding by inquiries among the soldiers and police. The entrance to the hall was besieged by somewhat over a hundred anxious expectants, a large majority of whom were ladies, and each of whom possessed a ticket similar to the above. Few, if any, of these had ever seen the Queen before, and it was somewhat amusing to hear the speculations in which they passed the time, regarding her personal appearance and style of dress. Some had heard that she was dumpy, and not at all like a queen; while others were of opinion that her portraits, so far from being flattering, did not do her any thing like justice. There was one who did not appear to be imbued with the proper respect for royalty, and who insisted with a democratic persistence that would not be checked, that the Queen was just like any other woman, and that she could indulge in a glass of ale as well as the next one. A lady, who happened to hear the remark, and who was standing beside the speaker, manifested considerable indignation, and gave a look that expressed, as plainly as a look could, that the aforesaid speaker was "very low." Now, whether she was indignant at the want of reverence manifested by the remark, or whether she supposed she was meant by the "next one," I am unable to say, and will not, therefore, venture an opinion on the subject; but it is a fact that she was very indignant.

A quarter past one was the hour specified in the ticket of admission, but it was nearly half-past one when the door of the grand hall was thrown open—a fact which shows plainly that they have not a very particular regard for punctuality in a palace. However, the door was opened at last, and that was something. Two of the officials of the Queen's household took the tickets, and we were permitted to enter the palace, the majority of us perhaps for the first time. We had to pass through two halls before coming to that which is called, by way of preeminence, the grand hall, and it is certainly worthy of the title. All that marble and statuary and mirrors and fresco painting, under the hands of ingenious architects and artists could do to make it magnificent, has been done. The only drawback, perhaps, is the insufficiency of light, and this want divests it of half its beauties. The palace itself is a splendid structure, and is deserving of all that is said for it in the guide books of London.

But here we are in the grand hall, with servants in knee breeches and red coats glittering in all the effulgence of gold lace, hovering about. Among these same servants is a very dignified old fellow in a blue coat with brass buttons, a white neck-tie, and a waistcoat of the same color—a terribly pompous individual, who holds his head so high that it is only by great exertion he can see any one near him. This character is no less a personage than the master of the outside ceremonies, which signifies that it is his duty to keep the crowd in order, and to preserve the sanctified decorum of the place. Show the slightest indication of a desire to go any further than the prescribed limits, and to use a homely but expressive phrase, he will come down upon you like a "thousand of brick." He is a rough customer—so rough that it is a wonder somebody don't put him in mind of it by an occasional castigation. His treatment of ladies is any thing but courteous; and the exhibition he made of himself on the day in question, was not of that kind which one would expect to see within the walls of a palace. But perhaps such exhibitions are only got up for the benefit and instruction of plebeians, and are never indulged in when any of the aristocracy are in his immediate neighborhood. He is, however, an efficient character in his place, and it may be after all that this roughness only arises from his strong desire to perform his duty to the utmost. But however strict he may be in this particular, the claims of friendship lead him into acts of partiality, which show that he is not altogether a Brutus in his line. His friends and favorites came in for the best seats, and those who were strangers, and who, ignorant of the state of affairs in this department of the palace, imagined that they were open to all alike, were very soon apprised that presumption of that kind was not to be tolerated.

"What are you going to do there?" he said to three ladies who were about to take a seat where they would have a better view of the Queen. "What are you going to do there?"

"Going to sit down," was the very natural reply.

"Well," said the old fellow, "that's a good idea."

The lady smiled as if she thought it was, and the official frowned as if he didn't at all believe what he said.

"Come back here! Who told you to go there?" he rejoined in a tone that was not to be mistaken.

'Nobody," replied the lady in a mollifying way; "but I supposed, seeing others go, I might do the same."

"Ah! indeed," he answered. "Did you? Well, I am afraid you can't. That's quite another thing. You can't sit there."

And so the three were obliged to stand aside, that his favorites might be accommodated. Now, it may have been all very well for him to show more partiality to his friends than to strangers, but his way of doing it was not exactly in accordance with good taste or a strict regard for the feelings of others.

The spectators have taken their places in front of the grand staircase down which the Queen is expected to come, and as the time passes they become more and more anxious. At last the royal carriages are seen approaching through the court-yard, and one of them draws up opposite the door which opens on the grand hall, ready to receive the sovereign. It is a fine establishment in its way, with plenty of gold fringe, and royal coats of arms, and small crowns and other regal appurtenances. A number of the household servants, almost covered with gold lace, now make their appearance, and flourish around the hall through which the ladies of the court are continually passing, on their way to St. James's. Some of these ladies, by the way, are remarkably handsome, and all are dressed in the most elaborate style of ornamentation. They have evidently a great contempt for high-necked dresses, if their feelings are to be judged by the excessive lowness to which they have attained. Their crinolines are wonders in their way, and excited the envying admiration of the fair spectators. But the Queen is said to be on her way, and all eyes are strained to catch a glimpse of her. Pshaw! it is not her, after all. It is merely a gouty old lord, who is making his way slowly down the grand staircase, and who has been mistaken as one of the *avant couriers* of her Majesty. Five minutes more elapse, and the crowd is becoming still more impatient. Now, however, she is certainly coming—no mistake this time—here is a forerunner whose particular duty it is to prepare the way for her approach, and here are six gentlemen, some of them with stars on their breasts—the sign which indicates the difference between a lord, a marquis, or any other member of the aristocracy, and a common man—here are six of them coming down the grand stairs, and according to the rule made and provided in such cases the Queen must soon make her appearance. As the forerunner and the six just referred to, who are dressed in something that looks like a military costume, show themselves, the lackeys at the foot of the stairs and in the hall become wonderfully active, and say something in a loud voice which sounds like the words "stand up," and which, it is to be presumed, is intended for the spectators. However, I am not certain as to the words, and will not, therefore, certify to them, no more than I would to the announcement made by the brakemen on railroads, when they intend to inform the passengers that they have arrived at a particular station; but I do know this—and the fact may be taken as presumptive evidence on this point—that the spectators did "stand up," and remained standing till she passed. The six marquises, or lords, or sirs, or whatever they are, have arrived safely at the foot of the stairs, and the Queen, leaning on the arm of Prince Albert, appears on the landing above. There she is at last, the ruler of the English people, the sovereign of Great Britain, and of colonial possessions whose extent exceeds the territories of any other nation in the world. There she is, a low-sized, and so far as you can judge of her figure, enveloped in a crinoline that Broadway in its most refulgent days never equalled, and probably never will be able to equal, a dumpy, roundabout little woman, in whose appearance, in whose walk, and in the expression of whose face there is about as little of what some call the attributes of royalty, as it is possible to conceive. To say that her portraits flatter her is downright absurdity—they don't flatter her at all—they have made a good-looking woman and written "Queen Victoria" below it, so that those who have seen her may not be mistaken in regard to who it is intended for. Now, in giving a true description, I wish to be historically accurate, although at the same time I'm in hopes that the royal lady, if she ever reads an American book, may not come across the volume in which this account is published. Keeping strictly, therefore, to historical accuracy, let me say, in the first place, that the stature of the Queen is considerably below the medium, that her face is so decidedly not handsome that it may be considered positively ordinary. To offset this, however, it is said that it is particularly pleasing when she smiles, while on the other hand, when she is determined to be unpleasant, the expression it assumes is of the most unprepossessing character. On this head I do not profess to be in possession of the most reliable information, as it is obtained altogether from hearsay. In describing the Queen's personal appearance, my desire is merely to present her to my readers as she looked to me, and I must not, therefore, be accused of writing with a prejudiced mind. The fact is, those who have written about her have been so far under the influence of partiality or prejudice that it would be unsafe to give credit to all they say. But, to continue: Her dress—in regard to which I must confess my utter ignorance of the details, and must, therefore, be excused for attempting any thing like a description—was white silk or *moire antique*, whichever the ladies please; but which it is only fair to suppose was of the richest, the best and the most appropriate material. It terminated in a grand train, which was upheld by two pages, bright-looking little fellows, about twelve years old. On her arrival at the foot of the stairs, she released herself from the arm of the Prince Consort, and relieving the pages from the train, took it up and threw it over her right arm. As she passed the spectators, she acknowledged their presence with a most gracious smile, one in which there was much kindness of feeling and goodness of heart expressed, whatever may be said to the contrary. All her "dumpiness" and want of beauty could not efface this, and you felt in looking at her that you were looking at a woman upon whom the vices of the Court had not and could not make any impression. Whatever ebullitions of feelings she may, as it is stated she does, sometimes exhibit, the fact that she is one of the most virtuous women that ever sat upon a throne cannot be denied. In fact, it is this leading point in her character that has gained her the affection of her people; for virtue in royalty is so rare a thing that it can never be too highly prized. The Court of Queen Victoria is in striking contrast with the courts of many of those who have sat on the same throne which she now occupies. In this regard she is a most exemplary woman, and to this is owing the title by which her people delight to call her. It is particularly pleasing to be able to speak in this way of any woman, and to have it in one's power to state a fact that no want of personal beauty can affect, and that cannot be compensated for by any amount of attraction. While on this subject, let me relate a little anecdote which I have heard here regarding the Queen, and which is said to be perfectly true. It appears that during one of her visits to her country seat on the Isle of Wight, the Prince of Wales got into a difficulty, which resulted in his being whipped by a little fellow less than his own age. His assailant was amusing himself in loading a miniature cart with sand, when the Prince approaching threatened to kick it over.

"Do it," said the boy, "and it 'll be worse for you."

True to his word, and undeterred by the threat, the scion of royalty did upset it with his foot; and true also to his promise, the boy did make it worse for him. The overthrow of the cart was the signal for a fight, in which the Prince came off second best, and was sent home with tears in his eyes. When brought before the Queen, however, he told what had actually happened, what he had done to provoke the boy and to bring on his own punishment. The royal mother thereupon sent for the little fellow, who, finding out the full extent of what he had done, was terribly frightened. When he made his appearance, however, she spoke to him kindly, said he had done right, and magnanimously provided for his education and support at her own expense, on discovering that his parents were in poor circumstances. A woman who could do such an act can well afford to be ordinary.

Prince Albert, who was dressed in military costume, is a tall and good-looking man. He is bald from the top of the forehead to near the crown of the head. His face is so German, that it would be impossible to mistake his nationality; in fact, both himself and the Queen look more German than English. She of course entered the carriage first, and when she had succeeded in adjusting her dress as well as she could, he took a seat beside her. But that dress, with such an amount of rebellious uprising crinoline beneath, would not be put down, and would surge and boil over on every side so as to completely envelope the lower half of the body of the Prince, leaving the upper part alone visible, like a wax-work bust in a barber's shop. When they were both seated, the royal carriage drove off, and the last we saw of the Queen, she was engaged in vain endeavors to suppress the swelling and rebellious crinoline. I would like to have seen her at the drawing-room; but the fact that I was not prepared with a court dress proved an insuperable bar to the indulgence of my desire.

Complying with the directions in the card of admission, the spectators left the palace, and once more made their way into the open street opposite the park. Here there was a considerable military force, the bands attached to which were performing the national anthem. A long line of carriages—over a thousand, I was informed—were drawn up on one side, and almost blocked up a number of the contiguous streets. Among these were those of the Marshal Pelissier,the Ministers of Austria, Prussia and other European nations, and the carriage of Mr. Dallas, our Minister at the Court of St. James. I regretted that my presence in the grand hall rendered it impossible to see the occupants of any of these establishments, and particularly do I regret my consequent inability to have seen Mr. Dallas; but if I had seen him, I could not have seen the Queen, and therein I must find whatever consolation I can. If I did not see him, however, I saw his carriage, as I have intimated, and that was something; and as people may be curious to know what kind of a carriage it is, they must be informed. Let me say, then, at the beginning, that it is so simple and unpretending, that there is really very little to be said about it. It is such a vehicle as you can see any day in Broadway, with a pair of fine horses attached to it, a driver in livery in that position where a driver generally sits, and a footman in that particular spot, where footmen have generally stood. The footman is also in livery, with an American eagle on every button, and both himself and the driver have their hats set off with a gold band and a cockade, or rosette, formed of the American colors. On the carriage doors are the arms of the United States, and, altogether, the vehicle is quite a respectable affair, simple and unpretending. And here I must close the account of my visit to Buckingham Palace, again expressing my regret that I had not seen Mr. Dallas, and was not provided with an opportunity of knowing whether he was habited in the early republican style of old Ben Franklin, or in the modern costume not set forth in the Court circular of the late Mr. Marcy.

Among the crowds of titled fashionables who visited the Niagara previous to her departure from England on the second telegraph expedition, were the members of a family which, but a few years ago, were at the head of one the greatest nations of the world.

Their history is one of the most remarkable on record, and furnishes another proof of the fact that there is no station in life free from those vicissitudes to which royalty and poverty are alike subject. These illustrious visitors were the Prince de Joinville, the Duc d'Aumale, the Duchesse d'Orleans, and the Duchesse d'Aumale, the exiled members of the Orleans family, and the rival aspirants with the Bourbons to the throne of France. They came unheralded and in the most unostentatious manner, and during their stay visited every part of the ship. The Prince de Joinville, who is *au fait* in naval matters, is a man forty-three or forty-four years old, about six feet two, with a frank and intelligent countenance. He wears a heavy pair of whiskers and mustache of a light brown color, dresses plainly and neatly, and his appearance and manners are those of a refined and courteous gentleman.

The Prince de Joinville is, as almost everybody knows, quite a sailor, and startled all England by a pamphlet which he wrote some years ago showing the defenceless state of her coasts, and the ease with which an enemy could be thrown upon her shores. He inspected every part of the ship, under the guidance of Lieut. Guest, who was at the time the senior officer on board. The engine room attracted his greatest attention, and the minuteness with which he examined into all the details—the throttles, the cut-off, and all those mysterious parts, which are known only to the initiated—showed that he was thoroughly conversant with the whole subject. The model of the ship particularly excited his admiration, and he was much pleased with her general appearance. He appeared to be thoroughly posted in regard to the particular duty on which she was detailed, and expressed his opinion pretty freely upon the nature and character of the enterprise. It was his belief that the cable should be lighter than it is, and that the outer covering or wire armor should be dispensed with. The strength which it received from this was, according to his ideas, not sufficient to compensate for the disadvantage arising from the greatly increased weight. He acknowledged that, by making the line without the wire armor it might become too buoyant; but he thought this difficulty might be removed by attaching some soluble material to it sufficiently heavy to sink it to the bottom, where the cable would remain even after the material itself should have been removed by the action of the water. The Prince had more to say on all subjects than any other of the party.

The Duc d'Aumale appears to be some four or five years the junior of the Prince de Joinville, and does not even look sufficiently like him to be of the same family. His hair is of a light red color, so are his whiskers, and he is less in stature by about three inches. Both brothers speak English with an unmistakably French accent; but, with this exception, they speak it well and fluently.

The ladies are both elegant and *distingué* looking, rather above than below the medium height, and are very unassuming and courteous in their manners. They are all free from that *hauteur* and reserve which are supposed to be the peculiar attribute of royalty, and are as cordial, as frank, and as sociable as the most unpretending republican could be. On leaving the ship they expressed themselves much pleased with all they had seen, thanked Mr. Guest again and again for his kindness, shook him warmly by the hand at parting, and expressed their hope in the success of the expedition.

INSPECTION OF THE PAYING-OUT MACHINE.

In the factory of Messrs. Easton & Amos, Gravel Lane, London, Mr. Everett was daily and nightly engaged in attending to the construction of the paying-out machinery; and when at last after weeks of unremitting labor it was ready for inspection, invitations were sent to the following gentlemen: Captain Hudson, of the Niagara; Capt. George W. Preedy, of the Agamemnon; Cap. J. Dayman, of the Gorgon; Mr. Joshua Follansbee, Chief Engineer of the Niagara; Mr. Faron, Chief Engineer, and Mr. McEllwell, Assistant Engineer of do; Mr. Hoare, Chief Engineer of the Agamemnon; Mr. Moore, Assistant Engineer of do; Mr. Morris, Mr. Samuel Canning, H. Clifford, H. Woodhouse, Mr. Brunel, J. S. Gilliatt, Rev. W. Mitchell, Messrs. C. & J. Johnson, Mr. J. Bower, Capt. Nolloth, R. N., Mr. C. W. Tafling, Mr. Kiddle, Mr. H. Stephenson, Mr. W. Brown, M. P.; Prof. Thompson, Mr. Gurney, M. P.; Rev. G. C. Schwabe, Mr. Pickering, Mr. Pender, Mr. Peabody, Mr. Logie, Mr. Le Breton, Messrs. Lampson, Johnston, Hornby, Harrison and Dugdale.

The majority of these gentlemen were present, and among them Mr. Brunel, who has gained such a world-wide reputation as an engineer, and who is one of the greatest scientific men of the day. Mr. Brunel is the son of the constructor of the Thames Tunnel, and is the architect of that eighth wonder of the world, the Leviathan. He is about forty years of age, of a plain, good-natured and most propossessing exterior. Like all true men of genius, Mr. Brunel is a modest and unassuming man, and is what might be called the *beau ideal* of a mechanic. Among the convocation of scientific men who assembled yesterday to examine and pass their verdict upon the machinery, he was the least conspicuous in personal appearance, and certainly the very last who would have been selected as the great English engineer. He was accompanied by his son, a perfect *fac simile* of himself, having, however, the advantage of being a couple of inches taller. The two were the most democratic in their manner, in their dress, and in their general appearance, of those present. Mr. Everett explained the principles and details of the machine to them both, after which the father and son had a little quiet tour of inspection to themselves. Mr. Brunel expressed himself much pleased with the whole affair, and was confident of its successful operation. The machine was running during the whole day, and accomplished all that was claimed for it. An illustrated and detailed description of it is given further on in this work.

The following letters were subsequently received from the gentlemen whose signatures are appended:

LONDON, April 23, 1858.

GEORGE SAWARD, ESQ., SEC. OF ATLANTIC TELEGRAPH CO.

SIR—I beg to say that I have attended at the works of Messrs. Easton & Amos every day during the construction of the new paying-out machinery, and saw it working on Thursday last. It is, in my opinion, well adapted to the intended purpose, and I have nothing to suggest that could render it more perfect. I am, dear sir, your most obedient,

HENRY CLIFFORD.

LONDON, April 30, 1858.

DEAR SIR—With reference to your request of the 19th instant, we beg to state, for the information of the Directors of the Atlantic Telegraph Company, that the machinery for paying out the cable is, in our opinion, well calculated to answer the intended purpose, and that we have no alteration to suggest. The apparatus for showing the speed of the ship, and for recording the total distance run, should of course be completed and fixed on board the Agamemnon and Niagara before the preliminary trials are commenced on board those ships, and the apparatus for showing the rate at which the cable is being paid out, and for registering the total quantity, should also be fixed on board. There will be ample time for this purpose, and no difficulty need be apprehended. We are, dear sir, yours truly,

T. LLOYD,
JOHN PENN,
JOSHUA FIELD.

CYRUS W. FIELD, ESQ., &c., &c., &c.

LONDON, April 24, 1858.

DEAR SIR—I have witnessed the operation of the machinery for paying out the Atlantic Telegraph Cable at the works of Messrs. Easton & Amos, in compliance with your invitation of the 19th inst. With the exception of the scrapers to clear the wheels of tar, not yet completed, and a guard for the cable as it enters upon the grooved wheels, which Mr. Everett informs me will be applied, I know of nothing further needed, and regard it as well adapted to the purpose for which it was designed. Very truly, yours,

JOSHUA FOLLANSBEE,
Chief Engineer United States Navy.

MR. GEO. SAWARD, SECRETARY TO ATLANTIC TELEGRAPH CO.,
No. 22 Old Broad Street.

Atlantic Telegraph Company,
22 Old Broad Street, London,
Engineer's Department, April 24, 1858.

To the Directors of the Atlantic Telegraph Co.:

Gentlemen—Since the report which I made to you in conjunction with Mr. Eyerett, of the 6th inst., in regard to the paying-out machinery and the result of the experiments relating thereto, a complete machine has been erected at the works of Messrs. Easton & Amos. The trials which have been made with this during the last few days have been perfectly satisfactory, and I have nothing further to suggest as an addition to, or an alteration in, the machinery, unless the experiments at sea should give rise to any modifications of our appliances prior to the departure of the actual expedition. I am, gentlemen, yours very faithfully,

CHARLES T. BRIGHT, Engineer.

While Mr. Everett was engaged in the construction of his machinery, Prof. Hughes was experimenting with his printing telegraph, on the whole length of the cable, while it was being coiled on the Niagara and Agamemnon. His instrument was not as perfectly adjusted as he desired, but he accomplished enough to show that it was the best adapted to the working of the cable, and with a few modifications, could be made to transmit from seven to ten words a minute under the most favorable electrical conditions of the line.

Every preparation was made to hasten the departure of the Telegraph Squadron on the trial trip, which it was decided should take place in the Bay of Biscay, and by the 29th of May the vessels were ready to sail. Before, however, describing their operations there, we will lay before our readers a detailed description of the vessels composing the Squadron, the mechanical and other arrangements which had been made for the great work, and all that is necessary to a proper understanding of the subject.

THE TELEGRAPH SQUADRON.

The vessels composing the Squadron were the U. S. frigate Niagara, H. M. steamers Agamemnon, Gorgon, Valorous, and Porcupine. As a description of the Niagara has been given in the narrative of the first expedition, it is merely necessary to mention her name.

The Agamemnon is one of the best line-of-battle ships in the British Navy. Her dimensions are as follows: Length between perpendiculars, 230 feet; breadth of beam, 55½, and depth of hold 24½ feet. The capacity of the ship is 3,102 tons, and her engines, of which she has two, are both 600 horse power. Her force at present numbers about 450, but her full complement, when on a war footing, is over 600. Her full armament consists of 91 guns, of which 34 are 8 inch shell guns on her lower deck, 14 on her spar deck, 32 pounders, and 36 on her main deck are also 8 inch. In addition to those, she carries on the forecastle six 32 pounders, and one heavy gun of 9,550 pounds, for throwing 8 inch solid shot. All the guns are made for firing shells. The Agamemnon was launched at Woolwich in the year 1852, and is said to be one of the fastest of the screw vessels of the British fleet. Her engines are known as the trunk, with horizontal cylinders, and their nominal horse power is capable of being worked up to 1,800. The motive force is supplied by four tubular boilers, which are made to resist a pressure of 17 pounds to the square inch. There are five furnaces under each of these, and the whole machinery is two and a half feet below the water line. The boilers, in addition to this, are protected from shot by the coal bunkers. As the engines and firerooms are nearer than usual to the stern, it accounts for the shortness of the shaft, which is sixty feet less than that of the Niagara. Its diameter is thirteen inches, and length forty feet, while the propeller is about eighteen feet in diameter, with a pitch of twenty feet six inches. Its weight is eight tons, exclusive of the gearing, and it is made of a composition called gun metal. The number of revolutions at the highest speed is fifty-four to the minute, and rate with a consumption of fifty tons of coal a day from nine to ten miles per hour.

The Agamemnon was Sir E. (now Lord) Lyon's flag ship, and took a part in the assault on Sebastopol on the 17th of October, 1855, from which she retired considerably damaged. On that occasion she approached within seven or eight hundred yards of the place, from which she retired with three or four of her ports knocked into one, several of her spars splintered, and with considerable other damage. To fit her for the work in which she is now employed, all her guns have been removed, and she has had frigate masts put in her. The following is a correct list of her officers, those with the asterisk prefixed having served on the last expedition: Captain, George W. Preedy; lieutenants, E. H. Murray, Hon. F. Fitzmaurice, F. C. B. Robinson, R. Gibson; master, H. A. Moriarty; paymaster, John N. De Vries; engineer, James Brown; assistant engineers, John Brown, W. B. Harvey, Edwin Pearce, Samuel Clements, William Smily, John Heffernan; surgeon, William D. Kerr; assistant surgeon, *W. W. P. Smyth; clerk, F. A. Pountney; carpenter, R. Rian; gunner, E. Snell; boatswain, Richard Farrell.

The Gorgon is one of the oldest steamers in the British navy, having been built some nineteen or twenty years ago. She is a comparatively small vessel, but at the time she was constructed she was regarded as one of the largest vessels in the whole English fleet, and as a wonderful specimen of naval architecture in her way. Her measurement is 1,111 tons, her armament six guns, which she carries on her spar deck; and her engines are 320 horse power. She accompanied the Niagara as an escort in the place of the United States steam frigate Susquehanna, which was in the last expedition, but which was prevented from accompanying this on account of the yellow fever having broken out on board of her while in the West Indies. The following is a list of the officers of the Gorgon: Commander, Joseph Dayman; senior lieutenant, J. B. Michell; lieutenant, J. B. Butler; master and pilot, C. Albert; paymaster, A. F. M. Roberts; surgeon, H. Gimlette; chief engineer R. E., Horne; clerk, Charles Wm. King; first assistant engineer, W. Pilcher; second assistant engineer, J. Spinks; third assistant engineer, P. Richmond; boatswain, H. Blake; carpenter, John Harcus; gunner, B. Howe; third assistants, R. Dillon, P. Baldwin.

The surveying steamer Porcupine is one of the smallest class of steamers in the English navy, and was built in 1844 for surveying purposes. Her engines are 132 horse power, and her measurement is 382 tons. She will also accompany the Niagara as a leading vessel to steer by, while the Gorgon will be employed when necessary only in towing, that is, in the event of any accident happening to the Niagara. The following is a list of the Porcupine's officers: Captain, Henry C. Otter; lieutenants, Albert Dent, Edward W. Hawes; master, William Stanton; surgeon, Francis McAree; second master, George Stanley; assistant paymaster in charge, Edmund B. Walker.

The steamship Valorous took the place of the Leopard, which accompanied the Agamemnon on the expedition of 1857 as her escort. She is reputed to be one of the finest side wheel steamers in the British navy, and carries an armament of sixteen guns. Her horse power is 400, her measurement 1,250 tons, and her full complement 220 officers and men. The following is a list of her officers: Captain, Wm. C. Aldham; lieutenants, R. Moore, G. S. Key, Hon. J. S. Fitzmaurice; master, S. Braddon; surgeon, A. Murray; paymaster, W. M. Shanks; chaplain and naval instructor, Rev. D. J. Boutflower; assistant surgeon, P. B. Mansfield; mates, Hon. E. L. V. Mostyn, W. H. Ryde, C. P. Heaslop; lieutenant, Rd. Williamson; assistant engineers, W. Farquharson, J. Broach, J. Scott, H. Walker, Robt. Gilchrist.

THE ENGINEERING AND ELECTRICAL CORPS.

The organization of this department on board both the cable ships was much better than it was in 1857, so that there could be no complaint in regard to its effectiveness, and the watches were arranged in such a manner that the machine need not at any time be left without proper attention. In addition to Mr. Everett and Mr. Woodhouse, there were Mr.

Joshua Follansbee, the chief engineer of the ship, Mr. M. Kellogg, and Mr. McEllwell, assistant engineers, all of whom kept watch. This made a force of engineers for this particular duty alone. Captain Kell had special charge of the coil, which he shared with Mr. Goodrich, master's mate, Mr. Fugitt, sailmaker, and Mr. Webber, the gunner of the Niagara.

On the Agamemnon were Mr. Amos, Mr. Clifford, Mr. Canning, and Mr. Bright, who were assisted by Mr. Hoare and Mr. Moore—two of the engineers of the Agamemnon. Mr. Amos did not go out on the expedition. The following is the numerical force of the staff on board both ships:

Engineers and assistants on Niagara,	5
Engineers and assistants on Agamemnon,	6

The electrical department was composed of the electricians, the operators and the splicers. Mr. De Sauty and Mr. Laws had the electrical force on the Niagara under their charge, while that on the Agamemnon was directed by Dr. Thompson and Mr. Bartholomew. The following table gives the number in each branch of the electrical departments on board both ships:

ON NIAGARA.	
Number of electricians,	2
Number of operators,	4
Gutta percha joiner,	1
Splicers of cable and assistants,	4
Total,	11

ON AGAMEMNON.	
Number of electricians,	2
Number of operators,	4
Gutta percha joiners,	2
Splicers of cable and assistants,	3
Total,	11

THE COILING PROCESS ILLUSTRATED.

As a great deal of importance is properly attached to the process of coiling, there is no part of the work which receives more care and attention, and which demands the exercise of a larger degree of vigilance. Some idea of it may be formed when it is known that every mile, every yard, every foot of the cable is laid down with as much precision, as much regularity, and as much neatness, as thread is wound upon a spool. The way the work of coiling is performed is exhibited in the following drawing, which was made on board the Niagara, and which presents an accurate and life-like representation of the scene.

Here the coilers are represented at work, while the manner in which the cable is drawn on board is also shown. The coiling is commenced

12

A A A—The cable payers.
B—Passage outside of the cable.
C—Roller over which the cable passes.

on the outer edge of the circus, or circle, and approaches nearer to the cone as each round is laid, until the cone is finally reached. Thus the first flake is laid, and flake succeeds flake till the coil is finished—that is, till it is carried as near the beams of the deck as possible—until, in fact, the space between the top of the coil and the deck beams is insufficient to allow the continuance of the work. Each measures from three to four miles in length, according to the diameter of the circus, and the number of flakes varies from one to two hundred, according to its height. On the Niagara a force of one hundred and twenty cable coilers was organized, and these were divided into two equal gangs—one gang for the forward and the other for the after coils. Each gang of sixty is next subdivided into two watches, who relieve each other every four hours. By this arrangement thirty men are employed at a time on one coil, and of these one or two is engaged on deck hauling the cable inboard over the rollers. One of these rollers is placed over the hatchway immediately over the cones, so that it is drawn with the greatest ease into the circus below. As it is thus transpaid down by the cable men on deck, it is seized by another who runs around the circle with it, paying out a portion to each one of the coilers by whom he is encircled, and who pack it as close as possible. The adhesive nature of the tar with which it is covered as a protection against the rust adds to its flexibility, and helps to keep it in its place when once laid. Each flake is as it were glued together, but not so firmly as to prevent its uncoiling without difficulty, when the process of paying out has commenced. The effect is rather beneficial than otherwise, as there is no danger on account of this adhesiveness of its being uncoiled faster than it is run out over the ship's stern, and consequently less liability to kinking. Under each flake are placed thin lath-like boards, at intervals of seven or eight feet apart, to prevent the possibility of one flake sinking through the interstices of the coil, and becoming confounded with the one immediately below.

Every precaution, as has been stated, is taken to secure the proper performance of this part of the work. Each gang of coilers has a foreman, and each foreman an assistant. The foreman inspects each layer of flakes, while the assistant follows close upon the heels of the payer, and sees that the men pack the cable closely. The payer himself is one of the coilers, each coiler taking his turn of hauling down and trotting round the circus every twenty minutes or half an hour, by which time it is supposed his arms will be pretty well tired. From two to two miles and a half of cable is coiled in an hour, and from fifty to sixty miles, when the men are obliged to work night and day. The kneeling position in which the coilers are placed would seem to indicate that they are engaged in devotional exercises, but they are supposed to be resting just at this particular time, having been seated for some two hours before they changed their posture. Each operative is provided with a seat of the most primitive description—sometimes a plain block of wood hollowed at the top so as to form a fitting receptacle for that part of the corporeal system which is to be deposited thereon. Others are less primitive, and occasionally assume the form of a stool of the most lowly dimensions, that the coiler may not be obliged to stoop too much. But after all, there is very little stooping, as each man is obliged to bend but once every time the payer goes round the circus. The work is not therefore very heavy, and the coilers make it more a labor of pleasure than any thing else. They are dressed in a regular uniform of duck, which is in glaring contrast with the tarred cable, the frequent contact with which does not tend to improve its color. As their hands are not exactly in that state of cleanliness in which a man would sit down to dinner, and as the tar makes them somewhat sticky, they are supplied with oil to lubricate them about once every two hours.

Those same cable coilers were wonderful fellows—as wonderful indeed as those who performed the work last year while the Niagara lay in the Mersey, and are therefore as deserving of as much attention. The cable circles, too, were the scenes of performances as interesting as extraordinary, and as amusing as before. I know there are sceptics who will sneer at such an assertion, and who imagine that where there is so much tar there can be little or no social enjoyment; but they are like all other unbelievers—they have no heart or soul for any thing, and what other men would find pleasure in has no allurement or interest for them, but is a dull, unmeaning blank. So much for the sceptics, and now for the sights and scenes among the cable men.

The wardroom circus is situated on the main or berth deck, and is generally an object of the greatest interest to visitors. On either side of it is a narrow passage, which was formed by cutting off about one-half of the officers' rooms. The privacy of both these miniature apartments is secured by means of a canvas wall, behind which, as behind a stage curtain, all those changes in the personal appearance of the occupant are affected which transforms the natural into the civilized man. Here he makes his toilet, and here, in this little room—seven by ten—he has his library of half a dozen volumes, his wardrobe, and all the other etceteras which make up the domestic part of an officer's world on shipboard. It requires no ordinary amount of genius to economize the little space in which he is cooped, and when nearly one-half the room is cut away, he is a prodigy indeed who can successfully manage with the other half.

Every morning about seven o'clock the cable coilers commence operations, and from that hour till six in the evening they never cease working. There are two watches of thirty men each, who relieve each other every four hours, and who are under the supervision of several directors or superintendents. When the first of these watches took possession of the circus and began their work, their uniform of duck was almost as white as snow, but hardly three days elapsed before it became as black as mourning weed, with here and there a patch of white gleaming through. "The Knights of the Black Hand," as the coilers were dubbed, rather like this change, and never omit an opportunity to improve upon it. Thus the backs of all of them are marked with the armorial bearings of their knighthood, the sign manual of their title of nobility. The emblem is stamped upon the wooden wall of the circus, among an array of artistic decorations and embellishments such as the world has rarely, if ever witnessed. The star-spangled banner is repeated again and again, with a patriotic persistency that never tires, while whole flocks of American eagles are soaring on tireless wing. These extraordinary exhibitions of artistic skill are got up without the aid of brush, pencil, or any of the usual instruments known to the world of art, and are to be regarded with still more consideration on that account. The forefinger of the right hand is employed as a substitute for the pencil, the brush, and the crayon, while the well-tarred palm of the left answers all the purposes of a palette. With such facilities as these present you would be astonished at the new wonders that are every day created within the circumference of the cable circus. Some of the artists devote their attention to illustrations of animated nature, and the specimens they give of the feathered tribe and other forms of animal life are without parallel in the works of Audubon, Cuvier, or any of the great naturalists. There are horses and deer such as Rosa Bonheur or Landseer never dreamed of, and probably never could, with all their wealth of genius, imagine. Dogs of the most remarkable dimensions, some with elephants on their backs, and others with eagles, attract the admiring gaze of the spectator, and share the praise with tom-cats, whose belligerent character is indicated by the swelled tail and raised back, infallible proofs of feline antagonism. Then there are fat porkers that would gladden the heart of a Cincinnati dealer to look at, and sheep with tails of the most remarkable dimensions. One portion of the circus is devoted exclusively to a grotesque procession of animals of every conceivable and inconceivable description, supposed to be on the march to some invisible Noah's ark. Fishes are to be seen out of their element, and apparently on the most sociable and companionable terms with the feathered denizens of the air. But the fancies of art do not stop here. They seek other fields for their flights, and illustrate the achievements of the champions of the ring, and the prowess of that enlightened portion of the community who patronize and maintain the manly art of self-defence. Prize fights are quite numerous on the boarded wall, and by way of variety, and to satisfy those whose refined natures and nice ideas revolt at such a vulgar way of settling private disputes or claims to personal superiority, duels with swords and pistols are also illustrated. The pugilists are in a large majority, however, and their tremendous muscular developments as compared with the skeleton-like forms of the duelists, would seem to convey the idea that their peculiar profession is good for the health. Now from all this there is but one conclusion to be drawn—that a cable circus is a remarkable promoter for the development of genius. But after all, the coilers have not much time to devote to works of art, and perhaps to this fact may be attributed the difficulty which the spectator sometimes finds in making out the exact character of the object intended to be represented. Occasionally a horse is mistaken for a dog, and were it not for the indispensable trunk the elephant might not be recognised at once. As for the pigs, sheep, and cows, it must be confessed that nature is not exactly copied, and that the aberrations of genius roam unrestricted through such extended fields of fancy, that it is impossible for ordinary minds to follow. No matter how much critics, however, may differ in regard to the quality or the truthfulness of these works of art, they must agree in one thing, that cable coiling is not the disagreeable occupation which some suppose, and that the cable coilers are as jolly, as pleasant, as jovial, as witty, and as humorous a set of fellows as were ever gathered together. While they coil flake after flake and layer after layer, they are as merry as the day is long, that is, in midsummer or thereabouts, when the day is longest, which makes all the difference in the world, so far as the force of the comparison is considered. Unpleasant work! Why, there never was work which was performed with greater alacrity and willingness. So eager were the men in regard to it, and so willing were they to offer their services, that when the demand was made for volunteers, the whole ship's crew came forward, and some difficulty was found in the selection of the necessary force. Every mile that is coiled, instead of wearying, appears but to give renewed strength to the coilers, and at the end of every four hours' watch they are apparently as fresh and vigorous as when they commenced. Each day, too, they have new jokes, new yarns, new conundrums, new Joe Millerisms, and a whole budget of new things in the jocular and humorous line. So exacting are they on this point, that an old joke is scouted at with indignation, and the joker himself severely censured for the attempt which he has made to impose on the good nature of his hearers. All the coils are distinguished by the same pleasant scenes, the same social features. In describing, therefore, one circle, we have, in fact, described all, but as there are some points of difference in that which is now being filled in the hold a brief reference to it may not be altogether unnecessary.

In making our way from the wardroom coil to that to which we propose to take our reader, the path is beset with difficulties to the uninitiated, and an attempt to reach it without a thorough knowledge of these is generally attended with a penalty, such as those who have tender feet and legs, or who are at all inclined either to lightness or heaviness in the upper regions, should avoid by securing the services of a guide. Leaving the wardroom coil behind us, we go forward on the main deck, pass the engine hatch on the left, and the ship's dispensary, the sailing master's, the purser's, and other rooms on the right. Pressing on still further, we reach the forward main deck coil, which will be one of the last filled up, and which is now only partially boarded up. A narrow passage on either side is the only means of egress to the fore part of the ship, where the cooking for the captain, officers, and men is carried on, and the odor from which tells us that interesting prelude to a more interesting performance is being enacted. But the way up to this point, that is, to the coil, is the easiest part of the passage—the most difficult has yet to be encountered.

By looking through the opening in the cone of the circle, where we now stand, we can get an indistinct view of that into which we will soon descend. It looks dark and gloomy, contrasted with the dim daylight which lights up this deck, and the occasional gleam from the forty or fifty candles by which it is faintly illuminated, serves but to make the prevailing darkness still more visible. Down through the centre of this cone, down through the centre of the cone of the circle on the orlop deck, down into the circle of the coil at which we are now endeavoring to get a glance, comes the deep sea line, black as the ink with which I write, and as it is hauled down it is packed away in flakes by the thirty men who sit around the circle. Close your ears as you look, and you have below you a scene which necromancer's craft never equalled; yes, in comparison with which even the boasted powers of his magic art appear insignificant. Through that blackened wire rope, as it is laid on the bottom of the great deep, will flash the subtle messenger of man, with a speed that outruns the sun in his course, and with which thought itself would run an unequal race. This is the necromancy of science, the creation of human genius, the very climax of human invention. Let your hearing return, and listen—that hearty laughter has no unearthly sound, but is as rollicking, as jovial and as cheerful as ever came out of mortal throat. Having given full liberty to one of your senses, you must now make another do double duty. You must open your eyes, and be just as wide awake as it is possible for you to be. Descending about ten feet we reach the orlop deck circle, which is almost similar to that on the deck above. Another descent—fourteen feet further down—and we stand upon the top flake of the rapidly increasing coil, the hold coil, the largest in the ship, which is to contain four hundred miles of the great sea line. We are now twelve feet below the water level, and in the lowest point of the vessel which it is possible for us to reach. An immense cone, larger than any that we have yet seen, stands in the centre of the circle like the peak of an extinct volcano. Around us is the magic, the necromantic circle, who are no more nor no less than thirty "Knights of the Black Hand" bearing the device upon backs, breasts, and sides, which attest their position on board ship as unmistakably as the red cross distinguished the crusader from his Saracenic foe. They are all out of the reach of daylight, and all the candles they can find places for are barely sufficient to chase away the darkness. Still there is plenty of light, not only to enable the coilers to see what they are about, but to enable them to coil as neatly, as rapidly, and altogether as successfully as those in the wardroom circus, between whom and themselves there is considerable rivalry. In point of wit, humor, fun, story-telling, ability, and all the other qualifications which are necessary to make what is called "a good follow," they are not a whit behind those same wardroom circus men; and although they may be somewhat below them in position, considering the distance the coils are apart, they are their equals in every respect, and their title to knighthood is just as well earned and as well graced. They can coil at the rate of two and a half miles an hour, and take as much pride in doing their work well. In fact, it would be impossible to decide which should have the palm. They are both well drilled, and for this due credit must be given to Mr. Fugitt, the sailmaker; Mr. Webber, the gunner; Capt. Kell, and Mr. Goodrich, master's mate, for their careful and attentive supervision of the coiling.

The following engraving, representing the coils in the forepart of the ship, is intended to show their exact proportion, and is according to a scale of twenty-five feet to an inch:

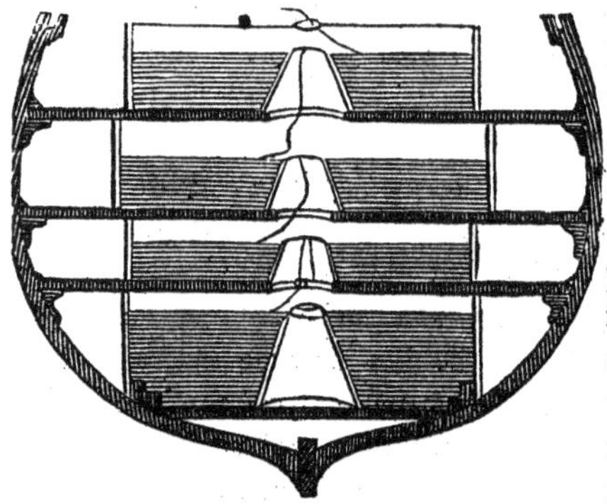

SECTION OF THE NIAGARA, SHOWING THE STOWAGE OF THE COILS IN THE FOREPART OF THE SHIP.

The base of the coil in the hold, it will be perceived, is not so regular and does not cover so much space as that of any of the others, on account of the construction of this part of the ship. The height from the floor to the deck above affords a large space for the coiling of the cable, and a much greater length is therefore placed here. This may be seen by reference to the table of coils. The same plan is observed in the construction of these four circles that has been described already, so that it is merely necessary to call attention to the fact.

THE CABLE CIRCUS, THE CONE AND FAIR-LEADERS.

The greatest vigilance and caution are required in the making of the coils, and in the paying-out process—in fact, every thing depends upon these two essential points, and any inattention to either is fraught with the most dangerous consequences to the success of the enterprise. The proper form of coil was at one time a subject of considerable discussion, and great difference of opinion prevailed in regard to the respective advantages of the circular and elongated, both of which had warm advocates. After satisfactory and conclusive trials the circular was finally adopted, and whatever merits the other form may have, it is now generally considered obsolete. The circular coils were the kind used on the Niagara and on the Agamemnon, with one trifling exception. The hold-coil on the latter was of an oval form, but far from being what is regarded as an elongated one. The construction of a proper receptacle for the coil was also a matter of much debate, and no inconsiderable amount of labor was expended before the present cable circus—or, as it is sometimes called, cable tank—was perfected. There were two things to be accomplished by its construction—the first was to prevent the cable from bulging out and the second to prevent it from becoming entangled in the centre. Then there was another and no less essential matter to be attended to to secure it from kinking, as it was unwound from the top or surface flake. Now, simple as the arrangements to secure these ends may appear, they did not reach their present state of perfection till the work of laying the Atlantic cable was entered upon. In the following engraving is presented a correct representation of the circus, the cone and the fair-leaders:

THE CABLE CIRCUS, THE CONE AND FAIR-LEADERS.

a—Large iron rings for fair-leaders and to prevent kinking.
B—Cone.
c—Pulleys with iron tricing lines for raising fair-leaders.
D—Portion of cone coiled.
E—Hatchway with the cable going up.

The circus is enclosed to a height of four or five feet, or as high as the coil rises—the enclosure being made of ordinary uprights or stancheons and rough boards. The floor is overlaid with common planking, upon which is placed a covering of zinc, for the protection of the deck, which would otherwise be stained by the tar with which the cable is saturated. The cone, which occupies the centre of the circus and coil, and is made of oak or some other hard wood, ranges, according to circumstances, from seven to nine feet in diameter at the base, and from three to five at the top. The particular part it is required to perform is to prevent the cable from becoming entangled in the centre of the circle, and to secure it a safe passage through the hatchway. The large iron rings, or fair-leaders, which encircle the cone, are intended to prevent the cable from kinking as it is unwound. The cable passes under these, and up between them and the cone, and in this way any tendency which it might have to kink is removed. The fair-leaders are secured by wire rope to the beams, and are capable of being lowered by means of pulleys, as the cable is reduced in paying out. The operative, who is represented in the act of lowering one of the fair-leaders by means of the wire rope, stands in a narrow passage, between the outer planking of the circus and the side of the ship.

THE COILS, ETC., ON THE AGAMEMNON.

There is perhaps no vessel in the British navy better adapted for the coiling and paying out of the cable than the Agamemnon. Her massiveness and great strength, as well as the peculiar advantages which she possesses for the stowage of the great sea line, were her chief recommendations. In 1857, the whole 1,250 miles which constituted her part of the cable were coiled in the forward hold, and it was feared at the time that she would be seriously damaged by the strain produced by so much dead weight in one part of the ship. A report was circulated then that she was "hogged," which, when translated into common English for the unlearned in nautical matters, signifies that she had broken her back, and was in an unfit state to go to sea. This report was, however, ascertained to be without foundation, and the ship was found, on investigation, to be in perfectly seaworthy condition.

The proportions of the ship, as given in the following engraving, are preserved as exactly and accurately as it is possible to do so, the scale being forty-six feet to an inch. The whole weight of the cable is thrown on the forepart of the vessel, between the fore and main masts; the machinery, stores, and coal, being in the after part, keep her on an even keel, and thus preserve that steadiness which is so necessary in the work she has to perform. With cable, coal, and all her sea stores on board, the Agamemnon drew about twenty-seven feet, which brought the water line almost to a level with the cable guard attached to the stern. An accurate idea may be formed of the way in which the cable was paid out from the several coils by reference to the engraving. The coil indicated by the letter A was first paid out, then coil B followed next in order, the hold coil C being the last reached. As the distance between all the coils and the paying-out machine (*c*) is over a hundred feet, the rollers (*d d d d*) are placed at regular intervals, to steady it in its progress. These rollers are made of iron, and are raised on a framework to the height of six or seven feet above the level of the spar deck. After the cable is delivered from the machine, it passes out over the wheel (*b*), which is secured by large wooden beams over the stern of the ship. This wheel, or sheave, as it is sometimes called, is about five feet in diameter, and has a groove five inches deep. As the forepart of the ship was of course lightened in proportion to the amount of cable paid out, the afterpart was lightened in an equal degree by the consumption of coal and by the removal of the ship's stores. Thus the equilibrium was preserved until the whole work was completed.

After the first coil, A, is exhausted, the line is taken from the coil B, through the hatches of the spar, main, and berth decks, its course being regulated by the iron rings or fair-leaders through which it passes, and which prevent its surging. These fair-leaders are different from those represented in another engraving in thus being fastened to the hatches, and cannot of course be raised or lowered. The part of the illustration representing the paying-out machine is necessarily on such a limited scale as to render any attempt to give the detail altogether impossible. It is, however, illustrated in another part of this work, and will be found, with a full description, under the appropriate head.

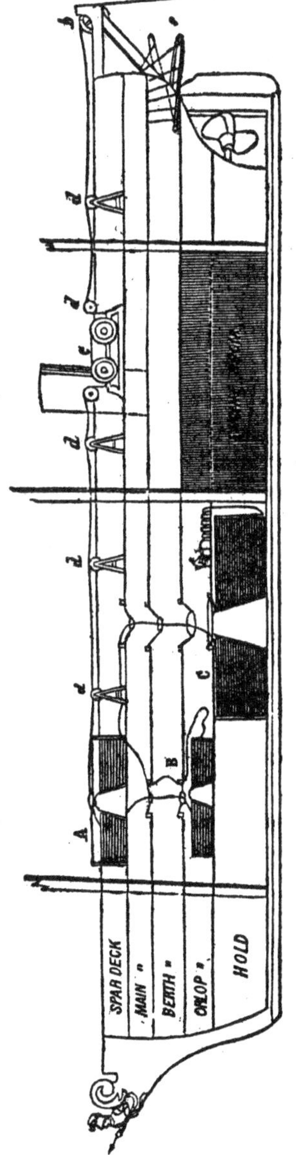

SECTION OF THE AGAMEMNON WITH CABLE ON BOARD.

C—Coil in Hold.—Length, 1,075 miles. *B—Coil on Orlop Deck.*—150 miles. *A—Coil on Spar Deck.*—225 miles. *Total Miles on Board.*—In hold, 1,075. *d d d, &c.*—Rollers placed along the decks to steady the cable. *e*—Cable guard. *f*—Screw.

THE COILS, ETC., ON THE NIAGARA.

The subjoined engraving is intended to show the internal arrangements and apparatus for the coiling and paying out of the cable, and may be regarded as substantially accurate in its details. At first view there appears to be very slight difference between the two cable ships, but it will be seen that the number of coils on board the Niagara is about double the number on the Agamemnon, and that the coil in the hold of the former is not so large as that in the hold of the latter by several hundred miles. The strain on this part of the Niagara, therefore, was not so great, and she was consequently better able to withstand the effects of a heavy sea. The number of coils on the Niagara was seven, and of these five were placed in the fore and two in the after part of the vessel. The sheaves were placed over the bow as well as in the stern, and there were the same contrivances in the way of rollers and fair-leaders. The strength of each deck, or that particular part of it on which the cable was coiled, was increased by large iron trusses, which extended from one side of the ship to the other, and which were the best kind of substitutes for stanchions. The removal of a large number of these stanchions was necessary to make room for the coils, and the trusses were designed to answer the same purpose—that is, as supports for the decks. The hatches in the forepart of the ship were made the centre of the cable circles, so that when the coil was exhausted in one the cable was drawn up from the circle beneath through the cone, which was hollow, and which had an opening at the base and at the top. The machine was placed as near the stern as possible, to facilitate the process of paying out; the sheaves were secured and held in their places by strong wooden beams.

THE CABLE GUARDS.

Among the precautions which were taken to prevent damage to the cable is that of the stern guards, which were placed over the screw of each of the ships. These guards were to prevent it from coming in contact with the screws, in which case it is almost needless to add the cable would be broken. In 1857, they were secured to the sterns with strong iron bars, which it was supposed would withstand the pressure or resistance of the water when the vessel was under way. This, however, was proved by experience to be a fallacious idea, several of the bars having yielded and broke under the pressure. In view of this fact Mr. Everett decided on adopting another style of guard, which would answer the same purpose, and which would also be free from the difficulty to which the other was subject. A glance at the engraving will give a correct idea of that which was adopted.

STERN GUARD OF THE NIAGARA.

This was a movable guard, and could be raised or lowered by means of the chains by which it was suspended. The hinge (*b*) was secured by

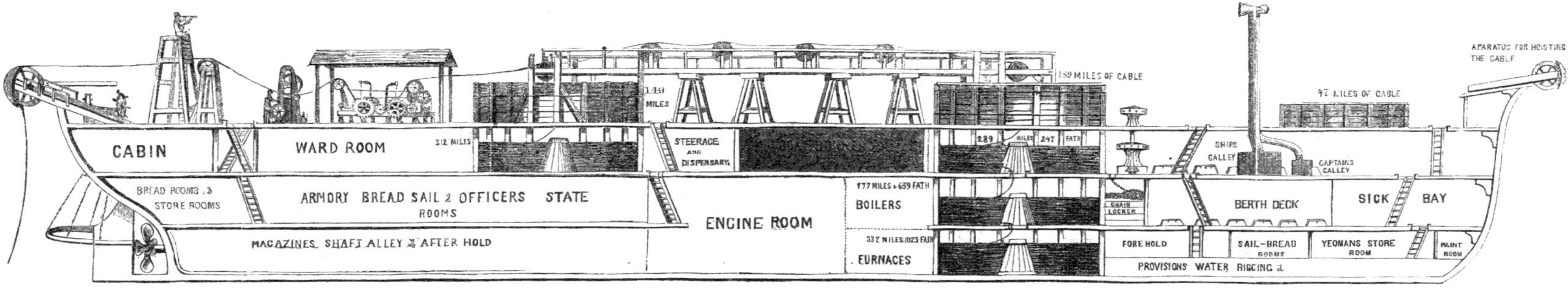

SECTIONAL VIEW OF THE NIAGARA.

a strong brass plate, which was fastened to the side of the ship with twelve copper bolts. The advantage of this movable guard will be readily appreciated. It could be raised to such a height when necessary as to entirely clear it from the water. Then it was intended, that if icebergs or other obstructions should render it necessary to back the ship, the guard should be immediately lowered, and lowered to such a depth as to prevent the cable being injured or broken by the screw. The length of the guard from the hinge (*b*) to the outer line (*d*) is 27 feet, and its greatest diameter athwart ships is 22 feet 6 inches. When hauled up, the extreme end (*d*) cleared the rudder-iron (*a*) about two feet. The stern sheave (*c*) over which the cable ran in its course before it reached the water was about four and a-half feet in diameter, and the groove at least five inches deep. A guard kept the cable from surging and working out of the groove.

The Agamemnon, as may be seen from the following illustration, is provided with a guard similar to that on the Niagara.

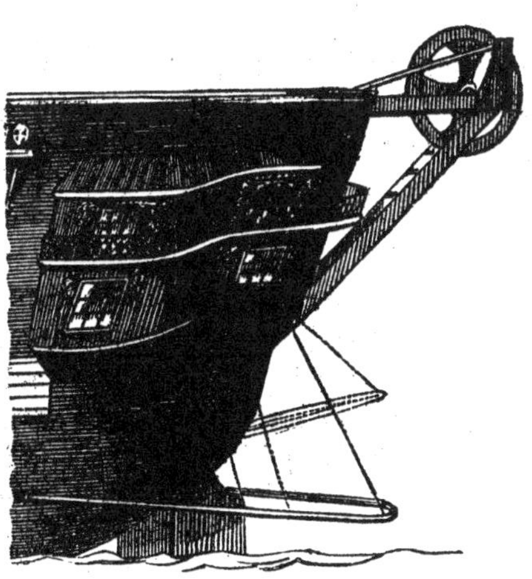

STERN GUARD OF THE AGAMEMNON.

A passage was left on either side of the wheel, to render it accessible when necessary, and this was rendered secure and safe by strong wooden railings, strengthened by iron uprights, the whole resting or constructed upon two massive beams, which ran in on the deck of the ship, where they were firmly attached.

The following engraving presents the stern sheave or wheel on a more enlarged scale.

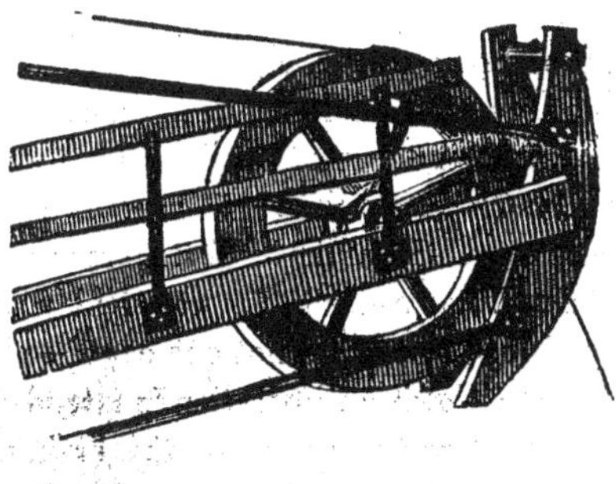

SECTION OF THE STERN GUARD OF THE AGAMEMNON

It was intended to put a cage around the propeller, like that which was attached to the Niagara in 1857, but the preference was given to a movable guard, so that in this particular both ships were alike.

THE MACHINE THAT LAID THE CABLE,

CONSTRUCTED BY MR. W. E. EVERETT.

As the success of the enterprise depended mainly upon the construction of the paying-out machinery, and its adaptability to the work it was intended for, a detailed description of its various parts becomes necessary to a perfect understanding of the subject. To render the matter more easy of comprehension, we have presented in the accompanying illustrations not only the prominent features, but the minor details of the machine. Before proceeding, however, to the description, we wish to make a few preliminary remarks, for the purpose of showing the nature of the work which it has to perform. It is needless, almost, to state that the machine used on the expedition of 1857, was so imperfect that it caused the parting of the cable. That fact has been established beyond dispute, but it may not be generally understood that the principal defect in the machine was in the form of brake used. The object of a brake is to counteract or diminish the speed of the wheels by increasing the pressure. This is done by tightening the wooden blocks which surround the periphery of the brake wheel, and inside of which the brake wheel revolves. As this tightening or pressure is increased or diminished, the sheaves round which the cable passes, and which are on the same shaft with the brakes, revolve with increased or diminished rapidity. This, then, is the object of the brake; but the brake to be fitted for this particular work must be self-releasing, so that after reaching the required pressure it cannot exceed it. It was the entire want of this essential requisite in the brakes of the machine used on the first expedition, that rendered it not only useless, but fatal to its success. In the construction of the machinery which was put on board the Agamemnon and Niagara, and which was designed by and made under the direction and supervision of Mr. W. E. Everett, this point received particular attention. In the first place the machine subserves two purposes—it is both winding in and paying out—while two separate machines were required last year for these operations. In the second place it was not so cumbersome, being about one-fourth the weight; and in the third place it occupied much less space. But the most important feature, and that by which it is most distinguished, is the self-releasing character of the brake, and the much greater ease with which it can be regulated and controlled. Of the large number of engineers who witnessed it in operation, not one expressed an unfavorable opinion.

The following illustration is intended to give a rear view of the machine, to show the action of the brakes, the way the cable enters and leaves the sheaves or four grooved wheels (*c c*), which are but partially seen, and the object of the dynamometer.

The first glance at this engraving will show at once the great difference in the form of the machine, as compared with that used before. While the old paying-out concern consisted of four, this has only two wheels, each of which has four grooves, the grooves being each four and a half inches deep. The surging of the cable out of the shallow grooves that marked the periphery of the former machine proved the necessity of making these nearly twice as deep. This is one of the lessons that was gained by experience and judgment. The dynamometer is intended not only to show the strain upon the cable, but also to release the cable from that strain should the self-releasing brakes through any accident have been unable to perform their part. The iron frame-work, on which the

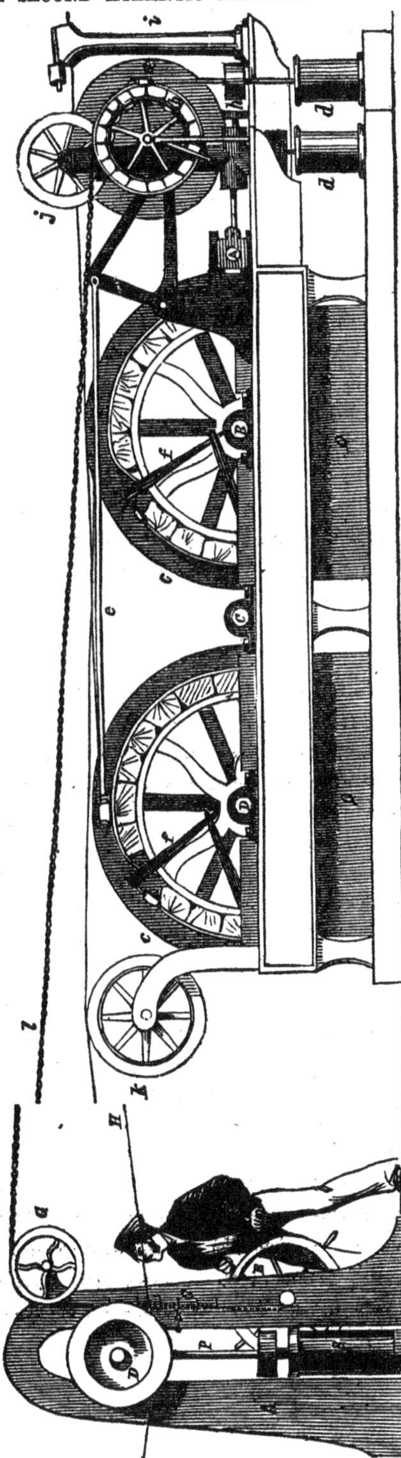

THE PAYING-OUT MACHINE.

(*A*) main shaft connecting with steam engine. When the machine is to be used as a "winding machine," a pinion wheel is shipped on it, a gear wheel on (*B*) connected with (*D*) by a pinion on (C)—(*a*) The guide wheel on which the cable takes one turn, regulated by the friction wheel (*b*) and weights.—(*dd*) Water cylinders. The piston rod on which the weights are put works in this, the water preventing sudden shocks by releasing of friction band, &c.—(*b*) A guide to lead the cable fair into the score of (*a*), with four pounds compression.—(*cc*) Four grooved wheels.—(*e*) Connecting rod between friction band and weights.—(*f*) Levers compressing friction bands.—(*g*) Water tank in which friction straps and wheels are immersed to prevent heating.—(*h*) Screw for throwing main shaft pinion into gear.—(*i*) Pillar of the compressor.—(*j*) Guide wheel which acts in connection with the dynamometer.—(*k*) Guide wheel.—(*l*) Chain.

machinery is placed, is represented by A, and the process is easily explained by the letters which mark the different parts. The large pulley (D) moves up and down in grooves, and is attached to the piston (F) moving in the water cylinder (B). The cable (H) which passes from the guide wheel (K) under the pulley to another wheel on the opposite side of the dynamometer, forms an angle under the pulley that is rendered more or less acute by the strain or pressure produced by the brakes. The greater the strain, the less acute the angle becomes, and the higher the pulley rises on the scale (C). Now this scale (C) is marked or graduated from twelve hundred to thirty-six hundred pounds. It is, in fact, a sort of a spring balance, the only difference being in the graduating of the scale, which in the dynamometer shows a numerical increase as you ascend, while in the spring balance the numbers become greater as you descend the scale. The weights by which the strain is increased on the cable at this point in proportion to the pressure on the brakes, are placed upon the rest, which is seen above the water cylinder (B). The other purpose which the dynamometer serves is as follows: By a simple contrivance it is made to act as a means of releasing the brakes when they have failed in releasing themselves. The man who stands behind is shown in the act of using this brake releaser. The wheel (E) which he holds in his hand, by being turned to the right or left, tightens the chain (C) which is attached to the triangular shaped frame on the paying-out machine. The tightening or drawing on this chain raises the weights, which are attached to a rod or shaft at the end of this triangle, and by thus raising the weights releases the brakes from the pressure. This process is more fully explained further on, in the description of the next illustration.

The tanks (*g g*) are always well supplied with water, to prevent the heating of the brake wheels from friction, an operation which consumes about two gallons an hour. It was proposed to use oil, but as oil was not considered better than water, considerations of economy prevailed, and the latter was adopted in preference. Beyond the brake wheels are the grooved sheaves (*c c*) round which the cable is passed four times, but which are only partially visible. These sheaves are each six feet in diameter, while the brake wheels are not more than four and a half. On the shafts (B B) are placed gear wheels which are connected with a pinion on C; but this gearing is never put on except the machine is to be employed in winding in, in which case a pinion wheel is put on the main shaft (A) in connection with a double forty-horse engine on the port side of the ship. None of this gearing is shown in the engraving, for the simple reason that its purpose can be easily understood without illustration, and also for the no less forcible reason that it would only help to make the drawing confused and complicated to no purpose. There are four brake wheels, the pressure on which can be increased by weights to two tons and upwards. The passage of the cable from the coil to the sea is so arranged that the slightest tendency to kink is stopped at once. From the very moment it leaves the circles till it passes over the bobbins and on the machine, it is subject to a greater or less strain, which keeps it straight throughout its whole course until it enters the water. After passing over several bobbins, it enters the compressor (*i*), which carries it safely to the guide wheel (*a*), on which it takes one turn, and on which it is subject to a still higher strain, regulated by the friction wheel (*b*). The strain produced by this and the compressor (*i*) is very slight, and only helps to straighten it out before it reaches the sheaves. From the guide wheel (*a*) it passes into the grooves and around the wheels or sheaves four times, after which it is delivered to the guide wheel (*k*); then going under the pulley, it reaches another wheel beyond the dynamometer, from which it is transferred to the sheave at the stern, the last part of the machinery it touches on its way into the ocean.

Upon the operation of the brakes, the success of the expedition, as we have already said, depends in a great measure. The greatest care and attention have therefore been given to their construction. The defects of those used last year have been pointed out already, and out readers will consequently be the better able to appreciate the way in which these are planned. For the principle on which they are made Mr. Appold is entitled to some credit; but material alterations and modifications were required before they could be adapted to the use to which they have been applied. In the following illustration is presented a perfect representation of the brake and its mode of action.

The shaft which is marked B in the preceding figure, and on which is placed the four grooved sheave, is shown by the letter *a* in the foregoing. The speed of the sheave and brake wheel is thus made uniform, a point which is of course absolutely essential in checking at any time the rate at which the cable is being paid out. That the simple action of the brake may be the better understood, we have, however, merely shown those parts which are necessary to that end, leaving out whatever would tend to complicate or confuse the drawing. The parts here presented are the shafts, the brake, the friction strap, the elm blocks, the levers, the connecting rods, the weights by which the strain on the cable is increased, the water cylinder, the chain connecting the shaft on which the weights are put, with dynamometer, portion of water tank, and a section of pillar to which the triangular part of the brake apparatus is attached. All of these may be easily distinguished by reference to the explanation at the foot of the engraving.

THE BRAKE WHEEL AND ITS CONNECTIONS.

(*a*) Shaft.—(*b*) Brake wheel.—(*c*) Friction strap to which is secured (*d d*).—(*d d*) Elm blocks; (*e e*) rods to relieve the upper part of friction strap of weights of lower part.—(*g g*) Levers.—(*h*) Connecting rod with weights (*i*) attached to friction strap (*c*) at (*s*).—(*j*) Water cylinder.—(*k*) Chain connecting weight with shaft (*l*) and wheel (*n*), to periphery of which is attached a chain connecting with the dynamometer in order to relieve the friction pressure.—(*o*) Pillar and shaft to which is attached (*p*).—(*t*) Portion of water tank.—(*r*) Lever stirrup or socket.—(*s*) Connection of rod and friction strain.

The periphery (*b*) of the brake wheel is twelve inches wide, and the whole, without the brake fixtures, is somewhat more than four feet in diameter. The shafts, as may be seen, are of a curved form, and the wheel is made of cast iron. On the periphery are the elm blocks (*d d*), which are bound together by a strong strap or band of iron (*c*). The blocks are secured by means of screws, the heads of which can be seen above the strap. The two ends of this strap, or band, are attached to the lever (*g*), which is held by the stirrup or socket (*r*). The tightening of the strap, and the consequent compressing of the elm blocks upon the periphery of the brake wheel causes it to revolve more slowly, and produces the same effect upon the sheave wheel over which the cable is passing. But while the brake wheel revolves the brake blocks are of course stationary, moving only sufficient for the purpose of compressing or releasing the brake wheel. The tightening or compressing is effected by increasing the weights on the piston, which can be raised to two tons if necessary. There are four brakes to the machinery, so that by putting ten hundred pounds on each piston the pressure can be increased to four thousand. Now as this weight is increased on the pistons, the pistons partially descend into the cylinder, pulling down to a proportionate degree the rod (*h*), which tightens the brake band (*c c*), thus producing the required strain upon the cable, which strain is indicated upon the scale of the dynamometer. As the shaft is drawn over to the right by the increase of weights upon the piston, the lever is acted upon as illustrated in the following:

The engraving is intended to represent the brake strap, the lever, and the stirrup. If you desire to compress by reducing the circumference of the strap (which is shown here without the elm blocks) you pull the lever (*c*) to the left hand, and by so doing move the other end of the strap (*b*) towards the right. This is a simple process and easily understood. As you pull on the lever (*c*) you draw upon the two ends (*b* and *a*) of the brake strap, but the distance travelled by *b* and *a* at the same time is not equal, and in this consists the principle of the tightening or compression. The end *a* being nearest the centre does not of course move over so much space as *b*, which is on the circumference, so that when the lever is moved, the end *b*, by travelling further than *a*, tightens the strap. But in the engraving of "the brake wheel and its connections," the rod (*h*) which is attached to the brake strap at *s*, performs this part of the operation—that is, the tightening of the brake strap. The junction of the ends of the strap at the lever (*g*) is on the same principle as that we have illustrated. As the rod is drawn to the right by the increase of weights on the piston, the same action is produced on the brake band as if the lever were used. The ends of the strap travel unequal distances, as has been shown, the outer one going over more space. The end of the lever is held in the stirrup or socket, against which it is pulled closer by the action of the rod (*h*) upon the straps. The action of the chain (*k m*) and wheel (*n*) is explained in the description of the dynamometer. When the brakes do not release themselves from the pressure of the weights on the piston rod, and exceed that pressure so much as to endanger the safety of the cable, the man at the dynamometer by a turn of the wheel raises the weights, and thus relieves the brakes. The rods (*e e*) are intended to relieve the upper part of friction strap of weight of lower part.

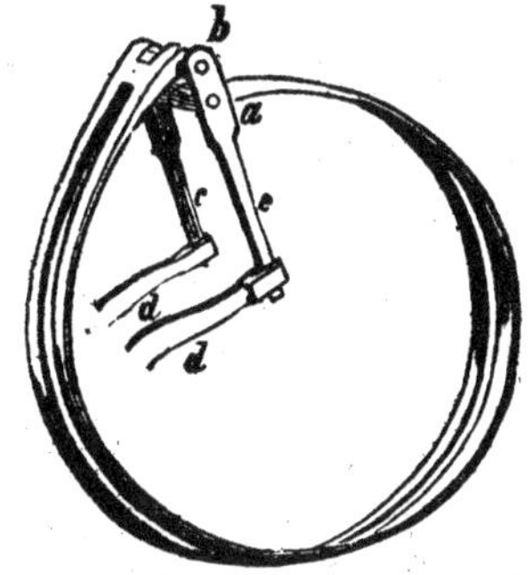

SHOWING THE ACTION ON THE BRAKES.

The following subjoined front view of paying-out machine is designed to show the sheave wheels, the guides, the compresser, and the scrapers, all the other portions being left out that these may be more distinctly seen:

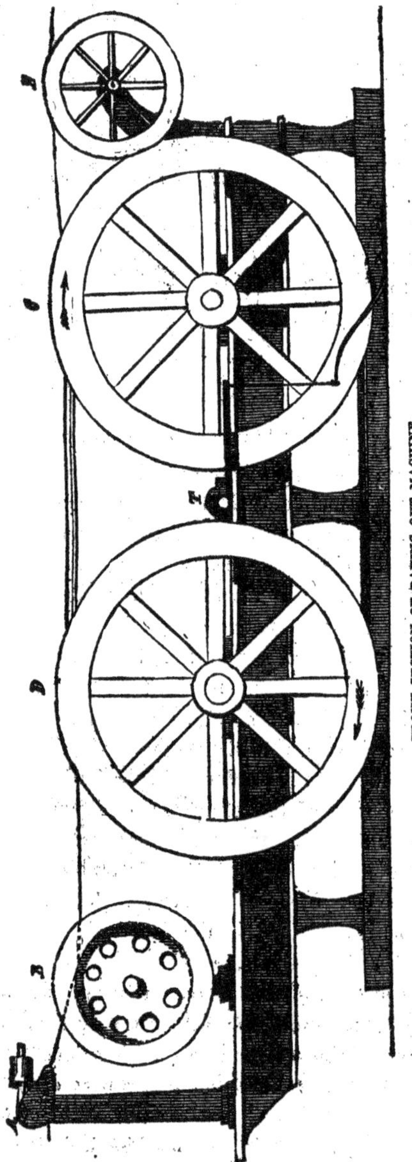

FRONT SECTION OF PAYING-OUT MACHINE.

The cable passes through the guide (*A*) on to a light sheet iron wheel (*B*)—placed for the purpose of steadying it on entering the groove of the large wheel—passes round (*C*) and back and under and over (*D*), thus making four half turns on each wheel—finally over the small wheel (*E*), thence under the dynamometer and over another wheel similar to (*G*) and overboard.

The cable first enters through the compresser or guide (A), takes one turn round the guide wheel (B), which is made of sheet iron, and which is governed and regulated by the friction wheel (*d*), and weighted as shown in the drawing of "the paying-out machine." From this it passes round C, and from C to D, and so on till it has passed four times over both, when it is received by the small guide wheel, from which it is transferred to the dynamometer. The scraper (T), which is secured on the shaft between the two wheels, is armed with eight teeth, four on each side, which fit into the grooves. These teeth clear out the tar as the wheels pass round, and thus prevent it from hardening and collecting in the grooves. The following is a representation of a sheave wheel, which will serve to give a clearer idea of its form and the form of the grooves than could possibly be given by a front view of the machine itself:—

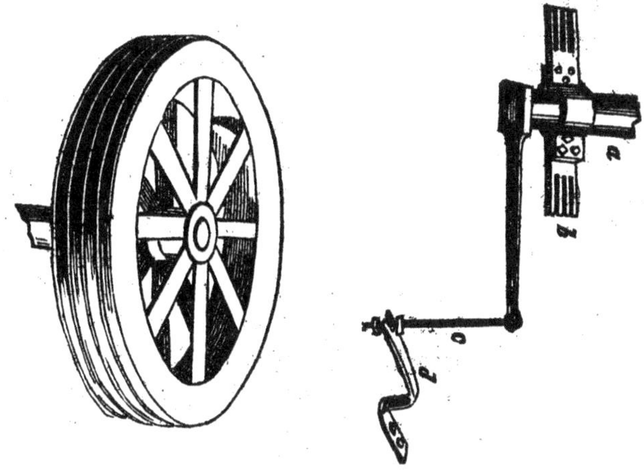

A SHEAVE WHEEL SHOWING THE GROOVES. THE SCRAPERS.

(*a*) Shaft.
(*b*) Fingers of scraper.
(*d*) Spring bolted to deck, to which is attached lever (*c*), but which releases it if any thing should overclog the grooves.

The object of the scraper has been already explained, but its form cannot be perfectly seen, on account of its position on the machine. The foregoing illustration, therefore, becomes necessary.

A is the shaft on which the scrapers are placed, and *b* the four teeth which enter the grooves of the wheel for the purpose of preventing the accumulation of tar. By means of the spring (*d*), which is bolted to the deck, and the lever (*c*), the scraper could be at once released, if the grooves were overclogged or filled up by any foreign substance getting into them.

THE CABLE BUOYS.

In addition to the mechanical contrivances which have been so fully described, two large buoys, each capable of sustaining a weight of five or six tons, were put on board the Niagara, so that in the event of her being obliged by stress of weather to slip the cable, it might be attached to this. This was to be effected by means of a wire cable eight or ten miles in length, one end of which was secured to the end of the submarine cable, and the other to the buoy, thus taking the great strain off it.

THE EXPERIMENTAL TRIP OF THE SQUADRON TO THE BAY OF BISCAY.

The 29th of May, the day on which the squadron sailed from Plymouth, on the experimental trip to the Bay of Biscay, was remarkably fine, and as there had been a continuous gale of some two weeks' duration, we entered upon the work before us with every prospect of a long spell of fair weather—a prospect in which we were not disappointed. Every thing necessary to the success of the trip was arranged two or three days previous to our departure. The machinery was in excellent working order, the buoys were provided with the necessary tackle, and the experience which the men had obtained by working at the cable proved of the greatest advantage in making the experiments. A consultation was had between the captains and the engineers of the company in regard to the point at which the vessels should commence their experiments, and after due deliberation it was decided that lat. 47, lon. 10, would be quite far enough. This is just on the verge of the Bay of Biscay, which bears such a terrible reputation for boisterous weather, and which it was supposed would afford every opportunity for testing the practicability of splicing and laying the cable in a rough sea, and under the most unfavorable circumstances. So lat. 47, lon. 10, was selected as the precise locality for the experiments. After leaving Plymouth Sound, therefore, the squadron made as direct a course as possible for this point. It was between four and five o'clock in the afternoon of the 29th of May when the four vessels got under way—the Agamemnon leading, the Gorgon, the Niagara, and the Valorous, following in regular succession. They started at a rate of five miles, and during their course out varied from that to a speed of eight miles per hour. The whole of Sunday no change was observed in the green color of the water denoting a greater depth, and the squadron kept on without making soundings. Monday, however, it had turned to a deep blue, showing that we had reached the great depths, although we had not yet arrived at the locality decided upon for the experiments. Signal was made by the Gorgon, under the command of Captain Dayman, to sound, and the whole squadron hove to to await the result.

We were now in latitude 47° 12′ N., long. 9° 32′ W., or about thirty miles distant from the point decided upon before starting from Plymouth, and, as it was subsequently shown by the soundings of the Gorgon, in 2,530 fathoms water. This, then, it was evident, was the place we were in search of, and it was determined that we should proceed to make our experiments at once. According to the memoranda drawn up by the engineers, the Niagara approached the Agamemnon within a convenient distance, when a line was passed in a boat to the Agamemnon, by which a hawser was hauled on board the latter, and by which also the two ships were fastened stern to stern. It must not be supposed from this, however, that they were actually in contact, for they were some seven or eight hundred feet apart, and as each vessel had steam up, there was no danger, with proper management, of their coming in collision. The two vessels now being firmly secured, the end of the telegraph cable was passed from the Niagara to the Agamemnon, where it was agreed the splice should be effected. The object of this experiment was to prove the practicability of accomplishing what is, or was considered, one of the most difficult operations of the whole expedition—the splicing and submerging of the cable in mid-ocean. The greatest interest was manifested on board our ship while the splicing was being performed on the Agamemnon, and every one was impatient to see the cable lowered from her stern, although the work was performed with praiseworthy celerity. It was about half-past five when the signal was displayed from that ship announcing that they were ready, and a few minutes after we could see the spliced portion hanging over the stern. Down it went until it disappeared below the surface, and the revolving cable wheel on the stern proved that it was on its way to the bottom, which lay at a depth of some twenty-five hundred fathoms beneath the ship. A length of cable having been paid out from the Agamemnon equal to the quantity used in passing the cable from ship to ship, so that the splice might be in the centre of the line formed by the cable between the ships, a flag was hoisted from the Agamemnon conveying intelligence of the fact to the Niagara. This was answered by a similar signal on the Niagara, when the two commenced paying out a quarter of a mile of cable each, at the rate of a mile an hour.

The cable used in this trial was a portion of that which had been laid last year, and which was much weakened by exposure. In some parts the outer wires, or protecting armor, was so oxidized, that the rust had rotted the hemp which covered the gutta percha. For this reason it parted several times during the experiments, but at the same time without interfering with their successful accomplishment.

A quarter of a mile, as has been stated, was paid out, and, in conformity with the "memoranda," the signals on both ships were hauled down, indicating that no more paying out should be done until they were again displayed. About ten minutes elapsed, when the flags were hoisted, and another quarter of a mile was let down into the sea at the same speed—a mile an hour. This process was repeated until a whole mile had been run out from the coil and over the machinery of each ship, making a total expenditure of two miles from both vessels. The process of paying out was performed by the engine connected with the machinery until the weight of the cable in the water was sufficient to turn the wheels. Mr. Follansbee, the chief engineer of the Niagara, had the engine under his charge all this time, and Mr. Everett took his stand at the dynamometer, where he regulated the pressure of the brakes. The Valorous and the Gorgon were obliged to play the part of lookers on, and with little profit or information, as they were of course entirely ignorant of the operations on board either of the cable ships.

While the first splice was being made, Captain Preedy, of the Agamemnon, sent the following despatch through the insulated conductor, to Captain Hudson—"We shall finish the splice in half an hour."

Throughout the experiments thus far the machinery answered our highest expectations, and proved its entire adaptability to the work. The brakes were under the most complete control, and the dynamometer, by showing the strain to which the cable was subject, placed it in the power of the man at the wheel to increase or lessen that strain as circumstances might demand or justify. In the expedition of 1857, the only difficulty was in the machinery. The wheels over which the cable passed would not revolve when required, and the strength of twenty men was exerted upon them in vain. Then the brakes, when put on, generally stopped the action of the whole machine, and brought a strain upon the line that was almost always fatal. Indeed, so patent had this fact become to all in the expedition, that it was doubted if a hundred miles of the cable could be successfully submerged, and the only wonder was that they had managed to get over three hundred miles out of the ship before it parted. Every one is agreed in regard to the qualities of the now employed paying-out machine. On that there is no difference of opinion, whatever there may be in regard to other matters connected with the Atlantic Telegraph enterprise. The strain, as indicated by the dynamometer, was equal to twelve hundred pounds, and this can be graduated from any amount between five hundred and fifty-five hundred, as the engineer in charge of the brakes may determine. It is now six o'clock, and the waiters have announced to the officers that supper is on the table; but it may be on or under the table just now for all any one cares; there is more interesting matter on hand, and until that is settled the supper may wait until it is cold. Looking at the cable as it comes out of the coil, passes over the paying-out sheaves, and descends from the stern, is the only thing worth attending to now, and the eager eyes of the sailors as they strain them in vain endeavors to see from the sides of the ship what is going on under the poop—an attempt to accomplish an impossibility—a sort of shooting-round-the-corner operation—proves only that the spirit of curiosity will try to surmount the most insurmountable obstacles. "Now it is going out grandly,"

PAYING OUT THE CABLE DURING THE TRIAL TRIP

some enthusiastic individual exclaims. A fact which a glance at both machine and cable proves beyond the possibility of a doubt. The machine revolves with the greatest ease; the indicator attached to it records the number of fathoms, and the cable comes out of the coil without exhibiting the slightest tendency to kink. Whatever speculations may be entertained about its kinking as it goes out of the ship, they are of very little account compared with the convincing ocular demonstration which is now presented. And this, too, is the experimental cable—the weakest, the most, imperfect, and the worst in every way on board the two ships. There is a number of men around the coil looking out for kinks, but they have not yet been able to detect a single one, and they may stop where they are for many hours to come before they will succeed. Captain Kell is overlooking this part of the work, and although about as wide awake as he can be, he can't see any thing. Lieutenant North, Lieutenant Macauly, Lieutenant Guest, Lieutenant Webb, Lieutenant Todd, Dr. Green, Dr. Hay, and all the lieutenants and doctors in the ship pay a visit to the coil, and they can't see a kink; and so it is concluded on board the ship that the thing that could be seen if it existed, can't be seen at all; "*argal*," that thing consequently don't exist.

The supper has been an hour on the table before the officers think it worth while attending to, and then they go to work so slowly at it you would believe it was a subject hardly worth discussing. The experiments that have been made form the topic of conversation, and there is but one general expression of opinion regarding them, which is one of entire satisfaction. The supper is quickly despatched, and, as the experiments are still going on, the poop is soon occupied by a crowd of spectators. Over a mile of cable has been paid out from each ship (both vessels being still seven or eight hundred feet apart and connected by the hawser), and operations are suspended till it has had ample time to reach the bottom, which is 2,530 fathoms down. The dynamometer at this point shows a pressure of 3,200 pounds upon the brake, which is a strain of a little more than a ton and a-half upon the cable. While they are still waiting for the sinking of the line, the Gorgon comes alongside, and Captain Dayman, who stands upon her wheel-house, announces in his loudest tones that they have sounded again and got 2,530 fathoms. Now this is deeper than any soundings that have been had upon the Atlantic Telegraph plateau, and the experiments which are made ought certainly to be regarded as thoroughly testing the practicability of laying the cable between Ireland and Newfoundland, the two immediate points of connection. This, however, was satisfactorily tested and proved last year, although it may be well now to state the fact for the benefit of those who are still inclined to be sceptical upon the subject.

Agreeably with the terms of the programme, or memoranda of the engineers, as it is called, the next thing is to prove the practicability of hauling in the cable on board both ships. The engine is put in gear with the paying-out machine, the action of which is reversed, so that it can be used as well for the purpose of winding in. Every thing being in readiness, the process of hauling in was commenced. The ship was backed very slowly until the cable was "up and down," which means at right angles with the water, in which position it appears there is less strain upon it than in any other. The wheels revolved very slowly as the line was drawn on board, and half a mile of it returned to the coil from which it had been taken about an hour before. At this point of the process a message was received, signed Bright, stating that it was that gentleman's wish the operation should be suspended until he had time to make a "new splice." It took about three hours to accomplish this, and when the work was finished a message was sent to Mr. Everett, to the effect that "all was ready." The paying-out process was resumed on the receipt of this message, and by half-past ten we had succeeded in submerging two miles. The strain upon the cable, as shown by the dynamometer, varied from thirty-six to forty-one hundred pounds, while this length was suspended from the stern. Again the action of the machine was reversed, and the hauling in process repeated, at a rate of a mile an hour. This Mr. Everett considered the highest speed at which it would be safe to work the machinery, in consequence of the weakness of the cable, which, it must not be forgotten, had been previously condemned and set aside as only fit to make experiments with. It was intended, however, before the close of the trip to use the new cable for the purpose of testing its strength, and to settle the disputed point as to the practicability of taking it up, should it be found necessary during the final expedition. About a quarter to twelve this night the hawser which held both ships stern to stern parted on board the Agamemnon, and thus concluded the experiments for the first day—Monday, May 31.

Second Day's Experiments.

Although the cable which kept the Niagara and Agamemnon together had parted, the two vessels were still kept in about the same position, and the work proceeded with little or no intermission. Something more than a mile and a-half was hauled in, when word was sent from the office of the electrician on the maindeck that the continuity was broken. Still the hauling in went on successfully; and as that was the matter with which Mr. Everett had more immediately to do, little attention was paid to the loss of the electrical continuity. Besides, it was the imperfect cable we were using, and it was never supposed that it would be of much service, if any, for electrical experiments. The hauling in, therefore, was continued till about half-past two A. M., when the end of the cable came up over the stern. Of the whole length paid out not more than one hundred and ten fathoms were lost. This concluded the experiments till after breakfast, when they were commenced with renewed energy.

At a quarter to nine A. M. a new hawser was passed from the Niagara to the Agamemnon, and both ships attached in the manner already described. The two ends of the cable were again spliced, and a quarter of a mile paid out from each ship, after which the hawser was released. Up to this time they had not allowed the cable to pass out of the Niagara faster than a mile an hour; but a change was now to be made in this respect, and it was concluded to see the effect of a more rapid movement of the machinery and an accelerated speed in the paying-out process. Two miles of it were permitted, in the language of the engineer's report, to "run quite freely," when the speed was gradually checked while an additional mile and about four hundred fathoms were being submerged. The ships were under way from the time the hawser was released, and continued moving, though at a comparatively slow rate, most of the time the line was passing out. It was now about half-past ten, and three miles had been transferred from the ship to the sea in the most satisfactory manner, as showing the admirable working of the machinery, and the ease with which it could be controlled. There was one point, however, which was not so satisfactory, and which it was seen would require the attention of the engineer before the departure of the ships on the final expedition. This was the excessive accumulation and hardening of the tar in the sheaves, which it is rightly feared may endanger the safety of the cable if some provision be not made in time. The necessity of making such provision as will obviate the difficulty is fully appreciated by Mr. Everett, who will devise some means by which it will be altogether prevented, or so counteracted as to render all danger therefrom a matter of impossibility. If the experimental trip made only this difficulty obvious, it was worth all the time and money and labor which have been expended. The accumulation of the tar in the grooves of the pulley or indicator of the dynamometer, and the grooves of the wheel leading to the stern, rendered the use of a scraper absolutely necessary to keep them clear. A man was accordingly appointed for this work; but while cleaning the groove of the indicator wheel, the tar was so hard and so thick that it broke the scraper, and forced it into contact with the cable, which was almost immediately severed at the point of contact. Here, then, was an additional experience of the greatest value in the successful accomplishment of the undertaking. It was made manifest, by the accumulation of the tar in the grooves, that some plan should be devised to obviate any difficulty from such a cause, and it was also shown that it was unsafe to trust a scraper in the hands of any man for the removal of the tar. The scrapers which were placed on the paying-out machine to keep the tar from collecting in the grooves of the sheave wheels are just the thing, but the abrasion and consequent wearing to which they are subjected will render an abundant supply of scrapers indispensable.

After paying out the length of cable stated (over three miles), the engineer gave the order to reverse the machine and to wind in. This was but the work of a few minutes, and soon after the order was given it was carried into execution. Not more than two hundred fathoms had been recovered from the sea before the line parted, and from the cause referred to.

The new cable was now brought into requisition for the first time, and the Agamemnon having been signalled, the ends were spliced as before in the case of the experimental line. At a quarter to five the wheels of the machine began to revolve, and by six, two miles and a half of cable were paid out, when a signal was observed on the Agamemnon conveying the unwelcome intelligence that it had parted. This, it was afterwards understood, was caused by a change which had been made in the paying-out machine of the Agamemnon, under the direction of Messrs. Bright and Canning. The wheel leading on to the machinery was made of cast, instead of sheet-iron, and was consequently much heavier and less adapted to the work for which it was designed—simply to act as a check in preventing the too rapid passage of the cable on the paying-out sheaves. Its unfitness for the purpose became so clearly apparent from this mishap—or fortunate accident, we should perhaps say—that it was at once removed, and the sheet-iron wheel, similar to that on the Niagara, substituted.

As nothing further could now be done in the way of paying out, it was concluded to haul in, and by half-past nine the whole of our portion of the cable was recovered. A glance at the indicator or dynamometer showed a strain of a little over two tons and a half, while the first quarter of a mile was passing over the stern sheave.

Third Day.

The last experiment which was to settle the practicability of buoying up the cable, was set down for this day. To appreciate the value of this experiment, it is necessary to know that serious fears were entertained about the capability of a buoy to retain its hold upon the deep sea line when exposed to the action of the sea in a gale. The force of the waves, it was urged, would act upon it in such a manner as to cause it to give way at the point where it is joined, or some other part of the cable that may be subject to the greatest strain. An immense buoy, shaped somewhat like a segar, capable of sustaining five or six tons, and sixteen or eighteen feet in length, was put on board of each ship. This was now brought into use on board the Niagara, and attached to the cable after three and a quarter miles had been paid out. Away it went from the side of the vessel, and the moment the weight of the cable suspended from it was felt, it assumed an erect position, about two-thirds or ten feet of its length appearing above the surface of the water. A smaller buoy, called the watch buoy, had been attached to it by a rope, and the two floated off from the Niagara, which continued paying out the cable until it gave way again at a part which inspection showed was completely destroyed by the rusting of the outer wire. This occurred about half-past nine A. M. At half-past ten the watch buoy was taken up, and the ship was proceeding in the direction of the cable buoy for the purpose of hauling it on board, also, when it was observed falling from its erect position, and lying its whole length on the surface. There was only one explanation for this. The cable had parted, and the buoy relieved from the weight of it, assumed a recumbent state. When taken up, it was observed that the three and a quarter inch rope-stopper had been cut off by the working or abrasion of the cable.

This was the last experiment on the memoranda, as we have said, but it was agreed to try another before starting for Plymouth. There were some miles of experimental cable left, and as it was desirable to know how fast the wire could be laid with safety, it was concluded to employ this with that view. The engine was set to work in submerging a sufficient length or weight of it to put the wheels in motion so that the machinery would work of itself. Less than half a mile of it was submerged in this way, when the engine was detached; the paying-out wheels, being subjected to the weight of the submerged portion, commenced revolving, and as a comparatively slight pressure was put upon the brakes, the cable went out at the rate of between seven and eight miles an hour, without exhibiting the least tendency to kink. Nothing could be more satisfactory or conclusive than this last experiment, as showing the high speed at which the line can be submerged with safety; and should it be adopted by the engineer, we shall accomplish the laying of our half of the three thousand miles in somewhat less than six days.

As there was nothing more to be done, the Telegraph Squadron made as direct a line as possible for Plymouth, where it arrived at six o'clock on Thursday, the 3d of June. During the passage the Agamemnon attempted another trial of speed with the Niagara, but with no better success than she had last year. She was, in fact, rather badly beaten, and had her new commander, Captain Preedy, only known the qualities of the Niagara, he would hardly have risked another defeat. Nothing like one's own experience, however.

Report of Mr. W. E. Everett in regard to the paying-out machinery and the submerging of the Cable.

UNITED STATES STEAM FRIGATE NIAGARA,
At Sea, June 3, 1858.

CYRUS W. FIELD, General Manager of the Atlantic Telegraph Company:

SIR:—For the information of yourself and the directors, I submit the following statement of experiments made during this trip.

Monday, 4 P. M., May 31, lat. 47° 12′ N., lon. 9° 32′ W., soundings 2,530 fathoms, this ship and the Agamemnon being attached stern to stern by a hawser, 180 fathoms of cable were veered out for the end to be taken on board that ship to be spliced. At 5·30, signal being made "all ready," in accordance with previous arrangement, one mile of cable was veered out. We then commenced hauling it in. At 6·30 had recovered half a mile, when Mr. Bright's message was received saying he desired to make a new splice. At 9·40 received message "all is ready," and again commenced paying out as before. At 10·34 P. M., two miles were out. After this amount was paid out, the strain upon the cable was 3,600 to 4,100 pounds. At 11·28 commenced hauling in, but very slowly, as the strain nearly approached the breaking point of the rope. At 11·45 the hawser securing the ships together parted on the Agamemnon, but the ships were retained nearly in the same relative positions by working the engine when required. At 1·40, having hauled in one mile·506½ fathoms, the continuity was reported broken. We continued to haul in until 2·15, when the end came, having lost of the two miles paid out 110 fathoms.

On Tuesday, at 8·40 A. M., the ships having been secured and splice made as before, a quarter of a mile was paid out, hawser released and ships started ahead slowly, at the same time the cable was allowed to run quite freely until two miles had been paid out, when a gradual restraint was applied until an additional one mile 387 fathoms had been paid out, making in all three miles 387 fathoms. At this time (10·23) commenced hauling in, and had recovered 190 fathoms when the cable parted. At 4·44 P. M., the two ends of the new cable having been spliced, we paid out 2½ miles at a rate which had been previously agreed upon, the electricians passing signals through the whole length of cable. At 6·15 P. M., the Agamemnon made signal the cable was parted. We at once commenced hauling in, the strain running up to 5,100 pounds during the receiving of the first quarter of a mile. At 9·20 the end came in, having lost 80 fathoms of the 2½ miles paid out.

Wednesday, June 2, at 7·30, experimental cable was again spliced, one quarter of a mile paid out, hawser released, and the ships started ahead. In a few minutes the Agamemnon made signal cable parted. We continued to pay out until 3½ miles were out. The ship was then backed, large buoy and watch buoy attached to the cable. Ship again run ahead, and when 300 fathoms had been paid out the cable parted on the machinery. The ship then made for the buoy with the hope of recovering the end of the cable; but while hauling in the watch buoy, the large buoy suddenly fell over, showing it had separated from the cable. Upon recovering it we found the rope-stopper (3½ inch rope) had been cut off by the cable. At 12·55, by the request of Mr. Woodhouse, we paid over the end of experimental cable, to ascertain how rapidly it could be run off the coil with safety, but no greater speed was attained than seven knots, as the cable was being often stranded on the machine by the accumulation of tar in the grooves, which was so hard that no scraper could be made to remove it at any speed. All the cable used to-day was that brought from Greenwich expressly for experimenting, and was long since condemned. Undoubtedly it has been much exposed to the weather, and stowed where considerable sand or dirt has been thrown upon it. With the cable which was recovered last year, and used by us during the experiment, we had no serious difficulty in keeping the tar out of the grooves, it being comparatively soft, though the amount was beyond what I could have believed. The amount of tar on this cable is much greater than that upon the cable intended to be laid down, therefore I believe we can make such provision as that it shall not become a serious obstacle.

The result of this experimental trip has demonstrated that we have the capability of hauling in the cable to a greater extent than I had expected. Not that I believe any great distance could be recovered, but in the general depth of water where the cable is to be laid, in good weather, should a fault go overboard before the ship could be stopped, I am of the opinion sufficient of the cable may be hauled in to remedy the fault.

The operation of the machinery generally is certainly satisfactory, and there is no alteration I can suggest other than in the tar scrapers, which will require modification. The amount of tar accumulating is so much beyond what could have been expected from last year's experience, owing to the repeated coatings it has received since it was unloaded from this vessel last October, that extraordinary provision will be required. As regards the attaching of buoys, we can attach them, but at a great risk of breaking the cable, and they should not be used in deep water except as a last resort.

The arrangements for coils, provisions for leading the rope, and all the other many particulars incidental to this work, which have been under the direction of Mr. Woodhouse, do not require any alteration, and fully meet the requirements. I am, respectfully, your obedient servant,

W. E. Everett.

THE SAILING OF THE SECOND, OR THE UNSUCCESSFUL EXPEDITION OF 1858.

THE Telegraph Squadron arrived, as has been stated, at Plymouth, after the experimental trip on the 3d of June, and having received a fresh supply of coal, started for mid-ocean on the 10th of the same month. The point in mid-ocean which had been decided on as the place of rendezvous was in lat. 52° 02′, long. 33° 18′.

Each vessel had about fifteen hundred statute miles of cable on board, making a total of three thousand, or a little more than fifty per cent. over the distance to be traversed by both. The weather had been very fine, and there was every appearance that it would continue so for some weeks. In fact, the summer had now fairly set in, and we felt hopeful in the assurance given us by Lieutenant Maury, that the month of June was the mildest of all the months in the year. We now looked forward with the most sanguine expectations to the time when we should land our end at the Newfoundland terminus, and with swelling hearts thought of the enthusiastic welcome which we knew would greet us when we returned to the commercial metropolis of the Union, after the successful accomplishment of the greatest work which has ever been conceived or attempted by the genius of man. The Sunday before our departure we were visited by a friend from New York (Rev. Henry Field), who told us with what interest and anxiety our people regarded the enterprise in which we are engaged, and how eagerly they awaited the moment when the first despatch from Newfoundland should apprise them that the cable was laid. That Sunday he preached a most appropriate sermon, in the course of which he made frequent reference to the great enterprise, and to its importance not only in a material but in a moral point of view, as bringing the nations of the earth into more intimate relationship with each other. The scene was certainly one that will not be forgotten easily, and the words of the preacher made a deep impression on the minds of his hearers.

On the 10th of June, as has been stated, we left Plymouth about ten o'clock in the morning, and took the direct course for the point of rendezvous, the four ships sailing in company. The Porcupine, which was the smallest steamer in the squadron, had been sent to St. John's with orders to meet the Niagara on her way to Trinity Bay, so that besides our own vessel and the Agamemnon there were but two others, the Valorous and Gorgon, the last of which was to act as our escort. There was no public demonstration at our departure, and with the exception of a few of the members of the company and their friends, there were none to bid us farewell. In a few hours we lost sight of the landmarks along the coast, and Eddystone light, which stands upon a reef of rocks out in the channel, and about seventeen miles from Plymouth, was rapidly disappearing below the horizon. About eight o'clock the land, which was gradually becoming more indistinct, was lost amid the evening shadows, but we could still see through the hazy twilight objects at the distance of four or five miles. For the two following days the weather continued very fine; but on the third, (Sunday, June 13,) the wind, which in the morning was moderate, freshened considerably towards evening, and at night blew a perfect gale. We were not a little surprised at this, especially as we had been led to believe, from the statements of those who were supposed to know something about the subject, that we were to have had nothing but gentle breezes and smiling skies. The delusion, however, was very soon dispelled, and before the end of the gale we were pretty well tired of our sea experience, and sighed most earnestly for what some poet songster, in an unaccountable fit of enthusiasm about the ocean, has called the "dull, tame shore." It was certainly a most severe gale; but in the Niagara we could not realize its severity, and it was only when we came to hear what wild work it was nearly making with the Gorgon and Valorous, and did make with the Agamemnon, that we began to have a proper idea of its true character. During the gale we had our spritsail yard and flying-jibboom broken, and the same sea by which this damage was done dislocated the right, or, as the sailors call it, the starboard wing of the American eagle, which forms the figure head of the Niagara. The injury, however, was repaired on the first opportunity, and the national bird restored to his pristine beauty and strength. It may be interesting to know that his mate on the stern, another terribly warlike-looking fellow, had not a feather ruffled, and looks as terrible and as warlike as ever. This was the only damage inflicted upon the ship by the gale; but the fearful havoc it made among the domestic utensils of the ward-room, and particularly those of a brittle kind, would have gladdened the heart of a dealer in crockery.

On the 19th of June we had a heavy sea and some bad squalls. The barometer fell as low as 28, and stuck there with such obstinacy as to render it doubtful whether it would ever rise again as high as 30. Each day was but a repetition of the day before, and the log-book was one unvarying record of the same particulars. One day it was "blowing heavy in squalls," and the next day it was "blowing heavy in squalls," and the only change was at the end of the gale, when the reader was informed there was "a fresh gale" and "heavy sea with squalls." We had managed to keep the Agamemnon in sight till Monday, June 21, when we lost her about 7 o'clock in the morning. The sea was heavier than we had yet seen it, and we found it impossible on that account to run down to her, as we were frequently obliged to do, in consequence of her drifting so rapidly to leeward. We were actuated in this solely by considerations for the safety of our own ship, which would have been much endangered by attempting to follow her under such circumstances. On the evening of the 21st of June, the wind moderated; the barometer began to rise rapidly, and there were other pleasant indications of an agreeable change in the weather. As the barometer rose the sea fell, and the following day, according to the stereotype phrase, was "all that could be desired." We had been buffeted about long enough, and were driven nearly three degrees further north than we wished, having drifted to lat. 54° 30′, when we never intended to go higher north than lat. 52. So much for the operations of the gale. We now set out for the rendezvous, and arrived there on the afternoon of the 23d, when we found the Valorous and Gorgon there before us—the former having reached it on the 21st, and the Gorgon on the morning of the 23d. An officer came on board from the Valorous, and informed us that they, too, had had very bad weather, and that they had not seen the Agamemnon since the 13th. We were also informed that the Gorgon nearly lost both her masts, and the Valorous her quarter boats. Captains Aldham and Dayman said that it was the worst weather they had ever experienced in the North Atlantic.

This night a thick fog set in, in which we lost sight of the two escorts. The next morning, at five o'clock, Lieut. Guest, who was officer of the deck at the time, spoke a packet ship bound from Liverpool to New York. She was not in sight more than ten minutes, on account of the fog, and had she not been quite close to the ship it is doubtful whether she would have been seen at all. When Mr. Guest first saw her she was looming up through the fog.

"Where are you bound for?" said he, as soon as she came near enough to speak her.

"To New York," was the answer.

"Please to report the United States frigate Niagara."

"Aye! aye!" responded a voice which it is supposed belonged to the captain; and he immediately asked in turn: "Where are the other vessels?"

"In company around us," Mr. Guest replied.

It was supposed by this time that the other vessels and the Agamemnon were close at hand, although not visible in consequence of the fog, and it was under this impression that Mr. Guest answered as he did. There was no time for a more lengthened conversation, and the object was to make it as laconic and as much to the point as possible. The last answer was received by the captain with a wave of his hat, to which a similar pantomimic return was made, and both vessels lost sight of each other almost immediately after.

Before the close of this day we had another gale, during which it blew in heavy squalls. The morning of Friday, June 25th, however, broke clear and pleasant, and about two o'clock in the afternoon, we saw the Valorous, the Gorgon, and the Agamemnon, all on the rendezvous. At half-past four o'clock we received a visit from Captain Preedy, from whom we learned that he had reached the rendezvous at twelve o'clock. He also reported severe weather, and said that during the gale, of which we have already spoken, the upper part of the main coil, which contained a thousand miles of cable, had shifted, and that for some time they were in a very perilous condition. About a hundred miles had to be removed and coiled on another part of the ship; and as soon as the coiling of this was finished he would be ready to make the splice and commence the work of paying out. Some idea of the effects of the gale on the Agamemnon may be conceived from the fact that the strain to which she was exposed by the great weight and peculiar nature of her cargo, opened her water ways about two inches and a half. The water ways are that part of the ship where the deck and the sides are joined, and when they part to any great extent, the vessel is considered in a dangerous state. Captain Preedy finding it impossible to keep the ship's head to the sea, on account of the shifting and working of the cable in the main coil, determined to scud before the gale, which he was obliged to do for thirty-six hours. The scene on board was reported to have been fearful. The ship rolled very heavily, and at one time nearly every man on deck was thrown off his feet; one man, a marine, was literally frightened out of his wits, and was crazy for some days. One man had his arm fractured in two places, and another had his leg broken. Every eye was turned on Captain Preedy, who, fully aware of the imminence of the danger, exhibited the greatest coolness and self-possession, and finally succeeded by his admirable seamanship in saving his vessel. It was peculiarly gratifying to see him once more, and to know that he was ready to go on with the work. In the midst of the fearful scene that took place on the Agamemnon a rather ludicrous incident occurred, which must not be omitted. One of the landsmen, who, it would appear, had very little experience of the sea, had not been seen for a long time, and his friends, anxious about him, searched all over the ship in their endeavors to discover his whereabouts; their efforts, however, were unsuccessful, and they were just giving up all hope of ever seeing him again, when some one suggested that the bread closet had not been looked into. The idea of his being in such a place was treated with contempt, but it was decided, however, to take a peep at it. The door was accordingly opened, and there, snugly ensconced in a corner, was the individual who had caused all the anxiety and trouble. It was never discovered why he went there, but some people are uncharitable enough to say that he had designs upon the provisions.

COMMENCEMENT OF THE WORK.

SATURDAY—JUNE 26.

The state of the weather was most propitious for the beginning of the work, and we all felt anxious to see the splice lowered into the water. It had been agreed upon that it should be made on the Agamemnon, and that as soon as they had begun to pay out a red flag should be hoisted as a signal that we should do the same. The splicing was one of the most important and at the same time one of the simplest operations connected with the work of laying the cable. The process may be divided into three distinct branches—the joining of the copper core or conductor, the insulation with gutta percha, and the splicing of the outer protecting wire. The gutta percha is stripped off the conductor to the length of about two inches on both ends, which are laid over each other, and bound with copper wire, as is seen in figure 4 of the annexed engraving:

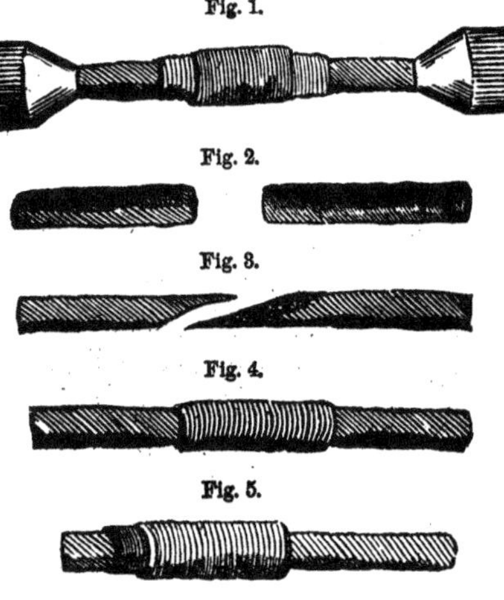

Fig. 6.

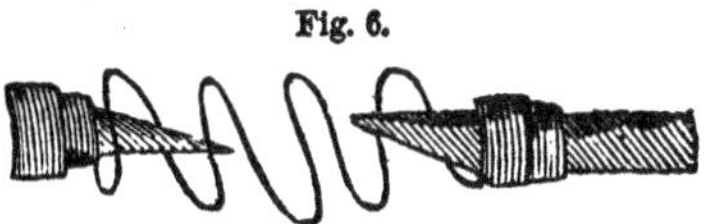

Over this again is laid another binding of copper wire, and the soldering repeated, so that the part which is spliced by being thus strengthened is made stronger than any other. This double binding is seen in figures 1 and 5, the ends having been previously prepared as they appear in figures 2 and 3. The great advantage of this manner of splicing will be at once perceived by reference to figure 6, which shows that in the event of the rupture of the splice the connection is still kept up by the single wire, which in this case being in contact with the several ends preserves the electrical continuity. Should there be any so skeptical as to disbelieve this, it ought to be sufficient for them to know that were the wire eleven times smaller than the small strand of seven wires which form the core, its power as a conductor of the electrical current is reduced only one thirty-seventh part in a whole mile. The splicing is completed by the insulation of the core with three layers of gutta percha, each of which is about as thick as ordinary foolscap. Layer after layer of this is laid on till it is brought to a uniform surface with the rest of the gutta percha insulation, after which the outer protecting wire is laid on and bound in a somewhat similar manner to the splicing of the conductor. To the splice when thus formed is attached a crescent-shaped piece of wood, about eight feet in length, through a groove, in which the cable is placed, and in which it is secured by a flat piece of sheet-iron of the same length and form as the wood. The spliced portion is in the centre of the wood, but to prevent any strain upon it a strong iron-bound loop is made of the cable at either end of the crescent, and these two loops are afterwards fastened by an iron shackle, which takes all the strain off the splice. This operation took about two hours, and the moment it was finished the hawser which held the two vessels was released, and the process of paying out commenced. The continuity was tested by the electricians and found to be perfect, and we had submerged something like two miles and a half of the cable when it parted on the machine. The cause of its fracture in this instance was very simple, and by proper attention might very easily have been avoided. The cable was allowed to run on the machine too slack, so that the leading on part of it got into the wrong groove, and in the endeavor to put it back into its proper position it was thrown off the wheels altogether, and, falling down on the tar scraper, was broken. The break of continuity was soon discovered on the Agamemnon, and both ships immediately returned and made a new splice, when the work of paying out was once more resumed. This time there was no running of the cable into the wrong groove, and the utmost caution and vigilance were exercised over the machinery. About half-past six nearly ten miles were paid out from both ships, and at eight the two vessels lost sight of each other. The electricians were at their post, and reported the continuity "all right." The cable was going out at the rate of five and six miles an hour, while the speed of the ship varied from four to five, so that by midnight thirty-one miles had been submerged. This certainly looked like work, and augured favorably for our success. Our hopes, however, were destined to be shortlived, for about ten minutes to 1 A. M. of the following morning the continuity was destroyed. How this was done could not be satisfactorily explained, but the general supposition on board the ship was that it was caused by the parting of the cable on the Agamemnon.

SUNDAY, June 27.—The continuity, as has been stated, ceased at ten minutes to one o'clock this morning, and after about thirty-one miles of cable had been paid out. The vessels had long since ran out of sight of each other, and it would, perhaps, require another day before they could return to the rendezvous. After the electric communication was severed the speed of the ship was reduced to less than two miles, and the cable paid out at a proportionate rate for three hours. This was considered a sufficient length of time to allow for the probability of its returning; but being now thoroughly convinced that it was gone forever, the action of the machinery was reversed, and they commenced winding in. About a hundred fathoms had been recovered when the cable parted, the amount lost in this second attempt being forty-two miles and 300 fathoms. The Gorgon was informed by signal of the disaster, and both vessels proceeded on their course to the rendezvous. The ill success which had thus far attended the expedition was very discouraging, and as we were altogether ignorant of the cause of the loss of continuity we were growing very doubtful about our chances of success. Some were under the delusion that the difficulty was created by the brakes, the prejudice against which still existed from the first expedition, when the cable was broken by the defective machinery; but this part of our paying-out machine was perfect, and realized all the expectations that were formed of it. It was impossible, however, to disabuse the minds of those who had conceived this prejudice of its injustice. It was their belief that the weights on the brakes, which never exceeded nineteen hundred pounds, produced a heavier strain than the cable was calculated to bear, and that it stretched until the inner core or electrical conductor parted, thus destroying the continuity. Finding prose too dull and heavy to express their feelings on the subject, they invoked the aid of the muse, and gave vent to their feelings in the following remarkable piece of composition:

Pay it out, oh! pay it out,
  As long as you are able;
For if you put the darned breaks on,
  Pop goes the cable.

It was intended to be a parody on the popular song of "Pop goes the Weasel," but after one verse the muse became exhausted, refused to get off another, and literally broke down. The brakes were put on in a poetical sense, and the composer found that he could not continue to "pay it out."

The Alice Munroe, a packet ship bound from Liverpool to Boston, was spoken about ten o'clock this morning, and a boat sent out with Mr. Field and Lieutenant Gherardi. Mr. Field gave a brief account to the captain of the proceedings of the expedition. He was also entrusted with a large number of letters to be put in the Post Office on his arrival in Boston, in the hope that our friends would hear from us before we could reach Newfoundland. A few hours after, the Alice Munroe was out of sight, and we resumed our course for the rendezvous.

MONDAY, June 28.—We were on the look out the whole morning and a portion of the afternoon for the Agamemnon and Valorous, and as there was no appearance of either of them, we felt somewhat apprehensive about seeing them at all this day. The Gorgon was also out of sight, but we naturally supposed that she was cruising around in the hope of falling in with one or both, as they very seldom lost track of each other. The weather was every thing we could desire; the sea was comparatively smooth, and it was just the very time to make a splice. The ill success of our two first attempts, it is true, was rather discouraging, but it was resolved that as long as we had sufficient cable to justify us in trying again and again, and sufficient coal with which to make the passage from the rendezvous to each side, we should not abandon the expedition. The failure which attended the first was purely the result of an accident, but it was very different with the second; and as no satisfactory or reliable explanation could be given as to the cause, our confidence in the ultimate success of the undertaking was terribly shaken. Various were the surmises and conjectures in regard to the subject. One was of opinion that too great a strain had been put upon the cable, and that either while on its way to, or resting on, the bottom, the conductor parted and the continuity was thus destroyed. Another believed that it was cut by lying on the top of a sharp rock; but the fact that the soundings both of Lieutenant Berryman and Commander Dayman prove that the bottom on this part of the plateau consists of ooze, is a sufficient refutation of this theory. Mr. De Sauty, one of the principal electricians, expressed his belief that the cable was broken on board the Agamemnon, while his associate, Mr. Laws, thought it had given way near the splice. Our anxiety to have this disputed point settled by the appearance of the Agamemnon became painfully intense, and the feeling was rather increased than diminished when she made her appearance. We had made up our minds upon two points—first, if the cable parted on the Agamemnon, the prevention of such an occurrence might be found in the increased vigilance and carefulness of those having charge of the work; second, but if it gave way on the bottom our ignorance of the cause must consequently render us totally unable to provide against it. What, therefore, was our dismay, when we heard from the Agamemnon that the break had not taken place on board that ship, and that they had supposed it happened on the Niagara. But this is anticipating, and we will, therefore, proceed in the regular order of our narrative.

The Agamemnon hove in sight at two o'clock in the afternoon, in company with the Valorous, and about two hours after the Gorgon became visible. There was no mistaking the line of battle ship, with her heavy massive hull looming above the horizon, as she was driven forward under an immense cloud of canvas. Nearer and nearer she came, until her two long white streaks could be plainly distinguished, and in little more than an hour from the time she was first seen she was within a few hundred yards of our ship, exchanging signals with us. The following question was asked from the Niagara as she came near enough to read our numbers:

"How did the cable part?"

To which she replied—

"The cable did not part—current ceased."

Thus were our worst fears realized—it must have given way on some part of the bottom, whether at or near the splice it was impossible to decide. The current had ceased. This was our case too—it was the same story on board of both vessels; but there was no use in further conjecture, or in repining over what could not now be avoided. There was but one course left, and that was to splice again and make another, and what we fondly hoped would be, a final attempt. Those on board the Agamemnon had evidently come to the same conclusion, as was shown by the signal which they displayed, and which, translated from the numbers, read as follows:

"Are you ready to splice?"

To this an affirmative was at once returned, and preparations were immediately made to enter once more upon the great work we had undertaken. Our confidence, however, as we have stated, in the prospect of success, was greatly impaired. The Valorous sent her two boats to the Niagara to receive the hawser which was to connect her with the Agamemnon preparatory to making the splice, and in the mean time a boat was sent from the Niagara to the last-named ship, with Lieut. North, Mr. Field, Mr. Everett, and Mr. De Sauty. At the interview of Mr. Field with the engineers on the British cable ship the following agreement was drawn up and signed:

AGAMEMNON, June 28, 1858.

Should any accident occur to part the cable before the ships have run one hundred miles from rendezvous—viz, N. lat. 62° 62′; W. long. 33° 18′—ships to return to rendezvous and wait eight days, when, if the other ships do not appear, then to proceed to Queenstown.

If ships (Niagara and Agamemnon) should return to rendezvous they will at once make the splice and proceed paying out, not waiting for either the Valorous or Gorgon.

CYRUS W. FIELD,
WM. THOMSON,
CHAS. T. BRIGHT,
S. CANNING,
W. E. EVERETT.

During the absence of Mr. Field the work of connecting the two vessels by a hawser, and of making the splice, was successfully and promptly performed, so that by half-past seven, the time at which the red flags were displayed on both ships, the process of paying out for the third time was commenced. The wheels revolved very slowly at first, as if they were living sentient beings, and were imbued with the general feeling of the caution which had taken possession of every one. A slight commotion of the water around the stern of each ship showed that they were both under way, although they hardly seemed to move. The engineers were determined that the cable should have a fair chance to reach the bottom before it was subject to any strain. As soon, however, as a sufficient length had been paid out the speed was slightly augmented, and by nine o'clock the distance was gradually increased at the rate of some five miles an hour, each ship going at two miles and a half in the same time. The evening, which in this northern latitude is so much lengthened out as to leave little or no night, was now setting in, and the mists, closing over the Agamemnon, like a huge veil, rendered her huge hull but dimly visible, while the upper portion of her lofty spars had entirely disappeared. The Valorous had taken her position on the starboard bow, and our little escort, the Gorgon, had resumed her post as our guide. It was a beautiful evening, more beautiful than any we had yet been favored with since we left Plymouth, and the severe gale through which we had passed, and which was yet fresh in our minds, gave us a more thorough appreciation of it than we might otherwise have felt. At ten o'clock the Agamemnon was dimly visible, and in less than half an hour we lost sight of her altogether, as she steamed on her eastward course. No accident had yet occurred to interrupt the work; but we almost dreaded to think of the future, lest it should have some other misfortune still in store for us. Nothing could be more satisfactory than the manner in which the machinery worked, and the process of paying-out was going on most successfully, but we could know nothing of the agencies that were at work, perhaps at the bottom of the ocean, to overthrow what little hope or prospect of success was yet left. Were there sharp pointed rocks lying on that plateau which Lieut. Maury had told us was a level plain, a great submarine prairie, or was it covered with a soft coating of mud or ooze, in which it had been said the cable might rest undisturbed for years, as on a bed of down? The soundings of Lieut. Berryman and Captain Dayman show that at least this part of the plateau is covered with this soft, and for our purpose, invaluable deposit.

It is now twelve o'clock, and the work is progressing in splendid style —in such splendid style, in fact, that, to use the frequent phrase on board, stock has gone up nearly a hundred per cent. The question is asked, if we can lay forty miles of it successfully, what is to prevent us from laying a thousand, should this fine weather continue?—and as we know of nothing, it is generally agreed that it is practicable. Ah, but then the cable is such a delicate thing, and is, therefore so liable to injury, for if, by any accident, a hole, through which it would be impossible to force even a hair, were to be made in it as far as the conductor, the insulation and electrical continuity of the whole three thousand miles would be gone forever. Then again the slightest accident arising from the carelessness of the men might defeat the whole undertaking just when we were within a hundred miles of Newfoundland. One thing, however, is certain—that every day which brings us nearer to our terminus reduces the risks and chances of failure, while the increasing prospects of success will render the engineers more vigilant and cautious. Looking at the magnitude of the enterprise and the wonderful results which must attend its successful termination, our triumph seems almost too much to expect, and we are hourly haunted with a dread that the worst has yet to happen. Every one who can spare the time from his other duties seems to regard the paying-out machine as under his special supervision, and visits it as often as those duties will allow. The same feeling prevails alike among the officers and men, and although there is a rule that none but the engineers shall be allowed to approach within a certain distance, yet they are content with a glance at its operations if they are satisfied that the cable is going out in good order. The parting of the cable, however, is not—as has been shown by our experience on this expedition—the only thing to be dreaded. There is yet another point which is a cause of as much, if not more, disquietude. Let the cable be laid across the plateau, yet, if the little strand of seven copper wires which compose the electrical conductor should be broken, the whole line is absolutely valueless, and the million and-a-half dollars expended in its purchase, might as well have been submerged in the ocean. There is no word perhaps in the English language which was fraught with such important meaning to those engaged on the first expedition as the term "continuity;" and even those who had not the slightest pretensions to scientific knowledge soon learned to appreciate its significance. We approach the electricians' office with a feeling of dread, lest at any moment some one may come out to inform the engineers that the continuity is lost. Let one of the operators inquire for either of the principal electricians and in a few minutes he will have a crowd of eager inquirers about him, all anxious to know if there is any thing wrong with the cable. Talk of the mental excitement of the gambler in comparison with that state of anxiety and suspense in which the mind is kept while the process of paying-out the cable is going on. The machinery may be working in the most satisfactory manner; but as we have shown, it does not depend on the machine alone, for there may be other agencies at work on the bottom of the ocean of which we are at present in ignorance. There is no reason as yet to say positively that there are; but the cause of the break of continuity the first time on this expedition still remains in uncertainty and doubt. The most reasonable theory is, that the outer wires were untwisted in the process of laying, and that the strand of copper wires of which the conductor is composed, parted under the excessive strain to which they were subjected. Whatever theories may be formed in regard to the way in which the continuity was destroyed, and whatever apprehensions may be felt in regard to the final success of the undertaking, the admirable manner in which the operation of paying-out is performed, and the gratifying reports which come from the telegraph office, are certainly calculated to inspire confidence and hope. Stepping upon the poop of our ship, one can trace the long black line of cable as it passes over the stern and enters the water. It is now going out at the rate of about five miles and a half an hour, while the speed of the ship is four and a half; so that the part that is now seen running out over the stern will take something like half an hour to reach the bottom, which lies at a depth of about two miles beneath us. The strain upon it is nineteen hundred pounds, which some say is too much, but which the engineers of the company insist is the very least that can be used. By reducing the weight to a still less amount they contend it would be impossible to prevent the cable from running out perfectly slack, and the loss of a much greater length than the surplus provided over and above the distance between the two points of connection in Ireland and Newfoundland. There is, in fact, a great difference of opinion on this point, and each party holds to its belief with the greatest tenacity. Says one party—those in favor of a strain being put upon the cable—" We might as well not attempt to lay it at all as to lay it without a strain; it would be expending cable to no purpose, and we should not have enough to reach land with."

" Yes," the other party reply, " but the difficulty is in your putting on too great a weight."

" Too great a weight!" is the rejoinder, " why certainly nineteen hundred pounds cannot be called too great a weight."

" You may think not; but look at the cable as it goes over the stern, and observe how many turns it takes before it reaches the water."

This is a feature which appears rather unfavorable, whatever may be the result, and it is well to speak of it here, on account of the importance which some attach to it. The number of turns the cable takes opposite to the twist is eleven in a length of one hundred feet, which is the distance between the stern and the surface of the water. Now, as it is contended, if it takes so many in a hundred feet, will not the outer wires be wholly unlaid before the cable reaches the bottom, and will not the whole strain be brought upon the gutta percha and the conductor?

Whatever party is right, those for or those against the strain, there is no difference of opinion in regard to the successful manner in which the work is going on to-night, or rather this morning, for it is now past one o'clock. The men are as watchful as men can be, and it will certainly be through no indifference or neglect on their part if any mishap should befall the cable. The coilers are in the circle wide awake and on the look out for kinks, with the determination to "squash" them the moment they make their appearance, while the tar gatherers, who look after the grooves of the different wheels over which the cable passes, are determined that none of the black and glutinous stuff shall interfere with its progress. Every thing is going on well; all appear to be doing their best towards the promotion of the undertaking; and having now laid some twenty-five miles successfully, there appear to be no reasons why we should not lay twenty five or a thousand more with equal success. And so with this conclusive argument we retire for the night, and after turning about from one side to the other for at least an hour, in our efforts to go to sleep, we at last succeed, and dream about cable laying, and the terrible effects of too great a strain, till the colored boy Thomas wakes us with the information that it is now seven bells, and that in half an hour breakfast will be on the table.

TUESDAY, June 29th.—The first question which every one asks on awakening is about the cable, and on being informed that it is all right, he is satisfied, until he gets his breakfast, when it is to be presumed he is still more satisfied. Such a question, however, is entirely superfluous, if the individual hangs up his hammock anywhere within the sound of the delightful and harmonious music made by the machine. He can hear for himself, and if he should happen to ask it is simply that he may have the pleasure of being informed of what he knows already, like most men who think they never can hear good news repeated too often. Every thing seems favorable at present for the success of the expedition; the weather never looked more propitious, and the barometer is up so high that it appears as if fixed for the remainder of the summer. The late gale was evidently the closing up of the windy season, which, in these latitudes, renders navigation rather an unpleasant occupation. Had the poet who was so anxious for "life on the ocean wave, and a home on the rolling deep," been with us in that eight days' blow, he would have been perfectly satisfied, and perhaps a little more desirous for a fixed habitation. We were not a little astonished at its duration when we remembered that it was in the mild and balmy month of June, which Lieut. Maury informs us is the best for laying the cable, if gales alone are to be taken into the account. His calculations, however, have proved in our case to be terribly astray, and have been partly the cause of the expedition sailing in this month. Had we but known what was in store for us, and that by delaying our departure for two or three weeks we would have escaped the most severe weather we have yet experienced, we certainly would not have sailed before the latter part of June or the commencement of July. However, as has been stated, we are at last favored with good weather, although not so pleasant as could be desired. It is very seldom during the day that the sun is visible, and the fog is one of our most frequent and unwelcome visitors. But no matter; let us lay the cable this time, and all these little annoyances will soon be forgotten.

At ten o'clock this morning, the length of the cable paid out was about eighty miles, and the whole amount submerged between the two ships, at least one hundred and sixty. This is certainly doing well, and as there is apparently nothing to prevent us from doing this way all the time, confidence is reviving rapidly. The continuity is still perfect, and the electricians report that the signals which are passing between the ships are very satisfactory. No messages are transmitted, as it was agreed before starting that none should be sent. The object of this is to prevent the possibility of those errors which might arise from imperfect manipulation of the operators, or difficulties from the substitution of a more complex form of instrument than is required merely for the transmission of signals. By adopting the present plan, the electricians have not only prevented the occurrence of mistakes from such a cause, but they have succeeded in securing the most perfect way of ascertaining the electrical condition of the conductor. Now it is merely necessary to look at the needle to be assured that the continuity is perfect and that the signals are passing through the whole length of the cable. A great deal of interest centres around the electricians' office, and although there are few, if any, who are scientific enough to understand the various operations that are going on therein, there are none who are disposed to undervalue their importance. The door is almost always shut, and the electricians pursue their work undisturbed; but it is impossible to exclude that spirit of inquiry which will satiate its thirst for information even through a keyhole. The office, which is of the most limited dimensions, has been fitted up alongside of the wardroom coil, and that part of the top of the coil which overlooks it affords a complete view of the movements of the electricians and of the instrument which tells them all about the continuity. The slender piece of steel which is attached to the centre of the dial that stands on the little bench before you, never fails to indicate the condition of the conductor. If there is no current passing through the cable, the piece of steel is perfectly motionless; but the moment a wave is sent through the conductor it exhibits unmistakable signs of activity, and refuses to return to its former quiescent state till the subtle current ceases to pass from ship to ship.

Various reports are current among the sailors in regard to the operations of the electricians and the mysterious performances which are supposed to be going on in the little office. The continuity is something they don't exactly understand, but they are fully aware of its importance, and know as well as the most learned that when it is gone the further laying of the cable is only a loss of time and a useless expenditure of money. Their interest in the work appears to increase every day, and although they will be the least gainers by its success they are none the less anxious to witness its triumphant termination. The cable guard—that is, the body of men by whom the cable was coiled—appear to have taken the whole enterprise under their special charge, and when among their associates who were not so fortunate as to have been enlisted in the service, speak in the tone of Sir Oracles upon every thing connected with the subject, and are regarded by some of their messmates as undisputed authority. There are certainly none on the ship more willing to do whatever is required of them, and none that should be more substantially remembered by the Atlantic Telegraph Company. They have performed the hardest part of the work, and as long as there was a foot of the cable to be coiled they were always ready. As the paying-out process does not require so many, their number has been reduced from over a hundred to about sixty, and the greater part of these are engaged on the coils, looking out for kinks—certainly an easy task compared with that on which they were formerly employed. There they stand, watching the cable as it is unwound at the rate of five and six miles an hour, and passes out over the cone on its way to the paying-out machine. Turn after turn is unwound, faster than a man can walk, until there is not more than six flakes left. The superintendent of the coil now calls out to the man who is at the speaking tube which extends to the engine room to "go slow," an order he immediately repeats through the tube to the engineer on watch. The speed of the ship is at once reduced, the cable is paid out at a diminished rate, and as the last flake goes up, and as the centre of the coil—where the turns are perhaps six times less than near its circumferences—is reached, the danger of kinking is entirely obviated. This process is performed every time a new flake is commenced, as the rate of paying out from the centre—where the turns are not more than seven or eight feet in diameter—cannot, of course, be carried on safely with the same rapidity as at those points where the diameter of the turns varies from ten to forty feet. The coil is already reduced to one-half its original size, and adding what was paid out at the fatal termination of the second attempt, nearly one hundred and thirty tons of cable have been deposited at the bottom of the ocean. The remainder will probably be payed out between twelve and one o'clock to-night, should no accident occur. Then there will be an exciting time, and the commencement on a new coil will be watched with intense interest, for the transfer from one cable circle to another is an operation which is sometimes attended with risk. All the preliminary preparations, however, have been made; the men thoroughly understand the nature of the operation, and it is almost impossible for an accident to take place. As there is considerable anxiety, however, exhibited in regard to its success, there won't be much sleeping done until it is all over. Although the machinery is working perfectly, and the angle the cable makes with the water shows that nothing is to be apprehended from the strain, the electricians' office is watched with an uneasy feeling, and the movements of the electricians themselves are eagerly followed, as if their very thoughts could be read therefrom. "Well, Mr. de Sauty," says one of the most anxious of the cable layers—"well, how is the continuity now?" "Capital, and the signals are coming out in grand style," he replies; and adds, "I hope they will continue so"—a hope in which it is almost needless to say every one indulges. The vessel was going about four miles and a half an hour at six o'clock, and the expenditure of cable is about a mile more, the strain being nineteen hundred pounds, or a little less than one-fourth the amount the cable is calculated to bear. Nine o'clock has struck, and the writer has just sat down in one of the little rooms of the wardroom to record the occurrences of the day in his note-book, when he hears a hasty step outside across the floor, and some one asking in a hurried, nervous manner for Mr. Laws. There is something in both that tells him all is not right, and in a few minutes more his worst fears are realized. The continuity is gone again, although the cable still goes out over the stern in the same style, and there is no indication, so far as appears from the operation of the machinery that there is any thing wrong. But the little magnetic needle in the electricians' office—the unerring indicator of the electrical condition of the cable—refuses to move, and the electricians, after going through all the tests, have at last to succumb. The continuity is gone, and they find it impossible to restore it, although they may use all the appliances of the wonderful science they have at command. It was subsequently, on the return of the squadron to Queenstown, found that the accident was caused by the parting of the cable a few feet from the stern of the Agamemnon.

After all hope of the continuity being restored was abandoned, a most satisfactory test was made in regard to the strength of the cable. The process of paying-out was stopped for about an hour and a half during which the Niagara was literally held by it, the wind blowing fresh all the time. A pressure of over four tons was put upon the brakes, and it absolutely seemed impossible to break the cable. At length it gave way, after holding the ship, as we have said, an hour and an half, and resisting a strain of over four tons which was put upon the brakes. The amount of cable paid out was 142 miles and 280 fathoms, and the total amount lost in the three attempts was 190 miles and 257 fathoms, while the distance run in the last attempt was 109 nautical miles. This is a loss of 21 per cent, or about two-fifths of the surplus which was allowed for excessive expenditure in laying the cable. We have now on board 1,090½ nautical miles, which, added to a similar length on the Agamemnon, makes a total of nearly 2,200 nautical miles.

THE STORM.

The severe gale through which we passed was so little felt on board our ship, that we could not realize its terrible force until we heard of its effects on the Agamemnon. As, however, those who were on board of her during the storm are best qualified to describe the scenes and incidents which occurred during those eight long and anxious days of its continuance, we will let them tell the story. The following vivid and thrilling account is from the pen of Mr. Wood, the special correspondent of the London Times:

At half-past twelve, on Monday morning, the 12th July, the Agamemnon anchored off Queenstown, after having, as your readers are now aware, failed in the attempt to submerge the Atlantic cable. The arrival of the Niagara must have made known the bare fact that the cable had parted, and the tremendous gales and unfavorable weather which all the squadron had to contend against, more or less, though only those on board the Agamemnon can be said to know the real nature of the peril which was encountered, and the long series of difficulties, mishaps, and misfortunes which marked almost the entire cruise from first to last. Not often have so many adverse and disheartening circumstances been crammed into a voyage of thirty-three days, and never have the enterprise, skill, and courage of all connected with the undertaking been more conspicuously displayed than in overcoming each obstacle as it arose, almost with every day. The next thing to success is to deserve it; and certainly, if any scheme was ever entitled to prosper from the perseverance and devotion of those engaged in carrying it out, that success was unquestionably due to the efforts of all on board the Agamemnon in favor of the undertaking. For once, however, fortune did not favor the bold. The attempt to lay the cable failed three times, and once in the most mysterious manner; and those on board have only the satisfaction of knowing that every thing that care and foresight could suggest was done. Beyond this consciousness that all has been achieved that was possible with such materials, no comfort is to be gleaned from the late attempts, except, perhaps, in the fact that as much wire or more still remains than the expedition was commenced with last year, and that both vessels will start again for another and a last attempt the instant they have filled up with coal—that is, by Saturday next at latest.

Your readers are already aware both the "wire" ships quitted England in the most unfavorable trim possible for bad weather. According to appearances at starting, however, bad weather seemed of all others the risk least likely to be encountered, so every thing had been foreseen, prognosticated, and provided for but a gale; that, of course, was out of the question. That traditional veteran, Brown, of the Translantic line, who had weathered so many storms in the Atlantic, showed how in June one never had occurred, while Jones proved how it wouldn't, and Robinson made "all serene" by demonstrating clearly how it couldn't happen. We might meet light winds and encounter some delay from calms and sultry weather, but a gale—a regular Atlantic storm—the very idea was food for laughter. So the wire squadron went to sea, with the two chief vessels laden almost to the water's edge, and in all other respects so little fitted for rough water, that, had a tithe of the tremendous weather they experienced been foreseen at home, not a ship would have moved from Plymouth Sound. The Agamemnon had 2,840 tons dead weight in her, a monstrous load for any ship of her tonnage, but made still more dangerous and overbearing by the manner in which it was stowed. In her hold was the main coil, a compact mass of 1,100 miles in length, and therefore 1,100 tons in weight. On her orlop deck, right forward, between the eyes, as sailors say, was another coil of 100 tons, while on her upper deck, and also right forward, was a coil of 236 tons. The latter was of sufficient size to interfere seriously with the proper working of the vessel from the deck, and the united weights of all, of course, brought the Agamemnon down by the head to an almost unsafe extent. The two small coils, it was said, counteracted the weight of the ponderous mass in the bottom of the ship, and certainly, if they did not tend to check the vessel's rolling, they made it easier and less dangerous to the masts. When the ship did roll, however, there was a constant struggle between the weights at the bottom and the weights at the top, and the ship's sides, as the levers along which the force of both was exerted and resisted, suffered in proportion. This, however, was not the evil of the upper deck coil, nor the reason which, after the bad weather had set in, made it an object of constant anxiety and almost of dread to all on board. It was bad enough to cruise with a dead weight forward of some 250 tons, a weight under which her deck planks gaped an inch apart, and her beams threatened daily to give way; but when to these evils was added the fear in bad weather that in some of her heavy rolls the whole mass would slip and take the vessel's side out, it will be seen that in the whole the precious coil was justly esteemed the *bête noire* of the entire affair—the millstone about the necks of all. However, as we have said, nobody thought of these things when on the morning of the 10th of June the squadron quitted Plymouth. It was then to be a yachting cruise—a mere summer-trip—and any talk of waterproofs and sou'westers would not have been more out of place in a drawing-room than on the deck of the Agamemnon. The day favored this illusion. The barometer stood at 30 64, the weather was hot and sultry, and after all sail had been set and re-set and every naval artifice adopted to catch the breeze that would not come, Captain Preedy reluctantly (for we had little more than coal for the voyage home) gave orders to get up steam. The Niagara, having plenty of coal, had the advantage of being always under steam, and the Valorous and Gorgon did mostly as the Agamemnon. Friday was the ditto of the previous day. The same coquettish breeze came fluttering through the rigging now and then, and it was "Hands, up screw and make sail," and "down screw and shorten sail," all day, till even Capt. Preedy wearied in his efforts to save fuel. Every one wished for a breeze, and there were some who, never having been at sea before, muttered rash hopes that they might rather meet an Atlantic gale; and their wishes were gratified as it turned out far more than the people who expressed them wished. Saturday the weather was cold and dull, but the breeze was so *prononcé*, that the screw was finally hoisted, and the fires raked out, while the Agamemnon, under royals and studding sails, went through the water at a rare pace, sending the foam from her bows and leaving a broad trail of still water upon the angry sea behind. What could be better?

It became less enjoyable towards noon, when the wind and sea got up as the glass went down, and the water grew darker, and the clouds on the horizon were merged into a dirty haze, thickening towards the sea, and boding very ill, indeed, to a summer cruise. Before evening came the sail on the ship was reduced to half, for the wind was up, with squally gusts of heavy rain, and the barometer had gone below 29, and was still falling rapidly. Such was the night; but Sunday told its own tale, for even those least versed in the boisterous premonitory symptoms of an Atlantic gale could see at a glance that we were in for it. The sky seemed a wretched mist—half rain, half vapor—through which the other vessels of the squadron loomed faintly like shadows, watery and unsubstantial as the Flying Dutchman. The sea had changed its bright crisp blue for a turgid foamy aspect, and the great waves of the Atlantic came rolling towards us in tremendous succession, like hills of water with their tops all jagged and broken by the fierce wind, and their white crests of foam blown out into a stream of feathery spray that almost hid the huge dark gulfs between them. The Agamemnon, however, still kept on her way, rolling and straining heavily, and giving all a fair foretaste of what they might expect when the gale set in worse, for the wind was fast going round to the southwest, and it was evident we were only at the beginning. There was Divine service that day on the main deck, and, as officers and men sat in respectful silence, every change in the fast increasing violence of the gale could be distinctly noted through the open hatchways. Heavy rain was falling, and a grayish-looking scud was flying across the sky with inconceivable rapidity; and every rope and shroud, tautened to the utmost, was humming with a loud and clear noise, as if ten thousand accordeons were going at once, while now and then, as the ship fetched up near the wind, her great sails flapped and slotted like peals of thunder, jerking the vessel with an uneasy vibration, as if the masts were coming out of her. Still, among the little congregation, no one moved more than was necessary to keep his seat as the ship lurched over, and the service proceeded as little disturbed by the war of elements outside as if all were assembled within the walls of a cathedral. Towards the end, however, Capt. Preedy looked up wistfully through the hatchway once or twice, scrutinizing the masts and sails with a keen glance, for the storm was getting worse and the air darker and thicker every minute, and the hoarse roar through the rigging was drowning every other sound. Service over, and it was "Hands, reef topsails;" then again, after a little lapse, the same cry; and yet again, till at four in the afternoon the Agamemnon was rushing through the foam under close-reefed topsails and foresail. At half-past four we caught the last glimpse of the Gorgon, as making a long stretch to windward she was lost in the misty darkness that marked the horizon. At five the Valorous began to drop astern, and by six she also had disappeared; but still the Niagara and Agamemnon held on together—the former under sail and steam, the latter, like all the English vessels, under sail alone. Of the two vessels specially appointed to convoy and assist, if necessary, the Agamemnon and Niagara, we saw no more till all danger was past and the squadron had re-assembled at the rendezvous some twelve days afterwards. On Sunday night the gale seemed at its worst. The ocean resembled one vast snowdrift, the whitish glare from which, reflected on the dark clouds that almost rested on the sea, had a tremendous and unnatural effect, as if the ordinary laws of nature had been reversed by the storm.

The Niagara, which had hitherto kept close, began to give us a very wide berth, and, as darkness increased, she too went out of sight, and it was every one for themselves. There must be many of your readers who know what a line-of-battle ship is in a gale of wind, though such experience would give them but a faint notion of how the Agamemnon went at it all that night. She strained and labored under her heavy burden as if she were breaking up, and the massive beams under her upper deck coil cracked and snapped with a noise resembling that of small artillery, almost drowning the hideous roar of the wind as it moaned and howled through the rigging, jerking and straining the little stormsails as though it meant to tear them from the yards. Those in the improvised cabins on the main deck had little sleep that night, for the upper deck planks above them were working themselves free, as sailors say, and, beyond a doubt, they were infinitely more free than easy, for they groaned under the pressure of the coil with a dreadful uproar, and availed themselves of the opportunity to let in a little light, with a good deal of water, at every roll. The sea, too, kept striking with dull heavy violence against the vessel's bows, forcing its way through hawse holes and ill closed ports with a heavy slush, and thence, hissing and winding aft, it roused the occupants of the cabins aforesaid to a knowledge that their floors were under water, and that the flotsam and jetsam noises they heard beneath were only caused by their outfit for the voyage taking a cruise of its own in some five or six inches of dirty bilge. Such was Sunday night, and such was a fair average of all the nights throughout the week, varying only from bad to worse.

Daybreak on Monday ushered in as fierce a gale as ever swept over the Atlantic. The barometer was lower, and, as a matter of course, the wind and sea were infinitely higher than the day before. It was singular, but at twelve o'clock the sun pierced through the pall of clouds and shone brilliantly for half an hour, and during that brief time it blew as it has not often blown before. So fierce was this gust that its roar drowned every other sound, and it was almost impossible to give the watch the necessary orders for taking in the close reefed foresail, which, when furled, almost left the Agamemnon under bare poles, though still surging through the water at speed. This gust past, and the usual gale set in—now blowing steadily from the southwest, and taking us more and more out of our course each minute. Every hour the storm got worse, until towards five in the afternoon, when it seemed at its height, and raged with such a violence of wind and sea that matters really looked serious, even for such a strong and large ship as the Agamemnon. The upper deck coil had strained her decks throughout excessively, and, though this mass in theory was supposed to prevent her rolling so quickly and heavily as she would have done without it, yet still she heeled over to such an alarming extent that fears of the coil itself shifting again occupied every mind, and it was accordingly strengthened with additional shores, bolted down to the deck. The space occupied by the main coil below had deprived the Agamemnon of several of her coal bunkers, and in order to make up for this deficiency, as well as to endeavor to counterbalance the immense mass which weighed her down by the head, a large quantity of coals had been stowed on the deck aft. On each side of her main deck were thirty-five tons, secured in a mass, while on the lower deck ninety tons were stowed away in the same manner. The precautions taken to secure these great masses also required attention as the great ship surged from side to side. But these coals seemed secure, and were so, in fact, unless the vessel should almost capsize—an unpleasant alternative which no one certainly anticipated then. Every thing, therefore, was made "snug," as sailors call it, though their efforts by no means resulted in the comfort which might have been expected from the term.

The night, however, passed over without any mischance beyond the smashing of all things incautiously left loose and capable of rolling, and one or two attempts which the Agamemnon made in the middle watch apparently to turn bottom upwards. In all other matters it was the mere ditto of Sunday night, except, perhaps, a little worse, and certainly much more wet below.

Tuesday the gale continued with almost unabated force, though the barometer had risen 29 to 30, and there was sufficient sun to take a clear observation, which showed our distance from the rendezvous to be 563 miles. During this afternoon the Niagara rejoined company, and, the wind going more ahead, the Agamemnon took to violent pitching, plunging steadily into the trough of the sea, as if she meant to break her back and lay the Atlantic cable in a heap. This change in her motion strained and taxed every inch of timber near the coils to the very utmost. It was curious to see how they worked and bent as the Agamemnon went at every thing she met head first. One time she pitched so heavily as to break one of the main beams of the lower deck, which had to be shored with screwjacks forthwith. It is dull work, however, writing a journal of such mishaps, and duller still to read it.

Suffice, then, to say that there was the same sea and less wind on Wednesday, heavy rain and sea on Thursday, with gusts and squalls and heavy rain on Friday.

Saturday, the 19th of June, things looked a little better. The barometer seemed inclined to go up and the sea to go down, and for the first time that morning since the gale began, some six days previous, the decks could be walked with tolerable comfort and security; but, alas! appearances are as deceitful in the Atlantic as elsewhere, and during a comparative calm that afternoon, the glass fell lower, while a thin line of black haze to windward seemed to grow up into the sky, until it covered the heavens with a sombre darkness, and warned us that, after all, the worst was yet to come. There was much heavy rain that evening, and then the wind began—not violently, nor in gusts, but with a steadily increasing force, as if the gale was determined to do its work slowly, but to do it well. The sea was "ready-built to hand," as sailors say, so that at first the storm did little more than urge on the ponderous masses of water with redoubled force, and fill the air with the foam and spray it tore from their rugged crests. By and by, however, it grew more dangerous, and Captain Preedy himself remained on deck throughout the middle watch, for the wind was hourly getting worse and worse, and the Agamemnon, rolling thirty degrees each way, was laboring heavily, and straining to a dangerous extent.

At four A. M., sail was shortened to close-reefed fore and main-topsail and reefed foresails—a long and tedious job, for the wind so roared and howled, and the hiss of the boiling sea was so deafening, that words of command were useless, and the men aloft holding on with all their might to the yards as the ship rolled over and over almost to the water, were quite incapable of struggling with the masses of wet canvas that flapped and plunged as if men and yards and every thing were going away together. The ship was almost as wet inside as out; and so things wore on till eight or nine o'clock, every thing getting adrift and being smashed, and every one on board jamming themselves up in corners or holding on to beams to prevent their going adrift likewise. At ten o'clock the Agamemnon was rolling and laboring fearfully, with the sky getting darker, and both wind and sea increased every minute. At about half-past ten o'clock three or four gigantic waves were seen approaching the ship, coming heavily and slowly on through the mist, nearer and nearer, rolling on like hills of green water, with a crown of foam that seemed to double their height. The Agamemnon rose heavily to the first, and then went down quickly into the deep trough of the sea, falling over as she did so, as almost to capsize completely on the port side. There was a fearful crashing as she lay over this way, for every thing broke adrift, whether secured or not, and the uproar and confusion were terrific for a minute; then back she came again on the starboard beam in the same manner, only quicker, and still deeper than before. Again there were the same noise and crashing; and the officers in the wardroom, who knew the danger of the ship, struggled to their feet and opened the door leading to the main deck. Here, for an instant, the scene almost defies description. Amid loud shouts and efforts to save themselves, a confused mass of sailors, boys and marines, with deck buckets, ropes, ladders, and every thing that could get loose, and which had fallen back again to the port side, were being hurled again in a mass across the ship to starboard. Dimly, and only for an instant, could this be seen, with groups of men clinging to the beams with all their might, with a mass of water, which had forced its way in through ports and decks, surging about; and then, with a tremendous crash, as the ship fell still deeper over, the coals stowed on the main deck broke loose, and, smashing every thing before them, went over among the rest to leeward. The coal dust hid every thing on the main deck in an instant, but the crashing could still be heard in all directions, as the lumps and sacks of coal, with stancheons, ladders, and mess tins went leaping about the decks, pouring down the hatchways, and crashing through the glass skylights into the engine-room below. Still it was not done; and, surging again over another tremendous wave, the Agamemnon dropped down still more to port, and the coals on the starboard side of the lower deck gave way also, and carried every thing before them. Matters now became most serious, for it was evident that two or three more such lurches and the masts would go like reeds, while half the crew might be maimed or killed below. Captain Preedy was already on the poop, with Lieutenant Gibson, and it was, "Hands wear ship," at once, while Mr. Brown, the indefatigable engineer, was ordered to get steam up immediately. The crew gained the deck with difficulty, and not till after a lapse of some minutes, for all the ladders had been broken away and the men were grimed with coal dust, and many bore still more serious marks upon their faces of how they had been knocked about below. There was some confusion at first, for the storm was fearful; the officers were quite inaudible, and a wild dangerous sea, running mountains high, heeled the great ship backwards and forwards, so that the crew were unable to keep their feet, even for an instant, and in some cases were thrown across the decks in a dreadful manner; two marines went with a rush head foremost into the paying-out machine, as if they meant to butt it over the side; yet, strange to say, neither the men nor machine suffered. What made matters worse, the ship's barge, though lashed down to the deck, had partly broken loose, and dropping from side to side as the vessel lurched, it threatened to crush any who ventured to pass it. The regular discipline of the ship, however, soon prevailed, and the crew set to work to wear round the ship on the starboard tack, while Lieutenants Robinson and Murray went below to see after those who had been hurt, and about the number of whom extravagant rumors prevailed among the men.

There were, however, unfortunately but too many. The marine sentry outside the wardroom door on the main deck had not had time to escape, and was completely buried under the coals. Some time elapsed before he could be got out, for one of the beams used to shore up the sacks, which had crushed his arm very badly, still lay across the mangled limb, jamming it in such a manner that it was found impossible to move it without risking the man's life. Saws, therefore, had to be sent for, and the timber sawn away before the poor fellow could be extricated. Another marine on the lower deck endeavored to save himself by catching hold of what seemed a ledge in the planks, but, unfortunately, it was only caused by the beams straining apart, and, of course, as the Agamemnon righted they closed again, and crushed his fingers flat. One of the assistant engineers, (Mr. Harvey,) was also buried among the coals on the lower deck, and sustained some severe internal injuries. The lurch of the ship was calculated at 45 degrees each way for five times in rapid succession. The galley coppers were only half filled with soup, yet, nevertheless, it nearly all poured out,

THE AGAMEMNON IN THE GALE OF JUNE, 1858.

and scalded some of the poor fellows who were extended on the decks, holding on to any thing in reach. These, with a dislocation, were the chief casualties; but there were others of bruises and contusions, more or less severe, and of course a long list of escapes more marvellous than any injury. One poor fellow went head first from the main deck into the hold without being hurt, and one on the orlop deck was "chevied" about for some ten minutes by three large casks of oil which had got adrift, and any one of which would have flattened him like a pancake had it overtaken him.

As soon as we had gone round on the other tack the Niagara wore also, and bore down as if to render assistance. She had witnessed our danger, and, as we afterwards learnt, imagined that the upper deck coil had broken loose and that we were sinking. Things, however, were not so bad as that, though they were bad enough, heaven knows, for every thing seemed to go wrong that day. The upper deck coil had strained the ship to the very uttermost, but still held on fast; but not so the coil in the main hold, which had begun to get adrift, and the top kept working and shifting over from side to side as the ship lurched, till some forty or fifty miles were in a hopeless state of tangle, resembling nothing so much as a cargo of live eels, and there was every prospect of the tangle spreading deeper and deeper as the bad weather continued.

Going round upon the starboard tack had eased the ship to a certain extent, but with such a wind and such a sea, both of which were rather getting worse than better, it was impossible to effect much for the Agamemnon's relief, and so, by twelve o'clock, she was rolling almost as bad as ever. The crew, who had been at work since nearly four in the morning, were set to clear up the decks from the masses of coal that covered them, and while this was going forward a heavy sea struck the stern, and smashed the large iron guard frame, which had been fixed there to prevent the cable fouling the screw in paying out. This guard, which, from its peculiar hooped shape, suspended round the stern by chains, the sailors had nicknamed "the crinoline," was about the most cumbersome and ill-contrived piece of mechanism which could possibly have been adopted. From the first hour every one had known that it was perfectly useless for the purpose it was intended to effect, and, what was worse than useless, that it was a source of positive danger also. Now that one side had broken, it was expected every moment that other parts would go, and the pieces hanging down either smash the screw or foul the rudder post. It is not over estimating the danger to say that had the latter accident occurred in such a sea, and with a vessel so overladen, the chances would have been sadly against the Agamemnon ever appearing at the rendezvous. Fortunately it was found possible to secure the broken frame temporarily with hawsers, so as to prevent its dropping further, though nothing could prevent the fractured end from striking against the vessel's side with such force as to lead to serious apprehensions that it would establish a dangerous leak under water. It was near three o'clock in the afternoon before this was quite secured, the gale still continuing and the sea running even worse. The condition of the masts, too, at this time were a source of much anxiety both to Captain Preedy and Mr. Moriarty, the master. The heavy rolling had strained and slackened the wire shrouds to such an extent that they had become perfectly useless as supports. The lower masts bent visibly at every roll, and once or twice it seemed as if they must go by the board. Unfortunately, nothing whatever could be done to relieve this strain by sending down any of the upper spars, since it was only her masts which prevented the ship rolling still more and quicker; and so every man knew that if once they were carried away it might soon be all over with the ship, as then the deck coil could not help going after them; so there was nothing for it but to watch in anxious silence the way they bent and strained, and trust in Providence for the result. About six in the evening it was thought better to wear ship again and stand for the rendezvous under easy steam, and her head accordingly was put about and once more faced the storm. As she went round she of course fell into the trough of the sea again, and rolled so awfully as to break her waste steam pipe, filling her engine room with steam and depriving her of the services of one boiler when it was sorely needed. The sun set upon as wild and wicked a night as ever taxed the courage and coolness of a sailor. There were, of course, men on board who were familiar with gales and storms in all parts of the world, and there were some who, with the writer of this article, had witnessed the tremendous hurricane which swept the Black Sea on the memorable 14th of November, when scores of vessels were lost and seamen perished by thousands; but of all on board none had ever seen a fiercer or more dangerous sea than raged that night and the following morning, tossing the Agamemnon from side to side like a mere plaything among the waters. The night was thick and very dark, the low black clouds almost hemming the vessel in; now and then a fiercer blast than usual drove the great masses slowly aside, and showed the moon, a dim greasy blotch upon the sky, with the ocean, white as driven snow, boiling and seething like a caldron. But these were only glimpes, which were soon lost, and again it was all darkness, through which the waves, suddenly npheaving, rushed upon the ship as though they must overwhelm it, and, dealing it one staggering blow, went hissing and surging past into the darkness again. The grandeur of the scene was almost lost in its dangers and terrors, for of all the many forms in which death approaches man, there is none so easy in fact, though so terrific in appearance, as death by shipwreck.

Sleeping was impossible that night on board the Agamemnon. Even those in cots were thrown out, from their striking against the vessel's side as she pitched. The berths of wood fixed athwartships in the cabins on the main deck had worked to pieces, chairs and tables were broken, chests of drawers capsized, and a little surf was running over the floors of the cabins themselves, pouring miniature seas into portmanteaus, and breaking over carpet bags of clean linen. Fast as it flowed off by the scuppers it came in faster by the hawseholes and ports, while the beams and knees strained with a doleful noise, as if it was impossible they could hold together much longer; and on the whole it was as miserable and even anxious a night as ever was passed on board any line of battle ship in Her Majesty's service. Captain Preedy never left the poop all night, though it was hard work to remain there, even holding on to the poop rail with both hands. Morning brought no change, save that the storm was still as fierce as ever, and, though the sea could not be higher or wilder, yet the additional amount of broken water made it still more dangerous to the ship.

Very dimly, and only now and then through the thick scud, the Niagara could be seen—one moment on a monstrous hill of water and the next quite lost to view, as the Agamemnon went down between waves. But even these glimpses showed us that our transatlantic consort was plunging heavily, shipping seas, and evidently having a bad time of it, though she got through it better than the Agamemnon, as of course she could, having only the same load, though 2,000 tons larger. Suddenly it came on darker and thicker, and we lost sight of her in the thick spray, and had only ourselves to look after, which was quite enough, for every minute made matters worse, and the aspect of affairs began to excite most serious misgivings in the minds of those in charge. The Agamemnon is one of the best line of battle ships in the whole navy, but in such a storm, and so heavily overladen, what could she do but make bad weather worse, and strain and labor and fall into the trough of the sea, as if she were going down headforemost?

Three or four hours more and the vessel had borne all which she could bear with safety; the masts were rapidly getting worse, the deck coil worked more and more with each tremendous plunge, and, even if both these held, it was evident that the ship itself would soon strain to pieces if the weather continued so. The sea, forcing its way through ports and hawseholes, had accumulated on the lower deck to such an extent that it flooded the stokehole, so that the men could scarcely remain at their posts.

Every thing went smashing and rolling about. One plunge put all the electrical instruments *hors de combat* at a blow, and staved some barrels of strong solution of sulphate of copper, which went cruising about, turning all it touched to a light pea green. By and by she began to ship seas. Water came down the ventilators near the funnel into the engine room. Then a tremendous sea struck her forward, drenching those on deck, and leaving them up to their knees in water, and the least versed on board could see that things were fast going to the bad unless a change took place either in the weather or the condition of the ship. Of the first there seemed little chance. The weather certainly showed no diposition to clear, on the contrary, livid looking black clouds seemed to be closing round the vessel faster and faster than ever. For the relief of the ship three courses were open to Capt. Preedy—one to wear round and try her on the starboard tack, as he had been compelled to do the day before; another, to fairly run for it before the wind; and, the third and last, to endeavor to lighten the vessel by getting some of the cable overboard. Of course the latter would not have been thought of till the first two had been tried and failed, in fact, not till it was evident that nothing else would save the ship. Against wearing round there was the danger of her again falling off into the trough of the sea, losing her masts, shifting the upper deck coil, and so finding her way to the bottom in ten minutes, while to attempt running before the storm with such a sea on was to risk her stern being stove in, and a hundred tons of water added to her burden with each wave that came up afterwards, till the poor Agamemnon went under them all forever.

A little after ten o'clock on Monday, the 21st, the aspect of affairs was so alarming that Capt. Preedy resolved at all risks to try wearing the ship round on the other tack. It was hard enough to make the words of command audible, but to execute them seemed almost impossible. The ship's head went round enough to leave her broadside on to the seas, and then for a time it seemed as if nothing could be done. All the rolls which she had ever given on the previous day seemed mere trifles compared with her performance then. Of more than 200 men on deck at least 150 were thrown down and falling over from side to side in heaps; while others, holding on to ropes, swung to and fro with every heave. It really seemed as if the last hour of the stout ship had come, and to this minute it seems almost miraculous that her masts held on. Each time she fell over her main chains went deep under water. The lower decks were flooded, and those above could hear by the fearful crashing, audible amid the hoarse roar of the storm, that the coals had got loose again below, and had broken into the engine room, and were carrying all before them. During these rolls the main deck coil shifted over to such a degree as to quite envelope four men, who, sitting on the top, were trying to wedge it down with beams. One of them was so much jammed by the mass which came over him, that he was seriously contused, and had to be removed to the sick bay, making up the sick list to forty-five, of which ten were from injuries caused by the rolling of the ship, and very many of the rest from continual fatigue and exposure during the gale. Once round on the starboard tack, and it was seen in an instant that the ship was in no degree relieved by the change. Another heavy sea struck her forward, sweeping clean over the forepart of the vessel, and carrying away the wood work and platforms which had been placed there round the machinery for under running. This and a few more plunges were quite sufficient to settle the matter, and at last, reluctantly, Capt. Preedy succumbed to the storm he could neither conquer nor contend against. Full steam was got on, and, with a foresail and foretopsail to lift her head, the Agamemnon ran before the storm, rolling and tumbling over the huge waves at a tremendous pace. It was well for all that the wind gave this much way on her, or her stern would infallibly have been stove in. As it was, a wave partly struck her on the starboard quarter, smashing the quarter galley and wardroom windows on that side, and sending such a sea into the wardroom itself, as literally almost to wash two officers off a sofa on which they were resting on that side of the ship. This was a kind of parting blow, for the glass began to rise, and the storm was evidently beginning to moderate; and though the sea still ran as high as ever, there was less broken water, and altogether, towards mid-day, affairs assumed a better and more cheering aspect. The wardroom that afternoon was a study for an artist, with its windows half darkened and smashed, the sea water still slushing about in odd corners, with every thing that was capable of being broken strewn over the floor in pieces, and some fifteen or twenty officers seated amid the ruins, holding on to the deck or table with one hand, while with the other they contended at a disadvantage with a tough meal—the first which most had eaten for twenty-four hours.

Throughout the whole of Monday the Agamemnon ran before the wind, which moderated so much that at four A.M. on Tuesday, her head was again put about, and, for the second time she commenced beating up for the rendezvous, then some two hundred miles further from us than when the gale was at its height on Sunday morning. Tuesday was a calm, fine day, though of course with a heavy swell on. Wednesday was also warm, fine, and calm, and for the first time for a fortnight we had a real summer day, and the reefs were shaken out of the topsails. Immediately the ship began to run before the wind. On Monday the shrouds of the main and fore masts were lashed in such a way as to give some support to the masts, and on Wednesday advantage was taken of the calm to "tauten" up the main rigging three inches, which for wire rope was a great gain. It was well that this was done in time, for on Wednesday, the 23d, the glass again went down; it was the old song of wind and rain, with heavy squalls, rough sea, and reefed topsails. So little was gained against this wind that Friday, the 25th, sixteen days after leaving Plymouth, still found us some fifty miles from the rendezvous. So it was determined to get up steam and run down on it at once.

As we approached the place of meeting, the Valorous hove in sight at noon, and in the afternoon the Niagara came in from the north, and in the evening the Gorgon from the south; and then, almost for the first time since starting, the squadron was reunited near the spot where the great work was to commence. The rendezvous actually agreed upon was 52° 2′ N. latitude, 33° 18′ W. longitude, but the place where the vessels met was in 51° 54′ latitude, 32° 33′ longitude, or about thirty miles more towards the English coast than had been agreed upon. The Valorous, it appeared, had been first on the real rendezvous. The Niagara was the next, arriving under steam two days before the Agamemnon, and the Gorgon, which had had a very bad time of it, and was also near losing her masts, was third. The Niagara seemed to have weathered the gale splendidly, though, nevertheless, with her, as with all others, it had been a hard and anxious time. She had lost her jibboom, and her spare spars and buoys for the cable had been washed from her sides and gone no man knew where.* On the evening of Friday, the 25th of June, the four vessels lay together side by side, and there was such a stillness in the sea and air as would have seemed remarkable in an inland lake; on the Atlantic, and after what we had all so lately witnessed, it seemed almost unnatural.

RETURN OF THE SQUADRON, AND ARRIVAL AT QUEENSTOWN.

According to the terms of the written agreement, which has been given in the narrative of the expedition, the whole fleet were to return after the two cable ships should have gone over one hundred miles towards their separate destinations, and it was in compliance with this explicit understanding that the Niagara proceeded to the point indicated therein. We arrived on the 5th of July, expecting to find the Agamemnon had got in before us. We were considerably disappointed, however, when we learned there were as yet no tidings of her, although she had over two hundred miles the start of us on her course. The supposition

* The correspondent of the London Times is incorrect in this statement. The Niagara lost her jibboom, but not her spare spars.—AUTHOR.

that she had not gone one hundred miles was greatly strengthened by her non-appearance, and we were forced to the conclusion, after two or three days, that she had really returned to the rendezvous, and was there awaiting us. Day after day passed, and yet there was no Agamemnon, no Valorous. Terrible stories were circulated about the missing ships; it was said that we had abandoned them, and that the Agamemnon had gone down. The London *Times*, with the most indecent haste, accused us of circulating reports throwing the discredit of the failure on the Agamemnon, and intimated that they must wait her arrival before they received reliable intelligence. At last the Agamemnon made her appearance, having returned, as we supposed, to the rendezvous in mid-ocean. The reliable intelligence had at length arrived, and it was ascertained that the cable had parted about twenty feet from her stern, and that she had gone a distance of one hundred and sixteen miles, or seven miles more than our ship. The reader will be somewhat surprised at the course pursued by her engineers in this instance, when he is informed that the agreement was made entirely on account of her not having a sufficient supply of coal. On leaving Plymouth she had but 450 tons, while the Niagara had 850, and although the reports in the London *Times* about our "water-logged" appearance, the strong probability of our going to the bottom, and the deplorable condition of our ship, were well calculated to arouse the fears of our people at home about our safety, we came out of one of the worst gales that has ever been seen in the North Atlantic, with no other damage to our noble ship than the loss of part of her bowsprit and one of the wings of the eagle which forms her figure-head. How the Agamemnon fared the reader is already aware. It is a strange fact that the breaking of the cable at the stern of the Agamemnon was never satisfactorily accounted for by the engineers in charge of the paying-out machinery on board that ship.

While the Telegraph squadron were lying in the harbor of Queenstown, meetings were held by the Board of Directors in London, at which it was proposed to abandon the enterprise, and, if possible, to sell the cable. The news of this proposition no sooner reached Mr. Field than he started with all possible dispatch for London. On his arrival there, he proceeded at once to the office of the Company, remonstrated with the despondent, upheld the wavering, and finally, by the force of his own unconquerable will, and the efficient aid of those who still hoped in the midst of defeat, succeeded at last in obtaining the consent of the Company to make another attempt. This effected, he returned to Queenstown, where immediate preparations were made for the sailing of the squadron on the last and successful expedition.

THE FINAL EXPEDITION OF 1858.

THE CABLE LAID.

The Niagara left the Cove of Cork for the telegraph rendezvous on the 17th of July, and arrived at her destination, or within a few miles of it, on the evening of the 23d, having made the passage in six days. As it had been previously decided that each ship should make the best of her way to mid-ocean, the vessels did not sail in company, the Gorgon and Valorous having started some hours before the Niagara, while the Agamemnon did not leave till three o'clock next morning. We saw none of the ships, therefore, till after our arrival at the rendezvous.

The weather, which had been, with one day's exception, very fine during our stay in Cork, looked heavy and threatening the evening of our departure. Great masses of leaden-colored clouds shut out the blue sky, and sent down shower after shower of drenching rain. Then sweeping in upon the land, they descended upon it in the form of a dense fog, concealing the inland mountains, and throwing out in strong relief the bold headlands of the iron-bound coast. The heavens had certainly a most funereal aspect, and overshadowed our prospects with a gloom that seemed to affect every one more or less. We were now on our way to make the second attempt to lay the Atlantic telegraph cable, and when we remembered the result of the first, we might be pardoned if we were somewhat dubious as to its termination; although, of course, we all "hoped for the best." Were we to pass through another gale before we should be able to make the splice, and when that splice was made, were our efforts to end in another inexplicable break of continuity, or fracture of the cable? These were questions that pressed rather heavily upon some of us, and converted a considerable number into confirmed sceptics. However, here we were outside of the Cove of Cork, bound for the telegraph rendezvous, and determined to resume the work with the same energy, if not with the same buoyant and sanguine feelings with which we entered upon it the preceding month. The sceptics still remained sceptical, and the hopeful sustained themselves with the idea that there was a chance of success yet.

The prospect of fine weather, which appeared so gloomy at the time of our departure, grew brighter as we increased our distance from the land; the gray sombre-looking clouds began to clear away, and the barometer, which had exhibited a very decided downward tendency, now began to rise, and continued rising till it had reached the gratifying altitude of 30° 40′ The only thing of which we had any just cause of complaint was the wind, and that blew from the wrong quarter with the most disgusting persistency. But it did not blow all the time, for we had some three or four days of the calmest weather, both before and after arrival at the rendezvous, that has ever been seen in these latitudes. To say that it was calm is not doing full justice to it—there was not a breath in the air, and the water was as smooth as that of a mill-pond. Even the wake of the ship scarce ruffled its surface, and the gulls—which have visited us almost daily, and to which our benevolent liberality has dispensed innumerable pieces of pork—throw an almost unbroken shadow upon it as they stoop in their flight to pick up the largest and most tempting. Those lazy-looking white clouds hanging over the western horizon have not changed either their form or their position for the last two hours, and that particular one to which the imagination has given the form of a human face, is just as grotesque and as much like a human face as it was an hour ago. The officer of the deck has been trying to persuade himself that those fleecy, vaporous affairs are "mares' tails," and that the breeze, of which they are regarded by the nautically learned as the sure forerunners, must soon come; but whatever may be the rules in such cases made and provided, they are certainly at fault this time, for there is no breeze, and not the remotest probability of any. The long streamer which is displayed from our main truck hangs lazily against the mast, and even the dog-vane, which tells from which quarter the wind comes, says nothing upon the subject. It is indeed a dead calm, and but for that never-ceasing swell, which has rightly been denominated "the pulse of the sea," our vessel would be as motionless as "a painted ship upon a painted ocean." The smoke which comes up from our engine fires through the huge chimneys rises like pillars, and spreads out in a broad canopy over the masts. "There comes a breeze dead ahead," says one of the sailors, pointing in the direction of the bow, and the clear and distinctly defined blue line which marks the horizon seemed to indicate the appearance of wind in that quarter; but an hour has passed since then, and still the dog-vane remains unmoved, the streamer hangs idly against the mast, and the canopy of smoke is becoming denser. The clouds have changed, it is true, but no wind will come from them. The human face has been converted into the head of an eagle, and those banks of white silver cumuli are very slowly changing their appearance.

So thoroughly has the calm affected every thing and everybody in and about the vessel, as to throw a sort of dreamy repose over all. It is impossible to get up a conversation on the most interesting topic, and you would imagine that our ship had ceased to be a part of the great world in which she moved, and that her living freight had nothing in common with the rest of humanity, but belonged to the unreal creations of dream land. And yet this is the very ocean, and we are within a few miles of the point where that terrible gale burst upon us, and those huge angry waves buffeted and tossed us about for eight or nine days. This settled, dreamy calm has rested on the ocean for four days, which are closed by sunsets as gorgeous as any ever seen under a tropical sky. The whole heavens are suffused with a golden glow from the descending sun, and as he disappears below the horizon it turns to a deep crimson, which is reflected in the unruffled ocean until there appears to be but one sky, and the ship seems suspended in space. The silver gray of evening brings us back again to the world; the golden glow and the deep crimson have disappeared, but the pleasant twilight remains, and will continue with us so long as to leave but a small portion of the twenty-four hours for the night. In fact the summer nights in these high latitudes are hardly entitled to the name, and what between the long twilight and early daybreak, have scarcely time enough to get rightly dark.

We have now been five days out, and if we have only ordinary luck we will certainly be at or near the precise point, which is marked by a dot on the chart of the North Atlantic, about half way between Ireland and Newfoundland. To-morrow evening, Friday the 23d, is fixed upon as the time of our arrival, and everybody is indulging in speculations as to the Agamemnon being there before us. In this all-absorbing question every thing else seems to be forgotten. We no longer hear of the prospects of the heroes and heroines of the romances and novels which have furnished topics for animated discussion for some days past, and no one seems to care whether the hard-hearted father has or has not been struck with remorse, and consented to make his lovely and amiable daughter superlatively happy by marrying the man of her choice. The dark designs of the schemer who has been baffled by the superior abilities of the lover (lovers are always a very superior class of men, although generally poor), have escaped that condemnation and sentence which all virtuous and high-minded readers are supposed to pass upon such characters, and even his terrible fate is hardly thought of in the great question which agitates the minds of all on board our ship.

We are about one hundred and thirty miles from the rendezvous, and at the rate we are now going we shall be at our post to-morrow evening, so that we may commence the work of laying the cable the following morning by daybreak.

Throughout the whole of Friday every one was on the lookout for the Agamemnon, but the best telescope on board failed to discover that ship, and so we lay as near that imaginary point called the Rendezvous, as the wind and surface current would permit. Saturday morning arrived, but with it no Agamemnon, and by seven o'clock, Saturday evening, we again made the rendezvous, having drifted considerably during Friday night. To be brief, we had no better success now than the day before; and as man is a somewhat restless animal, we became both restless and impatient in our desire to begin the work. The weather, which cannot be too highly eulogized, was magnificent for cable laying, and the barometer gave the strongest assurance of its continuance. Had she arrived on Sunday it would have been useless, as the religious scruples of our captain interpose an insuperable obstacle; and so we must patiently wait till Monday, the 26th. It was, however, somewhat consoling to learn that the Valorous had arrived on the morning of the 25th, although she had neither seen nor heard of the long expected ship. She was first seen at six o'clock, but as she came along under sail alone, she did not approach near enough to exchange signals till nine.

"I hope you are all well," was the purport of the signal made by our ship.

"Very well, I thank you," was the reply.

"Have you seen the Agamemnon?" asked the captain of the Valorous.

"No," replied Captain Hudson, and then asked in return if he had seen the Gorgon, but to this he received a negative response.

And after this brief interview and still more laconic conversation, the two ships separated. Monday afternoon, July 26, the Valorous was in sight, and the sea was as calm as we had yet observed it—so calm, to use the words of one of the crew, that it would be mere child's play to lay the cable under such circumstances. About ten o'clock Captain Aldham and one of his lieutenants paid us a friendly visit, and remained about an hour. The 27th was, so far as the weather was regarded, a perfect counterpart of the 26th. This day we were favored with another arrival, though not that we had first expected. The Gorgon was descried about two o'clock in the afternoon coming from the eastward, and it was but a few minutes after five when she came up. Now as two ships can hardly come together on the high seas without having something to say to each other, it is not to be expected that the Niagara and Gorgon would pass each other without indulging in some remarks. And so,

Captain Hudson and Captain Dayman had the following brief but pithy dialogue:

Captain H.—I hope you are all well on board?

Captain D.—All well, thank you—hope you are the same?

Captain H.—(Nodding an affirmative, and finishing the rest of the sentence by word of mouth)—Thank you.

Captains H. and D. (together)—Have you seen the Agamemnon?

A pause, and the question is repeated by Captain Hudson alone.

Captain D.—No, not since we parted. Have you any coal to spare? We have had head winds all the way out.

Captain H.—None at all. We have also had head winds. I think the Agamemnon could give you some, as she can't have burned much since she left.

Thus ended the conversation, and the Gorgon passed on to pay her respects to the Valorous, which was about two miles off our port quarter. Towards evening we observed both vessels had hoisted their ensigns, but the weather had become overcast and we could not discern any other ship. We also displayed ours, however, so that if it should turn out to be the Agamemnon she might be fully aware of our arrival. We felt confident that she had been seen by the Gorgon and Valorous, and that she would make her appearance next morning and answer for herself. Five days before we had made the rendezvous, and we were just beginning to get tired of waiting; and during that time what splendid days we have had—days which the Atlantic Telegraph Company could not purchase at ten thousand dollars apiece from that inexorable myth the Clerk of the Weather! However, according to Lieut. Maury, we can afford to be a little prodigal this month, and if we do lose a few days, why, after all, it can hardly be considered a loss when we come to reflect that July and August are the two best months in the year for cable laying. We are certainly entitled to some consideration after the gale through which we passed last month—a month we were led to believe was the mildest in the whole year.

On board of our ship every precaution has been taken to ensure success. The machinery has been put in proper running order, and the watches are all made out for the different departments. The captain and the first lieutenant, Mr. North, keep watch and watch, that is, they divide the day into alternate watches of four hours each, with the usual interposition of "dog watches," between four and eight in the afternoon. Mr. North, it may be remembered, was also first lieutenant of the Niagara last year, and has taken the most active interest in the enterprise. The duty which he performed in connection with Captain Hudson is an entirely voluntary one, as, according to the rules of the navy, he is not considered a watch officer, and his services are therefore given freely, and not in compliance with any obligations arising from his official position.

All we want now is a continuance of the fine weather we have had nearly the whole of this month, to lay the cable, for we still feel convinced of the practicability of the work, despite the unexplained break of continuity and fracture of the wire.

CEREMONY OF LAYING THE CABLE,

FIRST DAY—JULY 28.

We were right in our surmizes that there must have been some reasons for the Valorous and Gorgon displaying their flags, and our hopes that the Agamemnon had at last made her appearance, though invisible to us in consequence of the fog prevailing at the time, were now fully realized. About five o'clock this morning the mist began to clear away; and some ten or fifteen minutes after, our sister ship could be distinctly seen between two and three miles off our port quarter. Mr. Field had offered a reward to the man who would first discover her, and as may be supposed the crew were thoroughly wide awake, and on the lookout for the expected vessel. Two or three days before she came there were reports innumerable as to her having been seen, and at almost every point of the compass. The smallest speck of a cloud, barely visible through the best telescope on board, was converted into smoke by those who were determined to see her, even if she were a hundred miles away. "That certainly must be her," said one of the quartermasters, pointing at some imaginary object with the telescope, which he had just taken from his eye. "Yes, that's her, and no mistake this time."

"Where?" asked a dozen anxious querists all at once, and all as eagerly stretching out their hands for the telescope.

"There, there!" he replied, looking towards the cloudless horizon—"there! don't you see it, right there on the starboard bow, about three points?"

The man who had been most fortunate in securing the glass first, took a long observation at the point thus indicated, and after scanning it three or four times, announced in a tone of disgust that there was no smoke, and that it was "Cape Flyaway"—a nautical expression, which, literally translated, signifies "nothing."

The more energetic and enterprising would occasionally run up to the head of the topgallant-masts, and take a view of the horizon from that elevation, but with no better success than those who, of a less aspiring mind, remained on the deck, or kept their lookout from the forecastle or poop. Never was greater interest manifested in any ship than the proffered reward created in that vessel; and yet it was not the amount, but rather the distinction which the discovery would confer upon the man by whom it should be made. Then there was the excitement of the thing itself, and that alone would be sufficient to arouse the feelings of the most indifferent. Only those who have been at sea for any length of time can fully appreciate the value of this word, or how little it takes to get up an excitement at sea, where life is but one constant round of monotonous incidents which follow each other in as regular succession as the hours on a dial. The "reward," therefore, grew into all the magnitude of an important question, and with the addition of some whales, which occasionally indulged in spouting, served to make the time pass less heavily on our hands.

The arrival of the Agamemnon overtopped all other subjects, and knocked into a cocked hat the various opinions which had been circulated in regard to her engines having broken down. "There she is, sir," said the delighted sailor to the officer of the deck, when he observed her heavy-looking hull slowly emerging from the mist which still hung over her masts like a veil. "There she is, sir, on our port quarter." And there she certainly was—no mistake this time—there were the two white streaks, but still more conclusive than this—there was the cable-wheel over her stern, and there was the other over her bow. It was the Agamemnon, ten days out from Cork, having made the rendezvous the evening before, as we subsequently learned.

As has been stated, she was between two and three miles off our port quarter when first observed, and as there was no indication of either smoke or steam, we concluded that she had been saving her coal, and had sailed the greater part, if not the whole, of the way. This we afterwards found to be incorrect, as she had consumed two hundred of the five hundred tons with which she started, and had during the passage to mid-ocean met with head winds. She had also a repetition, on a small scale, of the bad weather we experienced during the month of June, but as it lasted only twenty-four hours, and as the wind did not freshen into a gale, there was no ground for alarm. One sea, however, made its way into the ward-room, and broke some of the bulkheads. But for the head winds she would have arrived two or three days sooner, and thus given us the advantage of the fine weather with which we have been so wonderfully favored since we left Queenstown, and, in fact, from the time the squadron left mid-ocean in June, up to the date of our re-appearance on the rendezvous this month. Here we are at last, however, ready to commence operations once more, and determined if success be possible, we will make every effort to secure and deserve it. Whatever other charges may be preferred against the enterprise by the dissatisfied, it cannot be said that those who are engaged in it have shown any want of perseverance or energy. Although they have met with failure after failure, and reverses that would have discouraged almost any other body of men, they have exhibited a determination that is deserving of all praise, and a hopefulness that no disasters could subdue. Preparations are now being made to resume the work, and although there are many who think it a useless expenditure of time and money, yet there are others who are sanguine as to the result. There is no want of energy certainly among our men, and if you could only witness the hearty assent that is given to the following inscription which has been made in chalk on the outside of one of the cable circles, you would say there is no want of enthusiasm in them :

" The wire will be laid, and we will go to New York."

About half-past nine o'clock the Agamemnon, having got up steam, was observed slowly approaching us, and in somewhat less than an hour after she crossed our bow, previous to taking her position on our stern, so as to be ready for splicing. All the preliminary preparations had been made on board the Niagara, and every thing was in readiness for the commencement of the work so far as she was concerned. The men were at their posts by the machinery, the stoppers were all arranged, the electricians were on watch in the long vacant office, the tar-tubs were put in their proper places, the scrapers adjusted, and nothing was left undone that human foresight could do. Within the boundaries of the rope that enclosed the machine, none but the privileged few were allowed to enter, and if any one did so, through ignorance, the inscription which was posted conspicuously in front, and which reads as follows, warned him against further intrusion :

" No one here except the engineer's watch."

This was certainly laconic, but if it was not sufficient for the purpose the marine who stood close by informed him that he must leave. This was not all, however, for if, under the impression that he was at liberty to talk to the operator in charge of the dynamometer, he was soon made aware of the absurdity of such an idea by another notice, to the effect that no conversation was allowed with that particular individual. Then, in addition to all this, the officer in charge of the platform, which was raised above two of the coils to facilitate the paying out of the cable, took care that none but those fully authorized should go up there. The curious were thus excluded from every point where they might interfere with the operations of those on watch, but still they had ample opportunities to witness all that was going on, and outside of the bounds they certainly indulged themselves to the utmost. There seemed to be a fascination for them in every thing connected with the process of paying out, but more particularly in the work of uncoiling the cable. The outside of the circle was crowded with spectators, who watched in silence the long black line as it unwound itself and passed over the machinery on its way into the great ocean depths. There they stood, hour after hour, looking at the removal of one flake after another, as if it were something new, and each mile served but to increase the attraction.

The Agamemnon has now taken her position about a hundred fathoms from the stern of the Niagara, and the hawser has been passed between the two ships previous to making the splice. Before the commencement of operations, however, Captains Preedy and Aldham came on board of our ship, and Mr. Field and one of the electricians visited the Agamemnon to make further arrangements in regard to the work before us. After the necessary time these are made, and it is concluded that if the cable should be broken after 150 miles shall have been paid out from each ship, both vessels shall at once proceed to Queenstown, there to await orders from the company regarding the final disposal and stowage of the cable. The captains have returned to their ships, the splice is made, and the work of paying out proceeds, while the two ships move so slowly through the water that their motion is hardly perceptible. The rate of the cable is certainly much faster than that of either of the vessels, for the simple reason that it has to descend to a depth of about two miles, and it will take a considerable time to do that. The announcement comes from the electrician's office soon after the splice has been lowered, that the continuity is perfect, and with this assurance the engineers go on more boldly with the work. In fact, the engineers may be said to be under the control of the electricians; for if they report any thing wrong with the cable they are brought to a stand, until they are allowed to go on with their operations by the announcement that the insulation is perfect and the continuity is all right. The sailors, who are somewhat in the dark as to the scientific definition of the term, are generally supposed to have a particular animosity to it, under the belief that it is it which causes all the difficulty. "Darn the continuity," said an old sailor, at the end of a scientific but rather foggy discussion which a nnmber of his messmates had on the subject—"Darn the continuity; I wish they would get rid of it altogether. It has caused a darned sight more trouble than the hull thing is worth. I say they ought to do without it, and let it go. I believe they'd get the cable down if they didn't pay any attention to it. You see," he went on, "I was on the last exhibition" (expedition he meant, but it was all the same—his messmates did not misapprehend his meaning), "and I thought I'd never hear the end of it. They were always talking about it, and one night, when we were out last year, it was gone for two hours, and we thought that was the end of the affair, and we would never hear of it again. But it came back, and soon after the cable busted. Now, I tell you what men, I'll never forget the night, I tell ye; we all felt we had lost our best friend, and I never heard the word continuity or contiguity mentioned but I was always afraid something was going to happen. And that's a fact."

This was conclusive on the minds of the majority of his hearers; but a number were of opinion that it was all right, and, at the risk of being considered humbugs, asserted their belief that whatever might be said against the continuity they couldn't do without it, and that because it was gone all the trouble had occurred.

The work of paying-out the cable was commenced at one o'clock. The speed of the vessel was gradually increased after sufficient had been lowered over the stern to reach the bottom, and by two o'clock five miles had left the ship, and she had gone two miles from the starting point. The observation taken by the Agamemnon and Niagara showed the position of both ships, as follows: Lat. 52° 09′, long. 32° 29′. To accomplish the work, the former has eleven hundred nautical miles, and three hundred tons of coal; while the latter had the same amount of cable and five hundred tons of coal. This will give our ship from ten to fifteen days' steaming; while the Agamemnon has sufficient for ten days, should she burn at the rate of thirty tons per day. But, if we should find that we have not enough to reach the land with, we will, if necessary, burn the spare spars; and should we be still further pressed, we will take down even the bulkheads for fuel. It is not very probable, however, that we shall be reduced to such straits. Mr. Follansbee, our chief engineer, assures us that we will have sufficient. Let us once get sight of Newfoundland, however, and though every ton of coal in our bunkers were expended, we will contrive to get into Trinity Bay and land the cable. We have already paid out a little over thirty miles of cable, although it is not yet seven o'clock, and the ship's speed varies from four to five miles per hour. There is a long distance yet, it is true, between this and Newfoundland, and thirty miles is a very small fraction of 882 miles—the distance from the point at which we made the splice to the telegraph station at the head of Trinity Bay. In this respect the Agamemnon has certainly had the advantage of us, as she will have but 813 miles to go—or sixty less than the Niagara. The depth of water here, according to the chart of soundings, is 1,550 fathoms; but the depth, so far as our experience testifies, presents little or no obstacle to the laying of the cable. The sea is smooth; the barometer well up; and if we can only do for the next seven days as well as we have done since one o'clock, we will be at Newfoundland by the 5th of

August, and to New York some time between the 15th and 20th of the same month. But we have been somewhat too hasty in our calculations, for our ship has just slowed down, and the propeller has ceased working for the last ten minutes. There must be something wrong to cause this interruption. Let us take a look at the machine. The cable still goes out, which certainly would not be the case if it had parted. Ah! the continuity! that's it—there's where the difficulty lies. And as the electricians are the only parties who can inform us on that point, we at once go in search of them. A visit to their office explains the whole matter. The continuity is not gone altogether, but is defective—so defective that it is impossible to get a signal through the cable. Still there is not "dead earth" upon it, and all hope, therefore, is not lost.

When dead earth, as it is termed, is on the conductor, then, indeed, the difficulty is beyond remedy, for it shows that the conductor must be broken, and is thrown under the influence of terrestrial magnetism. But the continuity is not gone, and although with darkening prospects, we are still safe while it remains, even imperfect as it is. The old adage, that "bad news travels fast," was never more fully realized than in this instance. The sad intelligence was known to every one on board the ship about fifteen minutes after it was announced to Mr. Field, and those who predicted the failure of the expedition fell back upon their prophecy, and hinted in a modest way at their own perception. It would be absurd to say that the occurrence was not discouraging; it was painfully so, for the hopes of some of us had really begun to revive, and we were gaining confidence every hour. Now nothing could be done. We must wait until the continuity should return or take its final departure. And it did return, and with greater strength than ever. At ten minutes past nine P. M. the electrician on duty observed its failing, and at 11.30 he had the gratifying intelligence for us that it was "all right again." The machinery was once more set in motion, the cable was soon going out at the rate of six miles an hour, and the electrical signals were passing between the ships as regularly as if nothing had occurred to interfere with or interrupt the continuity. No explanation could be given as to the cause of the accident, that was to be relied upon. It was supposed, however, that it had broken on board the Agamemnon, and that the end was secured and spliced before it could get out of the ship. This is favored by the fact that it would take an hour or so to make the splice, which was about the time that elapsed from the moment the continuity became imperfect till it was restored. Another reason, though probably not so good, was given —that the cable was subject to so severe a strain as to cause the parting of the copper wire or conductor, although the insulation remained perfect; and as soon as the strain was released the broken wires came together again, thus restoring the continuity. However it may have been, or by whatever scientific means it might be explained, the one fact was evident—the continuity was "all right," and we were satisfied. We were alarmed by no more unpleasant reports this night, and retired to bed—some to sleep, and some to spend a restless night in anxious fears about the safety of the cable and in feverish hopes of success.

As every thing relating to the electrical department must be of deep interest during the process of the work, we are determined to visit the electricians' office, which is situated in that little corner close by the wardroom coil—a point to which no one on board can look without apprehension when he reflects that at any moment a messenger may start from it with the dread announcement that the continuity has taken flight. That is where the subtle current which flows along the conductor, a part of which is now submerged in the great ocean depths, is generated, and where the mysterious apparatus by which electricity is weighed and measured, as a marketable commodity, is fitted up. In that little apartment, which will not hold more than five persons, one of the operators sleeps, because there is no room for him to sleep elsewhere, every available place being already occupied. The electricians' office is never left without a watch, day or night, and every movement of the little needle that tells the existence of the current in the cable is watched with the greatest interest. A brief description of what this apartment contains will give the reader an insight into all the operations that are performed therein.

A system has been devised for transmitting and receiving signals through the cable from ship to ship, during the process of paying out. This has been done by Mr. Laws and Mr. De Sauty, the two gentlemen who have charge of the electrical department on board our ship, and was accepted by the directors of the company, and made an order of the Board, by their minutes of June 7, 1858. It consists of an exchange of currents sent alternately during a period of ten minutes by each ship, which not only serve to give an accurate test of the continuity and insulation of the conducting wire, but also to give certain signals which are required to be sent when the ships are far apart. For instance, every ten miles of cable paid out is signalized from ship to ship, as also the approach to land or momentary stoppage for splicing, shifting coils, &c. The electrical apparatus employed on board the two vessels is not very complicated, and is simply composed of testing instruments, wholly different from those to be used for the transmission of messages when the ends of the cable shall be landed.

The electric current is generated by sand batteries consisting of plates of zinc and copper, about fourteen square inches each, arranged by pairs. These plates are immerged in a solution of sulphuric acid and water, mixed with saw dust, for the purpose of preventing the liquid from overflowing. Two hundred and forty of these pairs are in operation on board of each ship. The instrument used for sending the current thus created through the line is an ordinary commutator, in the form of a reversing key, by which the operator can, at will, send the zinc of copper current of the battery into the cable, and by so doing change the nature of the signals. The current next passes through an electro-magnetometer, an instrument very useful for the purposes of testing. It is composed of an electro-magnet, the armature of which can be "furthered" or "approached" by a small screw, so as to require a stronger or weaker current to attract it. It shows the charge as every current flows into the cable and the discharge as it comes out. Before entering the line the electric current is made to pass through a second instrument, called the marine galvanometer, which was invented by Professor Thomson, of Glasgow University, one of the directors of the company. The magnetic needle, which is placed in the centre of a coil of wire, instead of marking its own deflections as in ordinary galvanometers, has a little mirror fixed to it, the reflection of which creates a small spot of light according to the deflections, moving on a horizontal scale of white paper, placed at about eighteen inches from the instrument itself. This instrument reports accurately the force of the currents, not only in the sending, but also in the receiving from the corresponding ship.

Besides this marine galvanometer, the only other instrument in circuit when receiving is the ordinary galvanometer usually employed for testing. According to the nature of the current received, the needle is deflected to the right or the left of a point marked zero on the dial, and where the needle is in a vertical position when no current is passing through the coil of wire surrounding it. Every one of the deflections read on the galvanometer, as also the charge and discharge indicated by the magnetometer, are carefully recorded, so that if a defect of continuity or insulation occurred it might be visible by comparison with those received before.

These are all the instruments in the electrical department, and this is a simplified explanation of their various uses, so that the unscientific can understand them.

Second Day—July 30.

All through the night the sound of the machinery never ceased, and the continuity remained perfect. At half-past three o'clock this morning the last flake of the forward spar deck coil began to run out, and considerable anxiety is manifested in regard to the change to that on the forward main deck, which is immediately beneath. Every precaution, however, has been taken to guard against accident, and by a quarter to four the agony is over; the first turn of the new coil has been reached, and the cable is going out in splendid style. The interest is now transferred to the main deck, for there is nothing further to attract the attention in the appearance of the circle which has just become vacant—nothing but the thick tar that covers the floor, the broken cone, and the rings or fair-leaders through which the cable passes before it runs over the bobbins that lead to the machine. Yet it would be wrong to say that there is little of interest in this circle, for have we not successfully paid out all the cable it contained; and who doubts we would find more pleasure in looking at all the circles when empty? The ease with which the line runs out of the ship at this distance from the stern, for we are now about two hundred and seventy feet from that point, is calculated to infuse new confidence into every one who sees it, but it is, after all, a confidence terribly shaken by vague fears of the future. We have five or six days to run before we get into Trinity Bay, and in that time, which, in our state of suspense, seems so many years, what may not occur? We are afraid even to think of success, so often have our hopes been blasted by disappointment; the very thought of the magnitude of the undertaking brings with it a feeling almost akin to discouragement. We know that the risk is doubled by the employment of two ships, while at the same time it must be acknowledged our chances of success are increased by thus reducing the time one half. But, again, in running the distance between the two points which it is designed to connect, there is the probability that either or both vessels will get into a gale, and in that event the prospect of laying the cable becomes fearfully dubious. Such a gale as that we have had—an eight-day affair—would very soon put an end to the undertaking, and still the work appears easy and practical enough. Follow the course of the cable as it comes out of the coil, passes over the bobbins, round the sheaves of the paying-out machine, and so on till it goes overboard, and you will be fully impressed with its practicability. Yet what is the reason that all the attempts hitherto made have failed, you may ask? Why, if three hundred miles have submerged, is it not also possible to lay two or three thousand? This is a question which appears very simple, and which is yet rather difficult to answer. It is easy to say that the breaking of the cable is caused by defective machinery, but who is able to account satisfactorily for the break of continuity which occurred in June last, after forty miles had been paid out of both ships? This it is which raises the greatest doubts in the minds of all, and which makes even the most hopeful apprehensive as to the result. That word "continuity" has created more uneasiness and anxiety than any thing connected with the work, simply because it is seemingly beyond the control of scientific skill, and, once gone, cannot be restored by human ingenuity. At any moment we may hear that it has parted, and sleeping or waking, the fear that it will haunts us like a nightmare. Oh, how we long to see that bleak and barren, but to us, more desirable coast than any that ever met the gaze of enraptured voyager. What would we not give to be steaming up towards the head of Trinity Bay with the telegraph station in full view? Five or six days yet to run, at the end of which time we may be returning to Queenstown, again to bring the news of disaster and defeat. But we must not think of defeat now—we are bound for Newfoundland, and if Providence favors us, two or three weeks at the farthest will see us entering the bay of New York, after having successfully accomplished the greatest work ever undertaken by man. But let us see what progress we have made during the last twenty-three hours, for it is now twelve o'clock, and we have been paying out since one yesterday afternoon. The following table shows the distance run according to the different logs therein stated:

By observation,	89 miles.
By ship's log,	99½ miles.
By engineer's log,	102 miles.
By patent log,	105 3-10 miles.

The length of cable paid out, according to the indicator attached to the machine, is 131 miles and 900 fathoms, or a surplus over the distance run, as shown by observation, of 42 miles and 900 fathoms, which is equal to about 48 per cent. This is a ruinous expenditure, and if it should continue at the same rate for the next two or three days, we might as well abandon the undertaking at once, turn our ship's head toward England, and make the best of our way back. It must not be forgotten, however, that in starting, a large amount of slack was allowed, so as to prevent an undue strain upon the cable before some fifteen or twenty miles should have been paid out. Of course, it is almost needless to say that we will be forced into no such expenditure during the next twenty-four hours. Besides, we expect to be able to run out the cable at the rate of seven and eight miles an hour yet, and experience has proved the faster it is paid out the loss is proportionably diminished. There is sufficient to allow a surplus of thirty per cent.; and if that should not be enough, we can land the end at the entrance instead of at the head of Trinity Bay, as was proposed in the event of our having sufficient for the purpose. The depth of water during the last twenty-four hours has varied from 1,600 to 1,975 fathoms, but it appears to have no effect upon the laying of the cable—in fact, the great depth of water is one of the least obstacles against which we have to contend.

The electrician on watch has just reported to Mr. Field that he received a despatch at twenty-one minutes past two from the Agamemnon, which is now some two hundred and thirty miles off, and that they had paid out from that vessel 150 miles; and at thirty-six minutes past two we inform them by electric signals that we have laid the same length. This shows that she is ahead of us by fifteen minutes, which is equal to a mile and a half. We have thus far got along most successfully, but the remembrance of that unpleasant incident about the continuity still clings to our minds, and forbids us to indulge in any sanguine expectations. The weather, too, is beginning to look unfavorable; and, what is still worse, the barometer is falling, though slowly. A gale at this particular time would be a most unwelcome visitor, and we trust that although Lieutenant Maury was wrong in his meteorological calculations about the month of June, he will turn out to be correct on this occasion. The sky is overcast with gloomy-looking clouds, and the appearance of the horizon is very threatening and squally. The barometer has fallen half an inch, and has still a downward tendency, while the wind is slowly but steadily increasing. It is evident that we are in for it, unless those indications which have never deceived us before are at fault this time. The wind continues to increase towards evening, but up to seven o'clock it has not reached the magnitude of a gale. It is only blowing fresh—what sailors would call a stiff top-gallant breeze, and as long as it keeps at that we are all right, and have nothing to fear. Nine o'clock, and still no gale; but unless the barometer is astray, we will catch it some time during the night. Ten o'clock has just struck, but, strange to say, the wind is going down, and the sea is following the example. It is to be hoped it will stay down, and remain so till we get into New York, for we have had quite enough of it already, and have learned by experience that a smooth sea is preferable to "rolling billows" at any time. The night is clearing up, and through the patches of sky which are seen through openings in the drifting and broken scud, the quiet stars are peeping out. The would-be gale is literally used up, and we have a calm and beautiful night for the continuance of our work. Confidence is rising rapidly, and the bids in favor of its success are becoming quite heavy in the imaginary stock market which has been established on board. When it was reported that the continuity was not so perfect as we could wish, stocks went down with a terrible rush, and there were no bidders at any price. But twenty-four hours decided the matter; the Atlantic telegraph ran up to fifty per cent., and continued going up till it reached the remarkable figure of seventy-five. The cable is, indeed, the absorbing subject of conversation on board, and other things are only spoken of as they bear some relation to it. That group of sailors near the cook's galley are engaged in an animated discussion on the all-prevailing topic. One of the number is trying to persuade his messmates that it is impossible to lay it; but they lend him a rather unwilling ear, and are evidently more strongly inclined to the other view of the subject. Among them, too, is the same individual who delivered his opinion with such emphasis some time ago on "continuity," but who has since become a most sincere convert, and a firm believer in the faith that the cable can be laid. The very messenger boys are as deeply interested in the subject as the oldest tar on board, and at their head stands a bright-looking lad, who was rewarded the other day by Mr. Field for the look-out he kept for the Agamemnon. In the enthusiasm which has succeeded the hopeless despondency, and in which nearly the whole ship was sunk, a sort of veneration has sprung up for every thing with which the cable has been placed in contact. Some have designs upon the pieces of planking which formed the floor of the circles in which it has been or is coiled, and specimens of the cable itself are more highly prized now than they ever were before. Nothing is thought of during the day but the cable, and at night I believe two-thirds of the crew don't dream of any thing else. We have all become superstitious, and the man who has the most auspicious dreams is as eagerly listened to as if he were an infallible oracle.

"I dreamed last night," said one of these, "that we had laid the cable, and there was not a single break in it; and my dreams always come in true, as M. can tell you; for I told him a thing that he found out had happened exactly at the time revealed to me." This was considered by some as proof positive, while those who looked with contempt at prognostications, auspicious dreams, auguries, omens, and such like, smiled upon the dreamer with indulgent consideration. They were evidently pleased to listen, and although they would emphatically have contradicted the charge of being superstitious, the gratification which they manifested had somewhat of a leaning in that direction. Whether they are or are not superstitious, we hope the dream will be fulfilled, however, and that the Agamemnon as well as the Niagara will succeed in accomplishing her share of the work. If we should pass over another day in safety there will not be a single sceptic on board; for those who were the most incredulous are fast giving way before the strong evidence with which they have been presented in the last twenty-four hours. The feeling of confidence in the prospects of to-morrow is greatly strengthened by the facility with which all the operations are carried on, and by the admirable manner in which the paying-out machine works. Let the continuity remain perfect and there will be no difficulty.

Third day—July 31.

The desperate effort which was made yesterday by the barometer to get up a gale proved a total failure, and we have now one of the finest days for cable laying we have had during this expedition. The index hand pointed 29.64 still, but the wind would not come, the sea refused to rise without some provocation, and so the date of the storm was postponed indefinitely. There is, however, a thick mist, through which the Gorgon is indistinctly visible a short distance in advance on our starboard bow; but this is already beginning to disappear, and before noon the horizon will be perfectly clear. The first point of attraction is the coil, for if the cable is running from it freely you may be certain that all is right. The coilers who sit on the margin of each flake are amusing themselves in the intervals of their work by manufacturing little balls out of the tar, which has become hardened by exposure to the air, and throwing them down before each turn as it is taken up from the coil. As the cable passes out at the rate of from seven to eight miles an hour, it strikes these balls with considerable force while it courses round the circle, sending them before it with still greater speed. The rate at which they run depends to a great extent on their spherical form, and he who makes them roundest is generally the winner. As no bets, however, are offered or made, no pecuniary advantage accrues to any of the parties concerned. Occasionally a lump of chalk, a small potato, or a piece of wax candle is entered for the race, in which the chalk generally comes out ahead. As it is impossible for any accident to occur from this, and as it affords a harmless amusement to the men, without interrupting the work, they are not interfered with. They are always ready at the end of each flake to lead the cable into the centre, and perform the operation so well that a kink is almost a matter of impossibility. It is a pleasure to look upon their earnest, eager faces, and observe the care with which they handle the line while passing it from the outer edge of the circle to the cone. Although this operation requires to be repeated about fifty times a day, they always perform it successfully. If they allow a single kink to take place the expedition might be considered as at an end, for it would be next to impossible to remedy the damage. Not a man among them who does not know that, and who does not realize the full importance of the duty with which he is entrusted. The reader must by this time be aware that in paying out the cable, the greatest caution has to be observed to prevent it from kinking, and as there is a much greater tendency to kink near the cone, which is in the centre of the circle, than as you approach the circumference, the ship is always slowed down about five minutes before the last or outermost turn is taken up. As soon, however, as this critical part of the work is safely performed, word is passed to the engineer to "go ahead," and immediately after the huge propeller is again revolving with its former velocity.

Contrary to the predictions of some, the change from the forward main deck coil to that on the deck immediately below, took place at half-past five this afternoon. It was thought that we would not have it all paid out before midnight, but the speed had been somewhat increased during the last twenty-four hours, and the rapidity with which flake after flake passed out satisfied those on watch that the coil would be exhausted long before the time announced. At least an hour before the change was made the outer boundaries of the circle in which the cable lay was literally crowded with men, and never was greater interest manifested in any spectacle than that which they exhibited in the proceedings before them. There were serious doubts and misgivings as to the successful performance of this important part of the work, and these only served to increase the feeling of anxiety and suspense with which they silently and breathlessly await the critical moment. The last flake has been reached, and as turn after turn leaves the circle every eye is intently fixed on the cable. Now there are but thirty turns remaining, and as the first of these is unwound, Mr. Everett, who has been in the circle during the last half hour, gives the order to the engineer on duty to "slow down." In a few moments there is a perceptible diminution in the speed, which continues diminishing till it has reached the rate of about two miles an hour.

"Look out now, men," says Mr. Everett, in his usual quiet, self-possessed way. The men are as thoroughly wide awake as they can be, and are waiting eagerly for the moment when they shall lift the bight of the cable, and deliver it out safely. One of the planks in the side of the cone has been loosened, and just as they are about taking the cable in their hands, it is removed altogether, so that as the last yard passes out of the now empty circle, the line commences paying out from the circle below, or the "orlop" deck coil, as it is called. The men, who are no other than the coilers, or "Knights of the Black Hand," as they have not inappropriately been termed, have done their work well, and the applause with which they have been greeted by the crowd of admiring spectators is the most gratifying testimony they can receive of the fact. They have hardly passed the cable out of the circle before they are received with as enthusiastic a demonstration of approval as the rules of the navy will permit. Such a clapping of hands was never heard at the Academy of Music, and if they had only been indulged a little, they would have raised such a cheer as would have aroused old Neptune from the profoundest depths of his marine dominions. The hatches, which were covered over in the construction of the circle, are opened, and the daylight is thrown upon the top of the coil, from which the first flake is now being paid out. The same scene is presented as that exhibited in all the coils during the paying-out process, except that the rather dim daylight which penetrates to this deck renders the aid of candles a matter of absolute necessity. The removal of the hatches discloses to the view of those above the Knights of the Black Hand sitting, or rather crouching in a very unknightly manner, on the top of the cable, as the narrow space between it and the beams of the deck will not allow them to take a more erect or graceful position. Two dozen candles and a half-dozen lamps illuminate the circle: for, after all, it is hardly worth while saying any thing about the dubious instalment of daylight which is given here. It is certainly a strange spectacle, that cable paved circle from which the black line is rapidly ascending to the deck above, on its way to the bottom of the ocean—those men who seem to have been placed there for no other purpose than to look at it as it passes upwards—and lastly, that superintendent, who sits on the outside of the circle, and whose presence is necessary to make the scene perfect. But those men have been placed there for another purpose, and a most important one, too. There they sit, it is true, and in a rather uncomfortable position for the time being, but wait until the last turn of this flake is about leaving the circle, and you will see them display the greatest activity. Now they seize it in their hands and run with it towards the centre or cone, so as to prevent the possibility of a kink when the change from the long to the short turns takes place, and when this task is accomplished they return to their places, until they are again summoned forth to a repetition of the same operation.

In a few minutes the excitement attendant on this important operation ceases, but as we approach our destination, and our chances of success increase with every hour, the feeling of suspense and anxiety becomes absolutely painful. This is our third day, and since the two ships started from mid-ocean we have paid out a greater length of cable than was ever laid before. We hardly dare ask ourselves if we shall lay the line the whole distance—it seems too much to hope for—and we dread to think of the future. We count the day not by hours, but by minutes, and retire at night not to sleep, but to think through the tedious and weary moments of the all-absorbing subject. The sound of the machinery has become as familiar to us as that of our own voices, and when it is drowned in any other noise we listen with eagerness to hear it again.

The barometer is consulted hourly and its variations watched with a jealous eye, for we can now appreciate fully how much depends upon the weather. So far we have been greatly favored, but who can tell what another day may bring forth; and the weather-wise insist that the barometer never falls so low without a gale. The anticipation of such a thing is certainly not calculated to set one's mind at rest, beleaguered as it is by the fear that some untoward accident may happen to the Agamemnon which would cause the rupture of the cable.

At twelve o'clock to-day, we were in lat. 51 deg. 5 min., lon. 38 deg. 28 min., having made the following run:

	Miles.
Distance made good by observation, ...	137
By ship's log, ...	141¾
By engineer's log, ...	142¼
By patent log, ...	137 6-10.

—while the length of cable paid out during the preceding twenty-four hours was 159 miles 843 fathoms, showing a surplus of 22 miles over the distance run, which is an expenditure of seventeen per cent. The depth of water varied from 1,657 to 2,250 fathoms. Wind east by south-east. The Agamemnon informed us at a quarter to three o'clock, P. M., by telegraph signal, that they had paid out 300 miles of cable up to that time.

Fourth Day—August 1.

Confidence is growing stronger, and there is considerable speculation as to the time we shall reach Newfoundland. The pilot who is to bring us into Trinity Bay is now in great repute, and is becoming a more important personage every day. His opinion is solicited in regard to the weather, as he is supposed to know something about it in these latitudes, and he is particularly catechized on the navigation of the bay and the formation and character of the coast. We are really beginning to have strong hopes that his services will be called into requisition, and that in the course of a few days more we will be in sight of land. The night has passed without accident, the barometer is rising, and the wind has gone round to the north-west, a sure indication that we will have clear weather. But the sea is not at all so smooth as it was the day before; it is in fact so rough as to favor the belief that there must have been a severe gale a short time since in these latitudes. The wind is also very perceptibly increasing, and there are serious misgivings that we are going to have that threatened gale now. The condition of the vessel is such as to alarm us greatly for the safety of the cable, should it come on to blow very hard, as the large amount already paid out, and the quantity of coal consumed, have lightened her so much as to render her rather uneasy in a heavy sea. The barometer is still rising, and rising very rapidly, but the wind is increasing, and although it has not yet attained the magnitude of a gale, it is blowing rather fresh for us in the present unsettled state of our feelings. It is not a head wind, however, and that is greatly in our favor. Both wind and sea are nearly abeam, and the rolling motion which the latter creates brings a strain upon the cable which gives rise to the most unpleasant feelings. The sea, too, seems to be getting worse every minute, and strikes the slender wire with all its force. Every surge of the ship affects it, and as it cuts through each wave, it makes a small white line of foam to mark its track. The sight of that threadlike wire battling with the sea, produces a feeling somewhat akin to that with which you would watch the struggles of a drowning man, whom you have not the power of assisting. You can only look on, and trust either that the sea will go down, or that the cable may be able to resist the force of the waves successfully. Of the former there is very little prospect, but of the latter there is every reason for hope. The struggle has been going on now for several hours, and there is no more sign of the cable parting than when it commenced. The electricians report the continuity perfect, and the signals which are received at intervals from the Agamemnon, show that that vessel is getting along with her part of the work in admirable style. What more can we desire? Yes, there is something more; for, although we are doing so well, we are unreasonable enough to wish we were doing better, or rather to wish that we had done altogether, and were safe in Trinity Bay, after landing the cable. We are still more unreasonable to wish that we were steaming up the bay of New York; and that, after this terrible contest between fear and hope, we were once more at home and among our friends—at home, to tell them of all we have seen and all we have done—how we have failed or succeeded, as Providence only can determine. We have known what it is to be defeated again and again; and, although some of us have suffered much from anxiety and watching, we can hardly tell what an excess, what a wild delirium of joy, success may not create among us. But this is anticipating what may never happen; for, although we have been successful thus far, who can say we will continue so to the end?

It would seem impossible that where there is so much anxiety and mental uneasiness, the most ludicrous affair could excite even a smile; and why it should be otherwise let the philosophic say. An incident illustrative of this remark was afforded this afternoon, just about dinner time.

"Well," said a member of one of the messes, approaching some of his associates, "well, it is done at last."

"What is done?" said half a dozen, with the most impatient haste; "What is done, the cable?"

"The cable? No, dinner is done!" he replied, with a tone of disgust that showed, however his comrades might regard his remark, he certainly did not intend it as a joke. They laughed, however, as much as if it were intended for one, probably more because his explanation relieved their minds from the apprehension that it was really the cable he spoke of. However improbable it may appear, there are some who seem to think less of their own lives than they do of the tarred line now running over the stern; and there are few who would not risk their own safety to secure that of the cable. This is paramount to all other considerations, and every one feels that it is so, from the apprentice boy up to the captain.

We have made a better run to-day than during any twenty-four hours since we started. At 12 o'clock we were in lat. 50 deg. 32 min., long. 41 deg. 55 min., having made from 139 to 145 miles, as is shown by the following:

Distance run by observation,	. . . . . .	145 miles.
" Ship's log,	. . . . . .	139 "
" Engineer's log,	. . . . .	142 "
" Patent log,	. . . . . .	141 7-10

In running this distance we have paid out 164 miles 683 fathoms of cable, which shows a surplus of 19 miles 683 fathoms over the distance run by observation, or about 14 per cent. The depth of the water varies from 2,424 to 1,950 fathoms, and the wind, which blew from W. N. W., freshened very considerably. It did not, however, attain the force of a gale, and what was still more gratifying, began to fall as night approached, while the barometer continued rising.

Fifth Day—August 2.

At seven o'clock this morning a steamer was reported coming from the westward, and steering directly on our course. What vessel could it be? Not the Porcupine, which the British government despatched to Trinity Bay to look out for the Niagara on her arrival. No, it could not be the Porcupine, for she would not come out so far. It must be one of the Boston or New York steamers, which had followed the course of the Telegraph plateau for the express purpose of meeting and speaking the Niagara. Yes, it must certainly be from either of these places. A few minutes more, however, will place the matter beyond conjecture.

In half an hour from the time at which she was reported we discovered that she was a Boston steamer bound for Liverpool. On coming up to the Gorgon she slowed down, and finally stopped to make signals with our escort, from which she learned the mission on which we are employed, as well as the success that has attended us thus far. As it was impossible for the Gorgon to stop, the steamer turned off her course, and proceeded westward with her until she obtained all the information she could glean. Then stopping and waiting till we came up, she displayed a signal which we supposed indicated her number or name, but which we were unable to make out. Her deck was literally crowded with passengers, and from what we could see of them through the glass, it was evident that they were watching us with the greatest interest. Capt. Hudson had the telegraph flag displayed at the mizen, and as it is of somewhat gigantic dimensions, with the words "Atlantic Telegraph" wrought upon it in large letters, they had no difficulty in determining who and what we were. Then, too, if they could not discern the delicate line between our stern and the water, they must certainly have seen the wheel over which it was paid out, revolving with a speed that showed we were doing our work rapidly and well. The rate of paying out had reached seven miles an hour, and we were going through the water at from five to six. How different from the expedition of last year, when the speed of the ship hardly exceeded an average of four miles per hour! After watching us for fifteen or twenty minutes the steamer proceeded on her course, dipping her flag to us as she went—a compliment which was promptly returned. Less than an hour after she had disappeared below the horizon, and we could only trace her course by the black line of smoke she left along the sky.

There was a very heavy swell, like that left after a gale, during the whole of this day, and our ship rolled as she never rolled before, and as we had hardly considered her capable of doing. The cable, however, exhibited no sign of parting, and ran out at an angle with the water that showed that it was not affected by a strain greater than the eighteen hundred pounds which had been put upon the brakes. As for the machinery itself, nothing could be more perfect than the way it worked—no jarring, no irregularity of motion, but every thing in and about it was as steady and as perfect in its operation as clock-work. It has been running four days altogether, and is just as reliable now as when it was set in motion after the splice was lowered in mid-ocean. The tar which is pressed out of the cable as it passes over the grooved wheels, collects in large quantities; but the scrapers, which the wise foresight of Mr. Everett provided, prevent it from accumulating in the wheels and clogging their action. The brakes have never once failed, and never allow the strain upon the cable to exceed the pressure of the weights. They are properly called self-releasing, and although they can, by means of additional weights, be made to increase the pressure or strain upon the cable, yet, until those weights are still further increased, it is impossible to augment that strain in any other way. Whether we are successful or not, no fault can be found with the machinery. The ship may roll still worse than she does now—and that is bad enough—but it is not in the least affected by her motion, and pays out as steadily and as easily in a heavy swell as if there was not a ripple on the sea. The cloud of steam which rises from it, and which occasionally envelopes the operatives, proves how indispensable the use of water is in working the brakes, for the heat produced by the friction is so great, that if not kept down it would char and burn up the elm blocks in a very short time. Several gallons of water are consumed daily by the friction of the brakes, and thrown off in clouds of steam, sometimes as dense as that which is blown off by a locomotive. Large quantities of tar are pressed out of the cable as it enters and leaves the machine, and fall into tubs which are left near the machine for its reception. Of this stuff a couple of ordinary sized barrels full are collected each day and thrown overboard. It is all-pervading, and besmears every thing about it within a distance of twenty feet. The course of the cable is marked by one continuous black line, and small feathery-looking flakes of it are whirled through the air, besmearing every thing they touch. Some parts of the ship look as if a heavy shower of it had fallen, and in others it has become hard as it accumulated, and formed into little mounds. The front of the dynamometer has changed its original green color, and is now almost entirely black, while the operatives at work at and around the machine are covered with large patches of the same color. Yet with all its disadvantages it would be a difficult matter to get along without the tar, for it has proved the greatest preserver that could be found for the cable.

I have said that despite the bad weather and heavy sea the paying-out process was going on well, but during the night the continuity was again affected, and although it was restored and became as strong as ever, yet it was for about three hours a very unpleasant affair. It was subsequently found that the difficulty was caused by a defect of insulation in a part of the wardroom coil, which was cut out in time to prevent any serious consequences. There were only a few on board the ship, however, aware of the occurrence until after the defect was removed, and the electrical communication was re-established between the two ships: Both Mr. Laws and Mr. De Sauty, the two electricians on the Niagara, were of the opinion that the insulation was broken in some part of the wardroom coil, and on using the tests for the purpose of ascertaining the precise point, they found that it was about sixty miles from the bottom of that coil, and between three and four hundred from the part which was then paying-out. The cable was immediately cut at this point and spliced to a deck coil of ninety miles, which it was intended to reserve for laying in shallow water, and was therefore kept for Trinity Bay. About four o'clock in the morning the continuity was finally restored, and all was going on as well as if nothing had occurred to disturb the confidence we felt in the success of the expedition.

At noon we were in latitude 49° 52′, longitude 45° 37′, and had run, by observation, 154 miles, and by log as follows:

By ship's log, ...	144 miles.
By engineer's log, ...	141 6-8 "
By patent log, ...	141 3-10 "

The length of cable paid out was 177 miles 150 fathoms for the preceding 24 hours, which is a surplus of 23 miles 100 fathoms over the distance, or 15 per cent. The depth of water was from 2,385 to 1,600 fathoms. Wind north. The signals which have been received from the Agamemnon inform us that she is paying out at the rate of seven and eight miles an hour, from which we derive the assurance that she has fine weather, and that like ourselves, she is making the most of it. The night has set in fine; the barometer continues rising, and although the vessel still rolls considerably, we have had experience enough to tell us there is nothing to be feared from this motion. It is, however, impossible to throw off the feeling of uneasiness created by the interruption of the electrical communication, and those of us who have a more nervous temperament find it a difficult matter to sleep. The writer tried hard for something like four long hours to get into that blissful state of oblivion, but it was of no use; it was impossible to think of any thing else but the cable; and abandoning the attempt, he got up, and passed the remainder of the night in visits to the coil, to the machine, the stern of the ship, and the electrical department.

Sixth Day—August 3.

This is the anniversary of the day on which Christopher Columbus sailed on his voyage of discovery to America—is it to be still further signalized as one of those on which the work of connecting the Old and the New Worlds was accomplished? Heaven grant that it may be so, although it seems almost like presumption to hope. And yet there is a strong undercurrent of confidence that is often the precursor of success, although we are still about two hundred miles from land, and a kink in the cable, or a hole running through the gutta percha into the conductor—and through which you could not even force a hair—would render the labor of years utterly unavailing, we are so confident now, that we are calculating on seeing land to-morrow morning sometime about six o'clock, as the observation which was taken at noon to-day shows that it is not more than one hundred and fifty miles off.

The great work of this morning was the change from the fore hold coil to that in the wardroom, which are at least two hundred feet apart. This took place at eight o'clock in the morning, and as the time was known to all on board, there was even a larger crowd assembled to witness it than I observed at any of the other changes. It was considered a most critical time, and although the operation turned out to be very simple, it was anticipated by some with considerable uneasiness. The splice between the two coils had been made some hours in advance, and men were stationed all along the line of its course from the hold to the wardroom. Mr. Everett and Mr. Woodhouse were both on hand, the best men had been picked out to pass up the bight, or bend, when the last turn should be reached, and one man, named Henry Paine, a splicer, was specially appointed to walk forward with the bight to the after or wardroom coil. As the last flake was about to be paid out, the ship was slowed down, and by the time the last three or four turns came to be paid out, she could hardly be said to be moving through the water. The line came up more slowly from the hold, until they were nearing the bight, where it could not have been going out faster than half a mile an hour. One more turn and the bight comes up. There is not a sound to be heard from the crowd, who are watching it with eager and anxious faces from every point of view. No one speaks or has ventured to speak for the last minute, except the engineers, and they have very little to say, for their orders are conveyed in the most laconic style, and the quick "aye, aye!" of the men show that they understand the full value of time. "Now, men," says Mr. Everett, "look out for the bight," as those in the hold hand it up to the men on the orlop deck, and it is passed from hand to hand till it reaches the platform and long passage which has been built upon the spar deck for this part of the work. Here the bight arrives at last, and Paine takes it in his hand, paying out as he follows the line of the cable to the wardroom coil. How anxiously the men watch him as he walks that terrible distance of two hundred feet, and think that if he should happen to trip or stumble while he holds that bight in his hand, the great enterprise may end in disaster. It is not a difficult task, but how often have things that are so easily performed, been defeated by want of coolness. There is, however, such an easy self-possession about the man as he comes slowly after the long black line, that it inspires confidence. "All hands" have deserted the decks below, and follow him as he walks aft, and one in his impatience to get a glimpse of him, has nearly fallen through the skylight of the engine-room, in which he has smashed several panes of glass in the effort to save himself. "Pick up the pieces," says Paine, in a vein of quiet humor, as he proceeds on his course, without interruption, and coming up to the wheel, which is immediately above the wardroom, he straightens the bight, and the cable begins to run out from the top of the coil on the deck beneath. His work is done, and as the line passes out of his hands, he receives a round of applause from the hands of the spectators, who, but for those terrible navy rules, would have greeted him with a cheer that would have done his heart good. As it is, they must give vent to their feelings in some way, and the exclamations of "Well done!" "That's the fellow!" "By thunder, it's all right!" "Good boy, Paine!" are not a bad compromise after all. Besides, it might be rather premature at this time to indulge in any triumphant expression of feeling before we are even in sight of land.

All the signals we have received from the Agamemnon are most encouraging, and show that up to the present moment she has been as fortunate and successful as ourselves. If her per centage of loss does not exceed ours, she will doubtless land the end of her half of the cable at twelve o'clock to-morrow. As we have some sixty miles further to go before we reach the bay of Bull's Arm, which is at the head of Trinity Bay, we cannot accomplish our part of the work before seven or eight o'clock in the evening, and it is doubtful—on account of the condition of a portion of the cable which we have yet to pay out—whether we can do even that. The defective part, which was discovered yesterday in the wardroom coil, rendered it absolutely necessary to cut about sixty miles of it off, and to splice the severed end to the quarter-deck coil of ninety miles. This part of the line has been coiled so often, that it is bent and twisted to such an extent as to render it difficult to pay it out as fast as the other parts with safety. For this reason our landing will be delayed much longer than we expected, and it is hardly probable that we will be able to get into the bay of Bull's Arm before Thursday morning, the 5th instant.

The observation taken at noon to-day, places us in latitude 49 deg. 17 min., longitude 49 deg. 23 min., showing that we have run since twelve o'clock yesterday, 147 miles. Our run, according to the different logs, is as follows:

By ship's log,	137	miles.
By engineer's log,	138½	"
By patent log,	134½	"

In making this distance, 161 miles 763 fathoms of cable were paid out, which shows a surplus of 14 miles 613 fathoms expended, or an excess of ten per cent. The depth of water varied from 882 to 742 fathoms. Wind north-west.

At half-past two the Gorgon made a signal to us, which, translated from the numbers, reads as follows:

"I congratulate you on your success."

To this the following signal was sent:

"Accept my best thanks."

The weather was magnificent, and the surface of the ocean was hardly disturbed by a ripple. I have stated that the wind was W.N.W., and that is what the log of the ship says, but at times there was not enough to waft a feather, and the day was one of the mildest that this high northern latitude has ever seen. There was no indication of fog, unless the light summer haze that rested over the water could be tortured into the name. We saw several icebergs, some of the most gigantic dimensions, rising to an altitude of from fifty to a hundred feet. They were fashioned into a wonderful variety of forms, castles, towers, forts, Gothic church spires, columns, and one had a gigantic arch that seemed to rest on columns of emerald. The effect of the sun upon this was magnificent. The rays striking upon the clear green surface of the icy columns, the upper part of which were covered with a singularly fantastic fretwork, reflected themselves in all the hues of the rainbow. As our vessel proceeded on her course the position of the berg was entirely altered, and the great arch which we had seen but half an hour before, was transformed into a massive fort, with parapets and all the works of offence and defence. While looking at another, the crest of which rose above the water like a mountain peak, it fell apart, and sinking below the surface for a few moments, rose again in an entirely different form. One part resembled a large cliff with precipitous sides, in one of which was a miniature bay, on whose shores the swell of the sea broke in foam. The sky was one expanse of deep blue, except immediately over our heads, where a peculiarly beautiful corona of fleecy white clouds had rested. There was something so remarkable in its form and appearance, that those who felt inclined to look upon it as an auspicious sign, asserted that Heaven intended thus to crown our success, and mark its encouragement of the enterprise.

The calm that rested on the waters during the day was prolonged into the night, in the subdued darkness of which we can still discover some of the icebergs looming up above the water like immense rocks. There will be little sleeping on board the Niagara this night, for early morning will bring the long wished-for land in sight, and every one will be on the look-out.

Seventh day—August 4.

The morning of this day will be memorable in the history of the world, as that on which the Niagara first came in sight of the island outpost of the American continent, bearing to its shores one end of that great electric chain which is to destroy both time and distance, and bring the Old World into the closest communion with the New. It is an occasion only second to that on which the cable will be landed at the terminus of the great ocean line. And what a morning this is, so bright and so clear, within a few miles of the shores of a country which has been truly termed the land of fogs! There is not a breath of air, and were it not for its ever heaving pulse, the ocean would be as still and as motionless as the depths of the great plateau itself. As everybody is anxious to see the land, everybody is on the look-out. The men in the foretop are not satisfied with that elevation, and have gone up some fifty or sixty feet higher, while the main and mizen-masts have each a number of volunteers, every one of whom expects to be the first to report land. The forecastle has its look-outs too, although there is no prospect of their getting ahead of the others.

At seven o'clock land was reported from the main-mast, but the report was a little premature, for it was not really seen. About eight, however, the cheering cry of "land ho!" rang through the ship like a clarion note of triumph. Land at last, after six days of such anxiety and suspense as few men ever pass through—six days of weary watching, of feverish restlessness, and ending in nights that brought no repose. Land at last—yes, there it is, defined boldly and distinctly against the western horizon. Oh! friends at home, who believed we could not succeed, and who trembled as you read of that fearful gale, and the dangers through which we passed, had you seen the glowing faces, and the tears of joy that filled the eyes of all as we gazed upon the glad sight for hours, you too would have felt as we felt. With what deep earnestness we thought then of home, and how we conjured up before our mental vision the glad faces that would welcome us on our arrival! What a scene of wild excitement New York will present as the news that the "impracticable enterprise" has succeeded, and that in little more than a week the Niagara will make her appearance in its bay! But the voice of caution warns against too sanguine anticipations, and reminds us of the truth of the unwelcome proverb which everybody knows.

As we approach the land, we see more icebergs, some of which are floating in the bay, and others lying grounded on or near its shores. These bergs have assumed the most remarkable shapes, and are undergoing singular changes. There is one suspended in mid-air, over another, of which it is a perfect, though inverted fac simile. The land itself appears to be undergoing no less wonderful transformations, and where but a few brief minutes ago there was nothing visible but the rugged and wild-looking coast mountains, towns and villages have sprung up, as if the barren shores had been touched with a magician's wand and become an enchanted land. Far off, as far as the vision can reach, appears a stupendous railroad bridge, supported by a hundred abutments; but hardly has the eye rested on it before the abutments fade away, and a mountain with its peaks downwards and its base suspended in air takes its place. What strange land is this that startles the mind with its wonders? It is bleak, barren, rocky, foggy, mountainous Newfoundland, and there before us is the entrance to Trinity Bay, near the head of which the cable is to be landed.

The cities, and villages, and mountains suspended in mid-air with their peaks downward, are simply so many forms of the mirage, on which we have been gazing in bewildered astonishment for several hours past.

It is now half-past two o'clock, and we are entering Trinity Bay at a speed of seven and a half knots an hour, paying out the cable at a very slight increase on the same rate. The curve which it forms between the ship and the water proves that there is little or no strain upon it, and proves also another thing, that it can be run out at eight, nine, and I believe ten miles with the greatest safety. This, however, as I have previously stated, cannot be done with old cable that has been coiled so often as to have a tendency to kink, and there is, as has been already intimated, some of this kind which we will be obliged to pay out before landing. A signal, signifying "all well," has been received from the Agamemnon, which must now be on the point of landing her cable in Valentia Bay, Ireland, which is about 1,640 miles from our present position.

There is as yet no sign of the Porcupine, the steamer which was sent out by the British government to await our arrival, and render us any assistance we might require; and we fear she has gone round to St. John's, having abandoned all hope, after our failure in July, of ever seeing the Niagara. The only sign of life we have yet seen is that presented by a few fishing smacks, whose occupants seem to know who and what we are, but who, with one exception, have not exhibited the slightest enthusiasm. This individual waved his hat three or four times, and gave other indications of his pleasure at seeing us, and this is the only demonstration we have yet received of a private or public character.

A few minutes past five a steamer was reported in the bay, and soon after she was made out to be the Porcupine. In half an hour, her commander, Captain Otter, came aboard, and had a consultation with Mr. Field and Captain Hudson. He had, he said, given up all hope of seeing the Niagara, but had nevertheless posted look-outs on Bull's Island, which commands a view of the bay and a long distance out to sea. The minute he heard of her arrival he sent a telegraphic despatch to St. John's, to notify the people there of the fact. Mr. Field himself soon after went up to the telegraph station, which is fifteen miles from where our ship now is, with despatches for New York, and which, allowing for the difference in time between the two places, will be received there to-night at least an hour earlier than they are sent.

The Gorgon hoisted the American flag some hours ago at the fore, and the Niagara carries the English at the fore, while the telegraph flag floats from her mizen. Our progress up the bay is rather slow, on account of the condition of the cable, already alluded to; and it is now settled that we cannot get to our landing-place near the station before to-morrow morning. We are paying out the cable at three miles an hour, and as it is dark, the Porcupine goes ahead, and leads the way towards the Bay of Bull's Arm. The bleak mountains loom up through the night, and a huge bonfire, which has been built up in honor of our arrival on a neighboring hill, throws out columns of dense black smoke and great tongues of flame. It is a strange scene, of which our ship is now the centre, and in which she is the principal object. The moon has not yet risen, but it is not so dark as to prevent your seeing, though indistinctly, to a considerable distance. The after-deck coil, from which the cable is now going out, is illuminated with lamps, and about a dozen men are standing around the circle, ready to pounce upon any kinks that may make their appearance. The work is continued successfully to the end of this day; and as there are but a few more miles of cable to be paid out, it will be landed to-morrow morning.

According to observation to-day, the latitude was 48° 17′, longitude 52° 43′, showing the distance run to be 146 miles. The length of cable paid out was 154 miles 360 fathoms, the loss on which did not exceed 6 per cent. Depth of water from 742 to 200 fathoms.

LANDING OF THE CABLE.

Eighth Day—August 5.

At ten minutes past two this morning preparations were made for the landing of the cable, and the Niagara is brought to an anchor for the purpose. It is still quite dark, and we can only see the outlines of the hills which tower above us on every side, showing that we are in a completely landlocked harbor. We have just received the news from the electricians that a telegraphic despatch, or signal, has been sent from the Agamemnon, informing them that a thousand and ten miles of cable have been paid out from that ship up to the last hour. The intelligence is peculiarly gratifying at this time, and adds to the enthusiasm which every one feels. The operators have been at work all day and night, and still labor with as much zeal as at the commencement. Nobody has thought of going to bed, except a few who are so exhausted by their long watching as to render rest a matter of imperative necessity. Three of the Niagara's boats have been lowered, and two of these are to hold or buoy the cable at some distance from the stern of the vessel while the third receives a sufficient length to reach the telegraph station, which is about half a mile from the shore. As the Niagara has been brought to anchor, the cable is paid out over the machine with the aid of the little steam engine, which is put in gear with the paying-out sheaves. About a mile and a half is lowered and coiled in the boat, and by sunrise every thing is ready for the completion of the work. There is such a singular coincidence connected with this very part of the cable which is now about to be landed, that it deserves particular mention here. By reference to the account of the expedition of last year, it will be seen that the laying of the cable was commenced at Valentia Bay, Ireland, on the 5th of August, and that over three hundred miles of it had been paid out before it parted on the 11th of the same month. Some time after fifty or sixty miles were recovered, and this is a part of the same cable which is now about being landed. It is also somewhat singular that the cable was broken on the 29th of June last and spliced again on the 29th of July.

Before the landing of the cable, Captain Hudson notified the Captains of the Gorgon and Porcupine, and about five o'clock the boats of the Niagara were ranged in a regular line and connected with a hawser, to tow that on which the cable was coiled to the landing-place. The telegraph flag was displayed from the mizen truck, while the English flag was hoisted at the fore, and the American at the mizen peak. A similar compliment was paid to the American flag by the British vessels; and soon after our boats pushed off from the ship we observed others coming from the Gorgon and Porcupine to participate in the consummation of the great work. All the officers of the Niagara, with the exception of those on watch on the ship, were in the boats, the crews of which numbered altogether about sixty men. These, with the crews from the boats of the British ships, and all the officers, English and American, made a total of about one hundred men. The demonstration was certainly any thing but a pageant, for there were none of those accessories which make up what is generally understood by the word;

but there could be none who were imbued with a higher appreciation of the character of the occasion, nor who were better qualified to do it honor; and it is doubtful whether the presence of thousands would have added any thing to its importance or solemnity. It would be a difficult matter for one who has seen nothing but civic processions to form an idea of that which attended the last act in the completion of this enterprise. The scene, the circumstances, all conspired to render it totally different from any celebration the world has ever seen.

The Bay of Bull's Arm is an inlet of the sea at the head of Trinity Bay, from which it runs, between a range of irregular hills, a distance of about ten miles. Some of these hills rise to the dignity of mountains, which are in many places wooded down to the water's edge. The inhospitable nature of the climate, combined with the barren and rocky soil, is rather unfavorable to vegetation, and the forests are composed mainly of a stunted variety of pine, which seldom attains a height of more than 30 feet; while the turf, which in some places covers the rocks to the depth of three or four feet, is overspread with a thick growth of moss. The streams, which during the summer season become mere rivulets, are converted into foaming torrents by the freshets which follow the breaking up of the long and dreary winter. Judging from the hilly and mountainous character of this part of the country, and, indeed, of the whole island, the construction and establishment of railroads in the far distant future must prove a terribly expensive affair. The landing-place for the cable is a very picturesque little beach, on which a wharf has been constructed. A road, about the dimensions of a bridle path, has been cut through the forest, and up this road, through bog and mire, you find your way to the telegraph station, about half a mile distant. Alongside of this road a trench has been dug for the cable, to preserve it from accidents, to which it might otherwise be liable.

When the boats arrived at the landing the officers and men jumped ashore, and Mr. North, first lieutenant of the Niagara, presented Captain Hudson with the end of the cable. Captain Otter, of the Porcupine, and Commander Dayman, of the Gorgon, now took hold of it, and all the officers and men following their example, a procession was formed along the line. As the cable was covered with tar, the handling of it was rather objectionable, but there were none who, under the circumstances, refused to take a part in the landing. There were some, it is true, who would not at first put their bare hands to it, and who sought to protect them with gloves, or by covering the cable with moss. This movement, however, was rather unpopular; so the gloves were taken off, and although part of the moss adhered to the cable, there was little of it used afterwards. The road or path over which we had to take the cable was a most primitive affair. It led up the side of a hill a couple of hundred feet high, and had been cut out of the thick forest of pines and other evergreens. In some places the turf, which is to be found here on the top of the highest mountains, was so soft with recent rains that you would sink to your ankles in it. The road-maker or road-makers, whoever they were, had evidently done all in their power at the short notice they had to make it passable, and it is enough to say they succeeded to that extent, although we could not help wishing that they had not placed the stepping-stones so far apart, and had been a little more liberal in the use of timber. Well, it was up this road we had to march with the cable, and a splendid time we had. It was but reasonable to suppose that the three captains, who headed the procession, would certainly pick out the best parts, and give us the advantage of the stepping-stones, but it appeared all the same to them, and they plunged into the boggiest and dirtiest parts with a recklessness and indifference that satisfied us they were about the worst pilots we could have had on land, despite their well-known abilities as navigators.

This memorable procession started at a quarter to six o'clock, and arrived at the telegraph station about twenty minutes after. The ascent of the hill was the worst part of the journey, but when we got to the top, the scene which opened before us would have repaid us for a journey of twenty miles over a still worse road. There beneath us lay the harbor, shut in by mountains except at the entrance from Trinity Bay, and there, too, lay the steamers of the two greatest maritime nations in the world. On every side lay an unbroken wilderness, and if we except the telegraph station, at which we will soon arrive, not a single habitation to tell that man has ever lived here.

Never was such a remarkable scene presented since the world began. Even now, at the very point of its realization, it does not seem as if the work in which we have been engaged has been accomplished. Looking back on the past, the seven long days of anxiety and suspense appear but as one, and it is almost impossible for the mind to comprehend the great fact that the cable is really laid. It would seem like a dream, were it not for the visible, palpable evidence which we now hold in our hands, the electric chain which binds the two worlds together. No, it is not a dream, but a great reality, the announcement of which will startle the incredulous and unbelieving of both continents. The continuity, without which the cable would be utterly valueless, is as perfect now as it ever was. Mr. D. Laws and Mr. De Sauty, the two chief electricians, who have accompanied us from England, have "tasted" the current, and about a dozen others at the head of the procession have done the same thing. The writer himself is a witness on this point, and will never forget the singular acid taste which it had. Some received a pretty strong shock—so strong that they willingly resigned the chance of repeating the experiment.

About twenty minutes after we started from the beach we reached the station of the Atlantic telegraph on this side of the ocean, where we found some half dozen of the inmates awaiting our arrival. The station is a large frame building, two stories high, and eight windows wide. On the first floor is a kitchen, an office and a sitting apartment, dignified with the title of parlor. The door opens on the side of the house, and there is no means of exit from the front, for the simple reason that the first story is eight or ten feet from the ground. This singular arrangement is explained by the fact that the building is situated on the side of a hill, and that there is a considerable difference between the height of the front and back walls. The second story is divided into sleeping apartments separated by a single corridor, and the whole establishment will lodge about a dozen persons. A beginning has been made in the clearing away of the forest in the immediate vicinity of the house, and in the course of a year, they will have as pleasant and as comfortable a dwelling perhaps as any in Newfoundland, although it may not have all the luxuries of civilized life. Of the details of domestic life at the telegraph station more will be said hereafter. Meantime we must continue the particulars of our narrative.

On the arrival of the procession the cable is brought up to the house and the end placed in connection with the instrument. The deflection of the needle on the galvanometer gives incontrovertible evidence that the electrical condition of the cable is satisfactory. The question now is, how shall we properly celebrate the consummation of the great event? How, but by an acknowledgment to that Providence without whose favor the enterprise must have ended in disaster and defeat. Every one feels that this is all that is necessary to make the celebration complete, and to mark the undertaking as the work of two great Christian nations. When, therefore, they all gathered together before the telegraph station, they understood the purpose for which they were assembled. Captain Hudson took up his position on a pile of boards, the officers and men standing round amid shavings, stumps of trees, pieces of broken furniture, sheets of copper, telegraph batteries, little mounds of lime and mortar, branches of trees, huge boulders, and a long catalogue of other things equally incongruous.

"We have," said the captain, "just accomplished a work which has attracted the attention and enlisted the interest of the whole world. That work," he continued, "has been performed, not by ourselves; there has been an Almighty Hand over us and aiding us; and without the Divine assistance thus extended us, success was impossible. With this conviction firmly impressed upon our minds, it becomes our duty to acknowledge our indebtedness to that overruling Providence who holds the sea in the hollow of his hand. 'Not unto us, Oh Lord! not unto us, but to thy name, be all the glory.' I hope the day will never come when, in all our works, we shall refuse to acknowledge the overruling hand of a Divine and Almighty Power. It is He who can rebuke the winds and calm the seas. He works in a mysterious way for his people. His path is on the mighty waters. We have seen his power in the tempest; and when we have called upon Him in the time of trouble, He has heard our voice. And yet how ungrateful we are for all His favors, and how soon we forget Him when the trouble passes away like the summer cloud or the morning dew. On a solemn occasion like the present, we should feel more particularly our indebtedness to Him, and it is with a feeling of heartfelt gratitude we should acknowledge the many favors which He has bestowed upon us. There are none here, I am sure, whose hearts are not overflowing with feelings of the liveliest gratitude to Him, in view of the great work which has been accomplished through His permission, and who are not willing to join in a prayer of thanksgiving for its successful termination. I will, therefore, ask you to join me in the following prayer, which is the same, with a few necessary alterations, that was offered for the laying of the cable:

"'O, Eternal Lord God, who alone spreadest out the heavens and rulest the raging of the sea, who hast compassed the waters with bounds till day and night come to an end, and whom the winds and the sea obey—look down in mercy, we beseech Thee, upon us, Thy servants, who now approach the throne of grace, and let our prayer ascend before Thee with acceptance. Thou hast commanded and encouraged us in all our ways to acknowledge Thee, and to commit our works to Thee; and Thou hast graciously promised to direct our paths and to prosper our handiwork. We desire now to thank Thee, believing that without Thy help and blessing nothing can prosper or succeed, and we desire humbly to commit all who have been engaged in this undertaking to Thy care, protection and guidance. It has pleased Thee to enable us to complete what we have been led by Thy providence to undertake, that being begun and carried on in the spirit of prayer and in dependence upon Thee, it may tend to Thy glory, and to the good of all nations, by promoting the increase of unity, peace, and concord. May Thy hand of power and mercy be so acknowledged by all, that the language of every heart may be "Not unto us, O Lord; not unto us, but unto Thy name, give glory;" that so Thy name may be hallowed and magnified in us and by us. Thou hast controlled the winds and the sea by Thy almighty power, and granted us such favorable weather that we were enabled to lay the cable safely and effectually. Finally, we beseech Thee to implant within us a spirit of humility and childlike dependence upon Thee; and teach us to feel, as well as to say, "If the Lord will, we shall do this or that." Hear us, O Lord, and hear us in these our petitions according to Thy previous promise, for Jesus Christ's sake.'"

The "Amen" which followed the conclusion of this prayer showed what a sincere response it received from the hearts of all present, and the depth of feeling it excited. "You recollect," proceeded the Captain; "what our Saviour told his disciples, that if they had faith, even as a grain of mustard seed, they could move mountains. We have performed a work, or rather we are thankful to God for having performed a work for us, which has been ridiculed by a great many who regarded it as an impossibility. We have been peculiarly favored in being permitted to be His agents, and we are pleased to acknowledge that it was through His instrumentality the work was performed."

At the close of the foregoing remarks the audience of "cable layers" dispersed, some to amuse themselves in short excursions about the grounds adjoining the station, and others to explore the mysteries of the building itself. About an hour after, the captain, officers and men assembled on the beach where the cable had been landed, and where they re-embarked for their several ships. Up to this point, every thing had been conducted with silence and in a spirit of moderation, which some might consider ill-suited to the greatness of the work, and the feeling which the occasion might reasonably be supposed to call forth. Had such a scene occurred in the harbor of New York, it would have been impossible to restrain the wild enthusiasm and excitement of the people. And who is there under the circumstances that would desire to do so? But the men who laid that tarred line across one half of the Atlantic, and who had passed six days in anxious watching, in terrible suspense and in the midst of apprehension, one day hoping against hope, and the next fearing when the prospect appeared brightest, thinking of the one thing by day and dreaming of the one thing in their short and troubled sleep, until it seemed as if on that slender cable their very lives depended, and the accident that proved fatal to its safety were to put an end to their existence—these men were not devoid of enthusiasm. No, no; there was no want of enthusiasm among them; but it was determined that they should not give vent to it till the work was wholly accomplished—till the cable was landed, till they had carried the end in safety to the telegraph station, and till they had returned thanks to that Providence whose agents they were in the working out of the greatest achievement which has ever been conceived or performed by man. Want of enthusiasm! Oh, had the people of New York—of the United States—of the two worlds, heard the wild huzza that went ringing over the hills, chasing the deer from their coverts, sending thousands of startled sea birds out upon the ocean, as if the land no longer afforded them a place of security—had they seen the faces of these men, they would understand what enthusiasm is, and how unjust the suspicion that denied them the possession of an attribute only second to hope itself. A cheer it could hardly be called; it was one wild, prolonged shout of delirious joy, such as might welcome the disenthralment of a nation, or the union of two worlds—a union in which we all participate, you and I and every one of us, and the remembrance of which will live with us to the end. How eagerly we all waited for the word that told us the time had come when we might give vent to the feelings that had been so long restrained! And when the first lieutenant of the Niagara called upon us to give three cheers, what tongue could have remained, silent were it even the last sound it could utter?

"Now, men, three cheers," he cried; and the last word had hardly been spoken when the demand was responded to with an outburst that came from the very depth of the heart. "Hurrah! hurrah!! hurrah!!!" each louder and wilder than the last; and as the final cheer burst forth, the echoes took it up and repeated it again and again, till it seemed as if the wilderness around were peopled, and thousands of voices in every valley and on every mountain top joined in the glad shout of rejoicing. But three cheers are not enough—we must give another "for coming up"—that is for the last pull, for the landing of the cable. And still another is demanded, one which cannot be refused if it were the last cheer we should ever give. It is "One for America and England;" and it is called for by Captain Otter of the Porcupine, a gentleman whose earnest labors and whose untiring energy in his share of the work entitle him to the warmest praise. It was Captain Otter who surveyed the bay of Bull's Arm, and who guided us safely through all the intricacies of the passage the night of our entrance into Trinity Bay. To him and to Captain Dayman, of the Gorgon, who acted as our escort and pilot, from mid-ocean to the American termini, the line of the Atlantic Telegraph Company are largely indebted. It is doubtful if the British government could have selected from its long list of naval officers two who have proved themselves more capable of performing the work with which they were entrusted, or two who were more earnest in their exertions to promote the success of the great undertaking.

While the boats of the Niagara were on their way to that ship, they were cheered by the crews of the Gorgon and Porcupine, and at twelve o'clock a salute of twenty-one guns was fired from the former vessel.

As a large number of the men on board our ship had been at work all night, those who wished were allowed to "turn in," and there were very few who did not take advantage of the permission, and fewer still who did not enjoy their rest. They had worked hard and well, and took as deep an interest in the success of the work as those who had a greater stake in it.

MR. FIELD MAKES THE FIRST ANNOUNCEMENT TO THE NEW WORLD THAT THE CABLE IS LAID.

About eight o'clock on the evening of the 4th instant, while the Niagara was proceeding up Trinity Bay, and some seventeen or eighteen miles distant from the landing place, Mr. Field left the ship for the purpose of visiting the telegraph station, and if possible, of sending a despatch to the United States announcing the success of the enterprise. As the boat of the Porcupine was alongside, it was cheerfully placed at his disposal by Captain Otter, who had now undertaken to pilot the Niagara. Mr Field immediately set out, and as the Gorgon was on her way to the Bay of Bull's Arm, at the head of which the cable was to be landed, he went on board that vessel, and his boat was taken in tow. Here he was warmly received by Captain Dayman and his officers, who were in the full enjoyment of success. It was near two o'clock in the morning before he arrived at the beach, and as it was quite dark, he had considerable difficulty in finding the path that led up to the station. There was no house in sight, and the whole scene was as dreary and as desolate as a wilderness at night could be. A silence as of the grave reigned over every thing before him; while behind, at the distance of a mile, he could see the huge hull of the Niagara looming up indistinctly through the gloom of night, and the light of the lamps on her deck making the darkness still darker and blacker by the contrast. He entered the narrow road, and after a journey of what appeared to be twenty miles came in sight of the station, which stands about half a mile from the beach. There was, however, no sign of life there, and the house, in its stillness, seemed strangely in unison with every thing around. It had a deserted appearance, as if it had long since ceased to be the habitation of man. In vain he looked for a door in the front, there was no entrance there; he looked up at the windows in the hope, perhaps, of being able to enter by that way, but the windows of the lower story were beyond his reach, and the house having been partly built on piles gave it the appearance of being raised on stilts. A detour of the establishment, however, led to the discovery of a door in the side, and through this he finally succeeded in effecting an entrance. The noise he made in getting in, it was natural to expect, would arouse the inmates, but there seemed to be either no inmates to arouse, or those inmates were not easily disturbed. He stopped for a moment to listen, and as he listened he heard the breathing of sleepers in an apartment near him. The door was immediately thrown open, and in a few seconds the sleepers were awake, wide awake, and opening their eyes wider and wider as the wonderful news fell upon their astonished and delighted ears. They could hardly believe the evidence of their senses, and were bewildered at what they heard. The cable laid! when but a few short weeks before they had received the news of disaster and defeat, and they had looked only to the far distant future for the accomplishment of the great work. The cable laid, and they unconscious of it—they who had waited and watched so many weary days and weeks for the ships they had begun to believe would never come. What! and they were now in the bay—those same ships—within a mile of them! can they be dreaming? Dreaming! no—what they have heard is true, all true, and there is the living witness before them.

"What do you want?" was the exclamation of the first who was awakened, as he endeavored to rub the sleep out of his eyes.

"I want you to get up," said Mr. Field, "and help us to take the cable ashore."

"To take the cable ashore!" re-echoed the others, who were now just awaking, and who heard the words with a dim, dreamy idea of their meaning—"To take the cable ashore."

"Yes," said Mr. Field, "and we want you at once."

They were now thoroughly aroused, and directing Mr. Field to the bedrooms of the other sleepers—for there were four or five others in the house—they prepared themselves with all haste to assist in landing the cable. But the other inmates were already awake, and when Mr. Field made his appearance on the corridor which divides the sleeping apartments on each side of the house, he found them awaiting him in the lightest description of summer clothing. As they had neither pants, vests, coats, shoes nor stockings on, the curious will have no difficulty in discovering in what they were dressed. They were as amazed at seeing Mr. Field as if he were an apparition; and when they recovered themselves sufficiently to ask the meaning of such a strange visitation, they were thrown into another state of wonderment by what he related. When they learned all, they dressed, and prepared themselves for the work before them. Mr. Field found that the telegraph office would not be open till nine o'clock that morning, and that the operator of the New York, Newfoundland and London Telegraph was absent at the time. He also ascertained that the nearest station at which he could find an operator was fifteen miles distant, and that the only way of getting there was on foot. Now, fifteen miles in Newfoundland is about equal to twice the distance in a civilized country, and is a tolerably long walk; but it was something to be the bearer of such news to a whole continent, and so two of the young men willingly volunteered for the journey, bearing with them, for transmission to New York and the whole United States, the following despatch, which contained the first announcement of the successful accomplishment of the work, and the historical importance of which will justify its republication here:

United States Steam Frigate Niagara,
Trinity Bay, Newfoundland, August 5, 1858.

To the Associated Press, New York:—

The Atlantic Telegraph fleet sailed from Queenstown, Ireland, Saturday, July 17, met in mid-ocean, Wednesday, the 28th, made the splice at one P. M. Thursday, the 29th, and separated. The Agamemnon and Valorous bound to Valentia, Ireland, the Niagara and Gorgon for this place, where they arrived yesterday, and this morning the end of the cable will be landed. It is 1,696 nautical, or 1,950 statute miles from the telegraph house at the head of Valentia harbor to the telegraph house at the Bay of Bull's Arm, Trinity Bay, and for more than two-thirds of this distance the water is over two miles in depth.

The cable has been paid out from the Agamemnon at about the same speed as from the Niagara.

The electrical signals sent and received through the whole cable are perfect.

The machinery for paying out the cable worked in the most satisfactory manner, and was not stopped for a single moment from the time the splice was made till we arrived here.

Captain Hudson, Messrs. Everett and Woodhouse, the engineers, the electricians, officers of the ships, and, in fact, every man on board the telegraph fleet, have exerted themselves to the utmost to make the expedition successful, and by the blessing of Divine Providence it has succeeded.

After the end of the cable is landed and connected with the land line of telegraph, and the Niagara has discharged some cargo belonging to the Telegraph Company, she will go to St. Johns for coal and water, and then proceed at once to New York.

Cyrus W. Field.

HOW THE CREW OF THE NIAGARA CELEBRATED THE SUCCESS OF THE ENTERPRISE.

During the forenoon of the day on which the cable was landed, the greater part of the crew of the Niagara was permitted to go ashore and amuse themselves as well as they might in a perfect wilderness. And never did the crew of any vessel enjoy themselves with more zest under the circumstances,—it was different from their shore experience in other places, but the novelty only served to increase the pleasure.

Some amused themselves in explorations over the hills and through the forests; others in piscatorial excursions up the trout streams; others in swimming; while others commemorated the occasion by erecting a mast near the point where the cable was landed, and dignified the place with the title of "Niagara City." There were no lots marked out, it is true; no boundaries, nor any thing of that kind; but there may be at some future day, and if the inhabitants do not retain the name, they don't deserve to have a city—that's all. The portion of the crew who assisted in this work numbered about a hundred altogether, and among these was a considerable body of the firemen, under the charge of Mr. Sexton, the engineers' storekeeper. The high officiating personage on the occasion—in fact the founder of the future city—was John McMath, one of the sailors, and just the man to take the lead in such a movement. McMath resolved in his own mind that something more should be done to commemorate the great event in which he and his messmates had played a part, however humble, and acting upon this determination, he gathered a large number of the crew together, and addressed them on the subject. When they were all assembled he spoke in substance as follows:

"Now, boys, we are all here, and I want to say a few words to you. We have laid the cable. (Cries of yes, yes, and hurra). Yes, boys, we have laid the cable, and that's a fact, this time—no mistake now. (A voice—That's true, any way. Give us some more of that kind of talk, Mac.) It's down, and it'll stay down where we have put it. (Another voice—they'll have a job to lift it—that's all). Now, what I want to say to you is this—(Aye, aye). I want the people who come here to know, that the Niagara's boys have been here before them, and that it was they that laid the cable. No objections to that. (No, no, from a hundred tongues). Well, then, I have got something to propose. (What is it?—what is it?) I propose that we raise a mast on this very spot, and when we have got it up, that we shall call the place all round about "Niagara City." Are you all agreed? (Aye, aye, we're with you, Mac.)

At the close of this brief, but pithy and forcible address, they all unanimously decided that McMath should be the leader, and the better to perform his part he manufactured from the branch of a tree a boatswain's whistle, with which to direct the men in putting up the mast and rigging. Under his direction they went to work at the forest, selected the tallest pine, put a rope around it, and tugged and pulled till they dragged it up by the roots. They then cut off the branches, until nothing remained but the straight trunk of the tree, which they planted firmly in a deep hole they had dug for the purpose. This part of the work performed, they tore down several other trees to make yards for the mast. There was the main-yard, the maintop-yard, the maintop-gallant, and the main-royal-yard, and above these all floated the flag, which they extemporized for the occasion, and which bore the simple inscription "Niagara." At the close of their work, they gave three cheers, and separated, but the raising of the mast, and the founding of "Niagara City," furnished the subject of conversation among the crew for many days after.

HOME ECHOES OF THE GLAD TIDINGS.

The despatch which was sent to the Associated Press of New York did not, we understand, reach that city before the 5th, on account of the distance of the nearest station from the place where the cable was landed. That same day, however, and for a whole week, we continued to receive congratulations from all parts of the United States, and the British provinces. As they serve to show the feelings which our success called forth, and as they may be taken as the expression of the enthusiasm of the whole country, they will be read with interest. The following are pretty fair specimens of those received both at Trinity Bay and St. Johns:

[From New York.]

To Mr. Field:—

Despatch received. All well at home and store. Glorious.

C. W. Field & Co.

[From New York.]

To C. W. Field:—

Accept from your friends in New York their portion of the world's congratulations.

Peter Cooper.

St. Johns, N. B. August 7, 1858.

Trinity Bay, August 7, 1858.

[From New York.]

To C. W. Field, Esq:—

Sir—Your despatch has been received. I congratulate you, myself, and for the people of this city, on the success of the great work of uniting together the Old and New World, by the electric telegraph. Science, will, and perseverance have finally triumphed.

Daniel F. Tiemann.

Trinity Bay, August 7, 1858.

[From New York.]

To Cyrus W. Field:—

We have no facts in addition to your despatch of the 5th to the press. Every incident connected with the landing of the cable, or with the enterprise in any way, will be eagerly received by the public. Throughout the country there is intense anxiety to know all in relation to it, and the press desires the line kept open in the evening, so long as there are any facts of interest to warrant. PETER COOPER.

ST. JOHNS, August 9, 1858.

[From New York.]

Your family is all at Stockbridge, and well. The joyful news arrived there Thursday, and almost overwhelmed your wife. Father rejoiced like a boy. Mother was wild with delight; brothers, sisters—all were overjoyed. Bells were rung; guns fired; children let out of school, shouted, "the cable is laid"—"the cable is laid." The village was in a tumult of joy. My dear brother, I congratulate you. God bless you! DAVID DUDLEY FIELD.

ST. JOHNS, August 9, 1858.

[From New York.]

To CYRUS W. FIELD:—

Returned from country and received your message. Congratulate you with my whole heart on the success with which Providence has blessed the undertaking. Your name on every tongue. I need not say on what terms a household word. E. M. ARCHIBALD.

ST. JOHNS, August 9, 1858.

[From Astor House, New York.]

To C. W. FIELD:—

The Common Council of New York have resolved on a great celebration of the laying of the cable. The committee of arrangements desire to know the day on which the first message will be sent, in order to recommend a general illumination in the evening. Please send reply to the day. DANIEL F. TIEMANN, Mayor.

ST. JOHNS, August 11, 1858.

[From New York.]

To C. W. FIELD:—

Parties are pressing upon us messages to pay for them, and take their turn, when the line opens. What shall we do? Please reply.

W. G. HUNT.

The following despatch was sent by Mr. Field to the President, informing him of the landing of the cable:

TRINITY BAY, August 7, 1858.

To HIS EXCELLENCY JAMES BUCHANAN, PRESIDENT OF THE UNITED STATES, BEDFORD SPRINGS.

Your telegraph despatch duly received. We landed here in a wilderness, and, until the telegraph instruments are all ready and perfectly adjusted, no message can be recorded over the cable. You shall have the earliest intimation; but some days may elapse before all is perfected.

The first message from Europe will be from the Queen to yourself, and the first from America to Europe your reply.

With great respect, very truly, your friend, CYRUS W. FIELD.

To this the following reply was received:

TRINITY BAY, August 7, 1858.

[From Bedford Springs.]

To CYRUS W. FIELD, Esq.:—

MY DEAR SIR—I congratulate you with all my heart on the success of the great enterprise with which your name is so honorably connected. Under the blessing of Divine Providence, I trust it may prove instrumental in promoting peace and friendship between kings and nations. I have not yet received the Queen's despatch.

Yours, very respectfully, JAMES BUCHANAN.

TRINITY BAY, August 5, 1858.

[From Baltimore.]

To Mr. FIELD:—

Have you laid and operated the cable successfully? We can't believe the good news here. H. J. ROGERS.

ST. JOHNS, August 9, 1858.

[From Baltimore.]

To C. W. FIELD:—

Your despatch, announcing that the Atlantic telegraph cable has been laid, was delivered to me yesterday. I thank you for it, and congratulate you heartily on your success. J. H. T. MANNERS SUTTON.

ST. JOHNS, August 7, 1858.

[From Boston, August 6.]

To C. W. FIELD:—

DEAR SIR—The city authorities of Boston to-day ordered the firing of 100 guns upon the Common, and the ringing of bells for one hour from noon, in honor of the successful laying of the cable.

Respectfully yours, ALEXANDER H. PRICE.

ST. JOHNS, August 7, 1858.

[From Boston.]

To C. W. FIELD:—

Your despatch is received; universal joy is expressed; 100 guns fired this morning in honor of the success of the great event of the age.

NATHAN. P. BANKS.

ST. JOHNS, August 10, 1858.

[From Washington.]

To C. W. FIELD:—

SIR—Please advise the quickest route for sending you a flag-staff of oak, grown at Mount Vernon, for your company to commemorate.

JAS. C. RUCHETT.

TRINITY BAY, August 7, 1858
[From St. Johns, N. B.]
To Mr. FIELD :—

Accept the most hearty congratulations of Messrs. Jardine, Robertson, myself, and the inhabitants of this city generally. All join in congratulating you on your brilliant success. D. B. STEVENS.

ST. JOHNS, August 9, 1858.
[From Halifax.]
To CYRUS W. FIELD, Esq. :—

Greatest enthusiasm here—everybody full with joy. Salutes were fired during Saturday afternoon from the Citadel and flagship, and by the Halifax Volunteer Artillery, under Capt. Tremain. Every piece of bunting in the city displayed, and every bell ringing. In the evening all the public buildings and principal business establishments and private residences illuminated. Many magnificently and gayly decorated Telegraph offices shone forth with names of all prominent men celebrated in telegraph history, in which that of Mr. Field occupied the most conspicuous place. Immense torchlight procession, headed by the Mayor, Halifax Volunteer Artillery, and Engineer Company, paraded the streets until a late hour, discoursing sweet music to the amusement of citizens who, in vast numbers, promenaded the streets, cheering enthusiastically when passing the telegraph office. Many persons came in by railroad from the surrounding country to witness the demonstration. Double royal salute of forty-two guns each will be fired from Citadel, flagship, and by the Halifax Artillery, as Queen Victoria's message to President Buchanan is passing through Nova Scotia.

JESSE HOYT.

ST. JOHNS, August 6, 1858.
[From Toronto.]
To C. W. FIELD :—

His Excellency the Governor General desires to express his congratulations on the success of the accomplishing of the great undertaking of laying the Atlantic telegraph cable.

R. J. PENNEFEATHER, Governor's Secretary.

TRINITY BAY, August 7, 1858.
[From Montreal.]
To C. W. FIELD :—

I congratulate you most heartily—a flood of joy bursting forth from all parts of Canada at your indefatigable perseverance and final success.

O. S. WOOD.

A VISIT TO THE TELEGRAPH STATION.

The road which leads from the beach up to the telegraph station has already been described, and the reader is therefore aware that it is not the most inviting for those who are fond of rapid travelling. But it is a short road, and the passage over it is neither dangerous nor difficult, although the bog holes are but partially filled up, and the person who would undertake to walk over it with clean shoes would be somewhat disappointed at the end of his journey. At one end of this road, within a few feet of the beach, stood the telegraph station, before it was removed on the day the cable was landed. There was neither house nor log cabin there, and were the spectator not informed that the station had occupied a particular spot, he would have some difficulty in finding the precise place where it was located. The station was simply two upright poles planted in the earth, and rising to a height of about three and a half feet, and having a board three feet long and five inches wide nailed on top.. Upon this a small instrument for transmitting messages was placed, and on this instrument Mr. McKay, the Superintendent of the lines of Newfoundland, operated. He took it down soon after the cable was landed, put the instrument in his pocket, and literally speaking, walked away with the station. It would, however, have been a somewhat difficult matter to dispose of the Atlantic telegraph station in the same manner, and the man who should undertake the task would have had a herculean labor to perform. The reader has been made acquainted with the fact that it is built on the side of a hill; that it has but one door, and that opens on the side; that it is two stories high, with a parlor, a kitchen, and several bedrooms; that it is constructed mainly of wood; that it is five miles from the nearest house and fifteen miles from the nearest village; that an attempt has been made to clear away the wood which hems it in on almost every side, and finally, that it is in the midst of a perfect wilderness; but as yet he knows nothing of the wonderful domestic life that exists inside of that same house, and of the strange doings that take place therein, especially in the culinary departments. I may begin by stating that there are eleven occupants, and when I say that these occupants are all of the masculine gender, the reason why things are not as they ought to be in that house will at once become apparent. No man ought to be surprised, for instance, if the bread is not well baked, the meat not sufficiently cooked, the tea too weak or too strong, the potatoes—whenever they get them—boiled to smash, or not boiled at all, or if the fire requires to be kindled at least half a dozen times a day. Nor should they be astonished if the beds are not made till the occupant is just ready to get into them; and if, according to the same system, the table utensils are not cleaned till every thing is cooked and ready to go on the table. All this is explained by the fact that there are no women to attend to these things, and if the Telegraph Company should permit the operators to live as they now are, their relapse into a state of semi-barbarism, so far as the domestic usages of civilized life are regarded, is only a question of time. Imagine eleven or twelve young men thrown for the first time on their own resources, endeavoring to cook for themselves, to wash the dishes, to sweep the floor, to make the beds, to light the fires, and to perform the hundred and one little things of which men know nothing, but which, with those other "trifles," make up that greatest of all blessings—a comfortable and a happy home. Imagine, in fact, a man attempting to perform the part of woman in his clumsy, ungainly way, and you have some idea of what a house full of men can effect in this line, and of the condition of the domestic portion of the Atlantic telegraph station in particular. What a scene of confusion in the kitchen, what a terrible state of things in the half furnished parlor, without a sofa, and with a few boxes and trunks for seats! what a frightful chaos in the dozen little bedrooms up stairs, where the blankets and sheets and pillows are rolled up in one mountainous lump, or so twisted about as to furnish a good half hour's work to the occupant to get each into its proper place again! But with all this confusion, the electricians and operators are as fine a set of fellows as ever lived in one house, and live more cheerfully and happily in the midst of discomforts than many in the Fifth Avenue, who can boast of all the luxuries and appliances of civilized life. It would be unjust to bring them to account if their domestic education has been neglected; and if, among other things, they did not learn to bake bread and to cook a beef-steak properly, it is not their fault, although, in this instance, it is their misfortune. What matter if they do not know how long it takes to boil an egg, if they can translate the language of electricity, and send a message along the cable that now lies extended on the bed of the ocean between two continents? And if the company have not every thing provided for them, they can "wait a little longer" for the "good time coming"—a time that is to bring with it a piano and billiard table to while away their leisure hours—a time when the parlor shall no longer want a sofa, but when it shall shine forth in all the refulgence of a pier glass, one mahogany table, perhaps two—the company can afford to be liberal now that the cable is laid—a dozen handsome mahogany chairs, some ornaments for the mantelpiece, a stool for that piano, a substantial Brussels carpet with a handsome pattern, a hearth rug, new style, with a landscape, a lamblike lion, or ferocious tiger, in the centre; an accurate timepiece, in a neatly carved frame; and all the other articles that make up a well-furnished parlor. It may be asked what will they want with all these in the midst of a wilderness? The answer is very simple—they want them to keep them in mind of what civilized life is like, and of the homes which they have left behind in the Old World. With a parlor furnished in the manner described, they will require few other things, except some paintings to decorate the walls, and these the talented artist who belongs to the corps of operators will supply with his brush and palette.

Then, after the company have attended to the parlor, or rather before they have attended to it, they must look out for the kitchen arrangements, the culinary utensils, and all that. They must provide a pan or pans, so that the volunteer cooks may not be obliged to use the pot for the double purposes of boiling and frying; they must furnish more than one kettle, so that if the spout or handle should happen to be knocked off they may not be reduced to extremities. It will, however, assuredly be gratifying to the benevolent housekeepers of New York, and indeed of all Christendom, to know that the domestic difficulties which these same electricians and operators have encountered will soon be brought to an end, as a cook was on his way from St. Johns to take charge of the culinary department when we were about leaving that city. It is true the four occupants of the station who resided there before the arrival of the Niagara, did not take as much interest in the preparation of the house for the reception of the expected ones as they might have done, but, in extenuation of their neglect, it must be stated that they had given up all hope of ever seeing such a wonderful thing taking place, and as for the expected ones, they had long ceased to be expected. If, however, whether excusable or inexcusable, they did not attend to the few matters to which they could attend, there is no excuse for the company, should they neglect to furnish them with every thing necessary in the department now under our consideration, and to which we intend to direct their attention with all the particularity of which our knowledge of such matters will admit. In the first place, then, they must put a grate in the kitchen—that every cook considers almost indispensable. The next thing is an oven, and when this is put up, they will want toasting and roasting apparatus, chairs instead of hard boxes and harder blocks to sit upon—blocks which are particularly objectionable to men of tender and delicate feeling. It is needless to repeat the various things that the kitchen of the telegraph station will require to make it complete, but the directors of the company have only to get an inventory of what their own kitchens contain, to be aware of the wants of the operators and to be enabled to supply them. The cook, there is no doubt, will prove a perfect treasure to them, and that same cook will hear of efforts in cooking before he is long in the station that will astound him. Just think, oh! ye housekeepers of New York, who have been so often appealed to already, just think of Christian men putting a large lump of pork into a pot not big enough to hold one half the quantity; and that pot about one-third full of water! Is it any wonder that the water should all boil away, and that the bottom of the pot, becoming red hot, should set the pork in a blaze? Is it any wonder that this should occur, and that the cooks should throw a whole pailful of water, fill the pot to overflowing, and put out the fire altogether? What would you think of men who set out with the intention of making what they called a plum dumpling, and who were obliged, by their own incapacity and utter ignorance of the great art of cooking—an art that has immortalized a Soyer and a Murray—to leave the dumpling unfinished, and then endeavor to convert it into a series of pancakes? Just think of it, pancakes with plums in them, and those plums so battered and bruised that the stones would persist in appearing where they were not wanted, right on the top of the flattened surface. But the cook will set every thing to rights, and take care, when the pork is boiling, the fat does not get into the fire. He will also see to it, that when dumplings are commenced they do not end by becoming doubtful pancakes.

Now these little domestic mishaps and troubles are, after all, not such troubles as might be supposed, but furnish material for many a good joke to the dwellers at the station. They have plenty to eat, for the company are determined that, though there should happen to be a famine in Newfoundland, they shall not want. They have also a capital barrel of ale, and there is the best water in the island within a few feet of the building. There is no lack of fuel, for firewood is abundant all around them, and they can cut down sufficient in a day to last them for a month. In addition to all this, there is plenty of game in the valleys and on the mountains, while the sea, near the coast, swarms with fish, and the streams are alive with trout. Newfoundland is in fact the sportsman's paradise, and when the Nimrods of the United States come to find it out, they will rush there in crowds during the summer months. What do they think of catching forty trout in the course of an hour and a half, and of taking them all from the one spot, in a stream not more than two yards wide in its widest part? What do they think of performing this feat with a rod made of the crooked branch of a tree, without a reel, and the hook baited with a piece of mutton? This feat the writer himself performed, and he willingly testifies that the trout was the finest he ever tasted—vastly superior to the wretched affairs called brook trout, which many of the Broadway restaurants serve up at a dollar apiece. There are bears, too, in the island, affording fine sport for those who are fond of the rougher kind of game, and the wolves sometimes become so bold that they break into the farm-yards and kill the cattle. The deer, or the kariboo as it is called, affords very good venison, and there are several varieties of feathered game. All things considered, it will be seen from this that Newfoundland is not such a dreary, desolate place to live in, and that if the telegraph station is situated in the midst of a wilderness, it is one that is not devoid of attractions.

There is one particular part of the building which has not yet been alluded to, but which is, after all, the most important. This is the electricians' office, in which all the telegraphic instruments have been put up. There are the batteries, which bear the same relation to the wire conductor that the boilers bear to the steam engine; and there the delicate apparatus by means of which the weight or force of the electrical current is told to a nicety; there, too, the needle, which tells whether the continuity or insulation is perfect. There, in a word, are all the instruments which were put on board the Niagara, and which, having served their purpose well, have been transferred to the telegraph station at Trinity Bay. The office is also furnished with a clock which keeps Greenwich time, and in the event of its running down there are half a dozen chronometers by which to set it right again. Take it altogether, the electricians' office is the best arranged part of the whole establishment, and presents a strong contrast to the kitchen and parlor, both of which the company must have well furnished.

The telegraph house has been called "Cyrus Station" by the electricians, in honor of Mr. Cyrus W. Field, and will hereafter be known by that title. It could not receive a more appropriate one, and will help to perpetuate the name of a man who has done more than any other to make the Atlantic telegraph a grand reality.

DEPARTURE FROM TRINITY BAY AND ARRIVAL AT ST. JOHNS.

The Niagara, the Gorgon, and the Porcupine left Trinity Bay early on the morning of the 9th instant for St. Johns, where she arrived about six o'clock the evening of the same day. From what we had heard, it was evident that the whole population were moved by the greatest enthusiasm, and that they intended to make our visit the occasion of a grand demonstration. Indeed, sufficient evidence of this was to be found in the fact that the Speaker of the Colonial Legislature, Mr. Shea, had been deputed to wait upon Captain Hudson at Trinity Bay for the purpose of ascertaining what time they should set out, so that preparations might be made for the intended demonstration the day of their arrival. They proposed, he said, illuminating the city, getting up a regatta, and giving a ball in honor of the occasion. It was evident that the good people of St. Johns were determined to give us a hearty reception, and that when we left Newfoundland we should carry away a pleasant remembrance of their hospitality. The little steamer called the Blue Jacket, which brought Mr. Shea on his mission to Trinity

Bay, had about a dozen other gentlemen from St. Johns, whose impatience to see the Niagara before her arrival in that port could not be restrained. It was impossible for the captain to refuse the pressing invitations he received, and they were accordingly accepted; but he determined on remaining no longer than was necessary to take in a sufficient supply of coal for the homeward passage. We were all impatient to get to New York to see our friends again, and to tell them ourselves how the cable was laid, and all the incidents of the eventful week through which we passed. Every day that delayed our departure, therefore, seemed as long as two, and we thought, in our eager haste, that the fog which hemmed us in would never lift. At last, the weather having partially cleared up, we started, after a detention of four days in Trinity Bay, and made all the speed we could for St. Johns. The little Blue Jacket met us about a mile from the entrance of the harbor, with flags flying, and a large company of the residents of the city on board, and some four or five miles away to the south we could see Cape Spear light-house decorated with and almost concealed under a cloud of streamers. When at last we came within sight of St. Johns, and passed between the two lofty hills that form the outposts of the harbor, and which rise to the height of six or seven hundred feet, all the church bells in the city rang out their most joyful peals, the cannon thundered from their brazen throats a boisterous welcome, while cheer on cheer arose from the crowded wharves, the hillsides, and the shipping. Yet in the midst of all this our yearnings for home grew stronger and stronger, for while we fully appreciated their friendship and hospitality, we could not help thinking of those who were anxiously awaiting our return, and of the great city which we had left five months before. Our ship had hardly been anchored before she was boarded by several of the officials and citizens of the town. The cannon kept up their noisy demonstrations long after the crowds became tired of cheering, and at intervals could still be heard "the chiming of the bells." It was a grand festival in the city, the people abandoned their labor and kept holiday, and hundreds came pouring in from the country in their Sunday clothes. Never had St. Johns seen such a sight before, and the visit of the Niagara will be remembered hereafter as one of the greatest days in its annals. At night the public and other buildings were illuminated, and a very striking particolored transparency was displayed from the highest point of the market house. The office of the New York and Newfoundland Telegraph Company was also illuminated, and it may be added the operators were kept busy all night sending off despatches to New York. Over one of the buildings was the following inscription:

THE CABLE OF FRIENDSHIP,

MAY A WIRE NEVER BE BROKEN.

A wish to which every one, whether he is or is not a cable-layer, will heartily respond.

The rejoicing was kept up far into the night, and early morning caught some of the merry-makers still engaged in their festivities. The big guns got through with their part of the demonstration by dusk; but muskets, rifles, and other small arms kept at it till late in the evening. It was evident the quiet people of St. Johns had resolved to make a day of it, and they succeeded in making a night of it, too. One heard of nothing in the streets but the Niagara and the cable, and indoors it was all the same. The little city seemed to be actually beside itself with joy, and as if it had not done full justice, went at it the next day with as much zest as if it were but the beginning.

The following day Mr. Field was presented with an address at the Merchants' Exchange by the Chamber of Commerce. A deputation from that body was present, headed by their President, Walter Greive, Esq., who spoke as follows:

Sir—The Chamber of Commerce of St. Johns have the high gratification of welcoming you on your return to these shores, after the accomplishment of the grand undertaking in which you have been engaged for some years past. Personally known as you are, sir, to the members of the Chamber of Commerce, they have watched with deep interest your indefatigable perseverance in carrying out the vast scheme of the transatlantic telegraph; and whilst they sympathized with you in the disappointment you must have experienced at the failure of 1857, they felt assurred that your well-known energy, combined with the scientific skill of those gentlemen who were associated with you, would eventually succeed, if success were practicable. Devoting, sir, as you have done, your fortune, time and talents to this great enterprise, the Chamber of Commerce rejoice that you have seen the fulfilment of your most ardent wish; and they beg to express their fervent hopes that you may be spared many years to enjoy the fruit of your intense labor, and that you may receive on your return to your native land, such a welcome from your countrymen and friends as may in some measure compensate you for the days and nights of anxious care you have passed.

Mr. Field replied as follows, to the foregoing address:

Gentlemen—The address you have presented is deeply grateful to my feelings on this occasion. I will not affect to conceal from you that the successful result of laying the Atlantic telegraph cable fills me with great joy, while, I trust, I feel humbly thankful to the Giver of all Good for having permitted me to be an instrument in aiding the accomplishment of a work that is destined to promote the happiness and welfare of the human family. I have certainly made some sacrifices, and have had to contend with difficulties of no small magnitude. But when I find my friends coming forward, as you have done, to congratulate me in the hour of success, I am more than repaid for any toils I may have borne in the furtherance of this great work. But it would not only be ungenerous, but unjust, that I should for a moment forget the services of those who were my co-workers in this enterprise, and without whom any labors of mine would have been unavailing. It would be difficult to enumerate the many gentlemen whose scientific acquirements, and skill and energy have been devoted to the advancement of this work, and who have so mainly produced the issue which has called forth this expression of your good wishes on my behalf. But I could not do justice to my own feelings did I fail to acknowledge how much is owing to Captain Hudson and the officers of the Niagara, whose hearts were in the work, and whose toil was unceasing. To Captain Dayman of her Majesty's ship Gorgon, for the soundings so accurately made by him last year, and for the perfect manner in which he led the Niagara over the great circle arc while laying the cable; to Captain Otter, of the Porcupine, for the careful survey made by him in Trinity Bay, and for the admirable manner in which he piloted the Niagara at night to her anchorage; to Mr. Everett, who has for months devoted his whole time to designing and perfecting the beautiful machinery that had so successfully paid out the cable from the ships —machinery so perfect in every respect, that it was not for one moment stopped on board the Niagara until she reached her destination in Trinity Bay; to Mr. Woodhouse, who superintended the coiling of the cable, and zealously and ably co-operated with his brother engineer during the progress of paying out; to the electricians for their constant watchfulness; to the men for their almost ceaseless labor; and I feel confident that you will have a good report from the commanders, engineers, electricians and others on board the Agamemnon and Valorous—the Irish portion of the fleet—to the Directors of the Atlantic Telegraph Company, for the time they devoted to the undertaking without receiving any compensation for their services. And it must be a pleasure to many of you to know that the director, who has devoted more time than any other, was for many years a resident of this place, and well known to all of you, I allude to Mr. Brooking, of London; to Mr. C. M. L. Lampson, a native of New England, but who has for the last twenty-seven years resided in London, who appreciated the great importance of this enterprise to both countries, and gave it most valuable aid, bringing his sound judgment and great business talent to the service of the company; to that distinguished American, Mr. George Peabody, and his most worthy partner, Mr. Morgan, who not only assisted it most liberally with their means, but to whom I could always go with confidence for advice. I shall rejoice to find that the commercial interest of this colony which you represent, may be largely benefited by the close bonds that will now be drawn by the agency of the Atlantic telegraph between them, and the varied relations they hold throughout the world, and wishing you all every prosperity and happiness.

Later in the day Mr. Field was presented with another address by the President of the Executive Council of Newfoundland, in the Council Chamber, a large number of the members being present. Mr. Lawrence O'Brien, by whom the address was delivered, spoke as follows on behalf of the Executive Council:

We, the Executive Council of Newfoundland, have great and sincere pleasure in offering you our congratulations upon the success of the great project of the laying of the Atlantic telegraph cable. Intimately acquainted as we have been with the energy and enterprise which have distinguished you from the commencement of the great work of telegraph connection between the Old and the New Worlds, and feeling that under Providence this triumph of science is mainly due to your well-directed and indomitable exertions, we desire to express to you our high appreciation of your success to the cause of the world's progress, and our hearty sympathy in these feelings, inseparable from its present proved result. We recognize in this achievement the creation of new bonds of commercial and social union between the people of the two great nations thus marvellously connected; and we are gratified to remember the aid contributed towards this most important object by the Colony of Newfoundland, in the privileges conferred upon the company you represent. We sincerely trust the best expectations of the results of the enterprise to all interests connected with it may be immediately fulfilled, and that you, sir, individually, may reap from it an ample recompense for your many losses and sacrifices, from its inception to the present hour.

On behalf of the Executive Council of Newfoundland,

LAWRENCE O'BRIEN, *President.*

ST. JOHNS, August 9, 1858.

SIR—At the request of the Executive Council I enclose the copy of the address purposed to be presented to you by that body, and to request that you will be kind enough to intimate to me at what time it will suit your convenience to receive the Council for the purpose of its presentment.

Mr. Field replied as follows:

MR. PRESIDENT AND HONORABLE GENTLEMEN—I thank you with all my heart for this cordial manifestation of your good will. There is, however, nothing new to me in the present tone of your feelings. Upwards of four years ago, when I first laid before the Legislature of this colony the plan of uniting the two continents by means of telegraphic communication, I received your ready countenance, and in the charter of incorporation then passed, was unfolded the whole view, which has now arrived at its final accomplishment. The terms of that charter were liberal and encouraging. But had your councils been guided by a different spirit, the project would have been abandoned, and years perhaps might have passed without witnessing this happy union of the two worlds, with the beneficial consequences it is destined to diffuse. The exclusive privileges conferred by the colony on the New York, Newfoundland, and London Telegraph Company, have been the subject of hostile criticism, and it is therefore with satisfaction I observe the approving terms in which you refer to them. Every enlightened country recognizes a right of property in those who originate a work, where science or skill or capital has been invested. This protection is necessary to draw out the efforts of men in new works of public utility; for who would sow, if he couldn't reap? And while the individual has his reward, society is the gainer by his labors. In the exclusive privileges you have conferred on the company I represent, the principle of copyright only is involved, and I think there can now be no doubt that your policy has conserved the interests of the colony; while I confidently trust the future may be productive of much benefit to your people from the great work, which from the beginning to the present time has had your consistent and liberal support. I shall look with peculiar pleasure on the advantages you may derive from the proud position of this colony in the telegraphic connection with the Old and New Worlds, and shall be ever ready to promote your views of advancement by all means in my power.

An official visit was paid to Capt. Hudson, on board of his ship, by the Executive Council of Newfoundland, and a committee from the Chamber of Commerce, to congratulate him on the success of the undertaking in which he has played a part. Mr. Lawrence O'Brien addressed him on behalf of the Executive Council of Newfoundland, and Mr. Walter Greive on behalf of the Chamber of Commerce, to both of which the Captain made brief and appropriate replies.

At seven o'clock on the evening of Tuesday, the 12th instant, Governor Bannerman and his lady entertained a large company at dinner in the Government House. There were some sixty or seventy persons present, among whom were Captain Hudson, Mr. Field, Purser Eldridge, Drs. Green and Gunnell, Lieut. Boyd, Lieut. Gherardi and the author, from the Niagara; Commander Dayman, of her Majesty's steamer Gorgon; Captain Otter, of her Majesty's steamer Porcupine; Commander Paisley, of her Majesty's steamer Atlanta; Hon. Mr. Shea, Speaker of the Colonial Legislature; Mr. O'Brien, Chief Justice Brady, Mr. Kent, Colonial Secretary; Judges Little and Robinson, several officers of the garrison and prominent public officials. At the close of the dinner, Lady Bannerman retired, after which the company indulged in speech-making for about an hour, when they adjourned to the ball. The first toast given by the Governor was "The Queen of Great Britain and the President of the United States," which was drank with three times three. Then followed toasts complimentary to Mr. Field, Captain Hudson, Captain Otter, Captain Dayman and others, to which brief speeches were made in reply. When the Governor and his guests entered the Colonial building, in which the Provincial Legislature holds its sessions, and in which the ball was given, they were received with marked distinction by the large company present. The ball-room was handsomely decorated with American and English flags, and a portrait of Washington, in a wreath of evergreens, was suspended in the most conspicuous place. The ball, which was a most successful affair, was kept up till daybreak. It sustained the reputation of St. Johns for both the grace and beauty of the fairer part of the population, and it need not be wondered at if, some future day, we should hear of a union taking place between some of the sovereign citizens of the free republic and some of the fair daughters of Newfoundland—a union of a still stronger and more indissoluble character than even that established between the Old World and the New by the electric bond which now binds them.

The day after the ball there was a regatta on Lake Quidy Vidi, but as Captain Hudson had determined on starting for New York that afternoon, we were unable to wait for the termination.

HOMEWARD BOUND.

At length the hour of our departure arrived—we were at last homeward bound. We could hardly realize the fact that we were not again going to England, instead of New York, and that the cable was successfully deposited at the bottom of the ocean. For home, crowned with success! How slowly the ship appears to move, and the fog, that sets in thicker and thicker around us, seems as if it never would lift. But we have no reason to be dissatisfied, and though the hours were never more dull and monotonous, yet every delay only enhances the pleasure of meeting our friends again. How we measured the distance each day on the chart, and wished that it were only what it appeared on paper. How we tried to prove that we had overrun our reckoning, and were nearer to our destination than we really were. How we calculated on the wind, that would not come from any other point than that from which it was not wanted; and how eagerly we looked for any change in the sky that promised a favorable breeze. It is all useless, however, for here we are in our fourth day from St. Johns and three hundred and eighty-five miles from New York; but the fog would not clear, and the wind would not come, and without observation for two days, what could we do? Yes, here we are, over three hundred miles from New York, and it will hardly be credited, with a pilot on board—a New York pilot, Mr. William Maxwell, whom we have just taken from the Mary Taylor—the first pilot boat built by George Steers, as our ship was one of the last he ever constructed. Here was a piece of enterprise deserving of encouragement. Even at a distance we thought she was a New York boat, and we were not deceived when she came alonside. The pilot was soon aboard, and as the graceful little vessel which he had just left sailed by, one of her crew asked if we had been successful.

"Capt. Hudson," said he, "is the cable laid?"

"Yes," replied the captain, "the cable is laid."

It was the first he had heard of the fact, for the boat was twelve days out of New York; but it evidently took him by surprise. Pulling his cap off his head, he gave what was doubtless intended for a cheer, but which was nothing more or less than a perfect yell of delight. That satisfied him and it satisfied us, for it was worth a dozen hurras, both to hear and see the spirit with which it was done. An hour after the Mary Taylor was away beyond the horizon, and the base of a rainbow rested on the point where we had watched her till she disappeared.

On the 15th we sighted one of the European propellers bound to New York, but the fog soon after closed in and we saw no more of her. As Captain Hudson desired to speak her two guns were fired, to which she responded with two more, but she must have kept on her way, as we could not see her when the fog partially lifted. On the 17th we spoke the pilot boat Edwin Forrest, and asked if the Queen's message had arrived, to which we received a reply in the affirmative. This was enough—the cable was not only laid, but was in the best working order, and nothing more was necessary to complete our success. The pilot boat, as she passed astern, saluted us by firing a gun and dipping her flags, to which we responded by dipping ours. At five o'clock in the morning the tugboat is alongside. Home at last!

ARRIVAL OF THE NIAGARA AT NEW YORK.

It was about five o'clock in the morning of the 18th of August that the Niagara arrived off Sandy Hook, after one of the most eventful cruises on which ship had ever sailed. Already had the news of her arrival reached New York, and the waking city heard with a glad heart that the long expected ship had returned crowned with triumph. On her passage up the bay she was greeted with the thunders of cannon and the cheering of vast multitudes that had assembled on the wharves to welcome her home. The little tugboat, which had left her side early that morning with a few impatient passengers who would not await the return of the tide, reached the city hours before the historic ship herself. These passengers were Mr. Field, Mr. Everett, Mr. Woodhouse, Lieutenant the Baron de Boyé, of the Russian Navy, Mr. J. C. Eldridge, purser of the Niagara, Captain Matthew D. Field, who joined the vessel in Trinity Bay and the author. When leaving the Niagara, on board of which they had spent the most eventful period of their lives, the little company gave the captain, officers and crew, three hearty cheers. The rigging was immediately manned, and as the towboat started on her way to the city three thundering cheers greeted the passengers in return.

It was four o'clock in the afternoon when the Niagara steamed up the bay, and soon after anchored in the East River, opposite the Navy Yard. While lying here her captain, officers and crew, were visited by the public officials, and from morning to night her decks were so crowded as to render them almost impassable. The public enthusiasm was unbounded, and few thought of, or talked of, any thing else but the success of the great enterprise. The night before the arrival of the ship the city was illuminated, and although the news of the successful landing of the cable was now two weeks old, the public mind seemed as excited as ever at the wondrous achievement. The newspapers were filled with reports of the celebration of the event all over the country, and preparations were going on for the 1st of September, which had been appointed as the great day of jubilee and rejoicing. The 5th of August was justly regarded as the inauguration of a new era, an era bright with hopeful prospects for the whole human race. The thrilling announcement had been made to the world that time and space were no more, and that the great ocean itself no longer presented a barrier to the communion of the Old World with the New. All the various nations of the earth were brought together again as members of the one family, and the great idea of the unity of the race was re-established. Was it any wonder that the mind of the people of the freest land under the sun should be moved to its profoundest depth when the great principles which they promulgated were thus brought nearer to their practical realization? Not only the barriers of space and time were removed, but the entrance to the great domain of the Infinite seemed open to man, and the light that broke in from the other world tinged with its golden radiance the glorious promises of that good time which is yet to come, when wars shall cease, and peace and happiness shall reign over all the earth.

Already the rulers of the two countries which are thus united have exchanged congratulations, and their messages speak the language of friendship and goodwill—language that deserves to be recorded in letters of light for future generations.

THE QUEENS MESSAGE.

To the President of the United States, Washington.

The Queen desires to congratulate the President upon the successful completion of this great international work, in which the Queen has taken the deepest interest.

The Queen is convinced that the President wil join with her in fervently hoping that the electric cable which now connects Great Britain with the United States will prove an additional link between the nations, whose friendship is founded upon their common interest and reciprocal esteem.

The Queen has much pleasure in thus communicating with the President, and renewing to him her wishes for the prosperity of the United States.

THE PRESIDENT'S MESSAGE.

WASHINGTON CITY, August 16, 1858.

TO HER MAJESTY VICTORIA, THE QUEEN OF GREAT BRITAIN.

The President cordially reciprocates the congratulations of her Majesty the Queen, on the success of the great international enterprise accomplished by the science, skill, and indomitable energy of the two countries.

It is a triumph more glorious, because far more useful to mankind, than was ever won by conqueror on the field of battle.

May the Atlantic Telegraph, under the blessing of Heaven, prove to be a bond of perpetual peace and friendship between the kindred nations, and an instrument destined by Divine Providence to diffuse religion, civilization, liberty and law throughout the world.

In this view, will not all nations of Christendom spontaneously unite in the declaration that it shall be for ever neutral, and that its communications shall be held sacred in passing to their places of destination, even in the midst of hostilities?

JAMES BUCHANAN.

THE NIAGARA AS SHE APPEARED AFTER THE CRUISE.

The Niagara, as we have stated, was crowded with people after her arrival, and the greatest interest was exhibited in the cable circles and the paying-out machinery, none of which had been removed. Those who visited the ship had, therefore, a pretty fair opportunity of seeing all that was worth seeing, so far as the work of laying the cable is considered. The cones, the sheaves, the bobbins, the dynamometer, the rings or fair-leaders were all intact; and besides all these, two of the circles contained some eighty or ninety miles of cable coiled and ready for laying, all of which, however, was subsequently bought by a jeweler in New York, to be made up into ornaments. The flooring of two or three of the circles had been removed, but the remainder were as perfect as at any time while the work of submerging the cable in the depths of the ocean was in progress. There were three circles on the spar deck, two, which were forward of the engine hatch, had no cable, but the third, which was aft of the same part of the ship, had twenty or thirty miles in one coil. Above each of these a temporary staging was erected for the purpose of facilitating the paying-out process. While the work was going on no one was allowed on any part of this staging who had no business there—not even the officers of the ship. This rule was carried out to the fullest extent, and with the most despotic rigor. It was along this staging that the splicer, Paine, walked with the "bight" in his hand when the last fathom in the hold coil was paid out, and when the wardroom coil was reached. The covering of the engine-hatchway bore the marks of the curiosity of one of the men, who, in his exertions to get a glimpse of Paine while performing this feat, smashed the glass and nearly lost his life by his temerity. The iron bobbins over which the cable passed on its way to the machine, were not touched, and although an effort was made to remove the tar, it was found impossible to do so wholly, and traces of it could still be seen by the visitors. For six whole days and nights those same bobbins never stopped revolving, and they always saluted the ear with the self-same rattling sound—a sound, by the way, that was peculiarly pleasant, conveying as it did the information that the cable was going out successfully. Passing further aft, the visitor came to the great machine itself, and it is as perfect a piece of mechanism of its kind as was ever constructed. While it was in operation none but those on duty were allowed to go near enough to brush their skirts against it—they could hardly get sufficiently close to touch it with a six-foot pole, so strict were the regulations. No one dare transcend the written law which was displayed close by, informing all who had no business there that there they must not go. It was certainly a well guarded spot, and the sentry who kept watch near it was as rigid as an icicle—which means that he would sooner break than bend. Then, as if all this was not sufficient, the whole was inclosed with a rope that extended beyond the dynamometer, bringing that within the prescribed limits. All these regulations and rules, however, ended with the landing of the cable, and the machinery was as free to inspection as any part of the ship. The rope was removed, and the sentry no longer kept watch over the prohibited ground. The paying-out machine had done its duty, and done it well, and was, perhaps, as deserving of attention as any thing else on board the ship. It was perfect in every particular, so that those who were of a mechanical or scientific turn of mind could study it in all its details. There were the two sheaves, with the four grooves, in which the cable ran, and there the brake-wheels on the same shaft, so that the speed of the former could always be regulated by the latter. The end of the machine showed the levers which acted upon the brakes, and which by means of oblong weights of a hundred pounds each were made to increase the strain upon the cable. But all this has been so frequently explained already that the reader must be familiar with its action. The dynamometer, which stood within a few feet of the machine, of which it is an important part, was so simple in its construction and operation, that the visitor had no difficulty in understanding the principle on which it worked. Further aft was another wheel, which the cable passed over before it entered the sheave at the stern on its way into the ocean. The staging erected on this part of the ship was for the men who were stationed here, and whose duty it was to stopper the cable in the event of its breaking on or before it entered the machine. The moment the word was passed to these men that a fracture had occurred, they were at once to put on the rope stoppers, which were always at hand, and by which it was hoped to hold the cable until the fractured part could be spliced. Fortunately, their was no occasion for their services, and they had a merely nominal part to play.

From the forward deck coil to the stern the course of the cable was watched by more than a dozen men, while nearly thrice that number were stationed in the circle from which it was being paid out, to look out for and guard against kinks. The wardroom coil, containing some sixty miles of cable, was concealed beneath a covering of canvas, but as this covering could be partially raised, the manner in which the cable was coiled could be seen at a glance. On the port side of this coil was the electricians' office, but all the instruments had been removed, and the limits alone were traceable. As the visitor proceeded forward from this point he came to another circle, and looking through the hatchway, discovered two more on the orlop deck immediately beneath, and another still lower down in the hold. It was at this point that the greatest interest was manifested, as the last turn of the cable came out of the lower circle. This was the critical moment, and the visitor could imagine, as he looked down into the depth below him, how intense must have been the interest with which we awaited the moment when the bight came to be handed up through each of the circles until it reached the spar-deck above.

With all these arrangements on board of her the Niagara looked as much unlike a man of war as it was possible for her to look. There was nothing in fact belligerent in her appearance, except the four cannons which were intended as signal guns, and the twelve immense ports on her spar-deck. Those, therefore, who expected to see a man-of-war, were doubtless disappointed; but she has done more, during the great mission on which she was employed, to bring about the reign of peace, by drawing together in closer communion the several nations of the earth, than any mere man-of-war could have done. She has helped to lay the cable, and in what grander or nobler work could any vessel be engaged? This it is which has rendered her famous, and given her an interest in the eyes of the people of the United States, greater than if she had gained the most brilliant victory on record. She did not, perhaps, look as presentable to the eye of the naval critic as if each side of her deck were lined with guns; and the tar spots which frequently met the eye, may have seemed unsightly to what are called refined tastes, but they are preferable to blood stains; and it is to be hoped there may be more frequent employment for the cable machinery than for the cannon.

A. T. CO.'S STATION HOUSE.

OFFICIAL REPORTS.

MR. CYRUS W. FIELD'S DIARY.

NEW YORK, *August* 18, 1858.

TO THE DIRECTORS OF THE ATLANTIC TELEGRAPH COMPANY, London:

GENTLEMEN—For your information I herewith submit a copy of my diary since leaving Queenstown, Ireland.

SATURDAY, July 17, 1858.—Telegraph fleet sailed from Queenstown as follows:—The Gorgon and Valorous at 11 A. M., the Niagara at 7 30 P. M., and the Agamemnon a few hours later. All the steamers to use as little coal as possible in getting to the rendezvous. Up to 5 P. M. clear weather and blue sky; from 5 to 9 P. M. overcast, threatening weather and drizzling rain; from 9 to 12 P. M. overcast, hazy and squally.

SUNDAY, July 18.—The Niagara passed Cape Clear in the morning. Wind varying from W. by N. to N. N. W.; hazy atmosphere, cloudy and squally.

MONDAY, July 19.—Wind varying from W. to N. W.; hazy atmosphere, cloudy and rainy.

TUESDAY, July 20.—Wind from N. W. to N.; hazy atmosphere, cloudy and squally.

WEDNESDAY, July 21.—Wind N. W., with slight variations to the eastward. Cloudy.

THURSDAY, July 22.—Wind N. W. by W., blue sky and cloudy.

FRIDAY, July 23.—Wind from W. by S. to W. S. W. and N. N. W. Cloudy, hazy atmosphere and rain. Niagara arrived at rendezvous at 8 30 P. M., latitude 52° 5′ N., longitude 32° 42′ W.

SATURDAY, July 24.—Wind N. N. W. and N. by E. Hazy atmosphere cloudy and squally.

SUNDAY, July 25.—Valorous arrived at 4 A. M. Calm, hazy atmosphere, and cloudy.

MONDAY, July 26.—Calm, hazy atmosphere, cloudy. Capt. Oldham, of the Valorous, came on board of the Niagara.

TUESDAY, July 27.—Calm and hazy atmosphere. Gorgon arrived at 5 P. M.

WEDNESDAY, July 28.—Light wind N. N. W., some sea, blue sky and hazy atmosphere. Agamemnon arrived at 5 P. M.

THURSDAY, July 29.—Latitude 52° 9′ N., longitude 32° 27′ W. Telegraph fleet all in sight. Sea smooth. Light wind from S. E. to S. S. E. Cloudy. Splice made at 1 P. M. Signals through the whole length of the cable on board both ships perfect. Depth of water 1,550 fathoms. Distance to the entrance of Valentia harbor 813 nautical miles, and from there to the Telegraph House the shore end of cable is laid. Distance to the entrance of Trinity Bay, Newfoundland, 822 nautical miles; and from there to the Telegraph House at the head of Bay of Bulls' Arm, 60 miles—making in all 882 nautical miles. The Niagara has 69 miles further to run than the Agamemnon.

The Niagara and the Agamemnon have each about 1,100 nautical miles of cable on board—nearly the same quantity as last year. At 7 45 P. M. ship's time, or 10 05 P. M., Greenwich time, signals from Agamemnon ceased, and the tests applied by the electricians showed that there was a want of continuity on the cable, but the insulation was perfect. Kept on paying out from Niagara very slowly, and constantly applying all kinds of electrical tests, until 9 10 P. M., ship's time, or 11 30 Greenwich time, when again commenced receiving perfect signals from the Agamemnon.

FRIDAY, July 30.—Latitude 51° 50′ N., longitude 34° 49′ W. Distance run by observation last 23 hours, 89 miles; do. by ship's log, 99½; do. by engineer's log, 102; do. by patent log, 105.3. Paid out 131 miles 900 fathoms cable, or a surplus of 42 miles 900 fathoms over distance run by observation, equal to 48 per cent. Depth of water, 1,550 to 1,975 fathoms. Wind from S. E. to S. Weather thick and rainy, with some sea. Gorgon in position. At 3 50 A. M. finished the main deck coil, and commenced paying out from the berth deck.

467 miles from water, 1,465 fathoms.
547 " " " 1,080 "
577 " " " 465 "
747 " " " 200 "
793 " " Telegraph House at Bay of Bulls' Arm, Trinity Bay.

At 2 20 P. M. received signal from on board the Agamemnon that they had paid out 150 miles. At 2 36 P. M., had paid out from Niagara 150 miles cable, and informed engineers on board of Agamemnon of the same.

SATURDAY, July 31.—Latitude 51° 5′ N. longitude 38° 28′ W. Distance run by observation last 24 hours, 137 miles; distance run by ship's log last 24 hours, 141¾ miles; distance run by engineer's log last 24 hours, 142¼ miles; distance run by patent log last 24 hours, 137.6 miles. Paid out 159 miles 813 fathoms cable, or a surplus of 22 miles 843 fathoms over distance run by observation—equal to 17 per cent. Depth of water from 1,657 to 2,250 fathoms. Wind moderate, S. E. to S. W.; and from 6 A. M., N. W. by N. Weather cloudy, with rain and some sea. Gorgon in position. Total amount of cable payed out, 291 miles 730 fathoms. Total distance run by observation, 226 miles. Total distance run by patent log, 242.9 miles. Total distance run by ship's log, 241½ miles. Total distance run by engineer's log, 244¼ miles. Surplus cable paid out over distance run by observation, 65 miles 730 fathoms, equal to 29 per cent. 330 miles from water, 1,465 fathoms; 410 miles from water, 1,080 fathoms; 450 miles from water, 465 fathoms; 510 miles from water, 200 fathoms; 656 miles from Telegraph House. At 1 14 P. M. had paid out from Niagara 300 miles of cable, and informed engineers on board of Agamemnon of the same. At 2 45 P. M. received signal from on board the Agamemnon, that they had paid out from her 300 miles cable. At 5 37 P. M. finished the coil on berth deck, and commenced to pay out from the lower deck.

SUNDAY, August 1.—Latitude 50° 32′ N., longitude 41° 55′ W. Distance run by observation last twenty-four hours, 145 miles; distance run by ship's log last twenty-four hours, 139 miles; distance run by engineer's log last twenty-four hours, 142 miles; distance run by patent log last twenty-four hours, 141 7-10 miles. Paid out 164 miles 683 fathoms cable, or a surplus of 19 miles, 683 fathoms over distance run by observation—equal to 14 per cent. Depth of water, 1,950 to 2,424 fathoms. Wind moderate and fresh, from N. N. E. to N. E. Weather cloudy, misty with squalls and heavy swell. Gorgon in position and keeping our course very accurately. Total amount of cable paid out, 456 miles 400 fathoms. Total distance run by observation, 371 miles. Total distance run by patent log, 384.6 miles. Total distance run by ship's log, 380⅛ miles. Total distance run by engineer's log, 386¼ miles. Total amount of surplus cable paid out out over the distance run by observation, 85 miles 400 fathoms—equal to 23 per cent.; 185 miles to water, 1,465 fathoms; 265 miles to water, 1,080 fathoms; 305 miles to water, 465 fathoms; 365 miles to water, 200 fathoms; 451 miles to land, 511 miles to Telegraph House. At 3 05 P. M., finished paying out coil on lower deck, and changed to coil in the hold.

MONDAY, August 2.—Latitude, 49° 52′ N.; longitude, 45°′ 37 W. Distance run by observation last twenty-four hours, 154 miles; distance run by ship's log last twenty-four hours, 144 miles; distance run by engineer's log last twenty-four hours, $141\frac{3}{4}$ miles; distance run by patent log last twenty-four hours, 141.7 miles. Paid out 177 miles 150 fathoms cable, or a surplus of 23 miles 150 fathoms over distance run by observation—equal to 15 per cent. Depth of water, 1,600 to 2,385 fathoms. Wind north. Weather cloudy. Gorgon in position. The Niagara getting lighter and rolling heavily, it was not considered safe to carry sail to steady her, for in case of accident, it might be necessary to stop the ship as soon as possible. At 7 A. M. passed and signalled Cunard steamer from Boston to Liverpool. Total amount of cable paid out, 633 miles 500 fathoms; total distance run by observation, 525 miles; total distance run by patent log, 525.9 miles; total distance run by ship's log, $524\frac{1}{4}$ miles; total distance run by engineer's log, 528 miles; total amount of surplus cable paid out over distance run by observation, 108 miles 500 fathoms, or less than 21 per cent.; 31 miles from water, 1,465 fathoms; 111 miles from water, 1,080 fathoms; 151 miles from water, 465 fathoms; 211 miles from water, 200 fathoms; 297 miles from land; 357 miles from Telegraph House. At 12 38 A. M., ship's time, or 3 38 Greenwich time, imperfect insulation of cable detected in sending and receiving signals from Agamemnon, which continued until 5 48 A. M., ship's time, or 8.40 A. M., Greenwich time, when all was right again. The fault was found to be in the wardroom coil, on board of this ship, about 60 miles from the lower end, which was immediately cut and taken out of circuit.

TUESDAY, August 3.—Latitude, 49° 17′ N.; longitude, 49° 23′ W. Distance run by observation last twenty-four hours, 147 miles; distance run by ship's log last twenty-four hours, 137 miles; distance run by engineer's log last twenty-four hours, $118\frac{1}{8}$ miles; distance run by patent log last twenty-four hours, $134\frac{1}{2}$ miles. Paid out 161 miles 63 fathoms cable, or a surplus of 14 miles 763 fathoms over distance run by observation—equal to 10 per cent. Depth of water 742 to 1,827 fathoms. Wind N. N. W. Weather very pleasant. Gorgon in position. Total amount of cable paid out, 795 miles 300 fathoms; total distance run by observation, 672 miles; total distance run by patent log, 660.4 miles; total distance run by ship's log, $661\frac{1}{4}$ miles; total distance run by engineer's log, $666\frac{1}{2}$ miles; total amount of surplus cable paid out over distance run by observation, 123 miles 300 fathoms —less than 19 per cent. 74 miles to water, 200 fathoms; 150 miles to water, land; 210 miles to Telegraph House. At 8 26 A. M., finished paying out coil from hold, and commenced paying out from wardroom coil; 805 miles cable remaining on board at noon. At 11 15 A. M., ship's time, received signals from on board the Agamemnon, that they had paid out from her 780 miles of cable. In the afternoon and evening passed several icebergs. At 9 10 P. M., ship's time, received signal from the Agamemnon that she was in water of 200 fathoms. At 10 20 P. M., ship's time, Niagara in water of 200 fathoms, and informed Agamemnon of the same.

WEDNESDAY, Aug. 4.—Latitude, 48° 17′ N.; longitude, 2° 43′ W. Distance run by observation, 146 miles; distance run by ship's log, 149 miles; distance run by engineer's log, 149 miles; distance run by patent log, 142 miles. Paid out 154 miles 060 fathoms cable, or a surplus of 8 miles 360 fathoms over distance run by observation, equal to 6 per cent. Depth of water less than 200 fathoms. Weather beautiful, perfectly calm. Gorgon in position. Total amount of cable paid out, 949 miles 660 fathoms; total amount run by observation, 818 miles; total amount run by patent log, 802 4-10 miles; total amount run by ship's log, 810¼ miles; total amount run by engineer's log, 815½ miles. Surplus cable paid out over distance run by observation, 131 miles 660 fathoms, about 16 per cent.; 64 miles from the Telegraph House. Received signal from Agamemnon at noon that they had paid out from her 940 miles of cable. Passed this morning several icebergs. Made the land off entrance to Trinity Bay at 8 P. M. Entered Trinity Bay at 12 30 P. M. At 2 30 P. M. stopped sending signals to Agamemnon for 14 minutes, for the purpose of making splice.

THURSDAY, August 5.—At 1 45 A. M., Niagara anchored. Distance run since noon yesterday, 64 miles; amount of cable paid out, 66 miles 382 fathoms, being a loss of less than 4 per cent. Total amount of cable payed out since splice was made, 1,016 miles 600 fathoms. Total amount of distance, 882 miles. Amount of cable paid out over distance run, 134 miles 600 fathoms, being a surplus of about 15 per cent. At 2 A. M. I went ashore in a small boat, and awoke persons in charge of the Telegraph House, half a mile from landing, and informed them that the Telegraph fleet had arrived, and were ready to land the end of the cable. At 2 45 received signal from the Agamemnon that she had paid out 1,010 miles cable. At 4 A. M., delivered the following telegraphic despatch for the Associated Press, to be forwarded to New York as early in the morning as the offices of the line were open:

UNITED STATES STEAM FRIGATE NIAGARA,
TRINITY BAY, Newfoundland, August 5, 1858.

TO THE ASSOCIATED PRESS, New York—

The Atlantic Telegraph fleet sailed from Queenstown, Ireland, Saturday, July 17, to meet in mid ocean Wednesday, July 28. Made the splice at 1 P. M., Thursday, the 29th, and separated—the Agamemnon and Valorous, bound to Valentia, Ireland; the Niagara and Gorgon for this place, where they arrived yesterday, and this morning the end of the cable will be landed.

It is 1,696 nautical, or 1,950 statute miles from the Telegraph House at the head of Valentia harbor to the Telegraph House at the Bay of Bulls, Trinity Bay, and for more than two-thirds of this distance the water is more than two miles in depth. The cable has been paid out from the Agamemnon at about the same speed as from the Niagara. The electric signals sent and received through the whole cable are perfect.

The machinery for paying out the cable worked in the most satisfactory manner, and was not stopped for a single moment from the time the splice was made until we arrived here.

Captain Hudson, Messrs. Everett and Woodhouse, the engineers, the electricians, the officers of the ship, and in fact, every man on board the telegraph fleet, has exerted himself to the utmost to make the expedition successful, and by the blessing of Divine Providence it has succeeded.

After the end of the cable is landed and connected with the land line of telegraph, and the Niagara has discharged some cargo belonging to the Telegraph Company, she will go to St. Johns for coal, and then proceed to New York at once.

CYRUS W. FIELD.

The machinery for paying out the cable is certainly all that could be desired. The brakes are perfect. The greatest strain ever upon the cable was 23 cwt., and that only for a short time. The cable was paid out at an angle of from ten to nineteen degrees with the horizon, and at an average speed of six miles and a half per hour; and the average speed of the ship during the whole time the cable was being submerged, of five and two-third miles per hour.

The cable was well coiled, and ran out beautifully. Left with M. de Sauty, at his request, one and a half miles of the raised cable, and there is now remaining on board of this ship about sixty miles of the cable manufactured this year, and about twenty miles of the cable that was submerged last year and recovered.

For many interesting particulars in regard to the laying of the cable, I would refer you to the reports of the engineers and electricians.

At 5 15 A. M., telegraph cable landed. At 6, end of cable carried into Telegraph House, and receiving very strong currents of electricity through the whole cable from the other side of the Atlantic. Captain Hudson, of the Niagara, then read prayers, and made some remarks.

At 1 P. M., Her Majesty's steamer Gorgon fired a royal salute of twenty-one guns. All day discharging cargo, belonging to Telegraph Company, from Niagara and Gorgon. Telegraph House here not nearly finished. Received a large number of telegraph messages, congratulating us on the successful landing of the cable. Great credit is due to Commander Dayman, of Her Majesty's steamer Gorgon, for the careful and correct way in which he led the Niagara during the laying of the cable, keeping so near the line of the great circle arc. Too much praise cannot be awarded Captain Otter, of Her Majesty's steamer Porcupine, for the accurate and skilful manner in which he piloted the Niagara from the time he met us in Trinity Bay until our final anchorage near the shore where the cable was landed.

FRIDAY, August 6, at 2 A. M., steam-tug Blue Jacket arrived from St. Johns, and Mr. Brooking's partner was one of the passengers. M. De Sauty and myself urged him to have the Telegraph House finished as soon as possible. M. De Sauty purchased supplies from the Niagara, as they had hardly any provisions at the house, and the purser said they could have what they wanted at cost. At 11 A. M., received strong electric signals from the Telegraph House, Valentia. Arranging office, &c. Wrote the following despatch, to be forwarded to London as soon as the line was in operation:

BAY OF BULLS, N. F.

DIRECTORS OF ATLANTIC TELEGRAPH COMPANY, London:

Entered Trinity Bay at noon, Wednesday; landed cable at six Thursday morning. Ship at once to St. Johns two miles of shore cable, with ends prepared for splicing. Please request the Admiralty to permit the Gorgon, Com. Dayman, to accompany the Niagara to New York. When was the cable landed at Valentia? Please answer here by Telegraph, and forward by mail to New York my letters. CYRUS W. FIELD.

As I feel confident that it will be impossible for us to transmit promptly through one cable all the messages that will be offered, I hope that you will order another, manufactured in time to lay next summer.

The experience that has been had the last and present year, should prove of great value to your company.

Sent and received by telegraph a number of messages, among which were the following:

BEDFORD SPRINGS, PA., August 6, 1858.

To CYRUS W. FIELD, ESQ., Trinity Bay:

MY DEAR SIR:—I congratulate you with all my heart upon the success of the great enterprise with which your name is so honorably connected.

Under the blessing of Divine Providence, I trust it may prove instrumental in promoting perpetual peace and friendship between kings and nations. I have not yet received the Queen's despatch.

Yours, very respectfully,

JAMES BUCHANAN.

NEW YORK, August 6, 1858.

To CYRUS W. FIELD, Trinity Bay:

The city is intensely excited over your success. The news has reached all parts of the Union. Messages are offering for Europe. Shall we take them? Answer. J. EDDY.

ST. JOHNS, N. B., August 6, 1858.

To CYRUS W. FIELD, Trinity Bay:

Excitement here increasing. Parties in every moment for business. What tariff from here? D. B. STEVENS.

BOSTON, August 6, 1858.

To CYRUS W. FIELD, Trinity Bay:

DEAR SIR:—The city authorities of Boston to-day ordered the firing of 100 guns upon the Common, and the ringing of bells for one hour from noon, in honor of the successful laying of the cable.

Respectfully yours, ALEX. H. RICE.

TORONTO, August 6, 1858.

To CYRUS W. FIELD, Trinity Bay:

His Excellency, the Governor General, desires to express his congratulations on the success of the accomplishing of the great undertaking of laying the Atlantic telegraph cable. A. J. PENNEFEATHER, Governor's Sec'y.

Sent to the Associated Press the following messages:

TRINITY BAY, N. F., August 6, 1858.

To THE ASSOCIATED PRESS, New York:

The Atlantic telegraph cable was successfully landed here yesterday morning, and is in perfect order. The Agamemnon has landed her end of the cable, and we are now receiving signals from the Telegraph House, Valentia.

The United States steam frigate Niagara and her Majesty's steamers Gorgon and Porcupine leave for St. Johns to-morrow.

Due notice will be given when the Atlantic telegraph line will be open for business. CYRUS W. FIELD.

TRINITY BAY, N. F., Friday Evening, August 6, 1858.

To THE ASSOCIATED PRESS, New York:

Since our arrival here yesterday morning, I have been constantly receiving telegraphic messages asking for full particulars in regard to the laying of the Atlantic cable, to which it is impossible to reply, as every moment of my time will be fully occupied while I remain here; and I have handed to Mr. McKay, superintendent of the New York, Newfoundland, and London Telegraph Company's line, my daily journal, and given him full permission to send from the same any extracts that he might think of interest to the public, and especially those portions which will reply to the communications that I have received.

CYRUS W. FIELD.

Mr. McKay sent to the press the next day extracts from my journal.

SATURDAY, August 7.—Steamers Niagara, Gorgon, and Porcupine sailed, and returned on account of the fog. I visited lead mines to engage men to work on Telegraph House, cut wood, build road, &c. Electricians busy fitting up instruments. The following telegraphic messages, with many others, were sent and received:

TRINITY BAY, August 7, 1858.

To his Excellency JAMES BUCHANAN, President of the United States,

Bedford Springs, Penn.:

MY DEAR SIR:—Your telegraphic despatch is duly received. We landed here in a wilderness, and until the telegraph instruments are all ready and perfectly adjusted, no message can be recorded over the cable. You shall have the earliest intimation, but some days may elapse before all is perfected. The first message from Europe will be from the Queen to yourself, and the first from America to Europe your reply. With great respect, truly your servant,

CYRUS W. FIELD.

NEW YORK, August 7, 1858.

To CYRUS W. FIELD, Trinity Bay:

We have no facts in addition to your despatch of the 5th to the press. Every incident connected with the landing of the cable, or with the enterprise in any way, will be eagerly received by the public throughout the country. There is intense anxiety to know all in relation to it, and the press desires the line kept open at evening, so long as there are any facts of interest to transmit. Respectfully, PETER COOPER.

NEW YORK, August 7, 1858.

To MR. McKAY, Trinity Bay:

Please avail yourself liberally of Mr. Field's kind permission, and send us for morning papers from one to two thousand words from his diary. Add to it a circumstantial report of what has been done since the Niagara arrived at Trinity Bay. We will cheerfully pay the operators extra for their services.

There is a degree of excitement here which you cannot conceive of, and we want to meet public demand. D. H. CRAIG.

TRINITY BAY, August 7, 1858.

To THE ASSOCIATED PRESS, New York:

We landed here in the woods, and until the telegraph instruments are all ready, and perfectly adjusted, no communications can pass between the two continents; but the electric currents are received freely.

You shall have the earliest intimation when all is ready, but it may be some days before every thing is perfected. The first through message between Europe and America will be from the Queen of Great Britain to the President of the United States, and the second his reply. CYRUS W. FIELD.

SUNDAY, August 8.—Good signals being received through the cable. Religious service at Telegraph House at 5 P. M.

MONDAY, August 9.—Offered to remain at Trinity Bay with the electricians, if I could be of any service to them; but as I could not, left in the United States steam frigate Niagara at half past 5 A. M., for St. Johns. Her Majesty's steamers Gorgon and Porcupine sailing in company. At 6 P. M., arrived at St. Johns, where there was great rejoicing at the laying of the cable. Received here a great number of telegraphic messages, some of which I copy.

NEW YORK, August 9, 1858.

To CYRUS W. FIELD, St. Johns:

Your family are all at Stockbridge, and well. The joyful news arrived there on Thursday, and almost overwhelmed your wife. Father rejoiced like a boy. Mother was wild with delight. Brothers, sisters, all were overjoyed. Bells were rung, guns fired, children let out of school, shouted, "The cable is laid," "The cable is laid."

The village was in a tumult of joy. My dear brother, I congratulate you. God bless you. DAVID DUDLEY FIELD.

TRINITY BAY, August 9, 1858.

To CYRUS W. FIELD, St. Johns:

I have just joined up key and large coils, and am now sending to Valentia. Shall communicate again shortly. DE SAUTY.

TRINITY BAY, August 9, 1858.

To CYRUS W. FIELD, St. Johns:

It is necessary to pass many preparatory signals for adjustment of our instruments, needing some slight alterations. Do not expect her Majesty's message before the morning. Still exchanging good signals. DE SAUTY.

TRINITY BAY, August 9, 1858.

To CYRUS W. FIELD, St. Johns:

Receiving good recorded currents from Valentia,
Perfectly satisfactory. DE SAUTY.

TRINITY BAY, August 9, 1858.

To CYRUS W. FIELD, St. Johns:

I have received perfectly a communication from Valentia, and they get our signals there. Please send early, without fail, the fly-wheel. DE SAUTY.

NEW YORK, August 9, 1858.

To CYRUS W. FIELD, St. Johns:

DEAR SIR:—The Common Council of New York have resolved on a great celebration of the laying of the cable. The Committee of Arrangements desire to know the day on which the first message will be sent, in order to recommend a general illumination in the evening. Please send reply today.

DANIEL F. TIEMANN, Mayor.

ST. JOHNS, Tuesday, August 10, 1858.

Wrote to Messrs. T. H. Brooking, Sons & Co., in regard to completing Telegraph House and furnishing M. De Sauty with supplies.

ST. JOHNS, NEWFOUNDLAND, August 10, 1858.

Messrs. BROOKING, SONS & Co., St. Johns:

GENTLEMEN:—I have to request you will, as quickly as possible, brickway cell, and otherwise finish the house in Bay of Bull's Arms, belonging to the Atlantic Telegraph Company, and make such additions thereto as M. De Sauty may require. Also please furnish M. De Sauty with any supplies that he may order on account of the company. I remain, gentlemen, very truly your friend,

CYRUS W. FIELD,
General Manager Atlantic Telegraph Company.

Received an address from the Executive Council of Newfoundland, and also one from the Chamber of Commerce of St. Johns, and below you have copies of the same and my replies.—[These will be found in full in the account of the reception at St. Johns.—*Author.*]

The telegraph line to the United States was occupied every moment, and I gave the officers of the steamers the privilege of sending and receiving free, as many messages as they choose.

The Governor had a large dinner party at seven, where I met many of my oldest Newfoundland friends; and later in the evening there was a grand ball at the Colonial Building.

Sent and received many telegraph messages, of which the following are a portion:—

New York, August 11, 1858

To Cyrus W. Field, St. Johns:

Parties are pressing upon us messages, wishing to pay for them, and have them take their turn when the line opens. What shall we do? Please reply.

W. G. Hunt.

St. Johns, N. F., Wednesday, August 11, p. m

Wilson G. Hunt, Esq., New York.

Message received. I leave for New York in the Niagara this afternoon. Before I left London the directors of the Atlantic Telegraph Company decided unanimously that for several weeks after the cable was laid, it should be kept solely for the purpose of allowing several different electricians to try their various modes, and decide which could work through the cable with greatest speed and accuracy. Due notice will be given simultaneously, in Europe and America, when we are ready to receive business.

Cyrus W. Field.

St. Johns, Wednesday, Aug. 11, p. m.

To the Associated Press, New York.

Before I left London, the directors of the Atlantic Telegraph Company decided unanimously that, after the cable was laid and the Queen's and President's messages transmitted, the line should be kept for several weeks for the sole use of Dr. Whitehouse, Professor Thompson, and other electricians, to enable them to thoroughly test their several modes of telegraphing, so that the directors might decide which was the best and most rapid method for future use; for it was considered that after the line should be once thrown open for business, it would be very difficult to obtain it for experimental purposes, even for a short time.

Due notice will be given when the line will be ready for business, and the tariff of prices.

Cyrus W. Field.

St. Johns, N. F., Wednesday, August 11, 1858.

Vice Admiral Sir Houston Stewart, K. C. B., &c., Halifax, N. S.

Respected Sir:—I should consider it a very great personal favor if you would permit the Gorgon, Captain Dayman, to accompany the Niagara, Captain Hudson, to New York.

English officers and English sailors have labored with American officers and American sailors to lay the Atlantic cable. They were with us in our days of trial, and pray let them, if you can, share with us our triumph.

I know this would be agreeable to Captain Dayman and his officers. Please answer here. With high regard, your obedient servant,

Cyrus W. Field.

Trinity Bay, August 11, 1858.

To Cyrus W. Field, St. Johns.

We are doing our best. I do not think you can assist us by staying at St. Johns.

It is vulcanized India rubber, not vulcanite that is required.

De Sauty.

Trinity Bay, August 11, 1858.

To Cyrus W. Field, St. Johns.

Nothing to communicate, All progressing satisfactorily.

De Sauty.

TRINITY BAY, August 11, 1858.

To CYRUS W. FIELD, St. Johns.

Thanks for your kind message. All well and desire to thank you for your kindness to them. Sixteen yards vulcanized rubber cord, quarter of an inch diameter, required.

Not a second shall be lost in sending Queen's message.

Wish you a pleasant voyage.

DE SAUTY.

Left St. Johns, in United States steam frigate Niagara, at 4 30 P. M., for New York.

Her Majesty's steamer Porcupine, Capt. Otter, leaving at the same time for Plymouth, England. Weather pleasant; light S. W. wind.

THURSDAY, August 12.—On our way to New York. Thick weather; smooth sea; wind S. W.

FRIDAY. Aug. 13.—Thick weather in the forenoon; pleasant in the afternoon, with very light S. wind.

SATURDAY, August 14.—Calm; beautiful warm weather.

SUNDAY, August 15.—Thick and rainy in the morning; clear at noon, with light S. W. wind. Were at noon much surprised to hear that the chief engineer of the Niagara had just informed Captain Hudson that he had not coal enough left to take the ship to New York.

Fires were allowed to gradually go down, and proceed slowly under sail. The coal purchased at St. Johns turned out to be very poor for steam purposes, and has burned away much faster than was expected. At 5 P. M., more than 350 miles from New York, took on board from pilot boat No. 5, a New York pilot.

MONDAY, August 16.—Light head wind; thick weather; sailing very slowly, not more than two knots per hour, until 4½ P. M., when fires were lighted, and proceeded under easy steam towards New York.

TUESDAY, August 17.—Light west wind and very foggy in the morning; clear and pleasant in the afternoon, with wind from S. W. and S.

WEDNESDAY, August 18.—Passed Fire Island Light at 2 A. M., made Sandy Hook light at 4, and at about 6 chartered tugboat Achilles to take me to New York, where I arrived a little before 9 A. M.

The Niagara will cross the bar at high tide this afternoon, and arrive opposite the city at about 5 P. M. There is great rejoicing all over the country at the successful laying of the Atlantic cable.

One end of the Atlantic cable was landed from the Niagara on the Irish shore, August 5, 1857, and the other on the American side, August 5, 1858, from the same vessel.

The heavy shore end laid last year from Valentia still remains, and the main cable is to be spliced on to it, so that both ends have been landed from the Niagara.

The cable now laid in Trinity Bay is the same as was submerged last year, from the shore end of the Irish coast, and since recovered. The telegraph fleet sailed from Plymouth on the experimental trip May 29; the cable broke at the stern of the Agamemnon on the 29th of June, and the last splice was made on the 29th of July. The Atlantic Telegraph Company failed to lay their cable in August, 1857, and again in the second effort, June, 1858, but succeeded in the third attempt.

Sailed from Queenstown July 17, and would undoubtedly have arrived at New York yesterday (August 17), provided we had had on board a supply of coal.

Will you please to send me by mail a copy of the log of the Agamemnon from the time the splice was made until she arrived at Valentia, with the engineers' and electricians' reports of the laying of the cable from that ship?

At your unanimous request, but at a very great personal sacrifice to myself, I accepted the office of General Manager of the Atlantic Telegraph Company, for the sole purpose of doing all in my power to aid you to make the enterprise successful; and as that object has been attained, you will please accept my resignation. It will always afford me pleasure to do any thing in my power, consistent with my duties to my family and my own private affairs, to promote the interest of the Atlantic Telegraph Company.

I shall write you by the next mail in regard to the cable and machinery on board of the Niagara.

Rejoicing with you in the success which has, under the blessing of God, attended our united efforts to connect the Old and New Worlds by the electric telegraph, I remain, gentlemen, very truly, your friend,

Cyrus W. Field.

New York and Newfoundland Telegraph Station.

Report and Log of the Engineer, Mr. W. E. Everett.

United States Steamer Niagara, August 17, 1858.

To the Directors of the Atlantic Telegraph Company,
22 Old Broad Street, London.

Gentlemen:—I have the honor to enclose a copy of the engineer's log, which contains every particular of any importance connected with the paying out of the telegraph cable from this ship, and requires no explanation further than that the great percentage of loss from the time of making the splice to the next day at noon, was undoubtedly caused, to an extent, by the ship not running directly on her course, as for that day there was a difference of sixteen and a third miles between distance run by observation and patent log, while for the remaining part of the voyage they nearly coincided. Also, that the speed of the ship noted per hour must not be considered strictly correct, as it is not possible to log accurately by the ordinary means.

Nearly all of the stores were landed at the Telegraph House, Bay of Bulls' Arm, as they would be of much more service to the company there than any other disposition which could have been made of them.

There is now remaining on board about sixty miles of cable manufactured by Glass, Elliott & Co. during the present season, and about twenty miles of the cable recovered from Valentia Bay, most of which is not suitable for use.

The cable, machinery, and a few articles now on board, will be disposed of by the direction of Mr. Field.

It is almost needless for me to state, that each person connected with the undertaking has been untiring in his efforts to bring about so gratifying a result as the successful laying down of the Atlantic Telegraph Cable, and that Capt. Hudson and all the officers have made any and every sacrifice to further the great work. Accept my congratulations, and believe me, very truly, your obedient servant,

W. C. EVERETT.

Thursday, July 29.

Hour.	Dynamometer Strain.	Brake Strain.	Angle of Rope.		Amount per hour by Rotometer.		Speed of ship.	
A. M.			Horizontal.	Vertical.	K.	F.	K.	F.
10	—	—	—	—		200	—	
P. M.								
2	2000	1800	10° S.	25°	4	600	2	2
3	2050	1900	10° S.	21°	5	818	2	6
4*	2050	1900	18° S.	20°	5	800	2	6
5	2050	1900	10° S.	26°	6	060	4	2
6	2050	1900	10° S.	15°	5	818	4	6
7	2050	1900	10° S.	15°	5	241	4	4
8†	2050	1900	10° S.	15°	5	394	4	4
9	—	2000	10° S.	—°	2	413	2	
10	2050	1900	10° S.	20°	5	888	3	6
11‡	2050	1900	10° S.	18°	5	713	4	
12	2050	1900	11° S.	19°	5	520	4	2

Latitude 52 deg. 09 min., N.; longitude, 32 deg. 29 min., W.
Depth of water, 1,550 fathoms.

* 4.40 20 miles out.
† 9.55 40 miles out.
‡ 10.46 50 miles out.

Remarks.

July 29.—From 8 to meridian.—At 10 20, stem of ship being secured by hawser, commenced veering out cable to the Agamemnon to make splice. At 10 30 veered out 100 fathoms.

From 12 to 4 commenced paying out the cable. At 1 P. M. hawser was let go, ship steaming ahead slow. At 2 54, 10 miles of cable paid out. Smooth sea.

From 4 to 6, smooth sea. At 4 40, 20 miles paid out.

From 6 to 8, sea smooth. Light breeze on port beam. At 6 31 paid out 30 miles of cable. At 7 54 continuity reported to have ceased. Ship's speed reduced.

From 8 to 12.—At 9 11 continuity restored. At 8 55, 40 miles paid out. At 10 46, 50 miles paid out. Distance run at midnight, by patent log, 41 miles.

Friday, July 30.

Hour.	Dynamometer Strain.	Brake Strain.	Angle of Rope.		Amount per hour by Rotometer.		Speed of ship.	
A. M.			Horizontal.	Vertical.	K.	F.	K.	F.
1	2050	1900	—	—	5	713	4	2
2	2050	1900	—	—	5	763	4	6
3	2050	1900	—	—	5	550	4	2
4	2050	1900	11° S.	14°	5	213	4	2
5	2050	1900	10° S.	16°	6	210	4	6
6	2050	1900	5° S.	14°	6	420	5	2
7	2050	1900	8° S.	14°	6	533	5	4
8	2050	1900	2° S.	14°	6	580	5	2
9	2050	1900	10° S.	12°	6	170	5	0
10	2050	1800	10° S.	12°	6	813	5	2
11	2050	1800	6° S.	12°	6	600	6	0
12*	2050	1800	5° S.	12°	8	100	7	4
P. M.								
1	2000	1800	8° S.	12°	6	833	5	4
2	2000	1800	9° S.	11°	7	070	6	0
3	2000	1800	9° S.	12°	7	010	6	0
4	2000	1800	5° S.	11°	7	000	6	4
5	2000	1800	10° S.	12°	6	813	6	0
6	2000	1800	10° S.	12°	6	813	6	2
7	2030	1800	8° S.	12°	6	465	6	0
8	2030	1800	10° S.	12°	6	558	5	6
9	2100	1800	—	—	6	390	5	0
10	2100	1800	—	—	6	513	5	4
11	2100	1800	—	—	6	600	6	0
12	2100	1800	—	—	6	513	6	2

* 72 minutes.
Depth of water, from 1,550 to 1,975 fathoms.
Latitude, 51 deg. 50 min.; longitude 34 deg. 49 min.

Knots of cable paid out, 131,900 fathoms.
Knots run by ship, 89.
Loss per cent., 48.

Remarks.

From midnight to 4 A. M.—At 12 34, 60 miles of cable paid out; at 2 10, 70 miles. Sea smooth; very light breeze on port quarter. At 3 55 finished paying out coil on spar deck, and commenced on the forward berth deck circle.

From 4 to 8.—At 4 10, 80 miles of cable out; at 5 45, 90 miles; at 7 17, 100 miles. Light, fair breeze; smooth sea. At 8 A. M. had run 81½ miles by patent log.

From 8 to meridian.—At 8 50, 110 miles of cable out; at 10 27, 120 miles; at 11 55, 130. Distance by patent log, for the last 24 hours, 104.3 miles. Light wind aft. Smooth sea.

From 12 to 4.—At 1 10, 140 miles of cable out; at 2 36, 150 miles; at 4 02, 160 miles. Distance by patent log at 4 P. M., 23.4 knots.

From 4 to 6.—At 5 30, 170 miles of cable out. Strong wind and moderate sea aft.

From 6 to 8.—At 7 03, 180 miles of cable out. Fresh breeze and moderate sea on port quarter.

From 8 to midnight.—At 8 34, 190 miles of cable out; at 10 08, 200 miles; at 11 34, 210 miles. Wind and sea moderate, wind veered from port quarter to port beam. Distance run since noon by patent log, 46.8 miles.

Saturday, July 31.

Hour.	Dynamometer Strain.	Brake Strain.	Angle of Rope.		Amount per hour by Rotometer.		Speed of ship.	
A. M.			Horizontal.	Vertical.	K.	F.	K.	F.
1	2050	1800	Too dark to see cable outboard.		6	500	5	7
2	2050	1800			7	070	6	0
3	2000	1800	10° S.	13°	6	963	6	0
4	2030	1800	0° S.	12°	7	080	6	0
5	2000	1800	0° S.	12°	6	713	6	1

Hour. A. M.	Dynamometer Strain.	Brake Strain.	Angle of Rope. Horizontal.	Angle of Rope. Vertical.	Amount per hour by Rotometer. K.	F.	Speed of ship. K.	F.
6	2000	1800	0° S.	12°	6	000	5	4
7	2000	1800	5° S.	11°	6	300	5	6
8	2000	1800	9° S.	12°	6	818	6	0
9	2050	1800	2° S.	10°	6	550	6	1
10	2050	1800	8° S.	12°	6	253	5	7
11	2050	1800	2° S.	10°	6	170	5	7
12	2050	1800	3° S.	13°	7	560	6	4
P. M.								
1	2050	1800	8° S.	12°	6	683	5	4
2	2000	1750	5° S.	12°	7	200	5	6
3	2050	1800	6° S.	12°	6	300	6	0
4	2050	1800	8° S.	12°	7	818	6	0
5	2075	1800	10° S.	10°	6	498	5	7
6	2075	1800	10° S.	10°	5	908	5	4
7	2075	1800	9° S.	12°	6	580	5	6
8	2075	1800	7° S.	12°	6	663	5	0
9	2050	1800	4° S.	12°	6	420	5	5
10	2000	1800	Straight.	10°	6	523	6	0
11	2000	1800	5° S.	12°	6	770	5	7
12	2000	1800	4° S.	12°	6	623	5	7

Depth of water, 1,657 to 2,250.
Latitude, 51 deg. 5 min.
Longitude, 38 deg. 28 min.

Knots of cable paid out, 159 miles, 843 fathoms.
Knots run by ship, 187.
Loss, 17 per cent.

Remarks.

At 1 10, 220 miles of cable out; at 2 35, 230 miles; at 4 31, 240 miles. Fresh breeze and moderate sea on port quarter. Distance run by patent log since meridian Friday to 4 P. M. Saturday, 90.4 miles.

From 4 to 8.—At 5 34, 250 miles of cable out; at 7 11, 260 miles; at 8 11, ? miles, indicated by patent log since yesterday noon. Light breeze on port bow; sea moderate.

From 8 to meridian.—At 8 44, 270 miles of cable out; at 10 30, 280 miles; at 11 56, 290 miles. Distance run by patent log since Friday noon, 137.5 miles.

From meridian to 4 P. M.—At 1 14, 300 miles of cable out; at 2 35, 310 miles; at 4 02, 320 miles. Light head breeze; moderate sea. Rotometer 313 miles 700 fathoms.

From 4 to 6.—At 5 36, 330 miles of cable out; commenced orlop deck circle at 5 40. Very light breeze on starboard bow, with but little sea.

From 6 to 8.—At 7 12, 340 miles of cable out. Light head wind, with moderate sea. At 8, 44.3 miles run by patent log since meridian.

From 8 to midnight.—At 8 45, 350 miles of cable out; at 10 16, 360 miles; at 11 46, 377 miles.

Sunday, August 1.

Hour. A. M.	Dynamometer Strain.	Brake Strain.	Angle of Rope. Horizontal.	Angle of Rope. Vertical.	Amount per hour by Rotometer. K.	F.	Speed of ship. K.	F.
1	2075	1800	——	—	6	853	6	8
2	2075	1800	——	—	7	200	6	4
3	2075	1800	——	—	7	400	5	7
4	2075	1800	4° N.	12°	7	213	5	6
5	2000	1800	3° N.	10°	7	400	6	
6	2000	1800	3° S.	10°	7	110	6	
7	2000	1800	10° N.	10°	6	903	6	2
8	2000	1800	10° N.	12°	6	723	6	4
9	2075	1800	11° N.	12°	6	090	6	
10	2100	1800	10° N.	12°	6	400	6	
11	2100	1800	12° N.	12°	7	100	6	
12	2100	1800	10° N.	11°	8	613	6	
P. M.								
1	2030	1800	10° N.	12°	7	300	6	8

Hour.	Dynamometer Strain.	Brake Strain.	Angle of Rope.		Amount per hour by Rotometer.		Speed of ship.	
A. M.			Horizontal.	Vertical.	K.	F.	K.	F.
2	2030	1800	11° N.	13°	6	903	6	4
3	2050	1800	10° N.	11°	6	723	6	
4	2050	1800	11° N.	13°	7	010	6	
5	2050	1800	7° N.	12°	7	490	6	
6	2050	1800	7° N.	12°	7	313	6	
7	2000	1800	7° N.	14°	6	938	6	
8	2030	1800	9° N.	12°	7	485	6	
9	2050	1800	——	—	7	703	6	
10	2100	1800	——	—	7	300	6	
11	2075	1800	——	—	7	300	6	
12	2050	1800	——	—	7	313	6	

Latitude, 50 deg. 32 min.
Longitude, 41 deg. 55 min.
Knots cable paid out, 164, 683.

Knots run by ship, 145.
Loss, 14 per cent.
Depth of water, from 1,950 to 2,424 fathoms.

Remarks.

From midnight to 4.—At 1 15, 380 miles of cable out; at 2 36, 390 miles of cable out; at 3 59, 400. Fresh breeze on starboard bow; moderate sea.

From 4 to 8.—At 5 20, 410 miles of cable out; at 6 47, 420 miles of cable out; at 5 A. M., 90 miles run by the ship since Saturday noon. Moderate sea and breeze forward of starboard beam.

From 8 to meridian.—At 8 09, 430 miles of cable out; at 9 54, 440 miles of cable out; at 11 16, 450 miles of cable out. Distance run by patent log, from meridian to meridian, 141.2 miles. Ship rolling considerably; strong breeze and moderate sea on starboard beam.

From 4 to 6.—At 4 45, 490 miles of cable run out. Strong wind and heavy sea on starboard beam; ship rolling heavily.

From 6 to 8.—At 6 05, 500 miles of cable out; at 7 33, 510 miles of cable out. Distance run since noon, by patent log, 46½ miles. Fresh breeze and moderate sea forward of starboard beam.

From 8 to midnight.—At 8 50, 520 miles cable out; 10 10, 530 miles of cable out; at 11 38, 540 miles of cable out. Wind moderating; heavy sea; ship rolling badly.

Monday, August 2.

Hour.	Dynamometer Strain.	Brake Strain.	Angle of Rope.		Amount per hour by Rotometer.		Speed of ship.	
A. M.			Horizontal.	Vertical.	K.	F.	K.	F.
1	2050	1800	11° N.	13°	7	320	5	4
2	2050	1800	10°	14°	7	340	6	4
3	2030	1800	11°	13°	7	444	6	4
4	2030	1800	11°	13°	7	640	6	
5	2000	1800	15°	18°	7	337	6	
6	2075	2100	14°	18°	7	000	5	
7	2150	2100	12°	13°	6	818	4	6
8	2150	2100	12°	13°	7	100	4	6
9	2250	2200	10°	13°	7	150	5	4
10	2250	2200	8°	12°	7	030	6	
11	2350	2200	10°	12°	8	070	6	4
12	2150	2100	8°	12°	9	613	6	2
P. M.								
1	2000	1900	9°		7	863	6	4
2	1900	1900	0°		8	240	7	1
3	1850	1800	0°		8	260	7	
4	1850	1800	5°		7	313	6	6
5	1900	1800	Straight.		6	790	6	
6	1875	1800	9° N.		6	943	5	4
7	1875	1800	4°		7	573	6	
8	1870	1800	5°		6	613	5	4
9	1875	1800			6	743	6	
10	1875	1800	Could not see the cable		6	150	6	
11	1924	1800	over the stern.		6	240	5	2
12	1875	1800			6	130	5	6

Depth of water, from 1,600 to 2,885.
Latitude, 49 deg. 52 min., N.
Longitude, 45 deg. 37 min. W.

Knots of cable paid out, 177, 150.
Knots run by ship, 151.
Loss, 15 per cent.

Remarks.

From midnight to 4.—At 12 58, 550 miles of cable out; at 2 18, 560 miles of cable out; at 3 38, 570 miles of cable out. Wind and sea moderate. Distance by patent log, from noon Sunday to 4 P. M. Monday, 106½ miles.

From 4 to 8—At 4 53, 580 miles of cable out; at 6 20, 590 miles of cable out; at 7 45, 600 miles of cable out. Light breeze on starboard beam. Moderate sea. Ship rolling. At 5 20 commenced in new cable, which is very dry, leaving the circles, and four in number.

From 8 to meridian.—At 9 11, 610 miles of cable out; at 10 25, 620 miles of cable out; at 11 47, 630 miles of cable out. Light wind and moderate sea forward of starboard beam. Patent log at noon, 141.3 miles.

From meridian to 4.—At 12 50, 640 miles of cable out; at 2 03, 650 miles of cable out; at 3 16, 660. Light breeze on starboard beam. Ship rolling considerably.

From 4 to 6.—At 4 42, 670 miles of cable out; at 6 09, 680 miles of cable out. Light breeze and moderate sea forward of starboard beam.

From 6 to 8.—At 7 40, 690 miles of cable out. Wind and sea same as previous watch. Distance since noon by patent log, 47.7 miles.

From 8 to midnight.—At 9 09, 700 miles of cable out; at 10 46, 710 miles of cable out. Light wind and gently rolling sea, forward of starboard beam.

Tuesday, August 3.

Hour.	Dynamometer Strain.	Brake Strain.	Angle of Rope.		Amount per hour by Rotometer.		Speed of ship.	
A. M.			Horizontal.	Vertical.	K.	F.	K.	F.
1	1975	1800	—	—	5	963	5	0
2	1850	1700	—	—	6	818	6	0
3	1800	1700	—	—	6	500	6	0
4	1800	1700	—	—	6	000	5	4
5	1775	1700	10° N.	12°	6	593	5	6
6	1600	1600	8°	12°	7	260	6	0
7	1650	1600	8°	12°	6	963	5	4
8	1600	1600	8°	11°	4	603	6	0
9	1450	1400	0°	12°	5	709	8	0
10	1450	1500	5° N.	15°	6	203	4	4
11	1200	1200	—	11°	6	813	6	0
12	1200	1200	—	11°	8	200	5	0
P. M.								
1	1200	1200	5° S.	12°	6	580	5	4
2	1200	1200	8°	12°	6	508	6	0
3	1200	1200	4°	12°	6	330	6	4
4	1200	1200	4°	12°	6	850	7	0
5	1200	1200	—	11°	6	803	6	4
6	below 1200	1200	—	12°	6	590	6	2
7	below 1200	1200	10° S.	12°	6	593	6	0
8	below 1200	1200	4° S.	13°	6	643	6	2
9	1000	1000	—	—	7	400	7	6
10	900	1000	—	—	6	100	5	6
11	1000	1000	—	—	3	800	3	2
12	1000	1000	—	—	5	213	5	2

Latitude, 49 deg. 17 min., longitude, 49 23.
Knots of cable paid out, 161, 763.

Knots run by ship, 147.
Loss, 10 per cent.

Remarks.

From midnight to 4 A. M.—At 12 28 A. M., 720 miles of cable paid out; at 1 57 A. M., 730 miles of cable paid out; at 3 30 A. M., 740 miles of cable paid out. Light breeze on starboard beam; heavy swell; ship rolling moderately. Distance by patent log, from 8 P. M. to 4 P. M., 43.1 miles.

From 4 to 8.—Light breeze and sea forward of starboard beam. At 5 15, 750 miles of cable out; at 6 29, 760 miles of cable out; at 7 56, 770 miles of cable out.

From 8 to meridian.—At 8 26, cable all paid out from the forward circles, and commenced in the after circle. Total amount paid out 772 miles 700 fathoms. At 9 51 P. M., 780 miles of cable out; at 11 25 P. M., 790 miles of cable out. Set clock back 13 minutes. Distance run by patent log, 134.5 miles.

From meridian to 4.—Distance run by patent log, 24.5 miles. At 12 44, 800 miles of cable out; at 2 15, 810 miles of cable out; at 3 47, 820 miles of cable out.

From 4 to 6.—Nearly calm, with smooth sea during the watch. At 5 16, 830 miles of cable out.

From 6 to 8.—Distance run by patent log, from noon to 8 P. M., 50.3 miles. At 6 47, 840 miles of cable out.

From 8 to midnight.—Distance run by patent log, 15.7 miles. At 8 15, 850 miles of cable out; at 9 10, 860 miles of cable out; at 12, 870 miles of cable out. At 8 30 the Agamemnon made signals that she was in soundings.

Wednesday, August 4.

Hour.	Dynamometer Strain.	Brake Strain.	Angle of Rope.		Amount per hour by Rotometer.		Speed of Ship.	
A. M.			Horizontal.	Vertical.	K.	F.	K.	F.
1	1100	1000	Too dark to see cable.		6	410	6	2
2	1100	1000			6	623	6	4
3	1100	1000	8° S.	18°	6	120	6	0
4	1050	1000	4°	12°	6	170	6	6
5	900	900	4°	11°	5	703	5	6
6	900	900	—	11°	5	800	5	6
7	900	900	—	10°	6	718	6	2
8	900	900	—	11°	6	513	6	2
9	850	800	Straight.	13°	6	630	6	4
10	800	800	6° S.	18°	7	270	6	6
11	800	800	6°	12°	7	113	7	0
12	800	800	4°	11°	8	660	8	0
P. M.								
1	800	800	4° S.	12°	7	853	7	0
2	800	800	—	15°	7	560	7	0
3	1000	1300	—	80°	4	958	4	0
4	800	800	—	12°	8	513	3	0
5	800	800	4°	11°	5	820	5	6
6	800	800	Straight.	11°	6	253	5	6
7	600	600	—	—	6	140	5	6
8	600	600	—	—	3	600	2	6
9	400	400	—	—	4	683	1	6
10	400	400	—	—	2	733	2	6
11	400	400	—	—	4	320	3	0
12	400	400	—	—	4	190	3	0

Latitude, 48 deg. 17 min.; longitude, 52 deg. 43 min.
Knots of cable paid out, 154 miles 360 fathoms.
Knots run by ship, 146 miles.

Loss 6 per cent.
Depth of water from 742 to 200 fathoms.

Remarks.

From midnight to 4 A. M.—At 1 33, 880 miles of cable out; at 3 08, 890 miles; nearly calm, with smooth sea. Patent log, from noon Tuesday to 4 P. M. on Wednesday, indicated 91.6 miles.

From 4 to 8.—At 4 48, 900 miles of cable out; at 6 25, 910 miles; at 8, 920 miles. Distance by patent log, from Tuesday noon to Wednesday, 8 A. M., 115.7 miles.

From 8 to meridian.—At 9 29, 940 miles of cable out; at 10 50, 940 miles; at 12 43, 950 miles. Distance by patent log, for last 24 hours, 142 miles. Set the clock back ten minutes.

From meridian to 4.—At 1 28, 960 miles of cable out; at 3 10, 970 miles.

From 4 to 6.—At 5 10, 980 miles of cable out. Changed from wardroom to quarter deck coil at 4 50 P. M., in order to cut out a fault which had been developed yesterday, when rotometer indicated 978 miles 400 fathoms paid out. From noon to 4 P. M., by patent log, 21.6 miles.

From 6 to 8.—At 6 41, 990 miles of cable out. Distance run, by patent log, since noon, 41.1 miles.

From 8 to midnight.—At 9 38, 1,000 miles of cable out; at 12 06, 1,010 miles. At midnight the patent log indicated 58 miles run since noon.

Thursday, August 5.

Hour. A. M.	Dynamometer Strain.	Brake Strain.	Rotometer. K.	Rotometer. F.	Amount per hour by Rotometer. K.	Amount per hour by Rotometer. F.	Speed of ship. K.	Speed of ship. F.
1	400	400	1,018	600	4	00	2	6
2	—	—	1,016	600	3	00	2	0

Remarks.

From midnight to 4 A. M.—At 1 45 ship came to anchor off telegraph house, Bay of Bulls' Arm. At 1 A. M.—Distance run, by patent log, since noon of previous day, 62.6 miles. At 3 30, coiled 1¼ miles of cable aft, preparatory to the end being taken ashore in ships' boats. End of cable was landed ashore at 5.15 A. M.

Total amount of cable paid out since making splice in mid-ocean, 1,016 miles 600 fathoms. Total amount as per signal, per distance by the Agamemnon, 1,010.

Total distance run since making splice, 882 miles.

Total percentage of cable paid out over distance run, 15.

During the day 3 miles of cable was sent ashore, at the request of Mr. De Sauty, for future use.

THE LAYING AND LANDING OF THE CABLE ON THE EUROPEAN SIDE.

As the history of the final expedition would necessarily be incomplete without the narrative of the laying and landing of the cable on the European side, we feel gratified in being able to lay before our readers the following account, which was written by the reporter of the *London Times*, and which we copy from that paper:

In the face of difficulties and dangers, the magnitude of which cannot be properly appreciated by those not engaged in the work, the engineers engaged in this undertaking have, with almost untiring energy, adhered to their all but hopeless task with that perseverance which is sure, sooner or later, to lead to success. There were but few some twenty days ago who, after the unsuccessful return of the squadron to Queenstown, would have dared to predict such a speedy and glorious termination to all the trials and difficulties that the promoters of this undertaking have undergone. The final accomplishment of the scheme seemed indeed, up to the last moment, to hang upon a hair. Many serious difficulties had to be encountered during the six days and a half that the operations lasted, any one of which, had not chance favored us, might have ruined the expedition, and delayed the advance of ocean telegraphs perhaps more than half a century. But the difficult task has now been accomplished, and it only remains for us to accept the benefits which it will undoubtedly confer upon the community. Wonderful as the conception of conveying sensations from continent to continent, across the almost unknown depths of the ocean, may seem to us now, yet in a very little time people will forget the marvel while profiting by the fact; and without remembering the years of anxious toil and discouragement which those who have secured this boon to the community have undergone to secure success, the wonder will be, not that the undertaking has been carried out at all, but that it had not been accomplished long before. It has been the custom of mankind to honor the lives and celebrate the deeds of great statesmen, successful warriors, and eminent divines. Indeed, of such materials are the links in the chain of history chiefly composed. But those men who, by patient thought and persevering action, have achieved victories over matter which secure to the community permanent advantages, very often have their trouble for their reward. It is to be hoped that this may not be the case with those who have been mainly instrumental in bringing this great scheme to a successful termination.

It must be confessed that the prospects of success were very remote when the squadron left Queenstown on the 17th of last month. The amount of cable in the two ships had been reduced by nearly four hundred miles, and the recollection of three separate and most unaccountable breakages was still fresh in the minds of all who had accompanied the first expedition, and there was no reason whatever for supposing that the very same thing might not occur again. The cable might, and evidently did, as far as the contractors are concerned, fulfil all the guaranteed requirements; and the numerous accidents which occurred might be due to the cable having become injured during the gale. This supposition, though it may be gratifying to Messrs. Glass & Co., was no consolation to either the engineers or the shareholders. Under these circumstances it is not surprising that many regarded the prosecution of the scheme as a waste of the shareholders' money. However, in spite of the most vehement opposition, the majority of the directors determined to despatch the expedition to try their fortune again in mid-ocean before they abandoned the scheme altogether as impracticable.

Accordingly, on the morning of Saturday, the 17th of July, the Valorous, Gorgon, and Niagara, having completed coaling, steamed away from Queenstown for the rendezvous. The Agamemnon, having to wait for Professor W. Thomson, one of the directors, who took charge of the electrical department on board, did not weigh anchor until two o'clock on the following morning. As the ships left the harbor, there was apparently no notice taken of their departure by those on shore or in the vessels anchored around them; every one seemed impressed with the conviction that we were engaged in a hopeless enterprise, and the squadron seemed rather to have slunk away on some discreditable mission, than to have sailed for the accomplishment of a grand national scheme. It was just dawn when the Agamemnon got clear of Queenstown harbor, but as the wind blew stiffly from the south-west, it was nearly ten o'clock before she rounded the Old Head of Kinsale, a distance of only a few miles. The weather remained fine during the day, and as the Agamemnon skirted along the wild and rocky shore of the south-west coast of Ireland, those on board had an excellent opportunity of seeing the stupendous rocks which rise from the water in the most grotesque and fantastic shapes. About five o'clock in the afternoon Cape Clear was passed, and, though the coast gradually edged away to the northward of our course, yet it was nearly dark before we lost sight of the rocky mountains which surround Bantry Bay and the shores of the Kenmare River.

By Monday morning, the 19th, we had left the land far behind us, and thence fell into the usual dull monotony of sea life. Of the voyage out there is little to be said. It was not checkered by the excitement of continual storms or the tedium of perpetual calms, but we had a sufficient admixture of both to render our passage to the rendezvous a very ordinary and uninteresting one indeed. For the first week the barometer remained unusually low, and the numbers of those natural barometers, Mother Carey's chickens, that kept in our wake, kept us in continual expectation of heavy weather. With every little breeze of wind the screw was got up and sail made, so as to husband our coal as much as possible, but it generally soon fell calm, and obliged Captain Preedy reluctantly to get up steam again. In consequence of these continued delays and changes from steam to sail, and from sail to steam again, much fuel was expended, and not more than eighty miles of distance made good each day.

On Sunday, the 25th, however, the weather changed, and for several days in succession there was an uninterrupted calm. The moon was just at the full, and for several nights it shone with a brilliancy which turned the smooth sea into one silvery sheet, which brought out the dark hull and white sails of the ship in strong contrast to the sea and sky, as the vessel lay all but motionless on the water, the very impersonation of solitude and repose. Indeed, until the rendezvous was gained, we had such a succession of beautiful sunrises, gorgeous sunsets, and tranquil moonlight nights, as would have excited the most enthusiastic admiration of any one but persons situated as we were. But by us such scenes were regarded only as the annoying indications of the calm which delayed our progress and wasted our coal. In spite of the unusual calmness of the weather in general, there were days on which our former unpleasant experiences of the Atlantic were brought forcibly to our recollection—when it blew hard, and the sea ran sufficiently high to reproduce on a minor scale some of the discomforts of which the previous cruise had been so fruitful. These days, however, were the exception, and not the rule, and served to show how much more pleasant was the inconvenient calm than the weather which had previously prevailed. By dint, however, of a judicious expenditure of fuel, and a liberal use of the cheaper motive power of sail, the rendezvous was reached on the evening of Wednesday, the 28th of July, just eleven days after our departure from Queenstown.

The rest of the squadron were in sight at nightfall, but at such a considerable distance that it was past ten o'clock on the morning of Thursday, the 29th, before the Agamemnon joined them. We were as usual greeted by a perfect storm of questions as to what kept us so much behind our time, and learned that all had come to the conclusion that the ship must have got on shore on leaving Queenstown harbor. The Niagara, it appeared, had arrived at the rendezvous on Friday night the 23d, the Valorous on Sunday the 25th, and the Gorgon on the afternoon of Tuesday the 27th.

The day was beautifully calm, so no time was to be lost before making the splice; boats were soon lowered from the attendant ships, the two vessels made fast by a hawser, and the Niagara's end of the cable conveyed on board the Agamemnon. About half-past twelve o'clock the splice was effectually made, but with materials very different from carefully-rounded semicircular boards which had been used to inclose the junctions on previous occasions. It consisted merely of two straight boards hauled over the joining, with the iron rod and leaden plummet, attached to the centre. In hoisting it out from the side of the ship, however, the leaden sinker broke short off and fell overboard; and there being no more convenient weight at hand, a thirty-two pound shot was fastened to the splice instead, and the whole apparatus was quickly dropped into the sea, without any formality, and, indeed, almost without a spectator, for those on board the ship had witnessed so many beginnings to the telegraphic line that it was evident they despaired of there ever being an end to it. The stipulated 210 fathoms of cable having been paid out to allow the splice to sink well below the surface, the signal to start was hoisted, the hawser cast loose, and the Niagara and Agamemnon started for the last time for their opposite destinations.

For the first three hours the ships proceeded very slowly, paying out a great quantity of slack, but after the expiration of this time, the speed of the Agamemnon was increased to about five knots per hour, the cable going at about six, without indicating more than a few hundred pounds of strain upon the dynamometer. Shortly after six o'clock a very large whale was seen approaching the starboard bow at a great speed, rolling and tossing the sea into foam all around, and for the first time we felt the possibility of the supposition that our second mysterious breakage of the cable might have been caused after all by one of these animals getting foul of it under water. It appeared as if it were making direct for the cable, and great was the relief of all when the ponderous living mass was seen slowly to pass astern, just grazing the cable where it entered the water, but fortunately without doing any mischief.

All seemed to go well up to about eight o'clock; the cable paid out from the hold with an evenness and regularity which showed how carefully and perfectly it had been coiled away; and to guard against accidents which might arise in consequence of the cable having suffered injury during the storm, the indicated strain upon the dynamometer was never allowed to go beyond 1,700 lbs., or less than one-quarter what the cable is estimated to bear, and thus far every thing looked promising of success. But, in such a hazardous work, no one knows what a few minutes may bring forth, for soon after eight, an injured portion of the cable was discovered about a mile or two from the portion paying out. Not a moment was lost by Mr. Canning, the engineer on duty, in setting men to work to cobble up the injury as well as time would permit, for the cable was going out at such a rate that the damaged portion would be paid overboard in less than twenty minutes, and former experience had shown us that to check either the speed of the ship, or the cable, would, in all probability, be attended by the most fatal results.

Just before the lapping was finished, Professor Thomson reported that the electrical continuity of the wire had ceased, but that the insulation was still perfect; attention was naturally directed to the injured piece as the probable source of the stoppage, and not a moment was lost in cutting the cable at that point, with the intention of making a perfect splice. To the consternation of all, the electrical tests applied showed the fault to be overboard, and in all probability some fifty miles from the ship. Not a second was to be lost, for it was evident that the cut portion must be paid overboard in a few minutes, and in the mean time, the tedious and difficult operation of making a splice had to be performed. The ship was immediately stopped, and no more cable paid out than was absolutely necessary to prevent it breaking.

As the stern of the ship was lifted by the waves, a scene of the most intense excitement followed. It seemed impossible, even by using the greatest possible speed, and paying out the least possible amount of cable, that the junction could be finished before the part was taken out of the hands of the workmen. The main hold presented an extraordinary scene; nearly all the officers of the ship and of those connected with the expedition, stood in groups about the coil, watching with intense anxiety the cable, as it slowly unwound itself nearer and nearer the joint, while the workmen, directed by Mr. Canning, under whose superintendence the cable was originally manufactured, worked at the splice as only men could work who felt that the life and death of the expedition depended upon their rapidity. But all their speed was to no purpose, as the cable was unwinding within a hundred fathoms, and, as a last and desperate resource, the cable was stopped altogether, and, for a few mintes, the ship hung on by the end. Fortunately, however, it, was only for a few minutes, as the strain was continually rising above two tons, and it would not hold on much longer; when the splice was finished, the signal was made to loose the stopper, and it passed overboard safely enough.

When the excitement consequent upon having so narrowly saved the cable had passed away, we awoke to the consciousness that the case was still as hopeless as ever, for the electrical continuity was still entirely wanting. Preparations were consequently made to pay out as little rope as possible, and to hold on for six hours, in the hopes that the fault, whatever it might be, might mend itself before cutting the cable and returning to the rendezvous to make another splice. The magnetic needles on the receiving instruments were watched closely for the returning signals; when, in a few minutes, the last hope was extinguished by their suddenly indicating dead earth, which tended to show that the cable had broken from the Niagara, or that the insulation had been completely destroyed.

In three minutes, however, every one was agreeably surprised by the intelligence that the stoppage had disappeared, and that the signals had again appeared at their regular intervals from the Niagara. It is needless to say what a load of anxiety this news removed from the minds of every one; but the general confidence in the ultimate success of the operations was much shaken by the occurrence, for all felt that every minute a similar accident might occur. For some time the paying-out continued as usual, but towards the morning another damaged place was discovered in the cable; there was fortunately, however, time to repair it in the hold without in any way interfering with the operations beyond for a time slightly reducing the speed of the ship.

During the morning of Friday the 30th, every thing went well; the ship had been kept at the speed of about five knots, the cable paid out at about six, the average angle with the horizon at which it left the ship being about 15 deg., while the indicated strain upon the dynamometer seldom showed more than 1,600 pounds to 1,700 pounds. Observations made at noon showed that we had made good ninety miles from the starting point since the previous day, with an expenditure, including the loss in lowering the splice and during the subsequent stoppages, of 135 miles of the cable. During the latter portion of the day the barometer fell considerably, and towards the evening it blew almost a gale of wind from the eastward, dead ahead of course. As the breeze freshened, the speed of the engines was gradually increased, but the wind more than increased in proportion, so that before the sun went down, the Agamemnon was going full steam against the wind, only making a speed of about four knots an hour. During the evening topmasts were lowered, and spars, yards, sails, and indeed, every thing aloft that could offer resistance to the wind, was sent down on deck; but still the ship made but little way, chiefly in consequence of the heavy sea, though the enormous quantity of fuel consumed showed us that if the wind lasted, we should be reduced to burning the masts, spars, and even the decks, to bring the ship into Valentia.

It seemed to be our particular ill-fortune to meet with head winds whichever way the ship's head was turned. On our journey out we had been delayed and obliged to consume an undue proportion of coal for want of an easterly wind, and now all our fuel was wanted because of one. However, during the next day the wind gradually went around to the south-west, which, though it raised a very heavy sea, allowed us to husband our small remaining store of fuel.

At noon on Saturday, the 31st of July, observations at noon showed us to be in latitude 52 deg. 23 N. and longitude 26 deg. 44 W., having made good 120 miles of distance since noon of the previous day, with a loss of about 27 per cent. of cable. The Niagara, as far as could be judged from the amount of cable she paid out, which by a previous arrangement was signalled at every 10 miles, kept pace with us, within one or two miles the whole distance across. During the afternoon of Saturday, the wind again freshened up, and before nightfall it again blew nearly a gale of wind, and a tremendous sea ran before it from the south-west, which made the Agamemnon pitch to such an extent that it was thought impossible the cable could hold on through the night; indeed, had it not been for the constant care and watchfulness exercised by Mr. Bright and the two energetic engineers, Mr. Canning and Mr. Clifford, who acted with him, it could not have been done at all. Men were kept at the wheels of the machine to prevent their stopping as the stern of the ship rose and fell with the sea, for had they done so the cable must undoubtedly have parted.

During Sunday the sea and wind increased, and before the evening it blew a smart gale. Now, indeed, were the energy and activity of all engaged in the operation tasked to the utmost. Mr. Hoar and Mr. Moore, the two engineers who had the charge of the relieving wheels of the dynamometer, had to keep watch and watch alternately every four hours, and while on duty durst not let their attention be removed from their occupation for one moment, for on their releasing the brakes every time the stern of the ship fell into the trough of the sea entirely depended the safety of the cable, and the result shows how ably they discharged their duty. Throughout the night there were few who had the least expectation of the cable holding on till morning, and many remained awake listening for the sound that all most dreaded to hear—viz., the gun which should announce the failure of all our hopes. But still the cable, which, in comparison with the ship from which it was paid out and the gigantic waves among which it was delivered, was but a mere thread, continued to hold on, only leaving a silvery phosphorous line upon the stupendous seas as they rolled on towards the ship.

With Sunday morning came no improvement in the weather; still the sky remained black and stormy to windward, and the constant violent squalls of wind and rain which prevailed during the whole day, served to keep up, if not to augment the height of the waves. But the cable had gone through so much during the night, that our confidence in its continuing to hold was much restored.

At noon observations showed us to be in lat. 52° 26′ N., and lon. 23° 16′ W., having made good 130 miles from noon of the previous day, and about 360 from out starting point in mid ocean. We had passed by the deepest sounding of 2,400 fathoms, and over more than half of the deep water generally, while the amourt of cable still remaining in the ship was more than sufficient to carry us to the Irish coast, even supposing the continuance of the bad weather should oblige us to pay out the same amount of slack cable we had been hitherto wasting. Thus far things looked very promising for our ultimate success. But former experience showed us only too plainly that we could never suppose that some accident might not arise until the ends had been fairly landed on the opposite shores.

During Sunday night and Monday morning the weather continued as boisterous as ever, and it was only by the most indefatigable exertions of the engineer upon duty that the wheels could be prevented from stopping altogether as the vessel rose and fell with the sea, and once or twice they did come completely to a standstill, in spite of all that could be done to keep them moving, but fortunately they were again set in motion before the stern of the ship was thrown up by the succeeding wave. No strain could be placed upon the cable, of course, and though the dynamometer occasionally registered 1,700 pounds as the ship lifted, it was oftener below 1,000, and was frequently nothing, the cable running out as fast as its own weight and the speed of the ship could draw it. But even with all these forces acting unresistedly upon it, the cable never paid itself out at a greater speed than eight knots an hour at the time the ship was going at the rate of six knots and a half. Subsequently however, when the speed of the ship even exceeded six knots and a half, the cable never ran out so quick. The average speed maintained by the ship up to this time, and, indeed for the whole voyage, was about five knots and a half, the cable, with occasional exceptions, running about 30 per cent. faster.

At noon on Monday, August 2, observations showed us to be in latitude 52° 35′ N., longitude 19° 48′ W., having made good 127½ miles since noon of the previous day, and completed more than the half way to our ultimate destination.

During the afternoon an American three-masted schooner, which afterwards proved to be the Chieftain, was seen standing from the eastward toward us. No notice was taken of her at first, but when she was within about half a mile of the Agamemnon she altered her course, and bore right down across our bows. A collision, which might prove fatal to the cable, now seemed inevitable, or could only be avoided by the equally hazardous expedient of altering the Agamemnon's course. The Valorous steamed ahead, and fired a gun for her to heave to, which, as she did not appear to take much notice of, was quickly followed by another from the bows of the Agamemnon, and a second and third from the Valorous, but still the vessel held on her course; and as the only resource left to avoid a collision the course of the Agamemnon was altered just in time to pass within a few yards of her. It was evident that our proceedings were a source of the greatest possible astonishment to them, for all her crew crowded upon her deck and rigging. At length they evidently discovered who we were, and what we were doing, for the crew manned the rigging, and dipping the ensign several times they gave us three hearty cheers. Though the Agamemnon was obliged to acknowledge these congratulations in due form, the feelings of annoyance with which we regarded the vessel which, either by the stupidity or carelessness of those on board, was so near adding a fatal and unexpected mishap to the long chapter of accidents which had already been encountered, may easily be imagined. To those below, who of course did not see the ship approaching, the sound of the first gun came like a thunderbolt, for all took it as the signal of the breaking of the cable. The dinner tables were deserted in a moment, and a general rush made up the hatches to the deck, but before reaching it their fears were quickly banished by the report of the succeeding gun, which all knew well could only be caused by a ship in our way or a man overboard.

Throughout the greater portion of Monday morning the electrical signals from the Niagara had been getting gradually weaker, until they ceased altogether for nearly three-quarters of an hour. Our uneasiness, however, was in some degree lessened by the fact that the stoppage appeared to be a want of continuity, and not any defect in insulation, and there was consequently every reason to suppose that it might arise from faulty connection on board the Niagara. Accordingly Professor Thomson sent a message to the effect that the signals were too weak to be read, and, as if they had been awaiting such a signal to increase their battery power, the deflections immediately returned even stronger than they had ever been before. Towards the evening, however, they again declined in force for a short time. With the exception of these little stoppages the electrical condition of the submerged wire seemed to be much improved. It was evident that the low temperature of the water at the immense depth improved considerably the insulating properties of the gutta percha, while the enormous pressure to which it must have been subjected probably tended to consolidate its texture, and to fill up any air bubbles or slight faults in manufacture which may have existed.

The weather during Monday night moderated a little, but still there was a very heavy sea on, which endangered the wire every second minute.

About three o'clock on Tuesday morning all on board were startled from their beds by the loud booming of a gun. Every one, without waiting for the performance of the most particular toilet, rushed on deck to ascertain the cause of the disturbance. Contrary to all expectation the cable was safe, but just in the gray light could be seen the Valorous rounded to in the most warlike attitude, firing gun after gun in quick succession towards a large American bark, which, quite unconscious of our proceeding, was standing right across our stern. Such loud and repeated remonstrances from a large steam frigate were not to be despised, and, evidently without knowing the why or the wherefore, she quickly threw her sails aback and remained hove to. Whether those on board her considered that we were engaged in some filibustering expedition, or regarded our proceedings as another British outrage upon the American flag, it is impossible to say; but certain it is that, apparently in great trepidation, she remained hove to until we had lost sight of her in the distance.

Tuesday was a much finer day than any we had experienced for nearly a week, but still there was a considerable sea running, and our dangers were far from passed; yet the hopes of our ultimate success ran high. We had accomplished nearly the whole of the deep sea portion of the route in safety, and that, too, under the most unfavorable circumstances possible; therefore there was every reason to believe that unless some unforeseen accident should occur, we should accomplish the remainder.

Observations at noon placed us in lat. 5° 26′ N., lon. 16° 7′ 40″ W., having run 134 miles since the previous day.

About five o'clock in the evening the steep submarine mountain which divides the telegraphic plateau from the Irish coast was reached, and the effect of the sudden shallowing of the water had a very marked effect upon the cable, causing the strain on and the speed of it to lessen every minute. A great deal of slack was paid out to allow for any great inequalities which might exist, though undiscovered by the sounding line. About ten o'clock the shoal water of 250 fathoms was reached; the only remaining anxiety now was the changing from the lower main coil to that upon the upper deck, and this most difficult and dangerous operation was successfully performed between three and four o'clock on Wednesday morning.

Wednesday was a beautiful calm day; indeed, it was the first on which any one would have thought of making a splice since the day we started from the rendezvous. We therefore congratulated ourselves on having saved a week by commencing operations on the Thursday previous. At noon we were in lat. 52° 11′, lon. 12° 42′ W., 89 miles distant from the telegraph station at Valentia. The water was shallow, so that there was no difficulty in paying out the wire almost without any loss of slack, and all looked upon the undertaking as virtually accomplished.

At about one o'clock in the evening the second change from the upper deck coil to that upon the orlop deck was safely effected, and shortly after the vessels exchanged signals that they were in two hundred fathoms water. As the night advanced the speed of the ship was reduced, as it was known that we were only a short distance from the land, and there would be no advantage in making it before daylight in the morning. About twelve o'clock, however, the Skelligs Light was seen in the distance, and the Valorous steamed on ahead to lead us in to the coast, firing rockets at intervals to direct us, which were answered by us from the Agamemnon, though, according to Mr. Moriarty, the master's wish, the ship, disregarding the Valorous, kept her own course, which proved to be the right one in the end.

By daylight on the morning of Thursday, the bold and rocky mountains which entirely surround the wild and picturesque neighborhood of Valentia, rose right before us at a few miles' distance. Never, probably, was the sight of land more welcome, as it brought to a successful termination one of the greatest, but, at the same time, most difficult schemes which was ever undertaken. Had it been the dullest and most melancholy swamp on the face of the earth that lay before us, we should have found it a pleasant prospect; but, as the sun rose from the estuary of Dingle Bay, tinging with a deep soft purple the lofty summits of the steep mountains which surround its shores, and illuminating the masses of morning vapor which hung upon them, it was a scene which might vie in beauty with any thing that could be produced by the most florid imagination of an artist.

No one on shore was apparently conscious of our approach, so the Valorous steamed ahead to the mouth of the harbor and fired a gun. Both ships made straight for Doulus Bay, and about six o'clock came to anchor at the side of Beginish Island, opposite to Valentia. As soon as the inhabitants became aware of our approach there was a general desertion of the place, and hundreds of boats crowded around us, their passengers in the greatest state of excitement to hear all about our voyage. The Knight of Kerry was absent in Dingle, but a messenger was immediately despatched for him, and he soon arrived in her Majesty's gunboat Shamrock. Soon after our arrival a signal was received from the Niagara that they were preparing to land, having paid out 1,030 nautical miles of cable, while the Agamemnon had accomplished her portion of the distance with an expenditure of 1,020 miles, making the total length of the wire submerged 2,050 geographical miles. Immediately after the ships cast anchor, the paddlebox boats of the Valorous were got ready, and two miles of cable coiled away in them, for the purpose of landing the end; but it was late in the afternoon before the procession of boats left the ship, under a salute of three rounds of small arms from the detachment of marines on board the Agamemnon, under the command of Lieutenant Morris.

The progress of the end to the shore was very slow, in consequence of the very stiff wind which blew at the time, but at about three o'clock the end was safely brought on shore at Knightstown, Valentia, by Mr. Bright and Mr. Canning, the chief and second engineers, to whose exertions the success of the undertaking is attributable, and the Knight of Kerry. The end was immediately laid in the trench which had been dug to receive it, while a royal salute, making the neighboring rocks and mountains reverberate, announced that the communication between the Old and the New World had been completed.

The end was immediately taken into the electric room by Mr. Whitehouse, and attached to a galvanometer, and the message was received through the entire length

THE END.

SHAFFNER'S

TELEGRAPH COMPANION,

DEVOTED TO THE SCIENCE AND ART OF THE

MORSE AMERICAN TELEGRAPH.

VOL. I. JANUARY, 1854. No. 1.

Art. I.—THE AMERICAN ELECTRO-MAGNETIC TELEGRAPH.

By Hon. Amos Kendall.

An extract from an Argument submitted to the Supreme Court of the United States.

Seldom, if ever, has a more important case been brought before the Supreme Court of the United States for its decision.

It is important on account of the pecuniary interests involved in it; it is important as involving the fame of a distinguished citizen, and through him, to some extent, the fame of our common country. It is transcendently important in the principles of patent law which it presents for final decision by this tribunal.

It is now to be tested whether Prof. Morse is to share the fate of so many distinguished inventors, who have gone before him; whether individuals or the public, eager to possess the fruits of his mental labor before they rightfully become public property, shall be permitted to gratify their cupidity; whether Prof. Morse, like the inventor of the cotton gin, is to lose the profits of his invention, while thousands of his instruments, the originality of which no man doubts, resound throughout the land, almost in the presence of the tribunal which must decide upon his patents.

It is now to be tested, whether American courts are hereafter to consider patent privileges as the price paid by the Government for the fruits of mental labor, to be held as sacred from piracy, theft, or trespass, as any other species of private property; or whether, like the English courts for a long period, now happily at an end, they are still to confound them with odious monopolies, of what, before the issue of the special grants, had become the property of the public.

It is now to be tested, whether American courts, as the English courts so long did, are hereafter to look to machinery or instrumentalities as the only objects to be protected by patents, and avail themselves of errors or variances in structure or description, not fatal to the result, for the purpose of annulling patent rights; or whether they shall look through the means to the end, as the real object of protection, and in their decisions secure the results to the inventor, if arrived at by any mode intelligibly described by him, especially if the process be new.

We confidently assert, that if this court come up to the principles established by the highest courts in England, enough is *admitted* by our adversaries to entitle us to a decree in our favor.

A leading principle decided in England is, that when an inventor has by a new principle or a new application of a known principle, power or substance, produced a new result, or an improved result, and has intelligibly described the manner in which he uses those means, they being of his own invention, and has patented his means, nobody can deprive him of the exclusive use of his new principle, or new application, or new result, by any improved or different means.

At page 11 of Mr. Chase's printed argument, he asks, "What Morse actually invented?" and he proceeds to reply, "*He invented the first practically useful* MARKING *Telegraph.*" "The evidence in this case," says he, "I freely admit must satisfy the court, that though his patent and the practical application of his invention, were subsequent in date to some foreign patents and to the actual construction of some foreign telegraphs, still, his was the first practically usefully marking telegraph. *For that telegraph, beyond a doubt, he was entitled to a patent.*"

It is also admitted, that Morse invented the means by which this new and useful result was accomplished. "Morse," says the learned counsel, attached a marker to the armature of the magnet. He brought the paper and its revolving cylinder within the stroke of the marker. He adopted a contrivance for withdrawing the marker from contact with the paper at the instant of the cessation of the magnetic impulse. The combination of these contrivances, with the known means of operation from the distant station, enabled him to produce marks at a distance, &c."

Again: "It occurred to him [Morse] that the motion which previous discoverers and inventors had been able to produce by means of electro-magnetism, might be made to mark dots and horizontal lines. *A simple contrivance sufficed for this.*"

Though we by no means concede, that these admissions cover all of Morse's invention, or any considerable part of it, yet they cover enough to secure to him not only those means, but the new result obtained by their use. Having been the *first* to invent a *practically useful* marking Electro-Magnetic Telegraph by *any* contrivances, however simple, which "occurred to him," or were by him invented, and which he has intelligibly described in his patent, he is entitled to the exclusive use of *marking* for telegraphic purposes by any mode in which Electro-Magnetism is the essential agent. There are in fact two distinct grounds on which his general claim rests.

First. He makes a new application of a known power to produce an useful result.

Secondly. He produces a useful result never before produced by any power.

But for one branch of our argument, the two may be resolved into one,—*a new result produced by a new application of a known power,*—a result which our adversaries admit to be new and produced by means of contrivances which they admit to be his.

There are many cases in the English books tending to establish the principle that an inventor, who has produced a new result or a result in any degree useful by a new application of a known agent, may, by giving to the public an intelligible description of the means he uses, those means being of his own invention, secure to himself through a patent for the means, an exclusive right to the new application and its result against interference by any other means. The leading case, and the only one it is necessary to present in any detail, is that of Neilson's Patent for what was called *the Hot Air Blast.*

Cold air injected by a bellows had previously been used to produce heat in furnaces employed in the production and manufacture of iron. Neilson perceived that a large portion of the heat generated in the furnace, was absorbed in heating the cold air, and he conceived the idea that if the air could be heated before it went into the furnace, the heat of the furnace-fire absorbed in that process, would be saved, by which means the furnace could be made much hotter. To carry out his idea he constructed and patented a clumsy iron box placed between the blower and furnace through which the air must pass, and under the box he put a fire to heat the air in its transit.

His patent was denominated, a patent "*for the improved application of air to produce heat in fires, forges, and furnaces where bellows or other blowing apparatus are required,*" the only instrumentality described being the iron box with a fire under it between the blower and the furnace.

The discovery proved to be of vast public utility, and his mode of heating the air was greatly improved by various devices, among which was the substitution of iron pipes for his clumsy iron box. The parties who had substituted other modes for heating the air, maintained, as the appellants in this case do, that Neilson's patent was for *his mode of heating the air only*, and as they used different modes, they were not infringers.

Neilson on the other hand maintained, that being the first to conceive the idea, and having rendered it useful by *one* mode of his own invention, he was entitled to the exclusive right of using the hot blast by *all* modes during the existence of his patent. The opposing Council in that case, as our adversaries do in this, insisted that the patentee was entitled only to the mode described in his patent, that a patent covering all modes would be a patent for a principle; and they were alert as our adversaries are in this case, to point out how very little the patentee had invented. And little indeed it was in that case. The manufacture of iron was old; the furnace was old; the fuel was old; the blower was old; hot air was old; iron boxes were old;—not a single new thing was used by him—nothing equal to the "simplest contrivance" in Morse's Telegraph. He did nothing whatever in the way of invention, but to put a few old things together, and that not in a very satisfactory manner.

The reported litigation upon this patent occupies upwards of 150 pages in Webster's Reports of Patent Cases. It was contested with all the talent, zeal and perseverance which unlimited means could command: after appearing in various shapes in the English Courts, a case involving its validity and extent went by appeal from the Court of Sessions in Scotland up to the House of Lords.

A long, lucid, and most able charge was given to the Jury by the Court below, to which exceptions were taken; and upon those exceptions, the case was taken up. To show distinctly that the House of Lords decided upon the question now at issue, we are obliged to quote somewhat extensively from this charge to the jury. In that address the learned Judge spoke as follows: viz.

"It is quite true, that a patent cannot be taken out solely for an abstract philosophical principle: for instance for any law of nature, or any property of matter apart from any mode of turning it to account in the practical operations of manufacture, or to the business, and arts, and utilities of life. The mere discovery of such a principle, is not an invention in the patent law-sense of the term. Stating such a principle in a patent, may be a promulgation of the principle, but it is no application of the principle to any practical purpose; and without that application of the principle to a practical object and end, and without the application of it to human industry, or to the purposes of human enjoyment, a person cannot in the abstract, appropriate a principle to himself. But a patent will be good, though the subject of the patent consists in the discovery of a great, general, and most comprehensive principle in science or law of nature, if that principle is by the specification applied to any special purpose, so as thereby to effectuate a practical result and benefit not previously attained.

"The main merit, the most important part of the invention may consist in the conception of the original idea—in the discovery of the principle in science, or of the law of nature, stated in the patent, and little or no pains may have been taken in working out the best manner and mode of the application of the principle to the purpose set forth in the patent. But still, if the principle is stated to be applicable to any special purpose, so as to produce any result previously unknown in the way and for the objects described, the patent is good. It is no longer an abstract principle. It comes to be a principle turned to account, to a practical object, and applied to a special result. It becomes then not an abstract principle, which means a principle considered apart from any special purpose or practical operation, but the discovery and statement of a principle for a special purpose, that is, a practical invention, a mode of carrying a principle into effect. That such is the law, if a well-known principle is applied for the first time to produce a practical result for a special purpose, has never been disputed.

"It would be very strange and unjust to refuse the same legal effect, when the inventor has the additional merit of discovering the principle, as well as its application to a practical object. The instant that a principle, although discovered for the first time, is stated, in actual application to, and as the agent of, producing a certain specified effect, it is no longer an abstract principle; it is then clothed with the language of practical application, and receives the impress of tangible direction to the actual business of human life. Is it any objection then, in the next place, to such a patent, that terms descriptive of the application to a certain specified result, include every mode of applying the principle or agent so as to produce that specified result, although one mode may not be described more than another? Although one mode may be infinitely better than another, although much greater benefit would result from the application of the principle by one method, than by another—although one method may be much less expensive than another? Is it, I next inquire, an objection to the patent, that in its application of a new principle to a certain specified result, it includes every variety of mode of applying the principle according to the general statement of the object and benefit to be attained? You will observe that the greater part of the Defendant's case is truly directed to this objection. This is a question of law, and I must tell you distinctly, that this generality of claim, that is, for all modes of applying the principle to the purpose specified, according to, or within a general statement of the object to be attained, and of the use to be made of the agent to be so applied, is no objection whatever to the patent. That the application or the use of the agent for the purpose specified, may be carried out in a great variety of ways, only shows the beauty, and simplicity, and comprehensiveness of the invention. But the scientific and general utility of the proposed application of the principle, if directed to a specified purpose, is not an objection to its becoming the subject of a patent.

"That the proposed application may be very generally adopted in a great variety of ways, is the merit of the invention, not a legal objection to the patent."

* * * * * *

"I state to you the law to be, that you may obtain a patent for a mode of carrying a principle into effect; and if you suggest and discover, not only the principle, but suggest and invent how it may be applied to a practical result by mechanical contrivance and apparatus, and show that you are aware that no particular sort, or modification, or form of the apparatus is essential in order to obtain benefit from the principle, then you may take your patent for the mode of carrying it into effect, and are not under the necessity of describing and confining yourself to one form of apparatus. If that were necessary, you see what would be the result. Why that a patent could hardly ever be obtained for any mode of carrying a newly discovered principle into practical results, though the most valuable of all discoveries. For the best form and shape, or modification of apparatus, cannot, in matters of such vast range, and requiring observation on such a great scale, be attained at once; and so the thing would become known, and so the right lost, long before all the various kinds of apparatus could be tried. Hence you may generally claim the mode of carrying the principle into effect by mechanical contrivance, so that any sort of apparatus applied in the way stated, will, more or less, produce the benefit, and you are not tied down to any form."

* * * * * *

"I have to tell you in point of law, that under this patent not claiming any or the best contrivance for heating the air, and at the least expense and trouble, the result which actually followed, viz.: that persons in the trade and acting on the patent, contrived from time to time, a great variety of contrivances more or less valuable or costly, and at last came to settle generally into one form as better than others, was exactly the result which might be expected to follow under a patent of this general character, and that if the patent is good in law, then it gave no form of apparatus for heating air, but claimed the contrivance generally, of heating the blast for the effect and end of producing heat in the furnace. The only point for you is, will any contrivance which heats the blast, produce that beneficial effect and end?"

The subject was fully discussed by Counsel before the House of Lords, and by the Lords themselves, and that august Tribunal, so far as appears, without a dissenting voice, decided the law to be as laid down in the foregoing extracts from the charge to the Jury.

On that occasion Lord Campbell made the following remarks, viz.:

"The other exceptions, till we come to the 11th, turn upon the construction of the patent. Now in one stage of these proceedings, I certainly did entertain some doubt on that subject. But after the construction put upon it by the learned Judges of the Exchequer, sanctioned by the high authority of my noble and learned friend now upon the woolsack, when presiding in the Court of Chancery, I think the patent must be taken to extend to all machines of whatever construction, whereby the air is heated intermediately between the blowing apparatus and the blast furnace. That being so, the learned Judge was perfectly justified in telling the Jury, that it was unnecessary for them to compare one apparatus with another, because, confessedly, that system of conduit pipes was a mode of heating air by an intermediate vessel between the blowing apparatus and the blast furnace, and therefore it was an infraction of the patent."

Thus it was decided by the Courts of England and Scotland, including the House of Lords, substantially in the language of the exceptions, that the patentee, being the discoverer of a new principle, and the inventor of means, however simple and imperfect, by which he has rendered it in *some* degree *useful*, may "*claim or maintain that his patent is one which applies to all varieties in the apparatus which may be employed in heating air while under blast,*" and is "*not limited to a particular apparatus described in the specification*"—that it is "*in point of law no objection to the validity of such a patent that it included every mode of applying the principle or agent so as to produce the specified result, although one mode may not be described more than another, although one mode may be infinitely better than another, although much greater benefit would result from the application of the principle by one method, than another; although one method be much less expensive than another, and that this generality of claim, that is, for all modes of applying the principle to the purpose specified, according to, or within the general statement of the object to be obtained, and of the use to be made of the agent to be applied, is no objection whatever to the patent.*"

But it is distinctly laid down in the same case, that the patentee, if he wishes to enjoy his invention thus broadly, must take care in his specification not to confine himself to the single mode described by him; otherwise he will be confined to that mode. *Webster's Patent Cases,* pp. 679, 682, 688, 698, *Ex.* 6.

As well in the facts as in the law, there is a remarkable analogy between Neilson's patent for the hot air blast and Morse's patent for the Electro-Magnetic Telegraph. In Neilson's case the *ultimate* result was the manufacture of iron which was old.

In Morse's case, the ultimate result was the telegraphic communication of ideas from one mind to another, which was old.

In Neilson's case, the furnace, the fuel, the fire, the ore, the hot air, the blower and iron boxes, were old.

In Morse's case, the clockwork, the paper, dots and dashes, galvanic electricity, the battery, the circuit, the electro magnet, and the key were old.

Neilson put the old parts together in such manner as to heat the air in its transit, though he did not claim heating the air, without even a "simple contrivance" of his own invention.

Morse put the old parts together, by a port rule to regulate the pulsations of the electric current so as to make the dots and dashes of any desired length, by a contrivance to regulate the motion of the paper to receive them, by the pen or pencil in the first patent to delineate them, and the pen-point and grooved roller in his second patent to indent them, and by combined and local circuits.

In Neilson's case, the clumsy iron box in his combination, which was *the only patentable part* of his invention, was immediately abandoned in practice, being superseded by coils of pipe in which the air could be heated to a higher degree of temperature; but in the case of Morse, it is his own invented forms and combinations *now in use* unimproved, which make his Telegraph.

True, his port rule which forms *a part* of his invention, is not used, because, in common business, the end can be better attained without it; but this constituted a small part of his patentable invention.

Though the *whole* of Neilson's patentable invention was abandoned in practice, yet the British Courts of highest resort sustained his claim to the exclusive use of hot air applied to furnaces: And on what ground? On the ground, that *he was the first to devise and describe the means of applying the hot air*, no matter how bungling or imperfect those means were, if they were such as to make the application *to any degree useful.*

They decided that he was entitled to *the whole principle and effect*, because that was his real invention, and although it was necessary for him to devise and describe *some* plan by which the object could be attained, when he had described *one* such mode, *it carried with it all modes.* They do indeed lay down one exception to this rule, dependent however, on the patentee himself. It is where the patentee so frames his specification as to imply that he intends to confine himself to the mode described by him. In that event he is entitled to nothing beyond that particular mode. Neilson avoided that restriction, by declaring in his specification, that the size and shape of the box in which the air was to be heated, and the manner of heating the air, were immaterial. Morse avoids it by directly declaring, after he has described his machinery, that he does not propose to confine himself to it, but claims all modes wherein the same application of power is employed to attain the same end, both the application and end being new. And the Court will not fail to remark, that such a declaration, or something equivalent to it, was absolutely necessary to bring Morse's invention within the protection of the law as laid down in Neilson's case.

With this exposition, we confidently submit, that, upon the *admissions* of our adversaries, that by a few simple contrivances of Morse's invention, described in his specification, he has produced "the first practically useful Electro-Magnetic *Marking* Telegraph," he is entitled to the protection of this court against all other Electro-Magnetic *Marking* Telegraphs, whatever may be their form or modes of operation.

But our adversaries while admitting facts sufficient to entitle us to protection under the law as laid down in Neilson's case, resolutely contest the law itself. They sing us the old song with all its variations, that *principles*, *effects*, and *results* cannot be patented.

So, in the same sense, *Machines*, or *means* cannot be patented. An *abstract machine* is no more patentable, than an *abstract principle* or *result.* Go to the Patent Office with the most beautiful machine ever devised, seeming to perform evolutions more wonderful and sublime than those of the Heavenly spheres, and tell them you want a patent for it. They will ask you the very commonplace question, "*of what use is your beautiful machine? What* USEFUL RESULT *do you accomplish by it?*" If you reply "I don't know, I have not yet studied that out," they will tell you "you *must* know,—you *must* not only study that out, but you *must give us an intelligible description of it* before we can give you a patent."

Go to the Patent Office and tell them, that you have discovered a *principle*, or achieved a *result*, more important to the wealth, comfort, and happiness of mankind than all discoveries and inventions which have been made from creation down to this day, and ask a patent for it. They will ask you *how you apply* the principle so as to produce any useful result, or *how* you produce a result so astonishing? If you answer that you do not choose to tell, or have yet to study that out, they will tell you, that you must not only study it out, but give them an intelligible description of it, before they can give you a patent for it.

Every cause has its effect, and every effect its cause. Machines and their results in the eye of the patent law, cannot be separated. They come into existence together, and march, *pari passu*, hand in hand. They are the body and the soul. Without the soul the body is dead, and protection would be useless; without the body, the soul needs no human protection. It is *body and soul united*, which need the protection of human laws, and it is only body and soul united that such laws are designed to protect.

In the beginning of invention, every *new machine* produced a *new result*. They formed the basis of all subsequent improvements. By the principles of justice as well as patent law, the first inventor was entitled to be protected *both in his machine and his result*, in the one as well as in the other, both being his property, the fruits of his mental and manual labor. The second inventor by *an improved machine* might produce an *improved result*, and would be entitled to protection for his improvement and for his improvement only. It would be as unjust to let him deprive me of my result because he has improved it, as of my *machine* because he has improved that. He cannot build on my foundation without my leave, but having purchased my machine and results, he adds his improvements, and enjoys the whole together. The first inventor is entitled to the *whole* result; the second to his improvement upon it; so also the third, and so on. But gradations in results are not so easily distinguished as alterations in machinery, and as they both go together, the law attempts to define and protect an improvement in the result, through the improvement of machinery by which it is produced. When it speaks of a new and useful machine, it means a machine which produces a new and useful result; and when it speaks of a new and useful improvement, it means one that produces an improvement in the result. To understand the meaning of the law, we must look upon the machine and its result as *one*,—one in origin, one in object, and one in the eye of the law.

But our adversaries, like multitudes of others, separate machines from their results, and seem to think the former the only objects which the patent laws are designed to protect. We hold, on the contrary, that the ultimate object of the patent laws is, *the protection of results*, and so far as they are applicable to the protection of machines, the object is to *protect the result through protection of the machine.* Of what use is protection of the machine, if the result be not protected? Of what value is the machine to the patentee, or the public, except for the results it produces?

We need not tell this court, that patents in England were originally for new results, "new manufactures"—without regard to the manner in which they were produced. No specification of means or machinery was required. The fact that a man produced an useful result, was all that was required; and for the result only the patent was granted. This patent protected him against any person who should produce the same result by any means whatsoever.

What was the object of the specification afterwards required? Not, certainly, to enable others to deprive the patentee of his result by improving upon his means or substituting others; but simply to enable others to understand how he arrived at that result, that the public might have the full benefit of it after the expiration of his exclusive right. The first expedient resorted to for the purpose of enabling the public to avail itself of the invention after the patent had expired, was to require the patentee to instruct a certain number of apprentices in his art and mystery, who might go out and teach it to others. This was made a condition on which the exclusive use was guaranteed by a patent. This gave place to the written specification which was an improved mode of arriving at the same end.

There is a contract between the inventor and the public. The inventor says, I have accomplished an object never before accomplished, I have produced a result—"a new manufacture"—never before produced, of vast public utility. The government says to him, if you will make known the means by which you attain that end, so that the public will have the benefit of it after your patent expires, we will secure to you all the benefits of your result for fourteen years. The bargain is struck. The inventor reveals his secret; the government gives him a solemn contract of protection; and then, nine times out of ten, suffers him to be plundered, if not ruined by the uses made of the very secret he discloses!

Morse comes to the government with his ribbon of paper, imprinted with letters Roman, Greek, Hebrew or *Morsaic*, and says, I have produced this new and astounding result instantaneously, standing a thousand miles distant from the printing apparatus, and I ask a patent for it. A patent under the old English law would have given him the exclusive benefit of his result for the patent term; but the government says to him, "you must inform the public how you do this wonderful thing, and then we will give you a patent securing to you the exclusive use of it for fourteen years." Morse says "if I inform the public how I do it, you will let others, who perchance get their notions from my description, come in by some improvements real or pretended, and take from me all the benefits of my invention." The government assures him that the only object and legal effect of his description will be to enable the public to use his art after his patent expires. How far that assurance has been verified is shown by the open use of his invention on thousands of miles of line, in bold defiance of his patented rights.

It takes a long time to change the current of the public mind when it becomes concentrated in one deep channel, however devious from the line of right. You might as well attempt to make the Mississippi run straight by throwing pebbles into its curves, as to think by one or a hundred arguments to overcome unjust prejudices and opinions impressed on the public mind by the precedents of ages. In no portion of human affairs is this fact so conspicuous as in the profession of law, wherein most judges believe it their duty to think just as their predecessors did, and it is the pride of the lawyer that he is able to array a consecutive file of precedents extending back to black-letter age, since which a trifling error then originating, has, by the natural effect of adding precedent, accumulated like the rolling snow-ball, until it has become an enormous wrong.

We need not enter into a history of the English patent laws which are the ancestors of our own. It is sufficient to say, that the granting of patents for new inventions and for monopolies in trade and manufactures were in ancient times a royal prerogative in England, and there was no recognized distinction between patents for old things and for new. The royal prerogative was so enormously abused as to create a general abhorrence of patents of every sort, and the judges of England sought every pretext for declaring them void. At length they were all swept away with a few exceptions, by an act of parliament, and the prerogative of the king was limited to grants of exclusive privileges for limited terms to those only who devised or introduced some new manufacture, useful to trade, and beneficial to the public.

But the current of the judicial mind in England had long been running against all patents, and could not be suddenly changed. It still set against patents for new inventions, as it had done against the old monopolies; and when the specification was introduced, it was immediately perverted from its true object and used as a means of destroying a right, the protection of which was the sole object of the inventor in making it public. Even now, though a great change has been wrought in the judicial mind of England and America, the odium of the old monopolies in some degree attaches to patents, and something included in the specification which ought to have been omitted, or something omitted, which ought to have been included, though that instrument enables everybody distinctly to understand the invention, and how to use it, is seized upon as a pretext for annulling the grant altogether.

These are hard cases. The man's invention is his own; the government buys it of him for a price, and on a condition. He complies with the condition as well as he knows how, and under the instructions of officers of the government itself, appointed to advise and correct him if there be anything wrong in his papers. But some error is discovered by an astute lawyer in the specification, an error never thought of by him, nor suspected in the Patent Office, and his patent is declared void. The protection of the government is withdrawn from his invention, but his property is not restored. It is gone for ever, not from any fault of his, but because two public authorities, one in the Patent Office, the other in the courts, differ in opinion upon some point of his specification.

We trust the day is passed when pretexts were sought to get rid of these contracts between government and citizen. Morse comes and exhibits the result of his invention—*the printing of telegraphic characters at any distances.* All he asks is, that protection which the law would give him if no specification of means had ever been required. It is just that, and nothing more, which he has attempted to secure through his specification. It is just that, and nothing less, which his government has promised him. It is protection for *his art*—his *embodied* art, and our adversaries admit that "without doubt" such "an art can be patented,—the statute says so expressly."

Art. II.—GEOGRAPHY OF THE ATLANTIC OCEAN.*

THE WINDS AND THE CURRENTS—TIDES AND THE SEAS—DEPTH OF THE OCEAN—OCEAN TELEGRAPH PRACTICABLE.

THE time is probably not far distant when the popular will, no less than the enlightened good sense of the statesmen of the country will settle practically how far the government of the Union may be permitted "to provide for the general welfare," by the encouragement of science. Custom in such matters, whence no further usurpations can possibly arise, becomes almost as authoritative as a constitutional sanction; and unless we greatly misapprehend the character of the American people, few will be disposed to blame herein a leaning to the liberal

* From De Bow's Review.

side. The temptation to aid the national genius in the acquisition of those unfading laurels, awarded by universal consent to the successful discoverer of what is truly great and widely useful in these fields, might tempt the most rigid constructionist to relax here his rules, and admit, if possible, an exception to his political creed. The fame of one illustrious philosopher, one of the founders of American independence, is already blended with the history of human thought as well as political enfranchisement; and whether the spirit in which he pursued knowledge, or the magnitude of his additions to the common stock, are considered, it must be admitted that his example still modifies all legitimate inquiry into the august secrets of nature. The era of Franklin was but the dawn of modern science. The laws, the modifications, and the analogies of light, heat, chemical affinities, and electricity, in its Protæan forms, were then just emerging to human ken. The stone tables, on which, as on the leaves of a book, the earth's history are imprinted, were at that time united by unbroken seals. Observation had not yet accumulated a mass of records, nor been sufficiently extended to trace the varying intensities of the great powers of nature over the surface of the earth, and thus create a true philosophic geography. It is worthy of mention, that one of the most important features of our planet was pointed out by the great Franklin, and that he traced that portion of the ocean stream which rushes past our shores, and bestows on Western Europe its genial and temperate climate, its fertilizing showers, and abundant harvests. Since that period there have been travelers like Humboldt and Von Buch, who have measured mountains and gauged streams, watched the fires of the volcano, and explored the causes of those powers that sweep the surface or shake the depths of the earth. Every year the number of observers is increased; the circle of stations at which these investigations are prosecuted is continually widening; while commerce, allured by the promises of greater and more certain gains, bids fair soon to be pressed into the zealous service of science. Physical geography, the most attractive of the departments of the study of Nature, embracing the view and discussion of her phenomena on the widest field that man can grasp, by the aid of all the senses, and presenting subjects at once uniting the enjoyments of the imagination and the reason, and gratifying the passion for knowledge and the desire of profit, is now for the first time possible. The various *meters*, the delicate instruments of modern research, the product and realization in art of scientific progress, are now in the hands of every traveller. He reads off their scales the temperature of the air, the earth, and the ocean, the heights of mountains, the quantity of moisture contained in the air, and many similar relations are by their means accurately ascertained and measured, at every point whither man can penetrate. Governments have rivalled each other in fitting out expeditions for research and exploration; and if the cultivation of the sciences under the direct patronage of our own, notwithstanding such precedents, be questioned, as on another long vexed subject, we may suppose that the popular voice will incline to advance this cause, whenever it can be done in an incidental way.

The valuable volume of "Sailing Directions, by Lieutenant Maury," is but among the first fruits of what we may reasonably expect from the patriotic and liberal character of the officers of the navy and army. The younger officers are now as a class, admirably qualified, by their tastes and education, to second any system of scientific observation that may be adopted by the national authority. The Coast Survey and the Naval Observatory were the first steps made in this direction by the government, and they have already well repaid all that has been laid out in their maintenance and prosecution. The equipment and *materiel* of the Washington Observatory may be inferior to the imperial endowments of Pultowa or Greenwich, but the genius and untiring industry of its, superintendent has already given it a world wide celebrity. When the exacting and ceaseless duties of his station are considered, it is astonishing how he should have accomplished so much for the geography of commerce and navigation, as may be inferred from the articles in the "Sailing Directions," or when he found time for the arrangement and tabulation of the observations contained in thousands of log-books, the results of which gigantic labor we find in the same volume. We propose to look at what has been thus accomplished by Lieutenant Maury for commercial geography, under the three heads: first, the establishment of a regular system of observation, to be carried out by the various national and commercial marines of the world; second, the contributions already made to science by the materials collected under the direction, and arranged by the author; and third, the practical rules and directions which are therein laid down for the guidance of the navigator, with the results already obtained by following them.

These undertakings have received the sanction of the most distinguished physicists of the age, among them the illustrious Humboldt, who, in writing to a friend, (Dr. Flûgal, U. S. Consul at Leipzic,) says,—

"I beg you to express to Lieut. Maury, the author of the beautiful charts of the winds and currents, prepared with so much care and profound learning, my hearty gratitude and esteem. It is a great undertaking, equally important to the practical navigator, and for the advance of meteorology in general. It has been viewed in this light in Germany, by all persons who have a taste for physical geography. In an analogous way, anything of isothermal countries, (countries of equal annual thermal temperature,) has for the first time, become really fruitful. Since Dove has taught us the isotherms of the several months chiefly on the land—since two-thirds of the atmosphere rests upon the sea—Maury's work is so much the more welcome and valuable; because it includes at the same time, the oceanic currents, the course of the winds, and the temperature."

It is comparatively easy to map out the course of rivers over the land, and follow them from the glacier of the mountains to the ocean estuary, through their channels. This is but the visible half of the ceaseless circle which the waters make over the land. A far more difficult task it is, to track the viewless winds, and weigh the watery freights they carry from the ocean, and lay down so lowly and gradually in the fog, the dew, the shower, and the noiseless snow; or to pursue the oceanic currents that feed these thefts of the winds, and map out their path—

Parietibus textum cæcis iter.

The solution of the grand problems of physical science connected with navigation do not rest there; they overflow to other branches of human labor and interest. Agriculture, and the health and happiness of mankind, are blended with the course of the winds and the distribution of heat and moisture. The farmer as well as as the mariner, looks up and watches the appearance of the heavens; and plentiful crops and prosperous voyages equally depend on the agencies which set in motion the winds, and uplift the clouds from the ocean. The beauty and impressiveness of these signs, in which Nature addresses Man, render them worthy of the poet. Happy he who can read them aright.

THE LANGUAGE OF NATURE.—"The wind and rain, the vapor and the cloud, the tide, the current, the saltness, and depth, and temperature, and color of the sea, the shade of the sky, the temperature of the air, the tint and shape of the clouds, the height of the tree on the shore, the size of the leaves, the brilliancy of the flowers—each and all may be regarded as the exponent of certain physical combinations, and therefore, as the expression in which Nature chooses to announce her own meaning; or, if we please, as the language in which she writes down the operation of her own laws. To understand that language, and to interpret aright those laws, is the object of the undertaking which those who co-operate with me have in hand. No fact gathered in such a field as this, therefore, can come amiss to those who tread the walks of inductive philosophy; for in the hand-book of Nature, every such fact is a syllable; and it is by patiently collecting fact after fact, and by joining together syllable after syllable, that we may finally seek to read aright from the great volume, which the mariner at sea, and the philosopher on the mountain, see spread out before them.

Among the friends and collaborators of Lieut. Maury may be mentioned Dr. Buist, a distinguished *savant* of India, who announces, in the transactions of the Bombay Geographical Society, that the Assistant-Secretary, Mr. Macfarlane, "has made considerable progress in the construction of wind and current charts, founded on the information supplied by ships' logs, and on the principle of Lieut. Maury." What has been done for the Indian and the Northern Atlantic Ocean reveals the value of concert of observation among the navigators and meteorologists of the world. In a letter to Lieut. Maury, dated 17th November, 1851, Dr. Buist, after alluding to a vast mass of facts collected by observers in the Indian seas, observes:—

"Three years since, I began to perceive that we had certain classes of storms that occurred periodically, not only all over India, but all over the region to which my information extended, and that these were synchronous, or nearly so. I then began a series of maps, illustrative of the matter."

A system of stations and the co-operation of navigators is naturally suggested by what has already been done. It must be seen that a true science of meteorology is impossible from local observations. We may watch the height of the barometer, and record the amount of moisture in the air, set rain gauges for ever, and yet be merely accumulating facts that in themselves have no significance. The relations of the river, the rain, and the ocean, are not local; they belong to universal geography, and are, literally,

"General, as the casing air,"

the atmosphere which forms the invisible link in the mighty orbit of the waters about the earth. Nature herself seems here to refuse to be evoked by the efforts of the individual mind, and demands for the revelation of her secrets to be everywhere watched.

Towards the end of the year 1851, the idea of a conference between the meteorologists of Russia and those of the United States was suggested by Kupffer, a laborious meteorologist of the former country; and about the same time a proposition was made by the British Government that that of the United States should co-operate in making these observations at certain foreign stations, and according to instructions prepared by General Burgoyne, Inspector-General of Fortifications. This was felt to be an auspicious moment to secure concert of action among meteorologists on shore, and co-operation among navigators at sea everywhere; and Lieut. Maury then, in reply to the British proposition, suggested that sea and land should be included as the field, and that a general conference of meteorologists and navigators should be held to discuss the plans, draw up the forms, fix the standards, and select the instruments to be employed on this grand field of research.

A UNIVERSAL SYSTEM OF OBSERVATIONS.—The basis originally proposed by the British Government to that of the United States, is contained in the instructions drawn up by order of the Inspector-General of Fortifications, Sir John Burgoyne, the circular letter of Lord Palmerston to British consuls, and that of Lord Glenelg to Colonial Governors. Nineteen principal stations in the colonies of Great Britain were selected as the points of regular record. These were to be supplied with sets of instruments of similar construction. Twenty sets were to be sent to India, by the Board of Directors of the East India Company, and provision made of the same character for observations at Ascension, Rio de Janeiro, Callao and Valparaiso.

The circular addressed to the officers of the government of India, desires them—

"Upon the occurrence of any hurricane, gale, or other storm of more violence than usual, to note accurately the time of its commencement, the direction from which the wind first blows, whether in gusts or regular, and whether accompanied with rain, thunder and lightning, or other phenomena. Also, to note, with as much accuracy as possible, the changes of direction in the wind, and the time of occurrence of each; and lastly, the duration of the gale, and in what quarter the wind is when it ceases. The variations of the thermometer and barometer at each period noticed will also be of importance, if the means are forthcoming of making such observations."

On the transmission of these instructions to the United States government for the purpose of securing its co-operation in the plan, Lieut. Maury brought forward as an amendment a system of universal observation on sea as well as on land, and securing the assistance of the commercial marines of the civilized nations of the earth in carrying out its details. We copy the following from the paper of Lieut. Maury, on this subject:

"The importance of concert among meteorologists all over the world, and of co-operation between the observer on the shore and the navigator at sea, so that any meteorological phenomenon may be traced throughout its cycle both by sea and land, is too obvious for illustration, too palpable to be made plainer by argument; and, therefore, the proposition for a general conference to arrange the details of such a comprehensive system of observations, addresses itself to every friend of science and lover of the useful in all countries.

"The domain of this science of the atmosphere: its boundaries embrace the land and cover the sea.. To comprehend the laws which govern the movements of a machine so vast as it is, requires that its operations should be observed in all its parts and watched from all points at the same time. Its motions are freer and less obstructed over the water, than they are by the land and across the mountains. Indeed, the ocean itself may, in one sense, be regarded as a grand expression of meteorological agencies; therefore the good-will and friendly co-operation of private ship-owners and masters, in all maritime countries, is considered of great importance to the cause in hand."

The proposition for a universal system of observation, as suggested by Lieutenant Maury, was soon after submitted to the Royal Society, and, so far as an extension of these to the sea is concerned, it received a warm approval. The report adopted by the society recommends that instructions similar to those given to American shipmasters, according to the scheme submitted by Lieutenant Maury to the Bureau of Ordnance and Hydrography in 1842, be given "to every ship that sails" from British ports, with a request to transmit the results of them to the Hydrographer's Office of the Admiralty. The labors of the two greatest naval and commercial nations of the world, it is hoped, may be thus united in promoting the interest of navigation.

The additions that have been made to geographical science since American shipmasters have been engaged, under the guidance of Lieutenant Maury, in the business of watching and recording the course of the winds, the clouds, and the currents, have not been few or unimportant. The power of such discoveries in changing the course of trade is well illustrated by the influence of the Gulf Stream on the trade of Charleston. During the colonial times, the course of trade was to make that port the half-way house for vessels bound from England to the northern ports. If driven off the coast during the winter by gales and snow storms, they returned to Charleston, and there remained until spring. When Dr. Franklin taught the mariner to know when he crossed the banks of this ocean river, by dipping a thermometer into the water, it was, to use the graphic words of the navigators, as if blue and red lines were drawn on the ocean. This discovery shortened the passage to the west from sixty to thirty days. It changed the course of trade. Vessels, instead of running to Charleston to avoid a snow-storm, now stood off for a few hours, thawed out the ship and her crew in the warmth of the Gulf, and were ready for another attempt to make their port.

The view of the general circulation in the atmosphere, as traced by the investigations of Lieutenant Maury, is of the highest interest. The trade winds of the tropical seas have long been known, and form two links in the circuit of the winds around the earth. The ocean scenery of the region of the trades is among the most beautiful to the thoughts and the senses that can be conceived. The machinery of nature aiding so palpably the objects of man, and uniting lands divided so widely by the ocean; the canopy of flying clouds; the fresh and exhilarating breeze blowing day and night in one direction; the charming temperature and the moderate swell of the waves, make it the elysium of the mariner. The gentle spirit of the earth seems to be there bodily present; and the picture of a fleet hanging in the clouds, always an impressive object, becomes exquisitely poetic in its associations, when—

They on the trading flood,
Through the wide Ethiopian to the Cape,
Ply stemming nightly towards the pole.

These trade winds are the great evaporating winds of the ocean; and, as we learn from the investigations of Lieutenant Maury, the belt of the S. E. trades in the South Atlantic is not only more extensive than the N. E. trades in the South Atlantic, but the winds themselves are fresher in the south. The very natural conclusion is, that the increased water thus taken up goes to feed in part the rivers of the northern hemisphere. At the equator these surface winds meet, and form a belt of calms, a node of upward winds, the northeast trade wind becoming a northwest upper current, and the southeast trade a southwest wind in the upper regions of the atmosphere overlying the north torrid zone. At the tropics, two other nodes of calms and of downward currents are met, with the two descending nodes of the orbit of the winds. The prevailing surface winds should now blow in spirals from the southwest towards the north pole, and in similar spirals from the northwest towards the south pole. At the poles the upward current produces another region of calms, whence the winds begin from north and south other revolutions towards the equator. And this system of winds is the source of

THE RAINS.—"To evaporate water enough annually from the ocean to cover the earth, on the average, five feet deep, with rain; to transport it from one zone to another, and to precipitate it in the right places, at suitable times, and in the proportions due, is the office of the grand atmospherical machine. This water is evaporated principally from the torrid zone. Supposing it all to come thence, we shall have, encircling the earth, a belt of ocean 3,000 miles in breadth, from which this atmosphere evaporates a layer of water annually 16 feet in depth. And to hoist up as high as the clouds, and lower down again, all the water in a lake 16 feet deep, and 3,000 miles broad, and 24,000 long, is the yearly businesss of this invisible machinery. What a powerful engine is the atmosphere!

"In some parts of the earth the precipitation is greater than the evaporation; thus, the amount of water borne down by every river that runs into the sea may be considered as the ex cess of the precipitation over the evaporation that takes place in the valley drained by that river. In other parts of the earth the evaporation and precipitation are exactly equal, as in those inland basins such as that in which the city of Mexico, Lake Titicaca, the Caspian Sea, etc., etc., are situated; which basins have no ocean drainage. If more rain fell in the valley of the Caspian than is evaporated from it, that sea would finally get full and overflow the whole of that great basin. If less fell than is evaporated from it again, then that sea, in the course of time, would dry up, and plants and animals would all perish there for the want of water. In the sheets of water which we find distributed over that and every other inhabitable inland basin, we see reservoirs or evaporating surfaces just sufficient for the supply of that degree of moisture which is best adapted to the well-being of the plants and animals that people such basins. In other parts of the earth still, we find places, as the Desert of Sahara, in which neither evaporation nor precipitation takes place, and in which we find neither plant nor animal.

"In contemplating the system of terrestrial adaptations, these researches have taught me to regard the great deserts of the earth as the astronomer does the counterpoises to his telescope—though they be mere dead weights, they are, nevertheless, necessary to make the balance complete, the adjustments of this machine perfect. These counterpoises give ease to the motions, stability to the performance, and accuracy to the workings of the instrument. They are *compensations*."

A strong corroboration of the hypothesis that the southeastern trades are deflected into the upper regions of the atmosphere, is the fact that the occasional showers of dust to be met with in the Atlantic not far from the belt of calms of Cancer, and in the neighborhood of the Cape de Verd Islands, and sometimes extending to the northern coasts of the Mediterranean, contain the remains of infusoria, whose habitat is not Africa, but South America, and the southeast trade-wind region of South America. These remains cause the red fogs and sea-dust of the North Atlantic, the Cape de Verd Islands, and the dust-winds of southwestern Europe.

THE EQUATORIAL CLOUD-RING.—The graphic essay on the above subject, by Lieut. Maury, is well known; it forms part of his theory of the circulation of the atmosphere, and the following is his explanation of its formation:

"In a clear day at the equator, this cloud-ring having slid to the north or south with the calm belt, the rays of the sun pour down upon the crust of the earth, and raise its temperature to a scorching heat. The atmosphere dances above it, and the air is seen trembling in ascending and descending columns with busy eagerness to conduct the heat off, and deliver it to the regions aloft, where it is required to give momentum to the air in its general channels of circulation. The dry season continues; the sun is vertical; and finally the earth becomes parched and dry; the heat accumulates faster than the air can carry it away; the plants begin to wither, and the animals to perish. Then comes the mitigating cloud-ring. The burning rays of the sun are intercepted by it. The place for the absorption and reflection, and the delivery to the atmosphere of the solar heat, is changed; it is transferred from the upper surface of the earth to the upper surface of the clouds.

"Radiation from the land and the sea below the cloud-belt is thus interrupted, and the excess of heat in the earth is delivered to the air, and by absorption carried up to the clouds, and there delivered to their vapors to prevent excess of precipitation.

"In the meantime, the trade winds north and south are pouring into this cloud-covered receiver, as the calm and rain-belt of the equator may be called, fresh supplies in the shape of ceaseless volumes of heated hair loaded to saturation with vapor, which has to rise above and get clear of the clouds before it can commence the process of cooling by radiation. In the meantime, also, the vapors which the trade winds bring from the north and the south, expanding and growing cooler as they ascend, are being condensed on the lower side of the cloud stratum, and their latent heat is set free to check precipitation and prevent a flood.

"While this process and these operations are going on on the nether side of the cloud-ring, one not less important is going on on the upper side. There, from sunrise to sunset, the rays of the sun are pouring down without intermission. Every day, and all day long, they operate with ceaseless activity upon the upper surface of the cloud stratum. When they become too powerful, and convey more heat to the cloud vapors than the cloud vapors can reflect and give off to the air above them, then with a beautiful elasticity of character, the clouds absorb the surplus heat. They melt away, become invisible, and retain, in a latent and harmless state, until it is wanted at some other place and on some other occasion, the heat thus imparted."

THE GEOLOGICAL AGENCY OF THE WINDS.—The geological relations between the wind, the land, and the water, are shown to have an intimate connection with the fertility and habitable quality of each region. The largest portion of the surface swept by the southeastern trades is water; but those regions which lie to the northeast of South America and Africa, in the northern hemisphere, are deserts, and were it not for the inland seas of Europe and Asia, these regions would be still more extensive. In like manner, Australia occupies in the southern hemisphere a position opposite to the continent of Asia, and, being swept by winds borne over a vast extent of land, while in contact with the surface, is found to be mostly a desert. If this contental mass were removed so as to occupy the space in the South Pacific swept by the southeast trades, which blow as southwest winds over the basins of the great rivers and lakes of North America, the channel of the Mississippi would resemble that of the Australian rivers, and present a dry and dusty trough in the midst of a desert, the great lakes would be drained, and Niagara no longer resound with the whirl of its world of waters. If ever there was a time when the Andes and the Continent of South America were submerged, then the ancient winds that fell on the region of Central Asia, and the basins of the Caspian and Aral, were swelled with the waters that now are discharged, in part, by the Amazon and Orinoco into the ocean, and those seas were united, forming a Mediterranean of vast extent, and probably discharging its waters by an estuary more magnificent than the St. Lawrence. According to the circulatory scheme of the atmosphere, the winds that play over the torrid zone of one hemisphere become the surface winds of the temperate zone of the other hemisphere. Fill up the south torrid zone, the region of the southeast trades, with land, and the north temperate zone would become one vast Sahara. Such, in brief, is the aspect of the dry season in the geological cycle, happily not co-existing with man's possession of the planet.

"The Saltness of the Sea," is the title of another of the series of interesting papers contained in the present volume. We are unable to do more than to state that it is to this quality, in connection with the evaporation caused by heat and the passage of the winds over the water, that the currents of the ocean owe their extent and depth. By these agencies, a general circulation of the waters of the sea is maintained; and so complete is it, that the per centage of its salt is found to be nearly the same in every part of the globe.

Following the discussion of a general circulation of the waters through the entire ocean, is the argument so intimately connected with it, and now so deeply interesting both to philanthrophy and science, that a permanently open sea exists in the Arctic basin. The study of the currents of the ocean have led Lieut. Maury strongly to the conclusion, that the pole is surrounded by this sea instead of being piled by everlasting barriers of thick-ribbed ice. The report of Lieut. De Haven, the commander of the Grinnell Expedition, the first of the noble enterprises set on foot from the United States to aid in the discovery and rescue of the lost ships of Sir John Franklin, follows; and, in the midst of the dangers of the dreary cruise during the long nights of those two polar winters, a ray of hope, faint though it be, hangs over the track of the intrepid Kane, who has dared again the perils of the Arctic Sea, at the joint command of humanity and national glory.

DEEP SEA SOUNDINGS.—To determine the depth of the ocean, and approximately the outline of its abysses and shallows, will furnish data of the utmost value in completing the theory of the tides. We believe that American officers have been the foremost, and, with a few exceptions, the only investigators in this problem. Already they have contributed euough to make out a chart of the bottom of the Atlantic, which gives a general idea of the slopes and hollows of that ocean valley, and its transverse branches, the Caribbean Sea and the Gulf of Mexico. The first cruise of the "Fanny," the schooner despatched on this service of making these explorations, cleared up all doubts as to the non-existence of certain fancied rocks and shoals which had been long enough bugbears to navigators. The following is the list of rocks found to be purely imaginary during the cruise.

	Latitude North.	Longitude West.
Ashton Rock	33° 50′	71° 40′
False Bermudas	32 30	58 40
Nye's Rock	31 15	55 50
Van Keulen's Vigia	31 40	38 20
Joryna Rock	31 40	23 45
Steen Ground	32 30	21 15
Mary's Rock	19 45	20 45

Lieut. Berryman, in the United States brig "Dolphin," reports, in 1853, that nothing has been found at the places indicated:

	Latitude North.	Longitude West.
Eight Stones	34° 22′	16° 40′
Jean Hammond's Rock	36 56	19 50
Haugault's Rock	40 58	48 40
Daraile's Rock	40 52	54 42
Haugault's Breakers	41 7	49 23
35 Fathom Shoal	42 32	45 17
—— Rock	30 50	27 19

At some of these localities soundings were taken, with depths of from 2,200 to 4,600 fathoms. The greatest depth sounded in the Taney was in latitude 31° 59′ north, long. 58° 43′ west, on the 15th November, 1849, when 5,700 fathoms of wire were let out without reaching the bottom. The form of the deepest portion of the North Atlantic is that of a *y*, lying northwest and southeast the two divisions being in the former direction, and stretching from 20° to 40° north latitude, and from 40° to 60° west long. Just on the verge of one of the divisions of the *y*, the Bermudas rise from the sea, forming apparently a peak mostly submerged, of nearly six miles in height. The *y* form is preserved in the next higher shelf of the bottom, only the tail is prolonged, forming a long trough between the two continents of South America and Africa. Two lines of soundings have recently been run across the Atlantic by Lieut. Berryman, in the Dolphin; they confirm the supposition, that the depth of the North Atlantic is nowhere greater than 5,000 fathoms. No little practical difficulty is experienced in sounding these depths, and the best check, in fact it is indispensable, to observe the rate at which the wire or twine is delivered from the reel. Without this precaution, currents and counter-currents may operate on the line long after the plummet is on the bottom. The following is a series of deep sea soundings recently made from the brig Dolphin, Lieut. O. H. Berryman, and extracted from a letter of our author. It will be seen that it exhibits the profile of two lines carried across the North Atlantic.

DEPTHS OF THE OCEAN.

Date.	Lat. N. D. M. S.	Long. W. D. M. S.	Depth in Fathoms.	
Oct. 4, 1852	39 39 00	70 30 00	1,000	no bottom.
“ 7 “	41 12 00	62 38 00	2,200	bottom.
“ 9 “	41 40 00	59 23 00	2,600	“
“ 10 “	41 40 00	56 01 00	2,595	“
“ 11 “	40 36 00	54 18 30	3,450	“
“ 20 “	41 07 00	49 23 15	4,580	“
“ 24 “	43 40 00	42 55 00	2,700	“
“ 25 “	44 41 07	40 16 00	1,800	“
“ 26 “	33 08 00	16 10 00	2,950	no bottom.
Jan. 3, 1853	34 15 00	16 45 00	2,298	bottom.
“ 9 “	36 49 00	19 53 45	2,950	“
“ 9 “	36 59 00	19 58 00	2,500	“
“ 29 “	30 49 00	27 25 00	2,200	no bottom.
“ 30 “	30 45 00	27 31 00	2,480	bottom.
Feb. 3 “	27 05 00	28 20 26	1,700	“
“ 4 “	29 21 00	30 48 00	2,580	“
“ 5 “	31 17 00	33 08 00	2,400	“
“ 6 “	28 55 00	35 49 00	1,800	no bottom.
“ 8 “	29 13 30	41 20 50	2,270	bottom.
“ 9 “	31 16 00	43 28 00	2,089	“
“ 10 “	33 01 00	44 31 00	2,250	“
“ 11 “	32 29 00	47 02 00	1,950	no bottom.
“ 12 “	32 55 00	47 58 00	6,600	doubtful.
“ 13 “	33 03 00	48 36 00	3,550	bottom,
“ 15 “	32 47 00	50 00 00	3,240	no bottom.
“ 20 “	28 59 00	57 51 00	1,380	bottom.
“ 22 “	28 20 00	59 44 00	2,900	doubtful.
“ 23 “	28 04 00	61 44 00	3,000	bottom.
“ 24 “	28 23 00	64 17 00	2,518	“
“ 25 “	27 42 36	66 11 15	1,000	no bottom.
“ 26 “	26 49 00	66 54 00	2,720	bottom.
“ 28 “	28 16 00	69 24 00	2,950	“

THE CHARTS.—A series of charts has been compiled from the observations made by the numerous intelligent navigators engaged in the scientific enterprise set on foot by Lieut. Maury. The pilot chart is derived from these results. The ocean is divided into square districts, of five degrees in length on each side. The winds for each month in each district are then collated, and it is hence easy, knowing the prevailing set of the winds for each month, to decide upon the probability of finding in each district a favorable wind. The problem then assimilates to that of the engineer who is called on to make detours to avoid mountain masses in fixing on the best line for a road on land.

The thermal charts are of no little scientific import, and from hem we learn the office of the ocean in ameliorating the climates of the earth.

The chart of the trade-winds embodies the results of the observations made on these winds. One remarkable discovery has been made, and it is that the southeast trade region is wider than that of the northeastern trade in both oceans. The average line of division is about 9° north of the equator.

OCEAN TELEGRAPH.—The soundings reported in the preceding table establishes, beyond doubt, the practicability of laying a submarine electric cable on the bottom of the ocean.—ED.

THE ELECTRIC TELEGRAPH.

SPEAK the word, and think the thought,
Quick 'tis as with lightning caught,
Over—under—lands or seas,
To the far Antipodes.

Now o'er cities throng'd with men,
Forest now or lonely glen ;
Now where busy Commerce broods,
Now in wildest solitudes ;
Now where Christian temples stand,
Now far in Pagan land !

Here again as soon as gone,
Making all the earth as one.
Boston speaks at twelve o'clock,
St. Louis reads ere noon the shock ;
Seems it not a feat sublime—
Intellect hath conquer'd Time !
Sing who will of Orphean lyre
Ours the wonder working wire !

Art. III.—SUBTERRANEAN TELEGRAPH,

AS COMPARED WITH WIRES IN THE AIR.

OWING to the difficulties experienced in working wires on poles, or in the air, on account of atmospheric electricity, the minds of many are, at present, fixed upon a thousand plans to remedy the evils, and among these diversified speculations is a subterranean telegraph. At present we are unwilling to say but little upon the subject, knowing serious objections to any and all modes proposed; and as to that, which is surrounded with the least evil, we are unable to determine, except upon questionable theories.

An English writer thus refers to the subject, although we believe there are some subterranean telegraphs in France.

"It may be said that much of the alleged damage likely to ensue from the action of natural currents of electricity passing through the atmosphere, would be obviated by the use of wires buried in the earth; but when it is found in the case of even a single line of telegraph in Prussia, that mo re than one hundred miles of wire which were buried in the earth—owing to their defective insulation, and the difficulty experienced, and the time occupied in detecting the exact position of those defects, and in remedying the defects when discovered—have been abandoned, and the wires suspended on posts in their stead, the employment of subterranean wires for the sake *merely* of lessening the effects of atmospheric electricity cannot be recommended.

"And again, when we call to mind the great additional expense that must be incurred at the first outset, and the great difficulty and expense that must be encountered afterwards in submerging *additional wires*, when the increasing wants of trade demand such additions, it would appear unwise, in the present unsatisfactory evidence on the subject, to pursue very extensively the plan of burying the wires in the earth, in preference to their suspension in the air, unless money were of little or no importance, and the best possible insulation was demanded, whatever might be the cost."

We may be too fastidious in our views as to the practicability of a subterranean telegraph; but until there is more evidence upon the subject, and the plan thoroughly tested, we cannot refrain from entertaining a doubt as to the general feasibility, unless at a very great expense, and even then its economy is very questionable in America.

Our lines are very lengthy, and extend over lowlands and uplands, mountains and valleys, plains and swamps, spreading over every species of formation common to the earth. Through many sections of America, the expense of a subterranean system would be very great, and in fact so large, that the prospective income of many, if not all the lines, would never be commensurate with the hopes and wants of investing capitalists.

Extend our commerce to the port of Singapore; laden our ships with the natural products of Borneo, Malacca, and other islands of the Eastern Archipelago; admit them free of duty; open for competition the manufacture of gutta percha insulation; and then, and not until then, need we contemplate the beauties of a Telegraph Line, freed from the annoying hindrances of atmospheric electricity, particularly in the South and West, where Autumn is frequent in the production of the most gorgeous aurora borealis.

T. P. S.

GALVANIZED IRON.

We have seen, within the last half century, the most surprising changes in the condition of human affairs, brought about by the scientific application of established principles to practical uses. Not but that noble buildings, and beautiful statuary, and magnificent bridges, remain as monuments of the past; but it was not for antiquity to invent steamboats, or railways, or the Napier press, or the magnetic telegraph, or to equal even in architecture some of the splendid edifices which mark the progress of our age.

Magnetism, supposed to have but one power, and that a directive one,—to have but one practical use, that by which the navigator steers his bark in safety,—is now applied in the reduction of ores, and in the lifting of weights, and the writing of words, and by its ready obedience to a newly-discovered law, becomes the trusty amanuensis of the telegraphic conductor.

Galvanism, allied to electricity and magnetism, having the characteristics of both, with effects dissimilar, has also given its aid, under the direction of science, and we have its singular cements flowing through the vats of the laboratory, to form new *metallic combinations*, and to give strength, *durability*, and beauty to fabrics of indispensable necessity. The galvanic battery arms iron not only with the powers of the magnet, but gives it *security from corrosion*, and thus we have rapidly coming into use, materials with which, but a short time ago, we were entirely unacquainted.

Art. IV.—THE AMERICAN TELEGRAPH CONFEDERATION,

ORGANIZED AT WASHINGTON, MARCH 5TH, 1853—TO ASSEMBLE ANNUALLY—COMPOSED, BY REPRESENTATION, FROM ALL LINES IN NORTH AMERICA USING THE MORSE AMERICAN ELECTRO-MAGNETIC TELEGRAPH.

THE origin of this Association was the publication of a call, signed by the Presidents and others of a large number of the Telegraph Lines in the United States, inviting every company using the Morse system, to send one or more representatives to a Convention, to assemble at Washington City, March 5th, 1853. The object of the Convention as thus promulgated, was to act on such matters as might be of interest to the lines in common, without regard to the special interest of any given line or connection.

The Convention assembled, and embraced a representation from lines, amounting in extent to at least three-fourths of the wires in America. Various proceedings took place, and among them the adoption of a resolution, presented by Mr. Alvord of Missouri, organizing a General Committee on Confederation, to act in the interim of the Convention, with general powers. That committee, at an early day, after the adjournment of the Convention, issued the annexed circular address, which we republish for more general reflection. It embraces some very important facts, worthy of the daily consideration of every telegrapher, which too, must sooner or later be an integral on the final adoption of a universality of business system. Finding the business proper for this committee to act upon,—as contemplated by the Convention, too great to receive the necessary attention, the editor of the Companion was selected to act as Secretary, and as soon as possible, resigned his offices in the West to assume the new duties at Washington City, under the official direction of the committee appointed by the Convention as aforesaid.

The circular address of the Secretary, following that of the committee, will evidently startle the minds of every telegraph management throughout the country, and at the same time infuse a cheerful spirit, and new hope for success, in the prospect of realizing the immense saving, so emphatically exhibited by that document. The facts therein promulgated are worthy of immediate attention. The plans proposed ought to be adopted without delay, that the benefits may the earlier be accomplished. [EDITOR.

ADDRESS

To the Presidents of the several Companies using Morse's American Electro-Magnetic Telegraph, in the United States, Mexico, and the British Colonies in North America.

GENTLEMEN: In obedience to the directions of the Telegraph Convention, recently held in the City of Washington, the undersigned have the honor to transmit a copy of the resolutions adopted by them, and ask the concurrence and future co-operation of your respective companies.

The members of the late Convention, as well as from their observation and experience abroad, as by an interchange of views among themselves, were deeply impressed with the necessity of some organization to preserve harmony, and produce uniformity in the mode of doing business by the many companies using Morse's Telegraph. Obviously, this can be attained only by laying aside, for the occasion, all animosities and jealousies, which may have grown out of competition, or the violation of exclusive privileges, real or supposed, and waiving for that purpose only, but without abandoning, all conflicting claims. Acting upon these principles, the recent Convention was distinguished by the harmony and good feeling which characterized its sittings, giving promise of good to be derived from the annual recurrence of such assemblages.

It is, perhaps, a public misfortune, that all the principal telegraph lines of the country are not subject to one control, governed by one set of rules, and presenting in all cases an undivided responsibility.

As such an arrangement is obviously impracticable, it becomes important to the companies, and to the public, to secure by other arrangements, as far as practicable, the advantages which would result from a controlling power. Many evils have already shown themselves as incident to the present system, among which are the following, viz:—

1. The adoption of different abbreviations and signals on different lines, rendering their language measurably unintelligible to each other. On some lines it has even been proposed to change the elements of which some of the letters of Morse's Alphabet are composed. It requires no argument to prove that the tendencies of these practices is to produce utter confusion in the business of telegraphing; and if allowed to proceed, those engaged in it will become as unintelligible to each other, as were the builders of Babel after the confusion of tongues. This mischief cannot be obviated otherwise than by a concert of ac-

tion among the companies, and the adoption of one general system, setting their faces against any alteration therein, unless it be by common consent. As a basis for all future action, we earnestly recommend the adoption of the seventh and eighth resolutions, herewith transmitted.

2. Perhaps the greatest evil existing under the present system, is the absence of due responsibility on account of messages sent over the lines of two or more companies, which are unreasonably delayed, or never delivered at all. We all know that perfect certainty of prompt delivery is not attainable in the present condition of the telegraph lines generally; but it is not difficult to adopt and enforce such regulations, as will greatly lessen the disappointment and irritation so prevalent among the customers of the telegraph, in consequence of the failure of their messages to reach their destination, or their inability to procure information as to what has become of them.

The idea so prevalent among operators, that it is an injury to their line to let connecting lines know when they are down, is fatally erroneous. They receive messages and retain them, awaiting the repair of their line; and when the station whence the message came inquires after them, too frequently no answer is returned. The customer becomes impatient and irritated, and demands the refunding of his money, which is refused; whereupon he curses the telegraph and ceases to use it. None of us, it is confidently believed, have duly appreciated the injury done to all the telegraph lines by such short-sighted policy.

All this can be readily obviated. Let each line, when down, promptly inform every connecting line of the fact. If there be any other line by which messages appropriately belonging to the line thus down, can be promptly sent, let them be silently received and so forwarded; if not, let the customer be frankly told that a connecting line over which his messages must pass is down, and that it is uncertain when his message will reach its destination. If thus informed, he chooses to leave his message, he cannot complain of fraud or imposition.

The undersigned are perfectly satisfied, that incomparably more harm arises from the omission to give information in such cases, than from the failures themselves; and that multitudes abandon the use of the telegraph not because their messages have been delayed or lost, but because they can obtain no satisfactory explanation of the cause.

Intimately connected with these practices is the subject of refunding. Customers are put to great inconvenience in obtaining evidence that their messages have been delayed, mutilated, or lost, when the telegraph ought to know all about it. That the station from which the message is sent, is not in possession of the facts when messages are delayed or lost, is the fault of other stations or connecting lines, in withholding information which ought to be given.

These evils the Convention hope to mitigate by the rules laid down in their second, third, fourth, and fifth resolutions, which are earnestly recommended to the adoption of your respective companies.

To give greater efficiency to the principles therein laid down, the committee recommend that the following explicit instructions be given to the chief operator at the terminal station of every line, viz.:—

1. That when any line ceases to operate in whole or in part, for the space of one hour during ordinary business hours, notice thereof shall be given to all connecting lines, specifying what part of the line, if any, is still in operation; and that when the line again commences to operate, notice thereof be also given immediately to all connecting lines.

2. That operators of connecting lines, receiving such notices, shall immediately send them along their respective lines.

3. That when from any cause a message from another line or station cannot be forwarded, or, if it has reached its destination, cannot be delivered the same day, notice thereof shall be given to the station whence it came.

A strict observance of these rules would remove many causes of irritation which now beset the telegraph business, and would obviate much trouble now experienced in the matter of refunding.

The second resolution purports to regulate the principles on which moneys refunded shall be charged upon the several companies concerned. In the discharge of the duties imposed on the committee by the fourteenth resolution, they recommend the following rules for giving effect to the second resolution, viz:—

1. Where refunding is required by reason of an error of the telegraph, the whole amount shall be chargeable to the company on whose line the error was committed.

2. Where refunding is required by reason of delay in the transmission of a message, the whole amount shall be chargeable to the company on whose line the delay occurred, unless said company shall show that it was occasioned by providential or uncontrollable circumstances, of which the connecting lines were duly informed.

3. Where refunding is required by reason of neglect to deliver a message when received, the whole amount shall be chargeable to the company at whose station the neglect occurred.

4. In all cases where refunding is required, the manager of the station where money was paid in the first instance shall be sole judge of the justice of the demand; and if any dispute

arises as to what line is chargeable with the amount refunded, or any part of it, the question shall be referred to the Presidents or Principal Managers of the lines concerned; and if they disagree, the subject shall be referred by them to the Corresponding Committee, whose decision shall be final. *Provided*, that when any line refuses or omits to give information as prescribed in the third and fourth resolutions, the whole sum refunded shall be charged to such line.

The other resolutions adopted by the Convention do not appear to need any explanation. That uniformity may at once be introduced and preserved, it is recommended that they be all adopted, though they may in some particulars be considered objectionable, and that any desirable modifications be reserved for the next annual Telegraph Convention.

The Committee trust that all Telegraph Companies in North America using Morse's system will cause themselves to be represented in the next Annual Convention, by delegates formally chosen and furnished with credentials, and that they be authorized to pledge the faith of their respective companies to carry into effect the resolves of the Convention, so far as they may relate to the mode of doing business, their intercourse and responsibilities among themselves. It is only by receiving the vote of the Convention as authoritative, that it can become permanently useful.

In conclusion, we beg that, as soon as practicable, you will submit the resolutions of the late Convention, together with the recommendations of this Address, to your Company or Board of Directors, and communicate the result of their action thereon to our Chairman, that we may notify each Company of their adoption or rejection by the rest.

B. B. FRENCH,
AMOS KENDALL,
J. D. CATON,
J. K. MOREHEAD,
WM. M. SWAIN.

CIRULAR ADDRESS

TO ALL ELECTRIC TELEGRAPH COMPANIES IN NORTH AMERICA.

At the late American Telegraph Convention, in Washington City, the following resolution, among many others, was adopted, viz.:

"That it shall be the duty of the Corresponding Committee to encourage the establishment, at some central point, of manufactories or depôts of all the necessary materials, such as acids, instruments, stationery used and consumed in the conduct and management of telegraph lines."

Not being able themselves to attend to the details necessary to the efficient execution of this and other resolutions adopted by the Convention, the Corresponding Committee, deeming this matter particularly of great importance, appointed the undersigned their Secretary, with the understanding that he was to attend to the details which the Convention had imposed upon them.

Thus authorized by the Committee, the undersigned has given special attention to the subject of the foregoing resolution, which he interprets as follows, viz.:

1st. The organization of a system, by which all the lines in the country can procure the materials needed in the successful management of the Telegraph, *unadulterated* with baser substances.

2d. That the articles purchased might be obtained at the lowest price possible, resulting from a general wholesale arrangement.

3d. That a general uniformity might result therefrom, dispelling the necessity for continual experiments, originating from a scarcity of material in any section of the country, whereby the management necessarily resorts to supposed equivalents.

Considering the objects of the resolution to be as just recited, the Secretary has proceeded to make complete arrangements for carrying the same into immediate operation. He has visited the various cities in the East, and procured the prices from many firms, offering to supply the lines throughout the country with the materials consumed. The prices submitted are greatly under the amounts now paid in all parts of the country, and the proposals accepted are at least twenty-five per cent. less than the lowest price paid by any line heretofore. The multiplication of commissions by the dealers greatly increased the cost of the article, and with a view to save that increase of expenditure, the Secretary has, in every instance, sought proposals from the manufacturers. The great saving will be readily seen by an examination of the figures presented hereinafter. Not only is the price reduced, but the pure article is obtained, unadulterated and free from mixture with inferior qualities.

It must be remembered, too, that the great saving accruing under this arrangement, as well as the perfection of the materials purchased, contemplates the concentration of purchase through the arrangement of the American Telegraph Confederation. Some of the companies will not realize much saving, because their consumption is small. Every line throughout the country greatly needs the economy proposed, though ever so little. The benefits will be mutually enjoyed; none are excluded. The arrangements contemplate, that ever company or every line throughout the United States, Canadas, Nova Scotia or Mexico, can partake in the advantages proposed. It is the interest of all to unite; the larger the purchase, the less will be the sum to be paid; thus all will partake alike in the economy. The invitation is to all, and the earlier commenced the better. Many lines have, very probably, a supply on hand sufficient for the season, but when new orders are given, it is hoped the proposals beneath submitted will be accepted. The prices embraced in the schedule may not be much less than now paid by some lines, but much less than paid by other lines; besides, a good article is procured for the same amount paid for an inferior. Some lines are paying three hundred per cent. more than proposed in the schedule, and the consumption very large; to these lines the saving will be extraordinary. An examination of the prices will prove to be one-fourth, in the aggregate, less than the lowest price paid by any line in America. This may seem to be a bold assertion, but nevertheless it is true. The prices paid by the various lines have been procured, and there can be no mistake as to the correctness of the statements submitted.

It is proper to add, here, that a moderate commission is added to the price specified in the schedule, to be appropriated by the General Committee to defray the expenses necessary in carrying out the directions of the Annual Conventions. If the revenue thus accruing exceed the necessities of the Committee, a reduction will of course be promptly made. The Committee, under the resolutions of the Convention, will manage or direct the course of procedure in all matters, and will not fail to do all that may be possible for the general prosperity. The companies can safely repose confidence in the arrangements presented, as there are those entrusted with the charge, who will realize the advantages of the economy as shareholders in the respective lines, and not otherwise. The Committee is elected annually, and the Convention can adopt such rules and regulations as to its powers as may be deemed requisite and necessary. The prosperity of the cause is the aim in view. That the subject may the better be understood, a short review of the cost now paid and as proposed will doubtless suffice.

NITRIC ACID.

This article is one of the most costly in telegraph consumption, and none more impure as in general use; it is one of the important elements connected with the enterprise, and should be carefully considered, that the very best quality may be obtained for the objects in view. There are but few gentlemen connected with telegraphing who are expert chemists, and in consequence of which, the most base and adulterated ingredients have been mixed with acids and used in batteries instead of the quality required in the generation of effective electrical action. In fact, the most injurious effects have resulted from the use of mixed acids. Nitric acid is often diluted with muriatic and sulphuric acids, or, as commercially known, oil of vitriol. These baser acids reduce the cost of nitric in proportion to the ratio of mixture, and its utility is reduced upon the same scale. Muriatic acid acts powerfully upon zinc and platinum. According to the best authorities, it is much employed for making many metallic solutions; and in combination with nitric acid, it forms the *aqua regia* of the alchemists, so called from its property of dissolving gold, &c.

The mixture of acids does not only impose upon the lines a higher price for an inferior quality, but it brings into use agents powerful in decomposing the metals, and consequently shortens their duration in usefulness. The chemical action of the battery is a hundred-fold greater than the electrical. It should only be commensurate therewith. Science has settled the fact, that muriatic acid is not an auxiliary in the Grove battery. No one seeks it, but it is often forced upon the lines without their knowledge of the fact. Relative to the mixture of sulphuric acid, or oil of vitriol, with nitric acid, it may be said that there is no harm done, or that the two acids are used in the Grove series. That is true, but look at the relative value. Sulphuric is worth only one-fourth the value of nitric. Why then pay the price of the former for the latter? If they have to be mixed, let it be done at the offices, and let each kind be purchased at its proper value.

During the investigation of the quality of acids, by the Secretary, gentlemen proposed to furnish acids at most any price. In the West and South, the scale of acid mostly usd was No. 44, and anything under that was deemed worthless. In the East nearly as erroneous ideas prevailed. In fact, there are as many views entertained as to the kind or quality of acids as there are persons in the management of telegraph lines.

In procuring bids to furnish the acids, under this arrangement, the question proposed was, "At what price will you furnish nitric acid 44° Baumee's Hydrometer?" A druggist responded, "Nine cents." The question was then asked, "Are you willing to submit that acid to an expert chemist for examination?" He answered, "No," but was willing to test it with the acid used by nearly all the telegraph lines in the country, and it should be equal in quality.

He said that the lines generally required an acid that would act readily on the zincs; and a mixture of muriatic acid was the best means of accommodating the managers, as they pronounced it the quality required. A mixture with sulphuric acid or oil of vitriol elevates the scale of specific gravity, and therefore its measurement need not be feared by the dealer. Such are the means resorted to, by commercial trade, to gratify the singular ideas advanced by communities not expert in the science of chemistry. At least three-fourths of the acids heretofore used in the United States by the telegraph lines, are adulterated at least ten per cent., and thus the injury may be estimated proportionate with the scale of base mixture.

Consultation with practical telegraphers, and calculations based upon reliable data, show the quantity of nitric acid used in America to be about 32 carboys of 120 lbs. per week. The prices paid range from 9 to 15 cts. per lb., the average being 12 cts. per lb. This would make an estimated annual cost for nitric acid $23,961 60. The Secretary can have the quality of acid used by the lines unadulterated for 8½ cts. per lb., which would amount to an annual outlay, based upon the quantity estimated above, of $15,972 80. This makes a saving of $6,988 80 per annum! The saving will greatly exceed this, because several hundred offices have been and are now paying as high as 30 cts. per lb. for an inferior article to that offered now for 8½ cts.

The carboys are to be well made, strong, and capable of standing the hardships of transportation. They will be marked, and known as telegraph acids. The world generally entertains a great fear of the combustion of *aqua fortis* in transportation, and shippers manifest great indifference as to forwarding it. The acid will be shipped under an independent name.

SULPHURIC ACID.

The telegraph lines do not use the proportionate quantity of sulphuric acid contemplated by science and the early projectors of telegraphing. The cause of this inequality is owing to mistaken views entertained, mostly by young gentlemen, who have not a thorough knowledge of the necessary ingredients in the proper composition of a battery. Many use nitric acid diluted with water, in which to immerse the zincs, rather than be troubled with pouring out acids from separate carboys. By this process an acid costing 8½ cts. is used instead of one costing 2 cts.; in this, economy will be promoted by its abolition, and the restoration of principles settled by science and practice for years. Some gentlemen do not use any acid diluted with water, and claim it as a grand discovery in economy. Experience has taught that in such cases, the battery has to be enlarged, and it is inactive for more than an hour after its construction. Time has to be allowed for the acid to ooze through the porous cups, and a chemical action on the zincs is produced. A battery thus constructed will always be black, and more or less covered with a thick coating of the oxide of zinc. Sulphuric acid cleanses the zincs, and an opportunity is given for an even and steady action of the nitric acid upon the metal.

Science has devised the construction of the Grove battery. Experience has demonstrated its correctness. There should be two liquids, and two metals—one liquid to be nitric acid, and the other dilute sulphuric acid; and the metals platinum and amalgamated zinc. The plates of platinum are immersed in the nitric acid, and the zinc in the dilute sulphuric acid.

Rain water is the best with which to dilute sulphuric acid.

The quantity of sulphuric acid that should be used in America, for batteries as estimated under the head of Nitric Acid, would be about 50,000 lbs. per annum, which, at 2 cts. per lb., would amount to $1,000; the equivalents now used costing from 4 cts. to 10 cts. per lb., amounting to at least $2,500 per annum. In this, the result of arrangements made by the Secretary, the lines will make a saving of at least $1,500.

ZINCS.

To relate the many tricks resorted to in the manufacture of telegraph zincs, would require many pages. The impositions exceed those related of acids. Thousands of zincs used by the telegraph lines are composed of zinc, lead, tin-solder, and even iron, and every kind of base alloy. The commercial rates of zinc at present, in New-York, are quoted at 7½ to 8 cts. per lb. On examination of the rates quoted in different cities, it cannot be bought for less. How, then, can lines purchase a pure article for a less sum, after the expenses of moulding? There is no possibility for such to be the case; if bought for less, it must be alloyed. It is true that zinc rates very high at present, and the price is expected to be less in a few months. A proposal has been presented and accepted to supply zinc cups, warranted free from alloy, at 8 cts. per lb. This very favorable offer contemplates, like all other proposals, the patronage of the entire enterprise.

A few estimates will show the necessity of care in the purchase of zinc.

The quantity in daily use is about 1,100. These zincs, moulded of proper weight, will last, on an average, about two months. The locals will wear out in less time. The main battery, if properly amalgamated, will serve longer. According to this basis of calculation, the quantity consumed per annum will be 6,600, which, at 8 cts. per lb., would amount to $1,320. The lines have been paying all prices, ranging as high as 15 cts. per lb. At this price, full 8,000 miles of lines are paying at this time, and purchasing with them at least 20 per cent. of alloy. Estimating the average price paid to be 12 cents. per lb., the cost, as per quantity consumed, would be for 16,500 lbs. = $1,980, or $660 nett gain. These items are less than the calculations of others who have been consulted upon the subject. They are fully sustained by the reports of the various companies. At the price proposed, a pure metal is obtained, having passed through the analytical examination of a competent chemist. There will be no compounding of base metals, causing a torpid battery, but the pure and unalloyed material will be procured. The great result will not only be in saving of original outlay, but in securing a battery promoting the ends in view.

QUICKSILVER.

When Mr. Sturgeon and Mr. Kemp discovered the application of mercury by rubbing it on the zincs, causing them to last much longer, and the flow of electricity during the action of the battery to be more constant and regular, the scientific world rejoiced in the prospect of economy. Unfortunately, this saving is totally disregarded by many offices. This is, doubtless, the result of indifference and want of proper energy. The great benefits resulting from the amalgamation of zincs, ought to stimulate every operator to give the batteries the greatest attention in its fulfilment. The cost of the quicksilver is greatly less than the waste of zinc and acids by its non-use. It equalizes the chemical and electrical actions. The two harmonize, and the result is most effective. There is as much fraud or imposition in the sale of quicksilver as there is connected with the other items heretofore mentioned, and the telegraph lines seem to suffer the most. That which has been used by many lines is alloyed with lead, tin-foil, &c. Lead is worth 5 cts. per lb., and its mixture with quicksilver will enable the vendor to sell the lead at the rate of $1 per lb., that being the average price paid throughout the country. Those who have any doubt as to the correctness of this statement, can easily test its truthfulness by immersing a thin piece of lead or tin-foil in some quicksilver, and in a few moments the lead or tin will be dissolved, and appear as legitimate mercury. The alloy can exceed twenty per cent. and pass as genuine with many purchasers. Our lines have been cheated out of thousands of dollars by the mixture of these baser metals with quicksilver. The price paid heretofore, has been from 75 cts. to $2 per lb., mostly exceeding $1 per lb. The quantity used in America per annum, including mercury connections, is about 3,000 lbs., which at $1 per lb., would be $3,000, and at 65 cts. $1,950, or a saving of $1,050.

It will be seen from these figures that there will not only be a great saving in procuring a pure article, but also in the cost of purchase.

POROUS CUPS.

This article can be supplied to the lines at 62 cts. per dozen, made from the best New-Jersey clay. This clay is considered the best for porous cups that has been discovered in America, and an inferior quality will not answer as well. The best is the cheapest in the end. An inferior article made from brick clay can be purchased at 50 cts. per dozen. No arrangement has been made for purchasing such an article, they being deemed injurious to the proper construction of a battery.

TUMBLERS.

Various are the kinds of tumblers in use. Some thick and some thin, some costing $1.65 and some $2.50 per dozen. Some are so thin that they can scarcely bear the weight of the zinc and acids. In cold weather they easily break, thus causing a great expense. Tumblers can be furnished the lines at $2,00 per dozen, made of the best glass, and sufficiently strong for substantial use, and economical management. An inferior quality can be purchased at $1,60. No arrangement has been made for purchasing an inferior quality. The tumblers, zincs, and porous cups are all made to suit as pairs, and the full force of the battery will be brought into action by such an arrangement. A large zinc in a small tumbler occasions the use of a small quantity of dilute sulphuric acid, and its renewal must be more frequent. These questions will be carefully considered.

PLATINUM.

A line once supplied with a good article of platina, will not be required to renew the supply. If alloyed with inferior metal, it will not endure the nitric acid. If rolled into thin slips, the breakage is very great. If long and thick, the wear will be longer. There are various views entertained as to the utility of the thin or thick strip. Orders will be complied with. If thin be desired, it should be stated. If not specified, the plates will be rolled to the most approved thickness.

The very best imported platinum can be procured at $8,00 per oz., in plates rolled the required thickness. A quality inferior can be obtained, but the best imported cannot be had for less.

MESSAGE HEADS.

This item of consumption is one of no ordinary consideration. The great quantity used necessarily occasions a large expenditure. The amount employed by the Morse lines of America exceed 10,000,000 per annum, of which New-York City uses about 1,000,000. These estimates may appear large, but they are much less than the calculations of several gentlemen engaged in the active duties of telegraphing. Message heads are purchased by offices, and sometimes by the officers of the companies.

The prices paid range from $1,67 per 1,000 to $5,00 per 1,000. Several million are bought at $4,50 per 1,000. Estimating the average cost to be $2,50 per 1,000, the annual cost will be $25,000.

This large outlay ought not to be made without reflection, and the opportunity is now presented for making a very great saving. The Secretary can supply message heads, printed on good paper, equal to that used by any line in America, at $1,20 per 1,000. If all the lines would use the same paper as the Magnetic Company, the message heads could be furnished at $1,10 per 1,000. The proposals are arranged to meet the diversified opinions of companies.

The reduction in the cost of message heads, from the prices named to $1,20 per 1,000, will occasion a gain to the enterprise of a startling amount. The price paid now as an average is $2,50 per 1,000 on 10,000,000=$25,000; the price proposed $1,20 per 1,000 for 10,000,000=$12,000. Nett gain $13,000!

ENVELOPES.

The quantity of envelopes used is not as great as that of message heads; the amount will be considered 6,000,000. Of this, there are about 4,000,000 white, and 2,000,000 buff. The cost of the white will average $2,50 per 1,000. The cost of the buff will average $1,70 per 1,000. The cost of buff has ranged from $1,37 to $2,50 per 1,000. These estimates are upon white embossed, and printed buff envelopes. The annual cost, at the above prices, would be for white embossed $10,000; for buff and printed, at $1,70 per 1,000, would be $3,400; making an aggregate of $13,400.

The Secretary is now prepared to furnish white envelopes embossed, equally as good as the best now used by any line in the United States, at $1,60 per 1,000, and the buff printed at $1,20 per 1,000. If the buff are embossed, the price will be $1,10 per 1,000. The aggregate estimate upon these prices will be for the white envelopes $6,400; for the buff envelopes $2,400; making a total of $8,800. Nett gain, $4,600.

The prices now proposed are greatly under former rates. The proposal contemplates the supply of all the lines, and hence the reduced rates.

CLOCKS.

Arrangements have been made for procuring a superior quality of clock, from one of the most extensive manufactories in Connecticut. The face is about 12 inches in diameter, gilt frame, having the time of the hour, minute, second, and day of the month, all represented on its face, and to run eight days. Made to run lying on the table, hanging on the wall, or in course of transportation. The manufacturer says, he "will warrant them to keep the time correct, as to *day of month*, *hour*, *minute*, and *second*, and that he will start them with genuine Connecticut time, and tumble them over railroads, wagons, steamboats, drays, and by hand, and land them in Halifax, or St. Louis, still running, with the correct dial time of New-England. He will mark the moment of shipment, and its time of delivery will indicate how long the clock has been wandering to its new home." The price is $10 each. The stamp *American Telegraph* will be on the face of each one, and all will be warranted.

PENCILS.

The prices paid for pencils have been from 50 cents to $1,00 per dozen, and often a very inferior quality purchased. The number used per year exceeds 50,000. Supposing the average cost to be 60 cents per dozen, the total will be $2,500. The Secretary can furnish the best pencil made at 22 cts. per dozen, for Nos. 1, 2, 3, and 4. At this price, the cost in the aggregate will be $916,66. Nett gain $1,583 34. The pencils are to be well made, capable of making the finest point, without waste. They will be manufactured in Germany.

PENS.

There are millions of pens bought by the various lines. No one consulted places the aggregate less than 4,000 gross. Price paid from 60 cts to $1,25 per gross, average about 90 cts., total $3,600. These pens can be purchased for the lines at 30 cts. per gross. For the same quality, form and stamp, manufactured by the same firm in Birmingham, England, I paid in Louisville, St. Louis, &c. $1,25 per gross. It will be seen that on this small item the nett gain will be large. Thus, cost at 30 cents= $1,200 00. Nett gain, $2,400. They will be stamped in England, *American Telegraph Pens.*

BLACK INK.

The lines use a very large quantity of black ink, being about 4,000 quart bottles per annum. The best quality is retailed in New-York at 75 cts. per bottle. In the West and South it is sold at $1,00 to $1,25. Put the average at 80 cts. and the total will be $3,200. The same ink thus sold, the Secretary will fnrnish at 28 cts. per quart bottle, well corked, sealed and labelled. At this price the total will be $1,120 00, making nett gain $2,080. The ink will be labelled *American Telegraph Ink.*

The Secretary is not prepared to submit estimates of the cost of the many other kinds of materials required by the lines, such as red ink, inkstands, files, screw-drivers, battery brushes, instrument oil, magnet springs, screw-nuts, register paper, foolscap and letter paper, copper wire, plyers, solder, soldering-lamps, registers, magnets, keys, catgut, circuit breakers, lightning-protectors, repeaters, circuit-shifters, message-files, paper clips, &c., &c., embracing every thing used in the management of the telegraph. The subject has been sufficiently investigated to warrant the assertion, that in the purchase of every article a saving can be realized.

REGISTERS AND MAGNETS.

Relative to registers, magnets, keys, and other parts of the machinery, there will be vast improvements submitted. Not by the introduction of fanciful ideas or the application of new principles, but by the proper construction of machines, calculated to make them last, and prove serviceable, totally disregarding all freaks of fancy in the peculiar scroll, harp, fiddle, or banjo construction of the instrument. There is no reason why a machine should not wear twenty years, as certainly as the varieties of machinery common in mechanics. The re-supplying of lines every few years is a heavy tax. To re-supply the offices of America with machines will cost at least $75,000. The breakage of an instrument has frequently occasioned more loss than the price of a dozen, and generally, this loss is occasioned by the application of fanciful ideas, without regard to utility. The enterprise throughout the country may depend upon this subject receiving from the Committee the most careful consideration.

AGGREGATE ANNUAL EXPENSE.

Having considered the cost of the various materials common in the telegraph service, the annexed summary is presented, as being worthy of the most candid reflection.

Materials.	Present Cost.	Proposed Cost.	Nett Gain.
Nitric Acid	23,961 60	16,972 80	6,988 80
Sulphuric Acid	2,500 00	1,000 00	1,500 00
Zincs	1,980 00	1,320 00	660 00
Quicksilver	3,000 00	1,950 00	1,050 00
Message Heads	25,000 00	12,000 00	13,000 00
Black Ink	3,200 00	1,120 00	2,080 00
Envelopes	13,400 00	8,800 00	4,600 00
Pens	3,600 00	1,200 00	2,400 00
Pencils	2,500 00	916 66	1,583 34
Totals	$79,141 60	$45,279 46	$33,862 14

Nett gain, $33,862,14!! What argument could be more commanding? Look at this immense saving, and then who can doubt the general utility of a concentration of the purchase by the lines? Not only is the gain in money as presented, but the pure and unadulterated material is procured, and more efficient service obtained. Some of these estimates will appear large, but they are based upon an average scale, procured from reports of various lines. The lowest estimates have been taken in all cases where there was a difference of opinion, and experience will, beyond all doubt, establish the fact that the table of costs is really below the true sums now paid.

In procuring the articles from the Secretary, there will be no nitric acid mixed with oil of vitriol to increase its scale of degrees, and at the same time rated as equal in value to the pure article. No sulphuric acid with false gauging, and mixed with exhausted acid. No zincs, alloyed with lead, tin-solder, and iron. No quicksilver alloyed with 20 per cent. of lead, tin, or other base metals, destroying its usefulness and durability. No porous cups made of brick-dirt or clay, of density preventing a flow of nitric. No tumblers, almost as thin as wafers, causing breakage of 50 per cent. per annum. No platinum alloyed with metals of half value, thereby preventing durability. No message heads at enormous rates and waste of revenue. No envelopes at double prices for inferior quality, and of every species of paper. No pencils of inferior lead, causing a great waste in pointing.

Such are the views entertained by the Secretary, in the fulfilment of the important resolutions submitted to the American Telegraph Convention, as herein-before recited.

PRICES PROPOSED.

The following are the prices now proposed, and upon which the lines may depend in every particular, viz.:

Nitric Acid, per lb	8½cts.
Sulphuric Acid, "	2
Zincs, "	8
Quicksilver, "	65
Message Heads, per 1,000	$1 20
Envelopes, Embossed, per 1,000, White	1 60
" " " Straw colored, extra	1 60
" Printed " Buff	1 20
Pencils, per dozen	22
Tumblers "	2 00
Porous Cups "	62
Black Ink, quart bottles	28
Platinum, per oz.	8 00
Pens, per gross	30
Clocks, each	10 00

The straw-color envelope is a very superior article. The die will emboss that color of envelope better than the white. If generally adopted, the manufacturers contract to place watermarks in the paper, indicating it as the telegraph paper, and granting the lines its exclusive monopoly. The same idea will be proposed as to message-head paper.

CASH PRINCIPLES.

The Secretary has no power to contract debts without being individually responsible. The rates proposed are cash prices. No proposals were sought on the credit system, because no means could be devised to meet the case. The cash principle is the only plan to insure success.

The lines can estimate their supplies for the coming quarter, or year, and the whole shipped under one invoice. This will be a point in economy. The arrangements are such, that an order for all the materials, and for any quantity, and even for a million of message heads, can be placed in transportation within twenty-four hours after the time of its reception by the Secretary.

All orders must be addressed to the Secretary, at *Washington City*, and any requiring the action of the Committee thereon, will be promptly submitted.

That there may be increased confidence in the arrangements herein proposed, the Secretary will give such bonds as may be deemed necessary by the Committee.

The cost of the dies for embossing the envelopes will be $5 each. The cost of electrotypes to print the envelopes will be $1 to $2 each. The cost of electrotypes for printing message heads will be $1 to $2 each, and for duplicates 50 cents each. These expenses will be extra, and they will remain as the property of the Company.

Before closing, the Secretary would state that he is now wholly employed under the directions of the Committee, appointed by the late American Telegraph Convention, in carrying out the actions of that body. Their counsel will form his course of duty, and his energies will be untiring in the service of the enterprise. He feels too much interest in the general prosperity, to allow any part of his duty to remain unperformed. His determinations are, to render all service possible calculated to elevate the Telegraph, and the accomplishment of deeds tending to promote the general and universal weal.

Respectfully submitted.

TAL. P. SHAFFNER,

Secretary.

Editorial.

INTRODUCTORY.—The TELEGRAPH COMPANION, as now issued, is an improvement on the old series, or original issue. The quarto form was inconvenient.

The doctrines promulgated through this work will be relative to the Science and Art of Telegraphing. Many years' connection with the Morse American Electro-Magnetic Telegraph,—a participator in the struggles in its extension over thousands of miles of territory, even along the borders of, and before the doors of the red man's home, and an attentive student in the various legal investigations, in the courts of the country, have infused into our mind a firm conviction of its superiority and originality over all other Electric Telegraphs of the present age.

Our teachings will be, to sustain this conviction, being in accordance with the decrees of many of the most learned jurists of the land, and the sanction of the American people.

In promoting the ends in view, we do not desire to discuss them in a manner calculated to cast any disrespect upon other systems of Electric Telegraphs, but at the same time, a candid discussion of the merits and relative rights of the diversified systems must be expected. We speak thus frankly, that none may be deceived in the policy pursued.

The whole range of Telegraphing will be considered, embracing the manner of management, working and general policy, the construction and repair of lines, the various departments of operation, and qualities of materials consumed, and every thing requisite to elucidate the manual of Telegraphing.

We invite a fair consideration for the COMPANION, and a liberal encouragement. With these remarks, we submit the first number.

TAL. P. SHAFFNER.

TERMS AND TIME OF PUBLICATION.—The Companion will be published monthly, 48 pages in each number, octavo, making over 600 pages per annum. Terms—$2,00 per year, payable in advance.

The Companion, proper, will be wholly letter-press writings, and will embrace one number of the Compound Tariff Scale. The Tariff Scale will be a separate publication. The works will issue on the first of each month.

THE COMPOUND TARIFF SCALE will contain 32 octavo pages, and devoted entirely to Tariff affairs, being 30 pages of rule and figure work, and two pages of explanatory notes relative thereto.

Terms—$2,00 per year. It will be issued monthly, with all the corrections of Tariffs, and new offices established by the new lines built.

Companion and Tariff Scale.—The Companion will be sent to subscribers for $2,00 per year. The Tariff Scale will be forwarded at $2,00 per year. Both publications will be sent to one address for $3,00 per annum. We hope every Operator, and every Officer of the different Companies, will give us the necessary material aid in the publication of these important works. Merchants would find the Tariff a very useful book in the counting-room. Stockholders would find the Companion a useful book in obtaining a proper understanding of the art of telegraphing. We hope to have the co-operation of all in accomplishing the grand desideratum.

Our Publications again.—We desire it to be distinctly understood, that in the publication of these works we do not expect gain. They will cost more than the subscription. Already there has been expended nearly one thousand dollars, and the most unanimous subscription will not meet the outlay. We hope, however, the Companies will give all the aid possible. If the works pay expenses of printing, it is all we desire. Our labor and responsibility will be gratuitous in the premises.

Old Subscribers.—The subscribers to the Companion during the last year can have their choice in taking either of the works for the coming year at the same price. We will send to the Company subscribers the Tariff, knowing the object of their subscription to be for it. To the Operators we will send the Companion. If any change is desired, we will cheerfully comply.

Delay of Publication.—The delay has not been intentional, or for want of energy, but as a question of policy. The change of place of publication from Louisville to New-York, and the change of positions from the Presidency of the St. Louis and New-Orleans line, to the Secretaryship of the General Confederation, required a change in the order of things, to meet the necessities of the future. It is our purpose to publish the work, let the subscription be large or small.

The American Telegraph Confederation will hold the next annual meeting in Washington City, on the 6th day of March, 1854. A representation from every Morse line in the United States, Canadas, Mexico, Nova Scotia, or in other words, every line in North America, is expected to be represented there. We have already heard of the appointment of many delegates to attend that meeting, and we hope others will promptly act in the matter. Where Presidents or Superintendents have authority to represent their lines, it is hoped they will not fail to attend.

We would call attention to the official circulars in the present number, as involving important facts for the consideration of every Company.

Atmospheric Telegraph.—During our recent trip to Boston, we visited the rooms of the Atmospheric Dispatch Company, No. 24 Merchants' Exchange, State Street.

We had but little confidence in the practicability of the enterprise, prior to an examination of the machine and witnessing its operation. The tubes were made of lead, about two inches in diameter, and about twenty feet long. The feasibility of the invention for the uses designed was demonstrated by various experiments. Although the operation seemed to be perfect, yet we entertained doubts as to the ultimate success of a long line; but Mr. I. S. Richardson, the talented inventor, readily presented arguments, based upon fixed laws in philosophy, dispelling all fears. Important results will characterize this invention, though many difficulties will occur in its early progress. After fruition is attained, there will be hundreds claiming to be the original inventor. Like the history of Morse, men who were slumbering in ignorance for years later than his invention, have come forward and claimed to be *the* sole progenitor of the great art, conceived by Morse, and brought to perfection by the toil of years.

The Atmospheric Dispatch Company contemplate constructing a line from Boston to Worcester, as the first section of a line to New-York. The shares are $100 each, payable in calls of ten per cent., commencing on the 1st of February, 1854. Total capital stock, $500,000. The tube to be two feet in diameter, for conveying letters and packages to and from the said cities and intermediate places, allowing fifteen minutes to each transit.

Although we feel confident of successful results from the art invented, yet we cannot believe in the realization of all the hopes entertained by the worthy and ingenious inventor. If it accomplishes one-half, the triumph will be great. The achievement will rival in brilliancy the brightest star of this progressive age. It will be one of the most marvellous and resplendent gems that bedeck the illustrious escutcheon of American ingenuity.

TELEGRAPH MAGAZINE.—It has been announced that the Companion, published heretofore at Louisville, was to be united with the Telegraph Magazine, published in New-York. Such was the design of the proprietors of the two publications, but circumstances have occurred rendering the union inexpedient.

A BABY BATTERY.—While on a visit to Boston, not long since, we called on Messrs. Palmer & Hall, Telegraph Instrument Manufacturers, and were shown a baby battery, composed of zinc and copper, and dilute sulphuric acid. The plates were one-eighth of an inch square, and as thin as a common wafer. The action of the battery was sufficient to work the largest Relay Magnet. It was a beautiful exhibition, and its minuteness gave it no ordinary degree of novelty.

ALARM TELEGRAPH.—Houses are now being built, in cities, with telegraphs connecting each window and door with the bed-chamber; so that in case of the entry of burglars at night, an alarm-bell is sounded, waking up the residents, and advising a sudden retreat of the nocturnal invader. This is an important improvement, worthy of general use.

A NEW BATTERY.—We had the pleasure of examining a new galvanic battery, invented by Mr. Moses G. Farmer, Superintendent of the Electric Telegraph of the Boston Fire Department. Gallon Jars, large porous cups, and amalgamated zinc are used, differently constructed from Grove battery. The mode of application secures a constant battery for some thirty days without renewal. We hope to have a detailed account of the invention of Mr. Farmer, and if it proves more economical, and attains an electric current equal to the Grove battery, it will deserve the immediate consideration of the various Telegraph Companies.

Balize Telegraph Line.—This line extends from Algiers, opposite New-Orleans, to the Balize, at the mouth of the Mississippi river. It is owned by the Union Tow-Boat Company, and is well managed. The length is 120 miles. To commerce it proves to be of infinite value.

The Telegraphs in Canada.—In no section of America are there more lines in progress of construction than in the Canadas. We hear of some three thousand miles now being built. These lines will greatly aid the general system, and advance the prosperity of existing lines. As soon as we can collect proper material, we will give more definite news as to their extent.

Atlantic and Ohio Telegraph Line.—This Company has two wires from Philadelphia, through Harrisburg and other towns, to Pittsburg. A leased wire from the Magnetic Telegraph Company between Philadelphia to New-York, is worked by this Company as a more direct connection with the latter city. Mr. David Brooks has lately been elected Superintendent of the lines of this Company. Mr. Brooks is a gentleman well qualified for the station, and a thorough telegrapher. He is familiar with all the various departments, and his acts are characterized with excellent judgment. He labours for success by an economical and judicious management, laying aside all freaks of fancy, and adopting the useful. We most certainly wish him success, and that the prosperity of the line may be triumphant.

The Magnetic Telegraph Company.—This is the oldest Electro-Magnetic Telegraph Company in the world. It extends from Washington, through Baltimore and Philadelphia, to New-York. It has seven wires. The management of this line is somewhat peculiar, but well suited to its necessities. In a future number, a detailed account of the system will be given, believing that other lines can be benefited by the adoption of equivalent plans of operation. Wm. M. Swain, Esq., is the indefatigable and talented President.

Boston and Portland Line.—For many years the line between these two cities has been owned and managed by the Hon. F. O. J. Smith. Recently he sold the entire line, 120 miles, to the Maine Telegraph Company, which gives it a continuous wire from Boston to Calais, Me. The steamers' news is now sent direct from Halifax to Boston. We ardently hope that this line will realize a handsome revenue; but we cannot comprehend the necessity of connecting with an adversary in Boston. Morse lines ought to connect with each other. The policy adopted by Mr. Smith, a few years ago, refusing business from illegitimate lines, was universally condemned. We can see but little difference in the policy now adopted by Mr. Eddy, the Superintendent, in his separation from the Morse lines in Boston and connecting with the House line. The largest patronage received from other lines is from the Morse Companies. The return business is sent back, by Mr. Eddy, through a different line, and one too, limited in extent, connecting but few towns in the United States. The consummation of prosperity is only attained by an unbroken connection.

NEW MAGNETIC BATTERY.—A short time since we visited Providence, R. I., to witness the operation of a new battery in course of construction, designed to propel boats, or used as a motive power in mechanics generally, and to be applied to Telegraph lines. Mr. Calvin Carpenter, the inventor, has displayed a great deal of zeal and genius in the construction of the work. A patent has recently been granted him for the invention. We saw various experiments performed, and they were really wonderful. A small wire was placed in the circuit and instantly burnt into pieces. The power was great, and the current of electricity seemed to be even, and attaining what some gentlemen style quantity and intensity as verified by the diversified tests. The large battery, Mr. Carpenter estimates, is equal in strength of 100,000 pounds. In a future number we will give a minute description of the machine. To Mr. F. O. Gilbert, Manager of the Telegraph Office, and to Gov. Jackson, we are indebted for much information derived while at Providence.

IRON WIRE.—In the construction of Telegraph lines, a good quality of iron wire is more important than any other portion of material used. For the same reason that required the copper wire to be taken down from the early lines, demand the use of the very best iron wire that can be procured. We have seen all qualities used. Some worthless, and some very superior. Messrs. Dewey & Co., at Wheeling, Va., have probably manufactured the best wire employed for Telegraph lines west of the mountains. The wire was made from the Missouri Iron Mountain ore, which is doubtless superior to any other iron of America. We think so, because the wire manufactured from that ore has proved the most substantial.

Recently we were shown some specimens of wire from the extensive manufactory of Mr. Henry S. Washburn, at Worcester, Mass. It excelled all other wire that we have witnessed. The testings were startling and almost beyond belief. We have never seen wire of equal quality used by any line in America, though we understand that Messrs. Smith & Ward—who are very worthy and energetic gentlemen—have purchased a lot of the same wire for some new lines being constructed by them in Texas.

The question as to quality of wire will be presented to the General Committee, at Washington City, and we indulge the hope that some means will be adopted to aid Telegraph builders in procuring the very best wire in the construction or repairing of lines.

THE ST. LOUIS AND NEW-ORLEANS TELEGRAPH.—This line extends from St. Louis, Mo., to Nashville, Tenn., via Cairo, Ill., and Paducah, Ky. Length, about 400 miles. River crossings has greatly retarded the prosperity of this line. During the past summer, submarine cables have been laid across the various streams, and now the Company work successfully through cables across the Ohio, Mississippi, Tennessee and Merrimac rivers, making the most extensive submarine line in America. A reliable connection south of Nashville with New-Orleans, will enable the line to pay a handsome dividend at an early day. Col. Wm. Tanner is President.

NEW-ORLEANS AND OHIO TELEGRAPH.—The line of this Company extends from New-Orleans, via Vicksburg, Nashville, Louisville, Maysville, Cincinnati, Wheeling, to Pittsburg, connecting with the lines running to New-York, giving a direct intercourse thereto from New-Orleans. This Company has two wires from Louisville to New-Orleans, which makes not less than two wires from Boston to New-Orleans. The revenue of this Company is nearly $200,000 per annum, and is rapidly increasing. Col. Wm. Tanner is President. While the Company has the services of one in whom confidence can be so implicitly placed, as can be with Col. Tanner, there need be no fears of the property of the Company being wasted away, by wild and extravagant schemes, such as has marked the career of some other lines in America.

RAIL-ROAD TELEGRAPHS.—Since it has been established, that Telegraph lines greatly benefits the Rail-road routes by economy in running, and safety of lives, nearly all of the leading roads in the country are securing lines along their routes, and appropriating liberal sums for their use. The day is not far distant, when every Rail-road throughout the land will be compelled to adopt the use of the Telegraph in the running of their trains. We will discuss this question in future.

PITTSBURGH, CINCINNATI AND LOUISVILLE LINE.—The Company extends from Pittsburgh via Cincinnati to Louisville. Two wires the entire distance. This line is one of the best in the United States, having business connections with several long ranges. Mr. Jackson Duncan is Superintendent, and is actively engaged in the management of the line. Mr. Duncan is a practical man, well qualified for the office, and ere many months the Company will realize the advantage of having a Superintendent, who studies the economy as well as theory of operation. The man that can go out on the line, and partake with the men in the hardships of repairs, like Mr. Duncan, Mr. Brooks, Mr. Woods, and a host of others like them, are the men for Superintendents.

TELEGRAPH INCIDENT.—Early in November last, the wire of the Montreal Telegraph Line, near Northfield, Vt., was by some means caught by the locomotive of a train of cars, on the Vermont Central Rail-road, and stripped from the poles for a distance of fifteen miles. This demonstrates two facts: 1st, that the wire was good, and 2d, that the poles were totally worthless.

Boston Telegraph Offices.—The lines running into Boston have, nearly all, offices of their own, which necessarily occasions great inconvenience, and increased expense.

The Boston and New-York line has an office in building 76 State-street, up stairs. Bain line to Portland, in same office.

The Northern line to Montreal is in same building, first floor in rear.

The Vermont and Boston line has an office in same building, up stairs.

The Maine Telegraph line has an office on first floor, Traveller Building, 31 State-street.

Marine Telegraph line is in the Merchants' Exchange Reading Room.

The Boston, Lowell, Troy, House line, is in 77 State-street.

The New-York and Boston, House line, is in Traveller Building, 31 State-street.

The offices are very accessible; but the people must be well informed in telegraphing to know what route to patronize.

New-York and Boston Line.—This Company is styled "The New-England Union Telegraph Company." It has five wires, with many lateral branches. The wires embrace all of the Morse and Bain lines. The latter system has been totally abolished, and the Morse machines substituted.

This is one of the most important lines in the United States, connecting two of the largest cities in the Union. Unfortunately it has been allowed to go to wreck, and nearly the whole requires rebuilding. The insulation is mixed. Every kind, and nearly the very worst ever devised, is in use. It is astonishing to see such a state of affairs on an important line like this. It has not worked successfully for some time past, and never will until thoroughly repaired. Mr. Charles F. Wood, late of the Magnetic Office, in New-York, has been elected Superintendent. He has been for some time engaged in repairing. Mr. Wood is a finished telegrapher. He knows his duty, and he is nobly performing it. His perseverance is equal to the necessities of the task, and his fine judgment brought to use in the execution of his office, will produce results, crowning his efforts with the most cheering and triumphant success.

Wade Telegraph Lines.—These lines are those built and managed by J. H. Wade, Esq., of Ohio. One embraces the Cincinnati, Columbus, and Cleveland line; another, the Cincinnati and St. Louis line, and in addition, several branch lines and Rail-road routes. Mr. Wade is building an extensive range of lines along the Rail-roads in Ohio and Indiana. If there is a telegraph man in the United States deserving of credit for energy and good management, it is Mr. Wade. He has conducted his lines upon a liberal, yet economical scale. He does not falter in expending a dollar where ten-fold will result therefrom. Some managers of lines hold on to the dollar, and allow the line to go to wreck; others, again, spend every dollar for fancy and extravagant show. Not so with Mr. Wade. He is a saving man, energetic and just, possessing abilities equal to his position. Success has crowned his efforts, and his career as a telegrapher has been marked as conservative, and equal in skill to that of any other gentleman engaged in the enterprise.

New-York, Washington, and New-Orleans Line.—This Company is one of the pioneer lines in the United States. It was built by Mr. John J. Haley. The line extends from Washington City, via Richmond, Va., Raleigh, N. C., Columbia, S. C., Macon, Ga., Mobile, Al., to New-Orleans. A leased wire, belonging to the Magnetic Telegraph Company, connecting the line of the Company at Washington, direct with Philadelphia and New-York, is also under the management of that line. The office in New-York greatly increases the revenue of the line. Its income is very large. S. Mowrey, Jr., is President, and although new in the business, we have unlimited confidence in his superior judgment in the management of the line. It is one of the longest in the United States, and the difficulties of working are many. The most patient and energetic man will have times of sorrow; but we think Mr. Mowrey will never allow *fail* to enter his mind. He meets a liberal and hearty encouragement from the many gentlemen employed on the line, and his success may be considered as beyond doubt.

Texas Telegraph Line.—While Texas existed as a Republic, Prof. Morse presented his Patented Telegraph to the nation as a token of respect and esteem. He receives no consideration for lines constructed in the State of Texas.

We understand that Messrs. Smith and Ward are pushing forward the construction of many miles of lines in Texas. They have had to contend with many difficulties, but we are rejoiced to hear of their success. Their perseverance entitles them to great praise, and liberal realization of material relief.

Western Telegraph Line.—This line extends from Baltimore, via Frederick, Harper's Ferry, and Cumberland, to Wheeling, with a branch from Brownsville to Pittsburgh. It is about 360 miles long. The Company, last summer, made a contract to run a wire along the Baltimore and Ohio Rail-road. The line will be completed on or before January, 1854. This Company is paying a dividend, and the prospects for the future are very encouraging. Geo. R. Dodge, Esq., is President.

Bain Line from Lowell to Gardner.—A line of telegraph has been erected from Lowell to Gardner, Mass., via Fitchburg, on which the Bain system was designed to be worked. The revenue not being sufficient to sustain it, the property has been sold, and operations suspended. Some of the wire has been taken down. Small routes, or lines, having many offices, can only succeed with the use of the Morse system. Transferring work from one office to another, at will, is one of the principal elements of success.

Indiana and Illinois Line.—This range of lines is very extensive, running from Cincinnati to Dayton, Indianapolis, Terre Haute, Detroit, Chicago

&c., being in length over 700 miles. During the past year, it was leased for a term of years, to Mr. Ezra Cornell, who is one of the oldest telegraphers in America. He was on the first line built, and his experience and ingenuity enables him to surmount many difficulties that ordinary men would fail in their efforts to overcome. Mr. C., like many of the old telegraphers, has braved the storms and tempests, and we do hope the remainder of his career in the telegraph will be as brilliant and cheering as his pathway in the past has been rugged and gloomy.

YELLOW FEVER IN THE SOUTH.—This fatal disease has, during the past summer, swept over the Southern country with disastrous results. Towns and cities suffered sadly. In the midst of the epidemic, the telegraph lines were not excepted; many of the operators were the victims of the fever. Mr. B. P. Crane, Mr. Achilles Herbert, and others of the National lines in New-Orleans, fortunately recovered. Not so blessed were H. F. Watkins, chief operator at New-Orleans, W. H. Grogan, and T. S. Titcomb, formerly of the same office, and also W. Clayton, chief operator of the Mobile office, of the Washington line. They were victims of the fell destroyer. They were faithful and efficient officers. We record their early departure from among us, with pensive feelings, that useful men like those should be so early "borne from whence no traveller returns."

MAYSVILLE SUBMARINE CABLE.—We regret to learn that the electric cable, constructed for the Maysville, Ky., crossing, proved worthless, after applying the greatest energy to secure success. Cause of failure was over-heating the gutta percha, destroying its insulation, and thereby connecting the electric wires. Cables constructed on the same principle can be made effective by proper care and the use of suitable machinery. The reels were too small, and the twist proved fatal.

NEW-YORK, ALBANY AND BUFFALO LINE.—We are rejoiced to hear of the prospects of this line. The Company has several wires on their main line, and also a number of branch lines as feeders. Mr. F. H. Palmer, of New-York, is the Superintendent of the line from New-York to Utica, and Mr. O. E. Wood, Superintendent from Utica to Buffalo. These gentlemen are practical managers, and well versed in the art of telegraphing. If the line cannot succeed under the management of such gentlemen, there can be but little hope in the future. They are actively engaged in making repairs, and, ere long, the line to Buffalo from New-York can be relied upon as one of the most efficient and reliable in the United States. Mr. John Butterfield, of Utica, is President.

NEWFOUNDLAND TELEGRAPH LINE.—We understand that this Company has suspended further work in the construction of the submarine line to Cape Race, from Halifax, until spring. They are confident of success. The steamers to run in connection with this line, between Galway and America, are in course of construction. Unparallelled speed is expected in the running of these steamers.

House Lines.—The line of this system running from New-York to Washington, is doing a very fine business. Mr. Henry J. Rogers is the Superintendent. He is one of the oldest telegraphers in the United States, having been associated with Prof. Morse in the management of the first line in America, and is well versed in the science of electric telegraphs. Various improvements have been invented by him, and his diversified talents are equal to any emergency. We regretted that Mr. Rogers found it to be his interest to leave the "art that has worked so well" amid storm and tempest.

The line from New-York, via Albany, Buffalo, Cleveland and Cincinnati, to Louisville, is under the Superintendence of Mr. Anson Stager, of Buffalo. It is a long range of lines, and the difficulties of management must be very great. Fortunately, however, for the Company, Mr. Stager is well qualified for the position. He is a thorough telegrapher, understanding the working of lines as well as any other gentleman engaged in the business. His zeal and qualifications entitle him to richer rewards than are usually attained in the telegraph enterprise.

The business of the line from New-York to Louisville is very large and rapidly increasing.

Damage by Sleet.—The recent storms in the north greatly damaged the Telegraphs. The New-York, Albany and Buffalo suffered very much, but the line from Orwell, Vt., to White Hall, N. Y., and thence to Rutland, Vt., was totally destroyed. The wire was broken between nearly every pole. The damage was so great that fears are entertained that the repairs will not be completed before spring.

Telegraph Controversies.—We have received a communication, with a request for publication, from a friend, which reviews very critically the management of one of the lines in the United States. We would gladly publish it if we thought good would be the result. We desire to be cautious in meddling with the private affairs of Companies. We prefer to point out remedies for evils, without being too particular in noticing the localities of existing wrongs. Where an evil affects the general system of telegraphing, we will not fail to condemn, hoping to promote prosperity, and not foster contentions.

Correspondents.—We respectfully invite letters from telegraphers of all positions, relative to the mode of telegraphing, and all news pertaining to lines, and business thereon. Any question of the science is a matter of interest. Let every body write.

A Model Battery.—There is nothing about the telegraph business more essential in successful management, than care in the battery series. We always visit the batteries wherever an opportunity offers. Among those of the most beautiful and best arranged in the United States, is that in the New-York office of the New-England Union Company, under the management of Mr. Charles T. Smith. He has had as much experience in batteries as any other gentleman in the country, and he adheres to the settled doctrines of the Grove series. Experience of many years has demonstrated its superiority, and he delights in witnessing its perfection. It must afford the early projectors of electric telegraphs great pleasure, to find the old veterans in practical telegraphing, like Mr. Smith, dispel all the new doubtful schemes, and hold to that which has proved to be profitable and wholly successful for many years.

Cuba Telegraph Lines.—We see announced, through the press, the suspension of the further erection of the telegraph lines in Cuba, by the Government.

Western Telegraph.—The stockholders of the Texas and Red River Telegraph Company assembled at Shreveport, and organized by electing the following officers:

President—D. S. Welder. *Secretary*—J. G. Battle. *Directors*—B. P. Crane, D. F. Roysden, J. W. Morris, of Shreveport; L. R. Walmesly, T. H. Aives, of Natchitoches; H. Lynch, M. Ryan, T. C. H. Smith, of Alexandria.

The stock was very fully represented, and the best spirit prevailed. No doubt is entertained of the completion of the line at an early day. The yellow fever has greatly hindered the builders in its construction, but their energies are equal to the most extraordinary difficulties. The line is built by Messrs. Smith & Ward.

William Tanner, Esq.—We had hitherto neglected to mention the fact, that this gentleman, who has been so long and favorably known to the public as an editor and telegraph proprietor, has recently been elected President of the St. Louis and New-Orleans Telegraph Company, to fill the vacancy occasioned by the resignation of Tal. P. Shaffner, Esq., who goes to Washington City, as Secretary of the American Telegraph Confederation. Two better men for the posts they have been called to fill, could not be found; and we congratulate them both, upon their *upward tendency.*—*Pad. Penant.*

Submarine Telegraph Cables.—We shall, in future numbers of the Companion, discuss the various modes of crossing rivers. From sad experience we are convinced that masts are not the most reliable nor economical. The following notices, from the press, are a few pertaining to the electric cables submerged in the western waters. The newspapers throughout the country have favorably noticed these cables, and their superior excellence is evidenced from the tests applied. Though they pertain to our own work, yet we hope their republication will not be considered out of place, contemplating, as we do, to give the progressive movements in the entire telegraph enterprise, and the subject of submarine crossings is one of great importance to the prosperity of many lines. Since the construction of the cables, mentioned in the following notices, the same gentlemen have invented very great improvements thereon. Here are a few notices:

Submarine Telegraph at Paducah.—The great submarine Telegraph Cable, on the St. Louis and New-Orleans Telegraph Line, was laid across the Ohio river at this place, on Monday last, the 26th inst. We examined this strange piece of mechanism, a few days previous to the time it was deposited in its watery abode, and was not a little astonished at its wonderful strength.

The whole forms a cable of near two inches in diameter, and it is much the largest and most substantial cable of the sort *in the known world.*

We are told that the great cable across the channel from England to France, is inferior in size to this, and by no means as well insulated for electrical application; while, in point of strength, it will not compare at all with the one at this place.

This stupendous wire, which now conducts the lightning from shore to shore, beneath the bed of the majestic Ohio, is 4,200 feet in length, and the longest one to be found in the United States. It has been constructed by that amiable and accomplished gentleman, Tal. P. Shaffner, Esq., late President of the Company, and now Secretary of the American Telegraph Confederation, assisted by J. B. Sleeth, mechanical engineer. These gentlemen have made improvements in the construction of cables, both scientific and mechanical, which will entitle them to Letters Patent, and the country may well be proud of them, as men of skill and ability, in whatever they may undertake.

The wires on this line, we understand, have been exceedingly troublesome and expensive to the Company; upwards of $20,000 having been expended in unsuccessful efforts to cross the Ohio river in such a manner as to secure them against accident; but this great effort has accomplished the object, and there can be no future loss sustained, on account of breakage of masts, wires, &c.

We rejoice that the work has been successfully accomplished, and that it has proved fully equal to the most sanguine calculation our friend Shaffner had made of its utility. We had the pleasure of receiving the first dispatch which ever passed under the Ohio, on this mammoth cable, which run as follows:—

"Illinois Bottom, *July* 26, 1853.

"Col. Pike:—I send this through the great cable, successfully laid to-day.

"Shaffner."

Success to Shaffner! He may well be styled the "Lightning King," after this! May he live a thousand years, and succeed in everything which he undertakes, as he has in this instance! We regret to learn that he will soon go from amongst us, to engage in his new duties at Washington city; but even from that far distant point, we shall expect to hear from him occasionally through the medium of electricity, which seems to be his favorite element.

Submarine Telegraph Cable.—Tal. P. Shaffner, Esq., the former enterprising President of the St. Louis and New-Orleans Telegraph Company, arrived in our city on Tuesday last, and was engaged yesterday in laying the Submarine Telegraph Cable. It was put down about a half a mile above here, and was towed over to the other shore of the Mississippi by the steam ferry. Its length is about 3,710 feet.

From the size and great strength of the wire, we have no doubt it will withstand the swift current and snags of the old father of waters for a century to come. May unbounded success attend its projector.

There is another roll of this cable on our wharf, intended for the Merrimack river. We understand it will be laid in a few days.—*Cape Girardean Eagle.*

Shaffner's Lightning Ferry.—On Monday, the 26th July, Tal. P. Shaffner, Esq., whose pet is lightning, laid across the Ohio river, on the New-Orleans and St. Louis Line, about a mile below town, his great telegraph cable, the longest in America, and the largest in the world. This cable is 4¼ inches in circumference, fourteen hundred and forty yards long, and weighs eleven thousand pounds.

Last fall Mr. Shaffner constructed and laid across the Tennessee river, his first cable of this kind. During the winter and spring the freshets were greater than usual, and the great cable triumphantly resisted all forces coming in contact. The experiment confirmed the most sanguine hopes of the constructor, and Mr. Shaffner has commenced laying the cables at every crossing on the line. This line has more submarine telegraphing than any other line in the United States. Heretofore the companies have been much annoyed by the inefficacy of their submarine apparatus. Mr. Shaffner has been assisted in the construction of this cable by J. B. Sleeth, mechanical engineer.

The cable between England and France is inferior to this in strength and non-electric encasements.

We should not be surprised if Col. Shaffner will, before long, mount his pet and pass over to Europe, to offer his improvements to the trans-Atlantics. His energetic efforts and improvements in rendering subservient to man the fierce element, merits not only the admiration of the world, but a most fruitful reward.—*Paducah Journal.*

These are a few of the hundreds of notices of the cables crossing the Ohio, Mississippi, Merrimack, and Tennessee rivers. They have proved their efficiency. The torrents of the mighty floods roll over their powerful forms, and never in a single instance have they failed to perform their functions. We have received many letters from telegraphers, asking information upon submarine cables, and it will afford us great pleasure to give any aid in our power, tending to advance the enterprise. For near five years, amid storms, tempests, ice, and floods, we tried to conquer these mighty rivers. We feel proud in being able to enjoy the conquest.

COMPLIMENTARY.—We feel very much gratified in finding the following flattering good feeling entertained towards us, from the gentlemen connected with the St. Louis and New-Orleans Telegraph Line; some of whom have been associated with us for several years past. May richer blessings crown their efforts than was ever realized by them in times gone by. Their kind co-operation in the management of one of the most difficult lines in the country, will ever be cherished by us with the warmest affection. By request we insert the correspondence:—

MERITED CONFIDENCE.—The numerous friends of Tal. P. Shaffner, Esq., the great telegraph man of the West, will read the following complimentary correspondence with pleasure:—*Paducah Journal.*

LOUISVILLE, KY., *August 1st*, 1853.

On leaving the St. Louis and New-Orleans Telegraph Company, I cannot refrain from expressing to you, and the other gentlemanly officers of the line, my profound thanks for your liberal encouragement and energetic co-operation for, and in behalf of the line.

There is no telegraph company in the United States that can boast of a more true and faithful corps of officers than this, and I cannot refrain from expressing to you in this voluntary manner my sincere acknowledgments.

Your zeal, capacity, and moral worth, I trust will always be respected as pre-eminent, and equal to the full requirements of your station, and deserving of the same confidence you have so nobly won by your services for this company.

In resigning the Presidency of your company, I give place to one who is worthy of your confidence and esteem. Many years intimate association with Col. Tanner, my successor, has established in me an abiding assurance of his ability and integrity to serve the interest of the line with the utmost fidelity.

I leave you, gentlemen, to assume new duties in the East, called by the wishes of those deeply interested in the enterprise, though much I regret to part with you, so early after the triumphant re-election as your sole manager, by the late meeting of the stockholders.

In the hour of prosperity or adversity, weal or woe, the recollection of our past association in the fulfilment of our official relations, will be pleasant and felicitous.

With sentiments of high esteem for each, and all of you,

I respectfully bid you adieu,

TAL. P. SHAFFNER,

Late President of the St. Louis and New-Orleans Telegraph Co.

August 15*th*, 1853.

TAL. P. SHAFFNER, ESQ. :—Dear Sir :—We have each of us, at our respective stations, received your complimentary letter, announcing your withdrawal from the Presidency of this Company. We thank you kindly for the expression of confidence and regard for us, individually and collectively, as the corps of managers and operators on said line, and we assure you that those feelings of confidence and regard are fully reciprocated by us. Since our connection with this line, over which you have exercised a vigilant supervision, and exerted a most creditable enterprise, our intercourse with you has been one of uninterrupted pleasure. That we regret to part with you, it is unnecessary to add; but in our separation we beg you to rest assured that you have with you our warmest friendship and highest regard, and we shall ever cherish for you a most timely esteem. And with our best wishes for your future prosperity, good health and happiness, we are

Yours, most respectfully,

C. CARVILLE, GEO. D. SHELDON, *Nashville, Tenn.*
J. L. THOMAS, *Clarksville, Tenn.*
J. H. M'KENZIE, *Hopkinsville, Ky.*
E. J. MARSHALL, *Eddyville, Ky.*
SAM. B. HITT, *Smithland, Ky.*
H. B. MARSH, G. S. PIDGEON, J. B. SLEETH, *Paducah, Ky.*
W. H. BOLLARD, *Caledonia, Ill.*
M. B. HARRELL, HENRY CANDEE, *Cairo, Ill.*
HOMER PARR, *Cape Girardeau, Mo.*
JOHN M. WEBB, *Ste. Genevieve, Mo.*
F. M. COLBURN, T. E. SWEETS, *St. Louis, Mo.*

HON. AMOS KENDALL.—THE ARBITRATION.—It is known to the public, that recently an arbitration, on telegraph affairs, took place in the city of

Philadelphia. The case was one of difference between the Washington and New-Orleans Telegraph Company and the Morse Patentees, including their energetic agent, Hon. Amos Kendall. With a view of finally settling disputed points in a business affair, as to respective rights, the questions in dispute were amicably referred to three disinterested gentlemen, and their award to be final in the premises. These gentlemen were distinguished lawyers from New-York, Philadelphia and Charleston. The news reporter of Philadelphia was indiscreet enough to promulgate a slanderous news item for the press, charging Mr. Kendall with fraud, &c. The recollection of the base slander must mantle the news-reporter with shame and mortification. How a man can bring himself so low as to wantonly assail another in this wholesale manner, totally reckless of truth, is a question not easily solved. He stands behind a curtain, and is presumed to be just in his message to the world, never permitting a false statement to issue from his position. The flag entrusted to his charge, he trailed in the dust in heralding forth a fabricated statement, relative to this transaction.

With a view to place the matter before the country in its proper garb, we addressed a letter to Mr. Kendall, requesting information upon the subject. His letter nobly unfolds the bright page of truth. Here is the answer, viz.:

WASHINGTON, *Nov. 10th*, 1853.

TAL. P. SHAFFNER, ESQ.:—Dear Sir:—At your request, I proceed to state the practical results of the arbitration, lately held in Philadelphia, in which the Washington and New-Orleans Telegraph Company, Prof. Morse, the Messrs. Vails and myself were parties.

It was an amicable proceeding, in which the Company claimed that we had no right to a certain amount of stock acquired through the construction of the line, and we claimed a right to additional stock, in consequence of the putting up of a second wire on a portion of the line, which the Company denied.

Before the arbitrators entered upon the case, I called their attention to a telegraphic message in the New-York Herald, which appears to have been sent all over the Union, charging me, by name, with fraud in these matters.

The following is an extract from the award, viz.:

"*It being the opinion of the Referees, that* THERE HAS BEEN NO ACTUAL "FRAUD, and that the circumstances of the transaction are not such as to "induce the charging of these expenses on the parties in any other manner, "or to any greater extent, than they will bear them in common with all the "Stockholders of the Company."

The author of the libellous message thus finds his malice defeated by his own act, inducing an express acquittal of his charge.

Of the questions submitted, the Arbitrators decided the first in favor of the Company, and the second against them. By the first branch of the decision, Messrs. Morse, Vails, and myself are required to refund $20,000 in stock, and $2,200 in dividends; in all, ... $22,200 00

The second branch of the decision will give us additional stock, amounting to about 39,861 12

Balance in our favor, ... $17,661 12

The result in detail is as follows, viz.:

	To refund.	To receive.	Gain.
Prof. Morse,	$9,250 00	$16,608 80	$7,358 80
A. Vail,	1,387 50	2,491 32	1,103 82
G. Vail,	1 387 50	2,491 32	1,103 82
A. Kendall,	10,175 00	18,269 68	8,094 68
	$22,220 00	$39,861 12	$17,661 12

These results will, doubtless, be somewhat varied in the final settlement; but it is quite as likely that the amount accruing to us will be increased, as that it will be diminished.

I had proposed, for the sake of peace, to give up all claim to stock on the second wire, and all additional wires; but my proposition was not acceptable. If the malicious men who got up the difficulty are satisfied with the result, I assure them that I am.

There was the less reason for charging me with fraud in this matter, inasmuch as my accusers knew I was not the author of the arrangement of which they complained; but I look upon it as a compliment, that I was singled out as the object of attack. When a rogue is called a rogue, it creates no sensation; but when an honest man is charged with default, whether rightfully or wrongfully, all hell yells with delight.

With great respect,

Your obedient servant,

AMOS KENDALL.

ATLANTIC OCEAN TELEGRAPH.—We desire to say much upon this subject, but have not room in the present number. We publish an article on the Ocean-Sounding, as preparatory to a discussion of the question in future, There are several efforts being made for the construction of an electric telegraph cable across the ocean. We believe it can be done. There can be no doubt about it. This boldness we expect to be ridiculed. So were the founders of the telegraph. To our astonishment we find the editor of the *Telegraph Review*, Mr. Reid, indulging in a sneer at the enterprise. This was unexpected, although his good will towards us, has been, for a long time, deemed exceedingly questionable. We seek no controversy, nor will we permit ourselves to be drawn into one. We notice the article in the *Review*, because it is evidently intended to hinder the accomplishment of an enterprise, that is destined, ere the revolution of many years, to astound the world by its most triumphant success. Here is the article, viz:

"We now learn, that Mr. Shaffner is in concert with a former employee of an English Submarine Company, in endeavoring to form a Company to put a cable across the Atlantic. This will be a difficult work. Telegraph enterprise in this country has not been made so uniformly remunerative to stockholders, as to induce a connection with a colossal enterprise like this. The single fact of the immense weight of the cable, is enough to terrify an ordinary mind from contemplating it. The cable at Paducah weighs, at the average, of three tons per mile. The shortest stretch across the Atlantic is one thousand five hundred miles. Think of a coil, within the ribs of a vessel, weighing forty-five hundred tons! But great men are born for great necessities."

We understand this article to give the following reasons why a submarine line from America to Europe is impracticable, viz.:

1st. That it will be a difficult work.

2d. That telegraph stock in America has not proved very profitable, and that capitalists will be deterred from investing in a gigantic enterprise like this.

3d. The weight of the cable will be at least forty-five hundred tons.

4th. That no vessel is of sufficient tonnage to carry such a monster cable.

Relative to the first objection, we admit that the proper construction of an electric cable across the Atlantic Ocean will be difficult in the extreme. The crossing of the flooding waters of the inland has been difficult for years past. The same energy that has stretched a web of wire over forty thousand miles in the Western hemisphere, overland, and through its mighty streams, can master the difficulties in crossing the ocean. Tides may ebb and flow—the billows may surge with mighty power—the icebergs may tower their white mantled form, high in the skies, and sink deep in the briny sea—the heavens may let loose the loud rolling thunder, and the earth heave up its fiery lava; but, just as sure as these elements of nature exist, and worlds revolve, America and Europe will be connected by an electric cord.

To the second objection, we have to say that there is a cause for the unprofitableness of many telegraph lines. The rapidity in building, and recklessness of management, has been the progenitor of ill success. When the lines now constructed work with *fidelity*, the patronage will be sufficient to enable every line in the country to pay handsome dividends. In the construction and management of lines, apply the remedy, and the disease will be cured. Build or repair the lines strong, and insulate them well, and they will all prove profitable. Shun *extravagance* as you would a viper!

The third objection is singular, and we scarcely know how to answer it. We admit it will *weigh* very heavy; but we consider the great weight secures with it great *strength;* therefore his objection occurs to us, to be really an argument in favor of success.

The fourth and last objection is marvellous. If there was only one solitary vessel ploughing the mighty deep, then there would be something to reflect upon. After reading the objection, we proceeded forthwith to the harbor of New-York, to see if all the vessels of the world had vanished from the face of the earth. At one view we saw a forest of more than a thousand masts towering from vessels. We then felt relieved, and that all was safe. At the Merchants' Exchange, the marine registers evidenced the existence of thousands at sea, and our joy seemed to be full, that the laying of a cable need not be confined to only one poor vessel.

In the final cabling of the ocean we hope for success. We do not entertain faith in the various schemes blazoned forth in the press, but our arrangements contemplate solidity and reality.

In years gone by, Mr. Reid, with others, partook in the struggles of the telegraph. The electric telegraph was the "wonder of this wonder-teeming age," and but few entertained faith in its ultimate utility. Every person engaged in the business was ridiculed. The ignorance of that age has passed away. He who was an object of burlesque then, ought not to foster it now. The progressive march of the science ought to receive a cheering smile and not a scorn. We hope the Review will give the subject a more candid consideration.

EXTENSION OF MORSE'S PATENT.—The subject of the extension of the patents granted to Prof. Morse, by the United States, seems to be gravely considered by a portion of the American press. Of course, no one doubts its importance to the inventor and the people. The following notice, relative to the question, we copy from the *Scientific American*, viz:—

"EXTENSION OF PATENTS AND PATENT LAW SUITS.—A statement has lately appeared in one of our daily papers, to the effect that a number of interested capitalists with their seat of operations in the city of Washington, have formed an association, with a capital of $500,000, for the purpose of procuring the further extension of the Woodworth Planing Machine patent, also the Hayward Patent for manufacturing india rubber, and the Telegraph Patent, granted to Prof. Morse, April 11th, 1846. The intention is to accomplish this result by a special act of Congress during its next session. There must be some error in including the patent of Prof. Morse, inasmuch as it has yet seven years to run, and the extension, if any, should be granted under our general laws. It is possible, however, that the owners of the patent anticipating its rejection by the Commissioner of Patents, are thus providing in due season to supersede the general law by obtaining a special act. To be fully convinced of this, however, we shall need more light upon the subject, but, from information received from other sources, we are led to believe that large sums of money are being collected to obtain the extension of the two first patents. We are opposed to the further extension of these patents for the following reasons:—1st. Because the applicants for the extension have already amassed enormous amounts of money from these inventions. * * * 2d. We are opposed to the extension of these patents, because they have been so managed by the owners as to injure deeply the interests of inventors, and to cause the public to become dissatisfied with our whole patent system, which is one of the most noble institutions in our country. We have always advocated the interests of inventors, and have defended their just rights; but in opposing the extension of these patents we plant ourselves upon the foundation of the rights of the people, who, as well as inventors, are deeply interested."

The editor of the above paper expresses doubt as to an association of Prof. Morse in this Company, with a capital of $500,000, but proceeds to place him with inventors, whose patents he thinks ought not to be renewed. We deeply regret this species of procedure, upon the part of the editor, to arouse "public sentiment to bear forcibly upon Congress," against the merit of the Morse patent. He ought not to associate parties in an arrangement affecting so seriously the rights of persons, unless the evidence of the fact is complete. We can assure him, that so far as Prof. Morse, or any of his friends are concerned, there is no truth in the report he has seen fit to indicate in the article quoted above. Nor has there been any grounds for the origination of so base an imputation, other than a wilful misrepresentation by some one, who has probably been foiled in his propensity to plunder from Morse those rights seemingly guaranteed to him by the letters patent.

It occurs to us, and we express our opinion with due respect, that a high and elevated work, like the paper from which we have quoted, ought to be more careful and discriminating in assailing the reputation and property of citizens. The editor claims to be "the friend of inventors;" but we think his past career has manifested a very different disposition towards Morse. We have been often pained to see his paper joining with a part of the press in assailing the patents for the American Electro-Magnetic Telegraph.

The first objection to the extension of these patents seem to be correct, if *true*; but if not true, then a renewal ought to be granted by the commissioner. Such is the case of Prof. Morse. He has not "amassed enormous amounts of money." If he has not, the *Scientific American* ought to advocate the renewal of his patent.

The second objection is so sweeping, that we know not how to answer, so far as it may refer to the Morse patentees. We suppose, however, the objection must refer to the other patents, as there has not been any very great mismanagement of the Morse patents, unless an effort upon their part to prevent themselves from being robbed and plundered by reckless and unscrupulous speculators, be mismanagement.

The patent of Prof. Morse, granted in June, 1840, expires June 1854.* That he will apply for a renewal is beyond doubt; but as to his being connected with any combinations, either direct or indirect, to procure a renewal by any corrupt mode, particularly such a base one as indicated above, is wholly untrue. The renewal can safely rest upon its merits. The laws now existing are ample for the case, and no special acts will be needed. So just are his claims, that the Hon. Amos Kendall, his agent, has positively refused to receive any aid even from those who are engaged in the telegraph business. Again we say, we are confident in the belief that no effort has been, or will be made in any manner whatever, upon the part of Prof. Morse and his associates, in procuring any act through Congress relative to his patent, or any law tending to promote a renewal.

We hope the courteous editor of that valuable work on Science, will correct the misrepresentation made, and, in future, not assail the renewal of a patent, unless he knows his first objection is unquestionably verified. *Palmam qui meruit ferat.*

Notice.—The Companion, and the Tariff Scale, will be published and issued from New-York City by Messrs. Pudney & Russell, No. 79 John-street. Subscriptions can be forwarded to them, or to the Editor, at Washington City.

Articles designed for publication in the first thirty-two pages of the Companion should be in the hands of the Editor by the 1st of the month preceding that of publication. News designed for the editorial department should be forwarded to the editor on or before the 10th of the preceding month.

Corrections to be made in the Tariff Scale, should be given to the editor on or before the middle of the month preceding its issue.

SHAFFNER'S

TELEGRAPH COMPANION,

DEVOTED TO THE SCIENCE AND ART OF THE

MORSE AMERICAN TELEGRAPH.

VOL. II. APRIL, 1855. No. 2.

Art. I.—ELECTRIC INDUCTION.

BY PROFESSOR M. FARADAY, F. R. S.

[Presented to the Royal Institution of Great Britain.]

ON ELECTRIC INDUCTION—ASSOCIATED CASES OF CURRENT AND STATIC EFFECTS.

CERTAIN phenomena that have presented themselves in the course of the extraordinary expansion which the works of the Electric Telegraph Company have undergone, appeared to me to offer remarkable illustrations of some fundamental principles of Electricity, and strong confirmation of the truthfulness of the view which I put forth sixteen years ago, respecting the mutually dependent nature of induction, conduction, and insulation, (Experimental Researches, 1318, &c.) I am deeply indebted to the Company; to the Gutta Percha works, and to Mr. Latimer Clarke, for the facts; and also for the opportunity both of seeing and showing them well.

Copper wire is perfectly covered with gutta percha at the Company's works, the metal and the covering being in every part regular and concentric. The covered wire is usually made into half mile lengths, the necessary junctions being effected by twisting or binding, and ultimately, soldering; after which the place is covered with fine gutta percha, in such a manner as to make the coating as perfect there as elsewhere: the perfection of the whole operation is finally tried in the following striking manner, by Mr. Statham, the manager of the works. The half mile coils are suspended from the sides of barges floating in a canal, so that the coils are immersed in the water whilst the two ends of each coil rise into the air: as many as 200 coils are thus immersed at once, and when their ends are connected in series, one great length of 100 miles of submerged wire is produced, the two extremities of which can be brought into a room for experiment. An insulated voltaic battery of many pairs of zinc and copper, with dilute sulphuric acid, has one end connected with the earth, and the other, through a galvanometer, with either end of the submerged wire. Passing by the first effect, and continuing the contact, it is evident that the battery current can take advantage of the whole accumulated conduction or defective insulation in the 100 miles of gutta percha on the wire, and that whatever portion of electricity passes through to the water will be shown by the galvanometer. Now the battery is made one of intensity, in order to raise the character of the proof, and the galvanometer employed is of considerable delicacy; yet so high is the insulation, that the deflection is not more than 5°. As another test of the perfect state of the wire, when the two ends of the battery are connected with the two ends of the wire, there is a powerful current of electricity shown by a much coarser instrument; but when any one junction in the course of the 100 miles is separated, the current is stopped, and the leak or deficiency of insulation rendered as small as before. The perfection and condition of the wire may be judged of by these facts.

The 100 miles, by means of which I saw the phenomena, were thus good as to insulation. The copper wire was $\frac{1}{16}$ of an inch in diameter:—the covered wire was $\frac{4}{16}$; some was a little less, being $\frac{7}{32}$ in diameter:—the gutta percha on the metal may therefore be considered as 0.1 of an inch in thickness. 100 miles of like covered wire in coils were heaped up on the floor of a dry warehouse and connected in one series, for comparison with that under water.

Consider now an insulated battery of 360 pairs of plates (4 × 3 inches) having one extremity to the earth; the water wire with both its insulated ends in the room, and a good earth discharge wire ready for the requisite communications:—when the free battery end was placed in contact with the water wire and then removed, and, afterwards, a person touching the earth discharge touched also the wire, he received a powerful shock. The shock was rather that of a voltaic than of a Leyden battery; it occupied *time*, and by quick tapping touches could be divided into numerous small shocks. I obtained as many as 40 sensible shocks from one charge of the wire. If *time* were allowed to intervene between the charge and discharge of the wire, the shock was less; but it was sensible after 2, 3, or 4 minutes, or even a longer period.

When, after the wire had been in contact with the battery, it was placed in contact with a Statham's fuze, it ignited the fuze (or even 6 fuzes in succession) vividly :—it could ignite the fuze 3 or 4 seconds after separation from the battery. When, having been in contact with the battery, it was separated and placed in contact with a galvanometer, it affected the instrument very powerfully :—it acted on it, though less powerfully, after the lapse of 4 or 5 minutes, and even affected it sensibly 20 or 30 minutes after it had been separated from the battery. When the insulated galvanometer was permanently attached to the end of the water wire, and the battery pole was brought in contact with the free end of the instrument, it was most instructive to see the great rush of electricity into the wire ; yet after that was over, though the contact was continued, the deflection was not more than 5°, so high was the insulation. Then separating the battery from the galvanometer, and touching the latter with the earth wire, it was just as striking to see the electricity rush out of the wire, holding for a time the magnet of the instrument in the reverse direction to that due to the ingress or charge.

These effects were produced equally well with either pole of the battery, or with either end of the wire ; and whether the electric condition was conferred and withdrawn at the same end, or at the opposite ends of the 100 miles, made no difference in the results. An intensity battery was required, for reasons which will be very evident in the sequel. That employed was able to decompose only a very small quantity of water in a given time. A Grove's battery of 8 or 10 pair of plates, which would have far surpassed it in this respect, would have had scarcely a sensible power in affecting the wire.

When the 100 miles of wire in the air were experimented with in like manner, not the slightest signs of any of these effects were produced. There is reason, from principle, to believe that an infinitesimal result is obtainable, but as compared to the water wire the action was nothing. Yet the wire was equally well and better insulated, and as regarded a constant current, it was an equally good conductor. This point was ascertained, by attaching the end of the water wire to one galvanometer, and the end of the air wire to another like instrument ; the two other ends of the wires were fastened together, and to the earth contact ; the two free galvanometer ends were fastened together, and to the free pole of the battery ; in this manner the current was divided between the air and water wires, but the galvanometers were affected to precisely the same amount. To make the result more certain, these instruments were changed one for the other, but the deviations were still alike : so that the two wires conducted with equal facility.

The cause of the first results is, upon consideration, evident enough. In consequence of the perfection of the workmanship, a Leyden arrrangement is produced upon a large scale; the copper wire becomes charged statically with that electricity which the pole of the battery connected with it can supply;* it acts by induction through the gutta percha, (without which induction it could not itself become charged, Exp. Res. 1177,) producing the opposite state on the surface of the water touching the gutta percha, which forms the outer coating of this curious arrangement. The gutta percha across which the induction occurs, is only 0.1 of an inch thick, and the extent of the coating is enormous. The surface of the copper wire is nearly 8,300 square feet, and the surface of the outer coating of water is four times that amount, or 33,000 square feet. Hence the striking character of the results. The intensity of the static charge acquired is only equal to the intensity at the pole of the battery whence it is derived; but its quantity is enormous, because of the immense extent of the Leyden arrangement; and hence when the wire is separated from the battery and the charge employed, it has all the powers of a considerable voltaic current, and gives results which the best ordinary electric machines and Leyden arrangements cannot as yet approach.

That the air wire produces none of these effects is simply because there is no outer coating correspondent to the water, or only one so far removed as to allow of no sensible induction, and therefore the inner wire cannot become charged. In the air wire of the warehouse, the floor, walls, and ceiling of the place constituted the outer coating, and this was at a considerable distance; and in any case could only affect the outside portions of the coils of wire. I understand that 100 miles of wire, stretched in a line through the air, so as to have its whole extent opposed to earth, is equally inefficient in showing the effects, and there it must be the distance of the inductric and inducteous surfaces (1483), combined with the lower specific inductive capacity of air, as compared with gutta percha, which causes the negative result. The phenomena altogether offer a beautiful case of the identity of static and dynamic electricity. The whole power of a considerable battery may in this way be worked off in separate portions, and measured out in units of static force, and yet be employed afterwards for any or every purpose of voltaic electricity.

I now proceed to further consequences of associated static and dynamic effects. Wires covered with gutta percha, and then inclosed in tubes of lead or of iron, or buried in the earth, or

* Davy, Elements of Chemical Philosophy, p. 154.

sunk in the sea, exhibit the same phenomena as those described; the like static inductive action being in all these cases permitted by the conditions. Such subterraneous wires exist between London and Manchester, and when they are all connected together so as to make one series, offer above 1,500 miles; which, as the duplications return to London, can be observed by one experimenter at intervals of about 400 miles, by the introduction of galvanometers at these returns. This wire, or the half, or fourth of it, presented all the phenomena already described; the only difference was, that as the insulation was not so perfect, the charged condition fell more rapidly. Consider 750 miles of the wire in one length, a galvanometer *a* being at the beginning of the wire, a second galvanometer *b* in the middle, and a third *c* at the end:—these three galvanometers being in the room with the experimenter, and the third *c* perfectly connected with the earth. On bringing the pole of the battery into contact with the wire through the galvanometer *a*, that instrument was instantly affected; after a sensible time *b* was affected, and after a still longer time *c*: when the whole 1,500 miles were included, it required two seconds for the electric stream to reach the last instrument. Again;—all the instruments being deflected, (of course not equally, because of the electric leakage along the line,) if the battery were cut off at *a*, that instrument instantly fell to zero; but *b* did not fall until a little while after; and *c* only after a still longer interval;—a current flowing on to the end of the wire whilst there was none flowing in at the beginning. Again; by a short touch of the battery pole against *a*, it could be deflected and could fall back into its neutral condition, before the electric power had reached *b*; which in its turn would be for an instant affected, and then left neutral before the power had reached *c*: a wave of force having been sent into the wire, which gradually travelled along it, and made itself evident at successive intervals of time, in different parts of the wire. It was even possible, by adjusted touches of the battery, to have two simultaneous waves in the wire, following each other, so that at the same moment that *c* was affected by the first wave, *a* or *b* was affected by the second; and there is no doubt that by the multiplication of instruments and close attention, four or five waves might be obtained at once.

If after making and breaking battery contact at *a*, *a* be immediately connected with the earth, then additional interesting effects occur. Part of the electricity which is in the wire will return, and passing through *a* will deflect it in the reverse direction; so that currents will flow out of both extremities of the wire in opposite directions, whilst no current is going into it from any source. Or if *a* be quickly put to the battery and then to the earth, it will show a current first entering into the wire, and then returning out of the wire at the same place; no sensible part of it ever travelling on to *b* or *c*.

When an air wire of equal extent is experimented with in like manner, no such effects as these are perceived: or, if guided by principle, the arrangements are such as to be searching, they are perceived only in a very slight degree, and disappear in comparison with the former gross results. The effect at the end of the very long air wire (or *c*) is in the smallest degree behind the effect at galvanometer *a;* and the accumulation of a charge in the wire is not sensible.

All these results as to *time*, &c., evidently depend upon the same condition as that which produced the former effect of static charge, namely, *lateral induction;* and are necessary consequences of the principles of conduction, insulation, and induction, three terms which, in their meaning, are inseparable from each other, (Exp. Res. 1320, 1326,* 1338, 1561, &c.) If we put a plate of shellac upon a gold leaf electrometer and a charged carrier (an insulated metal ball of two or three inches diameter) upon it, the electrometer is diverged; removing the carrier, this divergence instantly falls; this is *insulation* and *induction*. If we replace the shellac by metal, the carrier causes the leaves to diverge as before, but when removed, though after the shortest possible contact, the electroscope is left diverged; this is *conduction*. If we employ a plate of spermaceti instead of the metal, and repeat the experiment, we find the divergence partly falls and partly remains, because the spermaceti insulates and also conducts, doing both imperfectly: but the shellac also conducts, as is shown, if time be allowed; and the metal also obstructs conduction, and therefore insulates, as is shown by simple arrangements. For if a copper wire, 74 feet in length and $\frac{1}{12}$ of

* 1326. All these considerations impress my mind strongly with the conviction, that insulation and ordinary conduction cannot be properly separated when we are examining into their nature: that is, into the general law or laws under which their phenomena are produced. They appear to me to consist in an action of contiguous particles, dependent on the forces developed in electrical excitement; these forces bring the particles into a state of tension or polarity, which constitutes both *induction* and *insulation;* and being in this state the contiguous particles have a power or capability of communicating these forces, one to the other, by which they are lowered, and discharge occurs. Every body appears to discharge (444. 987); but the possession of this capability in a *greater or smaller degree* in different bodies, makes them better or worse conductors, worse or better insulators: and both *induction* and *conduction* appear to be the same in their principle and action (1320), except that in the latter, an effect common to both is raised to the highest degree, whereas in the former, it occurs in the best cases, in only an almost insensible quantity.

an inch in diameter, be insulated in the air, having its end *m* a metal ball; its end *e* connected with the earth, and the parts near *m* and *e* brought within half an inch of each other, as at *s*; then an ordinary Leyden jar being charged sufficiently, its outside connected with *e* and its inside with *m*, will give a charge to the wire, which, instead of travelling wholly through it, though it be so excellent a conductor, will pass in large proportion through the air at *s*, as a bright spark; for with such a length of wire, the resistance in it is accumulated until it becomes as much, or perhaps even more, than that of the air, for electricity of such high intensity.

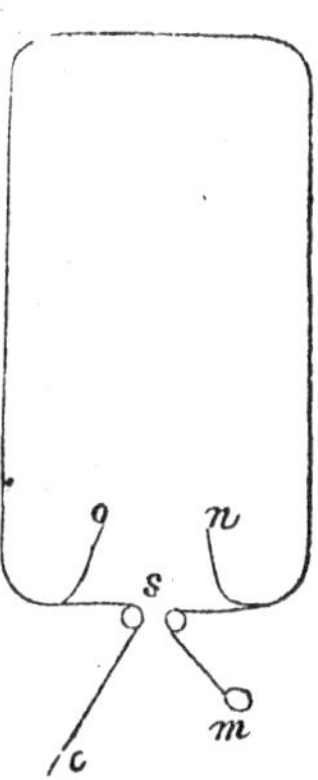

Admitting that such and similar experiments show that conduction through a wire is preceded by the act of induction (1338), then all the phenomena presented by the submerged or subterranean wires are explained; and in their explanation confirm, as I think, the principles given. After Mr. Wheatstone had, in 1834, measured the velocity of a wave of electricity through a copper wire, and given it as 288.000 miles in a second, I said, in 1838, upon the strength of these principles (1333), "that the velocity of discharge through the *same wire* may be greatly varied, by attending to the circumstances which cause variations of discharge through spermaceti or sulphur. Thus, for instance, it must vary with the tension or intensity of the first urging force, which tension is charge and induction. So if the two ends of the wire, in Professor Wheatstone's experiment, were immediately connected with two large insulated metallic surfaces exposed to the air, so that the primary act of induction, after making the contact for discharge, might be in part removed from the internal portion of the wire at the first instant, and disposed for the moment on its surface jointly with the air and surrounding conductors, then I venture to anticipate, that the middle spark would be more retarded than before: and if these two plates were the inner and outer coating of a large jar, or a Leyden battery, then the retardation of that spark would be still greater." Now this is precisely the case of the submerged or subterraneous wires, except that, instead of carrying their surfaces towards the inducteous coatings (1483), the latter are brought near the former; in both cases the induction consequent upon charge, instead of being exerted almost entirely at the moment within the wire, is to a very large extent determined externally; and so the discharge or conduction being caused by a lower tension, therefore requires a longer time. Hence, the reason why, with 1,500 miles of subterraneous wire, the wave was two seconds in passing from end to end; whilst with the same length of air wire, the time was almost inappreciable.

With these lights it is interesting to look at the measured velocities of electricity in wires of metal, as given by different experimenters.

	Miles per second.
* Wheatstone in 1834, with copper wire, made it	288,000
* Walker in America, with telegraph iron wire	18,780
* O. Mitchell, ditto. ditto.	28,524
* Fizeau and Gonnelle, (copper wire)	112,680
* Ditto. - - (iron wire)	62,600
† A. B. G. (copper) London and Brussels Telegraph	2,700
† Ditto. (copper) London and Edinburgh Telegraph	7,600

Here the difference in copper is seen by the first and fifth result to be above a hundred fold. It is further remarked in Liebig's report of Fizeau's and Gonnelle's experiments, that the velocity is not proportional to the conductive capacity, and is independent of the thickness of the wire. All these circumstances and incompatibilities appear rapidly to vanish, as we recognize and take into consideration the lateral induction of the wire carrying the current. If the velocity of a brief electric discharge is to be ascertained in a given length of wire, the simple circumstances of the latter being twined round a frame in small space, or spread through the air through a large space, or adhering to walls, or lying on the ground, will make a difference in the results. And in regard to long circuits such as those described, their conducting power cannot be understood, whilst no reference is made to their lateral static induction, or to the conditions of intensity and quantity which then come into play; especially in the case of short or intermitting currents—for then static and dynamic are continually passing into each other.

It has already been said that the conducting power of the air and water wires are alike for a constant current. This is in perfect accordance with the principles and with the definite character of the electric force, whether in the static, or current, or transition state. When a voltaic current of a certain intensity is sent into a long water wire, connected at the further extremity with the earth, part of the force is in the first instance occupied in raising a lateral induction round the wire, ultimately equal in intensity at the near end to the intensity of the battery stream,

* Liebig and Kopp's report 1850, (translated,) p. 168.
† Athenæum, 14th January, 1854, p. 54.

and decreasing gradually to the earth end, where it becomes nothing. Whilst this induction is rising, that within the wire amongst its particles is beneath what it would otherwise be; but as soon as the first has attained its maximum state, then that in the wire becomes proportionate to the battery intensity, and therefore equals that in the air wire, in which the same state is (because of the absence of lateral induction) almost instantly attained. Then of course they discharge alike, and therefore conduct alike.

A striking proof of the variation of the conduction of a wire, by variation of its lateral static induction, is given in the experiment proposed 16 years ago, (1333.) If, using a constant charged jar, the interval *s*, page 6, be adjusted so that the spark shall freely pass there, (though it would not if a little wider,) whilst the short connecting wires *n* and *o* are insulated in the air, the experiment may be repeated twenty times without a single failure; but, if after that, *n* and *o* be connected with the inside and outside of an insulated Leyden jar, as described, the spark will never pass across *s*, but all the charge will go round the whole of the long wire. Why is this? The quantity of electricity is the same, the wire is the same, its resistance is the same, and that of the air remains unaltered; but because the intensity is lowered, through the lateral induction momentarily allowed, it is never enough to strike across the air at *s*; and it is finally altogether occupied in the wire, which, in a little longer time than before, effects the whole discharge. M. Fizeau has applied the same expedient to the primary voltaic currents of Ruhmkorff's beautiful inducting apparatus, with great advantage. He thereby reduces the intensity of these currents at the moment when it would be very disadvantageous, and gives us a striking instance of the advantage of viewing static and dynamic phenomena as the result of the same laws.

Mr. Clarke arranged a Bain's printing telegraph with three pens, so that it gave beautiful illustrations and records of facts like those stated: the pens are iron wires, under which a band of paper, imbued with ferro-prussiate of potassa, passes at a regular rate by clock-work; and thus regular lines of prussian blue are produced whenever a current is transmitted, and the time of the current is recorded. In the case to be described, the three lines were side by side, and about 0.1 of an inch apart. The pen *m* belonged to a circuit of only a few feet of wire, and a separate battery; it told whenever the contact key was put down by the finger; the pen *n* was at the earth end of the long air wire, and the pen *o* at the earth end of the long subterraneous wire; and by arrangement, the key could be made to throw the electricity of the chief battery into either of these wires, simultaneously with the passage of the short circuit current through pen *m*. When pens *m* and *n* were in action, the *m* record was a regular line of equal thickness, showing by its length the actual time during which the electricity flowed into the wires; and the *n* record was an equally regular line, parallel to, and of equal length with the former, but the least degree behind it; thus indicating that the long air wire conveyed its electric current almost instantaneously to the further end. But when pens *m* and *o* were in action, the *o* line did not begin until some time after the *m* line, and it continued after the *m* line had ceased, *i. e.*, after the *o* battery was cut of. Furthermore, it was faint at first, grew up to a maximum of intensity, continued at that as long as battery contact was continued, and then gradually diminished to nothing. Thus the record *o* showed that the wave of power took time in the water wire to reach the further extremity; by its first faintness, it showed that power was consumed in the exertion of lateral static induction along the wire; by the attainment of a maximum and the after equality, it showed when this induction had become proportionate to the intensity of the battery current; by its beginning to diminish, it showed when the battery current was cut off; and its prolongation and gradual diminution, showed the time of the outflow of the static electricity laid up in the wire, and the consequent regular falling of the induction which had been as regularly raised.

With the pens *m* and *o* the conversion of an intermitting into a continuous current could be beautifully shown; the earth wire, by the static induction which it permitted, acting in a manner analogous to the fly-wheel of a steam engine, or the air-spring of a pump. Thus, when the contact key was regularly but rapidly depressed and raised, the pen *m* made a series of short lines separated by intervals of equal length. After four or more of these had passed, then pen *o*, belonging to the subterraneous wire, began to make its mark, weak at first, then rising to a maximum, but always continuous. If the action of the contact key was less rapid, then alternate thickening, and attenuations appeared in the *o* record; and if the introductions of the electric current at the one end of the earth wire were at still longer intervals, the records of action at the other end became entirely separated from each other. All showing most beautifully, how the individual current or wave, once introduced into the wire, and never ceasing to go onward in its course, could be effected in its intensity, its time, and other circumstances, by its partial occupation in static induction.

By other arrangements of the pens *n* and *o*, the near end of the subterraneous wire could be connected with the earth immediately after separation from the battery; and then the back flow of the electricity, and the time and manner thereof, were beautifully recorded; but I must refrain from detailing results which have already been described in principle.

Many variations of these experiments have been made and may be devised. Thus, the ends of the insulated battery have been attached to the ends of the long subterraneous wire, and then the two halves of the wire have given back opposite return currents when connected with the earth. In such a case the wire is positive and negative at the two extremities, being permanently sustained by its length and the battery, in the same condition which is given to the short wire for a moment by the Leyden discharge, p. 6; or, for an extreme but like case, to a filament of shellac having its extremities charged positive and negative. Colomb pointed out the difference of long and short as to the insulating or conducting power of such filaments, and like difference occurs with long and short metal wires.

The character of the phenomena described in this report, induces me to refer to the terms *intensity* and *quantity* as applied to electricity; terms which I have had such frequent occasion to employ. These terms, or equivalents for them, cannot be dispensed with by those who study both the static and the dynamic relations of electricity; every current where there is resistance, has the static element and induction involved in it, whilst every case of insulation has more or less of the dynamic element and conduction; and we have seen that, with the same voltaic source, the same current in the same length of the same wire gives a different result as the intensity is made to vary, with variations of the induction around the wire. The idea of intensity or the power of overcoming resistance, is as necessary to that of electricity, either static or current, as the idea of pressure is to steam in a boiler, or to air passing through apertures or tubes; and we must have language competent to express these conditions and these ideas. Furthermore, I have never found either of these terms lead to any mistakes regarding electrical action, or give rise to any false view of the character of electricity or its unity. I cannot find other terms of equal useful significance with these; or any which, conveying the same ideas, are not liable to such misuse as these may be subject to. It would be affectation, therefore, in me, to search about for other words; and besides that, the present subject has shown me more than ever their great value and peculiar advantage in electrical language.

The fuze referred to in page 3, is of the following nature: Some copper wire was covered with sulphureted gutta percha;

after some months it was found that a film of sulphuret of copper was formed between the metal and the envelope; and further, that when half the gutta percha was cut away in any place, and then the copper wire removed for about ¼ of an inch, so as to remain connected only by the film of sulphuret adhering to the remaining gutta percha, an intensity battery could cause this sulphuret to enter into vivid ignition, and fire gunpowder with the utmost ease. The experiment was shown in the lecture room, of firing gunpowder at the end of eight miles of single wire. Mr. Faraday reported that he had seen it fired through 100 miles of covered wire immersed in the canal, by the use of this fuze.

ART. II.—ATLANTIC AND PACIFIC OCEANS TELEGRAPH.

REPORT OF MR. FARLEY TO THE HOUSE OF REPRESENTATIVES OF THE CONGRESS OF THE UNITED STATES.

[IN volume one, of the Companion, we published an account of a proposed Telegraph, to connect the Atlantic and Pacific Oceans. The bill has been passed by both Houses of Congress and signed by the President. Proper energy will be devoted to its early completion, and the line, when done, will be of the utmost import to the nation. We earnestly solicit for this enterprise the energies and co-operation of our telegraph people. Messrs. Alden and Eddy deserve much credit for their successful efforts in getting the attention of Congress in the consideration of this important national enterprise.]—EDITOR.

The project contemplated in the bill is of transcendent public concern, and possesses the merits of *practicability* and *early completion*, if it can have the encouragement of the government. It provides—

Firstly. That a right of way shall be given through the public lands of the United States for the construction of a subterranean line of telegraph, (of at least two independent conductors,) from the Mississippi or Missouri rivers to the Pacific Ocean, at San Francisco, in California.

Secondly. That it be constructed by individual enterprise, and at individual expense.

Thirdly. That after its completion, in a specified and most permanent manner, the free use thereof, to the extent of eight thousand words per month, shall be tendered to the general government, and the enjoyment of that privilege secured to it in perpetuity, with the reservation to the government of the further *prior* use to any extent within the capacity of said line, at such rates of compensation for messages transmitted as Congress may by law provide.

Fourthly. That thereupon, and in consideration of such free use and said reservation, the government shall permit the parties to select from the public lands not before sold or appropriated, in the territories along and within fifteen miles of said line of telegraph, any quantity, not more than a section and in alternate sections, two millions of acres, which shall then be conveyed to them.

The citizens of the United States residing upon the Pacific coast have the strongest ties connecting them with the older States. They have established themselves there, organized a powerful State, and are rapidly creating a commerce reaching to the islands and the Asiatic coast. Their peculiar position gives them claims of an imperative character upon the protection and care of the government. Europe is extending lines of telegraph into Asia and Africa, and lines of great length have been constructed in India. When this proposed link shall be completed, the Pacific Ocean will be touched upon either shore by lines which, spanning continents, reach to the opposite shores of the Atlantic Ocean, and are destined, perhaps, to cross the latter and unite together.

The benefits which will follow the execution of this enterprise cannot be partial or sectional; they must necessarily be of incalculable national importance, and the moral influences resulting therefrom will be co-extensive with the world of civilization and commerce. The results of such a work can hardly be overrated, in the enlivening spirit which it will infuse into the business and other relations existing between the Atlantic and Pacific coasts, in its influence upon the varied interests of that vast population which is destined so soon to occupy every part of the territory embraced within the limits of the republic, and in the facilities which it will be able to render the government in peace and in war. While immense advantages must flow from the construction of the proposed line, your committee are not aware that a single evil can; and objections, if any there be, must be directed against the mode recommended to insure its success, rather than the object sought to be accomplished.

It may be contended that the precise point for the location of the line, at its eastern terminus, should be fixed in the bill: This is not important. It is left discretionary with the memorialist to commence from "such point on the Mississippi or Missouri rivers as they may hereafter select." It will undoubtedly be for their interest to start from some prominent point of population and business. The best route cannot be determined upon without an examination and survey; and as the public interests cannot suffer thereby, it is thought expedient to leave the eastern terminus and general direction of the line entirely open. The fact that from the point selected for an eastern terminus, wherever it may be, diverging lines running in any direction may and will be made to connect with it, is a sufficient answer to any desire for fixing it in the bill.

It has been said that the building of a telegraph line to the Pacific should be connected with that of a railroad; and, further, that the construction of a telegraph line, as an independent measure, will be marking out a line for the Pacific railroad. The force of these objections is not seen by the committee. If the telegraph is to await the construction of the railroad, it is evident that its completion must be postponed for some years, even if the latter be commenced immediately, while two years will suffice for the construction of the former. The plan of the memorialist cannot mark out the route for a railroad, or influence the decision of that question, for the reason that the *straightest* practicable line between the termini is the most desirable. It would cross mountains, valleys, and rivers, in directions utterly unsuitable and impracticable for the route of a railroad; its location would be controlled by other considerations than those of grades, bridges, excavations and embankments, which must enter so largely into the location of the former.

Connect the Atlantic and Pacific coasts by telegraph communication, and the impulse which it will give to business, and that great tide of emigration setting towards California, will add to the necessity for railroad communication. In this instance, the telegraph should precede the railway.

The bill provides that the telegraph line shall be completed within two years from its passage, and after such State legislation shall have been secured as may be necessary to authorize its construction in the States through which it may pass. The parties having had much experience in similar undertakings, have full confidence in their success and their ability to complete the work within the time specified. The benefits, therefore, which will accrue from this measure, are not to be postponed to an indefinite future; they are close at hand and within our immediate grasp.

The line is to be constructed in the most permanent manner, with two independent conductors, placed under ground, where they will be exempt from all the causes which operate to prevent the efficiency and reliability of lines constructed in the ordinary way. The wires are to be so completely protected by the insulating material, itself imperishable, that they will not corrode; and, being securely placed in the earth, no accidental breaking can occur. The electrical state of the atmosphere, or the most violent storms, can have no effect to interrupt the working of lines thus laid down. The plan proposed also includes the location of testing-tubes at intervals of five miles, and working stations at average distances of one hundred miles. Under such arrangements, should the line from any cause be interrupted, it could be speedily repaired. The parties are entirely confident that they will be able to work the line at *all* times as readily as air-lines are operated in the most favorable weather, and consequently that they can always transmit despatches directly through. This mode of construction, which has been attended with satisfactory success in Europe, will, it is confidently believed, secure all the advantages claimed for it by the memorialists, who have a practical knowledge of the building and operating lines of telegraph; being connected with the management of some of the best regulated telegraph companies in the country. The bill provides for two lines of wire, which will insure the transaction of a larger amount of business, and a degree of certainty and reliability to the government and the citizen in the transmission of despatches, which might, for obvious reasons, be sometimes interrupted, if the dependence was upon but *one* line of wire.

A subterranean line of two wires, such as the bill provides for, is estimated to cost eleven hundred and fifty dollars per mile. Calling the distance twenty-four hundred miles, the entire cost of the line, including the buildings necessary at the working stations, together with incidental expenses to be incurred in its construction, such as explorations and engineering, land transportation of materials, cost of supplies, and erection of forts to protect way stations, would be not less than two million seven hundred and sixty thousand dollars. The annual cost of operating the line is estimated at three hundred and fifty thousand dollars. Fifty operators will be necessary, and a force of two hundred and fifty other men will be required, constantly in the work of repairing and protecting the line. These men will be posted in small parties at the different working stations. It is proposed to have a double set of operators, so that the line may be worked by night as well as by day.

The value of the lands located along and near the telegraph line, if estimated as the government valued its bounty lands given to its soldiers in the Mexican war, when it commuted with them, giving one hundred dollars in scrip, or one hundred and sixty acres of land, would be only at the rate of sixty-two and a half cents per acre. Valuing the proposed grant of two millions of acres at the same rate, it would be worth twelve hundred and fifty thousand dollars, considerably less than one-half the estimated cost of the line. It should be remembered that the bill confines the grant to the *Territories*, while those soldiers had the right of locating in both Territories and States. It is thought, therefore, than the sum of twelve hundred and fifty thousand dollars, is a fair valuation of their worth, if estimated as aid in the construction of the line. These lands are so far remote that it must be years before they can became of value to the government. No person could afford to purchase them at the government price of one dollar and twenty-five cents per acre, and retain them until they became marketable; he never would realize the cost and interest. The value to the government of the privilege of transmitting without charge eight thousand words per month is, at the rates named in the bill, equal to a yearly interest account of one hundred thousand dollars, a sum equivalent to an annual interest at eight per centum on the value of two millions of acres of land, according to the foregoing estimate. In addition to this privilege, the government is to have the prior use of the line for all its business, without restriction, at rates to be established by itself.

The principle so frequently regarded of selecting alternate sections where grants have been made by the government, in aid of great works of public importance, is incorporated into this bill.

It may be inquired why the government is asked to aid in this enterprise? The answer is clear, and, we think satisfactory. Telegraphic lines are of recent origin, and the profits of their business uncertain. As an investment, they have not yet acquired that favor with the public which will induce the capitalist to take stock in a line like the proposed, running thousands of miles through a savage country. It is believed that the numerous telegraphic lines put in operation in this country, exceeding in their aggregate length the united lines of all other countries, have not, on the whole, been a profitable investment to those interested. This project does not hold out sufficient grounds for success as a profitable investment, to induce subscriptions, without government encouragement. Without that assistance it is not to be expected that a telegraph line, as an independent measure, can, for years to come, be carried through, with reasonable hopes of remuneration for the outlay of capital which would be required. A grant of land under the conditions named, will give to the enterprise a degree of confidence in the public estimation which cannot otherwise be created. It will give those engaged in it a credit and responsibility which will enable them to command means at once to carry on the work to an early completion, and overcome a great many obstacles which would be fatal to its success, if confined strictly to the efforts of private enterprise alone.

The aid of the government is invoked. Can it be granted with *safety* and *security* to the public interests? It is evident that it can. It is provided in the bill that no lands can be selected until *after* the completion of the line, and the free use of it tendered to the government. This condition is ample security. Again, it is provided that the line becomes forfeited to the government, in case of neglect on the part of the memorialists to operate it for a period of six months after its completion. The proposed grant in aid of the undertaking is not a *gift* of a portion of the public lands, but such a disposition of them as will confer great and lasting advantages to the citizen and the government. Looking at it in a pecuniary point of view, it is an investment by the government, upon which it will annually receive, in the transmission of its various orders, civil, military, and naval, a consideration of eight per centum on the value of the lands appropriated. This privilege, together with the "further prior use, to any extent within the capacity of the line, at such rates of compensation for messages transmitted as Congress may by law provide," are not of a temporary character; they are perpetual. The risk, labor, and responsibilityare all upon the side of the memorialists. The government incurs no expense in the construction of the line; in a word, it hazards nothing.

The committee report back the Senate bill with amendments, with a recommendation that they be adopted, and that the bill, thus amended, do pass.

ART. III.—THE ATMOSPHERIC TELEGRAPH.

REPORT OF MR. MALLORY TO THE SENATE OF THE UNITED STATES, ON THE ATMOSPHERIC TELEGRAPH.

[In the first volume of the Telegraph Companion, we noticed the plan of Mr. Richardson, for the establishment of a means of conveying substances between distant points by the force of air. The name "Telegraph," we consider as not appropriate. That word means to write from a distance. This new art conveys matter from a distance. We have not the room necessary to discuss the subject as to its practicability. Gentlemen of much scientific intelligence regard the invention as worthy of patronage. We concur in this opinion, and hope that Congress will, at an early day, advance the required assistance to put it in operation upon a large scale. We do not think it will interfere with the Electric Telegraph. If, however, it should prove useful, and wholly supersede the Telegraph, let it triumph. We believe in adopting the best of all things.]—EDITOR.

That Ithiel S. Richardson has obtained letters patent for what he denominates the "Atmospheric Telegraph;" but as these terms convey no distinct image to the mind, and but a very imperfect idea of the character and design of his proposition, your committee will briefly state them.

The idea of moving a piston within an exhausted cylinder by atmospheric pressure, and thereby transporting letters, merchandise, and even persons, is not new, and various experiments to attain this object have been made within the last thirty or forty years.

In 1810, Mr. Medhurst, a Danish engineer, proposed to carry letters and merchandise, by means of the rarification and compression of air, in a canal six feet high by five feet wide, containing a road of stone or iron. He was succeeded by the experiments of Mr. Pinkus, an American engineer; and about thirty years ago, John Vallance, Esq., of Brighton, (England,) took out a patent for a new method of carrying passengers and freight, which attracted much attention and speculation at the time, but which was considered more ingenious than practical. He proposed to construct from town to town, throughout the United Kingdom, air-tight cylinders of sufficient magnitude to enable ordinary wagons and cars to pass through them upon rail tracks by the alternate rarification and expansion of air.

Mr. Vallance seems to have constructed a model, and with it some experiments were made; but he probably realised the immeasurable space which too often separates theory from practice.

About the year 1838, public attention was arrested by the successful experiment at Chaillot (England) with the atmospheric railroad. Subsequently, about the year 1840, the atmospheric railroad was established between Kingstown and Dalkey, for the transportation of merchandise, passengers, &c., a distance of about thirty-five hundred yards, and this was followed by one in France.

Some ten years ago, Mr. W. H. James, son of the Mr. James so honorably identified with the origin of the British railroads, proposed a mode of carrying mails and small packages through air-tight tubes by atmospheric pressure, very similar to the plan under consideration.

He proposes to have two tubular passages, or carriage ways, running parallel to each other from end to end of any given distance. These tubular passages are to be placed either above or below the surface of the ground, as found most convenient, and to be constructed of metal, wood, brick-work, or any other suitable material. At one termination of these tubular passages, and between them, there is to be fixed an air exhausting and forcing machine, connected by means of curved tubes with each of the tubular passages; which machine is to be actuated by a steam-engine or any other suitable and competent power, and so arranged, that when put in motion it may cause the air to flow from one passage into the other with very great rapidity. A similar machine is to be placed at the other termination of the tubular passages, and connected thereto and worked in the same manner; or intermediate machines may be employed, if found necessary, so as to produce an extremely rapid and continuous current of air in both directions throughout the whole distance. The vessels or carriages for containing the letters or parcels to be transmitted are to consist of spherical-shaped vehicles, or bags, *formed of caoutchouc*, or other suitable materials, and are to be so constructed as to be perfectly elastic, and to retain their shape independently of what they contain, and capable of being *beaten* or *buffetted* about like a foot-ball or boxing-glove without injury; being of the least possible weight, and having at the same time the requisite strength. It is further proposed that these spherical bags or letter carriages should be about fifteen inches diameter when the tubular passages are about eighteen inches, and that each shall contain only about a hundred letters at a time, so as to have great surface in proportion to weight. It is *imagined* that, on being introduced into the current of air, they will be carried forward, one after the other, like so many small balloons in a strong gale of wind, without, perhaps, even rolling against or *touching* the inner circumference of the tubular passages.

The distinction between this method and that of Mr. Richardson is not one of principle, but of detail; but this distinction seems to involve the *impracticability* of the one, and the *practicability* of the other; while in Mr. James's plan the letters enveloped in spheroid caoutchouc bags of a diameter *three inches less than that of the tube* through which they pass, leaving thereby a *clear space upon all sides of an inch and a half for a free passage of air*, Mr. Richardson's *plunger exactly conforms to the tube*, and admits *not the passage of air beyond it*.

These various propositions are *all based upon certain well established facts and principles.*

The atmosphere presses with equal intensity in all directions, whether on vertical or horizontal surfaces. And this pressure may be taken to be equal to fourteen and three-quarter pounds to the square inch.

If we place upon the ground a tube of uniform diameter open at both extremities, and accurately adjust within it a piston capable of sliding in either direction, the piston of course remains stationary, the atmospheric pressure upon its surfaces being equal. But if we insert and confine the piston at one end, and, by means of an air pump at the other, exhaust the tube, the piston, upon being released, will pass through the tube at a speed equal to about (635) six hundred and thirty-five miles per hour, modified by its weight and friction.

Partial exhaustion would reduce this velocity; and if we insert the piston at one end, leaving it free to act, and work the air-pump at the other, the piston will move after a very slight rarification, dependent, as before stated, upon its weight and friction.

When the operation is performed in this manner, the air-pump has the control of the plunger's momentum, and may check or accelerate it at pleasure by the aid of a valve in the tube; and the pump, by exhausting the air in front of the advancing plunger, seems, in fact, to be drawing it onward, rather than clearing the way for the pressure of the following atmosphere.

Mr. Richardson exhibits a very beautiful model of his telegraph, which has been for some weeks past in one of the committee rooms of the Senate for inspection, and which your committee has frequently and carefully examined. It consists of a horizontal tube of one inch clear diameter, one-half of which is straight, while the other half contains curves, designed to represent the sinuosities of the tube passing over uneven ground. One small air-pump, placed near its centre, and communicating with either end of it, exhausts it at pleasure from left to right, or from right to left. A piston, or plunger, three inches long, and fitting the tube loosely, but followed by several detached disks, or washers of leather, which accurately fit it, is inserted in one end of the tube, separated by a cut-off; and a few strokes of the pump produce in the tube a partial vacuum. The cut-off is then reversed, and the plunger *set free on the side of the vacuum, relieved from the resistance of the air in the tube*, and, propelled alone by the pressure of the atmosphere, passes through it in a time wholly unappreciable by ordinary means. The cut-off may be dispensed with; for if the plunger, with its miniature mail-bag attached, be placed in one end of the tube, and the pump be worked, it will move (*supposing an absence of weight and friction*) with the first stroke of the pump, which destroys the equilibrium between the internal and external atmosphere;

and the degree of exhaustion necessary to produce this momentum must depend upon the weight and friction of the plunger and its attachments.

This model works admirably; and, without going into details of its construction, it seems to have *overcome all difficulties, and some which have been long supposed insuperable in the practicable operations of the* "Atmospheric Telegraph."

A mercurial barometer, whose base connects with the interior of the tube, instantly exhibits the changes in the rarification of the air within it, produced by every stroke of the air-pump; and this device is useful, enabling us to perceive at a glance, how slight a rarification of the atmosphere within the tube causes the piston, or plunger, with its "mail-bag," to move forwards.

Whatever differences of opinion may exist as to the properties of our atmosphere, its origin, its utmost limits from the earth, its laws of motion and expansion, sufficient reliable data are established to enable us to arrive at correct conclusions with reference to the principles involved in this proposition.

The density of the atmosphere decreases as we ascend from the earth, and whatever the height may be, we know that its pressure or weight on a square inch of surface is capable of supporting a column in the barometer tube about 30 inches high; and as mercury weighs 13,580 ounces, or 848¾ lbs. avoirdupois to the cubic foot, a simple proposition, 1,728 : 848¾ : : 30, gives 14.73 or 14¾ lbs. as the pressure of the atmosphere on every square inch of surface. Now, as mercury is about 10,800 times heavier than our air at the surface of the earth of medium density, a column of such air of equivalent weight to the atmospheric column would be 10,800 times 30 inches, which is about 27,000 feet. If we suppose a column of airiform fluid of this height to rest on a large exhausted receiver, as soon as a communication is formed between both, this tall column will force the air next the receiver in with a velocity equal to that acquired by a body falling *half the height of the fluid column* (as is supported by writers on natural philosophy); hence an atmospheric column (whatever height it may be) will force the air at the surface of the earth into an exhausted receiver with this velocity. Now, a body in falling 13,500, the half of 27,000 feet, will acquire, by the force of gravity, 932 feet at the last of its fall. This we easily found by dividing 13,500 by 16½, the fall in one second, the square root of the quotient gave nearly 29 seconds as the time of falling; this time, at the rate of 32⅙ of an increase of velocity per second gives the above. Nine hundrde and thirty-two feet per second is 635 miles per hour, as 932 × 3,600 and divided by 5,280 gives 635.

Assuming, then, that the tube is thoroughly exhausted, and the closely fitting plunger permitted to pass though it unresisted and free, and without weight or friction, by atmospheric pressure, it would preserve an uniform velocity throughout its whole extent, of 635 miles per hour.

But, in practice, a perfect vacuum is neither possible nor desirable; and it is believed that a degree of exhaustion, very easily attainable, will be amply sufficient for the accomplishment of a speed and power equivalent to the propulsion of fifty tons two hundred miles per hour.

The ordinary pressure of our atmosphere, as we have seen, may be taken at 14¾ pounds to the square inch; but wind, which is but atmosphere in motion, acts with a force dependent upon its velocity. When moving at thirty-five miles an hour, it exerts a force of six pounds on each square foot of an obstructing surface; at fifty miles an hour (the speed of an ordinary tempest) a force of 12⅓ pounds; and at one hundred miles the (hurricane's rate) 49⅓ pounds.

The weight of our atmosphere being found equal to that of a column of thirty inches of mercury, it follows that, at the hurricane velocity and pressure of 49⅓ pounds per square foot, the exhaustion or rarification indicated by the mercurial guage would only be about two-thirds of an inch; *and this result, we find, accords with the actual observations upon hurricanes.*

With these and other established data before us, we can approximate at least the degree of exhaustion of the tube necessary to cause a current of air to pass through it with twice or three times the velocity of a hurricane.

In addition to the model to which your committee has referred, Mr. Richardson has tested the working and capacity of his telegraph, by laying down a tube one mile long, of three inches clear diameter, and following the elevations and depressions of an ordinary ungraded field; and he has produced numerous certificates, from highly scientific and reliable sources, of its accurate performance and entire success. The certificates all say that the mile was traversed by the piston or plunger, to which was attached a weight of several pounds, in less than "*a minute;*" but it is understood that the time was much less than this, and that this expression was used as a maximum, and to preserve uniformity in the certificates.

Your committee do not deem it necessary to present, in this report, all the details which have determined its judgment; but the relation which the atmospheric pressure, of which it has spoken, bears to the weight to be moved and its velocity, is too important to pass entirely unnoticed.

It is found, upon level railroads, that eight pounds pressure moves a ton in weight.

Now, the piston, 24 inches in diameter, would expose 452 square inches of surface to be operated upon, by an atmospheric pressure of 14¾ pounds to the inch, equal to 6,667 pounds. And hence the moving power of the atmosphere upon the weight expressed in tons, would be as 8 to 6,667, or a moving force of 833 tons, on the supposition that friction would not interfere.

Many practical difficulties and objections will doubtless develope themselves whenever the "Atmospheric Telegraph" shall be established upon a large scale; such, for example, as wastage of power in the air-pumps, the wear and tear in the mail-bags, pistons, and interior suface of the tubes, by high velocities, the admission of air in the tubes, the effect of climate upon them, the expense of establishing them, &c., &c.; but your committee, after weighing these and other objections which have been suggested, deem it proper to recommend an appropriation, small in its comparison with the national interests involved in its success, to test its utility and capacity.

It is deemed expedient that the experiment should be made for a short distance upon an established mail route, in order that, if successful, it might constitute a part of a more extended work; and your committee has been disposed to prescribe a direct line between Washington and Baltimore. It has, therefore, concluded to leave the question to the Postmaster General, and report a bill accordingly.

It is impossible to foreshadow the multiplied and incalculable advantages which will result from such a mail carrier as Mr. Richardson's proposition discloses.

All the business pursuits and habits of our country were radically changed by the introduction of railroads.

Not only do we find men, whose ancestors for generations never travelled beyond their native counties, passing from State to State in the daily transaction of their affairs, identifying themselves with the various sections of the Union, and bringing it together by the multiplying bonds of mutual confidence, pursuits and self interests, but under the railroads' fruitful developing and creative influence, we find the pathless forest of the west, the rich river lands of the south, and the cold granite hills of the north, yielding vast treasures, hitherto locked in their unyielding grasp, to a free, happy and prosperous people. We find new States springing into existence at the call of the steam whistle; and in the train of the resistless iron horse, the people and products, of distant, widely separated lands, mingle together in the commercial marts of our country.

The hand of an all-wise Providence, guiding and controlling the destinies of men and nations by his inscrutable laws, enabled us to devise, in a happy moment, those iron links of brotherhood, the physical bonds, without which our widely extended and extending republic could hardly continue its beautiful, happy and glorious unity.

But railroads proved too slow for our progress; and the magnetic telegraph came to our aid in the abolition of time and space, for which the age seems to be struggling.

It was but yesterday, as it were, that the genius of Morse gave us the telegraph, and enabled us to write with a long pen from one city of the Union to another; and though it was received at first with doubt, nay, with derision, it is now one of the great facts, as well as one of the necessities of the age.

At this moment, when every man seems to be a special competitor against time; when Mammon is in the ascendant, and the dictum, that "time is money," impresses itself upon all the affairs of life; when hours, minutes and seconds, are pounds, shillings and pence, Mr. Richardson's proposition comes upon us to supply a link which is confessedly wanting.

It was but yesterday, as it were, that a speed beyond fifteen miles per hour upon railways, or beyond seven miles by ocean steam navigation, and the transmission of intelligence by means of electric currents, beyond a single mile, were denounced by philosophers, and proved by mathematicians, to be the chimeras of the dreamer; and yet our Union is reticulated and clamped together by railways, whose moral power transcends that of laws and constitutions, and upon which thousands are hourly demonstrating the philosopher's error; and by magnetic wires, wherein truth outstrips not only the mathematician's calculations, but even the lightning, and beats time itself.

The mail between Washington and New-York is now carried upon railroads in twelve hours. If your committee do not greatly err, the same mails may be carried between these cities in two hours, by the proposed atmospheric telegraph; and the expenditure now necessary for the transmission of one set of mails, would enable the Post Office Department to send six sets of mails every twelve hours.

The impulse which such a frequent, rapid and certain delivery of the mails between distant points would give to all the business of the country, is incalculable; operating with as much safety and unerring certainty in night as in day-light; unaffected by changes of seasons or weather—and exempt from liability to those mischances, accidents and delays which are daily retarding the delivery of the mails throughout the country, the atmospheric telegraph seems destined to become the exclusive mail carrier of the age.

ART. IV.—STEINHEIL ON MORSE'S TELEGRAPH.

CONDUCTIVE PROPERTY OF THE EARTH—VALUABLE DISCOVERIES IN EARTH CIRCUITS—EXTENSION OF MORSE'S TELEGRAPH IN EUROPE.

Letter from Prof. Steinheil of Munich.

MUNICH, *the 9th July*, 1854.

ESTEEMED SIR:—In answer to your favor of the 23d ult., and with reference to its contents, I send you herewith enclosed my Academical Discourse of 1838,* in which I have published my experiments on galvanic telegraphy made in 1837. In Schumacher's Austrian Annals of 1839, published in Stuttgard and Tubingen, you will find further notice of these original experiments, the principal results of which are, that I established the principles upon which an effective telegraphy must be based, and which even now, after 16 years, form the foundation of our present system. That on this occasion I found the conductive property of the earth for galvanic currents, by means of which the construction of galvanic telegraphs has been effected with one single conductor, and freed from all the inconveniences of double and multiplied conductors, such as resistance, contact, expense, &c.; that I demonstrated under what circumstances and modifications telegraphing may be effected between two telegraph stations, even without any metallic connection at all. Further records, with reference to this period, and my respective labors, you will find in Dr. Schellen's "Electric Telegraph, Brunswick, 1850, 8vo.;" in the Abbé Moigno's writings on Telegraphy in the Augsburg Gazette, &c.

Our government did not encourage, at that time, this promising enterprise any further, and, as pecuniary means were wanting, the experiments were compelled to be discontinued, until it was perceived from the newspapers what rapid progress, and what development, galvanic telegraphy had made in North America. It was not till 1849, when the net of railroads had reached so great an extension in Bavaria, that steps were taken to establish telegraphic lines. In order to ascertain with exactness what had already been done in this respect in Germany, I was commissioned by the Government to travel for this purpose through Germany, and I enclose my printed report, "*Description and Comparison of the Galvanic Telegraphs of Germany, April*, 1849."

In this document is also comprised the description of a railroad telegraph which I caused to be established, some years

* This discourse was translated and published in Sturgeon's Annals of Electricity, in March, 1839.

previous, between Munich and Augsburg. (See page 49, &c.) In the same year, 1849, I received from the Austrian Government an appointment in the department of the Ministry of Commerce, for the purpose of organizing, on a permanent system, the Austrian telegraphy, and was placed at the head of it. In a short time, under the powerful patronage of the intelligent minister Bruck, over 1,500 German miles of telegraphic connections had been constructed. Sixty stations had been furnished. *A treaty with Germany for a common system* (the Germano-Austrian Telegraph Union,) was entered into and ratified, and the Telegraph was made accessible to the public for its use, in all of which Austria constantly took the lead. Thus, the purpose which I had proposed to myself when I accepted the Directorship of Austrian telegraphy was soon attained, and I was enabled to accept a subsequent call from the Swiss Government in 1852, to organize the telegraphic net-work of that country on the same system. In six months, two hundred miles of connections were constructed; seventy-three stations established; the employees of the Post Office trained for telegraph service, by assembling them together and addressing them a course of lectures; the junction arranged with the Germano-Austrian Telegraph Union, and the lines delivered for public use. The whole enterprise, construction, public regulation, apparatus, school, &c., was accomplished with 400,000 francs. The conductors, however, are only made of iron wire, constructed after your plan in North America, for there they have mercantile ideas, and know how, with small outlay, to realize large profits.

The instructions for the telegraph operators in Switzerland I also inclose.

Since my mission to Switzerland, I have been called to Bavaria, and placed in a very pleasant and independent position, which enables me to realize my long cherished scientific wishes; and in accepting it, it is on the condition that I shall not be obliged to devote any more thought to telegraphy, to which problem I feel that I have already devoted sufficient time, since other subjects solicit my investigations.

In the inclosed *Instructions*, you will find the whole system of our Germano-Austrian Telegraphy developed in its most minute details. You will notice, at this period, the "Translators," which I devised in Vienna in 1850, and which were adopted by the Germano-Austrian Telegraph Union, in 1851; also the plan of loop-shaped construction of the telegraphic net-work, by means of which, freedom from interruptions increases in the ratio of the extension of the net-work. You will note also the introduction of very small chain batteries, the theory of which is given in pages 16–19 of the "Instructions;" and lastly, the teaching of the technical parts, by means of which the service is regulated, and the telegraphed net-work rendered accessible at any time and at any point in all its parts, (sectional circuits,) and at the same moment.

In said Instructions, you will find towards the close, information for acquiring the telegraphic art, which I introduced originally in Vienna, and which proved very practical, about 500 telegraphists having been trained by it.

In this way I have been able effectually to labor for the adoption of Morse's system throughout all Europe; and that I have thereby extended his well-earned fame, has been to me the source of peculiar pleasure, which I beg you to testify to Professor Morse in proper time, together with my most friendly respects.

With perfect esteem,
Yours respectfully,
DR. STEINHEIL,
Royal Ministerial Counsellor and Member of the Academy, &c.

TAL. P. SHAFFNER, Esq.,

ART. V.—FIRE ALARM TELEGRAPH.

MORSE TELEGRAPH APPLIED TO FIRE ALARMS, BY CHANNING AND FARMER—SUCCESSFULLY ESTABLISHED IN BOSTON—GREAT BENEFIT TO SOCIETY—ITS MODE OF OPERATION DESCRIBED.

WE have intended, for some time past, to describe this new and wonderful achievement in art. We now give a few facts for the consideration of the reader, and in a future number we hope to be able to give a full and perfect description of the system, so successfully put in operation by Messrs. Dr. Channing and Farmer, in the City of Boston.

A description of the system, as given in the present number, will show that the Morse Telegraph is ingeniously applied to mechanics, and the alarm system made complete. We do not fully understand in what consists the patent parts of the Fire Alarm Telegraph, as it is mostly included in the original Morse patent; but, we suppose it is in the ingenious arrangement for giving the signal, and the compiling of the different branches of mechanics to produce the desired result according to the described mode. We do not deem it material to discuss the question as to how much of the system is embraced in the

Morse patents, nor how much to Messrs. Channing and Farmer. It is enough for us to know, that it abounds in usefulness. No city in the world can do as well without as with it. It saves labor, time, and money. It promotes security of life and property. It lessens insurance and benefits the rich and poor. It prevents disturbances of society by riots, and diffuses a spirit of peace and safety throughout the entire people. Everything can be said in its favor, and nothing against it. Dr. Channing and Mr. Farmer have done much for the age, in devising the system and presenting it in a useful and practicable form.

We give some notices of the system from memorials and circulars upon the subject, which will be all that we can present to the reader's consideration at present.

"This system differs essentially from all other Fire and Police Telegraphs, and possesses advantages proved by constant experience for over two years, which place it beyond comparison with any other in point of rapidity, variety, and extent of communication. In a scientific point of view, its great and peculiar success is in its power of *acting* at great distances, itself producing effects which other systems have only sought to direct by instructions to agents. Practically, it is the only existing means of communicating a fact from as many points as may be desired to a Central Station; of giving instant alarm from thence by ringing bells in different places at the same moment, by one person; and of sending any instructions or making any inquiries between the Central Stations and the remote points.

The only telegraph of this description is established in Boston, and has been visited and examined with admiration by great numbers of practical and scientific men, both of this country and Europe, and recently has been examined by Committees from the City Governments both of New-York and Philadelphia. * * * * * *

The first peculiarity is, that it provides a sufficient number of Signal Stations to place one of them in the immediate neighborhood of every house in the city. These Signal Stations require no attendance, but are so arranged that any authorized person, by turning a small crank, may communicate an alarm from that neighborhood to the Central Office.

At these stations also, while the alarm is being rung on the bells, any one, by listening to certain intimations from the Central Office, may learn the precise neighborhood in which the fire or other trouble may have arisen.

These stations are not merely used in cases of fire or riot, but messages of any length, upon any subject, may be sent or received through them by any one acquainted with the telegraph key. They are constantly used as means of communication between the Central Office and remote points on occasions of municipal business.

Another peculiarity of the system is, that when an alarm has been notified to the Central Office from any one of the Signal Stations, it may instantly, by the pressure of a single finger, be rung upon any or all the alarm bells in the city, and this without the aid of watchmen or bell-ringers. There is no limit to the force of the blow that may be given to the bells, and an alarm may at the same instant be rung by one person in the Central Office from any desired number of bells, in any degree of loudness that they can produce.

This telegraph possesses one advantage which is peculiar to itself, in that it prevents any injury arising from the breaking of a wire, by having duplicate circuits between the Signal Stations and the Central Office, and between that office and the bells, so that if one part should be destroyed by storms or otherwise, the communication would remain uninjured.

Under this system, the moment a fire is discovered, the alarm is carried to the neighboring Signal Station, through which, by turning a crank, the fact of a fire and its locality is instantaneously communicated to the Central Office. When received there, the officer in attendance, by a motion of his hand, immediately tolls the district number on all the fire bells, and at the same time *taps* with the other hand to every Signal Station the number of the particular station where the alarm originated. Thus, in less than a minute from giving the alarm through the Signal Station, it may be rung on all the alarm bells in the city; and the firemen, by listening at the Signal Stations, may learn and be able to head their engines for the precise locality. All this is done by means of only one person at the Central Office.

To contrast this with the present condition of our city:* We have only eight points through which an alarm of fire can be communicated, and when once received, it must be entrusted at each station to bell-ringers, who must separately ring it from each bell-tower. Before a general alarm can be given, an often fatal delay must elapse, and the precise locality in a district can in no way be indicated. The difficulty of finding a fire, even after the district alarm has been rung, is too well known to require specific instances.

It would be absurd to attribute all the difference of loss by fires in the two cities to the possession of the Fire Alarm Telegraph by one, and not by the other. But after every consid-

* New-York City.

eration of difference of size and police organization, there remains no doubt that the small loss which Boston has sustained by fire during this last year, is mainly due to this valuable invention. According to the last Report of the Fire Department of that city, extending from September 1st, 1853, to September 1st, 1854, the whole amount of losses by fire has been ascertained to have been but $150,772. The losses in *our* city,* during the same period, must be estimated by millions."

We copy the following from a circular upon the American Fire Alarm Telegraph, which gives a description of the system ample for comprehension:

"Its object is to give an *instantaneous*, *universal*, and *definite* alarm in case of fire. This object, which has been hardly proposed by any other system, is fully accomplished by the Fire Alarm Telegraph. It presents, therefore, a claim to the attention of insurers, of property holders, and of municipal governments throughout the United States.

The Fire Alarm Telegraph consists essentially of two parts: First, *the Signal apparatus and wires*, by which the intelligence of a fire is communicated from any part of a city to the Central Station. Second, *the Alarm apparatus and wires*, by which the alarm bells in different parts of a city are struck from the Central Station by the touch of a single finger, without the intervention of hands, watchmen, or bell-ringers at the belfries or bell towers.

For example: there are in the City of Boston forty-three Signal Stations, or "*Signal Boxes*," distributed over the city, from any one of which the intelligence of a fire in the neighborhood can be communicated instantly to the Central Station by the simple turning of a crank. The operator at the Central Station—the sole watchman of the system—is then able, by simply depressing a key with his finger, to strike the District number simultaneously on twenty-two church, school-house, and engine bells in every quarter of the city; and not only this, but also to tap back on all the Signal Boxes the number of the Signal Box in the District from which the alarm proceeded. The engines are thus directed not only to the District, but actually to the very box originating the alarm. The time between the first discovery of a fire by the inmates of a dwelling, and its definite announcement from all the steeples and by all the Signal Boxes, is thus, on an average, not more than three minutes in the City of Boston at the present time, and is often within a single minute.

* New-York City.

The best example of a system of District Alarm, in which the bells are rung by hand, is probably that in the City of New-York. There the eight bell-towers are provided with watchmen, and are connected with telegraph wires, so that when one watchman discovers a fire he can notify it to all the others. There are thus only *eight* stations in the City of New-York from which an alarm can originate, whereas the Fire Alarm Telegraph provides forty-three Signal Boxes for the comparatively small territory of Boston, from any one of which the alarm is communicated instantly. The alarm system in New-York also requires eight watchmen constantly on the alert, who must each ring his bell according to the District number. The Fire Alarm Telegraph requires only one watchman at the Centre, who strikes any number of bells by the touch of a single finger. Moreover, in New-York, after the alarm is actually given, the engines are only directed to the District, which may be a mile or two square, and in which they may run about for half an hour without finding the fire. The Fire Alarm Telegraph, on the other hand, directs the engines to the District by the bells, and to the Signal Box, in the District from which the alarm came, by tapping its number, from time to time, on all the Signal Boxes in the city. The engines, therefore, may always be headed from the start to within at least two hundred and fifty yards of the fire. It may be added, that the adaptation of the Alarm apparatus to the eight bell-towers in New-York, and similar large bells in other cities, would furnish a much more simple and beautiful application of the Fire Alarm Telegraph than that in Boston, where twenty-two comparatively small bells are struck simultaneously.

The reports of the Fire Departments of New-York and Boston illustrate strikingly the practical operation of the two systems. In Boston, during the last year, there were a large number of *small* fires, many of which would have been destructive, if the first ten minutes had not been saved to the firemen by the Fire Alarm Telegraph. In 1853 there were 168 fires in Boston, with a loss of $268,621; while in New-York there were 335 fires, with a loss of nearly $5,000,000—that is, a *nine* times greater loss for each fire in New-York than in Boston. While the existence of immense warehouses, hotels, &c., in our cities, makes it impossible to guarantee them absolutely from large fires, it is all the more important to provide a system which shall give an immediate and certain alarm, when the only hope in the case of such conflagrations is confessedly in arresting them at the commencement.

A more detailed description will now be given of the American Fire Alarm Telegraph, in its various parts, and of the safeguards by which its permanence, and the regularity and certainty of its operations are insured.

The wires connected with the signalizing and alarm apparatus, forming the "Signal Circuits" and "Alarm Circuits," are carried over the houses, on the highest and most isolated of which they are supported by insulators held in brackets. The wires themselves are of the best Swedish iron, No. 9, and are to be erected in the most substantial manner. There are always duplicate wires, following different routes, between every two Stations, so that if one is broken from any cause, the second remains good until the first can be repaired. The ground is not used as any part of the circuit, so that the falling of a wire produces no false connection, and double insulation also results. These precautions are found to preserve the circuits practically intact. The wires, properly erected in a city, are very rarely interrupted from any cause; and the probability against the interruption of the two corresponding wires, between neighboring stations, at the same time, amounts almost to an impossibility. But, besides this, the Central Station is furnished with testing apparatus, by which the integrity of each circuit is constantly ascertained.

For convenience and security, the Signal Boxes and the Alarm Bells, in any great city, are not strung respectively upon one great Signal Circuit, and one great Alarm Circuit, but the number of circuits of each class is multiplied, all of them radiating from the Central Station, like the petals of a flower. Thus, Signal Circuits may traverse different parts of the city. To work on the bells, turn to one or more finger keys, which communicate back with the Signal Boxes, and tap on these occasionally *five* times; a little magnet and armature in each Signal Box gives a sharp click for every tap, and the firemen, who run to the nearest box and listen, know that the alarm comes from District *three*, Station *five*, and their pocket map tells them exactly where this station is, and the nearest route to it.

The machinery in the bell towers consists of a striking machine, carried by the water in the city pipes or by weight, and let off by telegraph at each blow. The blows are of any power required, there being no practical limit in this respect.

The advantages of the American Fire Alarm Telegraph may be recapitulated as follows:—

1. It furnishes an indefinite number of Signal Stations, scattered broadcast over a city, from which an alarm may be com-

municated. No time is lost, therefore, between the fire itself and the telegraph.

2. The operator, or the watchman at the Centre, receives the intelligence immediately, and forthwith strikes the District number on one or all the Alarm bells by telegraphic agency.

3. The number of the *Station*, from which the alarm proceeded, as well as the District, is telegraphed to the Fire Department, so that the engines are headed from the first, to almost the exact locality of the fire.

4. The arrangements of the system protect it from interruption, either by accident or design, and it works with equal certainty and promptitude in sunshine or storm, by day or by night.

5. It prevents almost entirely the occurrence of false alarms, which entail a great expense on a city, on account of the wear and tear of engines.*

6. It provides a system of organization, by which the whole Fire Department of a city is brought into communication with a single Centre, receiving directions from this Centre, either by the bells or Signal Boxes, and communicating back to it by a finger key, which, in addition to the crank, is placed in every Signal Box.

7. Telegraphic conversation may be held between any of the Signal Boxes and the Central Station, which is generally placed at the City Hall, for police purposes.

*The following facts are from official documents: The false alarms in New-York, in 1848, were 98; in 1847, 125; in 1849, 162; in 1853, 239. In 1846, '7 and '8, the false alarms were one-fourth of the alarms given, and in 1849, they were more than one-third.

In Boston, the average number of false alarms annually, for six years previous to 1850, was 50—about one-seventh the whole number of alarms given. Under the present system, in 1852, the false alarms were only 7, and, in 1853, only 10—an average, for those two years, of only one-twentieth of the alarms for fire. Both in New-York and Boston the expense of a false alarm is said to be about $100. The present number of annual false alarms costs the City of Boston $700 or $800, while in New-York the false alarms for 1849 cost the city more than $16,000, and at the same rate for 1850, over $23,000.

EPIGRAM.—A correspondent of the National Intelligencer has furnished to the editor of that print the following translation of an "epigrama," from the Latin, which recently appeared in the Southern Chronicle, viz:

On Morse, the Ceraunographer.—Nature Complaining of her Sons' Spoliations.

What daring men, cries Nature, will ye spare?
See Franklin force the clouds their bolts to bury;
The Sun resigns his pencil to Daguerre,
While Morse the lightning makes his Secretary.

ART. VI.—MAGNETO-ELECTRIC BATTERY.

TELEGRAPH BATTERIES USED IN AMERICA AND EUROPE—SUPERIORITY OF MAGNETO-ELECTRICITY OVER GALVANIC FOR TELEGRAPHIC PURPOSES, CLAIMED—ITS ECONOMY AND PRACTICABILITY—HENLEY'S IMPROVEMENT—TELEGRAPHS SUCCESSFULLY WORKED BY MAGNETO-CURRENTS.

IN AMERICA, nearly all the telegraph lines have been worked, from their commencement, by the Grove galvanic battery. It has proved to be the most successful over all others, and, with the Morse and House systems, it seems likely to be the most favored. Efforts have been made to devise another and a better battery—one that will not be so expensive, and that will require less labor in keeping it in order. Many improvements have been made in its construction and application. For the present, we will only mention one of the most important, which was devised by Mr. Anson Stager, while Manager of the Morse lines at Cincinnati, Ohio. He applied a battery commonly used for one line, to four others, and, in this manner, successfully worked five lines, each running in independent directions, and of unequal lengths. The battery had one ground or earth-wire. This was a great achievement, and one that will prove of material importance, if properly considered.

A modification of the Smee battery has been arranged by Mr. Charles T. Chester, and it claims particular attention on account of its cheapness and economy of labor in taking care of it. The Daniel battery has also been, to a limited extent, used by some lines. A few lines have worked the copper and blue vitriol battery on the local circuits. A few years ago, the sand battery was used on the Bain line, but was not wholly successful. The Magneto-electricity has never been satisfactorily produced in America to work a telegraphic line practically. Mr. Calvin Carpenter, of Providence, Rhode Island, has claimed to have invented a new and novel machine which can effect the desired end. To what extent, however, Mr. Carpenter has succeeded, we are not informed.

In England, the sand battery is in general use. The Gutta Percha Works of Mr. Statham has produced gutta percha cells, which renders the sand battery the most popular and serviceable. The telegraphs of England are mostly the needle system, and the quantity required is very moderate. On the Hamburg and Copenhagen line the sand battery has been used very satisfactorily. This line works the Morse system. We saw the sand battery used in France, Belgium, Denmark, Prussia, Austria, and Russia. We also saw many of the Daniel battery in use; but its construction was modified. The magneto-electricity, as proposed by Mr. Henley, is in service in England, Ireland and Scotland only. The Magnetic Company, or the English and Irish line, employs it, and with very great satisfaction. Mr. Henley is an expert of rare merit, and his ingenuity in constructing practical telegraph apparata entitle him to the most favorable consideration of the telegraph community. We give below his views as to the mode of generating an electric current suitable for telegraph purposes, which will give an idea of the true merits of the magneto-power. We saw the system very satisfactorily worked in England, and we think its claims are not overrated. How it would answer the American system, we are unable to say, nor can we express an opinion without a thorough trial. We give Mr. Henley's remarks, without further comment, at present.

"The Magneto-Electro Telegraph presents many very important advantages over all telegraphs hitherto invented. It is extremely compact and portable.

The instrument is worked by magneto-electricity, and from the simplicity of construction, is always ready for immediate use without the least preparation or trouble, and can therefore not only be used as a stationary telegraph, *but from its portability is peculiarly adapted for the use of guards on all lines of railways, who could, in the event of accident or any emergency, immediately apply the instrument to the existing telegraph- wires on any part of the line.* It is free from any expense whatever, after the first outlay, and not only dispensing with the cost and inconvenience of chemicals, repairs, and superintendence involved in the use of the voltaic batteries, but actually substituting for the present uncertain system of transmission one absolutely unerring, and that to an extent far beyond the power of any other telegraph, which has been proved by actual experiments on existing lines.

A very severe test of the capability of a telegraph is a damp state of the atmosphere, especially when the earth is used (as it always is now) as part of the circuit. Every supporting post, when its insulators become covered with moisture, conveys a great part of the current to the earth; but from experiments tried on the South Devon Railway, (known to be the worst insulated line in the kingdom,) and in the most unfavorable weather, the magneto-electric current from this machine was found to pass the whole distance of the line, and also through a great length of wire at each station, without any loss whatever;

this arises not from the electricity being of a different kind, but from its quantity and intensity being so adjusted that the wet posts should offer more resistance than the whole length of the metallic wire. The magneto-electric apparatus (18 inches long by 4 inches wide) will transmit a current much farther than twelve 24-cell batteries, occupying a space of 19½ square feet.

Another advantage is, that the needles never move sluggishly when worked from a great distance; they move as rapidly and distinctly through 500 miles as one mile; and the clockwork for alarums may be entirely dispensed with, quite sufficient sound being obtained to call attention from an adjoining room by the mere vibration of the needle between two bells, when moved by a machine many hundred miles off, and to persons acquainted with the trouble and annoyance attending the ordinary telegraph alarums, this will be considered no small advantage.

It is a well-known fact that the ordinary needle telegraph is entirely deranged by lightning; the polarity of the needles becoming displaced or destroyed, notwithstanding the protection of lightning conductors. With the Magneto-Electric Telegraph this can never occur; the only effect of the lightning is to deflect the needles as in the ordinary working.

One of the peculiar features of this invention is the use of electro-magnets, having four poles, formed by two segments of a circle, with a magnetic bar freely suspended within them; thereby doing away with the retarding force of springs or other contrivances generally resorted to, to cause the needle to point to any particular direction; and, by placing the needles on vertical axes with a horizontal dial, a very feeble current is quite sufficient to move them.

From the absence of springs and adjustments, this instrument is peculiarly adapted for working a one wire letter telegraph, or a recording telegraph, by which the message is marked or dotted on paper, and the dials for which can be substituted for the present.

The magneto-telegraph instrument is not affected by any variations in the state of the weather.

The permanent magnets are entirely protected from the loss of power by a peculiar and simple arrangement of the armatures, and the apparatus is free from the complications of the ordinary telegraphs for reversing and stopping the current, there being one unbroken circuit throughout.

The importance of being able to communicate *several thousand miles* with an instrument so portable and so simple, can readily be understood, when it is considered that the telegraph instruments at present in use, require for a distance of only three hundred miles the aid of several voltaic batteries, and in damp weather it is difficult with any number of cells to obtain a perfect communication.

From the advantages offered by this invention a considerable saving is effected in the cost of the wires, much smaller ones than those now in use being sufficient, and the additional wire required in other instruments for ringing the alarm bell being entirely dispensed with, as the wires conveying the messages serve for both purposes.

From the portability, economy, and impossibility of derangement of this instrument, which never requires any preparation or renewal, telegraphic messages will now be brought within the reach of more limited enterprise, such as dockyards, detached factories, mines, hospitals, and all other establishments and institutions, *both public and private*, as well as of individuals who, from the cost of the present system, are entirely precluded from the benefits of this rapid means of intercommunication; and railway companies having telegraphs already established, would find in the adoption of this instrument a considerable saving.

The magneto-telegraph instrument has been subjected to the severest trials, in all weathers, on existing lines of railway, in this country and on the Continent, and has received the unqualified approbation of many of the leading scientific men in Europe (including engineers of the highest repute) who have pronounced it to be the most simple, powerful, and economical instrument for telegraphic purposes yet invented. To illustrate its extreme simplicity, it is only necessary to state (*its action being entirely mechanical and free from all chemical agency*) that a boy twelve years of age is perfectly competent to superintend and effectually work the instrument."

We take the following notices of trials, in regard to Henley's magneto-battery. The first was in England, and the second was in France.

1st.—"Some interesting experiments have been made with Henley's Magneto-Electric Telegraph, from one side of the Serpentine to the other, near to the Kensington Garden's bridge, under the inspection of the following gentlemen:—Jury of Class 10—Sir John Herschel, Mr. Glaisher, Baron Seguir, Professor Schubarlt, Professor Potter, Professor Quetelet, Mr. Dobson, and another gentleman, both from Mr. Cubitt, the Engineer, Great George-street, Westminster.

"*First Experiment.*—Two lengths of gutta percha covered

wire were taken across and immersed in the water, and connected to the instruments; each length of wire had a portion of the gutta percha cut away from the wire; the wire well scraped to a bright surface, and allowed to remain under the water. The instruments worked well through the attractive power of the water.

"*Second.*—The water not having taken the expected effect of deviating the course of electricity, one length of wire was cut in two, and a long length of uncovered bright wire was inserted between, and again let fall into the water. The instruments again worked well.

"*Third.*—The wire was again cut asunder, and each end let fall into the water, a distance apart from each other, whereby the current had to be made complete by the water intervening between the ends of the wire; even through this defective insulation the instrument worked to the greatest satisfaction.

"*Fourth.*—A greater quantity of the gutta percha insulation was taken from off the wire which had not been cut, and the instruments continuing to work well, a correspondence was then commenced, and kept up for half an hour, from one side of the Serpentine to the other, between Mr. Dobson and the gentleman who was with him.

"Mr. Henley was highly complimented after the completion of the experiments, which occupied five hours.

2d.—"Two most successful and satisfactory trials have be en made with Henley's magnetic telegraph instruments, one on the wires of the Paris and Rouen Railway, at the office of the French Minister of the interior, in the presence of the Director in Chief of Telegraphs, and the other on the wires of the railway from Paris to Valenciennes. At the Paris end the Director in Chief of Telegraphs for the French Government superintended; while at Valenciennes were present the Belgian Minister of Public Works, Count Shekendorff; the Prussian Ambassador, M. Mosay; the Chief Engineer of the Belgian Railways, Baron Devaux; M. Quetelet, and M. Cabry, Chief Engineer of the Belgian Government. The distance is 180 miles, being the longest telegraphic line in France. After a most satisfactory series of trials on the single distance, first with the full power, and afterwards with one-twentieth of the power, the wires were connected so as to treble the total length of wire, making 540 miles to and from Paris and back—the magnetic message being communicated through the first wire, back by the second, through the third, and back again by the earth; and, contrary to what was antcipated, it worked through an enormous resistance as distinctly and rapidly as when only made to traverse the 180 miles with full power. The ordinary telegraph with battery power used by the French Government was then put in requisition; but not the slightest effect was produced. The government officers and others inspected the working operations from 10 to 3 o'clock, and expressed themselves perfectly satisfied with the success of the trial."

ART. VII.—MAGNETO-ELECTRICITY ON SUBTERRANEAN TELEGRAPHS.

SCIENCE OF MAGNETO-ELECTRICITY—APPLICATION TO SUBTERRANEAN TELEGRAPHS—SPEED OF MAGNETO AND FRICTIONAL ELECTRICITY—PRACTICABILITY OF SUBTERRANEAN TELEGRAPHS.

BY EDWARD B. BRIGHT, ESQ.

Secretary of the English and Irish Magnetic Telegraph Company, Liverpool, England.

[Substance of an address delivered before the British Association of Science and Art.]

In the paper now submitted to the Association, I propose to explain some peculiar features connected with the development and use of magneto-electricity and underground wires in long circuits for telegraphic purposes.

Magneto-electricity consists in the development of a species of the electric fluid discovered by Dr. Faraday, and resulting from the induction of polarity in a coil of insulated wire, when placed in propinquity to a magnet; the positive current manifesting its presence at one end of the coil, and the negative at the other, according to the position of the coil with reference to the poles of the magnet.

For practical purposes it is found that the greatest demonstration of magnetic power takes place when the coil of insulated wire is wound upon a soft iron rod, and applied to the poles of a permanent steel magnet; the process of excitation being exactly reversed, as compared with the polarization of an electro-magnet by galvanic power; for whereas, in the latter, the soft-iron centre of the coil is polarized by a current of electricity passing through the convolution of insulated wire wound around it, in magnetic induction the flow of electricity is occasioned in the helix of wire, by the temporarily developed polar state of the soft iron coil, when acting as the keeper to a magnet. In the use of galvanic electricity, the voltaic battery generates a current, which, on passing through the wire of the coil, communicates polarity to the iron centre; and in magnetic electricity, the core being polarized by near approach to a magnet, occasions the flow of electricity in the wire surrounding it. In early experiments, with a view to the application of this electricity to the telegraph, much difficulty was found from the apparently evanescent nature of the effect produced by its excitation; and although various attempts were made to introduce it into the commercial system of this country and America, none proved successful, until the invention of the system carried out in the operations of the Magnetic Telegraph Company.

The apparatus, founded on the magnetic principle, will therefore, I believe, interest all who have watched the extension of the telegraph in this country, differing as it does from the principle adopted by other companies, both at home and abroad, who all make use of the voltaic battery, generating their electric current by the decomposition of water and oxidation of metals, when subjected to the chemical action and excitation of acids or salts. I have already referred to the manner in which a magnetic current is produced in a coil when in proximity to a permanent magnet; and in continuance, should mention that the direction of the current is changed at will, by simply reversing the position of the coil, and its iron core, as regards the poles of the magnet, (as shown by experiment on apparatus,) an alteration of polarity resulting with each movement. Such changes in position are effected as shown by an upward or downward movement of a finger key, fixed upon an axis, to which the coil is attached; the soft iron centre of the coil is so adjusted as to move freely before the poles of the magnet without actual contact, and under the manipulation of an experienced clerk, as many as 400 to 500 changes of polarity may be induced in the coil in a minute. The electricity, when generated, is passed into the wire extending from the station by simple connections, and actuates the indicating apparatus fixed in the various instruments at a distance to which it communicates the magnetic sensation.

I have alluded to the evanescent effect of the magnetic fluid upon ordinary coils, and will now explain how, so to speak, this current is fixed in the present apparatus:—The electro-magnetic coils in the indicating portion of the machine have soft iron horns continuing their poles, which, by their elongation and position as regards one another, imbibe and fix a certain amount of polarity, termed residual magnetism, which remains in the iron after each change of the current passing through the helix. A small magnetic needle, on an axis, is so placed within the influence of the horns, that upon any alteration in their polarity, a corresponding movement of the magnetic needle takes place, forming the signal to be communicated, or actuating an alarm.

It was considered at first that the magnetic system was capable of but limited application, owing to the supposed quantitative nature of the current generated not possessing sufficient intensity to pass through long circuits; but experience does not show such to be the case: for with the improved apparatus now employed by the company, messages can be passed between Liverpool and Dublin direct, a distance of about 420 miles, the line of communication extending via. Portpatrick and Belfast, and signals can be interchanged when necessary between London and Dublin, a distance by the wire of 660 miles, without any break of circuit, or renewal of the magnetic circuit. The invariability of the current generated is a principal feature of the apparatus; and it is found that with careful treatment, no diminution of the current need take place. Generating magnets have been in use for three years, without change in the strength or polarity of the magnets employed—the magnetism induced being in consequence similar throughout—while, in an equal period, a dozen sets of voltaic batteries would have been worn out.

As most interesting phenomena have resulted from the application of the subterranean system of communication where long circuits are made use of, a cursory notice of the conditions involved in the production of the phenomena will not be out of place.

The Magnetic Company, in 1851, applied underground gutta percha covered wires for the purpose of communication between various towns. The gutta percha encasing the wires being protected from injury by various appliances, and buried two feet below the surface of high roads.

On extending this system throughout the United Kingdom, where circuits of several hundred miles were brought into operation, it was found upon communicating a current to such wires, that after the withdrawal of the excitation, (whether galvanic or magnetic electricity was employed,) an electrical recoil immediately took place at the end of the wire to which the current had been previously communicated. This recoil was apparently analogous in all respects to the discharge of electricity from a Leyden jar, except that the current flowing from the wire partook of a quantitative rather than an intense nature; thus, however, finishing the remaining link of comparison, and establishing the identity as regards primary characteristics of all species of electricity.

Although this phenomena, as analyzed by Dr. Faraday, has proved highly gratifying in a philosophical point of view, its existence interfered materially with the working of all the previous existing telegraphic apparatus, not having been at all contemplated or provided for; and up to this time, I am not aware that, as regards the galvanic system, any adequate remedy has been applied. The nature of the interference will be easily understood, when I mention that, with a letter printing telegraph, the surplus current has the tendency to carry the machinery on further, and to make other letters than those intended. With the chemical and other recording telegraphs, the surplus flow of electricity will continue nearly a minute, entirely confounding the marks representing one letter with the next. And lastly, with Cooke and Wheatstone's and other needle telegraphs, a beat more is made by the back current than intended with every letter formed.

In the magnetic telegraph, however, this current has been turned to account by the engineer of the company and myself, in an arrangement of the apparatus, by which the recoil current serves to keep the indicating needle at zero; consequently, under such conditions the effect of the recoil is neutralized, and it conduces to the effective working of the telegraph.

Another remarkable feature to be noticed in connection with the underground system, is the small comparative velocity with which the electric impulse is communicated through each conductor in long circuits.

In experiments conducted by my brother and myself upon a circuit of four hundred and eighty miles (480) of the underground wires, a *marked* difference between the communication of the electric impulse, and its arrival at the other end, has been observed; the interval required for the passage of the sensation amounting to rather more than a third part of a second.

The rate of transmission of the galvanic or magnetic fluids, through such conductors, is therefore only about 1000 (one thousand) miles per second.

Professor Wheatstone's experiments, showing the passage of *frictional electricity* through a short length of wire in a room, to take place at a speed approaching 300,000 miles per second, are well known, and incontestible.

A subsequent experiment, conducted by Prof. Walker, on some of the overground wires comprised in the American system, gives the velocity of the galvanic current, through two hundred and fifty (250) mile circuits, at about sixteen thousand miles (16,000) per second.

The underground wires, however, as just mentioned, give a far lower result; and hence it appears evident that the velocity of frictional electricity far exceeds the voltaic or magnetic current—owing, doubtless, to the far greater intensity and comparatively small quantitative development of the former.

The retardation experienced in underground wires, as regards the propagation of the electric impulse, is not, however, due to any resistance of the conducting medium; for, as it is found in the instance of the Leyden jar, that the frictional electricity communicated is temporarily absorbed by the metal in the interior of the jar; so the galvanic or magnetic currents, during their passage through the underground wires, are partly absorbed, until the mass of copper constituting the wire is saturated with electricity; and it would also appear that a definite time is occupied in the absorption of the electricity by the successive portions of the wire, such as is found to occur in charging a Leyden jar; and, until this process of impregnation has been completed, the sensation cannot be communicated to the other end of the conductor.

The retardation will, therefore, result not from resistance, but from the first portion of the charge communicated being absorbed, for the time, by the conductor through which it passes; for, in addition to the foregoing, copper wire conducts far more freely than the iron wire made use of in the overground wires.

Consequently, the speed with which an electric impulse is communicated varies with the energy or intensity of the current employed, and the nature or conditions of the conductor interposed.

I find the underground systems of wires are but very little affected by any flow of terrestrial electricity, as compared with the overground wires, owing, I believe, to the electrical 'status' of the latter being disturbed whenever the electric condition of the *atmosphere* changes as regards the earth, principally with the rising or falling of the dew; and during Aurora Borealis, while the subterranean conductors are, on the contrary, only affected to any extent when the magnetic condition of *one district* of the *earth's surface* differs as regards the terrestrial magnetism of another, and the wires form a connection between such districts, affording an easy path for an interchange to take place; and to the flow of such currents, the suspended wires are, of course, equally exposed.

Both overground and underground wires are, to a certain extent, subject to the inductive influence exercised by thunder storms in approaching or receding, the former being liable to direct percussion from lightning.

In concluding this notice of certain characteristics and phenomena of the English system, I cannot refrain from alluding, in a few words, to an article on telegraphs that appeared in the Quarterly Review of June, 1854, in which a very unjust and incorrect comparison is instituted between the American tariff for messages and the English rate of charge.

A message of fourteen words is instanced, and the Quarterly Review says:—

"Now, the London charge for the above, if forwarded to Liverpool, would be five and sixpence; but the American tariff for the same, on the Louisville and Pittsburgh Railroad, would be only one cent a word, or sixpence halfpenny, English." To prevent an erroneous opinion prevailing on this subject, which would be calculated to prejudice the English system, I refer to the "Abstract of the Seventh Census," printed by order of the American Congress, and published in 1853, which states* that the usual charge for transmission is twenty-five cents for ten words, or less, sent one hundred miles.

I will also quote the American Telegraph Tariff, published in April, 1854, by authority of Mr. Shaffner, the Secretary of the American Telegraph Confederation, which gives the charge for a message of ten words from Louisville to Pittsburg, as fifty cents, and an extra three cents for every additional word; or for a message, such as instanced by the Quarterly Review, two shillings and eightpence; and for a message of twenty words, three shillings and sixpence.

The English tariff, for a message of twenty words between Liverpool and London, in May last, was two shillings and sixpence, without charge for address or delivery within a short distance. So that, instead of the English charge being ten times that of America, as stated by the Quarterly Review, the English scale, prior to the publication of the number, was very considerably under the American rates for an equal distance.

The Quarterly Review further remarks, that "a message of ten words can be sent on O'Reilly's Line, from New-York to New-Orleans, for sixty cents, or two shillings and sevenpence." Such is not the case. The American tariff gives the charge for ten words from New-York to New-Orleans, at 240 cents, or ten shillings, the distance being about 1500 miles, or for twenty words, a pound sterling. The charge for twenty words from London to Queenstown, a distance of about 900 miles, is ten shillings, a lower rate, in proportion to distance, than the American scale for a like message, although a sub-marine cable is included in the circuit to Queenstown, and much greater risk of capital originally incurred in its submersion.

Both instances show, therefore, that the greater economy of system claimed for America by the Quarterly Review does not exist.

* Abstract of the Seventh Census, page 109. Pub. Washington, 1853.

Various other inaccuracies have crept into the article I have referred to, which do not, however, call for special refutation, though calculated to mislead any one forming an opinion upon the statements of the Review.

In conclusion, I shall be happy to show and explain the magnetic machines and system carried out at our offices in this town, to any scientific gentlemen wishing to have a practical view into the working of apparatus of such a nature.

ART. VIII.—ELECTRIC TELEGRAPHS IN EUROPE.

QUESTIONS PROPOUNDED BY TAL. P. SHAFFNER, ESQ., TO TELEGRAPHIC AND SCIENTIFIC GENTLEMEN IN EUROPE.

WITH a view to receive authentic information relative to the science and art of telegraphy in Europe, we hurriedly prepared the following questions, and presented them to many gentlemen, and from whom we received very interesting answers. The American reader will see from the questions that there is a difference of work, management and system in Europe, when compared with the American telegraphs.

We would gladly give full details of our observations while visiting the many telegraph lines of our transatlantic friends, but time and room will not permit.

We will give the essence of what we saw and learned, in the present and future numbers, as opportunities occur.

On arriving in England, we soon found that there was much to be learned, and we spared no pains in procuring all the information possible. Of course, our expenses were large, and the sacrifice of time very great. We shall be gratified to diffuse our knowledge among the American telegraphers, and hope they will be benefited thereby.

In the present number we give the answers of Messrs. Chas. T. Bright, Engineer of the English and Irish Magnetic Telegraph Company, and also the answers given by Mr. Edward B. Bright, Secretary of the same Company. These gentlemen did not give their views with the expectation of their publication; but we find them so exceedingly interesting, that we take the responsibility of publishing them for the benefit of others. If there should be found in them any imperfections, the reader must overlook the same, as they were not written for publication.

Messrs. Brights have charge of the Company's lines on which they are engaged. Their manner of business, and management generally, compare favorably with the best-governed lines of any country. They are gentlemen, well educated, and they understand their business thoroughly. We regard them as experts in all departments of telegraphing, and worthy of the most elevated consideration. We feel under many obligations to Messrs. Brights for their many attentions in presenting us with so much valuable information, and we assure them that their presence in America would be received with much pleasure and congratulation.

At the earliest opportunity we will feel pleased to reciprocate the favors shown us; and if it should be out of our power to return them equal favors, we hope it may fall to the lot of some generous American to square the account for us. We give the questions propounded by us, and then the answers by Messrs. Brights. In future numbers we will continue the subject by the publication of answers from other gentlemen.

QUESTIONS.

1. Do the wires of your company run over ground or under ground—and to what extent?

2. If on poles, what kind of timber do you find the most durable—and, if possible, please state about what age are the poles (or timber) thus employed?

3. Do you use any pitch, tar, or other matter on your poles, to increase their durability—and if so, what and how applied?

4. Please state what kind of insulators you use on your poles, and if possible, please give a drawing of them or samples of each, with your opinion as to their fitness or faults—also their cost?

5. Please state the expense of your poles, and what is the cost for digging holes, raising the poles, the putting on of insulators, and placing the wires on the poles?

6. What kind of wire do you use, and where mostly manufactured—and what is the price for the same, per pound?

7. Do you use galvanized wire, and what are its advantages or disadvantages?

8. Do you solder the joints of your wire—if not, do you find any difficulties arising from oxidation at joints?

9. Do you realise much difficulty in the use of either galvanized wire or other wire, on poles, from atmospheric electricity—on which the most, and at what seasons of the year?

10. Where you have wire on poles, do you find any difficulty arising from cross currents at the poles; that is, the current passing from one wire to another at the poles?

11. Are your instruments ever affected by induced currents; that is, the passage of the galvanic or magnetic electricity from one wire to another, by or through elements of nature other than material substances; and if so, to what extent?

12. Do you ever suffer from what may be denominated "heat lightning;" and if so, to what extent?

13. Do you suffer from atmospheric electricity, either accompanied or not accompanied with thunder, and to what extent? Also, how do you protect your iustruments from harm?

14. Do you know of the burning of any property through the agency of the electric wires; and if so, to what extent?

15. Are the telegraph poles ever struck and damaged by lightning; and if so, how often in a year, averaging for a scale of one hundred miles?

16. How high are your poles, and how many do you use per mile?

17. How many wires can you place upon one set of poles?

18. Do you find any difference in the working of the wires on the poles; that is, the upper, middle, or lower wires? If so, what is that difference in fair weather, warm or cold, wet or dry seasons, and in time of storm?

19. Do you fasten the wire at each pole; and if so, how?

20. Do your wires often break; and if so, what causes them to break?

21. How do you mend your breaks? How many persons are required, and what is the mode you adopt to make the joint?

22. Do your operators usually go on the line to repair breaks, or other damages to the line?

23. Do you have a police to repair the line; and what is the plan, or system, and the expense?

24. Does the snow in winter disturb the working of your lines on poles; and if so, what are the remedies?

25. Does much ice form on your wires; and do the wires break, caused by the weight of the ice?

26. Please state your mode of laying under-ground lines, and furnish drawings, or samples, if convenient?

27. Do you find any difference in the use of wires covered once or twice with gutta percha?

28. What are the difficulties presenting in laying wires covered only with hemp, over the gutta percha? and please state the different modes, with their respective costs.

29. What are the causes of breaks, and their frequency, with underground lines?

30. How do you discover the place of break in a subterranean line? Please give a drawing of the plan, and state the time usually required to make the repair. Please specify fully on the subject.

31. What is the cost of laying one, two, or more wires?—giving the cost of labor, depth of ditch, and the plan in detail.

32. In case of much rock on the surface, do you blast; and how do you lay the wires?

33. Where there are marshes, how do you lay the wires?

34. Do you suffer from the upheaving of the earth, in case of frost in winter, and to what extent; and what are the remedies to avoid it?

35. What seasons of the year do your wires suffer the least?

36. What are your plans for crossing small streams?

37. Do you suffer from cross or induced currents from one wire to another in underground lines?

38. Did you find any difference whatever in the working of the wires, by their increased number in any combination from one to ten or more underground? If so, what is that difference?

39. What is the relative quantity of battery you use on underground lines compared with lines on poles?

40. What battery do you believe the best, and what quantity required for a distance of one hundred miles? Please give the cost of the materials in items. Can you work more than one independent wire forming an independent circuit from the same battery? If so, how many—and by what arrangement and principle?

41. How often do you repair the battery; what is that repair, and its expense?

42. What are your plans for protecting your line and instruments from lightning?

43. What do you consider return currents; and to what extent do you find the existence of the same on both overground and underground lines? Please state all the points fully.

44. Have you discovered any difference in the time required in the transmission of a current on the overground or underground lines, or in submarine lines; and what are the facts respectively?

45. Have you found any advantages in the use of any given size wire for electric conductors, either over or underground; and what are they?

46. What is the difference in the practical use of a line of iron wire and one of copper, as far as you are able to judge?

47. Do your underground wires ever suffer from lightning?

48. Do you allow the Government any advantages in sending messages; and what are those advantages?

49. Has the Government given any grants, appropriations, or other advantages or benefits to the telegraphs, either in law or in its use?

50. Please give the mode of receiving messages from the public, and the various checks placed upon the message, and the time thus employed, commencing at the reception at the counter, and ending with its delivery at the destination.

51. Do you ever send messages not signed; or when written on any other paper than your printed forms?

52. Why do you require persons to use your printed forms, and has that been the practice from the commencement of the telegraph? Please give two blanks, thus used, one filled to illustrate the plan you follow, with all the explanations needed, to enable a stranger to understand the same?

53. Please give a form of your register books, upon which you enter the messages you send and receive, with explanations of their use. Also copies of your rules and regulations as to the company, and of working the line.

54. Please state the average salaries you pay for the respective officers required in your city and country offices.

55. Do you clothe your messengers?

56. Do you place any of your officers under oath or bonds, and is there any advantages to the public or company by so doing, and do the Government laws require it?

57. Are you often called upon to give copies of messages to persons, and do you retain copies in your office?

58. What is the cost of your printed forms respectively? And please furnish copies of every kind you use.

59. What rents do you average in the city and in the country?

60. How many hours per day do your clerks or operators work?

61. Do you employ female laborers, and if so, how and at what expense?

62. Have you ever paid damages by errors in messages? and has the responsibility ever been tried at law? and if so, please give the case.

63. Are you in the habit of sending free messages; and if so, to what extent? Also cypher messages, and what are your rules upon the subject?

64. Do you send news for the press at reduced rates?

65. Do you ever lose or mislay messages in their transmission; and if so, does it occur often?

66. Do you ever pay back money on account of delayed messages.

67. Do you ever give any class of messages preference in any manner?

68. Do you require pre-payment; and if not, on what kind of messages?

69. Are the operators allowed to answer messages, giving information to a patron, at a distant office?

70. How many clerks are required to attend one instrument in a city or country office?

71. What system of telegraph do you use, and the cost of the apparatus? and if possible, please give me the early history of its invention, and by whom? Please refer to any printed authorities, if any; and also to persons who are acquainted with any facts pertaining to its early history. Please give extracts, if you have any, from newspapers, magazines, or letters in your possession, pertaining to the above points, their date, and where they can be procured or examined.

72. Do you often make mistakes in messages; and if so, what causes the same?

73. Do you usually repeat back messages? and what are your rules respecting the sending or receiving of business on the line?

74. How many messages are you in the habit of sending,

before being answered of their proper reception from the office receiving?

75. How long has the plan of insurance been in use on your line, if at all; and is it any advantage to the Company or public? and if so, what is that benefit?

76. Do you insure on messages going beyond your line, and upon what plan? Please state the details, and give the forms adopted fully, whether going on your line or beyond, or from other lines.

77. Please give your opinions as to the use of magneto-electricity for telegraphing, and the expense of its application. How is it applied, and upon what length of circuit can it be employed?

78. Have you any mode of generating a continuous current of magneto-electricity; and do you think it could be continuously generated, giving an even or equal current, suitable for telegraphic purposes?

79. Do you work your wires charged continuously with electricity?

80. Are there any disadvantages arising from a continuous current, other than unfitness for your particular system; and if so, what are they?

81. What kind of submarine crossings do you consider the best, and how made, their cost, and by whom manufactured?

82. Do you consider there is any advantage in galvanizing the wires for cables, and to what extent?

83. Have you any facts relative to the extent of the action of the sea-water on the exterior wires? if so, please state them.

84. Do you know to what extent the sea-water acts upon the gutta percha? If any, please state the facts.

85. Do you consider there is any necessity for galvanizing the exterior wires for cables intended for fresh water crossings?

86. Please give me all the information you can as to the early history of submarine crossings, with plans and principles?

87. Supposing you needed ten conducting wires, how would you advise a cable or cables to be made?

88. Do you consider a cable of more than six conducting wires practicable; and if so, how constructed?

89. What is the weight of the cables of one, two, three, four and six wires, and the cost of each made of copper wire covered with one, two, or three coatings of gutta percha, being of Nos. 1, 2, 3, 4 and 5, as marked at the gutta percha factory, embracing the price of the respective materials?

90. Have you any information relative to the effect of lightning upon the submarine cables?

91. How do you protect cables from the dangers of lightning?

92. At what speed can a cable be manufactured?

93. Do you know of the use of gutta percha on lines overground, and how does it answer?

94. Supposing your line formed a circuit of two hundred miles, and there were fifty offices on that circuit, could you communicate with all the offices at one and the same time, and could they answer back respectively? And further, supposing one or more branch lines diverged from the main line at any one or more places, on which might be ten or more offices, can any one office on the main or branch lines communicate with all or any one of the offices on the main or branch line at the same time and at will, and be answered back at will? If so, by what arrangement?

95. Please state what were the first batteries used on the telegraphs in your country?

96. Please state what were the first telegraph lines erected in your country, how built, how long, when put up, when and how worked, by whom, and with what success? Also, what instruments were used on them?

97. Do you know any improvements in the art of telegraphing, either as to the lines or working, or as to the science not herein embraced, which would be beneficial to the enterprise if adopted?

98. Can you suggest any plan by which the telegraph can be made to serve the interest of the government of the country relative to army, police or other departments; and do you ever aid the police in the arrest of fugitives from justice?

99. Do bankers pay out money on messages from a distance, or delay protest; and are your messages recognized as evidence in court between parties as to contracts; and are your operators compelled, by law, to reveal in court the business of the line in any manner?

100. Can you give me any information relative to the early history and final invention of the different telegraphs? Please be particular, and give dates and the different stages of success, extracts from newspapers, magazines, books, etc., in which references are made to any or all of the inventions in question.

ART. IX.—ELECTRIC TELEGRAPHS IN GREAT BRITAIN.

FACTS PERTAINING TO THE SYSTEMS OF WORK AND GENERAL MANAGEMENT OF TELEGRAPHS IN ENGLAND, IRELAND, AND SCOTLAND.

BY CHARLES T. BRIGHT, ELECTRIC TELEGRAPH ENGINEER.

(*Answers to Mr. Shaffner's Questions.*)

Answer 1*st.*—Both. In its most important districts, from London to Birmingham, Manchester, Liverpool, Glasgow, Belfast and Dublin, the wires are laid underground. In some lengths there are duplicate lines, one above the other, underground. The following will show the extent of each description of telegraph in this company's system:—

UNDERGROUND WIRES.—From London to Liverpool, by Birmingham, Manchester, Bolton and Wigan, 250 miles, 10 wires. From Liverpool to Carlisle, 130 miles, 6 wires. Carlisle to Portpatrick, by Dumfries, 125 miles, 6 wires. Submarine cable from Portpatrick to Donaghadee, (22 miles,) 27 miles of cable used, 6 wires. From Donaghadee to Belfast, by Newtonards, 32 miles, 6 wires. From Belfast to Dublin, 105 miles, 6 wires. From Dumfries to Glasgow, and thence to Greenock, 115 miles, 6 wires. From Cork to Queenstown, 16 miles, 6 wires. Street-work in London, Liverpool, Glasgow, Dublin, and other towns, 13 miles, 12 wires, (average.) On Scottish Central, Great Northern Railway, and Haigh Colliery Lines, 8 miles, 4 wires. Total, 821 miles of line,—6,348 miles of wire.

Overground—Chiefly 6 wires.

On the Great Southern and Western Railway,	170	miles.
Midland Great Western Railway,	150	"
Dublin, Drogheda, and Belfast Junction and Ulster Railway Companies,	160	"
Belfast and County Down Railway,	40	"
Belfast and Ballymena Railway,	40	"
Ballymena and Coleraine Railway	30	"
Londonderry and Coleraine Railway,	50	"
" " Enniskillen Railway,	60	"
Kilkenny Railway Co,	30	"
Waterford and Limerick Railway,	80	"

Caledonian Railway,	200 miles.
East Lancashire Railway,	100 "
Killarney Junction Railway,	50 "
Portarlington and Tullamore,	30 "
Miles,	1,190
Wire,	7,200

The total mileage of the company is therefore a little above 2,000 miles, and the length of wire about 13,000. The works in progress will bring the mileage to nearly 2,500 miles, and the length of wire to above 15,000 miles.

Answer 2nd.—TELEGRAPH POLES.—All the magnetic companies' poles are larch. During the first seven years of pole telegraphs, (Cook's patent for his mode of fixing wires on poles, the precursor of all other systems of poles in England, was dated September 8th, 1842, and specified in March, 1843,) the timber used was, without any exception that I know of, Memel *squared* timber, chamfered down the sides. A table of the dimensions of these posts is given in Highton's book. Since the end of 1850, larch has been altogether used. All the companies have adopted the round wood in preference to the Baltic cut timber, from its being cheaper and more readily obtained, and if straight and well selected, stronger than the old wood.

We have no proof of the respective durability of the two woods, save from comparison of gate-posts, &c., where the woods have been exposed, as in telegraph poles, to *wet and dry*, and we are led to consider that the larch poles will last much longer. None of the larch poles fixed have given way as yet, of course; but most of the square poles fixed up to the beginning of '47, have become so much decayed immediately above and about the ground, as to make it necessary to lower them, which the height of the pole above the ground (14 feet) has generally allowed. The 4 feet buried in the ground being cut away, the pole is lowered to near the same depth. It must be borne in mind, when thinking of the safety of such short poles, that in England all the pole system is by the side of railways, and within their fence, and that persons who might injure the wires if fixed so low on the high-road, have a wholesome dread of trespassing on a railway.

On a few lines where the poles have not been high enough to admit of their being thus lowered, they have been cut off at the ground, and fixed in a cast-iron screw socket—similar to the dwarf-screw piles used for breakwater fastenings, &c., patented by Mitchell.

I do not stipulate for any particlar *age* of timber in purchasing larch poles, but only as regards the quality and dimensions. The age of the poles we use depends very much on the district we are passing through. In some parts the tops, and seven or eight feet of thick butt ends of poles, are used for sleepers, and for props in coal pits, and in others larch is only used for fencing; and here we use the entire tree, from the butt to such part of the top as suits us, for size, while in the former case one pole would be the middle of much finer and older wood.

The size I fix is 18 feet in length, by 9 inches diameter, at the lower end, and 5½ to 6 at the top, measured after being barked. Crossing poles vary from 20 to 28 feet, according to the height of the railway cutting.

Answer 3d.—I have the poles well charred, from the lower end to about a foot above the depth they will be fixed in the ground, and the charred part soaked in *gas tar* for about twelve hours, the poles standing in tanks of tar within a timber framing.

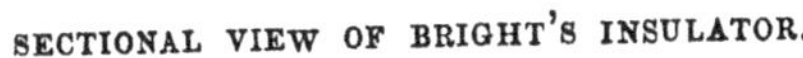

SECTIONAL VIEW OF BRIGHT'S INSULATOR.

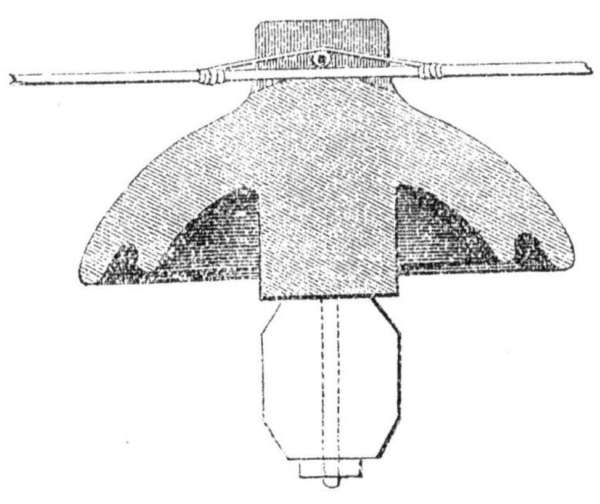

Answer 4th.—INSULATIONS.—The insulators first used by the Magnetic Company were of gutta percha, of the *surface* character of insulations, being simply two oblong pieces of gutta percha, about five inches in length, laid together while warm over the wire at the point of support, and fastened to the post by a small cast-iron chain, or shoe, screwed into the post.

These have been abandoned as not suitable to the long circuits the company works, and a glazed earthenware insulation, of the roof character, substituted and adopted in all the company's recent works.

I give a drawing to illustrate the insulations. You will see that the wires are so arranged upon the arms that any wire breaking will not fall upon the others.

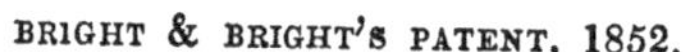
BRIGHT & BRIGHT'S PATENT, 1852.

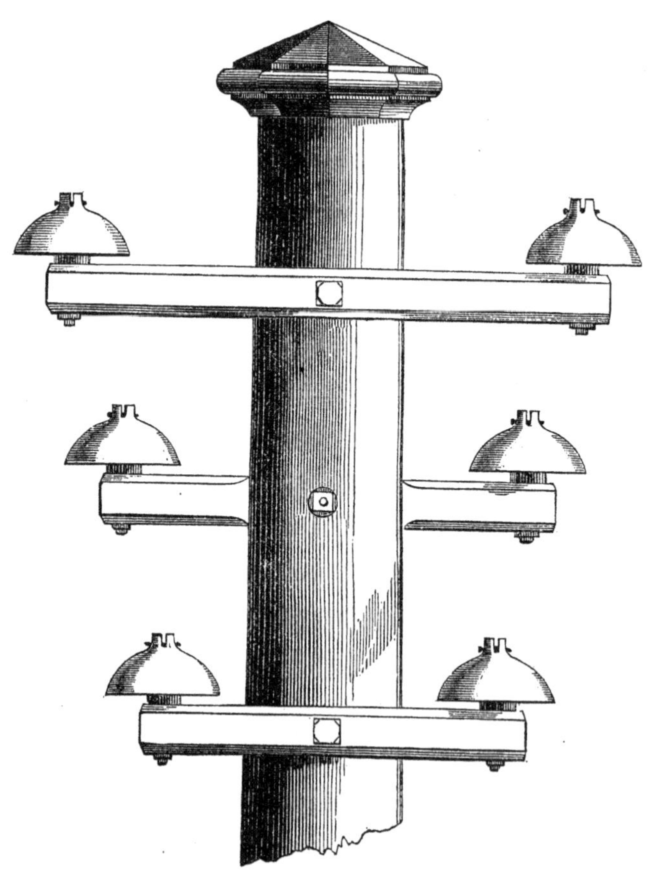

This system of pole telegraph was patented by my brother and myself, in October, 1852. The cost of each insulator, with bolt leaded in, nut and washer, is sixpence, delivered within two hundred miles. Of course, the apex of the cone in arranging the wires can be either above or below; but I prefer its being below, as the wires, in falling, keep clear of any insulators below.

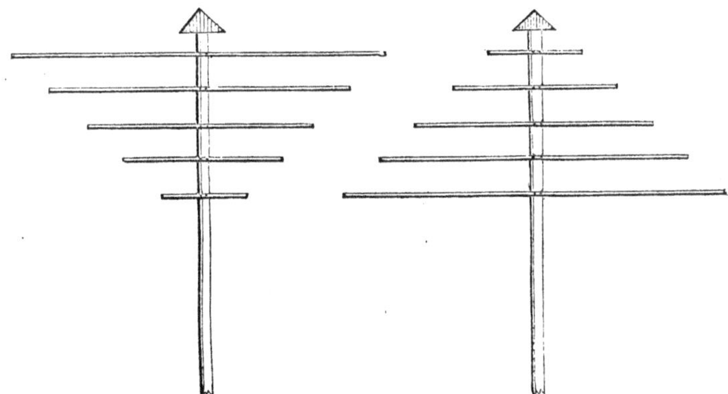

I find the insulators practically the best I have ever tried, though their size makes it necessary to have the poles well rammed.

COOK'S INSULATOR.

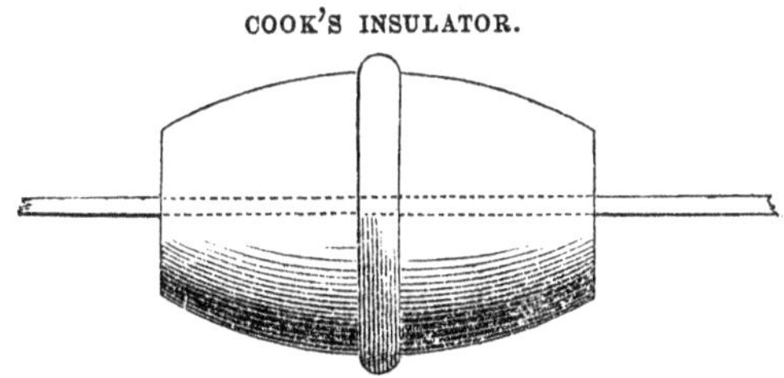

It may be interesting to describe the various methods of insulation used in England in the order of their adoption.

The first, known as Cook's Poll System, was by passing the wire through earthenware insulators of the size and form of an egg, slightly flattened at each end; but the system, though simple itself, was hampered with a method of winding of the wires at each quarter mile, by means of ratchet wheels. The system is described in Walker's Telegraph Manipulation. Cook's insulators were extensively used until 1848; but it was found that the surface was not sufficient, and an insulator, patented by Mr. Ricardo, but generally known as Physick's Insulator, was brought into use. It is described in the Mechanics' Magazine for 1850. The wire is supported by a hook, the upper part of which passes through a shed of earthenware, and is fastened by a nut at the top; above this, mastic was laid to insulate the hook from the post. This was found a very faulty insulator, the vibration of the wires, and other causes, breaking off the mastic.

CLARKE'S EARTHERN INSULATOR.

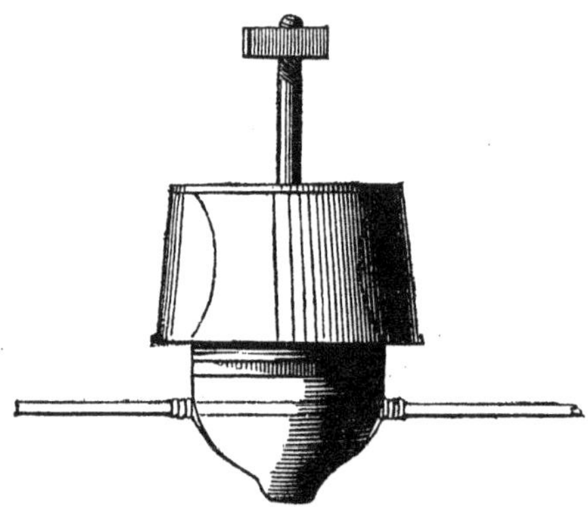

The next insulator is that known as Clarke's Insulator, having been patented by Mr. Edwin Clarke, the engineer of the Electric Telegraph Company, in 1850. It is described in one of the numbers of the Repertory of Patent Inventions, 1851; but as you may not have the work for reference, I have sketched it.

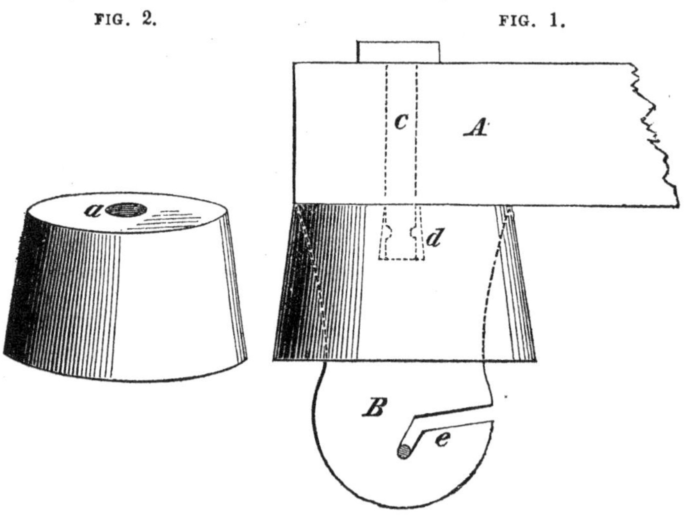

A is the arm to which the insulator is bolted by means of the bolt *c*, let into the earthenware at *d*—block *B* supports the wire by the slot *e* in the lower end of it. Between the arm and the earthenware is fixed, by passing over the bolt at the hole *a* in fig. 2 *a*, a zinc cap, of the shape sketched at 2. The size of the insulator is about twice that of the sketch. (Fig, 1.)

This insulator is now being discarded for one of the same form, and hanging down from an arm, but made of glass throughout, without any metal cap.

The object of the metal cap was, that the moisture might rather condense on it than on the earthenware; but it always seemed to me very hazardous to have a band of metal of such surface so near to the earthenware, and the result shows that the principle is faulty in practice; for the pent-house formed between the metal and the earthenware becomes so clammy with dew, or fog—without rain, which, of course, adds to it—that the insulator is a very defective one.

HIGHTON'S INSULATOR.

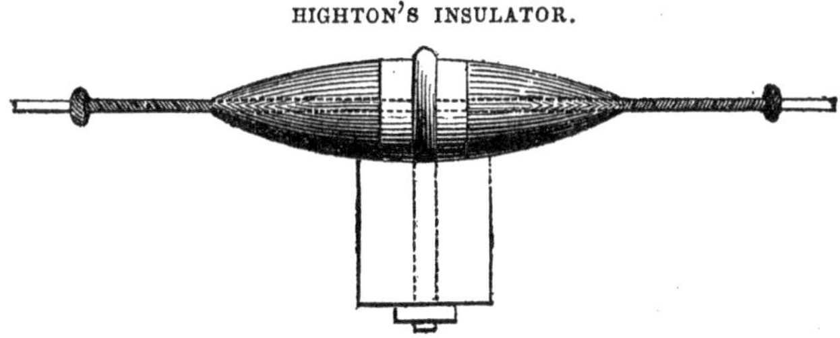

The British Company simply adopted a plan of lapping the wire with silk ribbon, for about six inches on either side of the point of support, and covering about five inches in the centre of the foot of ribbon with a piece of gutta percha, shaped like an elongated sphere; the whole is then varnished with brown, hard varnish. I believe this is very fair insulation for a few months, but the varnish soon comes off, unless frequently renewed, which is very expensive, and the silk decays and holds the moisture.

With Clark's and Physick's roof insulators the closeness of the sides was objectionable, on account of the clamminess thereby engendered, and the difficulty of cleaning.

In our roof insulator (page 183) we have spread the sides out, so as to widen the dry surface, and, by making more surface for the air to dry the insulator, the damp and dew is sooner dispelled. There is less lodgment for insects, and the insulator is readily cleaned. The double channel round the wire is to prevent the rain being blown up the insulator in high ground. I have adopted the method of fixing the insulator from below instead of from above, as I find it firmer, and there is no strain on the fixing of the bolt.

Other insulators besides those I mention have been invented; indeed nearly every patentee has had an insulator among his claims, but none of them have ever been used, except Brett and Little's, Nott's and Bain's, all of which were removed very shortly after their establishment on short lines.

One of the most extraordinary ideas on the subject of insulation is that of Highton, who, in his patent, dated January, 1852, proposes to run a wire down each post to the earth, from the central point between each pair of wires, so that any of the "electricity transmitted, as it escapes from the wire, may be intercepted by this communication with the earth, and so transmitted direct to the earth without the possibility of its entering an adjacent wire!" I have no doubt, a wet day would satisfactorily prove, that more than he wished would be intercepted. It has not been adopted.

Answer 5th—STRUCTURE.—Poles of the dimensions above mentioned, cost 3s. 6d. or 4s. each, barked, the knots planed off smooth, and the lower ends charred and tarred.

Twenty-five are generally fixed per mile (unless there are other supports, as walls, buildings, bridges, or viaducts;) the number used to be 30, and frequently 32, but it is now preferred to strengthen the poles, and sink them deeper, and by fixing only 25, to reduce the number of points of suspension for the wire, and thereby improve the insulation.

The expense of erecting the line in labor varies very much according to the price of wages in the district, the nature of the soil, the fitness of the weather, and the length of the days at the time, &c.; but it may be taken from £3 to £5 per mile. I am estimating for six wires.

Answers 6th & 7th—ON WIRES.—Galvanized iron-wire, number eight (Birmingham wire guage,) of the quality known as 'best annealed.' Cost, at present time, £23 10s. per ton, delivered within 200 miles, less 3 per cent. discount, for cash. Weight, 3 cwt., 1 qr., 18 lbs. per mile. Manufactured chiefly at Birmingham, London, and Liverpool.

I think the difficulty and cost of keeping ungalvanized wire, properly coated with paint, to prevent oxidation, renders it unsuitable for telegraphic purposes, otherwise it would be stronger, especially at the welds, than galvanized wire. Near large towns there are disadvantages in galvanized wire.

No. 8 has been universally erected in England, except on the length from London to Southampton, one of the earliest lines built, when No. 7 was adopted. It did not appear so much less broken by frost, &c., as to influence its being selected afterwards.

In very important circuits, I use stronger and more expensive wire, known as "best charcoal annealed," which is sold at the present time at £29 per ton.

The cost of wire has been gradually rising for a long time. In 1851, best annealed was quoted at £16, in 1852 it had reached £18 10s. and it has advanced steadily since that time. The wire is generally delivered in ¼ mile bundles.

GUAGE OF WIRE.—I do not know if your numbers of guage are the same as ours; perhaps the following table of our *lengths* of *one pound* may be a guide to you if they differ, in understanding the size—I mean by any number of guage I speak of.

	Ft.	In.		Ft.	In.
No. 1	4	0	No. 13	41	0
4	6	8	14	55	0
6	7	3	15	66	0
8	13	6	17	113	0
10	21	6	18	150	0
11	28	0	19	206	0
12	33	4	20	250	0

These figures are from personal weighing and measuring.

Answer 8th—MODE OF JOINTING.—I have all our joints soldered. Those made on the line are as in sketch below.

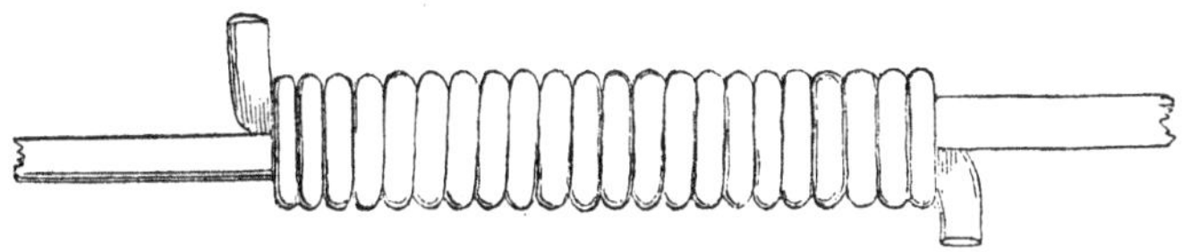

The ends of the wire to be joined are bent about ½ an inch; being laid together, they are lapped or bound with galvanized iron-binding wire (No. 20. B. W. G.) and soldered. I do not know any telegraph wires breaking at the *joints*, made after this fashion.

The wire used to be welded at the manufactory, and the weld more frequently gave way than any other part of the wire. Latterly, within the last two years, we have adopted a different plan—similar, I believe, to that used on many of the American lines. The two ends are laid side by side for about 5 inches, and each lapped four or five times round the other, with a space between each helix of about $\frac{3}{4}$ of an inch.

Answer 9th—ATMOSPHERIC ELECTRICITY, &c.—I have had no opportunity of observing any difference between galvanized and ungalvanized iron wire in their electrical statics during atmospheric variations; but I have no reason to suppose that there would be any difference—at all events, not so as to be perceptible on ordinary telegraphic apparatus.

We suffer most from atmospheric deflections in April, and the end of October and November. We have not arrived at any laws, nor does it seem, from the irregularity of the occurrence of these magnetic variations, that any definite laws can be established for their appearance or extent.

Some interesting experiments, carried on for some time on a pair of spare wires, between Derby and Birmingham, in 1848, are given in a paper read by Mr. Peter Barlow before the Royal Society in 1848, where the variations are tabulated for many days.

The term "deflection," which we use in speaking of the varying currents induced by magnetic storms, arises from Cooke and Wheatstone's needle telegraph, being at first so generally used in England, and the needle being *deflected* for awhile to one side or the other by the temporary continuousness of the atmospheric currents. The effects appear to be the same in this country and on the Continent as in America—at least I have not heard of any more violent or frequent deflections in America than in England.

[The facts above given, will inform the reader of the great difference in the atmospheric electrical hindrances in America and England. It must be remembered that in England the needle system is the telegraph employed. We are firm in the belief that in the Western, South Western and Southern States of America, the needle telegraph would ever be able to send a message of one hundred words successfully and uninterruptedly—compared with the American system. The atmosphere of England is never so highly charged with *adverse currents* of electricity, like we have experienced in the summer months, when the armature of our magnets are continually affected, though regulated with the most careful adjustments. We purpose referring to these questions in future numbers of the Companion.]—EDITOR.

Answer 10*th.*—In wet weather or long circuits we sometimes experience difficulty from currents passing from wire to wire at the poles, depending of course in extent on the degree of good or bad insulation of the line.

Answer 11*th.*—No.

Answer 12*th,* 13*th,* 14*th* and 15*th.*—Yes; the coils and other parts of our apparatus are sometimes fused and broken, and the needle demagnetized, but I have never heard of any property being burnt or injured through the agency of telegraph wires. I should expect that they have rather been the means of saving considerable damage by carrying off a great deal of electrical matter. I have occasionally had poles injured by lightning, but cannot supply any certain scale of average, not having kept record of each case.

I have had only two cases since the commencement of this year, in above a thousand miles of pole line. One of them was the most violent that has occurred in this country, 24 poles being more or less injured near Newry, on the Dublin and Belfast line, eight being split open and splintered to their bases, so as to be totally useless again.

A wire conductor, terminating in a spike, used to be let into all the squared poles; but since larch round poles have been introduced, it has been abolished.

We have violent electrical discharges, as often with as without thunder—of course more on long circuits.

We use lighting protectors with our instruments on pole lines. We have hitherto used two plates with sawteeth screwed into a mahogany base, the points being so close as nearly to touch—one is connected to earth and the other to line, and a small spiral, all of very fine copper wire (No. 40) forms part of the line circuit. The whole is covered with a glass cover. It is a very simple arrangement, and effective, but it is found objectionable on account of the wood sometimes warping and bringing the earth in contact with the line.

I am about introducing a protector, included in Bright and Bright's patent of 1852, formed of two wire brushes, (about the size of a nail brush, the wires being about ⅛ of an inch in length,) mounted on plates of brass ½ an inch thick—the top plate being capable of ready adjustment by a screw.

I have lately seen in Turnbull's work on the telegraph in America, that something after the same plan is in use there, and known as Carey's Protector, and I am curious to know the date of its introduction. I can easily understand the difficulty in adjustment, if the points are mounted in leather, as Carey's protectors are thus described.

I am under the impression that in your country lightning is far more frequent and injurious, and more violent than here. Perhaps this may partly arise from the wires passing through districts less populated, where there are not the same number of conductors in works, chimneys, towns, railways, &c.,—and I should like to know if you find the same average of discharges in your thickly populated districts, as in those where the towns are distant from each other. Say from Boston, to New-York and Baltimore and Washington, compared with some long line in a thin district.

[We have no doubt of the correctness of this opinion. We have not the opportunities of judging as to effects on the route mentioned above, as there is much the same state of settlement. We can mention some incidents quite curious and to the point. In the West we have large prairies, ranging in size from one to ten and fifty miles, without a tree. These prairies are sometimes separated by a skirt of woods, a mile (more or less) in width. These large open prairies may be considered as large open fields, with but few houses—say one every two or three miles—and but few trees. In sections of country thus situated, the atmospheric electricity is so troublesome to the telegraphs, that for many hours, during many days of the year, it is impossible to work. A few years ago, while acting as president of a telegraph line, (sole manager or engineer, as known in England,) we noticed the following facts :—

The line ran nearly north and south. The country, one hundred and twenty miles south of the northern station, was mostly of the barren growth—a small post oak. This timber is of slow growth, and contains a small quantity of sap, so little, in fact, that enough cannot be diffused to all the branches, and many die for want of nourishment. During the last twenty years we have noticed, with much care, the growth of this tree. In alluvial soil the trees, in a few years, grow twenty and more feet high. In the barrens the trees do not attain that number of inches in the same time. The barren section of 120 miles contains much of this slow growth timber. In the summer seasons the difficulties experienced on lines crossing prairie fields were witnessed on this section of the line; and, during the afternoons of July, August and September, many times it was not possible to work, owing to the superior influence of the atmospheric electricity over the most carefully arranged galvanic force.

In connection with this consideration, there are many circumstances which would enter into the formation of a correct judgment. These we have not the room to give at present.

On the southern section of the line aforesaid, for 160 miles, the country is not so open, and the timber is large, and of a kind which retains a great quantity of sap. This section is not so hilly, nor is the wire so exposed to the sun, running many miles through the thick woodlands. We never experienced the difficulties on this end of the line, as mentioned, relative to the northern part of the same line. While it was not possible to work on the northern end, we could successfully work on the southern. The two countries are widely different in natural formation and in product. The most southern section worked at times when the northern could not, on account of atmospheric electricity, or some unknown power. The winds and the storms are great enemies to the American lines. We have all our telegraphs built on poles. Trees are blown across our wires, and the line is either broken or buried in the earth. Notwithstand- the daily troubles occurring from the storms, yet the atmospheric difficulties are the most powerful and annoying. With our practical and money-making ideas, we have not properly studied this difficult problem. If they had the same difficulties to encounter in Europe we have no doubt some remedy would have long since been discovered. In America the dollar controls everything. Success in making money makes the man. It is thus that many men become great, while others of merit are passed unnoticed. Our people look for the dividends immediately, and unless they are large and often, dissatisfaction is manifested. Success in money-making elevates in estimation of the public a fool to the honors of the university. It makes kings, princes and potentates. A lottery ticket can make a nobleman in an hour. When the money is gone, the nobleman's blood cannot retain him in rank.

In making these remarks we may add, that while the American people do not apply the necessary theory and scientific talent in the conducting of our telegraphs, we think the European lines do not have the appliances of practical facilities equal to the American. They are in advance of us in theory. We are before them in practicabilities for the time being. Theirs are substantial and made for years, while many of ours are built and rotted within a year. Upon this subject we purpose speaking, to our American people in the language of figures, ere long. Daily observation tells us that we must change our mode of construction.]—EDITOR.

Answer 16*th*.—Answered under questions 2 and 5.

Answer 17*th*.—The size of poles I have described is intended for not more than 8 wires. *We* have no greater number any where on poles, except at a few junctions where different lines meet and pursue the same course for a short distance. They would probably bear 10, but I should not like to have so many in an exposed country without increasing the size. The greatest number of wires that I am acquainted with on one set of poles for any distance, is on the Eastern Counties Railway, where 18 wires are carried from London to Stratford. The London and North Western line has 13 wires, the greater part of the distance on one set of poles, and in many places for short distances many more.

Answer 18*th*.—I have not observed any marked difference arising simply from position of the wires. I should suppose the lower wires would be more affected by earth contact, and the middle wires with wire contact, while the top ones would be the best; but to ascertain this it would be necessary to have all the wires exactly on a par as regards their insulation, and a delicate galvanometer would scarcely then show much difference. I should imagine ordinary instruments would indicate no appreciable difference in their working, if the wires were otherwise equally insulated.

Answer 19*th*.—In our old method of insulation, the gutta percha held the wire at each pole. In our present plan, you will observe the pin, which passes over the wire across the slot in which the wire lays, has a piece of binding wire laid over it, and lapped and soldered around the wire, on both sides, so that while the wire has a little play at the point of support, it is held in case of breakage. If a wire is held by anything biting fast to the wire, the continual oscillation at that point injures the fibre and makes it very liable to give way there.

Answer 20*th*.—Not often after the first winter, which of course tries them more severely than any time after. Contraction by frost, weight of ice and snow, and accidental or malicious injury, are the general causes. I have known galvanized wires near manufacturing towns, broken by becoming so attenuated in some places in consequence of the destruction of the zinc by gradual deposit and decay, as to break by their own weight.

Answer 21*st*.—By line men kept on the line for the purpose, and for general maintenance of the poles and wires. The number employed varies on different lengths, according to the importance of the line as a commercial circuit, and consequent necessity or otherwise for immediate repair of any fault, and according to the convenience for speedily getting to any place in the length. On a straight line of railway, for instance, any point of a man's district may be much more readily arrived at than at one composed of many short branches, where the junctions and changes of trains make it difficult to travel so quickly. The average on my lines, is one to 70 miles of pole line.

Answer 22*d.*—No.

Answer 23*d.*—Answered under 21. The men's wages are from 18s. to 24s. per week. The latter for men of intelligence, capable also of repairing the instruments, or undertaking charge of works to small extent.

Answers 24*th* & 25*th.*—Our winters are not so severe, and our frosts so long in duration as to give us very much inconvenience in this way. Sometimes the wires break from the weight of the snow, when it collects to a great extent between the poles, but it is a rare cause of interruption. The greatest injury I remember being done by snow, was on the South Eastern line, where a considerable distance, above two miles I think, of poles and wires, were thrown down.

[In 1849-50, about two hundred miles of lines in the South Western States of America were broken in one day by sleet; many times a section of ten miles between every pole, the wire was found broken.]—EDITOR.

Answer 26*th*—SUBTERRANEAN LINES.- We have 820 miles of underground line; 670 of which, from London to Dublin, by Manchester, Liverpool, Carlisle and Belfast, is in a continuous line, the longest underground line by far in the world.

The chief part of this is laid in a trough of kreosoted Baltic timber, with a lid of galvanized roof iron, overlapping the groove by ½ an inch on each side, of the guage No. 14 in thickness.

It is drawn with six wires, but in some places 10 are laid.

SUBTERRANEAN TELEGRAPH—NO. 1.

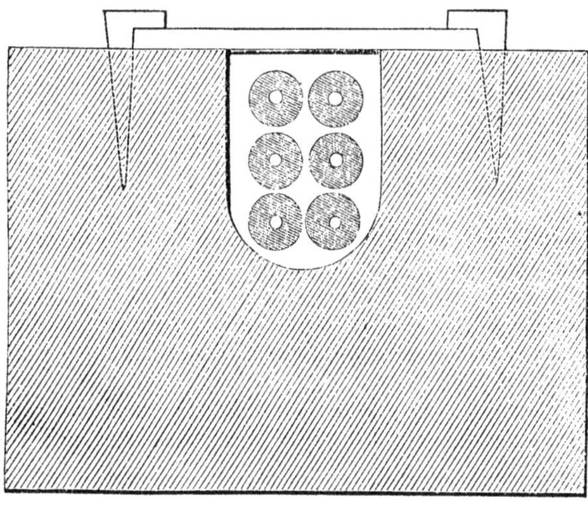

The line from Manchester to London, the first laid, has a wooden lid instead of the iron lid afterwards introduced. The district is easy of access by railway the entire distance, and the roads well attended to by the road; surveyors, (county, not *telegraph* officers) who inform us of any works, &c., to be done on the line of our wires.

The wires on this line, 10 in number, are covered with a serving of tarred jute as an additional protection, especially while laying, the expense being nearly covered by the saving in labor and carriage, in having the wires altogether in a rope, and wound on the same drum.

A full size section is given at fig. 2. The two plans are under the ordinary high road; but through the paved streets of towns, where the roads are often opened for laying gas and water pipes, drains, &c., and where, from the nature of the ground, the full depth of the trench cannot be made, the wires

SUBTERRANEAN TELEGRAPH—NO. 2.

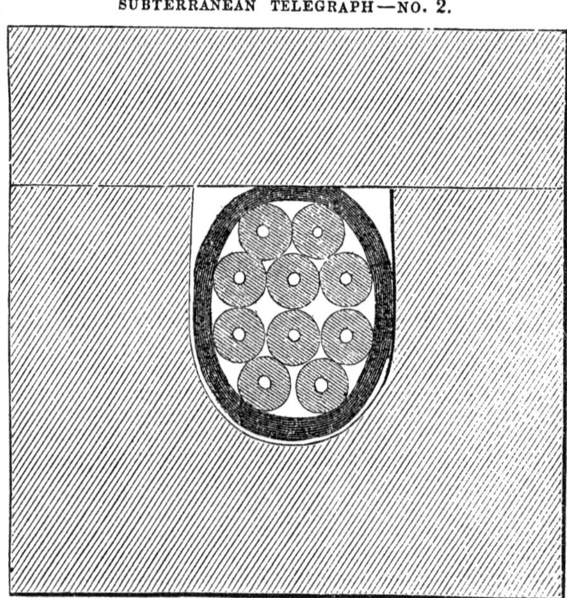

are laid in cast iron pipes.

The proportion of street work is generally about 3 miles out of every 100, but on some lines considerably more; between London and Manchester, we have 21½ miles laid in iron pipes out of 200.

Street wires used to be drawn through solid gas piping of about 3 inches diameter, the pipes being laid first, and the insulated wires drawn through afterwards. In doing this the insulating material was frequently injured; sometimes the wires were broken inside the gutta percha, or other insulating material, by the force necessary to pull them through, and occasionally they were drawn so tight that on the slight settlement of the ground, usual after the line has been laid a short time, some of the wires broke inside the insulating material, occasioning great difficulty and expense in detecting the fault.

The great proportion of the faults, however, were only abrasions of the insulating material; and though at the time the wires passed with all appearance of perfection through the ordeal of testing, and the streets were closed, and the pavement reinstated, before long the defects became so manifest as to interfere with the working of the apparatus, and the streets had to be re-opened, and the wires tested through length by length for the fault.

The wires required jointing at every other drawing point, and these points frequently proved defective, particularly in the old varnished cotton method of insulation and others, prior to the use of gutta percha.

In the beginning of 1852, having considerable lengths of street work to lay, I gave a good deal of attention to the subject, and determined on having the pipes cast longitudinally in two pieces, so that the wires could be *laid in* the under lengths, and the upper lengths then attached, instead of drawing, or threading them through solid pipes. I was the better able to carry this out, through the introduction of gutta percha, rendering the exclusion of moisture for the interior of the pipes of less moment. I tried various forms, rectangular, half-rectangular, with an arched lid, semi-cylindrical, with a flat sole, &c., but the form I found most generally useful and convenient, was that having the upper and under half exactly similar, making together a round pipe. I have the pipes cast in six foot lengths, and about 2 inches internal diameter, the substance being ⅜ of an inch,—the sides fitting clean together, without any flange, but fixed by small bolt and nut fastenings through semi-circular lugs projecting about 1½ inches from the side; one pair of lugs being about 9 inches from the faucet, and another pair two feet from the spigot end.

A pipe of these dimensions is much cheaper than the old 3 inch solid pipe, and more generally useful,—the halves being convenient for fixing to walls, viaducts, &c., over wires needing good protection in such places; and, from its circular form and smallness, it is very difficult to break, as a pick-axe, or other tool, cannot easily strike it full.

The process of laying in the wires is rendered much more expeditious and economical by the use of half pipes. I select a chronicle of some speedy operations in the middle of 1852, from the "Times" newspaper:—

"There is no greater annoyance in large towns than that which Parliament has granted to private Companies of ripping up their pavements at all times and places where it may be necessary for their interests. The authorities of a town pave their streets at great expense, and then comes a Gas Company, and then a Water Company, and then a Telegraph Company, to open deep trenches in some of the leading thoroughfares, interrupting the traffic, and creating great inconvenience. We have seen these trenches open in some cases six or eight days; but in the present instances we are glad to perceive that a great improvement has been introduced. The method adopted by the old Company has been to lay down a line of round cast metal pipes, through which the insulated wires are passed. This is necessarily a long and tedious operation, because considerable time is occupied, as each length of pipe is laid down, in passing the wire through it; but Mr. Charles Bright's plan is to use pipes split longitudinally into two halves. The under halves of the pipes are laid down in the trench, and then a large drum, on which the insulated wires are wrapped, is rolled along over the trench, and the wire is payed off easily and rapidly into its place—the upper parts of the pipes put on afterwards, and secured in their places by means of screws through small flanges, left outside for the purpose.

"So well has this mode succeeded, that in Liverpool the whole lengths of the streets, from Tithebarn Railway Station to the office in Exchange Street East, were laid down in a single night, (11 hours,) and in Manchester, the line of streets from the Railway Station in Salford to Ducie street, by the Manchester Exchange, in 22 hours. This was the whole time occupied in opening the trenches, laying down the telegraph wires, and re-laying the pavement; and while great credit is due to the Company on the ground of the little public inconvenience occasioned, no doubt they would find the benefit of it in economy of time and money."

Mr. Reid has invented an ingenious modification of the half pipe, of the rectangular form, which he has patented in company with Mr. Brett, and which we have used. I refer you for this to his patent, published in "The Repertory of Patent Inventions." Mr. Henley also has improved on the circular half pipe where it is intended only for subterranean work, which he has also patented; but both of them have top and under lengths differently shaped, and I find my original plan preferable for general purposes. All the telegraph companies have adopted the two piece pipe in place of the solid round pipe, except the old company. The depth of our trench is not less than 2 feet, but all obstacles, as drains, culverts, gas or water pipes, &c., are always passed *under*.

Answer 27th.—I have had no experience in laying underground wires with single covered gutta percha, having in common with all telegraphic engineers in this country considered the occasional small flaws and air bubbles which occur in single wire, and which are covered and made good by the second coating, a bar to its use, except about stations, &c., where it is not in close contact with the earth, and may be readily examined.

Answer 28th.—I do not think wire, covered with hemp only, could ever be laid so as to preserve good insulation, equally with that coated properly with gutta percha.

The wires through the streets of towns used, prior to the introduction of gutta percha, to be coated with a double serving of cotton, varnished, tarred, and enclosed in a leaden tube, which was passed through cast iron 3 inch piping. The wires were continually getting defective after being laid some little time, and we have only been able to have underground wires of any length in a good state of insulation, since the adoption of gutta percha; and that only within the last 5 years. Before that, the art of coating wires had not reached its present high state of practice, (which may be attributed to the perseverance, energy and science of Mr. Statham, the able Manager of the Gutta Percha Company;) and in one of its first trials in the most important lengths of street wires in London, it proved in a few months to be an utter failure.

Answer 31st.—Answered partly under 26. The cost of laying varies very much according to the hardness of the roads, the price of labour, the season at which the work is done, &c.; for six wires, according to the plan shown in sketch appended to question 26, a line along the old mail-roads varies from £180 to £200. The price of gutta percha has changed so much as to make estimates very little to be depended on for a long time. Last year No. 4 rose two pounds per mile in three months, and other guages in proportion. For ten wires, according to the plan with wooded lid shown above, and covered with hemp, the cost may be set down at about £230 per mile—this is on hard Macadamised roads.

I should never lay less than four wires under ground; the proportionate expense of cutting the trench, and for troughing, &c., being about the same for one as for ten, unless the scarcity of timber be much reduced, the expediency of which I doubt.

Wires laid without some protection, cannot be depended on very long, unless in a very favourable country. In Prussia, they appear to have formed the same opinion. We have had to re-lay a line from Manchester to Liverpool, which was originally laid without protection, though sunk to a good depth. A line of two wires laid from Dumfries to Stranrae, in Wigtonshire, by a now defunct company, called the Channel Submarine Company, has never been worked, and never will be.

The depth of our trench is two feet. In towns, and where gas and water pipes, &c., are laid, more according to the level of the mains and service pipes, which we keep under in all cases.

The only other company which have a line under ground of any length (the European and Submarine, from London to Manchester), have laid their wires less deep—from one foot to eighteen inches.

Answer 32*d.*—Where the road is rocky, we blast out about a foot deep, and lay the wires in iron pipes, packing up the trench with the shale and earth. We have had a great deal of rock crossing Shap Fell; on the road from Liverpool to Carlisle, we had a considerable length of solid rock; on the London line about Stoney Stratford, on that from Dumfries to Glasgow, near Abington, and through the Deloin Pass, and a good deal in Ireland.

Answer 33*d.*—Our wires are in every case, as yet, laid along the old mail-roads, which have been so carefully made and kept in repair throughout the kingdom for years past; we do not therefore ever pass through *marshes*, as the road would always pass over anything of the sort with a bridge or viaduct.* We have no telegraphs in England "across country" without regard to roads. For the same reason, we have no upheaving of the roads from frost; they are all too old and firmly set for any such disturbance. The only danger at all of the sort that I apprehend, is the *settling* of the roads in some places in the colliery districts, from seams of coal mines passing under the roads.

Answer 34*th.*—If you mean underground wires, at present, I cannot say which. I should imagine that seasons do not affect underground wires, save in induced currents, at all; with pole lines, spring, autumn and winter, are the worst times. I think about in the above order, summer is of course the best season for exposed wires.

Answer 36*th.*—See reply to 33—Our mail-roads always cross by bridges, and our wires are laid over them, frequently close under the parapet, about 6 inches deep, (as the crown of the bridge is generally shallow, to avoid much raise of the level of the road,) enclosed in wrought iron solid pipes, about an inch in diameter, by three-sixteenth in substance, which are threaded over the wires, for the short distance required.

Answer 37*th.*—CROSS, INDUCED, AND RETURN CURRENTS.—Under question 10, you have referred to *cross currents* as what we term "wire contact," that is, communicated by moisture, or otherwise from wire to wire.

Under 11, you speak of an *induced* current from wire to wire. I suppose, therefore, that by the latter you mean something that we have not yet experienced; at least not so as to be visible on our ordinary instruments, but which perhaps your continual current, or some peculiarity of your atmosphere, in some districts may have engendered.

[The American telegrapher will please observe the answers to Question 37. It is one of the greatest importance. It strikes at a question in philosophy about which our people have made more discussion than any other—their arguments being based upon theory. The answer given is full upon the subject. The author of the answer thoroughly understands the science and art of telegraphing; and when he speaks thus, we can depend upon the non-existence of that which American telegraph philosophers have mostly dreaded.]—EDITOR.

We have had no case of wire contact in underground wires; I should doubt our having any, unless in some case of a nail, or a portion of an iron cover, or of a tool being forced in between two wires, as the communication with the earth (or to use our term, the "earth contact") would be paramount.

We have had no experience of any induced currents from wire to wire in underground, any more than on pole lines.

Answer 38*th.*—I have not observed any difference; certainly our instruments are not in the least affected. You must bear in mind, that our wires have been laid only a short time. That from London to Liverpool has been completed 9 months—the North and Irish lines only six; and having been very much occupied with extensions, and opening out our present system, I have had little time for experiments with delicate galvanometers and other apparatus, but I speak here, and before, of my results as shown on working telegraph instruments.

Answer 39*th.*—I cannot speak for certain, as I have not had time to try. I have in reserve this, with a number of other experiments, when I have more leisure, and will acquaint you with the result.

You are aware that we use magnets only, and their induced currents, for our motive-power; and as my experience of batteries has, of late, been only for purposes of testing, etc., this and the two following questions will probably be much better answered by your other friends here.

Answer 42*d.*—Answered under 12, &c.

Answer 43*d*.—On overground lines they are very trifling, indeed, compared with underground; the conditions on which the wires are suspended and insulated, passing also through a medium, capable, to a certain extent, of absorbing any electricity developed in surplus, prevents the occurence of any effects appreciable by ordinary needle telegraphic instruments.

I look upon an underground wire as being exactly similar, on a large scale, to a Leyden jar, and I am borne out in this by the experiments of my brother and myself, and by those instituted by Faraday on the underground wires more recently laid by the Electric Telegraph Company. The magneto-electricity, as well as the galvanic (or chemical) electricity, evinces these phenomena, hitherto supposed to belong to properties appertaining peculiarly to frictional electricity.

The copper may be compared to the inner metallic coatings of a Leyden battery, the gutta percha to the glass, and the earth and moisture surrounding to the outer covering.

I was much interested in one of our experiments to observe, that the larger the size of the wire experimented upon, with the same battery power, the greater the amount of return current: a strong support of our opinion; as, had it arisen from an *elastic* return, owing to the wire being unable to receive as much electricity as was forced into it, as some supposed, of course a *smaller* wire (with the same power as that employed with the larger size) should have given out a *greater* amount of return current. If you experimentalize on No. 18 and No. 16, you will see this very clearly.

Answer 44*th*.—My brother tried some experiments, by connecting our underground wires together, which he will be better able to describe than myself. I am about to try, on a very extended scale (over all our wires joined together, and various lengths), the distance to which we *can get a current*, and will acquaint you with the result.

Answer 46*th*.—Practically, the difference is, that an underground line of copper requires considerably more power than a suspended line of iron. If we assume the difference of conducting power of the two metals to be in the proportion stated by Becquerel and others, then the vast resistance engendered by the (so to speak) Leyden jar condition of a well-insulated underground wire, is manifest.

Answer 45*th*.—No. 8 has been the only size of wire used overground. No. 7 has been tried on one line, but No. 8 was found to be sufficiently strong. No doubt, a much smaller wire would have sufficed (in the absence of any appreciable return current, as in subterranean lines,) for all ordinary conducting powers.

I have tried, with Mr. Statham, the Manager of the Gutta Percha Company, some important experiments on the conducting ratio of different sizes of gutta percha coated-wire, which show a considerable difference in conducting power of copper wire, leading me to the decision that, for any line of a length above one hundred miles, it is not expedient to use a size less than No. 16 copper wire (Birmingham wire guage).

I extract a few notes of our experiments on Nos. 18 and 16, as clearly showing the difference.

Fifty miles of No. 16, and fifty miles of No. 18, tested for continuity with a Galvanometer.

1st		Fifty miles of No. 18.	Fifty miles of No. 16.
With	3 pr. of plates,	45°	53°
	6 " "	62½	Full, so as not to be reckoned in degrees.
2nd		One hundred miles of No. 18.	Fifty miles of No. 16.
With	3 pr. of plates	29°	39°
	6 " "	50	59°

With needle of Galvanometer weighted.

3d		One hundred miles of No. 16.	Sixty-five miles of No. 18.
With	36 pr. plates,	17¼°	17¼°
	18 " "	10¼	10¼

The loss of conducting power appears, therefore, to be more than proportionate to the different area of metal.

Mr. Statham, who went to considerable pains in investigating the ratio of conductibility, and insulated many miles of various sizes, practically to demonstrate the differences, has made a very good wire for short distances, by which a saving may be effected in such lengths of underground lines, which he calls No. 7 Gutta Percha Covered Wire, the copper wire being 18 —the gutta percha being *double* covering, but not so thick.

Answer 77th —MAGNETO-ELECTRICITY.—I am naturally strongly in favor of the use of magneto-electricity. Its economy is undoubtedly the most prominent feature. A pair of magnets costing at Sheffield 30s. and perhaps 40s. to 45s. (according to the finish bestowed on the instrument,) by the time they are fixed and ready for use, will send a strong current on a well insulated suspended line for above 200 miles, and on an underground wire above a hundred. (I have had signals, but only weak ones, through 250 miles of underground wires with the class of instruments I am speaking of) while the six twelve-cell trough battery used in this country, which would be necessary to perform the same work, would cost £7 10s., besides the constant expense of renewal, &c.

A magnet, if the keepers are put on when the instrument is not in use, will retain its magnetizm for an indefinite time. I have not as yet had to re-magnetize any of our sending magnets, though we have instruments that have been in use since our incorporation in 1852, and some since the exhibition in 1851, where our apparatus carried off the highest medal the jury could allot.

I cannot speak as to what length of circuit magneto-electricity can be used, as I have not as yet tried with magnets of great power, beyond those we use daily.

We work the longest circuit that is daily worked in England—from Liverpool to Belfast and Dublin, an underground line, which, with a pole line would be equal, at least, to 800 miles, though I doubt if we could put a current of such power into any pole line, unless in very dry weather. The magnets here used, are the large horse-shoe compound magnets you have seen in our offices, about 15 inches from the poles to the back, about 5 inches in height, made of 12 plates, in breadth about 1½ inches. I have spoken with these for experiment through 530 miles of underground wire; but for our arrangement of circuits it would be unnecessary, and inconvenient, as we should have to lay more wires so as to connect up long direct circuits, which would be very little used.

These magnets cost nearly £7 each.

Answer 78th.—We have no mode in use, because it is not adapted to our system, the magnetic current we send being sufficiently long for our purposes.

I do not see much difficulty in keeping up a continuous current. Wheatstone patented one some years since, but it was complicated and comprised six compound magnets for each wire.

A simple reverser, which should change exactly as the coils changed their polarity, similar to that used by Billant, and a close arrangement of the poles of the permanent magnet, are the chief points.

By rotating a disc or plate, with coils on its axis between the poles, perhaps an equal current might be maintained.

I have not given much attention to the subject, as we do not use continuous currents here, and can obtain sufficient duration of the effects of the movement of a pair of coils for about 30 degress in the face of a permanent magnet, by having the receiving coils and their cores so arranged as to retain the residual magnetism until another current is sent.

Answer 79th.—We do not use our wires continuously charged with electricity.

Answer 80th.—I do not know of any practically, from having had no experience at all in the use of continuous currents. Glancing at the subject, I should think there must be some inconvenience wherever an iron core is used in the receiving coils by the residual magnetism retaining the keeper or magnet. This would be increased in an underground line, where the return current would follow so quickly on any break of current, as to make any rapid sending impossible. Is not the expense of maintaining battery much increased by their more frequent operation?

Answer 81st—SUBMARINE TELEGRAPHS.—I like the plan most generally adopted the best—that of covering the gutta percha wires first with tarred hemp, and afterwards with strong iron wires wound spirally round the rope. They have been made in England chiefly by Newall, of Gateshead. The cost varies very much of course, according to the size of wires used, &c.

Answer 82d.—I do not think there is. It weakens the rope, and in manufacturing is liable to injure the gutta percha wires by scaling, &c. We lost a galvanized rope between Portpatrick and Donaghadee in October, 1852, which was entirely recovered afterwards. A new one, ungalvanized, was laid in May, 1853 —the first successful attempt to connect England to Ireland after three failures by other companies and ourselves.

Answers 83d to *92d.*—I have either been unable to give reliable information on the subjects, or cannot just now go into them fully, and collect estimates. I shall be happy to do so hereafter, if you have not obtained full particulars from others.

Answer 93d—INSULATED WIRES ON POLES.—Gutta Percha wire has not been used in England upon poles. For my own part, I consider it would have all the disadvantages of both the overground and underground systems, with few of the merits of either. I speak of our abandoning gutta percha pole insulators under No. 4.

Answer 94th—COMBINING CIRCUITS.—We have no circuit with anything like that number of stations, so I cannot speak by experience; but I have no doubt if our present instruments could not overcome so great a resistance as that number of receiving coils in a long circuit would present, that apparatus could, without difficulty, be made that would be sufficient. We have no arrangement exactly such as you mention; but, at all our junctions we have switches for turning the branches into direct communication with the main lines.

Answer 95*th*—GALVANIC BATTERIES.—Trough batteries after Wollaston and Cruikshank's plans. Mr. Cooke modified them, and introduced the use of sand in the cells, which equalized the action, and made the batteries more convenient for carriage and use in offices. I speak of the first working telegraph—not experiments.

Answers 96*th* and 97*th*—FIRST ENGLISH TELEGRAPH.—Cooke and Wheatstone's Needle Telegraph. That with 5 needles, used on one or two lines at first—(the Norwich and Slough lines the only ones I remember at present)—but were shortly afterwards changed for the double needle as more convenient and economical. The first line—the Great Western to Slough—was fixed in 1839. It was erected on short standards, the wires being laid in a trough carried on them. It was worked a long time, but has since been changed for the suspended wire system. Its chief use was for the railway company's affairs, and partly for commercial business. Other lines followed rapidly after this—among the foremost, the Southwestern to Southampton, Gosport, Portsmouth, &c., with wires for government use in the Admiralty Department.

DIRECTIONS FOR INSULATING JOINTS IN GUTTA PERCHA COVERED ELECTRIC TELEGRAPH WIRE.

HAVE in readiness a few strips about ⅜ inch broad, of very thin Gutta Percha Sheet, also a little *warm* Gutta Percha about ⅛ inch thick, one or two hot tools, and a spirit lamp.

Remove the Gutta Percha covering from along the wire no further than may be necessary for making the joint in the wire. Having joined the wire, warm gently with the spirit lamp the bare wire and joint, and the Gutta Percha near to it; taper the Gutta Percha over the bare wire until the ends meet; warm this, and immediately apply one of the strips of thin sheet in a spiral direction over it. Press this covering well on until cool; then, with the spirit lamp, carefully warm the *surface*, and proceed as before to put on a second strip of the thin sheet, observing to wrap it in a direction reverse from the first strip, always making the commencement and termination of these coverings to overwrap the previous one. *It is safer to perform this operation a third time.*

Next, take a piece of the warm ⅛ inch sheet, and cover over the coats of thin sheet, again overwrapping the original covering of Gutta Percha, which should be heated so as to ensure perfect adhesion. Press it well on as it cools, and when cold, or nearly so, finish off the joint with a warm tool, working well together the old and new material at each end.

Lastly, and in general, avoid moisture, grease, or dirt, and be careful not to burn the Gutta Percha, which would prevent proper adhesion.

SHAFFNER'S

TELEGRAPH COMPANION,

DEVOTED TO THE SCIENCE AND ART OF THE

MORSE AMERICAN TELEGRAPH.

VOL. II. JULY, 1855. No. 3.

ART I.—ELECTRIC TELEGRAPHS IN GREAT BRITAIN.—NO II.

THE SCIENCE OF TELEGRAPHING—MAGNETO-ELECTRICITY—RETURN CURRENTS —ROYAL PROTECTION TO TELEGRAPHS—BUSINESS DEPARTMENTS AND OFFICE ARRANGEMENTS.

BY EDWARD B. BRIGHT,

Secretary of the English and Irish Magnetic-Telegraph Company, Liverpool, England.

(Answer to Mr. Shaffner's Questions.)

Answer 44th.—RETURN CURRENTS ON SUBTERRANEAN LINES. —In the course of a long series of experiments carried on last year by my brother and myself, inquiries were instituted with reference to the speed with which the galvanic or magnetic sensation is communicated through underground wires.

The result of the inquiry shows decidedly that the communication of the electric impulse through a length of 500 miles of underground gutta percha covered copper wire (16 guage) does not exceed 900 to 1000 miles per second—a speed far below that usually assigned.

Reasoning upon the issue of these experiments, and those previously tried in America, I have no doubt that the speed of any description of electricity varies greatly with the peculiar conditions and nature of the conductor used, and also with the length of the conductor interposed; and that a wire suspended in the open air, especially if insulated only at points of its support, (such as in a pole line) would offer far less resistance (cœteris paribus) than a wire undergound.

Submarine cables are similar, as regards electrical conditions, to subterranean lines, and the speed with which the electric impulse is communicated would be the same.

I have no doubt, however, that, as Professor Wheatstone's

experiments showed, the speed of electricity developed by friction (or machine electricity) is of *far* greater velocity, whatevre be the medium of communication interposed, than the species (voltaic or magnetic) used in telegraphic manipulation.

Answer 48th—PREFERRED MESSAGES.—It is provided in the royal charter granted to the company, that any communications handed to the company by government for transmission, are to be forwarded prior to any other messages, and at all times when the offices of the company are open. The government make considerable use of the magnetic telegraph, and their messages always take precedence, and are paid for according to the usual tariff for private messages.

Answer 49th—RIGHTS OF WAY FOR TELEGRAPHS.—Government has made no grant, as regards concession of property to telegraph companies; but gives to them power to open roads, and to pass their wires through or over any public way or public property without compensation, and subject only to certain formal notices to the local road surveyors, and to their approval of the subsequent re-instation of the surface of the road opened.

The various telegraph companies have availed themselves more or less of the power so conferred: the electric telegraph company by laying their wires through the streets of towns from the termini or stations of railways: this Company for some years past have extended the use of the clause to the construction of main lines along the high-road, in addition to street work; and recently the "European" Company have adopted a like plan. Finally the British Telegraph Company in several instances have carried pole lines for short distances (a few miles) over the highway, where they could not obtain permission to use the railways. There are many difficulties, however, in carrying wires along the turnpike roads overground, as the landlords of adjacent property have particular objection to the lopping of any branches that project, as is often the case for miles on both sides; and wires so placed are peculiarly open to malicious injury,.which could not well be guarded against.

ROYAL PROTECTION OF TELEGRAPHS.—Accidental or malicious injury is provided against in the Company's Act of Parliament, dated 1st August, 1851, 14, 15, Vict., Cap. CXVIII. I cite the clauses that particularly refer to this point:—

"LIV.—That if any person shall wilfully remove, destroy, or damage any electric telegraph, which shall or may have been lawfully erected, or any wire, standard, apparatus, or other part of such telegraph, or any works connected therewith, he shall be guilty of a misdemeanor.

LV.—That with respect to the offenders whose names or residences are not known, any officer, agent, or servant of the company, or any constable, police officer, or servant of any railway company, along or near to whose railway any electric telegraph, or any of the apparatus thereof, or any part thereof respectively, shall or may be erected or placed, or any constable or police officer, and all persons called by any such officer, agent, servant or constable as aforesaid, to his assistance, shall or may seize or detain any person who shall or may have broken, injured, or obstructed the working of any electric telegraph of or belonging to the company; or any of the wires, standards, instruments, apparatus, or other parts of any such electric telegraph, or who shall have committed any other offence against the provisions of this Act, and whose name or residence shall be unknown to such officer, agent, servant or constable, and shall or may convey such offender with all convenient speed before some justice, without any warrant or authority other than this Act; and such justice shall proceed with all convenient speed to the hearing and determining of the complaint against such offender."

I may instance, that, in November last, the wires of this (the magnetic) company were cut during the riots at Wigan. Having obtained information, I caused three men, Peter Moorfield, Peter Fairhurst and Thomas Bradshaw, to be apprehended, and obtained their committal to gaol to await trial.

We proved the charge against them at the Wirtedale Sessions, in January, 1854, and a verdict sentenced them to six months' imprisonment, with hard labor.

Answer 50th.—RECEPTION OF BUSINESS FROM THE PUBLIC.—All messages are handed to the company, written upon printed forms provided for the purpose. To all good customers small books of forms are issued. Larger books lie at the places of general resort (such as the exchanges, reading-rooms, &c., &c.); and any casual customers find forms ready at the company's offices upon counters of a height suited for writing, when standing, and subdivided into spaces, with fluted glass screens between each, to prevent any person seeing another's message.

The company's cashier quickly counts the words in the body of the message (the address not being included, but passing free), endorses the message and writes a receipt of the amount;

the customer is handed the *receipt*, upon the money being paid. Parties sending messages are advised to write them distinctly; and the cashier reads the message, in order to see that the writing is legible, before handing it through to the instrument room.

The cashier enters upon a list, opposite to the consecutive number of the message, the amount received; and, on being passed through to the instrument room, the lad receiving the message marks the number upon a similar list, and sends the message to the instrument for which it is intended. The clerk at the instrument then dispatches it to, or towards its destination, receiving an affirmative or negative signal after each word; if the latter, the word is repeated, not having been rightly understood by the receiving clerk at the distant station. So commencing the message, the *sending* clerk signals the number of words the message contains (previously inscribed on the paper by the cashier), and, as soon as completed, the *receiving* clerk's writer counts the number of words received, to see that the message is correct as to length; and, as will have been seen, the "understand " or " not understand " signals after each word, check the words themselves—admitting, when the system is carefully carried out, of little possibility of mistake.

In the foregoing I have embodied the routine observed in our *chief* stations. In small stations, where there is no great influx of messages, the checking is not carried out to such an extent.

As soon as the message has been sent, it is returned to the checking lad, who files it, and draws his pen through its consecutive number, to intimate that, as far as the due forwarding is concerned, the company have performed their duty, and it is his business to see that the signal clerk has endorsed upon the document the time at which he sent it, the station to which he signalled it, and his initials. By such an arrangement all chance of a message being mislaid is avoided; as, if the communication is not returned in a quarter of an hour, to have its number marked off the list, it is the duty of the checking clerk to enquire after it, and to ascertain why it has not been dispatched.

Very little time is lost in such an arrangement, and the chance of error of any nature greatly diminished.

CELERITY OF TELEGRAPHING.—Messages are forwarded upon a pair of wires by needle telegraph, at an average rate of 27½ words, of five letters each, per minute; and the more expert operators can pass 35 words in a minute; or as fast as the writer can possibly take them down.

The time occupied in forwarding messages, on an average of a thousand between Liverpool and London, averages 4½ to 5 minutes each (including any occasional delays that arise) counting from the time when handed to the company, by the customer, to the completion of their reception in the London office.

I cannot give any average for delivery, as that depends entirely upon the distance from the office to the address. Messengers are always in waiting, and one is immediately sent off with the communication in a sealed envelope upon arrival.

The order of precedence is determined by priority of handing the message ready written over the company's counter to the cashier.

Instances, well authenticated by the customers themselves, have occurred where the whole process from the handing of a message to the company, to its delivery to the party to whom addressed, has been accomplished in a minute and a half.

But this can only happen when the receiver's office is close at hand, and an instrument entirely disengaged at the moment the message was handed to the company.

Answer 51*st.*—OFFICIAL BLANKS FOR MESSAGES REQUIRED TO BE USED BY THE PUBLIC.—No. If messages are brought in to our offices on plain paper, the person bringing such is requested to copy the communication upon the printed forms provided. Otherwise the message would be refused by the company; though this is a contingency that does not arise, owing to the requirement being made without exception by each company.

If the customer cannot write, one of the company's clerks copies the message, reads it to the customer, keeps the original, and obtains the signature or mark of the person, at the foot of the company's paper. The message is then sent, the company being freed from onus.

Answer 52*d.*—Printed forms have been used from the establishment of the telegraph.

It has been found requisite for many reasons. In the first place, the difference of cost between plain and printed paper is of small consideration, as compared with the necessity that would devolve upon the company, to explain to customers the mode of arranging a message upon paper, to customers.

The defined position of the address from and to, and of the body of the message, materially aids the instrument clerk in forwarding the communication.

Moreover, for the security of the company as a trading concern, we consider it necessary to embody certain conditions and stipulations upon which alone we receive messages.

We also caution customers against indistinct writing, and

disclaim all responsibility for the same, and require, finally, the *signature* of the customer in authentication of his message, and *as subscribing to the company's conditions.*

INSURANCE FOR CORRECTNESS OF MESSAGES.—In the stipulations subscribed to, we mention, that in order to ensure accuracy, it is necessary that communications should be repeated from the station to which sent; and that an extra charge of half a rate is made for such repetition, the company holding themselves responsible to the extent of £5 upon such repeated messages. Further, another clause provides for the insurance of valuable messages to any amount upon payment of one per cent. upon the amount insured.

This latter regulation is *never acted upon;* and that of repetition seldom. No error has occurred in repeated messages.

When parties, as is frequently the case, hand us messages in French, German, Italian, or other foreign languages, we take them at the risk of the sender as to accurate transmission of the words.

Code signals for various descriptions of messages, and cyphers for short words of frequent occurrence, such as "the," "from," "and," "to," "in," "on," "you," "yes," &c., and for terminations, such as "tion," "ing," "ment," are much used by the staff to facilitate transmission.

The company's customers (especially the stock and other brokers and banks) use cypher to a great extent, one message out of four, on an average, being so written, the regulation being, that code words shall not exceed two syllables in length in order to prevent an abuse of the system by the introduction of words of a nature or length likely to delay the company's operators.

Of course the correspondents arrange their codes between themselves, each having a key, so that on arrival of the message at either end, it is translated.

Answer 57th.—WHEN COPIES OF MESSAGES ARE GIVEN.—We are very seldom called upon to furnish copies of messages. The company in all instances refuses to do so, unless upon the application of the person to whom the message is addressed; and in all cases requires a satisfactory reason.

MESSAGES RECEIVED AS EVIDENCE IN COURT.—We produce messages in courts of law upon an order of the sitting judge or magistrate; they are received as evidence in a court of law when recorded upon oath from the company's servants, connected with the reception of any communication so referred to.

FILING OF DUPLICATES OF MESSAGES.—We keep a duplicate of each message, (taken by means of carbon paper, in manifold,) each duplicate being numbered and put by with the others at the end of each day—the parcels being deposited in hampers sealed, and in a cupboard under lock and key. At the end of two years the messages are damped and mashed, until all trace of writing is lost.

Answer 58*th*—COST OF STATIONERY.—Our forms were much larger, and on a finer description of paper than at present used. But after a conversation with Mr. Shaffner, I have thought it best to change the size of the forms, and also the paper used; obtaining the present stationery at a geatly reduced rate.

Cost of Forms as under :—

Forms on which messages are written by customers, printed on both sides, with particulars, regulations, &c.	Five shillings and three pence per thousand, or $1 26.
Received message forms upon which communications are written for delivery,	*Same price as above.
Envelopes, printed with the words "Immediate," "By Magnetic Telegraph," and adhesive,	Five shillings per thousand, or $1 20.

Answer 59*th.*—Cannot give average—so much variation as to size, locality, &c.

Answer 60*th*—TIME OF CLERK LABOR.—Duty of clerks and messengers averages nine hours during day, and eight hours when on evening or night duty at the principal stations.

The older clerks take night duty in rotation. The younger clerks are always kept to day or evening work.

Answer 61*st.*—No.

Answer 62*d*—RESPONSIBILITY FOR ERRORS IN LAW.—We have never lost damages in any court—the question of responsibility has been occasionally tried. The most recent case is one in which the British Telegraph Company were implicated—the plaintiff being beaten.

I subjoin a copy of a press report from the Glasgow Chronicle, dated June 28th, 1854, of a suit instituted by Messrs. Dick and Martin, shawl manufacturers, Paisley, against the British Telegraph Company. Subjoined verbatim :—

"A manufacturing firm in Paisley, having lately sent a message by telegragh to their London agent, 'return all printed squares above five shillings,' and the message having been delivered with the word 'scarfs' substituted for 'squares,' which led to two days delay in the squares arriving in Paisley, the manufacturers brought a small debt action against the telegraph company, and their agent, Mr. William M'Intyre, jr., for £12 damages, as loss sustained by them in consequence.

"The defendant denied liability, pleading the message order as a special contract, which contained a condition, declaring that they would not be liable for mistakes. The sheriff took the case to avisandum for a week, and on Thursday last pronounced his decision, sustaining the defence."

The Chronicle remarks, that the decision must be regarded as of great importance, considering the continual risk of small mistakes occurring in the transmission of messages over long distances with several "repeats," and the ruinous amount of damages in which telegraph companies if liable might be involved. The agent for pursuers in this case was Mr. John Guy—for defendants, Mr. Thomas Campbell.

In this instance, the message had to travel over several companies' lines. The British company's wire not extending beyond Manchester.

Legal advisers, as a rule, do not like bringing forward such cases in the face of the conditions subscribed to by their clients upon the company's paper.

I consider that a claim cannot be well established except in a case of a repeated or insured message, as a claimant would be met with "Why did you not insure, if your message was of such consequence? Seeing that the company has a special provision for such cases! And in the case of any mistake or non-delivery of an insured message, the company would be willing to pay, upon proof, without going to law.

Answer 63*d*.—FREE MESSAGES.—No free messages, except those purely on the business of the company, and sent by the officers of the company, are allowed.

When directors or shareholders wish to send messages, they pay the ordinary tariff like any other customer, handing the message in over the counter in the usual form.

Answer 64*th*—TARIFF FOR PRESS NEWS.—Our rates to the press are far less than to the public. There are two district systems in operation as regards the transmission of intelligence for the news rooms and papers. Either they can supply themselves from their own agents, or contract for a supply from the company. In the former case, an universal tariff of sixpence per line of nine words is charged, whether between London and Liverpool, London and Glasgow, or London and Cork, &c., and by this system, of course, *special* news can be forwarded.

In the latter, the company having established agents and re

porters in the various towns with which we communicate, the press are furnished daily with a column and a half to two columns of the latest political, foreign, commercial, and market news, in return for a payment amounting on the average to a little over a farthing a line. But of course in this case the news forwarded is perhaps distributed in duplicate among the three or four news rooms and dozen papers of the town.

Answer 65*th*—REGULARITY OF BUSINESS.—This company, since the commencement of *working*, in February, 1852, lost four messages. In each case the amount paid was returned; none were insured. In one case, an action was brought but could not be sustained.

Answer 66*th*.—If, under any circumstances, a message is not sent in half an hour after being handed to the company, the superintendants are instructed to send word to the customers, giving the reason why the message has been delayed; it is then at the option of the party to withdraw his message and receive back the amount paid; or to allow the company further time to transmit it.

Answer 67*th*.—As previously mentioned, government communications take precedence.

Private (paid) messages come next in order, constituting the bulk of the company's business. Next to these rank news messages, whether forwarded by the agents of the company or of the press. In any great emergency, however, where a prompt order is necessary, a business message (usually *last* in order of precedence) is sent by an officer of the company before anything else, with a peculiar code or cypher prefixed to denote the extreme urgency of the message; and if any communication should be sent with such prefix without necessity, the officer sending it would be subjected to dismissal.

I may mention that the company's news messages are usually passed at hours in the day when the commercial business is slack.

Answer 68*th*—PRE-PAYMENT REQUIRED ON MESSAGES.—Prepayment is required upon all messages forwarded by the public; but good customers—sending many messages in the course of a day—are not usually called upon to pay at the time of sending each message; but an account is made up in the afternoon and sent round by a clerk, whose duty it is to collect in money for the cashier.

In cases of great exigency or emergency, persons are sometimes allowed to send messages "to be paid for by the receiver;" and *answers* are frequently pre-paid by those sending the messages requiring answers.

Answer 69th.—No. Answered in 63.

Answer 70th—OPERATING DEPARTMENT.—Three clerks to every two instruments, *i. e.*, an instrument while *sending* requires *one* clerk; and when *receiving*, two, one to read off, and the other to write down from dictation.

Answer 71st.—The apparatus belonging to, and used by, this company, is the magnetic telegraph, (the practical application of magneto-electricity to telegraphic apparatus,) and of course consists in principle of a needle telegraph, worked by the inductive influence exercised by magnets upon electro-magnetic coils, when placed in propinquity to the poles of the permanent magnets.

The electro-magnetic coils are so arranged that their cores of soft iron serve as a keeper (in facto) to the permanent magnet.

Professor Faraday is accounted the discoverer of the *principle*; and after many unsuccessful attempts to apply it to practical purposes, Steinheil, of Munich, (I believe,) was able to construct a magneto-electric machine to work between Munich and Bogenhausen.

Subsequently Professor Wheatstone endeavored to apply it, but failed, except as far as relates to ringing bells by an apparatus familiarly known as a "thunder-pump," from the pumping action of the machine, which consisted of a lever-handle, at the end of which two large electro-magnetic coils were fixed,—the axis allowing the coils to be attracted against a magnet; this apparatus engendered a strong current of electricity for ringing bells, but no indicating apparatus was contrived.

Mr. Henley afterwards managed by arranging a magnet-needle between a pair of horns of soft iron, projecting from the poles of a pair of small electro-magnetic coils—to obtain with the motion of the lever a backward and forward movement of the needles.

Since that time, various improvements have been introduced by my brother Charles and myself. The apparatus is found to answer every purpose as far as speed, certainty, invariability of action, and small cost of maintenance is concerned. The improved apparatus is moreover the only telegraph that I am acquainted with that works satisfactorily in connection with underground wires, as in its present form it is not at all affected by the induced currents that affect other apparatus. Cost varies, from £15 for small, to £36 for large.

Answer 72d.—Mistakes are of very unfrequent occurrence with us—averaging about 1 in 2,400 messages sent by this company, and two out of three are occasioned by the indistinct writing of customers. Others are caused by the similarity of sound between certain words, such as "hour," "our"—"one," done," &c. The immediate movement of our needles and their *dead-beat*, (*i. e.*, the absence of all vibration and oscillation,) greatly tend to prevent mistakes. In the ordinary galvanic telegraphs of Cooke, Highton, and others, the needle sways to and fro after each beat, occasioning confusion between letters, which are formed by combinations of "*beats.*" We also employ clerks in charge to check over all messages received or transmitted, to see that the context is correctly rendered, and the words rightly spelt.

Answer 73*d.*—At first we repeated all paid messages, but I found it led to more frequent error, as the clerks relied so much upon the repetition to correct any error, that they signalled in the first instance carelessly; and in any pressure of business the repetition being made still more hastily, they more frequently committed blunders.

I do not quite understand the latter part of the question, but suppose that answers 56–7; 66–7–8–9, will also apply to this.

Answer 74*th.*—As mentioned in answer 50, each word, on being forwarded through the instrument, is succeeded by an affirmative or negative signal from the receiving station. If the former, the word next in order is sent; if the latter, the word just sent is repeated.

Answer 75*th.*—The plan of insurance has been prescribed by this company for two years and a half, but, as mentioned in "52," the principle has not been adopted by customers.

Answer 76*th.*—If called upon to insure, the company would refuse to take such responsibility beyond their own lines, having no mutual arrangement with other companies on the subject. And in any case, it would be highly dangerous for one company to undertake responsibility for the working of another company; especially if the slightest ill-feeling existed on the part of either, as one might take advantage of such a system of insurance to ruin the other.

Answer 83*d*—PRESERVATION OF WIRE CABLES.—In reference to this question, I may observe, that tar is found to act as a great preservative in connection with iron, when immersed in salt water; hence, in making a cable, it is advisable to saturate the hemp surrounding the conducting wires with Stockholm tar, prior to laying on the outer casing of protecting wires. With a cable so constructed, it is advisable to select as *sandy* a bottom as possible; for the cable we laid between Donaghadee and Portpatrick, made on this plan, is found to have surrounded itself, when passing through sand, with a hard concrete, impervious to moisture, composed of sand and the tar that had oozed from the cable. There is an objection to galvanized wire, owing to its brittleness, interfering with the process of manufacture, and with the laying, by continual snapping; the galvanizing appears to make the wire in parts assume the crystalline condition in lieu of the fibrous.

Answer 91*st*—CABLES NOT LIABLE TO INJURY BY LIGHTNING.—A submarine cable, in connection with the underground system, is not, I apprehend, liable to injury from lightning, as such a cable would offer no more inducement, but at the same time far greater resistance to the exit of electricity through the insulating medium, from its wires, than the underground wires would evince. In the first place, the gutta percha coating of the submarine wires is considerably thicker than that around the land wires, and besides this, each wire in the cable is surrounded in addition by a thick non-conducting layer of closely packed tarred yarn.

The electricity, if ever it managed to get into the underground wires in any dangerous quantity, would naturally seek an equalization by the easiest path, and would make its way through the insulating coating of the subterranean wires to the moisture surrounding them, in preference to the cable.

It would, however, be extremely difficult for the electricity to pass into the wires, which are never brought above ground, save in the offices, when in connection with an instrument; and lightning would be opposed on entry by the thin coil-wire of the apparatus.

If submarine cables are used in connection with *overground* wires, it would be advisable to use every means of arresting, or rendering nugatory, a discharge of atmospheric electricity.

I should think several short coils of thin wire, consecutively interposed in the circuit on either side, would produce the required effect, especially when placed in an *earth* box; for any electricity that could pass without facing the coils and escaping to earth in transitu, would be comparatively harmless in the cable.

As it may be of some interest, I subjoin an extract from the London Times, May 26, 1853, relating to the submersion of our submarine cable between Donaghadee and Portpatrick.

"THE SUBMARINE TELEGRAPH BETWEEN GREAT BRITAIN AND IRELAND.

"This important line of communication has at length been successfully effected (as briefly announced in the Times yesterday), by a submarine cable, manufactured by the well-known masters, Messrs. Newell & Co., of Gateshead, and laid down, on Monday, between Donaghadee and Portpatrick.

"The cable consists of six communicating wires insulated in gutta percha, and protected, in the usual manner, by an outer covering of iron wire.

"It could not be laid, as was intended, during the previous week, owing to the gales from the east preventing the opening of the dock gates at Sunderland to let the vessel containing it pass out. As several previous attempts to lay a submarine telegraph across the Irish Channel had failed, every care was taken to ensure the successful termination of the present attempt; and the expedition, consisting of the screw steamer William Hull, (with the cable and apparatus on board) the Conqueror and the Wizard, left the Irish coast, having landed the end of the cable at a point about two miles to the south of Donaghadee harbor, and commenced the submersion of the cable, under the guidance of Captain Hawes, R. N., specially appointed by the Admiralty, who rendered great assistance in determining and directing the exact course to be pursued, without which, in all probability, the squadron could not have successfully overcome the swift tides and adverse currents prevalent throughout that part of the Channel.

"The party who accompanied the laying of the cable included Messrs. Newel, Mr. Statham, of the Gutta Percha Works, Mr. Bright, the Secretary, Mr. Charles Bright, the Engineer of the English and Irish Magnetic Telegraph Company, Mr. Reid, the well-known telegraph engineer, and Mr. Mosely. The cable was landed on Wednesday morning in a sandy bay (called Mora Bay), a little to the north of Portpatrick, which belongs to Mr. Blair, of Dunskey, who kindly accorded permission for the laying of the land wires through his estate; and as soon as the end had been taken up to the position assigned, the magnetic instruments were put in operation, and the following message was despatched:—

"'MORA BAY, PORTPATRICK, Monday, May 23.

"'The Directors of the English and Irish Magnetic Telegraph Company beg to acquaint His Excellency the Lord Lieutenant, that they have, this morning, successfully effected communication between the shores of Great Britain and Ireland, by means of a submarine cable from Portpatrick to Donaghadee.'

"The cable at each side was then buried in the trenches prepared for its reception, and instruments connected to serve as a means of communication for a short time, until the subterranean line of six wires, now being carried from the Company's station at Carlisle, through Dumfries, to meet the cable at Portpatrick, is completed to that spot; and an underground line is about to be extended from the Irish end of the cable at Donaghadee to Newtonards, the terminal station of the County Down Railway, along which the wires of the English and Irish Magnetic Telegraph Company are nearly completed to Belfast. At Belfast, the wires meet the Company's line of telegraph already completed over the Ulster Railway, and will be carried *via* the Belfast Junction and Dublin and Drogheda Railways, into the Company's offices, on College Green, Dublin, where their line from Galway (already working) and their Southern lineof telegraph, now in forward course of construction from Cork, will concentrate.

"The lines of the English and Irish Magnetic Telegraph Company, now working between Liverpool, Manchester, Blackburn, Bolton and Preston, and between Carlisle, Glasgow, Greenock and Edinburgh; and those now in forward progress between London and Manchester (consisting of ten subterranean wires), and between Preston and Carlisle, will join on at Carlisle; and the three capitals and chief towns of England, Scotland and Ireland will be thus brought into instantaneous communication with one another."

Answer 94*th*—ELECTRIC CIRCUITS FOR SUCCESSFUL WORKING.—I observe, in my brother's answer to this question, that he has merely referred to our existing arrangements with regard to circuits, and I would therefore add a few remarks.

It has been found in England that none but large towns yield any profit upon the working expenses of a telegraph; we therefore determined, in the outset, not to extend our wires to any points where a profit could not be obtained; hence our station list is small, and does not require more than five or six, or, at the utmost, eight stations in a circuit.

It is not, I consider, advisable to have too many stations in a circuit, continual interruption arising, combined with difficulty in obtaining that prompt attention to calls requisite.

Moreover, from the many connections, a circuit with a number of stations at all approaching that mentioned, would be much more likely to get out of order, from its integrity being disturbed.

In addition to this, an operator, in case the wires were occupied when he wished to forward a message, could not tell how long he might have to wait before the other stations would be sufficiently disengaged to allow him time to obtain the attention of the station he required, and to send his message; and the *calls* become very complicated when more than eight stations are in a circuit.

Many towns in this country have no demand for speedy communication by telegraph, although the charge for messages is low—about a shilling for twenty words (address not being counted, and porterage within a mile of station free) per hundred miles. This want of a demand is chiefly due to the facilities afforded by the postal arrangements, which are speedy and excellent, and partly to the steadiness of business and non-existence in many towns of any speculative trade.

We possess arrangements of a simple nature, ready for use whenever needed by the company, by which, even with a badly insulated line, any number of stations can be linked together, in immediate correspondence to and fro with one another, whether on the main line or branches.

Answer 98*th*—GOVERNMENTAL LINES IN ENGLAND.—The use of the telegraph in connection with the government and the police might be much more *systematized*, but at present great desultory use is made of the various telegraphs in this country by government, relating to the army, navy, and commissariat. In the southern districts government has had several lines constructed between the head-quarters of government and the chief naval depôts and arsenals, and have their wires worked by their own staff.

ARREST OF FUGITIVES FROM JUSTICE.—In many instances we have aided the police in arresting fugitives from justice. Sometimes telegraphing the exact dress, height, and personal appearance, with any special marks for identification of the party sought after.

In each case the company is merely the *carriers* of orders and instructions between the police of one city and another.

In the shipment of troops to the East, and prior to the departure of the naval squadrons, government made continual use of our wires, orders, countermands and directions following one another.

Answer 99th—BANKING BY TELEGRAPH.—The banks generally pass though certain codes known only to themselves and their correspondents—varying with each day. Such code-signals precede the *body* of the message. By this check on frauds, banks daily transact a large amount of business—chiefly relating to returning bills or stopping local notes. Sometimes remittances of twenty and even thirty thousand pounds ($140,000) are made by means of advice by telegraph from one bank to another. They frequently also inquire as to respectability of parties—managers holding applicants in conversation till the answer arrives.

MESSAGES RECEIVED AS EVIDENCE IN COURT.—Messages are received as evidence in court. The signature of the party sending the message being sworn to, and also that of the party receiving, (entered on the messenger's ticket.)

There is no law compelling evidence on the part of a telegraph company; but in all cases where necessary, that I am aware of, evidence has been given freely.

THE MERMAID'S LAST NEW SONG.

ON THE SUBMARINE TELEGRAPH, CONNECTING ENGLAND AND FRANCE.

BY DOUGLASS JERROLD.

THE mariners brave tidings bring
That they through Dover's Strait who steer,
If, of an understanding ear,
Thus ofttimes hear the mermaid sing,
When the blue deep is calm and clear:

A wonder have I seen below,
A marvel new and strange to me,
Who dwell beneath the rolling sea,
Amid the wrecks sunk long ago;
The wealth of Ocean's treasury.

There runneth an enchanted wire
O'er the sea-bed, from shore to shore,
Of nations that were foes of yore;
The conduit of a magic fire,
Lightning beneath the water's roar.

The skulls of ancient enemies
Around it lying, grimly frown;
There, where the slain of old went down,
Through wars of hoary centuries,
In many an action of renown.

The flash, amid those forms of death,
Flits quick as thought from land to land;
No hostile bolt, no deadly brand,
Nay: but a soft electric breath,
Warm like the grasp of friendly hand.

A kindly spirit guides its aim,
Benignant science bids it fly,
Conveying question and reply;
There's language in that social flame,
And France and England talk thereby.

'Mid antique arms, old gun, and sword,
Which insects of the sea o'erlay,
Of those long fall'n in savage fray,
The bony fingers with the chord,
That links the nations, gently play.

And sea-sprites, as they sport along
That nerve of wire, by human skill
Between two peoples made to thrill,
Sing joyously the Mermaid's Song,
To England, peace!—to France, goodwill!

ART. II.—BUSINESS FORMS IN THE ENGLISH TELEGRAPHS.

WE annex a series of blank forms used by the respective telegraph companies in Great Britain. They are herein presented in their adopted form, and about the same size, as those in use by the lines in England. We also give the blank receipts and account forms. We give a brief explanation of the forms respectively.

On pages 224–5, Document A, will be found a blank form, which is used by the public in the presentation of a message, to be transmitted by the telegraph company. The two pages re present the face of the blank form in which the message is written, and the heading is to be filled by the company's clerk. The patron signs the message. Document B, page 226, is printed on the back of the sheet on which the message is written, represented by Document A, on pages 224–5.

Document C, pages 228–9, is the form used by another company. Documents D, on page 227 and E, page 230, are forms printed on the back of the sheet, marked Document C, pages 228–9. These forms present the tariff of insurance and assumed responsibility. Pages 228–9, are on one side of the sheet, and pages 227—230, are on the other side of the official form. Document F, page 231, is the head or caption of a message as sent to the public. The face of the sheet is about the size of the usual letter paper, only half of the blank being represented by Document F, page 231.

Document I, page 232, is a blank used by the companies for messages received from a distant office, and which is to be transmitted further by another line. The size of this blank is the same as Documents A and C, only half of the sheet being represented. The forms at the bottom of the page are to be filled, and then sent to the next line. In order to prevent confusion, the blanks are printed in different coloured inks.

Document G, page 233, is the form of an account sent out with the messenger, accompanying a message for collection.

Document H, page 234, is the form of a receipt given the customer on the reception of his message for transmission at the counter of the company by the cashier.

Doc. A.

ENGLISH AND IRISH MAGNETIC TELEGRAPH COMPANY.

LIVERPOOL STATION, 2 EXCHANGE BUILDINGS.

No .... Date .... 1854.

Received .... }
Sent .... }

Code ....

No. of Words } ....

To Station. } .... By me .... Clerk.

Please to send the following Messages according to the conditions printed hereon.

Message,	"	"
Porterage,	"	"
Paid out,	"	"
Total	"	"

From	*To*
....	....
....	....
....	....
....	....
....	....

The Company will in every case guard as much as possible against mistakes, but cannot hold themselves responsible for any that may occur. } Signed

PLEASE TO WRITE DISTINCTLY.

Doc. B.

THE ENGLISH AND IRISH MAGNETIC TELEGRAPH COMPANY.

CONDITIONS AS TO UNINSURED MESSAGES.

The Public are informed that, in order to provide against mistakes in the transmission of MESSAGES by the MAGNETIC TELEGRAPH, every Message of consequence ought to be REPEATED by being sent back from the Station at which it is to be received, to the Station from which it is originally sent. Half the usual price for transmission will be charged for repeating the Message. The Company will not be responsible for mistakes in the transmission of unrepeated Messages, from whatever cause they may arise. Nor will the Company be responsible for mistakes in the transmission of a repeated Message, nor for delay in the transmission or delivery, nor for non-transmission or non-delivery of any Message, **whether repeated or unrepeated, to any extent above £5,** unless it be insured **at the rate of £1 per cent.**

Doc. D.

THE ELECTRIC TELEGRAPH COMPANY.

CONDITIONS AS TO UNINSURED MESSAGES.

The Public are informed that, in order to provide against mistakes in the transmission of MESSAGES by the ELECTRIC TELEGRAPH, every Message of consequence ought to be REPEATED by being sent back from the Station at which it is to be received, to the Station from which it is originally sent. Half the usual price for transmission will be charged for repeating the Message. The Company will not be responsible for Mistakes in the transmission of unrepeated Messages, from whatever cause they may arise. Nor will the Company be responsible for Mistakes in the transmission of a repeated Message, nor for delay in the transmission or delivery, nor for non-transmission or non-delivery of any Message, whether repeated or unrepeated, to any extent above £5, unless it be insured.

Correctness in the transmission of Messages can be Insured at the following rates in addition to the usual charge for repetition :—

	£ s. d.		£ s. d		£ s. d.
For any Sum up to £100	1 0 0	Above £400 to £500	5 0 0	Above £700 to £ 800	8 0 0
Above £100 to £200	2 0 0	£500 to £600	6 0 0	£800 to £ 900	9 0 0
£200 to £300	3 0 0	£600 to £700	7 0 0	£900 to £1000	10 0 0
£300 to £400	4 0 0				

and 20*s*. for every £100, or fraction of £100 above that sum ; and the Company will not be responsible for any amount beyond the sum for which the Message is insured and the rates paid.—**The Company will not be responsible in any case for delays arising from interruptions in the working of their Telegraphs.**

J. L. RICARDO, *Chairman.*

Doc. C.

STATION.

THE ELECTRIC TELEGRAPH COMPANY.

Prefix..........	Code Time.......... No..........	Message.......... " "
Received..........*m*	Date..........185	Repeating.......... " "
	Sent to..........*Station.*	Reply.......... " "
Finished..........*m*	by me..........*Clerk.*	Porterage.......... " "
		To be paid out.......... " "
		Total.......... " "

(All numbers must be written at length in words.)

PLEASE TO SEND THE FOLLOWING UNINSURED MESSAGE ACCORDING TO THE CONDITIONS ENDORSED HEREON.

FROM		TO	
Name and Address of the Sender of the Message.	....	**Name and full Address of the Person to whom the Message is to be delivered.**	....

....

....

....

Before Signing, please to see that the amount to be charged for the message is correctly entered above, & on the receipt, and read the endorsed Conditions.

Signature and Address of Sender. ....

The Company will not be answerable for Errors caused by indistinct writing.

Doc. E.

NOTICE.—Messages to be sent to any places beyond the extent of the Company's Lines or Stations, will be delivered by the Company's officers at their terminal Station mentioned in the subjoined request, to such parties as may have charge of the further means of conveyance; but it is expressly provided that the Company are in no case to be held responsible for the transmission or delivery of the Message beyond the terminal Station in such request mentioned.

(REQUEST.)

I request that this Message may be forwarded from the Company's Office at ....

(being the Terminal Station of the Company) by ....

to the address mentioned therein, subject to the above conditions, and have deposited ....

to be applied for that purpose.

Signed ....

Doc. F.

ENGLISH AND IRISH MAGNETIC TELEGRAPH COMPANY.

Code } Time } ______	**LIVERPOOL STATION,** 2 EXCHANGE BUILDINGS.	No. of } Words } ______

Received the following Message } At ______ h ______ m the ______ day of ______ 1854.

Signed ______ Clerk.

From	*To*
Name ______	*Name* ______
Address ______	*Address* ______

☞ **No inquiry respecting this Message can be attended to without the production of this paper.**

Doc. I.

ENGLISH AND IRISH MAGNETIC TELEGRAPH COMPANY.

From .... *Station.*	*Code Time*	.... *Station.*
To .... *Station.*	*No. of Words*	.... 1854.

FROM	TO
....	....
....	....

[The Form contains full space between these lines for a Message of fifty or more words in length. We omit the space.]

RECEIVED.	SENT.
Com : ...... *h.* ...... *m.* / *Fin* : ...... *h.* ...... *m.* — *Sd.*	*Com* : ...... *h.* ...... *m.* / *Fin* : ...... *h.* ...... *m.* — *Sd.* ....

Doc. G.

THE ENGLISH AND IRISH MAGNETIC TELEGRAPH COMPANY. **No.**

....1854.

Messenger's Name..

For..

H. M.

Sent out.... ....M.

Received at ....M.

Returned at ....M.

Signature of Receiver...

Charges to Pay..

Clerk's Initials...

N. B.—You are requested to give no fee or gratuity to the Messenger, and pay no charges beyond those entered in this sheet.

Doc. H.

ENGLISH AND IRISH MAGNETIC TELEGRAPH COMPANY.

LIVERPOOL STATION. Date..1854.

No.. Time received,.. No. of Words ....

From..

....

....

To..

....

....

Message	"	"
Portcrage	"	"
Paid out	"	"
Total	"	"

Signed ....*Clerk.*

ART. III.—COMPARATIVE CONDUCTIBILITY OF WIRE.

EXPERIMENTS ON THE CONDUCTIBILITY OF WIRE—IMPORTANT DISCOVERY IN TELEGRAPHY—GUTTA PERCHA WORKS IN THE WORLD—STATHAM'S FACTORY.

WE give below some experiments made by Mr. Statham, proprietor of the London Gutta Percha Works. There are four gutta percha manufactories now in existence:—one in London, one in Berlin, one in St. Petersburgh, and one in New-York; and of the four, the London works are far superior in every respect. Mr. Statham, who has labored so faithfully for many years in the production of the best means or mode of using gutta percha for electric telegraph purposes, has won for himself the admiration of the entire telegraphic community.

He has labored faithfully to devise the useful implements and auxiliaries required in the telegraphic art, and his success has been perfect. No one has done more for the art than Mr. S., and as a member of the profession, we feel grateful to him for the production of so much in the advancement of the telegraph enterprise. The London Gutta Percha Works manufacture gutta percha wares of all kinds, and his mode of insulating telegraphic wire is complete. Any company requiring wire for submarine, subterranean, or for office purposes, can safely depend upon Mr. Statham in forwarding the best article desired at an honest cost. He understands the subject much better than we who are more actively engaged in telegraphing; he has had facilities and experience superior to those which we have enjoyed, and his energies have impelled him to the consummation of the most useful and practical developments. We then, in view of these facts, recommend to all telegraph people, throughout the world, to procure gutta percha insulated wire from Mr. Statham. Inform him of the purposes of your wire, and he can best judge of the quality you need. What we here say, is wholly unsolicited by any one, and is the free and voluntary utterance of an opinion, produced by evidences enforcing conviction.

We refer to the following schedule, viz.,

EXPERIMENTS—*Showing relative resistance of No.* 18 *and No.* 16 *copper wire, insulated by double covering of gutta percha, and submerged in the Regent's Canal.*

Gutta Percha Works, 27*th May*, 1851.

No. 18.—Guage copper wire, covered with gutta percha to guage No. 7.

No. 16.—Guage copper wire, covered with gutta percha to guage No. 4.

An ordinary single needle instrument was employed—connected to earth, as usual in practice.

100 miles.	No. 18.	No. 16.	
With 3 pair plates	29°	39°	deflection of needle
6 do.	50°	59°	do.

The same instrument employed, but the needle slightly weighted.

Battery of 72 pairs plates.	No. 18.	No. 16.
100 miles	23°	30°
90 "	25°	
80 "	26½°	
70 "	28½°	
65 "	30°	

Battery of 144 pairs plates.	No. 18.	No. 16.
100 miles	35°	41°
90 "	37°	
80 "	38½°	
70 "	40°	
65 "	41°	

Battery of plates.	No. 18.	No. 16.
100 miles, 72 pr. plates	23°	30°
100 " 84	26°	
100 " 96	28½°	
100 " 102	30°	

ART. IV.—FRENCH NOTICES OF MORSE'S TELEGRAPH IN 1838.

PROOF OF THE EARLY INVENTION OF MORSE'S TELEGRAPH—NOTICES OF MORSE'S INVENTION BY THE PARIS PRESS—THE TELEGRAPH CONSIDERED BY THE ACADEMY.

In looking over the files of French papers, at the date of the presentation of *Morse's Telegraph* to the Academy of Sciences in Paris, September, 1838, we collected a few of the numerous notices of it, from which our readers can judge for themselves whether the Electro-Magnetic Telegraph was then considered an invention *well known*, or something *entirely new*.

From the Constitutionnel, Sept. 13, 1838.

"A foreign philosopher, M. Morse, of New-York, (who unhappily does not speak the French language, for we requested of him some explanations of his beautiful invention,) exhibited an *Electric Telegraph*. This instrument attracted the notice, and excited the curiosity of the whole Academy. M. Arago explained its mechanism, but in a manner too brief to enable us sufficiently to comprehend it.

Before speaking of it, we would see this telegraph in operation. We await elsewhere the future explanations which M. Arago has promised."

From the Courrier Francais, Sept. 13, 1838.

ACADEMY OF SCIENCES—SESSION OF 10th SEPTEMBER.

"Even before the opening of the session, an intricate apparatus, placed upon the table of the Academy, attracted all eyes. There was there seen a large magnet surrounded with electric conductors, some cylinders of brass, upon which paper was rolled up, and above all a cord, much intertwined, of galvanometer wire. It is the electric telegraph, established for sometime in the United States by Professor Morse, and which its author comes to submit for the approval of the Academy, and of France. Notwithstanding the exterior complication of this instrument, the general plan of it is very simple. A magnet, furnished with wires wound in a helix, which greatly increases its power; a wire conductor of indefinite length, which receives and transmits the current; some points of a pencil furnished with ink, which inscribes the dispatch in conventional black marks, and in which change of place forms an alphabet; such are the principles which lie at the basis of the electric telegraph. It appears that the system of Professor Morse unites the qualities of economy and certainty. It further offers this advantage, that it is not absolutelynecessary to have the persons employed permanently present at the place where the news is received, since the despatch inscribes itself. The strongest argument which presents itselt in favour of this invention of Professor Morse, is that it has already operated with complete success in the United States, through ten miles of conductors, or about four leagues.

Although we have seen the apparatus of Professor Morse, as well as many plans of German electric telegraphs, we by no means undertake to give here a description which would be superfluous to those who have examined these machines, and necessarily unintelligible to those who have not had this opportunity. We learn elsewhere that soon will be seen in action, in Paris, one of these telegraphs, upon a line of some extent. But while waiting for the realization of these promises, and even before the possibility of establishing long lines has been well established, the question of priority is contested with some warmth between the two worlds.

It is by no means easy to take positive ground in this contest.

There has been given to us even the first suggestions of some philosophers on this subject, as if in experimental science ideal machines were of the least value. It has been said that Franklin, and our celebrated musical composer Berton, had had *the idea* very strongly of electric correspondence at great distances. It appears that in the year 1794, a German philosopher, Reiser, gave a plan of an electric telegraph, by means of the ordinary machine, a plan which had been realized in Spain about 1798, by a Doctor Salva.

It is easily conceived that the invention of the galvanic battery, which dates in 1800, has given a new aspect to all these attempts. But ten years passed away ere any one attempted to take advantage of the immortal discovery of Volta. It was not till 1811, that Soëmmerring proposed an electric telegraph based upon the voltaic current, by means of thirty-five conductors, insulated from each other, which were to represent all the letters and cyphers possible. Its complication, even the inextricable intricacy of this apparatus consigned it to the region of impossibilities.

Ten years later, that is to say, about the year 1820, our countryman, the philosopher Ampère, attempted to find an electric telegraph in the discoveries of Oersted, as Soëmmerring had attempted to find it in those of Volta. Ampère gave the plan in a few words, which has been much better carried out since his time, in proposing as many magnet needles as there are letters of the alphabet, put in action by conductors, which are made successively to communicate with the battery by the touches of a key, which is depressed at pleasure.

Ampère thus saw that his process furnished the means of overcoming all distances.

Therefore, after the historical researches of M. Amyot, it must be admitted that the ideas of all those who have occupied themselves in England, in Germany, and even in Russia, in constructing the electric telegraph, have rested on the process of M. Ampère. The instrument of Professor Morse, shown to us, comes evidently within this category.* But can one award the title of inventor to an idea, very happy, it is true, but which the

*This is a mistake. Ampère's suggestion was the use of the *magnetic needle*, and this indeed is the basis of all the English, German, and even Russian telegraph systems. Morse's suggestion is entirely original with him. It is the use of the electro-magnet; it is a new basis of an electric telegraph, first suggested by him, and which he has successfully carried out. He is indebted to Ampère for nothing except the fact that an *intensity current overcomes all distances*. This is the fact discovered by Ampère, but which had been erroneously given, until recently, to Professor Henry.—EDITOR.

illustrious Ampère has only casually thrown out in his first memoir upon electro-magnetism.

We see then that in truth there does not yet exist the inventor of the electric telegraph.

The inventor will be the first *constructor*, (constructeur,) who will operate the machine upon a line of considerable extent.

Under this aspect of the matter, the palm might perhaps be given to the Baron Schilling, an amateur philosopher, who constructed at St. Petersburgh, in 1832-33, an electric telegraph which operated in a very satisfactory manner, for a considerable distance, and under the eyes of the Emperor. Schilling died a little after his first attempts, and the Russian government had abandoned an object which for it, above all, is of the greatest importance. The importance of sure electric telegraphs is readily comprehended for an empire which extends in Europe from Finland to the Black Sea.

After these experiments a multitude of attempts were simultaneously made, at many points. During the labors of Professor Morse in the United States, Professor Wheatstone disposed a telegraph to wire with electric relays in the vast cellars of the University of London; and Professor Steinheil, of Munich, corresponded regularly from his house with the botanic garden, by means of a telegraph with a thousand ingenious details in its construction. It seems this last philosopher has followed out the suggestions of the celebrated geometrician, M. Gauss. In France, M. Amyot appears to have attempted a degree of simplicity still superior: a single current, a single needle, which writes of itself on paper the correspondence which gives at the other extremity a simple wheel upon which a person has written it by the aid of points differently spaced, as in the cylinder organ of Barbary; such are the bases of his process. In short, at Caen, M. Professor Masson has lately announced that he has established with success an electric telegraph, operating by means of magnetic needles at the two extremities, on a line of about 600 yards.

These brief remarks which the telegraph of Professor Morse have suggested to us, will suffice to show that the question of the electric telegraph occupies at this time the attention of eminent minds so largely, as to lead us to expect with confidence to see it resolved. As M. Arago has well remarked in describing the apparatus of Professor Morse, the great difficulty lies in the establishment and placing of the conducting wires. Suspension in the air appears nearly impossible, for this mode is liable to all sorts of attack from malevolence. On the other hand, interring them in the ground would seem to present a greater inconvenience, which will arise in case they should become out of order among themselves, or broken in some part of the line. Nothing can point out the precise place where the evil exists. Would it be necessary to disinter the whole telegraphic line to repair a single point? Neither has one dreamt, at least in the apparatus where the wires are large and insulated, of the dangers which present themselves from the discharges of atmospheric electricity upon a line so extended. For example, from Paris to Bordeaux, one must admit, that many times in the year there is a storm more or less in the day upon the whole route, and can any one tell what effect will be produced at the termini, on the appearance of lightning at some of the intermediate points? This kind of despatch deserves serious consideration; at least it is a question as] yet unresolved. But however this may be, the Academy appears to take a great interest in the system of Professor Morse. Unhappily, this philosopher does not possess our language sufficiently to describe himself his system, of which he expects such great results, and the introduction of which among us is at the same time a scientific and political event. The electric telegraph and its splendid promises, has diverted our attention from other subjects treated at this session," &c.

From the "National," September 13, 1838.

ACADEMY OF SCIENCES, SESSION OF 10th SEPTEMBER, 1838.—TELEGRAPHY.—ELECTRIC TELEGRAPHS.

"It is a long time since we have spoken of electric telegraphs. Still, until to-day, the different notes addressed to the Academy upon this subject, at the same time curious and important, have indifferently attracted the attention of the philosophers of France. But in the session of this day, M. Arago, in presenting a novel electric telegraph in the name of M. Morse of the United States, dwelt in a manner altogether peculiar on the mechanism of this new system, which was operated in presence of the public. It will be difficult for us to give a very clear idea of it without the aid of a diagram. But we can do no less than record here some details of it, as possessing much interest, since perhaps in half a century France and Europe will be furrowed (sillonnées) with these new lines, which are, for the transportation of thought, what the most rapid railroads are for the transportation of merchandize.

* * * * *

This system presents one question for solution. Will it be best to suspend the conducting wires inhe air, or to put them beneath the ground? In the air, we shall sooner see if they are continuous, but at the same time, malevolence can cut them more easily. Beneath the ground, the advantages and disadvantages will be in an inverse ratio. The wires will be, it is true, protected from destruction, but when they shall have been broken, a great number of tubes must be broken open, before the place to be repaired can be found.

The apparatus of M. Morse is of the size of a small writing-desk; but it would have been not more than half the size, if the inventor had not wished to prevent the accidents by journeying, and the ravages of our amiable custom house officers."

From the "Journal des Debats," September 18, 1838.

ACADEMY OF SCIENCES.—SESSION OF 10*th* & 17*th* SEPTEMBER.

"The electric telegraph makes its way by degrees, and we do not despair very soon to see it take the place of the present machines with arms upon our buildings with as much advantage as steam has taken the place of the heavy horse-power of our factories. Professor Morse has submitted to the Academy a complete system of his invention, which has been in operation in the United States through a distance of many miles. The substantial difficulties which yet present themselves to the establishment of these admirable means of communication, as quick as lightning, cannot much longer resist the genius and skill of philosophers."

In an article published in the Journal des Debats of September 25, 1838, on the subject of lighting Paris, the author, M. Tournal, thus alludes to the exhibition of Professor Morse's telegraph to the Academy.

"Listen then; an example borrowed from some facts of another nature, will better illustrate my thought. Is it not true that when the invention of telegraphs, that marvellous invention which demonstrates to the most incredulous the possibility of a European union, men the most eminent believed in good faith that it was not possible in the nature of things to transmit thought with greater promptness, since in the most favorable circumstances, a half hour was sufficient to send a despatch from one end of France to the other, and a single signal could be sent from Paris to the Mediterranean in five minutes? Well, at this moment, numerous experiments, made with electric telegraphs, demonstrate irrevocably, that man can, by means of some copper plates and iron wire, send instantaneously a despatch over all parts of the European continent. These experiments have already been realized on a great scale at Munich and at New-York; and, can it be believed? an apparatus, very ingenious, adapted to one of the termini of the telegraph, completely dispenses with the presence of the superintendent, the despatches imprint themselves upon a strip of paper which is wound on a cylindrical roller. All those persons who were present at the session of the Academy of Sciences on the 10th of September, will testify to the authenticity of this discovery."

We see by the above extracts, what was the state of knowledge, and what were the opinions of the scientific world, in regard to the telegraph generally, and Morse's system in particular, in the year 1838.

It was with them a visionary scheme unworthy of the attention of the scientific minds of the Academy, until Morse's system was exhibited to the Academy, and explained with peculiar force, and with approbation by the celebrated Arago. Doubts were still entertained, amidst sanguine hopes that the electric telegraph would soon be proved a practicable enterprize. How was it then in France some years later? Eight years had passed, and the doubts of its practicability were not dispelled, at least to the satisfaction of the legislative mind of France. We give the following from the Paris correspondent of the National Intelligencer, in the summer of 1846:

"Professor Morse had the goodness to send me an account of the recent achievements of the electrical telegraph, with a copy of the Baltimore Sun, containing the President's message in the Mexican war, as it was magically transmitted to that paper. I sent the communication to *Pouillet,* the Deputy, author of the report heretofore mentioned to you, and he placed them in the hands of ARAGO, who submitted their very interesting contents to the *Academy of Sciences* and the *Chamber of Deputies.* In the chamber, on the 18th instant, when the proposed appropriation for an electrical telegraph from this capital to the Belgian frontier came under consideration, BERRYER opposed it on the ground that the experiment of the new system was not complete; that it would be well to wait for the full trial of what was undertaken between Paris and Rouen.

"ARAGO answered. *The experiment is consummated.* In the United States *the matter is settled irresistibly.* I received, three days ago, the *Sun* of Baltimore, with a letter of MR. MORSE, one of the most honorable men of his country, and here is the President's message printed from the telegraph in two or three hours; the message would fill *four columns of the Moniteur;* it could not have been copied by the most rapid penman in a shorter time than it was transmitted. The galvanic fluid travels seventy thousand leagues per minute."

"THE APPROPRIATION, OF NEARLY HALF A MILLION OF FRANCS, WAS PASSED *with only a few dissenting voices. The bill has been reported to the Chamber of Peers*, with a circumstantial and able recommendation from the pen of GABRIEL DELESSERT, chairman of the Committee of Peers."

It will be thus perceived that the electric telegraph had not been established in France, in 1846, while it was in full and active operation in this country, and, moreover, that it was the result of its success here that operated to its establishment in France. Morse's system is, at this date, established throughout the Continent of Europe thousands of miles, and is still in process of extension, and is fast superseding the needle and signal systems. Even in England, where the Morse telegraph has never been practically tried, it is about being introduced. We expect, in the future, to discuss the relative modes of telegraphing with a consideration to financial economy.

ART. V.—MEDITERRANEAN ELECTRIC TELEGRAPH,

UNITING EUROPE WITH AFRICA, EAST INDIES AND AUSTRALIA, VIA FRANCE, PIEDMONT, CORSICA, SARDINIA, ALGERIA AND EGYPT.

JOHN WATKINS BRETT, ESQ., GERANT.

WE append the substance of a circular, issued by the International Telegraph Company, relative to the extension of the line across the Mediterranean Sea. The whole management is under the direction of that wonderful and energetic telegrapher, John W. Brett, Esq., who has been the foremost man of the world in the extension of submarine lines and the general advancement of electric telegraphs.

In the advancement and promotion of this grand undertaking, connecting Europe with Africa, the French government has exhibited a degree of energy and character not surpassed by any other government. The Emperor of the French has had opportunities of witnessing the advantages to be derived from the extension of the electric telegraph, and with a spirit of enterprise that does honor to his power and country, he elevates the art in every way possible, for the general good of his people. Had the present emperor been on the throne in 1838, Professor Morse would not have met the sad fate he did when in France. After much expense in exhibiting his wonderful achievement in the invention of the electric telegraph,—producing the first available system known to man, he procured a patent from the French government. One of the conditions of the patent was, a requirement to put his invention into actual operation within two years. After much effort, Professor Morse effected an arrangement to fulfil this provision of the patent by the aid of one of the railways.

The fact becoming known to the government, Prof. Morse was served with information, prohibiting the erection of the line. This order continued in existence until after the expiration of his patent, and was then rescinded. These are the facts as near as we can give them. The king of the French ought to have abdicated long before he did. But he is gone! It would have been better to have informed Morse before he went to much expense, that his telegraph could not have been allowed in that country. We do not refer to this with a view to cast any unreasonable reflections upon the memory of the ex-king; but we refer to it, to show what difficulties Professor Morse had to contend with in the establishment of his telegraph, and also to illustrate the difference between the power of France in 1838, and that of 1855. The former was indifferent to the wants of the age, and the latter carefully studies and exerts himself to advance his country and promote the happiness of his people.

We will not say more at present upon this subject, and therefore refer the reader to the following, for further information relative to the extension of the electric telegraph, and the liberal consideration given to it by the French and Sardinian governments.

REPORT OF JOHN W. BRETT, GERANT.

GENTLEMEN :—We shall assemble on the 14th instant, to inaugurate the completion of the first portion of the submarine cable for the great Mediterranean and Indian line of telegraph, and it may be interesting to you, first, to recapitulate the various heads of the concessions, and, secondly, to inform you of the state of the works at the present moment.

The concessions were confirmed to me by the French and Sardinian governments, with the guarantees and privileges as above, on the 1st of June, 1853, allowing two years for the completion of the works, and an open communication for telegraphic correspondence in all languages, without restriction.

1ST.—THE CONCESSIONS

Give to the company the power to construct any number of telegraph lines (h e junction of the telegraph lines of

Italy, France, and England, at Spezzia,) across the Mediterranean, *en route* to India, with exclusive privileges for fifty years, dating from June, 1855.

STATE OF THE WORKS.

The first portions of the submarine cable intended to unite Spezzia with Corsica, and Corsica with Sardinia, is now completed (110 miles), allowing some 20 miles more than the actual distance, and it is confidently expected that these two portions will be laid down and in operation by the middle of July next, by which time the whole of the land lines (about 800 kilometers) in the islands of Corsica and Sardinia, will be finished.

About fifty miles of the second portion (150 miles) of the submarine cable is aleady completed, and it is confidently expected that this will be also laid down about the middle of August next, uniting the Island of Sardinia with the telegraph lines of the French Government at Bone, in Algiers, when the present undertaking of this company will be accomplished.

The company are at present under treaty with the English government for an extension of the telegraph to Malta; but as this extension would be purely a government line, it cannot be undertaken without some similar support from the British government to that already granted to this company by the French and Sardinian governments for the extensions to Algiers and the island of Sardinia; and they also confidently look forward to a fair support from the East India Company to enable them to extend the lines to Alexandria and India.

It must be borne in mind that, in addition to the difficulties attending the introduction of a system of telegraphs—in countries where all the necessary materials and labor had to be imported—other adverse circumstances have occured, not the least of which have been the enormous increase in the price of the materials and labor, and the extraordinary demands for freight (namely 90*s.* per ton,) owing to the demand of vessels for the government service. Notwithstanding these disadvantages, the works have been carried on energetically, both in the islands of Corsica and Sardinia, aided by the able superintendence of some of the most experienced and practical telegraphic engineers in Europe.

We must be allowed to add, that the thanks of the shareholders are due to Mr. Tupper, of the firm of Tupper and Carr, contractors for the cable, &c., and to Mr. Glass, of the firm of Kuper and Co., the manufacturers; also to Mr. Statham, of the gutta percha company, from whom, as from others, we feel indebted for the very able assistance received in forwarding the above works.

In conclusion, gentlemen, we must express to you the gratification we feel at the success attending our operations as far as they have gone, and we beg to assure you of our constant and unremitting efforts to carry out the undertaking, so as successfully to insure the interests of the shareholders and the advantages of an European telegraphic communication with the East.

I have the honor to be, Gentlemen,

Your most obedient and humble servant,

JOHN W. BRETT.

Since the issuing of the above circular, we had the pleasure of witnessing the shipping of the 110 miles of cable on the steam ship Persia, June 15th, 1854, at Greenwich, near London, designed for the section between Spezzia and Corsica. The rigging of the vessel was very beautifully dressed, with the flags of nearly every nation upon the face of the earth, and on referring to our notes, we find the United States flag was not there!

We attended the celebration, through the kindness of Mr. Brett, and we were much pleased to meet so many gentlemen interested in the extension of the electric telegraph. The cable was 110 miles, containing six wires. These electric wires were connected, making 660 miles, and through which the needle instruments were worked very successfully. During the day, we had only one desire, and that was to have there two of the Morse instruments with two expert operators, to convince the assembled gentlemen, that America was far in advance of them in the art of telegraphing.

The war in Europe is unfortunate for the extension of the telegraph. It has been a great hindrance to the success of Mr. Brett. Notwithstanding his promptness in making his cables, he cannot get vessels to lay them down. How *cheering will be the dawn of peace.*

ART. VI.—THE WORLD GIRDLE TELEGRAPH.

PRACTICABILITY OF A TELEGRAPH AROUND THE WORLD CONSIDERED—THE ROUTE GIVEN—THE COUNTRY PEOPLE AND CLIMATE.

TAL. P. SHAFFNER, PROJECTOR.

AN electric telegraph line or lines surrounding the globe, is now an enterprise of serious consideration, and, in our opinion, will, at an early day, be realized. When we say, that it is under serious consideration, we wish to be distinctly understood, that active arrangements are now being made to consummate that grand and stupendous undertaking. When we say that it will, at an early day, be realized, we desire to be understood as saying that, within a few years, probably not exceeding ten revolutions of the earth around the sun, we will see the earth girdled with an unbroken chain of electric flashes, controllable by man, and diffusing light and knowledge—cultivating peace and good-will to the nations of the globe. It may be deemed by some gentlemen as visionary—as a scheme for a few days' talk, or the wild and rattling fancy of an ill-arranged brain. The impossibilities, doubtless, arise in the minds of some, towering over the reach of human ingenuity. Natural formations of the earth's surface are supposed to contain formidable barriers, and even too much so to be overcome. Scientific difficulties are supposed to exist, preventing the consummation of the undertaking. No one doubts for a moment the advantages to be derived from the telegraph, if constructed to connect the continents across the Atlantic. No one doubts the benefits to the world that would flow from the construction of a telegraph, connecting the two hemispheres by lines, as proposed in the plan of the world's girdle telegraph. We do not deem it necessary to discuss the financial arrangement necessary to execute this great and magnificent undertaking. That must be a question resting upon a distinct basis. The advantages to the people of the earth are, of course, admitted by every person; and, therefore, any discussion upon that point we deem superfluous at the present time.

We propose to notice the two and only remaining difficulties, namely—the *scientific* and *natural* difficulties necessary to be over come in the construction of a telegraph around the world; and, first, the

SCIENTIFIC QUESTIONS.—It has been demonstrated, by several years' practical experiments, that a galvanic current can be sent on circuits varying in length from 100 to 1000 miles, on overground lines, and from one to six hundred, and, perhaps, a thousand miles, on subterranean or submarine lines. We can safely calculate on the successful working of a line six hundred miles, as a fact; and, therefore, we need not base a single argument upon a supposed theory, but wholly depend upon practical and unquestionably demonstrated history, in telegraphy.

If there should be formidable difficulties preventing the working of a line on a longer range than six hundred miles, we will have the chances of the efforts of science to overcome that difficulty, and its after realization. We have the knowledge of the working of a line six hundred miles; and, of course, nothing can dispel that practical law. As we can work successfully the distance mentioned, there is nothing to prevent the working of a line around the globe by the combining of circuits. The operator in London, St. Petersburg, or other cities, can work his circuit, and that will open and close his next, and that will repeat the same to the next; and, in this manner, circuits can be contrived to communicate, at will, any desired distance. In business messages, generally, the circuits can be worked separately, and dispatches can be repeated from point to point, as circumstances of economy may dictate. These are views not original now, but actually the daily operation of every telegraph line on the face of the earth. Why cannot the same practice be applied to a world girdle telegraph?

With the existence of these facts, well known to the scientific telegrapher, being the daily practice of nearly all telegraph lines, we do not see that, so far as the question of science pertains, there can be any doubt whether a line around the world can be successfully worked, for all purposes of trade between the people of all nations.

NATURAL OBSTRUCTIONS require more consideration than we have deemed proper to give the former proposition. We think it is eminently feasible, and, when attempted to be executed, must certainly be crowned with success. We are not sanguine upon the point, without being sustained, as we think, by evidence beyond question. We have devoted much energy and attention to the subject; we have carefully studied the natural and artificial difficulties in the way of its execution; the climate and the population of the countries through which the line must pass, have not escaped the calm reflection of the most earnest solicitude. The practicability of the enterprise may, perhaps, be better considered under the following questions, namely:—topography of the country, the climate, and the character of the population. These we will consider briefly.

We place the eastern coast of America as a starting point. The section connecting America with Europe, we believe, is a solved problem. The ocean section will be found discussed in the present number, under the head of the Transatlantic Telegraph; and we would refer to that article for further particulars as to what appertains to the section connecting the eastern and western hemispheres across the Atlantic Ocean.

It is not material, as to location, where the cable lands in Europe, whether in Ireland or on the western coast of Norway. If in Ireland, there is a telegraph the entire distance to St Petersburg, through England, Belgium and Prussia. If the cable lands on the west coast of Norway, then the line can be constructed to Stockholm, and from that city to the Alland Islands, and from thence along the coast of the Gulf of Finland to the city of St. Petersburg. We know very well that in Finland, north of the City of St. Petersburg, as far as the line will extend, the people are healthy, and cultivate their lands, as in other populous countries. The latitude is 61° north. Thus far, then, we have a country inhabited by people, and there can be no hindrance to the successful working of a telegraph. The face of the country is level, and well adapted to the easy construction of a line. From St. Petersburgh to Moscow the country is level, and government lines already exist. The line is composed of two wires, and runs with the railroad. From Moscow we propose to run to Vladimir, and to Nijhni Novgorod, on the Volga, a city of much importance in Russia. This is latitude 56° north.

Nijhni Novgorod.—This is a large and very important city, containing about 20,000 inhabitants, and in the summer months, during the fair, the population proximates 300,000. To this city traders from Europe and Asia assemble; and, in fact, people from all sections of the world are here to be seen engaged in merchandize. The city is well built, and contains a fortress and many public buildings. It is on the great highway to Asia, and is the centre of mercantile trade for a large section of the globe. We give a description of one of these fairs from an eye observer.

"The celebrated fair which is now held at Nijhni Novgorod, dates its proper institution from the year 1648, at which epoch it was established at Makarief, about fifty miles lower down the Volga than the site upon which it is at present held. In the year 1816, however, upon the occasion of the destruction of its buildings by fire, it was removed to its present site, where it is less exposed to the annual inundations of the great river, which had continually threatened its destruction while it was held at

Makarief. Since this time, the encouragement of the government, and its admirable position in the very centre of the vast inland navigation of the empire, have raised it to be, probably, the greatest place of exchange of merchandize actually exhibited upon the face of the globe.

But before we mingle with the busy throngs at this great gathering of the commercial world, it will be as well to make a few concise remarks concerning the races which compose the Russian people.

The Russian empire is inhabited by a number of nations and tribes of different origin and language, and of various degrees of civilization, from that of the refinement attained by a portion of the Slavonic race, differing in nothing from that of the most advanced people of Europe, down to the condition of the half wild man still roaming over the Siberian deserts, and subsisting by the use of the bow and arrow. Nevertheless, all the seemingly distinct races, which we find settled, or following still their pastoral or nomadic lives, between the Ural Mountains and the western districts of the empire, appear to derive their origin from two sources—from the great Caucasian family, and from the Mongolian tribes. From causes, however, the details of which belong to the history of barbarian conquests, to that of constrained and voluntary emigration, and to the effects of manners, morals and customs, upon the increase and decrease of numbers among particular races, the proportion of the population of Mongol origin, which was once considerable, is not now supposed to exceed a hundredth part of that of the entire empire.

The portion of the population belonging to the Caucasian family, inhabiting Russia Proper, has been divided, and, probly, very justly, into three branches, the Sclavonic, the Thule or Finn, and the Tatar. And it is, with tolerable exactness, ascertained, that the first of these, the Sclavonic, compose about nine-tenths of the whole of the population of Caucasian origin in the empire. The people of this race are, however, subdivided into Russians, properly so called, Lithuanians, Poles, Lettes, Wallachians, and Servians, the Russians of all these being so greatly predominant as to compose about two-thirds of the population of the empire, or amounting to about forty millions of souls. Those, indeed, of this branch of the grand Caucasian family may be considered to compose the more solid portion of the entire population.

In a word, the true Russian nationalit is formed, like our own, from the amalgamation of a variety of races, of which one chiefly stamps the character and shadows the destiny. Just in the same manner that all the races that successively settled in America, have mingled the elements of their character only to modify that of the Saxon; it is evident, that all the blood of all the races that have settled in this empire, will finally be confounded with, and only modify that of the predominant branch of the Sclavonic race of the grand Caucasian family which has given its name to the country and its inhabitants."

From Nijhni Novgorod, we propose to run the line to Kazan, passing over a fine country, and well cultivated, producing wheat, flax, hay, and other commodities. From Kazan the route extends over a country somewhat more undulating, until we arrive at Moukikaksinskaia, and then continuing through a country not quite so thickly settled until we come near Klanovskaia. The hills are few and very moderate in size. The woods are mostly the tall pine, and, to a considerable extent along the road, the birch is planted as ornaments, and in fact the whole country is beautiful and unequalled in its extent of scenery, pertaining to productive effects. It is not characterized with stupendous mountains, dashing streams over cataracts and of romantic vales; but, the rich waving fields of wheat, barley, flax, and the various products of the empire, can be seen for many miles in extent as one common plain. Crossing the river Ochausk, the largest of all the rivers rising in the Ural Mountains, we soon arrive at the

CITY OF PERM.—A very fine place of modern architecture. The result of the richest mines of the world has done much for this country. The roads are most substantially and beautifully constructed. We have no such roads in America. We have boasted of our national paved highway across the mountains, as one of the best in the world; but our national road cannot be compared to the Russian roads. A comparison between an ordinary stream, and the great father of waters, the Mississippi river, would be as proper.

The city of Perm contains about 5,000 inhabitants; who are mostly engaged in the smelting of iron, copper, and other mineral productions of the country. It is a commercial city, and ranks as one of great importance. From Perm we propose to extend this line to the Ural Mountains, passing many villages. Part of the route will pass over immense and solid fields of alabaster. The undulating hills are of a more variegated form, abounding in the fir tree and the cranberry, equalling the richest of the Newfoundland or American berries. We have omitted to speak about the large factories to be found in this country, one particularly, which has been the property of the Countess of Strogonoff, who, we have been informed, has held no less than 80,000 serfs. Vessels of various sizes are constructed on the streams, and being loaded with iron, copper, and products of different kinds, find their way to all parts of the world.

THE URAL MOUNTAINS.—The ascent to the Ural Mountains is very gradual. The highest peak is about 6,400 feet, the passes for the roads are about 2,100 feet above the level of the sea, and so gradual, that a railway can be easily constructed across the range of mountains in many places, with much less expense than has been incurred in crossing many of our ordinary ranges of hills. The pine, fir, larch, and silver-birch, are the common forest trees abounding on the mountains. The cedar is often found, and also the oak, in the direction of the route we propose for the telegraph, being about 56 degrees north latitude.

The Ural Mountains have a range of about twelve hundred miles, running from the Arctic Ocean to the Caspian Sea. They have great inequality of breadth, sometimes reaching seventy-five miles, and at other parts five to seven miles. Where they are broad, they abound in lakes, marshes and mineral springs. Thus far, there are no disadvantages to overcome, in the extension of either a telegraph line or a rail-road, at a less expense than over an equal extent of territory in the most favoured part of the United States.

Leaving the Ural Mountains, we proceed to Schadrinsk, Yalontorovsk, Ishim, Orlova, Tiokalinsk, Krasnoyarskaia, and to Omsk.

From the Ural Mountains to the city of Omsk, a distance of about five hundred miles, the country is much the same as Russia in Europe has been represented. The descent is very gradual, and the plains large, proximating much in appearance the American prairies, being occasionally skirted with woodlands. The roads, as throughout Russia in Europe, are well marked out by large guide-posts, painted white and black, and planted about every two-thirds of a mile, so that in winter, there is no probability of getting lost. Cultivation, throughout Russia in Asia, is not so extensive as in Europe, but there is much of the country under a high state of improvement. Although the country is in the same parallel of latitude as Moscow, the snow lies upon the ground, and the earth remains frozen for some five to six months in the year; and, as a writer says—

"Yet is this disadvantage in climate in a wonderful degree compensated, and its effects modified, by the earth's extreme fertility. The soil is here composed of a fine black mould, and very probably, as subsequent observation of similar soils, the origin of which could not be questioned, has induced me to think, of decomposed volcanic matter. Such, indeed, are the fertilizing qualities of this soil and their durability, that the composts, or the use in any way of stable or any other manure, is here unknown, although rye, barley, and oats, are cultivated in more than sufficient quantities for the consumption of the inhabitants. In the meantime, the surface of the ground is covered with a wild, coarse, long grass, which affords ample provision for herds of cattle during the year. In the summer they graze upon it at large, and fatten; and during the winter, they subsist upon the fallen grass of the past summer, which they rake from beneath the snow, where it lies withered in great abundance throughout the plains."

A writer on Siberia thus speaks of a night's dream and a day's observation, which leads the mind to contemplate the vastness of the Asian plains of Russia, and to the American it will forcibly remind him of the immense plains of the Far West of his own country.

"During the proper hours of the night, I seemed, as I slept, to float upon another Irtysch, whose silent banks and pine forests appeared converted into the seats of music and song, which resounded through such groves as might be formed by the olive and the sycamore, and the palm and the pomegranate, and wanted only exemption from the change, that we cannot but remember must come, to equal one of those blissful regions which poets write of, but which travellers never find. Gradually, however, the soft and harmonious sounds that had prevailed, grew confused and harsh, and the fresh groves became so full of light, that the eye could not without pain regard them, until, with the effort to recover the placid state of body and mind which the light seemed to have disturbed, I awoke.

Upon now opening my eyes, I found a scene before them, which, with the recollection of the state of the light before we fell asleep, confirmed the causes both of the agreeable and clear visions of the early portion of the night, and of the indistinct and confused scenes which succeeded them. The dim light of the moon and stars, which had shone through the first hours of our slumber, had passed away, and the full glare of day, as our faces were turned towards the east, was directly before us.

This morning was also among the more remarkable of those of our journey, on account of the magnificence of the spectacle which it presented to us. There was not a tree nor a shrub to be seen above the wastes of grass that appeared on all sides around, to make the least break in the uniformity of the plain. A hoar-frost covered the whole surface of the ground; and although the sun, when we opened our eyes, had not yet appeared above the horizon, the sparkling element, which sat upon every blade of grass, reflected the rays of the beautiful Aurora from the silvery bed of the wide plain. But as the sun approached the horizon, the face of the grassy steppe yet increased in splendour, and the scene in interest. As we cast our eyes around, without encountering a single object to obstruct the vision, it seemed as if we were gliding across an illuminated crystal plain. But as the bright orb began to appear above the line of the horizon, the chaste silvery scene gradually changed into golden hues, until the full reflection of his beams presented us with a spectacle too bright to behold.

Long after the bright orb "had ta'en his last leave of the weeping morn," and the spangled carpet of the plain had disappeared, and the ground recovered its wonted green, the same unbroken horizon appeared around. The first object that we saw above the level of the plain, looked like a distant vessel, wending her way across the waste of waters within Neptune's domain. It was a single tree, that braved the solitude of the steppe, and, bent by the winter tempests, appeared to the eye of the travellers like a ship under canvass in a stiff gale. * * *

There was nothing in the prospect around, that varied from that which constantly presented itself to us at the same hour. Nothing was to be seen but the silvery plain, and the red, grey, and blue of the different quarters of the heavens, all blending their colours insensibly with one another, without a cloud or fleeting rack to break the harmony of the view, or a breath of air to disturb the silence that reigned. A mariner would have been reminded of the scene which the ocean sometimes displays, when not the smallest ripple appears upon the surface of the water to arrest the reflection of the sun's brilliant rays, and not a cloud is seen in the sky. It reminded me of a calm I once experienced within the tropics, when all on board our bark watched anxiously for days for the first "cat's paw," to give us hopes of a breeze.

In both these positions, almost equally, the isolation to which we are exposed seems to leave the mind free to contemplate calmly the two greatest wonders that the creation displays, with more advantage than when we are surrounded by many objects that distract our thoughts or engage our attention—the great globe upon which we tread, and the far greater by which it is enlightened and fertilized. As we walk over the plain, or as we float upon the ocean, when no object breaks the evenness of the curve line of the horizon, the magnitude, the form, and the solidity of the globe which we inhabit, by the less familiar aspect in which they are now seen, than that in which we are accustomed to behold them, doubly impress us with their reality. Nay, often when the sun is rising or setting, whether the horizon which he is approaching or leaving be formed by the ocean or the plain, if we will forget for a moment the ideas we attach to our familiar expression of the rising and setting sun, and think only of our true relation to the bright orb, and of our rotatory motion, now bringing and now closing the day, we shall seem to observe more plainly the real character of our movement, and almost perceive the onward motion of the waters upon which we float, or of the firm ground upon which we tread.

With such scenes as these before our eyes, the coldest must feel what the poet alone can express. But nothing, perhaps, in a similiar position, is more striking than the contrast we are insensibly led to draw, between the durability of the grander objects of nature before our eyes, and the limited existence of the sentient being that is permitted to contemplate them.

Later in the day, we passed through a country abounding in morass land, and producing coarse high grass in greater quantities than usual. In several places we saw large herds of cattle and flocks of fat-tailed sheep, under the watch of Kirgeeze shepherds. The villages were, however, from twenty to five and twenty versts apart, and the way was unrelieved by any variety in the scene, and more wearisome than ordinary."

The route for the proposed telegraph will pass through Kainsk, Kolivan, Tomsk, Ashinsk, Krasnoyarsk, Kansk, Polavinotchezemhosskayah, Nij Oudinsk, Iamsk to Irkoutsk; latitude 51½° north. The city of Irkoutsk is about two thousand five hundred miles from St. Petersburgh, and about nine degrees south of that city; and the reader will please to remember, that we have kept south of north parallel 60° since leaving St. Petersburg. The country is much the same from the Ural Mountains to Irkoutsk; a hundred villages are passed, and cultivated fields are generally to be seen throughout the route, except occasionally in the more extended plains. Some of the villages are well constructed.

City of Tomsk, having a population of, at least, 10,000, ranks as a place of importance, and is rapidly growing.

" The departmental town of Tomsk is the capital of the district of the same name, in the great western government of Siberia. It is situated upon the right bank of the River Tom, which is one of the numerous tributaries of the Ob, and at about twenty or twenty-five versts from the point of junction of the tributary with the main stream of the grand river. It lies in the direct line between the Ural Mountains and the capital of Eastern Siberia—from each of which points it is about equally distant, and in the vicinity of some of the more productive mineral districts of the country. It is the residence of the governor of the department of which it is the capital, who is usually an officer of engineers, and superintends, in an especial manner, all the mining operations of the imperial government within the district.

Favored by these advantages, Tomsk has become, in point of wealth and population, superior to all the towns in Siberia, except the capital of the grand eastern government. Its population is about 10,000; and its wealth is probably greater than that of any town of an equal number of inhabitants in Russia Proper.

The town is built partly upon two hills, separated by a narrow vale, and partly upon low and even ground, and is divided into nearly two equal parts by a torrent which runs down the vale, and continues its course through the town along the bottom of a deep fissure in the ground, until it falls into the Tom. * * * * * *

In several shops of a superior class, were exposed the more valuable articles of merchandize, such as cloths, furs, cotton and linen goods, among which we found in one that we entered, which was kept by a Tatar merchant, articles of English, French, and German manufacture, as well as others of the coarser description of Russian goods. The prices, however, of every thing were from three to four times higher than we usually pay for the same articles in the west of Europe. Some were even valued as much as six times higher than the prices of London and Paris.

At the distance of a few hundred yards further, continuing the same street, we mounted the hill upon which stands the portion of the upper town, which is upon this side the ravine or fissure above mentioned. This brought us to the quarter occupied by the more wealthy portion of the inhabitants. The houses here also stand apart from one another. Some are of brick, and several are built after the model of those which are placed in the open parts of Moscow, and were painted with as much taste as is commonly displayed in the exterior decoration of houses in the towns in Russia. Some have walls painted straw-color, or a faint yellow, and others a pure white, and all have green roofs. They have all, also, their ends fronting the street, and their doors at the side in a spacious court, and several have gardens behind them. * * * *

The inhabitants of Tomsk may be divided into three orders,

in every one of which are found two or more classes. But that we may, in this account of the town, properly distinguish the voluntary colonist of every grade from the constrained inhabitants of a penal colony, who are not, in a civil sense, a part of the population, we shall have to regard the exiles of all orders and grades apart, though we shall find them mingled with all classes of the free population, under regulations which properly distinguish the political from the criminal exiles, and also the degrees of crime which the latter were sent into Siberia to expiate.

The first, then, of the three orders into which we must divide the population, may be considered to comprise all the civil and military authorities, from the governor down to the lowest *chinovnik*, or under civil official.

In the second order, we may place the principals and agents of the mining companies, and the merchants of the several grades, including, of course, the Tatars, and those of all religious faiths, with all who are employed in their service.

The third order will then consist of all the artizans and the inferior tradesmen and peasants, composed, for the most part, of the descendants of exiles, and the voluntary colonists for some generations back.

We will now divide the first of the above orders of the population—that is, all the *chinovnik*—into two distinct classes, in the same manner that conventual usages, with but slight variations, divide the same order of the people in all countries.

The first of these consist of the governor, and the general in command of the troops within the department, whose appointments are usually for a limited term, the *gorodnichii*, or chief of the police, the *ispravnik*, or judge, the post-master, the agents and engineers in the mining service, the chief architect, and several others whose appointments are permanent, or usually endure for a long period.

The second class of the same order of the people may be considered to be composed of all the under *chinovnik* in all the departments superintended by the above-mentioned superior officers. These are generally sent from Russia, after having been selected from among the classes whose attainments do not commonly exceed the acquirements of reading, writing, and the first elements of arithmetic.

In the second order of the people, the sole distinction is, between those engaged in the proper occupations that belong to mining, and those engaged in commerce.

In the third order, the varieties are yet less manifest. Here the artizan, inferior tradesman, and peasant or laborer, are, with but few exceptions, confounded with one another, by similarity of manners and conduct.

We come now to that important class which form so considerable a portion of the population of the country. But in order to introduce them in their proper character in this and other towns in Siberia, it is necessary to recur to the circumstances which attended their settlement in the country.

From the time of Peter the Great, exiles have been continually sent from Russia Proper into Siberia. The number which have been sent since that period up to the present time is uncertain; but the number that now annually pass the Ural Mountains is about 10,000, including many of the wives of the exiles, who voluntarily follow the fortunes of their husbands. But owing to the distance, which, save in the case of some who remain in the nearer governments, is not performed in less than two years, many of these never reach their destination; and thus the effective augmentation of the population by this means does not probably exceed 8,000 souls a-year.

The exiles are formed into five distinct classes; and every one receives the treatment in the country which is proportionate to the offence to be expiated.

The first class consists of those who are condemned for the highest crimes and offences against the laws of Russia.

The second class comprises all those who are found in a state of vagrancy throughout the country.

The third class consists of those condemned for minor offences against the laws.

The fourth consists of those condemned by the courts estabtablished in the villages, and, for the most part, for petty offences.

The fifth class is composed of serfs condemned by the order of the government, upon application from the proprietors of the estates to which they belong.

The exiles, generally, after the passage of the mountains, are distributed through the country, at various distances from the boundary of the colony, depending upon the character of their offences. Those who are condemned for the highest offences, are usually sent to the eastern provinces, but those who suffer for the lighter, remain in the western.

They now submit to a division into three classes only. Those of the first class are called *katorschniki*. They consist of such as are condemned for life, or for a long period, to work in the mines. They are considered as civilly defunct. Some of the most criminal of these are sent to the silver mines at Nertchinsk, in the government of Irkoutsk. Before the reign of Alexander criminals of this class labored for the rest of their lives beneath the ground, where they were at their decease interred; but at the present day their treatment is very different.

Those of the second class are called *loslannyje na raboto.* They consist of such as are condemned for a shorter period, and designed for colonists upon the expiration of their term of forced labor. These are employed in the service of the government in mere ordinary labor.

Those of the third class are called *loslannyje na poselenye.* They consist of such as are condemned for the lightest offences which incur the penalty of exile. They are considered upon their arrival in the country to have in effect already expiated their faults, and they are at once established by the government as proper colonists. Sometimes they are settled in villages already existing in the vicinity of the towns, and at other times they are placed in villages laid out and built expressly for their reception. They receive, moreover, the government aid in everything proper for their establishment, even to such a sum of money as is deemed necessary to accomplish that object; and for three years they are free from the taxes levied upon the older colonists. Almost the only inconveniences, indeed, which these exiles suffer, consist in their confinement to the villages in which they are settled, beyond the limits of which they are not permitted to pass the night, and in an interdiction from changing their avocation. They are, in effect, peasants *glebæ adscripti*, without the conditions of service to which the serfs of Russia Proper are subjected.

But the most remarkable feature in all that regards the settlement of the exiles, is the organization of the civil affairs of these new villages. At the head of every village is placed a simple soldier, ordinarily a Cossack, who administers justice and punishes all petty offenders, by thrashing them soundly with a stick. Nevertheless, in case of the commission of grave crimes, the administration of the law rests with the court of the nearest town, or is intrusted to the *zasidytelle*, who is here a sort of itinerent magistrate. This state of society, however, does not endure beyond the generation which succeeds that in which it is established. After this, a *starosta* is appointed, by whom justice is administered as in Rüssia.

It now becomes necessary to mention the important moral distinction in the classification of the exiles, in all that regards their position in the proper society of the places they inhabit at the different periods of their exile. This consists simply in the different conventional treatment, as well by the government as by the people, of those who have been exiled for state offences, and those who suffer the penalty of any other offences whatsoever. Thus, while the punishment of both is the same in regard to actual settlement, restraint, and civil dissabilities, and is proportionate alike to the gravity of the offence against the law; yet, as they become relieved from the first restrictions which follow their arrival, the difference of the position in which they severally stand in relation to the rest of the population, is very great. The criminal exiles remain for life under the moral ban, which neither pardon nor forgetfulness is able wholly to remove; while the political exiles, as soon as the first year or two of their exile removes the restraints which are first imposed in respect of the place of their abode and their confinement, enter, without any moral stain, into the society, wherever it is found, of the same rank as that to which they properly belonged when in their state of freedom in Russia.

Not any of either of these orders of exiles can engage in any trade or handicraft. Their proper avocation is the cultivation of the ground, which they may follow to any extent. * *

Everything within and without these houses, was upon a parallel scale, from the fitting up of the drawing-rooms, with their several articles of luxury imported from St. Petersburg, to that of the kitchen, and even to the stables in which the noble animal, so much abused by the peasant and *yemstchik*, has all the comforts that the most favored of his race enjoy in Western Europe. I entered but one of the kitchens, which was that of Gospodin Philomonoff. Eighty-two servants and dependents were sitting at the table to dinner; and I was told that sometimes there were about a hundred and twenty in the same house.

The provisions made by the three proprietors of these houses for the instruction of their children, was agreeable to the wants arising from the insulated position of their town, and commensurate with the arrangements throughout the different departments of their establishments. Gospodin Astaschaff, who had only a son, maintained an accomplished German gentleman in his house as tutor or *governor*, to apply the term equivalent to that in use here. Gospodin Philomonoff had daughters only for whom he had a governess of the same nation; and Gospodin Garrockhoff, who had both sons and daughters, had a German lady and gentleman as governor and governess. Thus, whatever the wants of the present generation, no fear can be entertained, that that which is to succeed will be full of all desirable knowledge, out of which, it is be hoped, will at least arise some reform in the present extravagant manner of living, which cannot be favorable either to the interests or morals of the Siberians. * * * * *

The costume of the inhabitants is as various in winter as in summer, and is regulated by the rank, or fortune, or profession of the parties. The military officers never put off their plumed caps; but the civilians wear fur caps of all forms and at all costs. The rest of the dress of all classes that is seen, consists of a simple *schouba* or pelisse, of which the material that it is composed forms the distinction. All who aspire to the first rank must be dressed in sable when walking or driving in fine weather for pleasure, and in bearskin when it is colder or when they are travelling. But those whose ambition does not affect this rank, or whose means are more limited, are content to walk, drive and travel in the colder weather, in wolf-skins. The under *chinovnik* dress in black lamb-skins; and they suffer much when they travel, from not being able to obtain better clothing to protect them against the cold. In the meantime, the peasants, whose condition is usually much better, dress ordinarily in deer-skins, which are said to be the warmest of any skins whatsoever. And they certainly are so, in proportion to their weight and the space they occupy, though the fur of the bear and that also of the wolf are, without doubt, much warmer. The men of the lowest of all classes, the actual criminal exiles, and others who work during the summer in the mines, dress at this season in common sheep-skins.

The winter dress of the Siberians sits picturesquely upon the peasants, who draw their *schoubas* tight around the waist with a scarf, but not upon men or women of any other class, owing to an absolute decree of fashion, which proscribes the girdle, and is obeyed by all except the peasants, by which the appearance of the dress is spoiled. Indeed, the *schouba* usually worn by all classes above the peasants, in walking, is made as ugly as can be imagined, by being put on with the sleeves, which it never wants, left dangling at the sides.

The peasant women wear precisely the same dress as the men, when abroad, save that a hood of the girdled *schouba* covers the head instead of a fur cap.

The *schouba* of the ladies is a true cloak, in which, however, they very rarely walk. If a morning visit is to be made merely across the street, the *sani* conveys them. And when their acquaintance with those they visit is not familiar, or when the rank or fortune is disproportionate, the formalities and etiquette are as rigorous as at St. Petersburg or Moscow. The head-dress of the ladies without doors is the same as in the larger towns in Russia. The bonnet that is worn in summer is merely lined with fur for the winter."

We have examined a meteorological table of the weather for December, and other months, and we find the climate not as cold as was experienced in the northern states of America in December, 1854. The table was prepared at Tomsk, and is a fair exhibit of the climate of that portion of Siberia through which the proposed line should run.

CITY OF KRASNOYARSK has some 8,000 population, having many public edifices, one of which is a cathedral costing over $1,000,000, being 187 feet in length, 96 feet in breadth, height of tower, 198 feet, height of dome, 182 feet. The church was built by voluntary subscriptions.

CITY OF IRKOUSTK.—We come now to speak of Irkoutsk, the capital of Eastern Siberia. It contains a population of 25,000 souls. The buildings are erected in the modern style, with large yards. That the reader may judge of the nature of the people and the city properly, we will quote a few sentences as written by an eye-witness:

"Irkoutsk, the capital of Eastern Siberia, is seated at the immediate point of the confluence of the Angara, the most considerable of all the rivers that fall into the Yenessei, and the broad and rapid torrent of the Irkout. It contains a population composed of the same social grades as the population of the town of Tomsk. It is the seat of the government of Eastern Siberia, and the place of residence and head-quarters of the governor-general over all the departments which are comprised in the great eastern division of the country. It possesses a handsome cathedral, nine churches, a government-house, and all the ordinary public buildings of a Russian governmental town, and a *gostinnoi dvor.*

There are seven public establishments for education in Irkoutsk, five of which are for the instruction of boys and two for girls. And there is also an independent seminary for the daughters of parents who can afford and prefer to give their children a private education.

The schools for the boys are of three distinct kinds, with different objects. One of them is designed for the sons of exiles of every kind, who are, without distinction, obliged by the law to be raised for soldiers. The boys are here educated, but not maintained, at the public charge. Another receives the sons of the *chinovnik*, who are educated, fed and clothed, at the expense of the crown, in the service of which they are afterwards employed.

Two higher schools have a common object, one of them

being but an elementary school of three classes, in which the children are prepared for the gymnasium, or higher school, which has seven classes. In this establishment there are usually about 150 boys, forty of whom are by special privilege, under regulations bearing reference to the positions of their parents, maintained, as well as educated, at the public expense. The scholars are, for the most part, sons of officers, merchants, and proprietors of mines or their agents. They receive a liberal education, and usually afterwards follow the profession or business of their fathers. Besides the head master, there are fourteen professors; and the branches of knowledge which are taught are the Russian, Latin, German, French and English languages, geography, mathematics, rhetoric, logic, physics, and drawing. All the boys, even though they should be the sons of peasants (of which there are many among the rest), if they pass a prescribed examination, are equally eligible to advancement, and may enter one of the universities of Russia under certain regulations. Those, for instance, who attain this privilege, but who have been educated at the public charge, are only eligible for Kazan, and are liable to serve the crown for eight years; while those who are educated at the expense of their parents may enter any one of the universities in Russia, according to their objects, the constitution and design of the universities being different; and they are liable for only six years' service.

It must here be remarked, however, that although, strictly speaking, the sons of the political exiles have no higher privilege than those of the criminal, who are ineligible to the higher class schools, the iron letter of the law has yielded to the force of natural claims, and the greater part of these enter the elementary school, which gives equal right to all to pass to the gymnasium, where they wear uniform, and receive the fourteenth or lowest grade of nobility, and become, finally, eligible to enter one of the universities of Russia.

The remaining school for boys is exclusively for the sons of the clergy, who are designed for the priesthood. At this period it contained no less than 150 scholars. All must have attained the age of fifteen before commencing their theological studies. They remain in the institution for six years, at the expiration of which time they are subjected to an examination, and advanced in proportion to the degree of proficiency which they have attained. A few of those who appear to have made the greatest advances in their studies, at the expiration of the prescribed period, are transferred to one of the four higher colleges at St. Petersburg, Moscow, Kieff or Kazan.

After this, such as aspire to the rank of bishops, become monks. Those who are next in reputation for their progress at the termination of their studies at the college, become eligible for the ministry; and upon their taking to themselves wives, they are ordained deacons, priests, and ministers. But those scholars who do not acquire such a reputation as is thought sufficient to entititle them to any of these privileges, are employed in the meaner ranks of the clerical order, or as mere assistants in the performance of the ordinary offices of the church.

One of the two public institutions for girls is maintained at the expense of the crown, and admits fifty children free. The other was founded by a millionare of Irkoutsk, and admits thirty or forty free."

The city of Irkoutsk is of very great importance. The climate of the country is good, latitude north, 51½. It is situated near lake Baikal and within a few miles of Chinese Tartary, and borders one of the best tea districts of the world. Maimatchin, in Chinese Tartary, on the boundary, is the great tea mart. From this place thousands of caravans proceed to Pekin, and to Nijhni Novgorod in Russia. Many weeks are thus employed in the transportation of the tea to these far distant mercantile cities. Could they have a railroad upon which to transport the products of the lands and the arts, what a great achievement it would be for the country and the nation! There is nothing to prevent the construction of a railroad from Moscow to Irkoutsk, and we believe, the early erection of the telegraph will open the way for the steam car? What a blessing it would be to Russia!

KIACHTA is on the boundary between Russia and China. It is a Russian town of about 2,000 inhabitants. Maimatchin is the Chinese town of some 1,500 people. These towns are within a half mile of each other, and yet the people of one cannot speak the language of the other. The trading carried on between the people of these two cities is very great. From official information we learn, that in 1850, the whole of the Russian wares exchanged here was 27,630,480 roubles, or, $20,722,860. In 1840 it was 19,501,281 roubles, or $14,625,061. These wares embraced the variety of furs, woollens, cottons, linens, leather, and other implements of arts, needed by society, including manufactures of iron, tin, copper, brass, lead, &c. The Chinese products consist of black tea, silks, &c., amounting to 11,697,357 roubles, or $8,773,023.

This data throws considerable light on the economical condition of the two empires,—great fertility to the north of the line and barrenness to the south; superior energy of the Russians over the slow and unprogressive Chinese. A traveler thus speaks of these places, and the grandeur of an Aurora Borealis, which he witnessed there.

"The two border towns of Russia and China, in every light they may be seen, are highly characteristic of the spirit of the people of the great empires to which they severally belong. North of the great line of demarcation, everything wears the appearance of youth, and rapid growth, and advancement towards the superior degrees of excellence which we trust that the people of the Russian empire are destined to attain. But we no sooner pass the threshold of the gate of the empire of the peculiar people whom we are now among, than the figure of age and social decrepitude stands before us; and were we not aware of the prevalence of a state of morals throughout the land that shocks every better principle that we have imbibed, the type now exhibited of Time's withering hand, might at least command our sympathy. * * *

The whole of the northern hemisphere first appeared tinged with a deep dull light, similar in color to red-hot iron shortly after it has been taken from the fire. This, however, soon spread in rays of brighter color, which seemed to dart like sunbeams across the zenith, until the entire heavens, from the horizon on one side to that on the other, was covered with these beams of light in rapid and continual motion, and change of shade and color, of which I know nothing in nature that might afford a simile to convey any just idea."

The face of the country surrounding Irkoutsk for many miles is slightly undulating, and the fertility of the soil is equal to that of any other part of Asia. Agricultural departments are extensively conducted, resulting in the filling of the graneries of the people. The products of the lands around Irkoutsk are very full, embracing wheat, barley, oats, hay, &c. The people never want for food. The cattle graze on the rich plains of grass, and hence, the living here is as good as can be found in any part of the world. Some travellers speak much against the dirt and filth of the people. We have read the like of Russia in Europe, and of America. There are travellers who expect to have the delicacies of London or Paris in every clime! We have heard much of the dirty huts of people living in camps and open shelters in the woods. We have seen all such in America, and yet, not occasion any especial wonder! The people about Irkoutsk, and in nearly the whole of Russia in Asia, are well disposed, and we have no fears of trouble from them in the maintenance of the telegraph. The churches, convents, hospitals and public edifices are constructed upon the most magnificent scale. The glitter of the golden domes give special wonder to the great inland cities. It seems most "pas sing strange," that Russia should be heralded forth throughout the world as a barbarous country. Other countries could improve by following in the footsteps of such people as Russians. At Irkoutsk there are charitable institutions, schools intended for the maintenance and education of female orphans. They receive such a training as will be likely to render them useful in life. With such a state of moral society, who can doubt the propriety of associating Siberia with the modern world by telegraph?

We have said as much of this part of Siberia as we deem necessary, and we now propose to consider the route to Yakoutsk and thence to the sea of Ochotsk. From Irkoutsk to the sea, there are two routes, by which a telegraph can be constructed;—one through Yakoutsk, and the other route along the old boundary between Russia and China. This route will, beyond doubt, be of much public use in the future, particularly as it borders the Amour River country, over which Russian jurisdiction now extends. As the northern route through Yakoutsk is the most traveled, and now the main government thoroughfare to the Pacific Ocean, we propose to consider that as the best and most feasible at the present time.

Route to Yakoutsk.—Leaving Irkoutsk, we bear north ward until we reach Yakoutsk, passing many small towns on the road, some of which are quite extensive. The road follows the Lena River and passes over a very fertile country, abounding in the richest products. The people between these two cities are descendants of a high rank of exiles, and they compare very favorably with the intelligent people of Russia in Europe. Of this country a traveler thus writes:—

"The country after this, during the day presented to us the same natural features, with intervals of arable land, which, as we perceived from the somewhat spare stubble of the preceding year, had borne crops of rye, barley, and oats.

Early on the day after that on which we commenced our journey, we arrived at a small village called Mansourskaia, where we breakfasted. After this, we found the country still improving in natural fertility and agreeable views. A long range of hills appeared on our left hand, at further and nearer distances, as we proceeded; and sometimes, upon our right, the river upon which we were to embark, a little further from its source, was seen wending its course through a still more varied country than any I had seen anywhere on this side of the Ural Mountains; unless, indeed, the shores of the Selenga, which, at the season at which I visited them, exhibited everything to great disadvantage, might be an exception.

We found the country now chiefly inhabited by the Bouriats; and the effects of their sobriety, generally, with its accustomed attendant, steady industry, were here, as on the opposite side of the Baikal, seen to great advantage, compared with the progress of the Russo-Siberians.

As the day advanced, we found the country flatter and the scenery tamer. Early in the afternoon, after crossing an alluvial plain, we arrived at the place of embarkation upon the great river we were to descend. Here we found a marshy point of land, forming the inner side of an elbow of the river. By the bank of the stream stood a number of huts and temporary sheds; and on the river, moored to the shore, were lying ten or twelve roughly constructed flat-bottomed craft. This little settlement is called the port of Mansursk. Immediately opposite to it is the village of Katschougskaia, seated upon more elevated ground; though the side on which we arrived has been chosen as more convenient for loading the craft which are to descend the river, as all the cargoes they carry come direct from Irkoutsk. At this point of the Léna is embarked all the merchandise designed for exchanging for furs, which are procured from the various tribes of the native inhabitants throughout the entire north-eastern districts of Siberia.

This mighty river, even here, at the distance of more than 4,000 versts from the Arctic Sea, into which its waters fall, is a deep and clear stream, of about the breadth of the Thames at London; and it is, at this season, perhaps, more rapid than any part of any navigable river in the world, except some portions of the Saint Lawrence, properly called the Rapids. It presents, as well here as at many other points of its course, the same peculiarity which has been noticed as prevailing with other rivers, both in Russia Proper and in Siberia, of high banks on the right hand along the course through which it flows, and more frequently low and marshy land which is often subject to inundations, upon the opposite shores.

The village of Katschougskaia possesses a church, which is painted in gaudy yellow, and has some of the better sort of Siberian houses ranged along the high bank by the river, which, together, give to the place rather a gay and agreeable aspect.

I visited this village during the time we were detained here. It is inhabited by Russo-Siberians and Bouriats, the latter being the most numerous. Its site has been well chosen; but it has nothing remarkable within it, and nothing differing from the ordinary Siberian villages inhabited by the same mixed races."

This same traveller passed down the river Lena, and of his voyage he writes the following:—

"As we lost sight of the village of Katschougskaia, we had steep hills on either side of our course, thinly covered with mixed woods, chiefly of the fir tribes; and there was here and there some small patches of cultivated land. During the second hour, we were driving through narrower passes of the river, between steep cliffs of red sandstone of considerable elevation. All that was here visible of the soil upon the banks of the river and upon the hills, was of the same color as the cliffs, and the woods were still of fir thinly sown.

Soon after we had swept through these narrow passages, we passed by the Russo-Siberian village of Korkinskaia, upon the right bank of the river. The position of this village seemed as isolated and desolated as could well be conceived.

Two hours after this, we passed the village of Ponomarefskaya upon the same side of the river. The country was now less hilly, and we observed a greater variety of vegetation in the natural forests; and there was also more cultivation to be seen at a distance from the banks of the river.

Before noon, we passed the village Yigolafskaya, upon our right hand; and three hours later, we brought up at Oustilguinskaya, a considerable village, with two churches, one of which was in a state of decay, and the other not quite finished.

The last-mentioned of these villages, the captain of our boat informed us, contained an industrious population and a manufactory of stockings and nightcaps, both of which articles were produced entirely by the hand. We stopped here for a short time to endeavor to obtain some milk for our supper, in which we were successful.

At a distance of twenty versts further, we passed the small village of Bolofskaya. Here the color of the soil along the inclined planes, more particularly upon the right bank of the river, indicated the existence of iron ore. During the afternoon we passed several of the smaller description of villages, and we found the country generally improving in aspect, with the firs in which it abounded of superior growth.

The face of the country, as we proceeded, continued to improve in appearance by the increase in the variety of the vegetation with which the hills were decked. The silver birch was now abundant, and there were more pines of a larger growth than we had before seen, distributed among the lesser species of the fir tribes. Before sunset we observed the first signs of the close of the winter sleep of the vegetable world, in the green tinge among the birches, where they were more thickly sown in the sheltered valleys. * * *

We had found the ice upon the shores as we proceeded every day in greater quantities. But it was lying in some of the coves, in fields undisturbed by the current that swept down the channel of the river; and in some places it was strewed in arge masses upon the shores on both sides. From this, it seemed evident that we were advancing more rapidly north wards than the genial summer heat. But if we were outstripping the effects of the sun in our progress, we had, however, the advantage of lengthening the day in a greater proportion, by the change of our latitude than by the advance of the sun. It was now the 15th, (our 27th) of May, and we were already north of the 55th degree, where the period that the sun at this season is below the horizon during the twenty-four hours little exceeds six hours; and when the sky was clear, the night was light enough to admit of our continuing our drift, without any necessity for mooring.

The next morning, we swept rapidly by the village of Urkutsk, upon the left bank of the river. Immediately after this, we passed the tributary river, Kuta, which here meets the parent stream. Salt, which is obtained from some low land near the sources of this river, is manufactured here, and sent through all the northern and eastern districts of Siberia.

The next day we had a return of the finest weather, with light and favorable winds. The thermometer at eight o'clock in the morning was at 11 degrees of heat, and at mid-day the rays of the sun were scorching, though we were still floating between banks of ice, or broken masses of the frozen element, which were lying along the shore upon either side. At twelve o'clock we passed the village of Markofskaya, with a church.

Throughout the greater part of our drift during to-day, the serpentine course of the stream, with the character of the hills, gave more than usual variety to the scenery around, and to the river very often the appearance of a lake. The hills were here steeper and higher than those we had before passed, and were covered with red pine forests, apparently of a "second growth;" but the woods were very open, and the trees were not large.

Nevertheless, the canoes that were to be seen at the villages, were made of single trunks of trees, rudely hollowed out, and were of large dimensions; and, as this attested the existence of very fine pine groves at some part or other of the river, we were led to inquire of the peasants where these groves were; but all the information we received was, that they did not go far to find them.

In the evening it became calm, and the scenery was greatly changed. We seemed now, from the distance which we were able to see before us, as if we were gliding into an open and champaign country; and the water was so still, that the hills and the forests that clothed them, were reflected upon its surface on either side, almost as distinctly as from an artificial mirror. In the meantime, our course was so gentle, though so rapid, that we were only sensible of being in motion, by the perpetual variations of the landscape.

The next day we were drifting in broader reaches of the river, and there appeared to be some slight diminution in the strength of the current. But the scenery presented the same features as during the last two or three days. * * *

Towards evening we approached a more mountainous country; and during the period of the dim light, in the short absence of the sun, we passed through a strait, which the navigators of the Léna have rightly named *Tchookhea*—the Magnificent. The natural objects here present the most striking of all the scenes which this mighty river exhibits. I saw them, unfortunately, but imperfectly; for I was not previously informed of our approach towards anything remarkable, and I was sound asleep when we passed through the grandest portion of the strait. Happily, however, I rose by accident, while we had yet a distant view of the remarkable objects by which it is formed. At the distance of ten or fifteen versts, by full daylight, it appeared like a vast rent in the range of mountains, which are here composed of granite rock. But this distance was too great to observe it from, to admit of the spectator speaking confidently of the breadth of the passage, or of anything further concerning it.

The whole country, indeed, at this part of the Léna, is magnificent in the extreme. It resembles some of the grander passes of the Rhine, near the sources of that river, with the advantage to the spectator, who may be navigating the Léna, of floating upon a far mightier stream. In some places, indeed, appear the boldest and most picturesque scenery that may, perhaps, be anywhere beheld, bordering any river in any land. The most striking that I saw to advantage was at the mouth of the River Ora, which falls by a narrow channel, between high and precipitous rocks, upon the left bank into the parent stream. It was such as we think we could gaze upon for ever. But there was a novelty which formed a portion of it of a very rare kind among the natural objects that mountain lands exhibit. The mother of the arts was here seen rather as a copyist of the works of men's hands than as the model to guide them. Perhaps Nature has nowhere produced anything more nearly resembling the works of men, than the prodigious rocks with which she has here bordered and overhung this great river. I was for a minute or two deceived, and believed we were looking upon the remains of the architectural works of some race of our species that might have inhabited the land, when the great mammoth trod the firm earth of the country, at this time watéred by the mighty Léna. The appearance, indeed, which is here presented of architectural ruins, has so near a resemblance to many remains of the productions of earlier ages of European history, that they will excite the wonder and interest of every traveller who beholds them. We seemed to look upon a vast fortress with several towers, one of which appeared even circular. The proper walls of the place, overhanging the water of the narrower stream, seemed to be supported by artificial stone work, resting upon jets or steps of the rock; and upon the side of the land, as far as the seeming walls were not hid from the view, was seen even the appearance of a lofty gate. Nay, even loopholes appeared to be pierced in several parts of the walls. If a race of genii were dwelling up this romantic river, and had been occupying themselves in constructing works in imitation of our ancient fortresses, they could not be said to have been unsuccessful. There is, indeed, a traditionary legend among all the native races in this part of Siberia, concerning this particular spot of the Léna, which relates that the bank of the Ora are inhabited by certain spiritual beings, whose will has great influence upon the destinies of men. Thus, all the navigators of the great river, who thread this pass when the season will permit, stay and bathe in the Ora, or at its mouth, which is thought to be complimentary and highly pleasing to the spiritual inhabitants of the vicinity.

"YAKOUTSK is the capital of the department of the same name, which is the largest of the provinces of Eastern Siberia. It lies in the latitude of 62 degrees north, and beneath the meridian of 129° 40 east of Greenwich. It is the most northern of the provincial capitals of Siberia, and is the place of residence of the civil governor of the department, and of an *ispravnik* and a *gorodnichii*. It possesses a population estimated at 4000 souls, composed of the mingled race of Russo-Siberians and Yakoutes, with a few pure Russians, who are chiefly officials in the service of the government and of the Russian Fur Company. * * *

Yakoutsk is at present the centre of the fur trade of Siberia, and is annually the depository of furs to the amount of upwards of two millions of rubles. Salt and talc are here also exchanged for merchandise.

Notwithstanding the somewhat heterogeneous materials which compose the population of this provincial town, to the eye of a stranger, the inhabitants appear to be almost wholly Yakoutes, on account of the features of the face, in particular, of that race being more distinctly marked than those which distinguish the proper Russians. The proportion of Yakoutes, however, of unmingled blood, does not exceed a quarter of the population. The mixed race, in the light in which they are chiefly seen by strangers, seem quite conformists to all Russian usages,—though this is not in all things in reality the case. At their homes, and in their domestic affairs, and in their language, they are Yakoutes; while in their religion, and in regard to the social rights which they have been admitted to enjoy, they are not now distinguished from their fellow subjects even of the pure Russian race. * * * * * *

But at the same time, while at Yakoutsk we find the best example of those happy consequences of this accommodating disposition of the Russians, it is here also, that in comparing the Russian conquest of the aboriginal inhabitants of the country with the conquests of other nations of which history affords us ample examples, we discover the more essential moral causes of the different results that the sequel of their several wars has produced. The Spaniards, whose conquests form the greatest contrasts with those of the Russians, carried before them the cross, for which they opened a passage by the sword, and by worse means, carrying on exterminating war against all who submitted not blindly to their authority, and embraced not the faith which was to them a religion of blood with no other moral than that which recognised the right of the strong to commit every kind of violence against the weak. The Russians, wiser, and better endowed with the true spirit of the religion they profess, have carried with them also the same emblem of peace and good-will from Heaven towards man. But the means by which they have opened the passage for the symbol of their faith, and by which they have planted it in new soils, has been justice and equal rights, for the firm establishment of which their tolerant spirit has been the pledge. Thus, while the Spaniards lighted the flames of war and hatred which are far from being extinguished even at this day, and afterwards converted to Christianity only in name the feeble remains of the people whom they nearly destroyed, the Russians have by their humanity subdued and reclaimed whole nations of far more barbarous races than any which the Spaniards encountered, and added them to the number of which their empire consists, and to whom their laws and their protection extend. * *

As we landed at Yakoutsk, there were a dozen or two men and women gathered upon the shores of the little port. The costume of the men we observed differed very little from that of the Siberians generally, but that of the women was novel to us. The men wore skins, cut in imitation of the caftan, trousers, fur caps, and short boots of untanned leather; but the women were dressed in very short caftans, also of skins, with a border of the breadth of half the length of the skirt in scarlet cloth and enormous bear-skin caps. They also had the short boots of untanned leather; but their legs were bare like those of Highland *men.* * * * * *

We found the streets of the town laid out with the same regularity as those of the greater part of the towns both in Russia and Siberia, and the town divided into two nearly equal parts by a brook of not very limpid water, for which space enough, however, has been left for a fine river to flow, with a public promenade on either side.

We counted during our walk, six churches, all of which had been painted in the usual yellow and green, but none of them had much remaining of this mark to distinguish them from the ordinary houses of the town. There is also a convent here, with a church belonging to it; and there are some remains of an old Cossack fortress, which is said to have been erected by the conquerors of Siberia so long ago as 1647. * * *

The weather had been extremely variable during the first days of our detention at Yakoutsk. Sometimes a scorching sunshine during the greater part of the day was succeeded by a cold wind and rain in the evening, and the thermometer did not, after our arrival, indicate more than 11 Reaumer degrees of heat, until the 7th of the month, when it rose to 13. On the ninth, it stood at 15 at eight o'clock in the morning, and at 16 at noon, and on the tenth at 16 in the morning, and 17 at noon, with every appearance of settled weather."

YAKOUTSK.—We have no correct data as to the temperature of the weather at Yakoutsk, there is every reason to believe that the summers are short and the winters very long. We have seen statements which represent that there are years when the frost never leaves the earth where the sun cannot reach it. Of course, we regard this as not to be wondered at in that far northern region. We have seen snow in Virginia lying in bank as late as the middle of June. In 1832 we very well remember seeing large quantities of snow lying in the field as late as the first of May, and in cultivating the land the snow was in the way of the farmers' progress. The snows remaining as late as the middle of June was where the sun did not reach it. With these facts existing in this country, we certainly expect the frosts to remain to a very late date in Siberia, as far north as Yakoutsk. But it is not material; the frost may be perpetual, and the snow may remain upon the earth for a century, and still the success of the telegraph would be certain. The colder and the more frozen climates are the best for the electric telegraph!

We have shown, that as far as Yakoutsk, the country is settled, the lands fertile, the people civilized and really useful in the cultivation of products, that the lands produce the varieties of grains, and that the face of the country being mostly level and abounding with timber, a telegraph can be constructed and maintained without any difficulty.

We have omitted to mention that the entire distance from the Prussian boundary in Europe, through Russia, across the Ural Mountains, to Tomsk, Irkoutsk, Yakoutsk to the sea of Ochotsk, is a post route, and every few miles a change of horses can be made at post stations! A traveller says:

"The next day after breakfasting upon the same dish on which we had supped on the previous night, we set off with fresh horses; and finding the same description of country, with a continuation of the same chain of small lakes, bordering with meadows and grassy slopes, that were perfectly dry, we encountered no obstruction, and reached the station Tshishikeiska, at the distance of thirty-two versts from that at which we had slept, at an early hour.

As far as the next post, Porotowska, at the distance of thirty-four versts, we passed over the same description of country, and had the same facility of travelling; and we found here a similar lodging to that in which we had passed the previous night.

Upon the third day of our journey, we set off at an early hour with fresh horses, and continued our way by the same chain of small lakes, which it was now quite evident were but the deeper parts of the bed of an ancient grand river, through which the current had ceased to flow, by the drying up of its sources, or a change in the course of the stream, or, possibly, by some geological phenomenon, such as the raising of the land caused by imperceptible volcanic action. Early in the day we arrived at the post of Tshuraptshinska, at the distance of thirty-two versts from that at which we had passed the second night of our journey; and soon after mid-day we reached Arilatska, at a further distance of thirty-two versts from the post last named. * * * * * *

The weather, during our journey up to this time, had been exceedingly fine, with the thermometer oscillating during the day between 16 and 21 degrees of heat. But during this afternoon the sun was obscured; and, a little before our arrival at this post, a storm of thunder, lightning and wind commenced, which, before our horses were relieved of their burdens, was attended with such torrents of rain as to make us think ourselves fortunate in being under cover."

Between Yakoutsk and the sea of Ochotsk, the route is much varied in its formation and products. The distance is about seven hundred miles to the port of Aian. The country next to Yakoutsk is very flat and swampy, full of marshes and ponds. The government road is very well improved, and the swamps are crossed by pole bridges, in the same manner as the marshes are in the western United States. Part of the route is hilly, and not a very agreeable country for travelling. The following description is from a traveller, who passed over Siberia, some two hundred miles north of the route intended to be followed by the telegraph.

" Until now, the spruce in its ordinary varieties had been sometimes the only kind of tree or shrub that was to be seen; and at other times the larch, with more kindly growth, flourished side by side with the several species of the hardier fir. Here and there, indeed, we had observed the pine growing, but only to the size, and in the form, of a mere shrub. But now we had the two first mentioned of these species among the innumerable varieties of the fir, of more luxuriant growth and in nearly equal quantities, and, at the same time, pines much larger in size than those we had seen before, and so rare and curious in form as to be worthy of particular remark. Not in a few instances merely, but during nearly the whole of this day's journey, we observed these trees growing as nearly as possible in the form of a bell turned upside down, and set upon its handle, which was represented by the trunk of the tree. The particular species appeared to be that of the common white pine, which, although I had seen it growing, both where scarce and where abundant, of all sizes, from the shrub up to the sovereign of the most magnificent forests, I never before observed it taking this form. Here, however, where it seemed to have robbed all the other species that appeared in its immediate vicinity of their fair share of the earth's foison and abundance—for none of any other kind which were near it exceeded in growth the smaller shrubs—its height did not exceed that of the spruce in favorable situations, or perhaps twenty feet, while the bowl of the bell that was formed must have been in many instances eighty or ninety, and in some cases above a hundred feet in circumference.

The weather had been fine since we reached the dry lands, and we enjoyed the first part of this day, as freer from the natural obstructions to travelling which the country offers, than any we had passed since the first days of our journey. We were continually ascending the hills in front of us; and, before midday, the streams had become mere brooks, though our way was now more precipitous, and more fatiguing for our horses.

Early in the afternoon we crossed the summit of the first ridge of hills of any considerable height forming the grand mountain range. Owing to the rugged character of the ground, and the winding of the ways through which we had passed, we had obtained but one view of the country around, and that had been at no great elevation. But here we were more fortunate; and we halted for a short time to refresh our wearied sense, so long fixed upon the same scenes immediately around us. We had now, indeed, an extensive view of the country through which we had passed, which presented to us an undulated and vast tract of land covered with its sombre groves, that seemed to want nothing but the variations in the color of the vegetation of more temperate climes to exhibit all the freshness and variety of the most luxuriant forests.

After this we passed over narrow plains or shallow valleys, in which the horses were sometimes up to their knees in snow, and at other times marching upon masses of ice, honeycombed upon the surface by the rays of the sun, though quite solid beneath. These are the glacial districts of these mountains, whence the streams of the lower country are supplied with water, when the sun has its full force in the height of summer. This source, however, of these streams is cut off with the earlier frosts, which usually occur towards the end of August; after which the lesser rivers are dried up. In some places we found rents in the ice like fissures in solid rocks; and through these the water was running over the ground in winding courses just in the manner that the brooks generally flow; and to pass them was difficult, on account of the thickness of the ice, which was from ten to fifteen feet. But in some places these unsubstantial banks of the streams were so worn beneath by the passage of the water, that, upon the horses approaching the edge of them, large sheets upon which we were marching broke off, and let us easily down; while the noise they occasioned in falling, made the hills echo with the loud sound from one extremity of the vale to the other. But what was most remarkable to observe upon these glacial fields, was the heat of the sun's rays reflected from the ice, which was greater than any thing of the kind I remembered experiencing, except the reflection from the sand in the hottest climates. Here, too, and far from the dry ground or trees, the quantity of the mosquitoes which swarmed until five in the afternoon exceeded any thing we had met with in the swamps. Altogether, the scenes and all we experienced during this day were novel in our travels; and the noise at all times of the ice melting sensibly around us—the occasional deep sounds caused by the falling of masses of the frozen element by the side of the streams—the crackling of the horses' feet as they crushed the honeycombed ice beneath them—the murmur of the running waters—the clouds of mosquitoes, and the excessive heat,—left an impression as indelible as that of the more disagreeable portions of the journey already described."

The country above described, is on the route formerly the government highway to the sea; but, it has been of late changed; it now runs from Yakoutsk to Aian, and not to the port of Ochotsk. Here is a description more appropriate to the telegraph route.

"For the endless firs, sown over the whole surface of the ground in larger or smaller quantities, depending upon the character and quality of the soil, and the elevation of the country, and exhibiting only the little varieties of color and foliage which their several tribes admit, we had now around us a mixture of the several perennial green-leafed trees that have been mentioned as growing in spare quantities in different parts of the country through which we passed during the journey, with a larger proportion of the lines of more luxuriant growth. Along the banks of some of the brooks we now found strawberries; and here and there we perceived open spaces, covered with a variety of shrubs, among which were mingled currant bushes, the fruit of which, though not sufficiently advanced to exhibit color, was evidently of the red sort. Our men were in raptures of delight at the sight of this fruit even in its present state, and picked and ate quantities of it; but we reserved our appetites for something more solid in prospect. A variety of flowers were also seen flourishing here among the brambles and underwood, amidst which the rose and the flag-iris were predominant.

This change in the appearanceof the country and the vegetation, was as unexpected as it was agreeable to us, seeing that we had yet scarcely recrossed the 60th degree of latitude, and it seemed to make some amends for our physical deprivations. * * * * * *

After descending this range of hills, we came into a vale of extreme fertility. The green and broad leafed trees that chiefly flourished here, were the lime and the birch; of the hardier species of the fir tribes which were more familiar to our eyes, we observed only the larch. The wood was open, and the trunks of some of the limes were from three to four feet in circumference, and the branches were much larger than the proportion which is usual to that size of trunk in most forest trees, but they had very few small boughs, and very little fresh foliage.

Along the banks of a slow rivulet by which our path lay, we observed shrubs of various kinds in full bloom, and growing with such luxuriance as in several places to obscure the view of the stream. Among these, the rose-trees were predominant. In many instances they reached to seven or eight feet in height.

* * * * * *

The next morning, as we advanced, we found the fertility of this plain greater than that of any portion of the country through which our path had hitherto lain. Early in the day we passed by several Yakoute huts, where we were plentifully supplied with cream. The distances from one another at which the several families that inhabited these houses were dwelling, in the midst of a country where there is no scarcity of pasture to maintain their cattle, which furnish the sole means of their subsistence, seemed indicative of their race being of a gloomy and unsocial disposition. We believed this, however, not to be the case; and we made inquiries of them why they lived so far apart. But in reply we heard only the same reasons that are often given in very different countries, for the conservation of usages that ought long since to have been abolished, that such was the custom of their fathers.

Attached to all the houses that we passed by, after crossing the last hills, there were larger portions of pasture-ground than we had before seen; and the grass, though of a coarse description, was here growing most luxuriantly. By the stream, the abundance of wild productions of the several kinds with which we were familiar, still more surprised us. The rose-bushes, which were everywhere in great plenty, were in some instances from six to nine feet in height. Early in the day, we crossed several times a stream of a chalky colour; and we observed that, whenever the stones broke its smooth course, appeared a foam like soap-suds, which covered the surface of the water as far down as the eye could reach."

Such is the nature of the country through which the proposed telegraph will pass; some of it is unfavourable, having but few settlements, and inhabited by people uneducated. Notwithstanding all the unfavourable features of the country, there are no formidable obstructions to the construction of a telegraph. We have built lines in America over worse country, climate more unfavourable, and among people no better than the phlegmatically disposed Siberians. We have not forced upon the reader wholly our own views, but we have given the information gained from a multiplicity of authorities. The distance from Irkoutsk to the sea of Ochotsk, is about 2,800 miles, and estimated to be about 6,550 miles from Moscow.

The port of Aian is superior as a harbor for vessels, and is destined to be a town of great importance; and, we suppose it will be the great Russian mart on that sea. From Aian, we propose to run the line around the sea of Ochotsk, north to the Cape Iamsk, and thence across the narrow neck of sea to Cape Utkaloka, in Kamtchatka.

Arriving in Kamtchatka, we will extend the line to a convenient point for connection with the Aleutian Isles. We can also run south to Petropavlovski, the principal fortress and town in Kamtchatka. For the benefit of the reader, we give a few facts on the Peninsula, which will serve to show that the country is not a range of desolate hills, covered with perpetual snow, and inhabited by barbarians.

"KAMTCHATKA comprises the whole of that great peninsula which stretches out from the coast of Asia at its north-eastern extremity, and is washed by the Pacific Ocean on the east and the sea of Ochotsk on the west. It lies between the 51st and 64th degree of north latitude, and between the 155th and 164th of east longitude. It is between 700 and 800 miles in length, and about 250 in breadth at its centre near the latitude of 55 degrees, but not above eighty or ninety at either of its extremities. The most remarkable natural features of this great peninsula are its volcanic mountains, which rise at intervals throughout a vast range, which stretches from its southern to its northern extremity, and appears to be but a continuation of the volcanic range which forms the Kurile Islands, and extends even to Japan and the islands along the eastern coasts of the Asiatic continent. It has only one navigable river, called the Kamtchatka, which falls into the Sea of Kamtchatka near the centre of the peninsula, but it has many less considerable streams. The coasts and all the river of Kamtchatka abound in fish and water-fowl. The sea is frequented by whales of several species, and by walruses and seals in great abundance, besides cod and herring; and in the rivers are found great quantities of salmon. Geese and ducks, also, of several species, frequent the coasts and the rivers during the autumn and spring in great numbers.

The peninsula is inhabited by three aboriginal tribes, the Kamtchatdales, the Kouriaks, and the Ohlutors. The first of these occupy the southern, and the other two the northern districts of the country. But the whole of the native population is not supposed to exceed 4,000 or 5,000 souls.

The climate of Kamtchatka is much milder than that of the continent in the same parallel of latitude, owing, without doubt, to the influence of the sea on both sides of it. The maximum of cold in the southern districts does not exceed 20 degrees.

The country politically forms a part of the government of Ochotsk, and is comprehended within the grand province of Eastern Siberia. Its capital town is called Petropavlovski, or the town of St. Peter and St. Paul, and is seated in the bay of Avasha. * * * * *

The Kamtchatdales, however, live in villages like the Russians in winter, when they hunt and procure furs, some of which they exchange with the traders for useful articles, but the most part for *vodka* and tobacco. * * *

The imperial government, in conjunction with the Agricultural Society of St. Petersburg, has established two superintendents of agriculture, who travel and distribute seeds sent from Russia, and collect information concerning the condition and capabilities of the country.

On one occasion at the government-house, the commandant, whose interest seemed fully engaged in the advance and prosperity of the country under his government, exhibited a specimen of cloth manufactured by two Kamtchatdale girls of the interior of the country, and also some specimens of the plants from which it was made. The cloth was not very fine, but was said to be extremely durable. The plant which furnished the raw material is called *Krapeva* by the natives. It very much resembles our stinging nettle, but is of larger growth and of a fibre much stronger. Those which were exhibited were upwards of six feet in length. Specimens of the cloth had already been sent to St. Petersburg; and the agricultural society there had forwarded some rich presents to the two ingenious girls. *

The government has not been unmindful that moral culture, if it do not precede, must at least march hand in hand with material progress of any kind; and the true elements of proper civilization, the means of instruction, have been afforded the natives of the southern districts of the peninsula. Several schools have in effect been established; one at Milkova, 320 versts from Petropavlovski, and the other at Clutchifskoi, 600 versts from the capital. And besides these there are other small schools for young children, attached to the churches, which have been erected and endowed in different parts of the country."

The middle district of the peninsula is described as being very fertile, comprising an extensive valley, lying for

"The most part between two ranges of hills, and watered by the River Kamtchatka. Here the soil is composed of fine mould, similar to that which we have seen prevailing in Siberia; and its natural productions are abundant, consisting of all the varieties of the fir and the birch, of a finer growth than any to be found in the same latitude upon the Asiatic continent. It was the general opinion, that all this part of the country would produce hemp, flax, and the principal culinary vegetables. Ships of 100 tons burden may advance 200 versts up the river which here fertilizes the country. Raspberries, strawberries, whortleberries, currants, and cranberries, abound also in the same district. There is likewise much grass in the lower lands; and many forest trees flourish on the drier soils, such as larch, poplar, willow, cedar, and juniper.

The wild animals most abounding in the peninsula are, bears, lynxes, sea and river otters, reindeer, foxes of different colours, wolves, and martens or sables. The natives exchange annually about 100,000 of the skins with the Russian traders, for various articles of merchandise. Ducks, geese, and other birds of passage, are plentiful in spring and autumn.

Of the fish with which the rivers abound, salmon of several kinds is the most remarkable.

Herrings are as plentiful in spring and autumn, as upon the coast of Europe and America. Smelts are likewise plentiful at the same season. * * * *

There is little doubt that the peninsula is rich in mineral deposits, but it has been very imperfectly explored. The natives are said to know of districts which abound in the precious metals, but which they judge it prudent to conceal, lest it should tend to increase the number of the Russians in their country, and by and by lead, as they seem to have a somewhat obscure presentiment, to their being forced to labour in the mines."

Iron ore, coal and other valuable mines, exist to a very great extent throughout the entire country!

"There is, perhaps, no country in the world that is of more purely volcanic formation than Kamtchatka. The whole peninsula must be considered to be composed of but one vast range of volcanic mountains, and the *debris* which remains of the substances emitted during their eruption at different periods in the geological history of our planet. Many of them still are in a state of action. * * * * *

From the crater of the Avasha, which is immediately behind Petropavlovski, have been thrown at the same time stones, lava, and water; and from the two mightiest in a state of action, Klutchewsky and Assachninsk, the ashes have been thrown beyond a hundred versts."

Much of the country is fertile, though abounding with hills and valleys. The river bottoms are cultivated, and produce the useful commodities of the inhabited countries. The people are very civil, and though not so rapid in life as the inhabitants of the modern world, yet, they would be less offensive to a telegraph line. Our readings on Kamtchatka teaches us to believe, that a telegraph can be as easily constructed, as across the great chain of mountains in America. Having now noticed the route of the proposed telegraph across the continents of Europe, and Asia, to the Pacific Ocean, on the eastern shores of Kamtchatka, we will examine the route to America across the Pacific Ocean.

We do not deem it necessary to discuss the advantages or disadvantages of the route around, and crossing Behring Straits. Many gentlemen regard that as the best for the telegraph. There are no mountain icebergs there to destroy the electric cable; there are no great slides of ice to break asunder the subterranean wires, as has been wildly imagined, and there are no elements in nature to injure the successful working of a line by that route. We do not propose to run by the Behring Straits, because it will cost less to run the line direct over to America, along with the chain of Aleutian Isles, which seem to have been placed there by the hand of nature, to aid the girdling of the world with the telegraph. We have no doubt of the practicability of both routes, but as these telegraph isles are so beautifully arranged, and located at short distances from each other, and within a moderate climate, we have fixed upon that direction as the best for the purposes in view.

ALEUTIAN ISLES.—Proceeding from the eastern coast of Kamtchatka with the electric telegraph to the American continent, we propose to occupy these islands. They are in the possession of Russia. Many of them will not be used, because their respective proximity preclude the necessity. Such of them as may be deemed advantageous, will be employed for the enterprise. Many of them are surrounded with shoal water, broken and projecting rocks, rendering them inaccessible. There are many fine islands among them, well suited for the landing of a cable. If deep water be required, there are those that can be approached with deep water. If shallow water be required, then we can select those suited for that purpose. If inhabited islands should be required only, then we can select those alone, and if not, we can select those few upon which there are no people.

The inhabitants of these islands are very well informed, and are perhaps better disposed, than the people of any other part of the northern hemisphere. Their pursuits are directed, mostly in fishing and hunting. Cattle are grazed on some of them, and the products of the earth are, also, cultivated to a moderate extent.

The Aleutian Isles are divided into four divisions—the *Blignie* group is composed of four islands, the *Rat Islands* compose several more, the *Andréanoff* Isles compose another group, and the next are the *Fox Islands*, composed of several which extend to the Aliask Peninsula of the American continent.

We do not deem it necessary to go into details, as to the character of these islands. That can be done in the future. They are scattered across the Pacific Ocean, from Kamtchatka to America, at distances varying from one to fifty miles apart, and they are from one to eighty miles in length. Some of them are quite low, and others are composed of immense mountains, exceeding in height the great Ural Mountains. Some of the higher peaks are covered with perpetual snow. Some contain volcanoes and abound with hot springs. The volcanoes continually issue smoke, and one of the higher peaks contain a large lake of boiling water.

These islands have been examined, and we have before us very correct data as to their topographical features, the geological formations of the earth, the latitude and the longitude of each; the depth of the water around each, the products, the inhabitants, and the climate of the whole. With this information we think we can safely come to proper conclusions, as to their fitness for the purposes of the telegraph. We have studied them very carefully, and the line can be carried by this route with the utmost facility.

Landing the line upon the western end of the Aliask Peninsula, which projects many miles into the ocean, from America, we will follow its most favourable formations. The length of the peninsula is 330 miles, and from 25 to 90 miles in breath. On this peninsula are high mountains, and a peak towering high in the heavens, on the summit of which is a volcano, that will equal in grandeur the Hecla, Vesuvius and Ætna. There are not many inhabitants on the land, perhaps not more than 10,000, but they are good and useful people.

The line will run around the head of Cooke's Inlet, proceeding south along the coast, to the British possessions, latitude 54° 40. The whole country between Cooke's Inlet and the British boundary is of varied formations, mostly hilly, having a few streams entering the ocean. The streams can be easily crossed, and the mountains in the interior are gradual in ascent, rendering them accessible to travellers, sufficiently so, at least, for the construction of a telegraph. The coast is more or less populated, having some 11,000 people scattered over the country.

The lands are capable of producing wheat, barley, oats, &c., and the climate favours their growth. With a better management of the people from that which is exercised over them now by the Fur Company, will make the inhabitants advance in the cultivation of the products of the earth. Their main commodity is fur, and that is the marketable article. If they would devote more attention to the cultivation of grains, the country would very soon change in its appearance, and where the fox and other fur tribes inhabit, the plough would occasion the coast to be beautified with the useful products of the earth.

Passing from the Russian territory in America across the British, to the United States, at 49° 50, we enter a country well understood by the people of the present age. We do not deem it necessary to speak of this country, nor of the people ; as the character of both are well known to be favourable to the construction of a telegraph. The maintenance of the line is another question. In that we shall have trouble from the Indians. The rapid settlements of the whites along the coastwise territory, will occasion, perhaps, the hostility from the savage tribes; but a few years will dispel these fears. The Indians will be compelled to go into the interior, and the coast will be thickly settled by the enterprising whites. Ten years will perhaps place a million of people in this country, scattered all along the coast! Proceeding along the coast of the Pacific Ocean, south to San Francisco, all the important towns will be placed in communication with the Atlantic, European and Asiatic people.

At San Francisco the line will connect with the great Atlantic and Pacific Telegraph, which is under arrangement of construction by the American people. For the particulars as to the plans of this gigantic enterprise, reference is requested to the article upon that subject in the second number of the present volume of the Companion.

From St. Louis, Missouri, we will have two connections with the Atlantic Ocean; one through the States and the other through Canada, via Chicago. If the Atlantic Ocean telegraph starts from Labrador, a line on the north side of the St. Lawrence can be run to make a connection, and another through the Provinces, Newfoundland, and thence to Labrador. These connections can be readily completed, as much of the lines are at present in operation.

We have devoted room enough to the consideration of this subject in the present number. Facts have been given sufficient to convince any one that a telegraph can be constructed around the world. We have shown that the country through which the line will run is well suited for the construction of the telegraph, that the climate is not unfavorable, and that the people are not barbarous, as has been slanderously promulgated to the world by conceited writers, but by people who are the best in the world, inhabiting the entire country, except, perhaps, the American coast where the savage tribes of Indians roam. There is no part of the route more covered with lakes, swamps, and inundations, than some parts of America where we have constructed lines of telegraph, and where they have been in operation for many years. We are sure there is no country through which the line will run so unfavorable, so difficult either to build or maintain a telegraph, as upon Newfoundland, where the energy of our people is rapidly approaching the Atlantic coast with the electric wires. As to the Atlantic Ocean section, we refer the reader to the article on that subject in the present number of the COMPANION. We have been as brief as we possibly could in the discussion of the subject. We have omitted many facts which would greatly favor the proposition, but we could not say all in a volume of less than five hundred pages. A route of thirty thousand miles over a country presumed to be but little known, circling the whole earth, cannot be discussed within a few pages. We do not address these remarks to the mind limited by narrow boundaries, poisoned with envy, selfishness, and prejudice. We seek for the consideration of those persons who are imbued with a liberal state of patriotism, and a zeal commensurate with the progressive state of the age. They alone can grasp with justness and competency the vastness of this magnificent and stupendous enterprise. That it will be consummated, we have no doubt. That it will subserve the welfare of all nations, and be calculated to bless generations to come, we earnestly believe. So far as we can devote our energies to the realization of these hopes, we intend to prosecute the cause to the end of life, or until the enterprise is complete, and the world circled with one continuous stream of the electric flame!

ART. VII.—THE TRANSATLANTIC SUBMARINE TELEGRAPH.

EUROPE AND AMERICA TO BE CONNECTED BY THE ELECTRIC TELEGRAPH—A COMPANY FORMED—PROGRESS OF THE ENTERPRISE.

JOHN W. BRETT, OF EUROPE,
TAL. P. SHAFFNER, OF AMERICA, } GERANTS.

THE connection of the eastern and western hemispheres, by electric telegraph, has been a subject of grave discussion for many years. More than a year ago, we announced to the American people that we were engaged in the earnest prosecution of that undertaking, and that we intended to adhere to it until success was triumphant. Of course, we have many times calculated the cost of the enterprise, as regards money, time and life. So far as we command these requirements, the undivided energies of our future life will be directed to this object. That we shall ultimately be successful, there can be no doubt. We care not for opposition, as we are confident none can arrest us in the satisfactory prosecution of the enterprise. There may be a few ambitious persons who are ready to grasp a favorable opportunity to make a noise, for a prospective gain, hoping to have their silence bought; but we can assure all such, that any vain boasting of great wealth and power, only occupies in our mind that consideration which is generally allotted to the music of "sounding brass and tinkling cymbal."

In order to consummate this vast undertaking, we need no high-sounding names of men who have figured in the affairs of state, in the Bourse, Lombard-street, Wall-street, or in any department of fancy life. A select group, of men from any one section of the world, will not be sufficient to carry out an enterprise of such magnitude. In its management the best and most experienced telegraph skill that can be employed from the whole world will be required in its prosecution. Money will be indispensable in its aid; but money, without the experience and knowledge of the science and art of telegraphing, will be of no avail.

It is often the case, that gentlemen embark in telegraphing, and because they are possessed of a few dollars, they imagine that in a few hours a thorough knowledge of the art and science of telegraphing can be comprehended. That which requires the devotion of years to obtain by the practical telegrapher, a man of money sometimes conceives he can grasp—with his self-conceited genius—in a few days. Such men are to be dreaded in any enterprise. They are like so many vampires upon the cause, however important. Public welfare never receives their solicitude; but, it is their own selfish ends that must be gratified before all others, even at the sacrifice of the public weal. All such men we are determined to eschew, and give no concern in the management of this grand undertaking. We would much prefer seeing the whole enterprise fail, than in the hands of speculators, who enter into the company solely for speculative gain, for the present, regardless of the future.

We are not particular in our feelings as to the proper place of running this submarine cable, though we are firm in the conviction, that it will be best to adopt the Greenland and Iceland route. Nevertheless, we desire that all shall be thoroughly examined and judged upon, before the final adoption of any. We desire to see a cable stretched from continent to continent, that will endure all time; one that will never fail, and be the means of advancing the interests of the people of all nations. We hope to see its management liberal and international. We do not seek any advantages for the American people, and we hope none will be sought for the people of any other country. The communication should be free to all alike and co-operatively under the shield of every nation of the globe. We hope to see it beyond the possibility of interruption through the power of the elements of nature; and also free from that most dreadful destroyer, the god of war. It is the uplifted sabre of this monster that gives us more fear than the combined elements of natural creation. With the pledged faith of nations, that this intellectual flame shall not be quenched, we can confide in the triumphant creation of a power, that can say, "there shall be peace and good will among men."

In this great undertaking we have with us that noble and intrepid submarine telegrapher, John Watkins Brett, Esq., of Europe. His name has ornamented the pages of European history, and the annals of years near at hand will record his deeds great in America. His energies have no bounds, and his abilities are equal to any emergency in the prosecution of these advancements of the electric telegraph. His devotion to the extension of the telegraph in Europe and Africa entitle him to the gratitude of nations, and particularly the governments most directly interested. In the erection of the Transatlantic Telegraph Mr. Brett will share largely, and his superior experience, judgment, and energy, will be of pre-eminent service in its consummation. We are not saying too much when we assert, that Mr. Brett stands foremast as a submarine telegrapher, and has no rival. With such aid we have no fears of a failure. We do not deem it necessary to give a full statement as to the plan of carrying out this enterprise. That will be promulgated in the future. Until all the routes are thoroughly examined, and all questions properly considered, we do not deem it proper to even form a fixed opinion. We have given the different routes much study; yet there are circumstances which may change any opinion we may have formed in the past; consequently future examinations must determine the best route to run the transatlantic submarine telegraph.

We give the following letter, which explains itself, and leave the further discussion of the subject for the future.

ATLANTIC OCEAN TELEGRAPH.

METROPOLITAN HOTEL,
New-York, February 2, 1855.

TO THE EDITORS OF THE EVENING POST:

Gentlemen:—You did me the honor to notice my proposed world-girdle telegraph, for which I thank you. I am also under obligations to the press throughout the land for copying your editorial upon the subject. A discussion of the scientific questions involved in the project of the telegraph across the ocean I do not deem at the present time opportune, for many reasons; nevertheless, it is well for the enterprise to be under public consideration.

I have seen in the *Louisville Courier* a notice purporting to originate with the *Philadelphia American*, relative to the telegraph across the Atlantic Ocean, in which the route I propose is regarded as a scheme of folly. The editor says:

"If we do not get a telegraphic communication with Europe before this line is constructed, we fear that a perpetual separation must exist. The account says, that there must be no submarine section of more than five hundred miles; yet the map tells us that the distance between Iceland and Norway is eight hundred and fifty miles. The stupidity of the whole affair is evident; for the map will show any one that Iceland is nearer to Scotland than to Norway; and as for running telegraph lines into Russsia, Chinese Tartary and Kamtchatka, instead of to England, that seems particularly absurd. The three submarine sections, from Labrador to Greenland, from thence to Iceland, and from thence to Norway, are either impracticable or useless; for, if practicable, science will teach any one that the same reasons will make the direct line from Newfoundland to Ireland practicable. If Mr. Shaffner went to Europe on any such mission as that above stated, he has spent a great deal of money for nothing."

With your permission, gentlemen, I will briefly consider these points of difference in opinion, with a little more regard, however, for courtesy and respectful language than characterizes the editorial from the *American.*

It is a settled fact in philosophy that a galvanic current is arrested in its transit through a long submarine or subterranean wire. So great has this new impediment been experienced in Europe, that the most learned savans have been active in new discoveries to find a remedy. The difficulty may be overcome, ultimately. I will not say that a galvanic or magnetic electric current can never be sent from Newfoundland to Ireland; but I do say that, with the present discoveries of science, I do not believe it practicable for telegraphic service.

The distance between these two points is about 1,800 miles; and, allowing for a slack of a cable, the length of the electric wires will be at least 2,500 miles! As experience thus far has proved the impracticability of transmitting a current at will on a submarine or subterranean wire of 1,000 miles in length, how is it possible to transmit it 2,500 miles? The most extended submarine wire ever experimented upon is the Mediterranean telegraph cable, on which I witnessed many experiments, with a view to ascertain the necessities of an oceanic line. The length was 660 miles. On that distance success was evident. We have no knowledge of the successful working of a line in length as great as 1,000 miles, embracing submarine and subterranean wires; and if we have not the evidence of the practicability of transmitting telegraphic intelligence over a line of this length, it occurs to me that I should, indeed, be guilty of great "stupidity" were I to talk about a line direct from continent to continent—a distance of at least 2,500 miles! Nevertheless, new discoveries may at an early day overcome this formidable barrier in the science of telegraphing.

As to the Greenland route, I would say that the editor of the Philadelphia American has certainly exhibited great unfairness. On reference to the map, any one can see that the longest section is from America to Greenland, being about 500 miles. From Greenland to Iceland, or from Iceland to the Faroe isles, or from the Faroe isles to Norway, that distance is neither exceeded nor equalled. Estimating, however, the sections to be each as much as 660 miles, I am within the bounds of practicability and certainty. These facts must prove one of two points, viz: that the Philadelphia editor was either ignorant of the existence of the Faroe isles, or wilfully omitted to mention them. They are nearly half way between Iceland and Norway, and are embraced in my grants from Denmark.

Again: this unfair editor urges objections to this route because it does not run direct to England. It is in contemplation to extend the line, if necessary, from the Faroe isles, not only to Norway, but also to North Scotland, and thence south to England. The great business relations between America and Great Britain cannot be overlooked; but I am not one of those who believe that England is the only place of importance upon the face of the earth. We have a large trade with that great country, but we have also a respectable trade with the nations on the continent.

I regard this question with an American proclivity, and in the negotiations with the governments of Europe, while I have consulted as well their interests and convenience, I have had in view the welfare of my own before that of any other country. And in the preservation of the rights of the people of America to transmit intelligence over the lines proposed by me, I have, also, not forgotten that there are other nations of the earth. As an evidence of my sincerity in this respect, and my regard for reciprocity between the people of the whole world, I give an example illustrative of the course which I have marked out for myself in all my treaties with the governments of Europe. The following clause, taken from my letters-patent, granted by his Majesty the King of Denmark, I presume will be sufficient to demonstrate the end I have in view:

"That the government of Denmark will forever defend and preserve the rights of the citizens of the United States, and the people of all nations, to transmit messages over the line herein contemplated, provided the said messages are not calculated to promote war, insurrection, riot, or the violation of peace among nations."

The editor of the *Philadelphia American* will see from the above, that I have not only considered the good of my own country, but also that of England. I could not regard the people of Great Britain with more favor than those of the German States, of France, and other powers of the Continent.

Supposing it was practicable to work at will a line of telegraph from Newfoundland, the French islands, or any other part of the American coast, direct to Ireland, I would not consider it worthy of American patronage unless the rights of our people were duly protected by fixed treaties with Great Britain. In case of war between the United States and Great Britain, the American people would have no opportunity of sending or receiving intelligence by telegraph. All communication between the people of this country and the nations of Europe would be cut off. The line would be in the sole service of the British Government in transmitting orders from the War Office in London to their forces in the provinces, exclusively in their own interests, and to the ruin of this country.

In the consummation of this important enterprise most formidable difficulties will doubtless arise, and they may possibly be too great ever to be overcome; but a small share of the indomitable energy so characteristic of the country in the successful achievement of bold enterprises may safely be relied upon to accomplish this grand and magnificent project, notwithstanding it has been so sneeringly characterized by the *Philadelphia American* as a "scheme of folly."

The *American* says that the Greenland route, as sections, is "either impracticable or useless," and, "if practicable, science will teach any one that the same reasons will make the direct line from Newfoundland to Ireland practicable." He gives no reason why the line would be "useless." I suppose he considers his *ipse dixit* to be sufficient to determine that question. The reason for making what he calls a direct line practicable amounts to this, viz: if it is practicable to work a telegraph cable five hundred miles submarine, it is also practicable to work twenty-five hundred miles! This is not the fact, however, and it is for the editor of the *American* to prove it. To show how ridiculous this proposition is, I will apply it to our own daily experience, viz: If it is practicable to work a line direct with one circuit from Boston to New York, it will work also from Boston direct to New-Orleans. This has never been done, and is yet to be proved practicable! Boston can work to New-Orleans by the combining of electric circuits; but we cannot have stations to combine circuits in the ocean. By the Greenland route I believe America can telegraph, by the connection of the galvanic circuits, with London, Paris, Copenhagen, St. Petersburgh, &c.

I am fully aware of the vastness of this undertaking. For years it has been the object of my desire, and I am now solely devoted to its consummation. Conflicting opinions and jealousy cannot arrest or temporarily postpone the girdling of the world with a telegraph. When Prof. Morse first said his telegraph could work around the globe, little did he dream of ever witnessing it, or even living to see the plan so favorably considered by the great powers of the earth. He may yet live to send the first despatch, and receive by the electric flash the congratulations of nations for giving birth to the most wonderful achievement of man.

Very respectfully, &c.,
TAL. P. SHAFFNER.

RELATIVE CONDUCTING CAPACITIES OF METALS.—The annexed table exhibits the relative capacities of the metals mentioned to conduct voltaic electricity. They are the results of experiments instituted by M. Becquerel:—

Metal	
Copper wire	100.
Gold	93.6
Silver	73.6
Zinc	28.5
Platinum	16.4
Iron	15.5
Lead	8.3

ART. VIII.—AMERICAN PRESS ON THE WORLD GIRDLE TELEGRAPH.

[We give the following notices from the American press on the World Girdle Telegraph. We have seen hundreds of the like, and they manifest the most confident hopes of the consummation of the enterprise.]—EDITOR.

[*From the New-York Post.*]

SHAFFNER'S WORLD-GIRDLE TELEGRAPH.

"We announced several months since the departure of Tal. P. Shaffner, Esq., the editor of the American Telegraphic Magazine, for Europe, to make arrangements for the construction of a telegraph around the world. He has recently returned from his expedition, the results of which possess more than ordinary interest.

We learn from Mr. Shaffner that his recent tour in Europe was undertaken for the purpose, first, of acquiring a thorough knowledge of the different modes of telegraphing and constructing lines in the Old World; second, to negotiate with the Danish government for the exclusive right to lay a line over Greenland, Iceland, and Faroe isles, and Denmank, for the term of one hundred years; third, for the acquisition of similiar rights over Norway, Sweden, and Russia. With these and other rights, which he proposed to himself to secure, the success of his plan to girdle the world with the electric telegraph no longer appears visionary or impracticable.

The route of his proposed line is as follows:

Starting from the coast of Labrador, the width of the sea to Greenland is about five hundred miles. From the point of landing, the line is to extend under ground around Cape Farewell to a point on the east coast of Greenland, favorable for a submarine connection to Iceland. A subterranean line across to the eastern coast of that island will connect with a submarine wire running to the Faroe isles, and thence to Norway, landing at or in the vicinity of Bergen. Mr. Shaffner informs us that the land and climate of Greenland and the isles are well, and even better adapted to the construction of the telegraph than those of the United States. Greenland abounds with mineral wealth, and he thinks the telegraph will tend to develop the unappreciated resources of that country. By this route there will be no submarine section of more than five hundred miles, and the loss or failure of one section will not destroy the others. In a line direct from Ireland to Newfoundland the failure of any part occasions a loss of the whole.

After landing on the coast of Norway it is intended to run

the line to Christian, the capital of Norway, and from thence branches to Copenhagen and Stockholm. The Danish government has bound itself to furnish proper connections with the governments on the continent and Great Britain. Consequently, it will not be necessary to run a cable from the Faroe isles to the Shetlands, Orkneys, and to north Scotland. Treaties with the Emperor of Russia contemplate the extension of the line from Stockholm, in Sweden, to St. Petersburgh, across or along the coast of Finland. By the construction of this section America will be able to transmit intelligence direct to Russia, and thus establish most intimate relations between the subjects of the Czar and the sovereigns of the United States.

Leaving St. Petersburgh, Mr. Shaffner proposes to run his line to Moscow, or connect at the latter place with the imperial lines already in operation—from thence to Kazan, across the Ural Mountains, into Asia, passing through Omsk, Kolivan, Kansk, Oudinsk, to Irkoutsk, near Lake Baikal. This is near the great tea country in Chinese Tartary, from whence the Russian tea is brought overland on wagons. The trade in this tea, which is said to be the best in the world, is very large, and the telegraph, it is supposed, will tend to increase it materially.

From Irkoutsk it is intended to run the line to the sea of Ochotsk, either north the Yakoutsk, or south with the Amour river, and thence along the coast of the sea of Ochotsk to Iamsk, and across the Gulf to Cape Utkoloka, Kamtchatka, and thence along the Aleutian isles to Aliaska peninsula or Cooke's inlet, in North America. From this point the line will be run along the Pacific coast to Oregon, and south to San Francisco, California. This range is entirely south of the latitude of St. Petersburgh, and in fact the line can be carried around by Behring's Straits, and be south of the Arctic circle.

From San Francisco Mr. Shaffner proposes to run the line along the best route to the Salt Lake, and thence to the western boundary of Missouri, where it will intersect the existing section of the California line, built by him a few years ago. Joining the great lines in America, the earth will be girdled with one continuous and unbroken flame of electric light.

In the ocean or submarine department of the great work Mr. Shaffner has associated with him Mr. John W. Brett, who has been the projector and successful constructor of the vast ranges of submarine and subterranean lines of the Old World.

The consummation of this great enterprise will be productive of consequences which the human imagination strives in vain to realize. It will enable us to communicate daily with every civilized nation on the face of the globe, and many not so civilized; for, as soon as possible after the completion of the main trunk, branch lines will be extended to Japan, Pekin, Nankin, Canton, and other cities of China.

We are informed by Mr. Shaffner that he expects but little trouble in maintaining the line through Russia in Europe, in Asia, or America. The roads are good and well improved; the climate is most favorable for the enterprise; and with the aid of the Emperor he thinks there will be no formidable hindrance. The military system is very perfect throughout the empire, and will constitute an ample guarantee against any troubles which telegraphic science cannot provide against.

In the negotiations of Mr. Shaffner in Europe he has been singularly fortunate, and his efforts have been crowned with flattering success. Depending upon his energy, he has succeeded where the most skilful diplomats have failed. He informs us that he had one great element of strength; that was, he was an *American*. His Majesty the King of Denmark intimated to him that he would not have considered the proposition had it come from a citizen of any other nation; but he informed Mr. Shaffner that he granted the patents under the belief that there were no obstacles in nature that could be a barrier against the genius and enterprise of his countrymen."

[*From the New-Orleans Crescent.*]

A WORLD GIRDLE.

"It is singular to notice how, in the history of the world, almost every great achievement of science has been at some time, long previous to its discovery, prefigured and prophesied by the pen of genius; has been foretold and partially described in fable, romance or poetry. For truly great minds live always in advance of their own age, and are chiefly great in that they see as probable and possible those things which to all other men are chimeras. Hardly any of the great inventions of the world but have been more or less fully and accurately pictured centuries before they were made practicable. Thus the winged wonders, which Ariosto and Spenser delighted in creating, now fly through the air as balloons, or thunder over the earth as locomotives, or plough the deep as steamships,

"Steadying with upright keel"

against wind and wave. Things that were the fables of a past age are the facts of the present, and what were once dreams have become realities.

In the Midsummer Night's Dream, Shakespeare makes *Puck* say:

"I'll put a girdle round about the earth
In forty minutes."

It is in proof of our statement that an American citizen, of the present day, is engaged in receiving subscriptions and making arrangements to perform actually what Shakespeare faintly foreshadowed, and to accomplish that which, if it had been advocated a century ago, would have constituted sufficient grounds for a writ *de lunatico inquirendo* against the enthusiast. Thus the fancies and fables of genius render themselves the facts of after-time.

This world girdling scheme to which we have referred is not dependent upon any new discovery in science, and is actually but the extension of our present telegraph system. But such an extension! It contemplates bringing us into neighborly converse and propinquity with those inhabitants of the antipodes that are far deeper under our feet than any Artesian wells ever sunk or to be sunk; it contemplates daily mails from the great tea countries of Chinese Tartary and regular news from the Faroe Islands and Cooke's Inlet. It is more grand and gigantic in its proportions than any scheme of the present day, and seeks to tie together, in commercial and friendly relations, the whole civilized world; if completed as contemplated, the reader in this city will be able each morning to peruse the records of yesterday's proceedings on the Bourse, the publications of the papers in St. Petersburgh, the successes of the armies in China, the news at Honolulu, and the state of the weather in Greenland. It will girdle the world like a new equator, and make Cancer and Capricorn mere figments of a fool's brain.

The Columbus of this telegraphic feat contemplates starting from the coast of Labrador, and laying an unbroken wire, five hundred miles in length, among the walruses and whales of the North Sea, to Greenland. The wire will cross Greenland and stretch again eastward to the Faroe Islands, from whence it will reach the continent in the vicinity of Bergen, in Norway. Thence, sweeping on towards the circumference of the globe, the wire will reach Stockholm, and coast along Finland to St. Petersburgh. Leaving the city of the Czar, it will trend towards the Ural Mountains; leap across them into Asia; pass through the provinces of Omsk, Oudinska, Kansk, Kolivan, and the great tea country of Chinese Tartary; stretch away to the sea of Ochotsk and across the gulf to Kamtchatka; thence along the Aleutian Islands to Cooke's Inlet, in North America. Then running down the Pacific coast to Oregon and San Francisco, the line will strike to the east by the Salt Lake, and touch civilization at the western boundary of Missouri.

This gigantic scheme for crossing oceans, and islands, and continents; for bringing savage and civilized nations into daily communication; for outstripping the winds and annihilating time; for girdling the globe with one uninterrupted flame of electric fire; is not a scheme only, but a practical plan towards the accomplishment of which treaties and agreements have already been made—for the fulfilment of which scientific men are now daily laboring. A few years time is expected to see its accomplishment in full, and the present year is looked forward to as sufficient for a connection with Europe. The mind refuses to take in at once all the consequences of so grand an enterprise. American, European and Asiatic interests would be joined, and the great occurrences of one day, in this country, would be known to-morrow in the capitals and remote provinces of the whole world as would their day's business be published here. The scheme is worthy of our go-ahead countrymen, to whom there is not known any such word as fail.

Shakspeare's strange prophecy grows to its fulfilment, and the telegraph will yet do what Puck promised to accomplish."

[*From the Portland Argus.*]

THE TELEGRAPH.

"The Magnetic Telegraph is among the most important and wonderful inventions of modern times. Since 1774, when Le Sage, a Frenchman, made the first known attempt to render electricity available for the transmission of intelligence, there have been almost constant experiments to effect this desirable result. From 1820 to 1850, no less than sixty-three varieties of telegraph were invented, of which only those of Morse, Bain and House are much in use. In 1832, Prof. Morse, an American, commenced his experiments for an electro-magnetic telegraph, and was able publicly to announce his invention in 1837. Upon his petition, Congress appropriated $30,000 to test the practical advantages of the invention, and in 1844, the first line from Washington to Baltimore (40 miles) was established and put in operation. During the succeeding year, 1845, this line was extended eastward to Philadelphia, New-York and Boston. The line was constructed by stretching copper wires upon posts from 15 to 20 feet high, and placed at distances from 12 to 15 rods apart. The high cost of copper wire has caused it to be superseded by that of iron; the latter, however, must be six times heavier than the copper, to afford equal constructing power. About 250 pounds of iron wire are required to the mile, which, with posts, labor, &c., make the cost of constructing an ordinary telegraph, about $150 per mile.

Later experiments tend to show that wire, or a rod of iron, from three to five eighths of an inch in thickness, and weighing a ton to the mile, possesses very decided advantages over the smaller wire. It is less liable to be broken, and the mass of metal gives free passage to electrical currents, without insulation, and without being interrupted by the hardest rains. It is not sensibly affected by rust, and considering the less amount of repairs required, the rods are but little more costly than small wires. The rods will undoubtedly be found to be vastly superior for lines through a wild country, as from the valley of the Mississippi to California.

The average performance of the Morse instruments is said to be from 8,000 to 9,000 letters per hour, and the usual charge is twenty-five cents for ten words or less, for the distances of one hundred miles.

The amount of business which can be done on one of these lines is immense. As an example, it is stated that 154,514 messages were sent over the line from New-York to Washington in six months, for which $68,499 23 were paid. It may be safely stated, that from 500 to 1000 messages can be sent and received over a single line in a day.

Besides the advantages of the telegraph to business men for private correspondence, there is the more important public benefit which it affords for communicating intelligence through the newspaper press. By its aid, the Portland papers are usually enabled to publish all the important foreign and domestic news as early as those of Boston and New-York. The proceedings of Congress appear in the morning papers of Portland, just as early as those of Washington, where Congress sits. These advantages, which the public thus derive, can hardly be overestimated, although they seem to be lightly valued.

Newspapers are expected to be furnished at the old prices, notwithstanding the largely increased cost of publishing them, arising from the advanced prices of labor and material, in addition to the heavy expenses of the telegraphic communications.

The cost of dispatches to the New-York associated press is $64,000 per year. Yet the advantages of the telegraph, so overbalance the outlays it requires, that it has extended with wonderful rapidity.

In 1853, there were in operation in this country and in Europe, 27,168 miles of telegraph, without reckoning the lines then in process of construction in Austria, Russia, Spain, Bavaria, and some other States, and 16,735 miles of this were in the United States. The aggregate length of lines now constructed and in operation, can scarcely fall short of 40,000 miles—more than half of which is in this country.

A submarine cable across the English channel from Dover to Ostend, connects Great Britain with the continent of Europe, and places most of her principal capitals in telegraphic communication with each other. Lines are also progressing toward India and Africa, and the Crimea. In this country, some eighty lines form a net-work of wires connecting nearly all important points upon the Atlantic side of the continent; and it is now seriously contemplated to connect this Atlantic system with the Pacific coast, by means of a direct line across the country. A charter has been granted for the purpose, at the present session of Congress, to Messrs. Alder & Eddy, citizens of Maine, who are to undertake the project as a private enterprise, and great confidence is expressed that they will be able to accomplish it.

But this is not all. The telegraph is not only thus rapidly creeping over the two continents—bringing their extreme points in hourly communication with each other; but strenuous efforts are being made to connect these two systems of telegraph, by a line running from one to the other; and thus to girdle the earth with the lightning messengers.

There are two projects for accomplishing this result. One proposes to connect the Eastern point of Newfoundland with the Western point of Ireland, by a submarine cable, running directly across the ocean between them. The distance is 1,800 miles, and allowing for slack of cable, would require a wire 2,500 miles in length.

Recent soundings have showed that there is not a great depth of water between these points; that the bed of the ocean is not swept by currents, and that it is otherwise favorable to the security of the wires, and to the feasibility of putting them down. The great obstacle to the success of this project, is the scientific fact, that the electric current is arrested in its transit through long submarine or subterranean wires. The greatest length of submarine and subterranean wire ever yet experimented upon, is the Mediterranean Telegraph cable, which is 660 miles in length, and has been successfully operating, until some remedy is found (and the scientific are now actively in search for it) for the exhaustion of the galvanic current by transmission for long distances, under ground or under water. This project of sending messages under ocean upon a conducting wire 2,500 miles in length, must, so far as we are able to judge, be deemed impracticable. Future discoveries may render it possible.

The other project presents no insuperable obstacle, that we can discover. It proposes to run a line from the Northern point of this continent to Greenland, thence to Iceland, thence to the

Faroe Isles, thence to Norway; or from the Faroe Isles to the Orkney Isles, and thence to North Scotland. The longest water space by this route is from America to Greenland, estimated at 500 miles. It certainly does not exceed 660 miles; the distance which the magnetic current has already been made to operate.

The projectors of this line have been engaged for some time in experimenting, with a view to its construction; and have perfected negotiations for the right of way, in part at least, and are still actively and confidently prosecuting the work.

T. P. Shaffner, Esq., of New-York, has recently, through the press, warmly enlisted the public in favor of this magnificent enterprise, and inspired the hope that it will ere long be accomplished.

What a result! The earth encircled by a telegraphic wire, and its remotest inhabitants brought in hourly communication with each other! Stupendous achievement, indeed! Its beneficial results in harmonizing and humanizing the great family of man, and elevating them into one brotherhood, cannot be estimated or appreciated. We can, however, in a measure appreciate the advantage of reading, in our morning papers, an account of all the important events which transpire in the world, during the previous day, as we now read those of the extreme South or West."

[*From the Kentucky Rifle.*]

"On our first page will be found an article from the New-York *Post*, in reference to Tal. P. Shaffner's grand project of belting the earth with an electric telegraph.

Mr. Shaffner, as the Post informs us, has demonstrated beyond question that the scheme is practicable; and the fact that Tal. P. Shaffner is at the head of this magnificent enterprise, is a sufficient guaranty for its complete success.

What a bold, what a splendid achievement in science! The earth bound up in a net of iron nerves, diffusing intelligence to its remotest corners, and lighting up the world in a blaze of electric glory!—Truly this will, if accomplished, be regarded as the proudest victory of genius.

[*From the Boston Traveler.*]

A GIRDLE ROUND THE GLOBE.

"Tal. P. Shaffner, Esq., the editor of the American Telegraphic Magazine, has just returned from his expedition to Europe, where he has been making arrangements for the construction of an electric telegraph around the world. One great object of his visit was to negotiate with the Danish Government for the exclusive right to lay a line over Greenland, Iceland, the Faroe

Isles, and Denmark, for the term of one hundred years; and the acquisition of similar rights over Norway, Sweden and Russia.

The scheme is a bold one, and is certainly large enough for any capacity. The route the wire is to take is already sketched: Starting from the coast of Labrador, the width of the sea to Greenland is about five hundred miles. From the point of landing the line is to extend underground around Cape Farewell, to a point on the east coast of Greenland, favorable for a submarine connection with Iceland. A subterranean line across the eastern coast of that island will connect with a submarine wire to the Faroe Isles, and thence to Norway. By this route there will be no submarine section of more than five hundred miles. Treaties with the Emperor of Russia contemplate the extension of the line from Stockholm, in Sweden, to St. Petersburgh.

Mr. Shaffner proposes to run his line to Moscow, and thence into Asia, piercing Chinese Tartary, extending to the Sea of Ochotsk, and by the way of Kamtchatka, reaching Cooke's Inlet in North America. From this point the line will be run along the Pacific coast to Oregon, and south to San Francisco, California, &c., &c.

Joining the great lines in America, it is eloquently remarked that 'the earth will thus be girdled with one continuous and unbroken flame of electric light.'

In the ocean, or submarine department of the great work, Mr. Shaffner has associated with him Mr. John W. Brett, who has been the projector and successful constructor of the vast range of submarine and subterranean lines of the old world."

PRICES OF SUBMARINE CABLES.—The prices of submarine cables fluctuate with the cost of material and labor. The following were the prices for 1854, which we procured in London :—

No. of Miles.	Weight.		Price per Mile.
6	8 tons,	not galvanized	£410
5	7 "	"	380
4	6½ "	"	320
4	6½ "	galvanized	410
3	5½ "	not galvanized	275
2	4½ "	"	240
1	3 "	"	195
1	2 "	"	100
1	2 "	galvanized	120

The above prices will change, of course, according to times. Add to the above the duty and cost of transportation to America, and the expense of cables for our rivers will be known.

ART. IX.—HONORABLE TESTIMONIALS TO PROFESSOR MORSE IN EUROPE.

LETTER FROM PRUSSIA—MORSE TELEGRAPH ADOPTED IN GERMANY—DR. STEINHEIL.

WE mentioned, in our last number, that Professor Wheatstone and a few other persons of high scientific attainments in England were disposed to consider Professor Morse's claims to priority and originality in the telegraph as doubtful, and this on the ground, as they intimated, that Professor Henry had some sort of undefined claims in the matter. The "defence by Professor Morse," published in our last, has, we think, effectually disposed of this mistake. But whatever may be said by the *illiberal* of England, the sentiment towards Professor Morse on the Continent has been, and is still, in striking contrast.

We have had frequent and conclusive proof in our own personal intercourse with the highest officers and philosophers in the various continental governments, that his name is held in the highest honor.

In a late visit to Prof. Morse, we were shown a letter to him from one of our highly esteemed ambassadors to one of the courts of Europe, which we have been allowed to copy, and which shows in a just light the sentiment held in regard to the inventor of the telegraph by the commanding intellects of the old world. It is as follows:—

Extract of a letter from the Hon. D. D. Barnard, late minister plenipotentiary of the United States of America to the court of the King of Prussia, to Prof. Morse, dated July, 1854:—

"I have been an indignant observer from the beginning, of the outrageous piracies to which you have been subjected at the hands of your countrymen, and the infamous course of a portion of the public press of this country towards you in reference to your wonderful invention of the telegraph. It was, therefore, with peculiar satisfaction that during my residence abroad I was accustomed to hear your name pronounced with emphasis and honor everywhere on the Continent where I chanced to be, and in whatever circle, whenever the subject of the electric telegraph was named. I became entirely satisfied that the general sentiment of the European world did not fail nor hesitate to award to you the chief merit of this grand invention, and that your name was as sure of unrivalled immortality in connection with it, as that of Galileo or Newton with astronomy, or that of Bacon with philosophy. I spoke to you briefly of this when I had the pleasure of meeting you, but I have wished to express to you the same thing in a more substantial form."

"In Germany, after the most mature and elaborate investigation, by the aid of the profoundest learning and wisdom of the age, your telegraph was adopted in a general convention of all the States assembled expressly to consider that subject. And I can give you the assurance, (without attempting to detail particular conversation,) that had you visited Berlin while I was there, and where I hoped to have seen you, you would have met from such a man as the *illustrious Humboldt* and from the *King of Prussia* himself, such a distinguished and honored reception, as would only be accorded from such quarters, to the few who have made themselves eminent and immortal by such rare benefactions of their genius to the world, as have satisfactorily passed the ordeal of trial and time. Regretting the necessity I am under of writing thus briefly, and wishing you all honor and prosperity,

"I am, very dear Sir,

"Most truly yours,

"D. D. BARNARD.

"To S. F. B. MORSE, ESQ."

But in connection with this testimonial, we have another which reflects so much credit on the heart of one of Europe's most estimable scientific men, that we cannot refrain from giving it to our readers.

Prof. Steinheil, of Munich, it is well known invented an ingenious electro-magnetic telegraph in 1837, although subsequent to, yet independent of Morse's. The name of Steinheil stands high on the continent of Europe, as connected with the wide diffusion of the telegraph, and its efficient and economical administration. His writings on the subject of telegraphy are profound and thorough, replete with sound and intelligent views. He was one of the promoters to the great Telegraph Convention held in Vienna, in 1849, which resulted in the adoption of Morse's Telegraph for the Austro-Germanic Telegraph Union, and which is alluded to in the Hon. D. D. Barnard's letter. To Steinheil's advice and influence is owing the decision of the Convention.

When we were in Paris last summer, anxious to learn from Dr. Steinheil himself the position in regard to telegraphs which he held, we addressed him a letter, to which he courteously replied from Munich, under date of June 9, 1854. After giving the date of his own invention, (1837,) and his various labors for the establishment of telegraphs in Europe, under the commission of various governments, he says—"In this way I have been enabled effectually to labor for the adoption of Morse's system throughout all Europe, and that I have thereby extended his well-earned fame, has been to me the source of peculiar pleasure, which I beg you to testify to Professor Morse, in proper time, together with my most friendly respects."

When we consider that Dr. Steinheil must have resisted all the natural sympathies for his own mental offspring, urging him to a different course, in order to bring about this result, we can, to some extent, appreciate the nobleness of heart which could make a sacrifice of any mere selfish predilection in favor of another inventor—a stranger and a rival.

We scarcely know how to express our feelings of admiration, in view of such an example of genuine disinterestedness. No wonder that Steinheil is so universally beloved throughout all Europe.

[*From the North British Review.*]

ART. X.—HISTORY OF COOKE'S AND WHEATSTONE'S TELEGRAPH.

FAVORABLE NOTICES OF MORSE—COOKE AND WHEATSTONE AS THE INVENTORS OF THE ENGLISH NEEDLE TELEGRAPH CONSIDERED—INTRODUCTION OF THE TELEGRAPH IN ENGLAND AWARDED TO COOKE.

[WE copy the following from the *North British Review*, for February, 1855, being extracts from a very able article on the early history of the electric telegraphs. We omit much of the article, and only copy so much of it as relates to Morse's, Cooke's, and Wheatstone's inventions. We think the facts disclosed will very much startle the telegraph pirates of America. We thank the Review for the just consideration given to the American invention. The chastisement awarded to the Quarterly Review for the publication of a patched article on telegraphs, regardless of the truth of history, meets our hearty concurrence. On reading the following, in the Review, we were much surprised to learn the true merits of Mr. Cooke, and in future we will give his claims that just commendation which his services so eminently deserve.

We earnestly solicit for the article a reading. The award of the jury is plain and positive in its meaning. The concurrence by Cooke and Wheatstone gives it an unquestionable character of authority.]—EDITOR.

"We come now to the most interesting part of our subject, namely, the history of the introduction of the electric telegraph into England. We regret that this question has not been discussed by Dr. Lardner, who is better fitted to do it skilfully and honestly than any person we know. He has declined, however, on account of the space which such a discussion would have occupied, and the little interest which it would have inspired in 'the masses to whom his Museum is addressed.' So com pletely, indeed, has he shunned the subject, that he has hardly mentioned the names of the individuals to whom we are indebted for the introduction of this noble instrument into England. In the pages of a Review, however, such a discussion cannot be evaded, and we regret that a recent attempt to vitiate the history of the electric telegraph in England should give this discussion a controversial character.

About two years ago we became possessed of a printed document, containing the views, or rather the decision, of two of our greatest men upon this very subject; and we intended to have placed this decision before our readers without any argument of our own, on the basis of the few observations which we meant to oppose to the vitiated history to which we have referred. We have been fortunate enough, however, to obtain, only this day, the copy of a pamphlet which states the grounds upon which the above decision was pronounced, and which informs us, that all the documents and drawings relating to the subject are now in the press.

Mr. William Fothergill Cooke, to whom we owe the introduction of the electric telegraph into England, and who was the first English inventor of the telegraph apparatus, held a commission in the Indian army. Having returned from India on leave of absence, and on account of ill-health, he afterwards resigned his commission and went to Heidelberg to study anatomy. In the month of March, 1836, Professor Möncke, of Heidelberg, exhibited an electric telegraphic experiment, in which electric currents, passing along a conducting wire, conveyed signals to a distant station by the deflection of a magnetic needle enclosed in Schweigger's galvanometer or multiplier. The currents were produced by a voltaic battery placed at each end of the wire, and the apparatus was worked by moving the ends of the wires backward and forward between the battery and the galvanometer. Mr. Cooke was so struck with this experiment, that he immediately resolved so apply it to purposes of higher utility than the illustration of a lecture, and he abandoned his anatomical pursuits, and applied his whole energies to the invention of a practical electric telegraph. Within three weeks, in April, 1836, he made his first electric telegraph, partly at Heidelberg and partly at Frankfort. It was of the galvanometer form, consisting of six wires, forming three metallic circuits, and influencing three needles. By the combination of these signals, he obtained an alphabet of twenty-six signals. Drawings of the instrument are given in the work which we have alreday mentioned as in the course of publication. Mr. Cooke soon afterwards made another electric telegraph of a different construction. He had invented the *detector*, for discovering the locality of injuries done to the wires, the *reciprocal* communicator, and the *alarm*. All this was done in the months of March and April, 1836; and in June and July of the same year, he recorded the details of his system in a manuscript pamphlet, from which it was obvious, that in July, 1836, "he had wrought out his practical system from the minutest official details up to the records and extended ramifications of an important political and commercial engine."

When his telegraphic apparatus was completed, he showed it in November, 1836, to Mr. Faraday, and he afterwards submitted it and his pamphlet, in January, 1837, to the Liverpool and Manchester Railway Company, with whom he made a conditional arrangement, with the view of using it on the long tunnel at Liverpool. In February, 1837, when he was about to apply for a patent, he consulted Mr. Faraday and Dr. Roget on the construction of the electro-magnet employed in a part of his apparatus, and the last of these gentlemen advised him to consult Professor Wheatstone. He accordingly went to him on the 27th February, 1837. The following is Mr. Cooke's account of the interview and its results:—"He politely invited me to King's College, where I found, that in connection with about four miles of wire, he was in the habit of using two galvanometers of different constructions in his experiments on the effects of electric currents in deflecting magnetic needles. He had no apparatus of any kind for giving signals; but he had two keyboards, one of which was occasionally used in our experiments.

"What he had done towards inventing the practically electric telegraph was confined to the 'permutating principle' of his keyboard. This principle, which diminished the requisite number of wires, was engrafted on my reciprocal telegraph, and became very valuable in connection with later improvements; but though diminishing the number of wires, the permutating keys by themselves, and without the later improvements, would have been more complex than my first galvanometer keys; for each of the latter gave two signals by a single needle, (the plan now adopted on the Blackwall Railway,) while the former required the concurrent action of at least two keys and two needles.

"Though Professor Wheatstone was, when I first consulted him, in possession of a valuable principle, he had gone no further. Excepting the permutating principle, he was practically behind Möncke; for the latter had an instrument for giving signals, and Mr. Wheatstone had none. Even had all his apparent intentions been worked out, he would not then have fulfilled any of the fundamental conditions of the practical electric telegraph,—the power of detecting injuries to the wires by fracture, water, or contact,—of attracting attention at the commencement of the communication,—of sending signals alternately backwards and forwards by the same apparatus, and of exhibiting the signals to the operator, as well as to the recipient. In a word, he had no detector, no alarm, no reciprocal communicator."

The result of this interview was the formation of a partnership in May, 1837, when it was agreed that in the joint patent, Mr. Cooke's name should stand first; that Mr. Wheatstone should pay £80, and Mr. Cooke £50 of the expense of the patent, and that an allowance of £130 should be made to Mr. Cooke for his past experiments.

After these arrangements were completed, and the invention had become the subject of conversation, it was ascribed to Mr. Wheatstone alone. Mr. Cooke's name, though standing first in the patent, and though undoubtedly the original inventor, was never mentioned, and to such a length did this go, that in an account of the electric telegraph, published in *Chambers's Edinburgh Journal* for the 25th July, 1839, and obtained from conversation with Mr. Wheatstone, Mr. Cooke's name never appears. The inventions of Mr. Alexander Bain, a most meritorious individual, the inventor of electric clocks, and of the beautiful electric telegraph which we have explained, were all ascribed to Mr. Wheatstone; and the members of the different scientific societies and coteries in London, the dispensers of contemporary fame, and to whom Mr. Cooke and Mr. Bain were unknown, were the tools by which these acts of injustice were perpetrated. Mr. Cooke, a soldier, an educated man, and a gentleman, was represented as a mechanic, and Mr. Bain as a workman, who had pilfered the inventions of Mr. Wheatstone.

The day of retribution, however, came, as it always comes, both in defence of Mr. Cooke and Mr. Bain. Mr. Cooke attempted in vain to have these erroneous impressions effaced by the help of Mr. Wheatstone himself, but having failed, he insisted upon having it ascertained by arbitration, "in what shares, and with what priorities and relative degrees of merit the said parties hereto are inventors of the electric telegraph, due regard being paid to the original projection thereof, to the development of its laws and properties, to the practical introduction of it into the United Kingdom, since the improvements made upon it since its introduction there, and to all other matters which the arbitrators, or any two of them, shall in their discretion think deserving of their consideration." The arbiters were Sir Isambard Brunel, named by Mr. Cooke, and Professor Daniell, of King's College, by Mr. Wheatstone, both colleagues of Mr. Wheatstone in the Royal Society, and Mr. Daniell, a brother professor of Mr. Wheatstone in King's College,—an important remark, the reason of which will soon appear. Mr. Cooke was a member of none of the London societies or coteries, but felt himself safe, as he might well do, in the high talents and established character of Sir Isambard Brunel.

In the course of five months, the arbiters examined all the documents submitted to them, and on the 27th April, 1851, they made the following award:—

"As the electric telegraph has recently attracted a considerable share of public attention, our friends, Messrs. Cooke and Wheatstone, having been put to some inconvenience by a misunderstanding which has prevailed respecting their relative positions in connection with the invention. The following short statement of the facts has, therefore, at their request, been drawn up by us, the undersigned, Sir M. Isambard Brunel, engineer of the Thames Tunnel, and Professor Daniell, of King's College, as a document which either party may at pleasure make publicly known.

"In March, 1836, Mr. Cooke, while engaged at Heidelberg in scientific pursuits, witnessed for the first time, one of those well-known experiments on electricity, considered as a possible means of communicating intelligence, which have been tried and exhibited from time to time, during many years, by various philosophers. Struck with the vast importance of an instantaneous mode of communication to the railways then extending themselves over Great Britain, as well as to government and general purposes; and impressed with a strong conviction that so great an object might be practically attained by means of electricity, Mr. Cooke immediately directed his attention to the adaptation of electricity to a practical system of telegraphing; and, giving up the profession in which he was engaged, he from that hour devoted himself exclusively to the realization of that object. He came to England in April, 1836, to perfect his plans and instruments. In February, 1837, while engaged in completing a set of instruments for an intended experimental application of his telegraph to a tunnel on the Liverpool and Manchester Railway, he became acquainted, through the introduction of Dr. Roget, with Professor Wheatstone, who had for several years given much attention to the subject of transmitting intelligence by electricity, and had made several discoveries of the highest importance connected with the subject. Among these were his well-known determination of the velocity of electricity when passing through a metal wire;—his experiments, in which the deflection of magnetic needles, the decomposition of water, and other voltaic and magneto-electric effects, were produced through greater lengths of wire than had ever before been experimented upon; and his original method of converting a few wires into a considerable number of circuits, so that they might transmit the greatest number of signals, which can be transmitted by a given number of wires, by the deflection of magnetic needles.

"In May, 1837, Messrs. Cooke and Wheatstone took out a joint English patent, on a footing of equality, for their existing inventions. The terms of their partnership, which were more exactly defined and confirmed in November, 1837, by a partnership deed, vested in Mr. Cooke, as the originator of the undertaking, the exclusive management of the invention in Great Britain, Ireland, and the colonies, with the exclusive engineering department, as between themselves, and all the benefits arising from the laying down of the lines, and the manufacture of the instruments. As partners, standing on a perfect equality, Messrs. Cooke and Wheatstone were to divide equally all proceeds arising from the granting of licenses, or from sale of the patent rights,—a per centage being first payable to Mr. Cooke as manager. Professor Wheatstone retained an equal voice with Mr. Cooke in selecting and modifying the forms of the telegraphic instruments; and both parties pledged themselves to impart to each other, for their equal and mutual benefit, all improvements, of whatever kind, which they might become possessed of, connected with the giving of signals, or the sounding of alarums, by means of electricity. Since the formation of the partnership, the undertaking has rapidly progressed, under the constant and equally successful exertions of the parties in their distinct departments, until it has attained the character of a simple and practical system, worked out scientifically on the sure basis of actual experience.

"Whilst Mr. Cooke is entitled to stand alone as the gentleman to whom this country is indebted for having practically introduced and carried out the electric telegraph as a useful undertaking, promising to be a work of national importance, and Professor Wheatstone is acknowledged as the scientific man, whose profound and successful researches has already prepared the public to receive it as a project capable of practical application, it is to the united labors of two gentlemen, so well qualified for mutual assistance, that we must attribute the rapid progress which this important invention has made during the five years since they have been associated.

"Mc. Id. BRUNELL,
J. F. DANIELL.

"*London*, *27th April*, 1841.

"*London, 27th April,* 1841.

GENTLEMEN,—We cordially acknowledge the correctness of the facts stated in the above document, and beg to express our grateful sense of the very friendly and gratifying manner in which you have recorded your opinion of our joint labors, and of the value of our invention. We are, gentlemen, with feelings of the highest esteem, your obedient servants,

"WILLIAM F. COOKE.
"C. WHEATSTONE.

"Sir M. Isambard Brunel and
J. F. Daniell, Esq., Professor, &c. &c."

With such a distinct verdict from so distinguished a jury, we should have thought that this controversy was for ever closed. The parties expressed their satisfaction, and it was to be presumed that the two arbiters, whose European reputation was at stake, had conscientiously discharged their duty to the real claimants and to the public. This, however, was not the result of the award. Mr. Cooke claimed nothing more than was adjudged to him, while Mr. Wheatstone again attempted to monopolize the honor of being the inventor of the electric telegraph. His numerous scientific friends propagated the tale, and against such odds the real and little-known inventor had no chance of protection. An humble inventor or discoverer in the provinces, or in the private circles of the metropolis, has no chance against the combination and partisanship of London institutions; but as has happened before, a day of retribution again arrives for the protection of the helpless and the establishment of truth. In the eagerness to seize the bubble-reputation, it often bursts in the grasp. In the present case, a fact transpires in the ardor of pursuit which speaks volumes on the subject.

Under these circumstances, Mr. Cooke applies for redress to Mr. Wheatstone, his partner in a lucrative concern, and on the 16th January, 1845, thus addressed him:—

"It is now nearly two years since I remonstrated with you on the endeavors which your friends were making to undermine the award of Sir Isambard Brunel and Mr. Daniell, of April, 1841; but as these remonstrances were met by the assurance of your solicitor (made in your name and by your expressed desire) in his letter of the 20th May, 1843, that there was no truth in the report that you denied your full consent to the declarations contained in the printed paper,—an assurance further confirmed by his letter of the 27th June, in these words—'Mr. Wheatstone does not desire to escape from a single conclusion which the award warrants;'—all I could do, was to express myself satisfied with an explanation so unqualified.

"The same cause of complaint has, however, been repeatedly obtruded upon me since. And I *now hear from your own lips, that you have absolutely armed yourself with a letter from Mr. Daniell to counteract a certain construction of the award, which you consider objectionable.*

"This is indeed an alarming document to hold in reserve; and how Mr. Daniell could reconcile any such letter with the character of a judge, remains to be explained."

If the letter from Mr. Daniell, thus singularly referred to, is a real document intended to affect the history of science, and the rights of an individual, Mr. Cooke and the public ought to call for its production. It will reveal a fact, hitherto unsuspected, that the arbiters did not agree on their verdict, and that Mr. Daniell conceded something to Sir Isambard Brunel in favor of Mr. Cooke, and against Mr. Wheatstone. In this there was nothing wrong. It happens in almost every arbitration when two individuals are appointed by two contending parties, that each concedes something to the other to obtain a harmonious settlement; and it would not be unjust if each arbiter were to leave on record, in the hands of their respective friends, a memorandum of the points which have been thus conceded. But if one of the arbiters does this without the knowledge of the other, and puts it in the power of his friend, at any future time, to bring it forward in support of his original and rejected claims, that arbiter has acted *unjustly, illegally, and dishonorably;* and society should protect itself by marking such conduct with its severest rebuke. If this letter should ever fall down upon Mr. Cooke's neck, above which it is now suspended, we shall then *conjecture* for ourselves the amount of concession which Sir Isambard Brunel must have made against his own client, to balance the concessions made by his brother arbiter; for we are sure that he has left no letter in the hands of Mr. Cooke to assist him in escaping from a single conclusion of the award. But if this letter is brought forward to alarm Mr. Cooke, the friends of Professor Daniell may well be anxious about the result, and we think it is their duty to demand its production. We have ample faith in the honor of Professor Daniell, and we willingly adopt the liberal sentiment of Mr. Cooke, that if he "did express himself, incautiously in writing to his friend, no one acquainted with his manly and upright character, can suppose that he intended to sanction a clandestine use of his letter to assist Mr. Wheatstone," or to injure Mr. Cooke. Ignorant though we be of the nature of this singular document, we have no difficulty, if it was written by Professor Daniell, in predicting its contents. Its object, doubtless, was to sweeten the bitter pill of the award. It was an opiate tenderly administered to disappointed vanity,—a curb, perchance, to that morbid appetite for fame, which respects neither individual rights nor social feelings. By this anticipation of its purpose, we at once protect the character of its author, and the rights of the individual which it has been brought forward to assail.

The future history of this remarkable partnership is soon told. Mr. Cooke pursued, with unflinching ardor, his scheme of making the electric telegraph a work of "national importance," and being prepared by his own inventions, and by the joint invention in Cooke and Wheatstone's patent, he took steps, in the autumn of 1845, to organize a joint-stock company, which he effected in 1846. This company, under the name of the *Electric Telegraph Company*, applied to Parliament in the session of 1846 for a bill of incorporation. This bill was opposed by Mr. Alexander Bain of Edinburgh, who asserted in his petition that he had invented an Electric Clock, and an Electric Printing Telegraph,—that he had communicated these inventions confidentially to Mr. Wheatstone, and that the latter had claimed them as his own. Notwithstanding this opposition, the directors of the company carried their bill, though not without difficulty, through the House of Commons; but when it came to the House of Lords, Mr. Bain's statement and the evidence which he gave in its support made such an impression on the members of the Lord's Committee, that on the afternoon of its third sitting, the Duke of Beaufort, as chairman, intimated to the counsel of the Electric Telegraph Company that they should make an arrangement with Mr. Bain, "hinting," as Mr. Cooke says, "pretty plainly, that their bill might be thrown out if they declined to do so." Mr. Bain accordingly received, we believe, £12,000, and thus, to Mr. Wheatstone's extreme displeasure, became associated with the Company, binding himself to give them the use of his inventions. "About the same time the directors had, unluckily, made an arrangement with a Mr. Henry Mapple, in ignorance that this person had a similar controversy with Mr. Wheatstone respecting an improved alarum and a telegraphic rope," and "in consequence of these untoward circumstances, Mr. Wheatstone sent in an account of his expenses, and retired altogether from the company's service."

Let us now see under what obligation, and how richly rewarded, Mr. Wheatstone left the service of the company. So early as the 12th April, 1843, Mr. Cooke entered into an agreement, by which he was to pay Mr. Wheatstone a royalty varying from £20 to £15 per mile for every ten miles of telegraph he should complete during the year, £20 for the *first* ten miles, and £15 for the *sixth* ten miles, and all beyond it, Mr. Wheatstone assigning to Mr. Cooke all the letters patent of Cooke and Wheatstone, and all future patents for improvements. In 1845, when the electric telegraph company was in contemplation, and when many lines of telegraph had been already laid down by Mr. Cooke, he entered into a new agreement with Mr. Wheatstone, by which he bought up his royalty for £30,000, together with all arrears of royalty due at the date of the agreement.

Thus liberally rewarded for half of the joint patent held by Mr. Cooke and himself, one would have thought that all farther controversy was at an end. The company succeeded beyond their most sanguine expectations, and Mr. Wheatstone became discontented with his reward. He claimed to be the inventor of the electric telegraph! He forgot the rights of his partner and benefactor as conceded and signed by himself,—and as adjudicated by Sir Isambard Brunel and Professor Daniell. He forgot the concession of £12,000 by the Lord's Committee to Mr. Bain for his electric clock and his beautiful electric telegraph; and those eminent individuals ceased to be named but as mechanics and workmen, whom he had taken into his service! Mr. Cooke, whose forbearance we cannot but admire, maintained a dignified silence as long as the injuries which were done to him were whispered in private, or circulated in scientific coteries. The time, however, at last came, and the crisis in Mr. Wheatstone's history as well as in his, when he was dragged before the public by a representative of Mr. Wheatstone's feelings as well as opinions, and compelled to appeal to its tribunal, in a voicc as articulate as the railway whistle or the electric thunder.

An article on the Electric Telegraph appeared in the Quarterly Review for June, 1854, in which the claims of Morse and Steinheil, and Cooke and Bain, are unceremoniously thrown overboard, and Mr. Wheatstone pronounced the inventor of the Electric Telegraph!! That such a perversion of scientific history, and such a violation of recorded truth, should have appeared in such a respectable journal, has greatly surprised us, and we confess that we feel as much for the author who has permitted himself to be a dupe, as we do for Mr. Cooke, whom that dupe has so wantonly made a victim. Roused by this attack upon his honor, and this attempt to wrest from him not what he claims, but what was given to him by the solemn decree of two of the most distinguished men of the day, and one of them Mr. Wheatstone's particular friend, Mr. Cooke has been driven to write the pamphlet to which we have referred, and to publish in support of its statements a volume of documents, illustrated by numerous plates.

Having been the first individual who introduced the eelectric telegraph into England,—having been the first constructor of a working telegraph and various pieces of valuable telegraph apparatus, invented by himself,—having availed himself of Mr. Wheatstone's talents for completing the particular telegraph patented by Messrs. Cooke and Wheatstone,—having paid Mr. Wheatstone £30,000 for his interest in the joint patent,—having established beyond the power of challenge his claim to "*stand alone as the gentleman to whom this country is indebted for having* PRACTICALLY INTRODUCED AND CARRIED OUT THE ELECTRIC TELEGRAPH AS AN USEFUL UNDERTAKING, Mr. Cooke succeeded, in 1846, in establishing the ELECTRIC TELEGRAPH COMPANY, of which he is now one of the principal directors.

Mr. Cooke was fortunate in obtaining the co-operation of such a man as Mr. Lewis Ricardo, M. P., by whose zeal and sagacity this company has attained its present gigantic magnitude. By the outlay of *three quarters of a million of money*, this company has covered England and Scotland with a complete net-work of telegraphs, extending along 5480 miles of railway lines, and employing no less than 24,000 miles of wire.

INVENTION OF THE MORSE TELEGRAPH.

DEDICATED TO THE NEW-YORK SKETCH CLUB.*

BY W. H. COYLE.

HERE from the city's surging roar shut out
By academic walls, are gathered in
A gifted group, at Arts high festival,
Painters and sculptors, orators and bards,
High born disciples of the Beautiful—
The noble brotherhood of Genius:
Each bringing offerings of homage to
The altar of his heart's fidelity.
These are the city's solitary men;
Not sordid, battling with the multitude,
For gold, or glory with its blood-bought plume,
Not aspirants for venal spoils or power;
But leading gentle, quiet, cloister'd lives,
Young hermits in imagination's cells—
Patient, yet panting to adorn the domes
And galleries of the outer world,
With glorious trophies of the ideal.

* At a late meeting of the Club, in the University Building, a room formerly occupied by Prof. Morse, while perfecting his invention of the Telegraph, was the same in which was assembled the festive association. Brilliant speeches were made upon the occasion, one of which referred to the great invention of the Electro-Magnetic Telegraph, by Morse, which occasioned the delivery of the beautiful poem, here published, by Mr. Coyle. It is a rich tribute,—embracing ideas and language most excellent.

Toil on, brave brothers—though the weary night
Of penury and cold indifference
Be long and dark, faint not upon your path—
For in the Orient, soon the morning star
Shall rise, and golden dawn, with radiant smiles,
Beckon you onward to immortal day!

Not many years ago, in this same hall,
Musing an Artist sat; he was not old
In age, yet pondering on a problem
Which became a restless, ever-present thought,
Had furrow'd with deep lines his fever'd brow,
But still like a Chaldean seer, or some
Grey-bearded necromancer studying
The mystic circles of astrology,
Or alchymist, he fed the crucible
Of his wild, burning hopes, and sleepless worked
The wizard spells of his philosophy.
E'en he forsook the first love of his youth
Painting, that sweet Madonna of the mind,
At whose pure shrine he bent the knee of fresh
And early worship, and turned coldly from
Her costly gems which flashed upon his walls,
To render fealty to his soul's new queen.
One mighty purpose loomed before his life—
Spectral, and vast and vague, but taking form
With each day's intimacy, till at last
He grappled with its mystery, and like
A giant wrestled for the victory!
Out on the wild sea, 'mid the hurtling storm,
Where hissed the lightning's blinding blaze, and shook
The strong ship like an aspen to her keel
Beneath the thunder crash, was born the great,
Sublime conception; and upon the shore
It haunted him amid the city's hum,
And would not leave him—till, Prometheus-like,
He dared to steal from heaven the sacred
Fire, and animate his own creation!

The hour at last had come—Silence and night
Had hushed the Babel-city to deep sleep.
Around the walls of the magician's room,
A circuit ran three miles, of air-hung wires;
And on a table stood the sealed jar
Where coiled the fearful fiery messenger.
Trembling he wrote "Eureka!" when a flash
Electric, like a ray swift travelling
From the sun, thrill'd thro' each palpitating,
Iron vein, and lo! upon a spotless
Scroll unrolled, a hand invisible wrote
The winged word, "Eureka!" The artist's dream
Was realized; and now blooms on his brow,
The laurel of his country's gratitude!

MARCH 8th, 1855.

ART. XI.—PROTEAN RUBBER INSULATOR.

[THE following communication has been sent to us for consideration. We publish it, with the drawings; also, the letters of commendation. We have heard the insulator highly approved. Mr. Eddy, the able superintendent of the Eastern Lines to the British Provinces, has well tested its merits on a very large scale. By such practicable experiments reliance can be entertained and confidence inspired. We would rather have the practical tests on a well managed telegraph line, conducted by a competent superintendent, than the certificates from every Professor of schools in America. Mr. J. M. Batchelder is the proprietor of the patent, and supplies lines with the insulator.]—EDITOR.

THIS insulator, which has been introduced during the past year, possesses those properties that have been long sought for by all persons engaged in the practical management of lines of electric telegraph. The great value of the Protean Rubber for the insulation of telegraph wires is shown by its

ELECTRIC PROPERTIES.—In this particular it is equal to the best kinds of glass. A plate electrical machine has been made of it, and electricity is more readily excited than it is in the common cylinder or plate-glass machines.

It does not absorb moisture:—The material is hard, and of fine and uniform texture, and moisture cannot penetrate below the surface in the slightest degree.

Dew is not deposited so quickly upon its surface as it is upon glass or porcelain. This quality gives it especial value during the early hours of the morning, and when fogs prevail.

DURABILITY.—This substance is not injuriously affected by exposure to air and moisture, or by the ordinary changes of the weather; it does not become soft at a less temperature than 280° F. It is not liable to those molecular changes which so soon affect gutta percha, and entirely destroy its insulating properties.

ECONOMY.—The first cost of this insulator is greater than that of many kinds now in use, but the saving of battery expenses, and a less expenditure for repairs will, it is believed, insure its use by those who have full knowledge of the difficulties and loss of income caused by the present defective system of insulation.

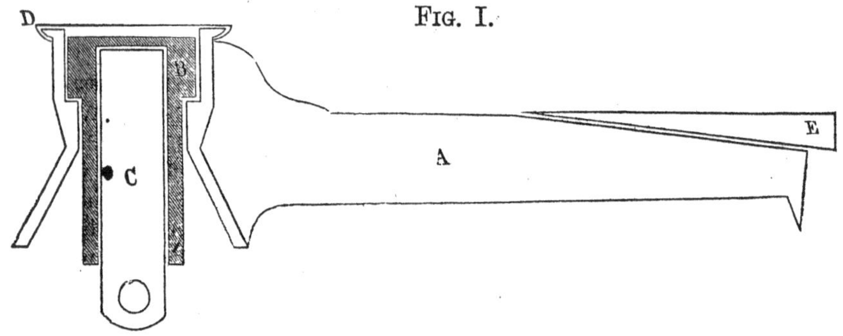

FIG. I.

FIGURE I. is a vertical section of a side insulator. A, iron support; B, protean rubber cap; C, suspension pin; D, cover; E, wedge. The rubber while baking contracts upon the iron pin, so that it cannot be drawn out, and obviates the necessity of using sulphur or other cement.

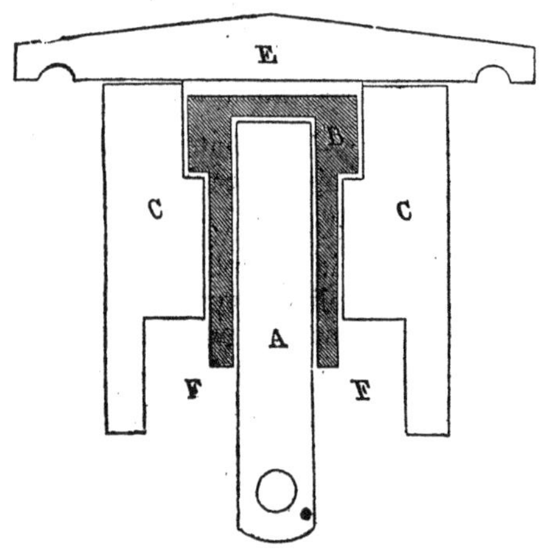

FIG. II.

FIGURE II. Represents another form of side insulator. A, is the suspension pin, with its rubber covering B, inserted in a round hole at the end of a wooden arm or support, C; E, cover; F, circular, open space.

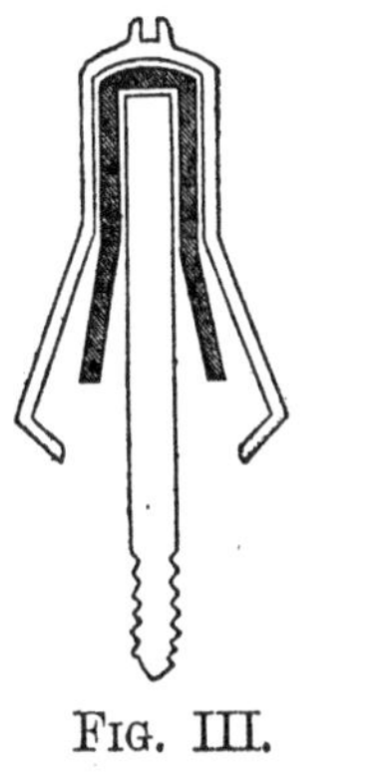

FIG. III.

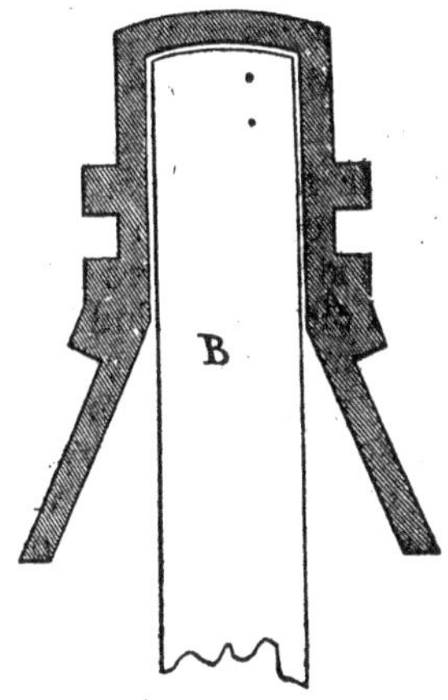

FIG. IV.

FIGURE III.--Top insulator. The shield is of cast iron, the support of wrought iron, with the rubber cap intervening. The re-entering angle at the base of the shield prevents rain, when driven by the wind, from entering the inside of the shield.

FIGURE IV.—Top insulator. The cap A is composed wholly of rubber, and is mounted upon an iron screw bolt B; or it may be supported upon a stout pin of wood, in which case the cap is shrunk on, no cement being used. If the wooden pin swells the cap is not injured.

PORTLAND, *October* 10*th*, 1854.

J. M. BATCHELDER, ESQ.,

SIR,—Having given some attention to the insulation of telegraph wires upon India rubber as prepared by you, I can say that, in my judgment, it is better adapted for insulating purposes than any other material in use.

It is a perfect non-conductor; it is lighter and much stronger than glass, and for insulating wires in the air it has great superiority from the fact that moisture does not gather so readily upon its surface, and it is capable of being made upon iron so strong that only extraordinary violence can break it.

One hundred insulators of this material put up by me last season have proved satisfactory, and our company has used the present season nine thousand of them.

We are continuing to order insulators of the same kind for air lines in preference to all others.

Respectfully yours,

JAMES EDDY,

Supt. Maine Telegraph Co.

PLACERVILLE, CAL., *February* 24, 1854.

MR. J. M. BATCHELDER,

DEAR SIR,—I am perfectly satisfied with the insulators; they fully answer my expectations, and are in fact the best I ever saw. If any country in the world will test the qualities of an iusulator, it is this, where we have incessant rain for a week at a time, and often the wind blowing a perfect hurricane. During the worst rains that we have had this winter, the line has worked as perfectly as in the dryest weather; in fact, we can perceive no difference between wet weather and dry in the working of the line. We use fourteen cups Grove's battery, seven at each end—distance one hundred and fifteen miles.

Your obedient servant,

J. E. STRONG,

Supt. Alta California Telegraph Co.

BOSTON, *March* 15, 1854.

MR. J. M. BATCHELDER,

DEAR SIR,—I believe protean rubber to be the very best substance known for insulating either air or subterranean telegraph lines.

Yours, very truly,

MOSES G. FARMER,

Supt. Telegrayhic Fire Alarms.

TO OUR PATRONS.

In consequence of a sudden attack of fever, we have no opportunity of presenting, in the present number, the many editorials which we had expected.

We leave by the first steamer for Europe, and will return some time during the summer.